Variational Problems and Applications

Variational Problems and Applications

Editor

Savin Treanta

MDPI • Basel • Beijing • Wuhan • Barcelona • Belgrade • Manchester • Tokyo • Cluj • Tianjin

Editor
Savin Treanta
Applied Mathematics
University Politehnica of
Bucharest
Bucharest
Romania

Editorial Office
MDPI
St. Alban-Anlage 66
4052 Basel, Switzerland

This is a reprint of articles from the Special Issue published online in the open access journal *Mathematics* (ISSN 2227-7390) (available at: www.mdpi.com/journal/mathematics/special_issues/Variational_Problems_Applications).

For citation purposes, cite each article independently as indicated on the article page online and as indicated below:

LastName, A.A.; LastName, B.B.; LastName, C.C. Article Title. *Journal Name* **Year**, *Volume Number*, Page Range.

ISBN 978-3-0365-6589-7 (Hbk)
ISBN 978-3-0365-6588-0 (PDF)

Contents

Muhammad Bilal Khan, Hatim Ghazi Zaini, Savin Treanţă, Mohamed S. Soliman and Kamsing Nonlaopon
Riemann–Liouville Fractional Integral Inequalities for Generalized Pre-Invex Functions of Interval-Valued Settings Based upon Pseudo Order Relation
Reprinted from: *Mathematics* **2022**, *10*, 204, doi:10.3390/math10020204 . . . . **153**

Yating Guo, Guoju Ye, Wei Liu, Dafang Zhao and Savin Treanţă
Optimality Conditions and Duality for a Class of Generalized Convex Interval-Valued Optimization Problems
Reprinted from: *Mathematics* **2021**, *9*, 2979, doi:10.3390/math9222979 . . . . **171**

Savin Treanţă
On Well-Posedness of Some Constrained Variational Problems
Reprinted from: *Mathematics* **2021**, *9*, 2478, doi:10.3390/math9192478 . . . . **185**

Alexander Kuleshov
A Remark on the Change of Variable Theorem for the Riemann Integral
Reprinted from: *Mathematics* **2021**, *9*, 1899, doi:10.3390/math9161899 . . . . **197**

Savin Treanţă and Koushik Das
On Robust Saddle-Point Criterion in Optimization Problems with Curvilinear Integral Functionals
Reprinted from: *Mathematics* **2021**, *9*, 1790, doi:10.3390/math9151790 . . . . **201**

mathematics

Editorial

Variational Problems and Applications

Savin Treanţă [1,2,3]

[1] Department of Applied Mathematics, University Politehnica of Bucharest, 060042 Bucharest, Romania; savin.treanta@upb.ro
[2] Academy of Romanian Scientists, 54 Splaiul Independentei, 050094 Bucharest, Romania
[3] Fundamental Sciences Applied in Engineering—Research Center (SFAI), University Politehnica of Bucharest, 060042 Bucharest, Romania

1. Introduction

Over the years, many researchers have been interested in obtaining solution procedures in variational (interval/fuzzy) analysis and robust control. In order to formulate necessary and sufficient optimality/efficiency conditions and duality theorems for different classes of robust and interval-valued/fuzzy variational problems, various approaches have been proposed. In this regard, we provide the Special Issue "Variational Problems and Applications" to cover the new advances in these mathematical topics. In this Special Issue, we focused on formulating and demonstrating some characterization results of well-posedness and robust efficient solutions in new classes of (multiobjective) variational (control) problems governed by multiple and/or path-independent curvilinear integral cost functionals and robust mixed and/or isoperimetric constraints involving first- and second-order partial differential equations. In response to our invitation, we received 30 papers from many countries (Romania, China, India, Saudi Arabia, Australia, Egypt, Yemen, Germany, Pakistan, Thailand, Russia), of which 14 were published.

2. Brief Overview of the Contributions

In a review conducted by Treanţă [1], nonlinear dynamics, generated by some classes of constrained control problems that involve second-order partial derivatives, were comprehensively reviewed. Specifically, necessary optimality conditions were formulated and proved for the considered variational control problems governed by integral functionals. In addition, the well-posedness and the associated variational inequalities have been considered in this review paper.

Olteanu [2] briefly reviews a method of approximating any real-valued nonnegative continuous compactly supported function defined on a closed unbounded subset by dominating special polynomials that are sums of squares. This method also works in several-dimensional cases. To perform this, a Hahn–Banach-type theorem (Kantorovich theorem on an extension of positive linear operators), a Haviland theorem, and the notion of a moment-determinate measure were applied. Second, completions and other results of solving full Markov moment problems in terms of quadratic forms are proposed based on polynomial approximation. The existence and uniqueness of the solution are discussed.

Treanţă and Das [3] introduced a new class of multi-dimensional robust optimization problems (named (P)) with mixed constraints, implying second-order partial differential equations (PDEs) and inequations (PDIs). Moreover, they defined an auxiliary (modified) class of robust control problems (named $(P)_{(\bar{b},\bar{c})}$), which is much easier to study, and provided some characterization results of (P) and $(P)_{(\bar{b},\bar{c})}$ by using the notions of a normal weak robust optimal solution and robust saddle-point associated with a Lagrange functional corresponding to $(P)_{(\bar{b},\bar{c})}$. For this aim, they considered path-independent curvilinear integral cost functionals and the notion of convexity associated with a curvilinear integral functional generated by a controlled closed (complete integrable) Lagrange 1-form.

Citation: Treanţă, S. Variational Problems and Applications. *Mathematics* **2023**, *11*, 205. https://doi.org/10.3390/math11010205

Received: 19 December 2022
Accepted: 23 December 2022
Published: 30 December 2022

In 1961, Kestelman first proved the change in the variable theorem for the Riemann integral in its modern form. In 1970, Preiss and Uher supplemented this result with the inverse statement. Later, in a number of papers (Sarkhel, Výborný, Puoso, Tandra, and Torchinsky), the alternative proofs of these theorems were provided within the same formulations. In [4], Kuleshov showed that one of the restrictions (namely, the boundedness of the function f on its entire domain) can be omitted, while the change of variable formula still holds.

By considering the new forms of the notions of lower semicontinuity, pseudomonotonicity, hemicontinuity and monotonicity of the considered scalar multiple integral functional, Treanţă [5] studied the well-posedness of a new class of variational problems with variational inequality constraints. More specifically, by defining the set of approximating solutions for the class of variational problems under study, he established several results on well-posedness.

Guo et al. [6] studied the derivation of optimality conditions and duality theorems for interval-valued optimization problems based on gH-symmetrical derivatives. Further, the concepts of symmetric pseudo-convexity and symmetric quasi-convexity for interval-valued functions are proposed to extend the above optimization conditions. Examples are also presented to illustrate corresponding results.

The concepts of convex and non-convex functions play a key role in the study of optimization. So, with the help of these ideas, some inequalities can also be established. Moreover, the principles of convexity and symmetry are inextricably linked. In the last two years, convexity and symmetry have emerged as a new field due to considerable association. In the work of Khan et al. [7], the authors studied a new version of interval-valued functions (I-V·Fs), known as left and right χ-pre-invex interval-valued functions (LR-χ-pre-invex I-V·Fs). For this class of non-convex I-V·Fs, they derived numerous new dynamic inequalities interval Riemann–Liouville fractional integral operators. The applications of these repercussions are taken into account in a unique way.

Lai et al. [8] introduced a new class of interval-valued preinvex functions termed as harmonically h-preinvex interval-valued functions. They established new inclusion of Hermite–Hadamard for harmonically h-preinvex interval-valued functions via interval-valued Riemann–Liouville fractional integrals. Further, they proved fractional Hermite–Hadamard–type inclusions for the product of two harmonically h-preinvex interval-valued functions. In this way, these findings include several well-known results and newly obtained results of the existing literature as special cases. Moreover, applications of the main results have been demonstrated with some examples.

The principles of convexity and symmetry are inextricably linked. Because of the considerable association that has emerged between the two in recent years, we may apply what we learn from one to the other. In the study of Khan et al. [9], the main aim is to establish the relationship between integral inequalities and interval-valued functions (IV-Fs) based upon the pseudo-order relation. Firstly, we discussed the properties of left and right preinvex interval-valued functions (left and right preinvex IV-Fs). Then, we obtained a Hermite–Hadamard (H–H) and Hermite–Hadamard–Fejér (H–H–Fejér) type inequality and some related integral inequalities with the support of left and right preinvex IV-Fs via a pseudo-order relation and interval Riemann integral. Moreover, some exceptional special cases have been discussed.

In Alnowibet et al. [10], a hybrid gradient simulated annealing algorithm is guided to solve the constrained optimization problem. When trying to solve constrained optimization problems using deterministic, stochastic optimization methods or using a hybridization between them, penalty function methods are the most popular approach due to their simplicity and ease of implementation. There are many approaches to handling the existence of the constraints in the constraint problem. The simulated-annealing algorithm (SA) is one of the most successful meta-heuristic strategies. On the other hand, the gradient method is the most inexpensive method among the deterministic methods. In previous literature, the hybrid gradient simulated annealing algorithm (GLMSA) demonstrated efficiency and effectiveness in solving unconstrained optimization problems. In Alnowibet et al. [10], the GLMSA algorithm is generalized to solve the constrained optimization problems. Hence, a new approach penalty function is proposed to handle the existence of the constraints. The proposed approach penalty function is used to guide the hybrid gradient simulated annealing algorithm (GLMSA) to obtain a new algorithm (GHMSA) that finds the constrained optimization problem. The performance of the proposed algorithm is tested on several benchmark optimization test problems and some well-known engineering design problems with varying dimensions. Comprehensive comparisons against other methods in the literature are also presented. The results indicate that the proposed method is promising and competitive. The comparison results between the GHMSA and the other four state-Meta-heuristic algorithms indicate that the proposed GHMSA algorithm is competitive with, and in some cases superior to, other existing algorithms in terms of the quality, efficiency, convergence rate, and robustness of the final result.

Data-mining applications are growing with the availability of large data; sometimes, handling large data is also a typical task. Segregation of the data for the extraction of useful information is inevitable for designing modern technologies. Considering this fact, the work of Alrasheedi et al. [11] proposes a chaos-embedded marine predator algorithm (CMPA) for feature selection. The optimization routine is designed with the aim of maximizing the classification accuracy with the optimal number of features selected. The well-known benchmark datasets have been chosen for validating the performance of the proposed algorithm. A comparative analysis of the performance with some well-known algorithms proves the applicability of the proposed algorithm. Further, the analysis was extended to some of the well-known chaotic algorithms; first, the binary versions of these algorithms are developed, and then a comparative analysis of the performance is conducted on the basis of the mean features selected, the classification accuracy obtained and the fitness function values. Statistical significance tests have also been conducted to establish the significance of the proposed algorithm.

In the work of Peng et al. [12], the reverse space-time nonlocal complex modified Kortewewg–de Vries (mKdV) equation is investigated by using the consistent tanh expansion (CTE) method. According to the CTE method, a nonauto-Bäcklund transformation theorem of nonlocal complex mKdV is obtained. The interactions between one kink soliton and other different nonlinear excitations are constructed via the nonauto–Bäcklund transformation theorem. By selecting cnoidal periodic waves, the interaction between one kink soliton and the cnoidal periodic waves is derived. The specific Jacobi function-type solution and graphs of its analysis are provided in this paper.

Lai et al. [13] obtained characterizations of solution sets of the interval-valued mathematical programming problems with switching constraints. Stationary conditions, which are weaker than the standard Karush–Kuhn–Tucker conditions, need to be discussed in order to find the necessary optimality conditions. The authors introduced corresponding weak, Mordukhovich, and strong stationary conditions for the corresponding interval-valued mathematical programming problems with switching constraints (IVPSC) and interval-valued tightened nonlinear problems (IVTNP), because the W-stationary condition of IVPSC is equivalent to the Karush–Kuhn–Tucker conditions of the IVTNP. Furthermore, they used strong stationary conditions to characterize the solution sets for IVTNP, in which the last ones are particular solutions sets for IVPSC, because the feasible set of tightened nonlinear problems (IVTNP) is a subset of the feasible set of the mathematical programs with switching constraints (IVPSC).

In the work of Cipu and Barbu [14], the authors are concerned with solutions for Sturm–Liouville problems (SLP) using a variational problem (VP) formulation of regular SLP. The minimization problem (MP) is also established, and the connection between the solution of each formulation is then proved. Variational estimations (the variational equation associated with the Euler–Lagrange variational principle and Nehari's method, shooting method and bisection method) and iterative variational methods (He's method and HPM) for regular RSL are presented in the final part of the paper, which ends with applications.

Acknowledgments: I am thankful to the editors and reviewers of the *Mathematics* journal for their help and support.

Conflicts of Interest: The author declares no conflict of interest.

References

1. Treanţă, S. Recent Advances of Constrained Variational Problems Involving Second-Order Partial Derivatives: A Review. *Mathematics* **2022**, *10*, 2599. [CrossRef]
2. Olteanu, O. Markov Moment Problem and Sandwich Conditions on Bounded Linear Operators in Terms of Quadratic Forms. *Mathematics* **2022**, *10*, 3288. [CrossRef]
3. Treanţă, S.; Das, K. On Robust Saddle-Point Criterion in Optimization Problems with Curvilinear Integral Functionals. *Mathematics* **2021**, *9*, 1790. [CrossRef]
4. Kuleshov, A. A Remark on the Change of Variable Theorem for the Riemann Integral. *Mathematics* **2021**, *9*, 1899. [CrossRef]
5. Treanţă, S. On Well-Posedness of Some Constrained Variational Problems. *Mathematics* **2021**, *9*, 2478. [CrossRef]
6. Guo, Y.; Ye, G.; Liu, W.; Zhao, D.; Treanţă, S. Optimality Conditions and Duality for a Class of Generalized Convex Interval-Valued Optimization Problems. *Mathematics* **2021**, *9*, 2979. [CrossRef]
7. Khan, M.B.; Zaini, H.G.; Treanţă, S.; Soliman, M.S.; Nonlaopon, K. Riemann–Liouville Fractional Integral Inequalities for Generalized Pre-Invex Functions of Interval-Valued Settings Based upon Pseudo Order Relation. *Mathematics* **2022**, *10*, 204. [CrossRef]
8. Lai, K.K.; Bisht, J.; Sharma, N.; Mishra, S.K. Hermite-Hadamard-Type Fractional Inclusions for Interval-Valued Preinvex Functions. *Mathematics* **2022**, *10*, 264. [CrossRef]
9. Khan, M.B.; Treanţă, S.; Soliman, M.S.; Nonlaopon, K.; Zaini, H.G. Some New Versions of Integral Inequalities for Left and Right Preinvex Functions in the Interval-Valued Settings. *Mathematics* **2022**, *10*, 611. [CrossRef]
10. Alnowibet, K.A.; Mahdi, S.; El-Alem, M.; Abdelawwad, M.; Mohamed, A.W. Guided Hybrid Modified Simulated Annealing Algorithm for Solving Constrained Global Optimization Problems. *Mathematics* **2022**, *10*, 1312. [CrossRef]
11. Alrasheedi, A.F.; Alnowibet, K.A.; Saxena, A.; Sallam, K.M.; Mohamed, A.W. Chaos Embed Marine Predator (CMPA) Algorithm for Feature Selection. *Mathematics* **2022**, *10*, 1411. [CrossRef]
12. Peng, J.; Ren, B.; Shen, S.; Wang, G. Interaction Behaviours between Soliton and Cnoidal Periodic Waves for Nonlocal Complex Modified Korteweg–de Vries Equation. *Mathematics* **2022**, *10*, 1429. [CrossRef]
13. Lai, K.K.; Mishra, S.K.; Singh, S.K.; Hassan, M. Stationary Conditions and Characterizations of Solution Sets for Interval-Valued Tightened Nonlinear Problems. *Mathematics* **2022**, *10*, 2763. [CrossRef]
14. Cipu, E.C.; Barbu, C.D. Variational Estimation Methods for Sturm–Liouville Problems. *Mathematics* **2022**, *10*, 3728. [CrossRef]

mathematics MDPI

Article

Variational Estimation Methods for Sturm–Liouville Problems

Elena Corina Cipu [1,2,*] and Cosmin Dănuţ Barbu [1]

[1] Department of Applied Mathematics, University Politehnica of Bucharest, Spl. Independentei, No. 313, RO-060042 Bucharest, Romania
[2] CiTi, Faculty of Applied Sciences, University Politehnica of Bucharest, Spl. Independentei, No. 313, RO-060042 Bucharest, Romania
* Correspondence:corina.cipu@upb.ro

Abstract: In this paper, we are concerned with approach solutions for Sturm–Liouville problems (SLP) using variational problem (VP) formulation of regular SLP. The minimization problem (MP) is also set forth, and the connection between the solution of each formulation is then proved. Variational estimations (the variational equation associated through the Euler–Lagrange variational principle and Nehari's method, shooting method and bisection method) and iterative variational methods (He's method and HPM) for regular RSL are unitary presented in final part of the paper, which ends with applications.

Keywords: BVP nonlinear problems; variational methods; estimating nonlinearities; Green function

MSC: 34A12; 34A45

Citation: Cipu, E.C.; Barbu, C.D. Variational Estimation Methods for Sturm–Liouville Problems. *Mathematics* **2022**, *10*, 3728. https://doi.org/10.3390/math10203728

Academic Editors: Simeon Reich and Alessio Pomponio

Received: 31 July 2022
Accepted: 7 October 2022
Published: 11 October 2022

1. Introduction

Nonlinearities are different from linear type by a function, an operator or a system that is nonlinear or is the case in which only some characteristics of it are known. The existence of the solution and the dependence of conditions for solving some classes of differential equations described by an operator is specified by the general framework of the Sturm–Liouville problem, with parametric conditions at the limit. The general framework of the Sturm–Liouville problem with parametric conditions at the limit is specified in the first part of the paper. The existence of the solution and the dependence of conditions is specified through the connection between the differential operator and Green's function. Based on the properties of Green's function, the operator used to analyze the behavior of the solution of the parameters given by the boundary conditions is specified. Variational problems derived from the initial RSLP are outlined with different type conditions in order to estimate the solution.

Let be the operator $L = -\frac{d}{dx}\left[p(x)\frac{d}{dx}\right] + \rho(x)$ as part of the regular Sturm–Liouville problem (RSL). The Sturm–Liouville (SL) problem expressed by the differential equation and the boundary conditions

$$a(x)\frac{d^2u}{dx^2} + b(x)\frac{du}{dx} + c(x)u - \lambda d(x)u = 0, \tag{1}$$

$$\begin{aligned} B_1 &: a_1u(a) + a_2u'(a) = 0,\ |a_1| + |a_2| \neq 0, a_1, a_2 \in \mathbb{R}, \\ B_2 &: b_1u(b) + b_2u'(b) = 0,\ |b_1| + |b_2| \neq 0, b_1, b_2 \in \mathbb{R} \end{aligned} \tag{2}$$

could be written as

$$Lu + \lambda s(x)u = 0,\ \ x \in (a,b) = I, \lambda \in \mathbb{R} \tag{3}$$

with $p(x) = a(x)$, $\rho(x) = -c(x), s(x) = d(x)$ in case $b(x) = a'(x)$ and with integrant factor $\mu = ke^{\int_a^x \frac{b(t)}{a(t)}dt}$, $p(x) = \mu a(x)$, $\rho(x) = -\mu c(x), s(x) = \mu d(x)$ in case $b(x) \neq a'(x)$ (see [1,2]).

The Sturm–Liouville equation is regular in the interval $[a,b]$ if the functions verify the condition $p(x) > 0$ and $s(x) > 0, \forall x \in I$ or $s \equiv 0$ and the operator $L : \mathcal{H} = \mathcal{L}^2(I) \cap \mathcal{C}^2(I) \to \mathcal{L}^2(I)$ is self-adjoint with real eigenvalues and orthogonal eigenfunctions in space $\mathcal{L}_s^2(I)$ according to the inner product

$$\langle f, g\rangle = \int_a^b fg \, \mathrm{d}x f, g \in \mathcal{L}^2(I); \langle f, g\rangle_s = \int_a^b sfg \, \mathrm{d}x \text{ in } \mathcal{L}_s^2(I). \tag{4}$$

and for a given λ, there exist two linearly independent solutions of a RSL equation in the I interval, $\mathcal{L}^2(I) = \left\{ f : I \to \mathbb{R}, \int_a^b |f(x)|^2 \, \mathrm{d}x < \infty \right\}$.

We denote $D(L)$ as the domain of L that is defined by

$$\begin{aligned} D(L) &= \{\mathrm{y} \in C([a,b]), y'' \in \mathcal{L}^2(I), \text{ y satisfies } B_1, B_2\} \text{ for general case} \\ D(L) &= \{\mathrm{y} \in C([a,b]), (py')' \in C([a,b]), \text{y satisfies } B_1, B_2\} \text{ for regular case.} \end{aligned} \tag{5}$$

The adjoint operator, L^*, associated to the operator L verifies $\langle Lf, g\rangle = \langle f, L^* g\rangle, \forall f, g \in \mathcal{H}$ and L is self-adjoint if $L = L^*$. Additionally, the operator L is symmetric if $\langle Lf, g\rangle = \langle f, Lg\rangle, \forall f, g \in D(L)$. For the operator defined for SL problems, one obtains

$$\langle g, Lf\rangle - \langle f, Lg\rangle = [p(f'g - fg')]|_a^b, \forall f, g \in D(L)$$

and the condition $\langle Lf, g\rangle = \langle f, Lg\rangle$ holds if $p(fg' - f'g)|_a^b = 0$ verified in $D(L)$ and the Lagrange identity is expressed by

$$gLf - fLg = [p(fg' - f'g)]', \forall f, g \in D(L).$$

Remark 1. *L for SL problems is the self-adjoint operator if*

$$p(u'v - uv')\big|_a^b = p(b)u'(b)v(b) - p(a)u'(a)v(a) = 0. \tag{6}$$

For example, for $p(b) = p(a)$ and periodic conditions

$$u(a) = u(b) = A, u'(a) = u'(b) = B$$

or antiperiodic conditions

$$u(a) = -u(b) = A, u'(a) = -u'(b) = B$$

the operator L is self-adjoint.

The RSL eigenvalue problem is to find $v \in D(L)$ such that for $Lv + \lambda v = 0$ with λ, the eigenvalue associated with v is the eigenfunction. For RSL problems, all the eigenvalues are real and positive [3–5], and there exists an infinite number of eigenvalues. The sequence of the eigenvalues $(\lambda_n)_n$ is considered such that $\lambda_0 < \lambda_1 < \ldots < \lambda_n < \ldots$ with $\lim_{x\to\infty} \lambda_n = \infty$. For each eigenvalue λ_n, the corresponding eigenfunction v_n is unique up to a constant factor and has exactly $n-1$ zeros in interval (a,b). The set $V = \{(v_n)_n, v_n \in D(L)\}$ is complete in the $D(L)$ space, and the solution of RSL is represented by a generalized Fourier series of the eigenfunction

$$u = \sum_{n=1}^{\infty} c_n v_n(x). \tag{7}$$

2. General Framework of SLPs

In this section, we will mention certain conditions that the functions defining the operator L fulfill for different SL or RSL problems.

A second method to find the solution of a RSL problem, different from the generalized Fourier series development, is described using the Green function and two linear independent solutions. The section ends with the analysis of the Fourier equation with different types of boundary conditions.

Remark 2. *For Sturm–Liouville problems, we consider two types of assumptions that are usually used (see [4])*

General assumptions:

(1) $p(x) \in C([a,b])$, *differentiable in* $x = a$, $p(x) \neq 0\ \forall x \in (a,b]$ *with* $p(a) = 0$, $p'(a) \neq 0$. *For* $p(x) = (x-a)\varphi(x)$, *we suppose* $\varphi \in C([a,b])$, $\varphi(x) \neq 0, \forall x \in [a,b]$

(2) $\rho, f \in C([a,b])$.

RSL assumptions

(1) $p(x) > 0$ *and* $s(x) > 0$ *or* $s \equiv 0$ *on* $[a,b]$;

(2) $p, \rho, s \in C([a,b])$;

(3) $a_1, a_2, b_1, b_2 \in \mathbb{R}$;

(4) p, ρ, s *continuously differentiable on* $[a,b]$.

Known equations, such as Fourier, Graetz–Nusslet, Collatz and Airy equations, for which RSL assumptions are verified, are given in Table 1, and the first eigenvalues and eigenfunctions are depicted in Figures 1 and 2.

Table 1. Examples of regular Sturm–Liouville problems.

Equation	Associated Functions	Name
$-u'' + \lambda u = f, x \in (a,b)$	$p \equiv 1,\ s \equiv 1,\ \rho \equiv 0$	Fourier
$-(xu')' = 2\lambda x(1-x^2)u, x \in (0,1)$	$p(x) = x, s(x) = 2x(1-x^2)$	Graetz–Nusselt
$-x^6u'' + (3/4)x^4u = \lambda u, x \in (1,2)$	$p(x) = x^6, s(x) = \dfrac{3}{4}x^4$	Collatz
$-u'' + xu = \lambda xu, x \in (0,1)$	$p(x) = x, s(x) = 2x(1-x^2)$	Airy

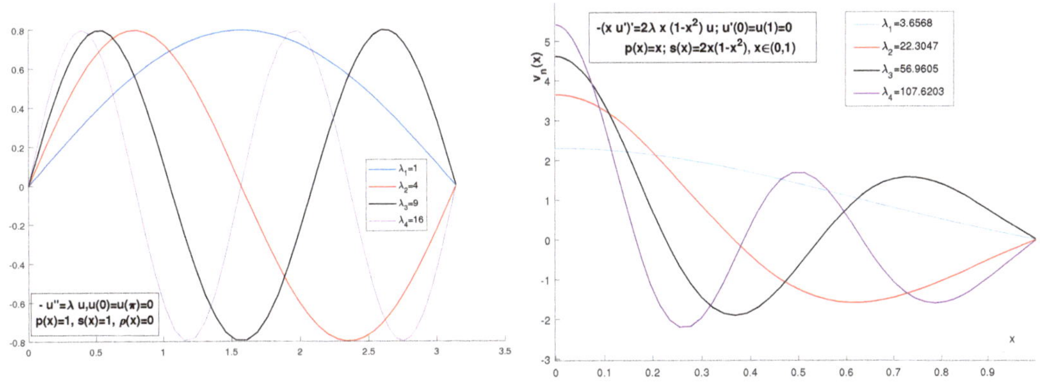

(**a**) Fourier equation, Dirichlet conditions

(**b**) Graetz–Nusselt, Robin conditions

Figure 1. (**a**) Fourier equation; (**b**) Graetz–Nusselt equation.

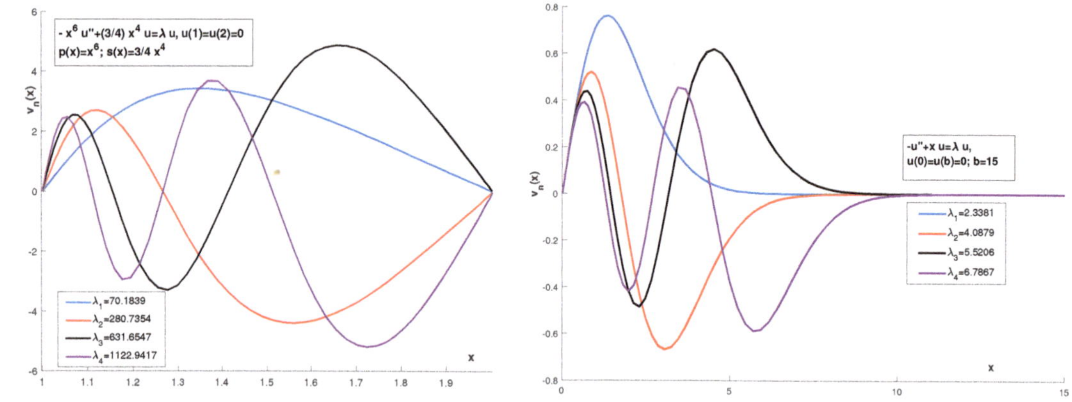

(a) (b)

Figure 2. (**a**) Collatz problem; (**b**) Airy problem.

Some other known equations, such as the Legendre differential equation, Chebysev's differential equation or Bessel equation, must be transformed into the Sturm–Liouville form that we considered in (3). These forms are specified in Table 2. Other SL equations for which general assumptions are fulfilled are exemplified in Table 3.

Table 2. Examples of differential equations and their SL form.

Type	Equation	Sturm–Liouville Form
Legendre	$-u'' - \dfrac{2x}{1-x^2} + \dfrac{\mu}{1-x^2}u = 0,$	$-((1-x^2)u')' + \mu u = 0$
Chebysev	$-(1-x^2)u'' - xu' + n^2u = 0$	$-(\sqrt{1-x^2}u')' = \dfrac{n^2}{\sqrt{1-x^2}}u$
Bessel	$x^2u'' + xu' + (\lambda^2 - n^2)y = 0,$	$-(xu')' + \dfrac{n^2}{x}u = \lambda^2 xu$

Table 3. Examples of Sturm–Liouville problems.

$-(\sin(x)u')' + \cos(x)u = \lambda x^2 u, x \in (0,b)$	$p = \sin(x), \rho = \cos(x)\, s = x^2$
$-(x^2u')' - x\sin(x)u = \lambda xu, x \in (0,b)$	$p = x, s = 2x(1-x^2)$

For an example of a singular SL, a discontinuity on the middle of the interval is considered $[a,b]$, $x_0 = (b-a)/2$, with $\rho(x) \equiv 0$ and $p(x) = \begin{cases} 1, x \in [0, x_0) \\ c^2, x \in [x_0, 1] \end{cases}, c \neq 0, c \neq 1.$

The problem to solve is $Lu + \lambda u = 0$, $u(0) = u(1) = 0$ and with $u(x_{0-}) - u(x_{0+}) = 0$, $u'(x_{0-}) - c^2u'(x_{0+}) = 0$ transmission conditions.

The *asymptotic behavior* of the eigenvalues leads to $\dfrac{\lambda_n}{n^2} \to \left(\dfrac{2\pi c}{1+c}\right)^2$, as $n \to \infty$.

2.1. *Resolvent Operator and Green Function*

This RSL problem is solved using a Green function solution for the resolvent operator $R(\lambda) = (L + \lambda I)^{-1}$ of the form

$$R(\lambda)f = \frac{\varphi_\lambda(x)}{\omega(\lambda)} \int_a^x f(t)\psi_\lambda(t)dt + \frac{\psi_\lambda(x)}{\omega(\lambda)} \int_x^b f(t)\varphi_\lambda(t)dt \quad (8)$$

where ψ_λ, φ_λ are non-trivial classical solutions of $(L+\lambda I)f=0$ which satisfy

$$\begin{aligned} a_1\varphi_\lambda(a)+a_2\varphi'_\lambda(a)=0 \\ b_1\psi_\lambda(b)+b_2\psi'_\lambda(b)=0 \end{aligned} \tag{9}$$

A simple normalization that eliminates some complexity can be specified by requiring

$$\begin{aligned} \varphi_\lambda(a)=a_2, \varphi'_\lambda(a)=-a_1 \\ \psi_\lambda(b)=b_2, \psi'_\lambda(b)=-b_1 \end{aligned} \tag{10}$$

Then, the Wronskian $\omega(\lambda)=v_1(x)v'_2(x)-v'_1(x)v_2(x)$ of these solutions is a function that depends only on λ:

$$\omega(\lambda)=(p\varphi'_\lambda)\psi_\lambda-\varphi_\lambda(p\psi'_\lambda) \tag{11}$$

Therefore, $\omega(\lambda)\neq 0, \forall x\in[a,b]$ or $\omega(\lambda)\equiv 0$. The Wronskian vanishes if $\{\varphi_\lambda,\psi_\lambda\}$ is a dependent set of functions of x, which is precisely when both functions satisfy $(L+\lambda I)h=0$ as well as the specified conditions at $x=a$ and $x=b$, meaning λ is an eigenvalue of L (see [6]).

For the RSL case, the equation $Lu=0$ has two linear independent solutions, v_1 and v_2 such that $a_1v_1(a)+a_2v'_1(a)=0$, $b_1v_2(b)+b_2v'_2(b)=0$, the Green function $G: [a,b]\times[a,b]\to\mathbb{R}$,

$$G(x,y)=\begin{cases} v_1(y)v_2(x)/m, & a\le y\le x\le b \\ -v_1(x)v_2(y)/m, & a\le x\le y\le b \end{cases}, \tag{12}$$

$m=p(x)\omega(\lambda)$ has the properties

(i) $G\in C^1([a,b]^2)$, $G(x,y)=G(y,x)$ and satisfies the boundary conditions according to each variable;

(ii) $G\in C^2([a,b]^2\backslash M)$,with $L_\rho G\equiv -p(x)G_{xx}(x,y)-p'(x)G_x(x,y)+\rho(x)G(x,y)=0$ over $[a,b]^2\backslash M$ and $M=\{(x,y)\mid x=y\}$;

(iii) $G_x(y^+,y)-G_x(y^-,y)=\lim\limits_{\substack{\varepsilon\to 0\\ \varepsilon>0}}[G_x(y+\varepsilon,y)-G_x(y-\varepsilon,y)]=\dfrac{1}{p(x)}$, G_x is discontinuous on M.

Now let T be the operator $Tu(x)=\int_a^b G(x,y)u(y)dy$ defined on $C[a,b]$. Using the properties of the Green function G and the continuity of u, one obtains that $Tu\in C^2[a,b]$ and is the solution of the equation $Lu=f$. The function Tu satisfies the same boundary conditions as $u\in C^2[a,b]$, then $T(Lu)(x)=u(x)$, and T is the inverse operator of L. The problem of eigenvalues and eigenfunctions $Lu+\lambda u=0$, $B_1u(a)=0; B_2u(b)=0$ becomes $Tu=\mu u$, with $\mu=-1/\lambda$. For results for the construction of the operator T for fractional SLPs, see [7,8].

Remark 3 (Rayleigh quotient). *The eigenvalues of the operator L are lower bounded by a real constant. The smallest eigenvalue of the SL eigenvalue problem satisfies*

$$\lambda_0=\min_{\substack{u\neq 0\\ u\in D(L)}}\frac{\langle Lu,u\rangle}{\langle u,u\rangle_s}=\min_{\substack{u\neq 0\\ u\in D(L)}}\frac{-p\,uu'|_a^b+\int_a^b p(u')^2+\rho u^2dx}{\int_a^b u^2s\,dx} \tag{13}$$

and the minimum u_0 is achieved if u_0 is the eigenfunction corresponding to λ_0.

2.2. Sturm–Liouville Fourier Problems

Consider the operator $L=-\frac{d}{dx}\left[p(x)\frac{d}{dx}\right]+\rho(x)$ and nonhomogeneous equation $Lu+\lambda s(x)u=f(x)$ with functions $p(x)$ smooth, $\rho(x)$ positive, and also (i) $p(a)=0$ or $p(b)=0$ or both or (ii) the interval I is infinite. In this section, we study the Fourier problem

$$-u'' + \alpha u = f(x), x \in (a, b), \text{BVP conditions (2) and (3)}$$

with different type of boundary conditions. For example, in the case of Dirichlet conditions $u(a) = u(b) = 0$, the operator $L = -\frac{d^2}{dx^2} + \alpha$ in space $C_0^\infty(I)$ is self-adjoint.

In *Example 1*, we study the case for $\alpha = 0$. Additionally, for the case $\alpha = n^2 > 0$, general solutions of the homogeneous equation are $v_n(x) = A\exp(nx) + B\exp(-nx)$, and for boundary conditions $u(a) = u(b) = 0$, the RSL solution is $v = 0$.

In *Example 2*, for $\alpha < 0$, we consider different cases, shown in Tables 4 and 5.

Table 4. Examples of Sturm–Liouville problems with $a = 0, b > 0, x \in (0, b)$, case 1: $a_1 \cdot a_2 = 0$.

case 1.1a	$a_1 \neq 0, a_2 = 0$	$b_1 \neq 0, b_2 = 0$	$u(0) = 0, u(b) = 0$
case 1.1b	$a_1 \neq 0, a_2 = 0$	$b_1 = 0, b_2 \neq 0$	$u(0) = 0, u'(b) = 0$
case 1.1c	$a_1 \neq 0, a_2 = 0$	$b_1 \neq 0, b_2 \neq 0$	$u(0) = 0, b_1 u(b) + b_2 u'(b) = 0$
case 1.2	$a_1 = 0, a_2 \neq 0$	$b_1 = 0, b_2 \neq 0$	$u'(0) = 0, b_1 u(b) + b_2 u'(b) = 0$

Table 5. Examples of Sturm–Liouville problems with $a = 0, b > 0, x \in (0, b)$, case 2: $a_1 \cdot a_2 \neq 0$.

case 2.1	$a_1 \neq 0, a_2 = -a_1$	$b_1 = 0, b_2 \neq 0$	$u'(0) = 0, b_1 u(b) + b_2 u'(b) = 0$
case 2.2	$a_1 > 0, a_2 = -1$	$b_1 = 0, b_2 \neq 0$	$a_1 u(0) - u'(0) = 0, b_1 u(b) + b_2 u'(b) = 0$

Example 1. *Let us consider the RSL equation $-u''(x) = f(x)$, with general solution $v(x) = mx + n$ for the homogeneous equation and associated Green's function*

$$G(x,y) = \begin{cases} x\,(b-y)/b, 0 \le x \le y \\ y\,(b-x)/b, y \le x \le< b. \end{cases}$$

Using the superposition principle, the solution of the problem defined for $u(0) = A, u'(b) = B$ is $u(x) = v_1(x) + v_2(x)$, $v_1(x) = (b-x)A + xB$ and

$$v_2(x) = \int_0^b G(x,y)f(y)dy = \frac{1}{b}\left[(b-x)\int_0^x yf(y)dy - \int_x^1 y(b-y)f(y)dy\right].$$

Changing the boundary conditions in the previous problem, we now consider

$$-u''(x) = f(x), B_1 : u(0) - u'(0) = 0, B_2 : u(b) + u'(b) = 0.$$

Solving the initial value problem $-u''(x) = f(x), B_1 : u(0) = A, u'(0) = A$, one finds the solution $u(x) = A(1+x) - \int_0^b (x-y)f(y)dy$ and boundary condition B2 leads to $u(x) = \int_0^b G(x,y)f(y)dy$ *with* $G(x,y) = \begin{cases} (1+x)\,(b+1-y)/(b+2), x < y \\ (1+y)\,(b+1-x)/(b+2), y < x. \end{cases}$

Example 2. *For $\alpha = -n^2$ and $a = 0, b = \pi$, general solutions of the equation are $v_n(x) = A\cos(nx) + B\sin(nx)$ with $\lambda_n = n^2$ the eigenvalues and for $u(0) = u(\pi) = 0$ the eigenfunctions are $v_n = \sin(nx)$. The general solution is a Fourier series:*

$$u(x) = \sum_{n=1}^{\infty} B_n \sin(nx), B_n = \frac{\langle f(x), \sin(nx)\rangle}{\langle \sin(nx), \sin(nx)\rangle} = \frac{2}{\pi}\int_0^\pi f(x)\sin(nx)dx \quad (14)$$

Case 1.1

According to Table 4, for cases 1.1, we consider $a_2 = 0$ *and* B_1 *is* $u(0) = 0$ *and the eigenfunctions* $v_n = \sin(\sqrt{\lambda_n} x)$. *The eigenvalues corresponding to cases 1.1a and 1.1b are* $\lambda_n = \left(\frac{n\pi}{b}\right)^2$ *and* $\lambda_n = \left(\frac{(2n+1)\pi}{2b}\right)^2$, *respectively. For problems P1c*

$$P1_c : -u''(x) = \lambda u + f(x) \text{ in } (0,b); u(0) = 0, b_1 u(b) + b_2 u'(b) = 0 \tag{15}$$

the general solution is $u(x) = \sum_{n=1}^{\infty} c_n v_n(x)$ *with the eigenvalues determined by the equation* $\tan(\sqrt{\lambda_n} b) = -\frac{b_2}{b_1}\sqrt{\lambda_n}$. *The determination of the first eigenvalues is graphically presented in Figure 3.*

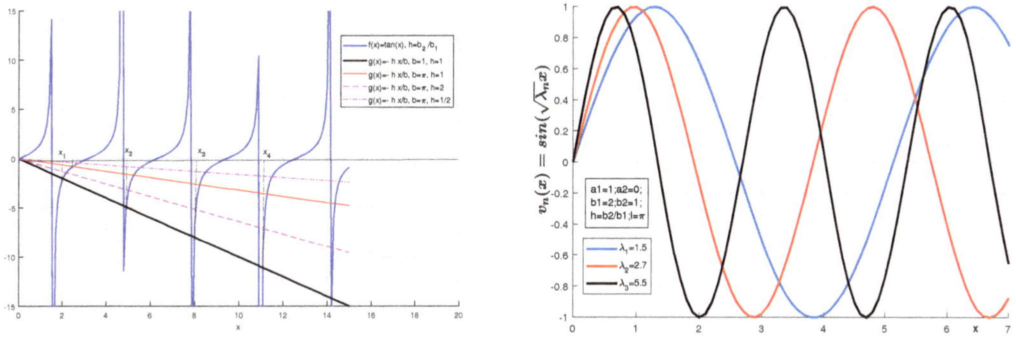

(**a**) Eigenvalues determination (**b**) The first corresponding eigenfunctions

Figure 3. The eigenvalues determination and the corresponding eigenfunctions example (15).

Case 1.2

The eigenfunctions corresponding to case 1.2 are $v_n = \cos(\sqrt{\lambda_n} x)$ *with the eigenvalues determined by the equation* $\tan(\sqrt{\lambda_n} b) = \frac{b_1}{b_2\sqrt{\lambda_n}}$.

Case 2

The eigenfunctions corresponding to case 2.1 are $v_n = \sqrt{\lambda_n}\cos(\sqrt{\lambda_n} x) + \sin(\sqrt{\lambda_n} x)$ *with the eigenvalues determined by the equation* $\tan(\sqrt{\lambda_n} b) = -\frac{(b_1+b_2)\sqrt{\lambda_n}}{b_1 - b_2\sqrt{\lambda_n}}$. *If b has the form* $\frac{(2n+1)\pi}{2}\cdot\frac{b_2}{b_1}$, *then* $\lambda_n = \frac{b_1}{b_2}$ *is the eigenvalue for the problem. In Figure 4a, the determination of the first eigenvalues is graphically presented as the roots of the function* $\tan(x) + \frac{(b_1+b_2)x}{b_1 b - b_2 x}$ *with notation* $x = \sqrt{\lambda_n} b$ *and in Figure 4b, the corresponding eigenfunctions are plotted.*

For case 2.2, the eigenfunctions are $v_n = \frac{\sqrt{\lambda_n}}{a_1}\cos(\sqrt{\lambda_n} x) + \sin(\sqrt{\lambda_n})$, *and the eigenvalues are the solutions of the nonlinear equation* $\tan(\sqrt{\lambda_n} b) = \frac{(a_1 - b_1)\sqrt{\lambda_n}}{a_1 + \sqrt{\lambda_n}}$.

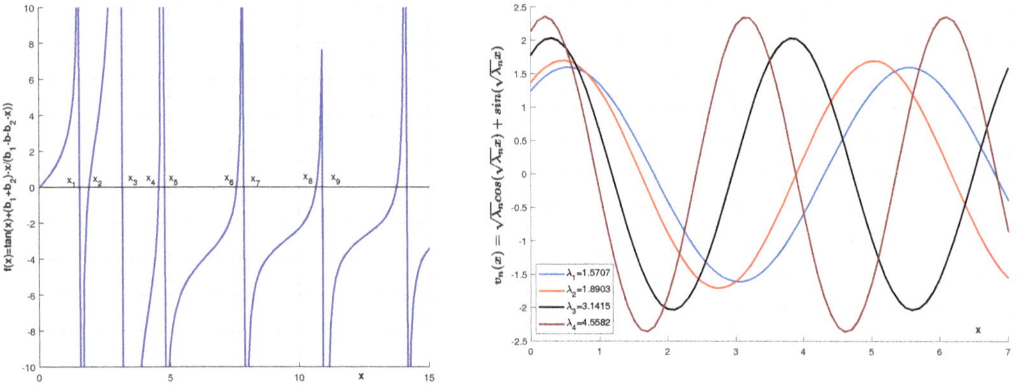

(**a**) Eigenvalues determination

(**b**) The first corresponding eigenfunctions

Figure 4. The eigenvalues determination and the corresponding eigenfunctions example 2.1.

Example 3. *The conditions can be considerably weakened with respect to continuity and differentiability. In some cases, changes of variables, dependent and independent, may transform a problem from singular to regular; see [4].*

For construction of the solutions, the Dirac function is used. Green's function verifies $-\frac{d}{dx}\left[p(x)\frac{dG(x,y)}{dx}\right] + \rho(x)G(x,y) = \delta(x-y)$, *and expresses the response under homogeneous boundary conditions to a forcing function consisting of a concentrated unit of inhomogeneity at* $x = y$.

For the problem $-u''(x) = \lambda u(x) + f(x)$ *in* $(0,b)$; $u(0) = u(b) = 0$, $\lambda = n^2$, *the solution is* $u(x) = \int_0^b G(x,y)f(y)dy$ *using the Green function*

$$G(x,y) = \begin{cases} \dfrac{\sin(nx)\sin(n(b-y))}{n\sin(nb)}, 0 \le x < y \\ -\dfrac{\sin(n(b-x))\sin(ny)}{n\sin(nb)}, y < x \le b. \end{cases}$$

That leads to the representation

$$u(x) = \frac{\sin(nx)}{n\sin(nb)}\int_0^x \sin(n(b-y))f(y)dy - \frac{\sin(n(b-x))}{n\sin(nb)}\int_x^b \sin(ny)f(y)dy.$$

Remark 4. *Using the definition of the norm convergence, namely: "A sequence* $(\varphi_n)_n$ *in* $\mathcal{L}_s^2(I)$ *converges to* $\varphi \in \mathcal{L}_s^2(I)$ *if* $\lim_{n\to\infty}\|\varphi_n - \varphi\|_s = 0$, *i.e.,* $\varphi_n \to \varphi$ *in* $\mathcal{L}_s^2$ *norm", some sequences* $\delta_n(x)$ *could be used instead of* $\delta(x)$ *in order to obtain the Green function.*

Starting from the definition $\delta(x-y) = \begin{cases} 0, x \ne y \\ \infty, x = y \end{cases}$ *and use some properties (see [6,9]):*

δ *is symmetric with* $\delta(ax) = -\frac{1}{|a|}\delta(x)$, $\delta(x) = \lim_{n\to\infty}\delta_n(x)$, $\delta_n(x) = \frac{n}{\sqrt{\pi}}e^{-n^2x^2}$, $\delta_n(x) = \frac{\sin^2(nx)}{n\pi x^2}$ *or* $\delta_n(x) = \frac{n}{\pi(1+n^2x^2)}$, *also*

$$\delta\left(x^2 - a^2\right) = \frac{1}{|2a|}[\delta(x+a) + \delta(x-a)] \text{ and } \int_{-\infty}^{+\infty} f(y)\delta(x-y)dx = f(x).$$

3. Variational RSL Problems

We define problem P_1 as follows:

$$-(pu')' + \rho u + \lambda s u = f,\ \text{on } (a,b) \tag{16}$$
$$B_1 u(a) : a_1 u(a) + a_2 u'(a) = 0 \tag{17}$$
$$B_2 u(b) : b_1 u(b) + b_2 u'(b) = 0$$

and the set $V = \{v \in C^1([a,b]), v' \text{ piecewise continuous on } [a,b], B_1 v(a), B_2 v(b) \text{verified}\}$.
For $v \in D(L)$, we have $\int_a^b pu'v'dx + \int_a^b (\rho + \lambda s)uvdx = \int_a^b fvdx,\ \forall v \in V$ (see [10,11]).

Variational problem (VP$_1$) associated to the problem $P1$ is as follows: find $u \in V$ such that $a(u,v) = l\,v, \forall v \in V$ with

$$a(u,v) = \int_a^b pu'v' + (\rho + \lambda s)uv\,dx\,, \forall u, v \in V;\ l\,v = \int_a^b fv\,dx, \forall v \in V. \tag{18}$$

The functional $F : V \to \mathbb{R}$, $Fv = \frac{1}{2}a(u,v) - lv$, $\forall v \in V$ expresses the difference between the internal elastic energy and the load potential.

Lemma 1.

(i) *$l : V \to \mathbb{R}$ is linear;*

(ii) *Let $a : V \times V \to \mathbb{R}$ with λ positive eigenvalue of RSL (P_1), then $a(u,v)$ is bilinear functional, positive and symmetric.*

Proof. (i) Let $v_1, v_2 \in V$ and $\alpha, \beta \in \mathbb{R}$, then $l(\alpha v_1 + \beta v_2) = \alpha\, l v_1 + \beta\, l v_2$ is the result that is obtained from the properties of the scalar product.

(ii) Let $u_1, u_2, v \in V$ and $\alpha, \beta \in \mathbb{R}$ then

$$\begin{aligned} a(\alpha u_1 + \beta u_2, v) &= \int_a^b p(\alpha u_1 + \beta u_2)'v' + (\rho + \lambda s)(\alpha u_1 + \beta u_2)vdx \\ &= \alpha \int_a^b pu_1'v' + (\rho + \lambda s)u_1 vdx + \beta \int_a^b pu_2'v' + (\rho + \lambda s)u_2 vdx \\ &= \alpha\, a(u_1, v) + \beta\, a(u_2, v) \end{aligned}$$

Let $u, v_1, v_2 \in V$ and $\alpha, \beta \in \mathbb{R}$, then

$$\begin{aligned} a(u, \alpha v_1 + \beta v_2) &= \int_a^b pu'(\alpha v_1 + \beta v_2)' + (\rho - \lambda s)u(\alpha v_1 + \beta v_2)dx \\ &= \alpha \int_a^b pu'v_1' + (\rho + \lambda s)uv_1 dx + \beta \int_a^b pu'v_2 + (\rho + \lambda s)uv_2 dx \\ &= \alpha\, a(u, v_1) + \beta\, a(u, v_2) \end{aligned}$$

Let $u \in V$, then

$$a(u,u) = \int_a^b p(u')^2 + (\rho + \lambda s)u^2 dx = p\int_a^b (u')^2 dx + \int_a^b (\rho + \lambda s)u^2 dx$$

The weight function $p(x)$ in $[a,b]$ is positive and in RSL(P_1) conditions, $\rho + \lambda s$ is a positive function in $[a,b]$ accordingly $a(u,u) \geq 0$, $\forall u \in V$, and hence $a(\cdot,\cdot)$ is positive. Let $u, v \in V$, then

$$a(u,v) = \int_a^b p\,u'v' + (\rho + \lambda s)\,uv\,dx = a(v,u)$$

Consequently, $a(\cdot,\cdot)$ is symmetric. □

Minimization problem (MP_1) associated to (VP_1) is as follows.
Find $u \in V$ such that $Fu = \min_{v \in V} Fv$ with

$$Fv = \frac{1}{2}\int_a^b p(v')^2 + (\rho + \lambda s)v^2 dx - \int_a^b fv\,dx \tag{19}$$

Theorem 1.

(1) *$u \in V$ is the solution of (VP_1) if u is solution of (MP_1);*
(2) *$u \in \mathcal{H} = C^1([a,b]) \cap C^2((a,b))$, u solution of (VP_1), then u solution of (P_1).*

Proof. *(1)* (i) Let $u \in V$ be the solution of (VP_1), then $a(u,v) = lv, \forall v \in V$. For any $w \in V$, denoting $v = w - u \in V$, we have

$$\begin{aligned} Fw - Fu &= \frac{1}{2}a(u+v,u+v) - l(u+v) - Fu \\ &= Fu + Fv + a(u,v) - Fu = a(u,v) + F(v) \\ &= a(u,v) - lv + lu + F(v) = \frac{1}{2}a(v,v) \geq 0 \end{aligned}$$

meaning that

$$Fu = \min_{w \in V} Fw \text{ i.e. } u \text{ solution of } (MP_1)$$

(1) (ii) Let $u \in V$ be the solution of (MP_1), then $Fu = \min_{w \in V} Fw$; therefore, $Fw - Fu \geq 0, \forall w \in V$.

Using $w = u + tv$, $t \in \mathbb{R}$, one finds $F(u+tv) - Fu \geq 0, \forall t \in \mathbb{R}$ meaning

$$\frac{1}{2}a(u+tv,u+tv) - l(u+tv) - \frac{1}{2}a(u,u) + lu \geq 0, \forall t \in \mathbb{R}, \forall u,v \in V$$

$$\frac{1}{2}a(u,u) + t\,a(u,v) + \frac{t^2}{2}a(v,v) - lu - t\,lv - \frac{1}{2}a(u,u) + lu \geq 0,\ \forall t \in \mathbb{R}, \forall u,v \in V$$

$$\left[\frac{1}{2}a(v,v)\right]t^2 + [a(u,v) - lv]t \geq 0\,\forall t \in \mathbb{R}$$

Using the positivity of the term $a(v,v)$, one finds

$$[a(u,v) - lv]^2 \leq 0 \quad \Rightarrow \quad a(u,v) = lv \quad \forall v \in V$$

meaning the u solution of (VP_1).

(2) Let $u \in V \cap \mathcal{H}$ solution of (VP_1), then

$$\begin{aligned} &\int_a^b pu'v' + (\rho + \lambda s)uv\,dx = \int_a^b fv\,dx \\ &\int_a^b pu'v'\,dx + \int_a^b (\rho + \lambda s)uv\,dx = \int_a^b fv\,dx \\ &(pu')v\big|_a^b - \int_a^b (pu')'v\,dx + \int_a^b (\rho + \lambda s)uv\,dx = \int_a^b fv\,dx \\ &(pu')v\big|_a^b + \int_a^b \left[-(pu')' + (\rho + \lambda s)u - f\right]v\,dx = 0,\ \forall v \in V \end{aligned}$$

In case of a self-adjoint operator for L, such as in the case of periodic or antiperiodic boundary conditions, we have

$$(pu')v\big|_a^b = p(b)u'(b)v(b) - p(a)u'(a)v(a) = 0,\ \forall u,v \in V$$

and one obtains $\int_a^b \varphi v\, dx = 0, \forall v \in V$ for $\varphi(x) = -(pu')' + (\rho + \lambda s)u \in C(a,b)$ that is $\varphi \equiv 0$ over interval (a,b).

This means that the u solution of P_1 also verifies the boundary conditions. □

The theorem proved above transfers the search space of the solution u of the problem P_1 to the search space for the solution of the problem MP_1, where the existence is ensured through the Lax–Milgram theorem for a coercive quadratic form, even more general from the Lions–Stampacchia theorem, where $a(\cdot,\cdot)$ is of a symmetric positive bilinear form.

4. Variational Approaches for VP of RSL

4.1. Nehari Variational Method

Let $u \in C^2([a,b])$ and $F : [a,b] \times C^2([a,b]) \times C([a,b]) \to [a,b]$ be a function that has continuous second-order derivatives with respect to all of its arguments. According to the Euler–Lagrange variational principle, a necessary condition for the functional

$$J(u) = \int_a^b F(x,u,u')dx, \tag{20}$$

to be stationary at u is that u is a solution of the Euler–Lagrange equation (see [3])

$$\frac{\partial F}{\partial u} - \frac{d}{dx}\left(\frac{\partial F}{\partial u'}\right) = 0, \quad a \le x \le b \tag{21}$$

with the Dirichlet conditions $u(a) = A$ and $u(b) = B$.

For a nonlinear RSL problem,

$$-u'' = f(x,u^2), f \in \mathcal{H}, x \in (a,b) = I; u(a) = A \text{ and } u(b) = B, \tag{22}$$

for $\mathcal{H} = \{f \in C([a,b] \times [0,\infty]) | f \text{verifies (ip1), (ip2) and boundary conditions}\}$.

$$\begin{aligned}&(\text{ip1}) : f(x,y) > 0 \text{for } y > 0\\ &(\text{ip2}) : \exists v, y^{-v} f(x,y) \text{ is a non-decreasing function of} y \in [0,\infty)\end{aligned}$$

For the problem (22), looking for the extremum value of the functional

$$J(u) = \int_a^b \left[(u')^2 - \int_0^{u^2(x)} (f(x,y)dy)\right] dx, \tag{23}$$

for the set $V_{a,b} = \{u | u \in C([a,b]), u' \text{piecewise continuous in} [a,b], u(a) = u(b) = 0\}$ the functional $J(u)$ is not bounded. Using the Nehari method, a new condition on the function f and u is imposed:

$$\int_a^b (u')^2 dx = \int_a^b u^2 f(x,u^2)dx, \tag{24}$$

which is satisfied by the solutions of (22).

Let us consider the set $\mathcal{V}_{a,b} = \{u | u \in V_{a,b} \text{verifies (24)}\}$. For I given, let $\mu(a,b) = \inf_{u \in V} J(u)$. Then $\exists u \in \mathcal{V}_{a,b}$ such that $J(u) = \mu(a,b)$ and also (see [12]),

for $u \in \mathcal{V}_{a,b}$ with $J(u) = \mu(a,b)$, $w = |u| \in \mathcal{V}_{a,b}$ is a positive solution of (22).

The function $\mu(a,b)$ is continuous with respect to both arguments and

$$\mu(a,b) = \inf_{c<d \in [a,b]} \mu(c,d) \text{ with } \lim_{b \to a} \mu(a,b) = \infty. \tag{25}$$

Remark 5. *For a partition $\Delta_n : a = x_0 < x_1 < \cdots < x_{n-1} < x_n = b$ of the interval I, over each subinterval $[x_i; x_{i+1}]$, consider $u_i \in \mathcal{V}_{x_i,x_{i+1}}$ normalized with the Nehari condition and*

$$\text{For } x \in [x_i; x_{i+1}] : u(x) = (-1)^i |u_i(x)|, J(u) = \mu_{n-1}(x_1, x_2, \ldots, x_{n-1}) \tag{26}$$

$$\text{For } \Delta_n \text{ given} : \mu_{n-1}(x_1, x_2, \ldots, x_{n-1}) = \sum_{i=1}^{n} \mu(x_{i-1}, x_i), \tag{27}$$

then the solution $u(x)$ is in $V_{a,b}$ and is vanishing $n-1$ times over interval I. Additionally, if $|u'_k(x_k)| \neq |u'_{k+1}(x_k)|$ then $\mu_{n-1}(x_1, x_2, \ldots, x_{n-1})$ is not a minimum of $\sum_{i=1}^{n} \mu(x_{i-1}, x_i)$.

4.2. Variational Estimations for RSL

In the following, two variational estimation methods are presented, the shooting method and bisection method, consisting in solving the variational equations associated to the problem given.

Shooting method:

$$(P_2) \begin{cases} -(pu')' + (q + \lambda s)u = 0, & x \in [a, b] \\ u(a) = 0, u(b) = 0 \end{cases} \tag{28}$$

For λ eigenvalue and $u_\lambda(x)$, the corresponding eigenfunction $u_\lambda(a) \neq 0$ and $y = \dfrac{u_\lambda}{u'_\lambda(a)}$ is the normalized eigenfunction with $y'(a) = 1$, which is the solution for the variational equation associated to (28) with the initial value conditions:

$$(VIP) \begin{cases} -(py')' + (q + \lambda s)y = 0, & x \in [a, b] \\ y(a) = 0, y'(a) = 1 \end{cases} \tag{29}$$

with $y(b) = 0$ (see [4]).

Algorithm of the shooting method:

Step 1 Determine an interval of an eigenvalue and make a guess;
Step 2 Solve VIP (P_2) and find the eigenfunction $u = u_\lambda(x)$;
Step 3 If $u_\lambda(b) = 0$ or $|u_\lambda(b)| < \varepsilon$ given, then Stop.
Else, find λ the root of $u_\lambda(b) = 0$ in a given interval and update λ.
GO TO Step 1.

Bisection method

For SL eigenvalue problem (P_3) with functions and constants satisfying RSL assumptions (1)–(4):

$$(P_3) \begin{cases} -(pu')' + (q + \lambda s)u = 0, & x \in [a, b] \\ B_1u(a) : a_1u(a) + a_2u'(a) = 0 \\ B_2u(b) : b_1u(b) + b_2u'(b) = 0 \end{cases} \tag{30}$$

the related variational initial value problem VIP_3 is

$$(VIP_3) \begin{cases} -(pu')' + (q + \lambda s)u = 0,, & x \in [a, b] \\ u(a) = -\dfrac{a_2}{\sqrt{a_1^2 + a_2^2}};\ u'(a) = \dfrac{a_1}{\sqrt{a_1^2 + a_2^2}} \end{cases} \tag{31}$$

For the eigenvalue λ denoting u_λ, the corresponding eigenfunction has $u_\lambda(0) \neq 0$, and $y = u_\lambda$ is the normalized u_λ eigenfunction such that $a_1y(a) + a_2y'(a) = 0$. In this case, λ is the eigenvalue for P_3 if $F(\lambda) := B_2y(b) = b_1y(b) + b_2y'(b) = 0$.

The function $w_\lambda(x) = \dfrac{\partial u_\lambda}{\partial \lambda}$ satisfies the variational initial value problem $(VIVP_3)$.

$$(VIVP_3)\begin{cases} -(pw')' + (q+\lambda s)w + sw = 0 \\ w(a) = 0,\ w'(a) = 0 \end{cases} \tag{32}$$

and $F(\lambda) = b_1 u_\lambda(b) + b_2 u'_\lambda(b)$ is a continuously differentiable function on λ with $F'(\lambda) = b_1 w_\lambda(b) + b_2 w'_\lambda(b) \neq 0$.

Remark 6. *Under RSL assumptions (1)–(4), if λ is the eigenvalue of (P_3) and $y = u_\lambda$ is the corresponding normalized eigenfunction, then there exists $(\lambda_{\inf}, \lambda_{\sup})$ containing λ such that $F(\lambda_{\inf})F(\lambda_{\sup}) < 0$ and the approximate sequence $(\lambda_n)_n$ is convergent, $\lambda_n \to \lambda$ and $y_n = u_{\lambda_n}$ are the corresponding eigenfunctions obtained by solving $(VIVP_3)$ such that $y_n \to y$ and $y'_n \to y'$.*

For instance, the solution of the problem

$$(EP_3)\begin{cases} -(p(x)u')' + \rho u(x) = f(x), & x \in (0,1) \\ u(0) = 0,\ u(1) = 0 \end{cases} \tag{33}$$

with $p, \rho, f \in C([0,1])$ verifying (RSL) conditions (1)–(4) is obtained solving the associated

$$(VI-EP_3)\begin{cases} -(py')' + \rho y = f(x), & x \in (0,1) \\ y(0) = 0,\ y(1) = s \end{cases} \tag{34}$$

The solution of (EP_3) is determined such that $u_s(x) = u_p(x) + sv(x)$ with $u_s(1) = 0$ and u_p is a particular solution of $Ly = f$ and v satisfies

$$Lv = 0,\ v(0) = 0;\ v'(0) = 1.$$

4.3. Iterative Variational Methods for RSL

Among analytical estimation methods, the variational iteration method (VIM or He's methods, see [13]) and homotopy perturbation method (HPM) (see [14,15]) are considered to find approximations for the nonlinear equation

$$Lu + \lambda s(x)u = f(x, u, u'),\ x \in (a,b) = I, \lambda \in \mathbb{R}, \tag{35}$$

under different boundary conditions (Dirichlet, Neumann or general case $B_1u(a), B_2u(b)$).

4.3.1. He's Variational Method (VIM)

For the nonlinear Equation (35), we define N as the nonlinear operator such that (35) becomes

$$Lu + Nu = g(x),\ x \in (a,b) = I, \tag{36}$$

and the correction functional for the general Lagrange multiplier method is

$$u_{n+1}(x) = u_n(x) + \int_0^x \mu(t,x,\lambda)[Lu_n(t) + N\tilde{u}_n(t) - g(t)]dt, \tag{37}$$

with $\tilde{u}_n$ considered as restricted variation, $\delta\tilde{u}_n = 0$, and $\mu(t,x,\lambda)$ a Lagrange multiplier determined through the calculus of variations from (37); see [10,16].

$$\delta u_{n+1}(x) = \delta u_n(x) + \delta\int_0^x \mu(t,x,\lambda)[Lu_n(t) + N\tilde{u}_n(t) - g(t)]dt. \tag{38}$$

4.3.2. Homotopy Perturbation Method (HPM)

For the nonlinear Equation (35) we define the operators $\mathcal{L}$ and N for $q \in [0,1]$

$$\mathcal{L}[\Phi(x,q)] = -\frac{d}{dx}\left[p(x)\frac{d}{dx}\Phi(x,q)\right], \tag{39}$$

$$N[\Phi(x,q)] = -\frac{d}{dx}\left[p(x)\frac{d}{dx}\Phi(x,q)\right] + (\rho+\lambda s)(x)\Phi(x,q) - f(x,\Phi(x,q),\Phi_x(x,q)), \tag{40}$$

given by the maximum order of derivation from the equation and by the form of the equation; see [14,17]. We write the zero-order equation associated with the initial equation:

$$(1-q)\mathcal{L}[\Phi(x,q) - u_0(x)] = hqN[\Phi(x,q)] \tag{41}$$

with h as a nonzero parameter, u_0 as a first analytical approximation of the function u with conditions

$$\Phi(x,0) = u_0(x); \quad \Phi(x,1) = u(x), x \in [a,b]. \tag{42}$$

where u_0 is a initial function that verifies the boundary conditions $B_1u(a) : a_1u(a) + a_2u'(a) = 0$, $B_2u(b) : b_1u(b) + b_2u'(b) = 0$ could be obtained from polynomial approximation developing the function f.

We develop $\Phi(x,q)$ by a Taylor series in the vicinity of the origin in relation to the second variable

$$\Phi(x,q) = u_0(x) + \sum_{1}^{\infty} u_m(x)q^m; u_m(x) = \frac{1}{m!}\frac{\partial^m \Phi}{\partial x^m}(x,q)\bigg|_{q=0} \tag{43}$$

A good choice for h (in relation to the error obtained compared to the initial equation) leads to $u(x) = u_0(x) + \sum_{m=1}^{\infty} u_m(x)$.

The equation of order m:

case $m = 1 \rightarrow \mathcal{L}[u_m(x)] = hN[u_{m-1}]$
case $m \geq 2 \rightarrow \mathcal{L}[f_m(x) - f_{m-1}(x)] = hN[u_{m-1}]$

with boundary conditions $B_1u_m(a), B_2u_m(b)$.

For the approximation of order 1, we have

$$-[p(x)u_1'(x)]' = h\underbrace{\left\{-[p(x)u_0'(x)]' + (\rho(x)+\lambda s(x))u_0(x) - f(x,u_0(x),u_0'(x))\right\}}_{\varepsilon_0(x)} \tag{44}$$

with $\varepsilon_1(x,h) = N[u_1(x)]$.

The parameter h at step 1 is chosen such that the value of $\max_{x\in I}|\varepsilon_1(x,h)|$ is the smallest possible and becomes the next value of ε_1, but also could be taken as $h = 1$. Iteratively, for $m \geq 2$

$$Lu_m + \lambda s(x)u_m = f(x,u_{m-1},u'_{m-1}),\ x \in I;\ B_1u_m(a), B_2u_m(b) \tag{45}$$

with start condition u_0 being known and stop condition $\max_x|u_m - u_{m-1}| < \epsilon$.

4.3.3. Applications

Let us consider a nonlinear RSL, such as the following problem:

$$-u''(x) + \lambda u(x) = f(x,u,u'), x \in [0,b];\ B_1u(0), B_2u(b). \tag{46}$$

The corresponding correction functional (37) to the problem (46) for the variational iteration method leads to the general Lagrange multiplier

$$\text{for } \lambda > 0, \mu(t,x,\lambda) = \frac{1}{2\alpha}\left(e^{\alpha(t-x)} - e^{\alpha(x-t)}\right) = \frac{1}{\alpha}\sinh\alpha(t-x), \alpha = \sqrt{\lambda} \quad (47)$$

$$\text{for } \lambda < 0, \mu(t,x,\lambda) = -\frac{1}{\alpha}\sin\alpha(t-x), \alpha = \sqrt{-\lambda} \quad (48)$$

and for $f(x,u,u') = g(x)$, one finds

$$u_{n+1}(x) = u_n(x) + \frac{1}{\alpha}\int_0^x \sinh\alpha(t-x)\left[-u_n''(t) + \alpha^2 u_n(t) - g(t)\right]dt, \lambda > 0, \quad (49)$$

$$u_{n+1}(x) = u_n(x) - \frac{1}{\alpha}\int_0^x \sin\alpha(t-x)\left[-u_n''(t) + \alpha^2 u_n(t) - g(t)\right]dt, \lambda < 0 \quad (50)$$

with $u_0(x) = A + Bx$. Particularly, for $g(x) = x$, the first step leads to

$$u_1(x) = u_0(x) + \frac{1}{\alpha}\int_0^x \sinh\alpha(t-x)[\lambda A + (\lambda B - 1)t]dt, \lambda = \alpha^2, \quad (51)$$

$$u_1(x) = u_0(x) - \frac{1}{\alpha}\int_0^x \sin\alpha(t-x)[\lambda A + (\lambda B - 1)t]dt, \lambda = -\alpha^2 \quad (52)$$

from where

$$u_1(x) = 2A + 2Bx + \frac{\alpha^2 B - 1}{\alpha^3}\sinh(\alpha x) - A\cosh(\alpha x) - \frac{x}{\alpha^2}, \lambda = \alpha^2, \quad (53)$$

$$u_1(x) = 2A + \frac{\alpha^2 B - 1}{\alpha^3}\sin(\alpha x) - A\cos(\alpha x) + \frac{x}{\alpha^2}, \lambda = -\alpha^2, \quad (54)$$

For $n > 1$, we have

$$u_{n+1}(x) = u_n(x) + \frac{1}{\alpha}\int_0^x \sinh\alpha(t-x)\left[-u_n''(t) + \alpha^2 u_n(t) - t\right]dt, \lambda > 0, \quad (55)$$

$$u_{n+1}(x) = u_n(x) - \frac{1}{\alpha}\int_0^x \sin\alpha(t-x)\left[-u_n''(t) + \alpha^2 u_n(t) - t\right]dt, \lambda < 0 \quad (56)$$

Constants A and B are determined from the boundary condition imposed to the last function u_n computed, and for $u(x) = u_n(x)$, boundary conditions are imposed, resulting in a system for the constants A, B. Thus, the solution of the problem is obtained.

In the case of using HPM, Equation (44), with $\lambda = \alpha^2$, for the first step becomes

$$-u_1''(x) = h(-u_0''(x) + \lambda u_0(x) - x) = h\varepsilon_0(x) \quad (57)$$

and for case $m \geq 2$

$$-[u_m'' - u_{m-1}''](x) = h(-u_{m-1}''(x) + \lambda u_{m-1}(x) - x) = \varepsilon_m(x,h). \quad (58)$$

One obtains

$$u_1(x) = -h\left(\frac{\lambda A x^2}{2} + \frac{(\lambda B - 1)x^3}{3}\right), \quad (59)$$

$$u_2'' = h(1-h)(\lambda A + (\lambda B - 1)x) + hx - h^2\left(\frac{\lambda^2 A x^2}{2} + \lambda\frac{(\lambda B - 1)x^3}{3}\right) = -\varepsilon_1(x,h). \quad (60)$$

from where

$$u_2 = h(1-h)(\lambda A\frac{x^2}{2} + (\lambda B - 1)\frac{x^3}{6}) + h\frac{x^3}{6} - h^2\left(\frac{\lambda^2 A x^4}{24} + \lambda\frac{(\lambda B - 1)x^5}{603}\right). \quad (61)$$

The solution will be $u(x) = u_0(x) + u_1(x) + u_2(x) + \dots$.

Additionally, if we consider the nonlinearity in (46) through function $f(x,u,u') = g(x)u$, that is, for $g(x) = -x^2$, $x \in (-l,l)$ we are in the harmonic oscillator case ($\lambda < 0$), then the following correction functional appears

$$u_{n+1}(x) = u_n(x) + \frac{1}{\alpha}\int_0^x \sinh\alpha(t-x)\Big[-u_n''(t) + (\alpha^2 - g(t))u_n(t)\Big]dt, \lambda > 0, \quad (62)$$

$$u_{n+1}(x) = u_n(x) - \frac{1}{\alpha}\int_0^x \sin\alpha(t-x)\Big[-u_n''(t) + (\alpha^2 - g(t))u_n(t)\Big]dt, \lambda < 0 \quad (63)$$

as an eigenfunction of the equation Hermite polynomials appears.

For $B_1u(-l) : u(-l) = 0; B_2u(-l) : u(l) = 0$ and ($\lambda < 0$)

$$u_1(x) = A + Bx - \frac{1}{\alpha}\int_0^x \sin\alpha(t-x)\Big[t^2(A+Bt) + \alpha^2(A+Bt)\Big]dt, \quad (64)$$

$$u_{n+1}(x) = u_n(x) - \frac{1}{\alpha}\int_0^x \sin\alpha(t-x)\Big[-u_n''(t) + (\alpha^2 + t^2)u_n(t)\Big]dt, \quad (65)$$

$$-u_1''(x) = h\Big(-u_0''(x) + (x^2 + \alpha^2)u_0(x)\Big) = h\varepsilon_0(x) \quad (66)$$

and for case $m \geq 2$

$$-\big[u_m'' - u_{m-1}''\big](x) = h\Big(-u_{m-1}''(x) + (x^2 + \alpha^2)u_{m-1}(x)\Big) = \varepsilon_m(x,h). \quad (67)$$

The two methods are fast convergent methods.

Variational iteration methods, such as VIM and HPM, could be used also for nonlinear propagation problems in which the temporal variable is considered, for example, for the coupled pseudo-parabolic equation, or the one-dimensional coupled Burgers equation numerically studied in [18]. The nonlinear coupled Burgers equations are also studied in [19] as an application of EOHAM (extension optimal homotopy asymptotic method) in which homotopy is combined with perturbation techniques. The Newell–Whitehead–Segel equation (NWSE) was also studied using the VIM technique and He's polynomials [20].

5. Conclusions

In the first part of the paper, definitions and results are presented connected to regular and singular Sturm–Liouville problems. Some types of direct singular SLPs were solved in [5,21] and a study of the inverse SLP algorithm was made. We defined in a different manner the SLP, and different boundary conditions were considered. All the figures were made using Matlab codes, the academic versions.

In the core of the paper, the variational formulation (VP) through a bilinear functional positive and symmetric is made. The minimization problem (MP) is also outlined through the functional of energy, and the equivalence of the formulations under some conditions imposed for RSL problems is proved.

Variational estimations are in the final part of the paper through the construction of the solution trough variational equations associated to the problem, such as the shooting method and bisection method, or using a sequential analytical approximate solution that is constructed according to the accuracy established. Here, we present He's variational method and the homotopy method. In the closing part, a is taken into account and the sequentiality of the transition from one step to another is specified for both methods. Al-Khaled et al. (see [22]) solve numerically a SLP using the general Sinc–Galerkin and Newton method but for different types of boundary conditions. In the paper, He's method, the Adomian method and Lagrange multiplier for special ODEs were given in detail, numerical results being obtained for Duffing and Titchmarch equations. We considered our applications the interval $(0,b)$ and general conditions $B_1u(0), B_2u(b)$ for a linear and a nonlinear case of $f(x,u,u')$.

In [23] spectral problems of the nonlocal SLP with an integral $B_2u(b)$ were studied. Kernel of the operator, properties of the first eigenvalue and oscillation properties of eigenfunctions to the nonlocal problem were expressed. Additionally, the solution of the Cauchy problem for the SL equation on a star graph was constructed in [24].

For fractional differential equations, VIM could also be a very powerful instrument, in which Equations (36) and (37) are written using the Caputo fractional derivative, see [25]. This is our intention for the new study.

Nonlinear RSL problems could appear in the case of non-Newtonian fluid flows. Variational estimation methods are efficient techniques for finding analytical approximate solutions for a class of problems and also for optimal problems when looking for a minimum, using the functional of energy.

Author Contributions: Conceptualization, E.C.C.; methodology, E.C.C. and C.D.B.; software, E.C.C. and C.D.B.; validation, E.C.C. and C.D.B.; formal analysis, E.C.C.; investigation, E.C.C. and C.D.B.; writing—original draft preparation, E.C.C. and C.D.B.; writing—review and editing, E.C.C. and C.D.B.; supervision, E.C.C. All authors have read and agreed to the published version of the manuscript.

Funding: This research received no external funding.

Acknowledgments: The authors want to thank to the referees who allowed us to improve ourselves and our article.

Conflicts of Interest: The authors declare no conflict of interest.

References

1. Dautray, R.; Lions, J.L. *Mathematical Analysis and Numerical Methods for Science and Technology*; Springer: Berlin/Heidelberg, Germany, 2000.
2. Fowler, A.C. *Mathematical Models in the Applied Sciences*; Cambridge University Press: Cambridge, UK, 1997.
3. Tyn Myint-U, T.; Debnath, L. *Linear Partial Differential Equations for Scientists and Engineers*, 4th ed.; Springer: Berlin, Germany, 2007; ISBN 0-8176-4393-1.
4. Guenther, R.B.; Lee, J.W. *Sturm-Liouville Problems. Theory and Numerical Implementation*; CRC Press: Boca Raton, FL, USA, 2019; ISBN 9781138345430.
5. Perera, U.; Böckmann, C. Solutions of Sturm-Liouville Problems. *Mathematics* **2020**, *8*, 2074. [CrossRef]
6. Hassana, A.A. Green's Function Solution of Non-Homogenous Regular Sturm-Liouville Problem. *J. Appl. Comput. Math.* **2017**, *6*, 362. [CrossRef]
7. Klimek, M. Spectrum of Fractional and Fractional Prabhakar Sturm–Liouville Problems with Homogeneous Dirichlet Boundary Conditions. *Symmetry* **2021**, *13*, 2265. [CrossRef]
8. Razdan, A.K.; Ravichandran, V. *Fundamentals of Partial Differential Equations*; Springer: Singapore, 2022. [CrossRef]
9. Guo, H.; Qi, J. Sturm–Liouville Problems Involving Distribution Weights and an Application to Optimal Problems. *J. Optim. Theory Appl.* **2020**, *184*, 842–857. [CrossRef]
10. Altintan, D.; Ugur, O. Variational iteration method for Sturm-Liouville differential equations. *Comput. Math. Appl.* **2008**, *58*, 322–328. [CrossRef]
11. Johnson, C. *Numerical Solution of Partial Differential Equations by the Finite Element Method*; Cambridge University Press: Cambridge, UK, 1987; ISBN 0521345146.
12. Chen, C.N. A survey of nonlinear Sturm-Liouville equations. In *Sturm-Liouville Theory: Past and Present*; Amrein, W.O., Hinz, A.M., Eds.; Pearson D.P.: Basel, Switzerland, 2005; pp. 201–216.
13. He, J.H.; Wu, X.H. Variational iteration method: New development and applications. *Comput. Math. Appl.* **2007**, *54*, 881–894. [CrossRef]
14. Hayat, T.; Khan, M.; Ayub, M. On the non-linear flows with slip boundary condition. *Z. Angew. Math. Phys.* **2005**, *56*, 1012–1029. [CrossRef]
15. Yusufoglu, E.; Bekir, A. On the extended tanh method applications of nonlinear equations. *Int. J. Nonlinear Sci.* **2007**, *4*, 10–16.
16. Neamaty, A.; Darzi, R. Comparison between the Variational Iteration Method and the Homotopy Perturbation Method for the Sturm-Liouville Differential Equation. *Bound. Value Probl.* **2010**, *2010*, 317369. [CrossRef]
17. Zhang, T.-T.; Jia, L.; Wang, Z.-C. Analytic Solution for Steady Slip Flow between Parallel Plates with Micro-Scale Spacing. *Chin. Phys. Lett.* **2008**, *25*, 180. [CrossRef]
18. Nadeem, M.; Yao, S. Solving system of partial differential equations using variational iteration method with He's polynomials. *Int. J. Math. Comput. Sci.* **2019**, *19*, 203–211. [CrossRef]
19. Fiza, M.; Chohan, F.; Ullah, H.; Islam, S.; Bushnaq, S. An extension of the optimal homotopy asymptotic method with applications to nonlinear coupled partial differential equations. *J. Math. Comput. Sci.* **2019**, *19*, 218–229. [CrossRef]

20. Nadeem, M.; Yao, S.; Parveen, N. Solution of Newell-Whitehead-Segel equation by variational iteration method with He's polynomials. *J. Math. Comput. Sci.* **2020**, *20*, 21–29. [CrossRef]
21. Herron, I.H. Solving singular boundary value problems for ordinary differential equations. *Caribb. J. Math. Comput. Sci.* **2013**, *15*, 1–30.
22. Al-Khaled, K.; Hazaimeh, A. Comparison Methods for Solving Non-Linear Sturm–Liouville Eigenvalues Problems. *Symmetry* **2020**, *12*, 1179. [CrossRef]
23. Liu, Z.; Qi, J. The Properties of Eigenvalues and Eigenfunctions for Nonlocal Sturm–Liouville Problems. *Symmetry* **2021**, *13*, 820. [CrossRef]
24. Kanguzhin, B.; Aimal Rasa, G.H.; Kaiyrbek, Z. Identification of the Domain of the Sturm–Liouville Operator on a Star Graph. *Symmetry* **2021**, *13*, 1210. [CrossRef]
25. Nagdy, A.; Hashem, K.H. Numerical solutions of nonlinear fractional differential equations by variational iteration method. *J. Nonlinear Sci. Appl.* **2021**, *14*, 54–62. [CrossRef]

mathematics

Review
Markov Moment Problem and Sandwich Conditions on Bounded Linear Operators in Terms of Quadratic Forms

Octav Olteanu

Department of Mathematics and Informatics, University Politehnica of Bucharest, 060042 Bucharest, Romania; octav.olteanu50@gmail.com

Abstract: As is well-known, unlike the one-dimensional case, there exist nonnegative polynomials in several real variables that are not sums of squares. First, we briefly review a method of approximating any real-valued nonnegative continuous compactly supported function defined on a closed unbounded subset by dominating special polynomials that are sums of squares. This also works in several-dimensional cases. To perform this, a Hahn–Banach-type theorem (Kantorovich theorem on an extension of positive linear operators), a Haviland theorem, and the notion of a moment-determinate measure are applied. Second, completions and other results on solving full Markov moment problems in terms of quadratic forms are proposed based on polynomial approximation. The existence and uniqueness of the solution are discussed. Third, the characterization of the constraints $T_1 \leq T \leq T_2$ for the linear operator T, only in terms of quadratic forms, is deduced. Here, T_1, T, and T_2 are bounded linear operators. Concrete spaces, operators, and functionals are involved in our corollaries or examples.

Keywords: polynomial approximation; unbounded subsets; Markov moment problem; positive operators; solution; existence; uniqueness; sums of squares; Banach lattices

MSC: 41A10; 46A22; 46B42; 46B70; 47B65

Citation: Olteanu, O. Markov Moment Problem and Sandwich Conditions on Bounded Linear Operators in Terms of Quadratic Forms. *Mathematics* **2022**, *10*, 3288. https://doi.org/10.3390/math10183288

Academic Editor: Stefano De Marchi

Received: 30 July 2022
Accepted: 7 September 2022
Published: 10 September 2022

Publisher's Note: MDPI stays neutral with regard to jurisdictional claims in published maps and institutional affiliations.

1. Introduction

We begin by recalling a few general remarks on approximation theory and its applications. A first fact is that the results of the present review paper focus on the existence and uniqueness of the solution of the solution for a large class of Markov moment problems. The involved solutions are bounded linear operators T mapping $L^1_\nu(F)$ into an order-complete Banach lattice Y, where ν is a moment-determinate positive regular Borel measure on the closed unbounded subset $F \subseteq \mathbb{R}^n$, $n \in \{1,2,\ldots\}$. The uniqueness follows from the density of polynomials in $L^1_\nu(F)$ (Lemma 1) via the continuity of the operator T. Of note, our first result (Lemma 1) also works for $n \geq 2$, when, unlike the case $n = 1$, there exist moment-determinate measures ν on $\mathbb{R}^n$ for which the polynomials are not dense in $L^2_\nu(F)$ (according to [1]). Thus, for $n \geq 2$, Lemmas 1, 2, and 3 are no longer valid if we turn $L^1_\nu(F)$ into $L^2_\nu(F)$. Moreover, Lemma 1 holds true for any closed (unbounded) subset of $F \subseteq \mathbb{R}^n$. Hence, the nonnegative polynomials on F are dense in the positive cone of $L^1_\nu(F)$. If $F = \mathbb{R}^n$ or $F = \mathbb{R}^n_+$, special convex cones of nonnegative polynomials (which are sums of squares) are dense in the positive cone of $L^1_\nu(F)$ (Lemmas 2 and 3). These remarks lead to the characterizations in terms of quadratic forms in the case $n \geq 2$, which is the main contribution of this review paper. Going back to our aim on the applications of approximation theory, in [2] an interesting connection of a moment problem on $[0,1]$ (the Hausdorff moment problem) with fixed point theory was pointed out. As a rule, fixed point theorems use an iteration process. In [2], this iteration involved a rational function. The solution of the Hausdorff moment problem under attention is regarded as the fixed point of a transformation appearing naturally from the context. In [3], deep results on the uniqueness of the solutions for moment problems were carefully discussed. The article [4] provided approximation results on various locally compact spaces not necessarily related to the moment problem. In references [5] and [6], the geometric and iterative aspects of optimization theory were emphasized. The article [7] provided several interesting functional equations and new simple proofs of related inequalities involving logarithmic convexity and proposed new conjectures on the subject. In the article [8], an iterative method and its related algorithm, accompanied by a convergence analysis, for solving an optimization problem were discussed. As a general remark, recall that determining the element of minimum norm of a closed convex subset in a Hilbert space, not containing the origin, is also a passing to the limit process associated with an iteration geometrical method. This method can be adapted for a more general setting. The article [9] provides an iterative method for solving and approximating the solution of an operator equation, starting from Newton's global method for convex monotone increasing (or decreasing) operators. Sometimes, the usual iteration defining Newton's method leads to an iteration $A_{k+1} = \varphi(A_k)$, where A_k are self-adjoint operators acting on a Hilbert space and φ is a contractive convex mapping. As is well-known, the convergence of the sequence generated by Newton's method generally only works locally. For convex monotone operators of the C^1 class, it works globally, with the control of the norm of the error (providing the velocity of the convergence). The key point of the article [9] is that the convergence of the sequence of the successive approximations associated with the contraction mapping φ can be handled more easily than that provided by Newton's method. The contraction constant of φ can be determined quite easily. In particular, if the matrices have real entries, the result holds for functions of symmetric matrices. In the end, recall the connection between optimization (such as the best approximation by the elements of a closed subspace of a Hilbert space) and Fourier approximation. This is a useful remark that can be used in controlling the mean square error $g - h_2^2$ between the solutions g, h of the reduced moment problems $\langle g, \psi_j \rangle = y_j$, $\langle h, \psi_j \rangle = m_j$, $j = 0, 1, \ldots, m$ in terms of the squares of the errors $(m_j - y_j)^2$, $j = 0, 1, \ldots, m$. Here, all the involved functions g, h, ψ_j are elements of the Hilbert space $L^2_\mu(F)$, and $F \subseteq \mathbb{R}^n$ is a closed subset:

$$\psi_j(t) = t^j := t_1^{j_1} \cdots t_n^{j_n}, \; t = (t_1, \ldots, t_n) \in F, \; j = (j_1, \ldots, j_n) \in \mathbb{N}^n,$$

where y_j are the exact values of the moments, determined in the experimental stage, while m_j are the modified values for y_j, perturbed by external influences in the real-life measuring stage. Another important field in approximation theory is provided by Korovkin-type theorems and their applications. The article [10] presents such an application in approximating a Kantorovich-type rational operator by means of Korovkin's classical approximating result and completing technique. Associated inequalities are established as well. The papers [11,12] refer to the aspects related to or like those of the moment problem, being inverse problems, as the moment problem is as well. The references [13,14] contain a polynomial approximation on the unbounded subsets discussed in the beginning of this introduction. Another direction of applying these approximation results is that of characterizing sandwich conditions on bounded linear operators defined on $L^1_\nu(F)$ (where ν is moment-determinate) only in terms of quadratic forms (see below). Another well-known application of approximation theory arises from Krein-Milman theorem, which leads to approximation by convex combinations of the extreme points of a compact convex subset in a locally convex space. Such results lead to representation theorems and possible applications for optimization (see the references [14–17]).

Before stating our work on the multidimensional Markov moment problem and the related results studied in Section 3, we recall some basic notions and related terminology on compatible structures on usual spaces, which are used in the sequel. The motivation for this is that all concrete spaces of functions and self-adjoint operators have such natural structures. For complete and related information, see the monographs and books [18–27].

An ordered vector space is a real vector space X endowed with an order relation compatible with the algebraic structure expressed by the following two properties:

$$x, y \in X, \qquad x \leq y := x + z \leq y + z \text{ for all } z \in X,$$
$$x \leq y := \alpha x \leq \alpha y \text{ for all real } \alpha \in [0, \infty).$$

An order relation with the above two compatibility properties is called a linear order relation on X. An ordered vector space X with the property that for any $x_1, x_2 \in X$ there exists the least upper bound $sup\{x_1, x_2\} = x_1 \vee x_2$ for the set $\{x_1, x_2\}$ is called a vector lattice. In a vector lattice X, the following basic notations are used:

$$x^+ := x \vee \mathbf{0}, \quad x^- := (-x) \vee \mathbf{0}, \quad |x| := x \vee (-x), \; x \in X.$$

All the usual vector spaces have such a natural order relation. If X is an order vector space, one denotes by X_+ the convex cone with a vertex at $\mathbf{0}$, defined by $X_+ := \{x \in X; x \geq \mathbf{0}\}$. This cone is called the positive cone of X. In the function spaces and in the spaces of symmetric matrices with real entries, as well as in the space of self-adjoint operators acting on an infinite-dimensional Hilbert space, there exist natural norms, which make them Banach spaces. Generally, the structures given by the norms are compatible with the algebraic and order structures on the Banach spaces appearing in applications. An ordered Banach space is a Banach space X endowed with a linear order relation such that the positive cone X_+ is topologically closed and the norm is monotone increasing (isotone) on X_+ :

$$x_1, x_2 \in X, \; \mathbf{0} \leq x_1 \leq x_2 := \|x_1\| \leq \|x_2\|.$$

A Banach lattice is a Banach space X, which is also a vector lattice, such that the norm is solid on X :

$$x_1, x_2 \in X, \; |x_1| \leq |x_2| := \|x_1\| \leq \|x_2\|.$$

Almost all Banach function spaces have a natural structure of a Banach lattice. From the above definitions, clearly, any Banach lattice is an ordered Banach space. The converse is false. A first example of an ordered Banach spaces that is not a lattice is the space $\mathcal{SM}(n \times n)$ of all symmetric $n \times n$ matrices with real entries. The order relation on this space is given by:

$$A, B \in \mathcal{SM}(n \times n), \; A \leq B \text{ if and only if } \langle Ah, h \rangle \; \leq \; \langle Bh, h \rangle \text{ for all } h \in \mathbb{R}^n.$$

From this definition, we infer that $A \leq B$ if and only if $B - A$ is positive semidefinite. The norm of the symmetric matrix A is: $A = \sup_{h \leq 1} |\langle Ah, h \rangle|$. Here, by $\|h\|$ we denote the Euclidean norm of the vector h. These definitions and notations make sense and have motivations in the infinite-dimensional case. Namely, if H is an arbitrary infinite-dimensional real or complex Hilbert space, a linear operator $A : H \to H$ is called a symmetric operator if $\langle Ax, y \rangle = \langle x, Ay \rangle$ for all $x, y \in H$. A linear symmetric (continuous) operator is called a self-adjoint operator. Of note, any symmetric linear operator acting on H is continuous and therefore self-adjoint thanks to the closed graph theorem. The last definition makes sense for linear operators $A : D(A) \to H,$ where $D(A) \subseteq H$ is a vector subspace of H, called the domain of definition of A. In this case, $\langle Ax, y \rangle = \langle x, Ay \rangle$ holds for all $x, y \in D(A)$. To avoid the inconvenience arising from the fact that the real vector space of self-adjoint operators is not a lattice as well as the noncommutativity of the multiplication (composition) of self-adjoint operators (and of symmetric square matrices), the following subspace has been studied. Let $A \in \mathcal{A}(H)$, where $\mathcal{A}(H)$ is the real vector space of all self-adjoint operators acting on H. We define:

$$Y_1(A) := \{V \in \mathcal{A}(H); AV = VA\}, \; Y(A) := \{W \in Y_1(A); UW = WU \;\; \forall U \in Y_1(A)\}.$$

Then, $Y(A)$ is an order complete Banach lattice and a commutative real algebra of self-adjoint operators (according to [22]). $\mathcal{P} = \mathbb{R}[t_1, \ldots, t_n]$ is the real vector space of all polynomial functions with real coefficients of n real variables $t_1, \ldots, t_n$.In what follows, F is a closed, unbounded subset of $\mathbb{R}^n$, and $\mathcal{P}_+(F)$ is the convex cone of polynomials $p : F \to \mathbb{R}$, with $p(t) \geq 0$ for all $t \in F$. We denote by $\mathcal{P}_{++}(F)$ a convex subcone of $\mathcal{P}_+(F)$ whose elements are special nonnegative polynomials. For example, $\mathcal{P}_{++}(\mathbb{R}^n)$ can be the convex cone of all sums of polynomials of the form $p_1 \otimes \cdots \otimes p_n$, where:

$$(p_1 \otimes \cdots \otimes p_n)(t_1, \ldots, t_n) := p_1(t_1) \cdots p_n(t_n),\ t = (t_1, \ldots, t_n) \in \mathbb{R}^n, \\ p_i \in \mathcal{P}_+(\mathbb{R}),\ i = 1, \ldots, n. \tag{1}$$

We recall that:

$$p \in \mathcal{P}_+(\mathbb{R}) \Leftrightarrow p = q^2 + r^2 \tag{2}$$

for some polynomials q, r and

$$p \in \mathcal{P}_+(\mathbb{R}_+) \Leftrightarrow p(t) = q(t)^2 + tr(t)^2 \text{ for all } t \in \mathbb{R}_+ := [0, \infty). \tag{3}$$

for some $q, r \in \mathbb{R}[t]$. We denote by $\mathbb{N} := \{0, 1, \ldots\}$ the set of all nonnegative integers. If F is a closed unbounded subset of $\mathbb{R}^n$, then $C_c(F)$ is the vector space of all real-valued continuous compactly supported functions defined on F. In the sequel, all the involved vector space and linear operators (or functionals) are considered over the real field.

The classical moment problem can be written as follows: being given a sequence $(y_j)_{j \in \mathbb{N}^n}$ of real numbers and a closed subset $F \subseteq \mathbb{R}^n$, $n \in \{1, 2, \ldots\}$, find a positive regular Borel measure μ on F such that $\int_F t^j d\mu = y_j$, $j \in \mathbb{N}^n$. This is the full moment problem. The existence, uniqueness, and construction of the unknown solution μ are the focus of attention. The truncated (or reduced) moment problem requires the interpolation moment conditions only for $j_k \leq d$, $k = 1, \ldots, n,$, $j = (j_1, \ldots, j_n)$, where d is a given positive integer. The numbers y_j, $j \in \mathbb{N}^n$ are called the moments of the measure μ. When a sandwich condition on the solution is required, we have a Markov moment problem. The moment problem is an inverse problem since the measure μ is not known. It must be found, starting from its moments. Instead of real number moments, one can work with elements $y_j \in Y$, $j \in \mathbb{N}^n$, where Y is an order complete Banach lattice of functions or self-adjoint operators. If the y_j are operators, we have an operator-valued moment problem. When Y is a Banach lattice of functions, we have a vector-valued moment problem. The requirement for Y to be order-complete is motivated by the necessity of applying Hahn–Banach-type theorems in order to obtain a linear positive extension $T : X \to Y$ of the linear operator $T_0 : \mathcal{P} \to Y$, satisfying the moment conditions $T_0(\varphi_j) := y_j$, $j \in \mathbb{N}^n$, $\varphi_j(t) = t^j = t_1^{j_1} \cdots t_n^{j_n}$ from $\mathcal{P}$ to an ordered Banach space X containing both spaces $\mathcal{P}$ and $C_c(F)$. When a sandwich condition $T_1 \leq T \leq T_2$ is required on the extension T, where T_i, $i = 1, 2$ are given bounded linear operators mapping X into Y, we have a Markov moment problem. In this case the positivity of T on X_+ is replaced by the condition $T_1 \leq T$, while the requirement $T \leq T_2$ controls the norm of the solution T. As in the case of a scalar-valued linear solution, we now study the existence, the uniqueness, and eventually the construction of a/the linear solution T satisfying the interpolation moment conditions and the sandwich condition. A basic result in solving the classical moment on unbounded closed subsets is the Haviland theorem [28]. In [29], the result of Kantorovich on the extension of positive linear operators preserving linearity and positivity was reviewed and proven. This a Hahn–Banach-type result. The references [30–43] point out various aspects of the moment and related problems. Unlike other unbounded subsets of $\mathbb{R}^n$, $n \geq 2$, the expression of nonnegative polynomials on a strip in terms of sums of squares is known due to M. Marshall's theorem [39]. Using the polynomial approximation ensured by Lemma 1 and Theorem 1, proven below, the Markov moment problem in terms of quadratic forms is solved (see Theorem 3 below). Applications of Hahn–Banach-type extension theorems to the study of the isotonicity (increasing monotonicity) of continuous convex operators on the positive cone X_+ were published in the article [44]. References [45–48] focus mainly on several aspects of the truncated or full Markov moment problem. The rest of this paper is organized as follows. Section 2 summarizes the basic methods and results used along the proofs of the theorems in the present paper. Section 3 is devoted to the results: polynomial approximation on unbounded subsets in some L^1_ν spaces, applications of such results accompanied by other theorems to the existence and uniqueness of the solution of the Markov moment problem on an unbounded closed subset, and characterizations of the sandwich condition for bounded linear operators. All these applications of approximation-type results are partially or completely formulated in terms of quadratic forms. Section 4 concludes the paper.

2. Methods

Here are the basic methods used directly or as background of this paper:

(1) Polynomial approximation on closed unbounded subsets $F \subseteq \mathbb{R}^n$. in spaces $L^1_\nu(F)$, where ν is a moment-determinate positive regular Borel measure on F. Here, we use notions on the determinacy of measures, Kantorovich theorem on the extension of positive linear operators, Haviland theorem, and measure theory standard results. However, the key point is the notion of a moment-determinate measure and its use in the proof of Lemma 1. Bernstein-approximating polynomials are applied in the proofs of Lemmas 2 and 3.

(2) The characterization of the existence and uniqueness of the solution for full vector-valued Markov moment problems on unbounded subsets and their consequences for scalar Markov moment problems.

(3) The characterization of the sandwich-type conditions for a large class of bounded linear operators on $L^1_\nu(\mathbb{R}^n)$, only in terms of quadratic forms.

3. Results

3.1. On Polynomial Approximation on Unbounded Closed Subsets $F \subseteq \mathbb{R}^n$ in Spaces $L^1_\nu(F)$, Where ν Is a Moment-Determinate Positive Regular Borel Measure on F

In the sequel, the following approximation lemmas are applied

Lemma 1. *Let $F \subseteq \mathbb{R}^n$ be an unbounded closed subset and ν be a moment-determinate positive regular Borel measure on F, with finite moments of all natural orders. Then, for any $x \in C_c(F)$, $x(t) \geq 0$, $\forall t \in F$, there exists a sequence $(p_m)_m, p_m \geq x$, $m \in \mathbb{N}$, $p_m \to x$ in $L^1_\nu(F)$. Consequently, we have:*

$$\lim_m \int_F p_m(t)d\nu = \int_F x(t)d\nu,$$

where $\mathcal{P}_+ = \mathcal{P}_+(F)$ is dense in $\left(L^1_\nu(F)\right)_+$, and $\mathcal{P}$ is dense in $L^1_\nu(F)$.

Proof To prove the assertions of the statement, it is sufficient to show that for any $x \in (C_c(F))_+$ we have

$$Q_1(x) := inf\left\{\int_F p(t)d\nu; p \geq x,\ p \in \mathcal{P}\right\} = \int_F x(t)d\nu.$$

Obviously, one has

$$Q_1(x) \geq \int_F x(t)d\nu.$$

To prove the converse, we define the linear form

$$T_0 : X_0 := \mathcal{P} \oplus Sp\{x\} \to \mathbb{R},\ F_0(p + \alpha x) := \int_F p(t)d\nu + \alpha Q_1(x),\ p \in \mathcal{P},\ \alpha \in \mathbb{R}.$$

Next, we show that F_0 is positive on X_0. In fact, for $\alpha < 0$, one has (from the definition of Q_1, which is a sublinear functional on X_1):

$$p + \alpha x \geq 0 := p \geq -\alpha x := (-\alpha)Q_1(x) = Q_1(-\alpha x) \leq \int_F p(t)d\nu := T_0(p + \alpha x) \geq 0.$$

If $a \geq 0$, we infer that:

$$0 = Q_1(0) = Q_1(\alpha x - \alpha x) \leq \alpha Q_1(x) + Q_1(-\alpha x) \implies$$
$$\int_F p(t)d\nu \geq Q_1(-\alpha x) \geq -\alpha Q_1(x) := T_0(p + \alpha x) \geq 0,$$

where, in both possible cases, we have $x_0 \in (X_0)_+ := T_0(x_0) \geq 0$. Since X_0 contains the space of the polynomials' functions, which is a majorizing subspace of X_1, there exists a linear positive extension $T : X \to \mathbb{R}$ of T_0 (cf. [29]), which is continuous on $C_c(F)$ with respect to the sup-norm. Therefore, T has a representation by means of a positive Borel regular measure μ on F such that

$$T(x) = \int_F x(t)d\mu, \; x \in C_c(F).$$

Let $p \in \mathcal{P}_+$ be a nonnegative polynomial function. There is a nondecreasing sequence $(x_m)_m$ of continuous nonnegative function with compact support such that $x_m \nearrow p$ pointwise on F. The positivity of T and Lebesgue's dominated convergence theorem for μ yield

$$\int_F p(t)d\nu = T(p) \geq \sup T(x_m) = \sup \int_F x_m(t)d\mu = \int_F p(t)d\mu, \; p \in \mathcal{P}_+.$$

Thanks to Haviland's theorem [28], there exists a positive Borel regular measure λ on F such that

$$\lambda(p) = \nu(p) - \mu(p) \Leftrightarrow \nu(p) = \lambda(p) + \mu(p), \; p \in \mathcal{P}.$$

Since ν is assumed to be M-determinate, it follows that:

$$\nu(B) = \lambda(B) + \mu(B),$$

for any Borel subset B of F. From this last assertion, approximating each $x \in (L^1_\nu(F))_+$ by a nondecreasing sequence of nonnegative simple functions and using Lebesgue's convergence theorem, one obtains, first for positive functions, then for arbitrary ν-integrable functions, φ :

$$\int_F \varphi d\nu = \int_F \varphi d\lambda + \int_F \varphi d\mu, \; \varphi \in L^1_\nu(F).$$

In particular, we must have

$$\int_F x d\nu \geq \int_F x d\mu = T(x) = T_0(x) = Q_1(x).$$

The conclusion is: $Q_1(x) = \int_F x(t)d\nu$. This ends the proof. $\square$

Using Bernstein polynomial of n real variables when Lemma 1 is applied to $n = 1$, for $F = \mathbb{R}$ and Fubini's theorem we derive the following multidimensional polynomial approximation result.

Lemma 2. *Let $\nu = \nu_1 \times \cdots \times \nu_n$ be a product of n positive regular Borel-moment-determinate measures on $\mathbb{R}$, with finite moments of all orders. Then, we can approximate any nonnegative continuous compactly supported function $\psi \in X = (C_c(\mathbb{R}^n))_+$ with the sums of products:*

$$p_1 \otimes \cdots \otimes p_n,$$
$$(p_1 \otimes \cdots \otimes p_n)(t_1, \ldots, t_n) := p_1(t_1) \cdots p_n(t_n).t = (t_1, \ldots, t_n) \in \mathbb{R}^n,$$

where p_j is a nonnegative polynomial on the entire real line, $j = 1, \ldots, n$, and any such sum of special polynomials dominates ψon $\mathbb{R}^n$.

Lemma 3. *Let $\nu = \nu_1 \times \cdots \times \nu_n$ be a product of n positive regular Borel-moment-determinate measures on $\mathbb{R}_+$, with finite moments of all orders. Then, we can approximate any nonnegative continuous compactly supported function $\psi \in (C_c(\mathbb{R}_+^n))_+$ with the sums of products:*

$$p_1 \otimes \cdots \otimes p_n,$$
$$(p_1 \otimes \cdots \otimes p_n)(t_1, \ldots, t_n) := p_1(t_1) \cdots p_n(t_n).t = (t_1, \ldots, t_n) \in \mathbb{R}_+^n,$$

where p_j is a nonnegative polynomial on the entire nonnegative semi axes, $j = 1, \ldots, n$, and any such sum of special polynomials dominates ψ on $\mathbb{R}_+^n$.

Proof. Let $f \in (C_c(\mathbb{R}_+^n))_+, K_i = pr_i(supp(f))$, $a_i = infK_i, b_i = supK_i$, $i = 1, \ldots, n$, $K = [a_1, b_1] \times \cdots \times [a_n, b_n]$.

The restriction of f to the parallelepiped K can be approximated uniformly on K by Bernstein polynomials B_m in n variables. Any such polynomial B_m is a sum of the products of the form $q_{m,1} \otimes \cdots \otimes q_{m,n}$, where each $q_{m,i}$ is a polynomial nonnegative on $[a_i, b_i]$, $i = 1, \ldots, n, m \in \mathbb{N}$. B_m can be written as:

$$B_m = \sum_{\substack{k_i=0,\ldots,m, \\ i=1,\ldots,n}} q_{m,k_1} \otimes \cdots \otimes q_{m,k_n},$$

where q_{m,k_i} is a nonnegative polynomial on $[a_i, b_i]$, $i = 1, \ldots, n, m \in \mathbb{N}$. By the Weierstrass–Bernstein uniform approximation theorem, we have:

$$\|f - B_m\|_\infty := \sup_{t \in K} |f(t) - B_m(t)| \to 0,\ m \to \infty.$$

By an abuse of notation, we write $q_{m,i} = q_{m,k_i}$. We need a similar approximation, with sums of tensor products of nonnegative polynomials p_i, $p_i(t_i) \geq 0$, for all $t_i \in \mathbb{R}_+$, $i = 1, \ldots, n$ in the space $L^1_\nu(\mathbb{R}_+^n)$. To this aim, the idea is to use Lemma 18 for $n = 1$, $F = \mathbb{R}_+$, followed by Fubini's theorem. We define $q_{0,m,i} = q_{m,i} \cdot \chi_{[a_i, b_i]}$, $i = 1, \ldots, n$ and $f_i(t) = q_{m,i}(t), t \in [a_i, b_i]$, $f_i(t) = 0$ for t outside an interval $[a_i - \varepsilon, b_i + \varepsilon]$ with small $\varepsilon > 0$, the graph of f_i on $[b_i, b_i + \varepsilon]$ being the line segment of the ends of the points $(b_i, q_i(b_i))$ and $(b_i + \varepsilon, 0)$. We proceed similarly on an interval $[a_i - \varepsilon, a_i]$. Clearly, for $\varepsilon > 0$ small enough, f_i approximates $q_{0,\,m,i}$ in $L^1_{\nu_i}(\mathbb{R}_+)$ as accurate as we wish. On the other hand, f_i is nonnegative, compactly supported, and continuous on $\mathbb{R}_+$, so that Lemma 1 ensures the existence of an approximating polynomial p_i with respect to the norm of $L^1_{d\nu_i}(\mathbb{R}_+)$, $p_i(t) \geq 0$ for all $t \in \mathbb{R}_+$, $i = 1, \ldots, n$. According to Fubini's theorem, the preceding reasoning yields $p_1 \otimes \cdots \otimes p_n$, which approximates $f_1 \otimes \cdots \otimes f_n$, and $f_1 \otimes \cdots \otimes f_n$, which approximates $q_{0,m,1} \otimes \cdots \otimes q_{0,m,n} = q_{0,m,k_1} \otimes \cdots \otimes q_{0,m,k_n}$. The approximations hold for finite sums of these products in $L^1_\nu(\mathbb{R}_+^n)$. Moreover, finite sums of functions $q_{0,m,1,} \otimes \cdots \otimes q_{0,m,n}$ approximate f uniformly on K because their restrictions to K define the restriction to K of approximating Bernstein polynomials $(B_m)_{m \in \mathbb{N}}$ associated to

f. Since f and $q_{0,m,1}, \otimes \cdots \otimes q_{0,m,n}$ vanish outside K, we infer that the following norm $\| \|_1$ in $L^1_\nu(\mathbb{R}^n_+)$ is evaluated as:

$$\left\| f - \sum_{\substack{k_i=0,\dots,m,\\ i=1,\dots,n}} q_{0,m,k_1}, \otimes \cdots \otimes q_{0,m,k_n} \right\|_1 = \int_K \left| f - \sum_{\substack{k_i=0,\dots,m,\\ i=1,\dots,n}} q_{m,,k_1} \otimes \cdots \otimes q_{m,k_n} \right| d\nu \le$$

$$\sup_{t\in K} |f(t) - B_m(t)| \cdot \nu(K) \to 0,\ m \to \infty.$$

The conclusion is that f can be approximated in $L^1_\nu(\mathbb{R}^n_+)$ by the sums of products $p_1 \otimes \cdots \otimes p_n$, where p_i is nonnegative on $\mathbb{R}_+$ for all $i = 1, \dots, n$. This ends the proof. □

Example 1. *For any $\alpha \in (0, \infty)$, $d\nu = e^{-\alpha t} dt$ is a moment-determinate positive Borel measure on $\mathbb{R}_+$, according to [14]. The application of Lemma 3 shows that for the product measure:*

$$d\nu = exp\left(- \sum_{j=1}^{n} \alpha_j t_j \right) dt_1 \cdots dt_n =$$

$$exp(-\alpha_1 t_1) dt_1 \times \cdots \times exp(-\alpha_n t_n) dt_n,\ \alpha_j > 0,\ j = 1, \dots, n,$$

the polynomials are dense in $L^1_\nu(\mathbb{R}^n_+)$. In particular, the measurev is moment-determinate on $\mathbb{R}^n_+$. A similar consequence follows from Lemma 2, for the measure

$$d\mu = exp\left(- \sum_{j=1}^{n} \alpha_j t_j^2 \right) dt_1 \cdots dt_n,\ \alpha_j > 0,\ j = 1, \dots, n.$$

In this case, the polynomials are dense in $L^1_\mu(\mathbb{R}^n)$; in particular, μ is a moment-determinate measure on $\mathbb{R}^n$.

3.2. Solving Markov Moment Problems in Terms of Signatures of Quadratic Forms

The approximation results reviewed in Section 3.1 allow the extension of sandwich conditions on the solution T, preserving the interpolation moment conditions, from the subspace of polynomials to the entire space $L^1_\nu(F)$ for moment-determinate measures ν. The results stated in the sequel complete theorems previously published in [13,14,16].

Theorem 1. *Let F be a closed unbounded subset of $\mathbb{R}^n$, Y an order-complete Banach lattice, $(y_j)_{j\in\mathbb{N}^n}$ a given sequence in Y, and ν a positive regular moment-determinate Borel measure on F, with finite moments of all orders. Let $T_1, T_2 \in B(L^1_\nu(F), Y)$ be two linear bounded operators from $L^1_\nu(F)$ to Y. The following statements are equivalent:*

(a) *there exists a unique bounded linear operator $T \in B(L^1_\nu(A), Y)$ such that $T(\varphi_j) = y_j$, $j \in \mathbb{N}^n$, and T is between T_1 and T_2 on the positive cone of L^1_ν;*
(b) *for any finite subset $J_0 \subset \mathbb{N}^n$ and any $\{a_j\}_{j\in J_0} \subset \mathbb{R}$, we have*

$$\sum_{j\in J_0} a_j \varphi_j \ge 0 \text{on} F \Rightarrow$$
$$\sum_{j\in J_0} a_j T_1(\varphi_j) \le \sum_{j\in J_0} a_j y_j \le \sum_{j\in J_0} a_j T_2(\varphi_j).$$

Proof. We define $T_0 : \mathcal{P} \to Y$ by

$$T_0\left(\sum_{j\in J_0} \lambda_j \varphi_j \right) := \sum_{j\in J_0} \lambda_j y_j. \tag{4}$$

Here, $J_0 \subset \mathbb{N}^n$ is an arbitrary finite subset, and $\lambda_j,\ j \in J_0$ are real coefficients. With this notation, point (b) says that

$$T_1(p) \le T_0(p) \le T_2(p),\ p \in \mathcal{P}_+(F). \tag{5}$$

In other words, $U_1 := T_0 - T_1,\ U_2 := T_2 - T_1,\ U_i : \mathcal{P} \to Y,\ i = 1,2$ are positive linear operators on the positive cone $\mathcal{P}_+(F)$ of the ordered vector space $\mathcal{P}$, and $U_1\big|_{\mathcal{P}_+(F)} \le U_2\big|_{\mathcal{P}_+(F)}$. According to the Kantorovich extension result for positive linear operators, there exists a positive linear extension V_1 of U_1 from $\mathcal{P}$ to a dense subspace X_1 of $X := L^1_\nu(F)$ since $\mathcal{P}$ is a majorizing subspace of $X_1 := \{f \in X;\ \exists p \in \mathcal{P},\ |f| \le p\}$. Clearly, the space X_1 contains both subspaces $C_c(F)$ and $\mathcal{P}$. Then, $V_1 + T_1$ extends T_0 to a linear operator:

$$W_1 : X_1 \to Y,\ W_1 := V_1 + T_1 \ge T_1 \text{ on } \mathcal{P}_+(F).$$

Using Lemma 1, the continuity of T_1, T_2, and the inequalities $\mathbf{0} \le U_1 \le U_2$ on $\mathcal{P}_+$, we infer that for any sequence of nonnegative compactly supported functions $(g_l)_l,\ g_l \to \mathbf{0}$, there exists a sequence of polynomials $(p_l)_l,\ \mathbf{0} \le g_l \le p_l$ for all $l,\ p_l - g_l \to \mathbf{0},\ l \to \infty$. These yield:

$$p_l = (p_l - g_l) + g_l \to \mathbf{0},\ l \to \infty. \tag{6}$$

On the other hand, (5) and (6) lead to:

$$\mathbf{0} \leftarrow T_1(p_l) \le T_0(p_l) \le T_2(p_l) \to 0.$$

Thus, $W_1(p_l) = T_0(p_l) \to \mathbf{0}$, which further implies

$$\mathbf{0} \le W_1(g_l) \le W_1(p_l) \to 0.$$

Thus, $W_1(g_l) \to \mathbf{0}$ for any convergent to zero sequence of elements from $(C_c(F))_+$. Now, let $(g_l)_l$ be an arbitrary sequence in $C_c(F),\ g_l \to \mathbf{0}$. Then, $g_l^+ \to 0,\ g_l^- \to 0$, and the preceding reasons imply $W_1(g_l^+) \to \mathbf{0},\ W_1(g_l^-) \to \mathbf{0}$. Therefore, $W_1(g_l) = W_1(g_l^+) - W_1(g_l^-) \to \mathbf{0}$. The conclusion is that the linear operator W_1 is continuous on $C_c(F)$. It admits a unique linear continuous extension $T \in B(X,Y)$, since $C_c(F)$ is dense in X. Hence, T is continuous and defined on the entire space $X = L^1_\nu(F)$, verifying $T(\varphi_j) = T_0(\varphi_j) = y_j,\ j \in \mathbb{N}^n$. If $\psi \in X_+$, there exists a sequence $(g_l)_l$ of functions in $(C_c(F))_+$ such that $g_l \to \psi$ in X. If $(p_l)_l$ is a sequence of polynomial functions, $g_l \le p_l$ for all $l,\ p_l - g_l \to \mathbf{0}$, then the continuity of the operators T_1, T, T_2 on X and the inequalities (5) yield:

$$T_1(\psi) = \lim_l T_1(p_l) \le \lim_l T_0(p_l) = \lim_l T(p_l) \le \lim_l T_2(p_l) = T_2(\psi),\ \psi \in X_+.$$

This ends the proof. □

If the nonnegative polynomials on F are expressible in terms of sums of squares, theorem 1 allows the characterization of the existence and uniqueness of the solution in terms of quadratic forms. The following consequences hold. We start with the simplest case, when $F = \mathbb{R}$.

Corollary 1. *Let $X = L^1_\nu(\mathbb{R})$, where ν is a positive regular moment-determinate Borel measure on $\mathbb{R}$, with finite moments of all orders. Assume that Y is an arbitrary order complete Banach lattice and $(y_n)_{n\ge 0}$ is a given sequence with its terms in Y. Let T_1, T_2 be two linear operators from X to Y such that $\mathbf{0} \le T_1 \le T_2$ on X_+. The following statements are equivalent:*

(a) *There exists a unique bounded linear operator T from X to Y, $T_1 \le T \le T_2$ on X_+, $\|T_1\| \le \|T\| \le \|T_2\|$ such that $T(\varphi_n) = y_n$ for all $n \in \mathbb{N}$;*

(b) *If $J_0 \subset \mathbb{N}$ is a finite subset and $\{\lambda_j; j \in J_0\} \subset \mathbb{R}$, then*

$$\sum_{i,j\in J_0} \lambda_i\lambda_j T_1(\varphi_{i+j}) \le \sum_{i,j\in J_0} \lambda_i\lambda_j y_{i+j} \le \sum_{i,j\in J_0} \lambda_i\lambda_j T_2(\varphi_{i+j}).$$

Proof. We apply Theorem 1 to $F = \mathbb{R}$ as well as the explicit form of nonnegative polynomials on the real axes (2). One uses the obvious equality:

$$q = \sum_{j \in J_0} \lambda_j \varphi_j \Rightarrow q^2 = \sum_{i,j \in J_0} \lambda_i \lambda_j \varphi_i \varphi_j = \sum_{i,j \in J_0} \lambda_i \lambda_j \varphi_{i+j},$$

Here, $J_0 \subset \mathbb{N}$ is an arbitrary finite subset, $\lambda_j \in \mathbb{R},\ j \in J_0$. It remains to prove that

$$\|T_1\| \leq \|T\| \leq \|T_2\|.$$

The positivity of the linear operators $T_1, T, T_2,\ T - T_1,\ T_2 - T$ on X_+ and their continuity yields:

$$\pm T_1(x) = T_1(\pm x) \leq T_1(|x|) \leq T(|x|),$$

which implies $|T_1(x)| \leq T(|x|),\ x \in X$. Since Y is a Banach lattice, we infer that the inequalities:

$$\|T_1(x)\| \leq \|T(|x|)\| \leq \|T\| \|x\|,$$

hold for all $x \in X$. This proves that $\|T_1\| \leq \|T\|$. Similarly, we show that $\|T\| \leq \|T_2\|$. This ends the proof. □

Here is the scalar-valued version of Corollary 1.

Corollary 2. *Let ν be a positive regular moment-determinate Borel measure on $\mathbb{R}$, with finite moments of all orders. Assume that h_1, h_2 are two functions in $L^\infty_\nu(\mathbb{R})$ such that $0 \leq h_1 \leq h_2$ almost everywhere. Let $(y_n)_{n \geq 0}$ be a given sequence of real numbers. The following statements are equivalent:*

(a) *There exists a unique $h \in L^\infty_\nu(\mathbb{R})$ such that $h_1 \leq h \leq h_2$ $\nu-$almost everywhere and $\int_{\mathbb{R}} t^j h(t) d\nu = y_j$ for all $j \in \mathbb{N}$.*

(b) *If $J_0 \subset \mathbb{N}$ is a finite subset, and $\{\lambda_j; j \in J_0\} \subset \mathbb{R}$, then:*

$$\sum_{i,j \in J_0} \lambda_i \lambda_j \int_{\mathbb{R}} t^{i+j} h_1(t) d\nu \leq \sum_{i,j \in J_0} \lambda_i \lambda_j y_{i+j} \leq \sum_{i,j \in J_0} \lambda_i \lambda_j \int_{\mathbb{R}} t^{i+j} h_2(t) d\nu.$$

Proof. The implication $(a) := (b)$ is obvious. To prove the converse, we apply Corollary 1 to the case $Y = \mathbb{R},\ T_i(f) := \int_{\mathbb{R}} h_i(t) f(t) d\nu,\ i = 1, 2$. The linear positive (hence, continuous) functional T is represented by a function $h \in L^\infty_\nu(\mathbb{R})$ according to the measure theory results from [9]. The moment interpolation conditions from Corollary 1 must be written as

$$\int_{\mathbb{R}} h(t) t^j d\nu = T(\varphi_j) = y_j,\ j \in \mathbb{N}.$$

To finish the proof, we must show that $h_1 \leq h \leq h_2$ $\nu-$almost everywhere in $\mathbb{R}$. According to Corollary 1, we already know that:

$$\int_{\mathbb{R}} h_1(t) f(t) d\nu \leq \int_{\mathbb{R}} h(t) f(t) d\nu \leq \int_{\mathbb{R}} h_2(t) f(t) d\nu,$$

for all $f \in \left(L^1_\nu(\mathbb{R})\right)_+$. Writing this for any $f = \chi_B$, where $B \subseteq \mathbb{R}$ is an arbitrary Borel subset with $\nu(B) \in (0, \infty)$, the following conclusion holds:

$$\int_B (h(t) - h_1(t)) d\nu \geq 0,\ \int_B (h_2(t) - h(t)) d\nu \geq 0,\ B \in \mathcal{B},\ \nu(B) > 0.$$

Here, $\mathcal{B}$ is the sigma algebra of all Borel subsets of $\mathbb{R}$. Now, a well-known measure theory argument [9] leads to $h_1(t) \leq h(t) \leq h_2(t)$ for almost all $t \in \mathbb{R}$ with respect to the measure $d\nu$. This ends the proof. □

If in Corollaries 1 and 2 we take $\mathbb{R}_+$ instead of $\mathbb{R}$, the following statements hold, via proofs like those shown above.

Corollary 3. *Let $X = L^1_\nu(\mathbb{R}_+)$, where ν is a positive regular moment-determinate Borel measure on $\mathbb{R}_+$. Assume that Y is an arbitrary order-complete Banach lattice and $(y_n)_{n\geq 0}$ is a given sequence with its terms in Y. Let T_1, T_2 be two linear operators from X to Y such that $0 \leq T_1 \leq T_2$ on X_+. The following statements are equivalent:*

(c) *There exists a unique bounded linear operator T from X to Y, $T_1 \leq T \leq T_2$ on X_+, $\|T_1\| \leq \|T\| \leq \|T_2\|$ such that $T(\varphi_n) = y_n$ for all $n \in \mathbb{N}$;*

(d) *If $J_0 \subset \mathbb{N}$ is a finite subset and $\{\lambda_j; j \in J_0\} \subset \mathbb{R}$, then*

$$\sum_{i,j\in J_0} \lambda_i\lambda_j T_1\left(\varphi_{i+j+k}\right) \leq \sum_{i,j\in J_0} \lambda_i\lambda_j y_{i+j+k} \leq \sum_{i,j\in J_0} \lambda_i\lambda_j T_2\left(\varphi_{i+j+k}\right),\ k \in \{0,1\}.$$

Corollary 4. *Let ν be a positive regular moment-determinate Borel measure on $\mathbb{R}_+$, with finite moments of all orders. Assume that h_1, h_2 are two functions in $L^\infty_\nu(\mathbb{R}_+)$ such that $\mathbf{0} \leq h_1 \leq h_2$ almost everywhere. Let $(y_n)_{n\geq 0}$ be a given sequence of real numbers. The following statements are equivalent:*

(c) *There exists a unique $h \in L^\infty_\nu(\mathbb{R}_+)$ such that $h_1 \leq h \leq h_2$ $\nu-$almost everywhere, and*

$$\int_{\mathbb{R}_+} t^j h(t)d\nu = y_j \text{for all } j \in \mathbb{N}.$$

(d) *If $J_0 \subset \mathbb{N}$ is a finite subset and $\{\lambda_j; j \in J_0\} \subset \mathbb{R}$, then:*

$$\sum_{i,j\in J_0} \lambda_i\lambda_j \int_{\mathbb{R}_+} t^{i+j+k} h_1(t)d\nu \leq \sum_{i,j\in J_0} \lambda_i\lambda_j y_{i+j+k} \leq \sum_{i,j\in J_0} \lambda_i\lambda_j \int_{\mathbb{R}_+} t^{i+j+k} h_2(t)d\nu,\ k \in \{0,1\}.$$

Example 2. *If, in Corollary 4, we take $d\nu = e^{-t}dt$, $h_1(t) := te^{-t}$, $h_2(t) :=$ **1/2**, then $d\nu$ is moment-determinate* [14],

$$\int_{\mathbb{R}_+} t^{i+j+k} h_1(t)d\nu = \int_0^\infty t^{i+j+k+1} e^{-2t} dt = 2^{-(i+j+k+2)} \int_0^\infty u^{i+j+k+1} e^{-u} du = 2^{-(i+j+k+2)}(i+j+k+1)!,$$

$$\int_{\mathbb{R}_+} t^{i+j+k} h_2(t)d\nu = 2^{-1}(i+j+k)!.$$

Thus, condition (b) must be written as follows:

$$\sum_{i,j\in J_0} \lambda_i\lambda_j 2^{-(i+j+k+2)}(i+j+k+1)! \leq \sum_{i,j\in J_0} \lambda_i\lambda_j y_{i+j+k} \leq \sum_{i,j\in J_0} \lambda_i\lambda_j 2^{-1}(i+j+k)!,\ k \in \{0,1\},$$

where $J_0 \subset \mathbb{N}$ is an arbitrary finite subset and λ_j, $j \in J_0$ are arbitrary real numbers.

We go on with the two-dimensional case, starting with the Markov moment problem on a strip. The motivation is that the explicit expression of nonnegative polynomials on a strip in terms of sums of squares is known due to following M. Marshall's result [39].

Theorem 2. *If $p(t_1,t_2) \in \mathbb{R}[t_1,t_2]$ is nonnegative on the strip $F = [0,1] \times \mathbb{R}$, then $p(t_1,t_2)$ is expressible as:*

$$p(t_1,t_2) = \sigma(t_1,t_2) + \tau(t_1,t_2)t_1(1-t_1),$$

where $\sigma(t_1,t_2), \tau(t_1,t_2)$ are sums of squares in $\mathbb{R}[t_1,t_2]$.

From Theorems 1 and 2, the next result also holds. Let $F = [0,1] \times \mathbb{R}$, ν be a positive regular Borel M-determinate (moment-determinate) measure on F, and $X = L^1_\nu(F)$, $\varphi_j(t_1,t_2) := t_1^{j_1} t_2^{j_2}$, $j = (j_1,j_2) \in \mathbb{N}^2$, $(t_1,t_2) \in F$. Let Y be an order-complete Banach lattice and $(y_j)_{j\in\mathbb{N}^2}$ be a sequence of given elements in Y.

Theorem 3. *Let $T_1, T_2 \in B_+(X,Y)$ be two linear (bounded) positive operators mapping X into Y. The following statements are equivalent:*

(a) *There exists a unique (bounded) linear operator $T : X \to Y$ such that $T(\varphi_j) = y_j$, $j \in \mathbb{N}^2$, where T is between T_1 and T_2 on the positive cone of X, $\|T_1\| \le \|T\| \le \|T_2\|$;*

(b) *For any finite subset $J_0 \subset \mathbb{N}^2$ and any $\{\lambda_j; j \in J_0\} \subset \mathbb{R}$, we have:*

$$\sum_{i,j\in J_0} \lambda_i\lambda_j T_1(\varphi_{i+j}) \le \sum_{i,j\in J_0} \lambda_i\lambda_j y_{i+j} \le \sum_{i,j\in J_0} \lambda_i\lambda_j T_2(\varphi_{i+j}),$$
$$\sum_{i,j\in J_0} \lambda_i\lambda_j \left(T_1\left(\varphi_{i_1+j_1+1,\, i_2+j_2} - \varphi_{i_1+j_1+2,\, i_2+j_2}\right)\right) \le$$
$$\sum_{i,j\in J_0} \lambda_i\lambda_j \left(y_{i_1+j_1+1,\, i_2+j_2} - y_{i_1+j_1+2,\, i_2+j_2}\right) \le$$
$$\sum_{i,j\in J_0} \lambda_i\lambda_j \left(T_2\left(\varphi_{i_1+j_1+1,\, i_2+j_2} - \varphi_{i_1+j_1+2,\, i_2+j_2}\right)\right),\ i = (i_1,i_2),\ j = (j_1,j_2) \in J_0.$$

Unfortunately, similar results cannot be proven for moment problems on $\mathbb{R}^n$ and $\mathbb{R}^n_+$. This is a motivation for reviewing the following result [13].

If $F \subseteq \mathbb{R}^n$ is an arbitrary closed unbounded subset, then we denote, by $\mathcal{P}_{++}$, a subcone of $\mathcal{P}_+$ generated by special nonnegative polynomials expressible in terms of sums of squares.

Theorem 4. *Let $F \subseteq \mathbb{R}^n$ be a closed unbounded subset; ν be a positive regular Borel-moment-determinate measure on F, having finite moments of all orders; and $X = L^1_\nu(F)$, $\varphi_j(t) = t^j$, $t \in F$, $j \in \mathbb{N}^n$. Let Y be an order-complete Banach lattice, $(y_j)_{j\in\mathbb{N}^n}$ be a given sequence of elements in Y, and T_1 and T_2 be two bounded linear operators mapping X into Y. Assume that there exists a subcone $\mathcal{P}_{++} \subseteq \mathcal{P}_+$ such that each $f \in (C_c(F))_+$ can be approximated in X by a sequence $(p_l)_l$, $p_l \in \mathcal{P}_{++}$, $p_l \ge f$ for all l. The following statements are equivalent:*

(a) *There exists a unique (bounded) linear operator*

$$T : X \to Y,\ T(\varphi_j) = y_j,\ j \in \mathbb{N}^n, \mathbf{0} \le T_1 \le T \le T_2\ \ X_+,\ \|T_1\| \le \|T\| \le \|T_2\|;$$

(b) *For any finite subset $J_0 \subset \mathbb{N}^n$ and any $\{\lambda_j; j \in J_0\} \subset \mathbb{R}$, the following implications hold true:*

$$\sum_{j\in J_0} \lambda_j\varphi_j \in \mathcal{P}_+(F) := \sum_{j\in J_0} \lambda_j T_1(\varphi_j) \le \sum_{j\in J_0} \lambda_j y_j,$$
$$\sum_{j\in J_0} \lambda_j\varphi_j \in \mathcal{P}_{++} := \sum_{j\in J_0} \lambda_j T_1(\varphi_j) \ge \mathbf{0},\ \sum_{j\in J_0} \lambda_j y_j \le \sum_{j\in J_0} \lambda_j T_2(\varphi_j).$$

The application of Theorem 4 and Lemma 2 yields the following result.

Theorem 5. *Let $\nu = \nu_1 \times \cdots \times \nu_n$, $n \ge 2$, ν_j being a positive regular $M-$determinate (moment-determinate) Borel measure on $\mathbb{R}$, $j = 1,\ldots,n$, $X = L^1_\nu(\mathbb{R}^n)$, $\varphi_j(t) = t^j, t \in \mathbb{R}^n$, $j \in \mathbb{N}^n$. Additionally, assume that ν_j has finite moments of all orders, $j = 1,\ldots,n$. Let Y be an order-*

complete Banach lattice, $(y_j)_{j\in\mathbb{N}^n}$ *a given sequence of elements in* Y*, and* T_1 *and* T_2 *two bounded linear operators mapping* X *into* Y*. The following statements are equivalent:*

(a) *There exists a unique (bounded) linear operator* $T : X \to Y$, $T(\varphi_j) = y_j$, $j \in \mathbb{N}^n$, $0 \le T_1 \le T \le T_2$. *on* X_+, $\|T_1\| \le \|T\| \le \|T_2\|$;

(b) *For any finite subset* $J_0 \subset \mathbb{N}^n$ *and any* $\{\lambda_j; j \in J_0\} \subset \mathbb{R}$*, the following implication holds true:*

$$\sum_{j\in J_0} \lambda_j\varphi_j \in \mathcal{P}_+ \Rightarrow \sum_{j\in J_0} \lambda_j T_1(\varphi_j) \le \sum_{j\in J_0} \lambda_j y_j.$$

For any finite subsets $J_k \subset \mathbb{N}$, $k = 1,\ldots,n$ *and any* $\{\lambda_{j_k}\}_{j_k\in J_k} \subset \mathbb{R}$*, the following inequalities hold true:*

$$0 \le \sum_{i_1,j_1\in J_1}\left(\cdots\left(\sum_{i_n,j_n\in J_n}\lambda_{i_1}\lambda_{j_1}\cdots\lambda_{i_n}\lambda_{j_n}T_1\left(\varphi_{i_1+j_1,\ldots,i_n+j_n}\right)\right)\cdots\right),$$

$$\sum_{i_1,j_1\in J_1}\left(\cdots\left(\sum_{i_n,j_n\in J_n}\lambda_{i_1}\lambda_{j_1}\cdots\lambda_{i_n}\lambda_{j_n}y_{i_1+j_1,\ldots,i_n+j_n}\right)\cdots\right) \le$$

$$\sum_{i_1,j_1\in J_1}\left(\cdots\left(\sum_{i_n,j_n\in J_n}\lambda_{i_1}\lambda_{j_1}\cdots\lambda_{i_n}\lambda_{j_n}T_2\left(\varphi_{i_1+j_1,\ldots,i_n+j_n}\right)\right)\cdots\right).$$

A similar result holds for products of n moment-determinate measures on $\mathbb{R}_+$, $n \ge 2$ via Theorem 4 and Lemma 3, also using the explicit form of nonnegative polynomials on $\mathbb{R}_+$ written in (3).

3.3. Characterizing Sandwich Conditions on Bounded Linear Operators in Terms of Quadratic Forms

Lemma 2 leads to the following characterization.

Theorem 6. *Let* ν, X *be as in the statement of Theorem 5,* Y *a Banach lattice, and* T_1, T, T_2 *bounded linear operators mapping* X *into* Y*. The following statements are equivalent:*

(a) $T_1 \le T \le T_2$ *on the positive cone* X_+;

(b) *For any finite subsets* $J_k \subset \mathbb{N}$, $k = 1,\ldots,n$ *and any* $\{\lambda_{j_k}\}_{j_k\in J_k} \subset \mathbb{R}$, $k = 1,\ldots,n$*, the following inequalities hold:*

$$\sum_{i_1,j_1\in J_1}\left(\cdots\left(\sum_{i_n,j_n\in J_n}\lambda_{i_1}\lambda_{j_1}\cdots\lambda_{i_n}\lambda_{j_n}T_1\left(\varphi_{i_1+j_1,\ldots,i_n+j_n}\right)\right)\cdots\right)$$

$$\le \sum_{i_1,j_1\in J_1}\left(\cdots\left(\sum_{i_n,j_n\in J_n}\lambda_{i_1}\lambda_{j_1}\cdots\lambda_{i_n}\lambda_{j_n}T\left(\varphi_{i_1+j_1,\ldots,i_n+j_n}\right)\right)\cdots\right) \le$$

$$\sum_{i_1,j_1\in J_1}\left(\cdots\left(\sum_{i_n,j_n\in J_n}\lambda_{i_1}\lambda_{j_1}\cdots\lambda_{i_n}\lambda_{j_n}T_2\left(\varphi_{i_1+j_1,\ldots,i_n+j_n}\right)\right)\cdots\right).$$

Proof. Statement (b) says that $\mathrm{T}_1(\mathrm{p}) \le T(p) \le \mathrm{T}_2(p)$ for all $p \in \mathcal{P}_{++}(\mathbb{R}^n)$, where $\mathcal{P}_{++}(\mathbb{R}^n)$ is the subcone of $\mathcal{P}_+(\mathbb{R}^n)$ formed by all polynomials that can be written as finite sums of the polynomial defined by (1), with $p_i \in \mathcal{P}_+(\mathbb{R})$, $i = 1,2,\ldots,n$. Hence, the implication $(a) := (b)$ is obvious. For the converse, according to a measure-type result [9], for any $\psi \in X_+$ there exists a sequence $(g_l)_{l\in\mathbb{N}}$ of functions from $(C_c(\mathbb{R}^n))_+$, with $\psi = \lim_l g_l$. On the other hand, Lemma 2 implies that there is a sequence of polynomials $(p_l)_{l\in\mathbb{N}}$, $p_l \in \mathcal{P}_{++}(\mathbb{R}^n)$ for all l such that $p_l - g_l \to 0$, $l \to \infty$. Thus,

$$\psi - p_l = (\psi - g_l) + (g_l - p_l) \to 0.$$

This means that $\psi = \lim\limits_{l \to \infty} p_l$. From (b), we know that $T_1(p_l) \leq T(p_l) \leq T_2(p_l)$ for all $l \in \mathbb{N}$. Now, the continuity of the three involved operators T_1, T, T_2 yields

$$T_1(\psi) = \lim_l T_1(p_l) \leq \lim_l T(p_l) = T(\psi) \leq \lim_l T_2(p_l) = T_2(\psi), \; \psi \in X_+.$$

This ends the proof. □

Using Lemma 3 and the form of nonnegative polynomials on $\mathbb{R}_+$ (3), the next result holds too.

Theorem 7. *Let* $X = L_\nu^1(\mathbb{R}_+^n)$, $\varphi_j(t) = t^j, t \in \mathbb{R}_+^n$, $j \in \mathbb{N}^n$, *where ν is as in Lemma 3, Y is a Banach lattice, and T_1, T, T_2 are bounded linear operators mapping X into Y. The following statements are equivalent:*

(a) $T_1 \leq T \leq T_2$ *on the positive cone* X_+;
(b) *For any finite subsets* $J_k \subset \mathbb{N}$, $k = 1, \ldots, n$ *and any* $\{\lambda_{j_k}\}_{j_k \in J_k} \subset \mathbb{R}$, $k = 1, \ldots, n$, *the following inequalities hold:*

$$\sum_{i_1, j_1 \in J_1} \left(\cdots \left(\sum_{i_n, j_n \in J_n} \lambda_{i_1} \lambda_{j_1} \cdots \lambda_{i_n} \lambda_{j_n} T_1\left(\varphi_{l_1 + i_1 + j_1, \ldots, l_n + i_n + j_n} \right) \right) \cdots \right)$$

$$\leq \sum_{i_1, j_1 \in J_1} \left(\cdots \left(\sum_{i_n, j_n \in J_n} \lambda_{i_1} \lambda_{j_1} \cdots \lambda_{i_n} \lambda_{j_n} T\left(\varphi_{l_1 + i_1 + j_1, \ldots, l_n + i_n + j_n} \right) \right) \cdots \right) \leq$$

$$\sum_{i_1, j_1 \in J_1} \left(\cdots \left(\sum_{i_n, j_n \in J_n} \lambda_{i_1} \lambda_{j_1} \cdots \lambda_{i_n} \lambda_{j_n} T_2\left(\varphi_{l_1 + i_1 + j_1, \ldots, l_n + i_n + j_n} \right) \right) \cdots \right),$$

for all $(l_1, \ldots, l_n) \in \{0, 1\}^n$.

4. Discussion

The present paper provides recently published results and a new way to present them. Such results refer to the Markov moment problem, which motivated the polynomial approximation on unbounded subsets stated in the beginning of the previous section. Instead of looking for the explicit form of nonnegative polynomials on unbounded closed subsets F of $\mathbb{R}^n$, $n \geq 2$ (which has been proven to not always be expressible in terms of sums of squares), the approximation by finite sums of special polynomials pointed out in Lemmas 2 and 3, followed by the passing to the limit process, solved partially or completely, respectively, the problems discussed in the present work. With respect to our own previous similar results, this review paper comes with generalizations and improvements in the theorems, which clearly needed to be improved. We did not see a simpler method in the literature that was able to solve polynomial approximation on unbounded subsets (which is important as a separate subject) and the applications emphasized in this paper. It is a work in the settings of analysis and functional analysis over the real field. The presentation of some statements completes or generalizes the published results on the subject. As a direction for future work, it would be interesting to study what these theorems say in the cases when the codomains Y are concrete Banach lattices.

Funding: This research received no external funding.

Data Availability Statement: Not applicable.

Acknowledgments: The author would like to thank the reviewers for their comments and suggestions, which led to an improvement in the presentation of the paper.

Conflicts of Interest: The author declares no conflict of interest.

References

1. Berg, C.; Thill, M. Rotation invariant moment problems. *Acta Math.* **1991**, *167*, 207–227. [CrossRef]
2. Berg, C.; Durán, A.J. The fixed point for a transformation of Hausdorff moment sequences and iteration of a rational function. *Math. Scand.* **2008**, *103*, 11–39. [CrossRef]
3. Fuglede, B. The multidimensional moment problem. *Expo. Math.* **1983**, *1*, 47–65.
4. Bucur, I.; Paltineanu, G. De Branges type lemma and approximation in weighted spaces. *Mediterr. J. Math.* **2021**, *18*, 120. [CrossRef]
5. Cobzaş, S. Ekeland, Takahashi and Caristi principles in quasi-pseudometric spaces. *Topol. Appl.* **2019**, *265*, 106831. [CrossRef]
6. Cobzaş, S. Geometric properties of Banach spaces and the existence of nearest and farthest points. *Abstr. Appl. Anal.* **2005**, *2005*, 259–285. [CrossRef]
7. Raşa, I. Convexity Properties of Some Entropies (II). *Results Math.* **2019**, *74*, 154. [CrossRef]
8. Pakkaranang, N.; Kumam, P.; Cho, Y.J. Proximal point algorithms for solving convex minimization problem and common fixed points of asymptotically quasi-nonexpansive mappings in in CAT(0) spaces with convergence analysis. *Numer. Algorithms* **2018**, *78*, 827–845. [CrossRef]
9. Balan, V.; Olteanu, A.; Olteanu, O. On Newton's method for convex operators with some applications. *Rev. Roumaine Math. Pures Appl.* **2006**, *51*, 277–290.
10. Özkan, E.Y. A New Kantorovich-Type Rational Operator and Inequalities for Its Approximation. *Mathematics* **2022**, *10*, 1982. [CrossRef]
11. Kim, Y.-T.; Park, H.-S. Fourth Cumulant Bound of Multivariate Normal Approximation on General Functionals of Gaussian Fields. *Mathematics* **2022**, *10*, 1352. [CrossRef]
12. Mennouni, A.; Zaouia, S. Discrete septic spline quasi-interpolants for solving generalized Fredholm integral equation of the second kind via three degenerate kernel methods. *Math. Sci.* **2017**, *11*, 345–357. Available online: https://link.springer.com/content/pdf/10.1007/s40096-017-0237-x.pdf (accessed on 2 July 2022). [CrossRef]
13. Olteanu, O. On Markov Moment Problem and Related Results. *Symmetry* **2021**, *13*, 986. [CrossRef]
14. Olteanu, O. On Hahn-Banach theorem and some of its applications. *Open Math.* **2022**, *20*, 366–390. [CrossRef]
15. Olteanu, O. Convexity, Markov Operators, Approximation, and Related Optimization. *Mathematics* **2022**, *10*, 2775. [CrossRef]
16. Olteanu, O. *Convexity, Extension of Linear Operators, Approximation and Applications*; Cambridge Scholars Publishing, Lady Stephenson Library: Newcastle upon Tyne, UK, 2022.
17. Phelps, R.R. *Lectures on Choquet's Theorem.*, 2nd ed.; Springer: Berlin/Heidelberg, Germany, 2001.
18. Akhiezer, N.I. *The Classical Moment Problem and Some Related Questions in Analysis*; Oliver and Boyd: Edinburgh, UK, 1965.
19. Berg, C.; Christensen, J.P.R.; Ressel, P. Harmonic Analysis on Semigroups. In *Theory of Positive Definite and Related Functions*; Springer: New York, NY, USA, 1984.
20. Schmüdgen, K. The Moment Problem. In *Graduate Texts in Mathematics*; Springer International Publishing AG: Cham, Switzerland, 2017; p. 277. [CrossRef]
21. Krein, M.G.; Nudelman, A.A. *Markov Moment Problem and Extremal Problems*; American Mathematical Society: Providence, RI, USA, 1977.
22. Cristescu, R. *Ordered Vector Spaces and Linear Operators*; Academiei: Bucharest, Romania; Abacus Press: Tunbridge Wells, UK, 1976.
23. Niculescu, C.; Popa, N. *Elements of Theory of Banach Spaces*; Academiei: Bucharest, Romania, 1981. (In Romanian)
24. Choudary, A.D.R.; Niculescu, C.P. *Real Analysis on Intervals*; Springer: New Delhi, India, 2014. [CrossRef]
25. Niculescu, C.P.; Persson, L.-E. *Convex Functions and Their Applications, a Contemporary Approach*, 2nd ed.; CMS Books in Mathematics; Springer: New York, NY, USA, 2018; Volume 23.
26. Rudin, W. *Real and Complex Analysis*, 3rd ed.; McGraw-Hill Book Company: Singapore, 1987.
27. Singer, I. *Best Approximation in Normed Linear Spaces by Elements of Linear Subspaces*; Springer: New York, NY, USA, 1970.
28. Haviland, E.K. On the momentum problem for distribution functions in more than one dimension. II. *Am. J. Math.* **1936**, *58*, 164. [CrossRef]
29. Kutateladze, S.S. Convex Operators. *Russ. Math. Surv.* **1979**, *34*, 181–214. [CrossRef]
30. Berg, C.; Christensen, J.P.R.; Jensen, C.U. A remark on the multidimensional moment problem. *Math. Ann.* **1979**, *243*, 163–169. [CrossRef]
31. Berg, C.; Szwarc, R. Self-adjoint operators associated with Hankel moment matrices. *J. Funct. Anal.* **2022**, *283*, 109674. [CrossRef]
32. Stoyanov, J.M.; Lin, G.D.; Kopanov, P. New checkable conditions for moment determinacy of probability distributions. *Theory Probab. Appl.* **2020**, *65*, 497–509. [CrossRef]
33. Cassier, G. Problèmes des moments sur un compact de $\mathbb{R}^n$ et décomposition des polynômes á plusieurs variables (Moment problems on a compact subset of $\mathbb{R}^n$ and decomposition of polynomials of several variables). *J. Funct. Anal.* **1984**, *58*, 254–266. [CrossRef]
34. Schmüdgen, K. The K-moment problem for compact semi-algebraic sets. *Math. Ann.* **1991**, *289*, 203–206. [CrossRef]
35. Putinar, M. Positive polynomials on compact semi-algebraic sets. *IU Math J.* **1993**, *42*, 969–984. [CrossRef]
36. Putinar, M.; Vasilescu, F.H. Problème des moments sur les compacts semi-algébriques (The moment problem on semi-algebraic compacts). *Comptes Rendus Acad. Sci. Paris Ser. I* **1996**, *323*, 787–791.
37. Vasilescu, F.H. Spectral measures and moment problems. In *Spectral Analysis and Its Applications (Ion Colojoară Anniversary Volume)*; Theta: Bucharest, Romania, 2003; pp. 173–215.

38. Choquet, G. Le problème des moments (The moment problem). In *Séminaire d'Initiation à l'Analise;* Institut H. Poincaré: Paris, France, 1962.
39. Marshall, M. Polynomials non-negative on a strip. *Proc. Am. Math. Soc.* **2010**, *138*, 1559–1567. [CrossRef]
40. Tagliani, A. Maximum entropy solutions and moment problem in unbounded domains. *Appl. Math. Lett.* **2003**, *16*, 519–524. [CrossRef]
41. Inverardi, P.N.; Tagliani, A. Stieltjes and Hamburger Reduced Moment Problem When MaxEnt Solution Does Not Exist. *Mathematics* **2021**, *9*, 309. [CrossRef]
42. Stochel, J. Solving the truncated moment problem solves the full moment problem. *Glas. Math. J.* **2001**, *43*, 335–341. [CrossRef]
43. Lemnete, L. An operator-valued moment problem. *Proc. Am. Math. Soc.* **1991**, *112*, 1023–1028. [CrossRef]
44. Niculescu, C.P.; Olteanu, O. From the Hahn–Banach extension theorem to the isotonicity of convex functions and the majorization theory. *Revista de la Real Academia de Ciencias Exactas Físicas y Naturales Serie A. Matemáticas* **2020**, *114*, 171. [CrossRef]
45. Norris, D.T. Optimal Solutions to the L∞ Moment Problem with Lattice Bounds. Ph.D. Thesis, Department of Mathematics, College of Arts and Sciences, University Colorado Boulder, Boulder, CO, USA, 2002.
46. Gosse, L.; Runborg, O. Resolution of the finite Markov moment problem. *Comptes Rendus Acad. Sci. Paris* **2005**, *341*, 775–780. [CrossRef]
47. Lemnete-Ninulescu, L.; Zlătescu, A. Some new aspects of the L-moment problem. *Rev. Roum. Math. Pures Appl.* **2010**, *55*, 197–204.
48. Olteanu, O. Application de théorèmes de prolongement d'opérateurs linéaires au problème des moments e à une generalization d'un théorème de Mazur-Orlicz, (Applications of theorems on extension of linear operators to the moment problem and to a generalization of Mazur-Orlicz theorem). *Comptes Rendus Acad. Sci. Paris* **1991**, *313*, 739–742.

mathematics

Article

Stationary Conditions and Characterizations of Solution Sets for Interval-Valued Tightened Nonlinear Problems

Kin Keung Lai [1,*,†], Shashi Kant Mishra [2,†], Sanjeev Kumar Singh [2,†] and Mohd Hassan [2,†]

1 International Business School, Shaanxi Normal University, Xi'an 710119, China
2 Department of Mathematics, Institute of Science, Banaras Hindu University, Varanasi 221005, India
* Correspondence: mskklai@outlook.com
† These authors contributed equally to this work.

Abstract: In this paper, we obtain characterizations of solution sets of the interval-valued mathematical programming problems with switching constraints. Stationary conditions which are weaker than the standard Karush–Kuhn–Tucker conditions need to be discussed in order to find the necessary optimality conditions. We introduce corresponding weak, Mordukhovich, and strong stationary conditions for the corresponding interval-valued mathematical programming problems with switching constraints (IVPSC) and interval-valued tightened nonlinear problems (IVTNP), because the W-stationary condition of IVPSC is equivalent to Karush–Kuhn–Tucker conditions of the IVTNP. Furthermore, we use strong stationary conditions to characterize the several solutions sets for IVTNP, in which the last ones are particular solutions sets for IVPSC at the same time, because the feasible set of tightened nonlinear problems (IVTNP) is a subset of the feasible set of the mathematical programs with switching constraints (IVPSC).

Keywords: nonlinear programming; switching constraints; stationary conditions; interval-valued optimization

MSC: 90C30; 90C33; 49K10

Citation: Lai, K.K.; Mishra, S.K.; Singh, S.K.; Hassan, M. Stationary Conditions and Characterizations of Solution Sets for Interval-Valued Tightened Nonlinear Problems. *Mathematics* **2022**, *10*, 2763. https://doi.org/10.3390/math10152763

Academic Editor: Savin Treanta

Received: 28 June 2022
Accepted: 1 August 2022
Published: 4 August 2022

1. Introduction

Mathematical programming problems with equilibrium constraints (MPEC) [1] and mathematical programming problems with vanishing constraints (MPVC) [2] have recently found considerable attention in the area of optimal control, mathematical equilibrium, truss topology, and other research fields [3] due to a wide range of applications in real-life problems.

Singh et al. [4] established Lagrange-type duality results and saddle point optimality criteria for mathematical programs with equilibrium constraints for differentiable functions. Pandey and Mishra [5] established Wolfe and Mond–Weir-type duality results for mathematical programs with equilibrium constraints using convexificators. Pandey and Mishra [6] obtained optimality and duality results for semi-infinite mathematical programs with equilibrium constraints using convexificators. Pandey and Mishra [7] established that the Mordukhovich (M) stationary conditions [7] are strong KKT-type sufficient optimality conditions for the nonsmooth multiobjective semi-infinite mathematical programs with equilibrium constraints. Mishra et al. [8] obtained duality results for mathematical programs with vanishing constraints for differentiable functions. Mishra et al. [9] showed that Cottle, Slater, and Mangasarian–Fromovitz constraint qualifications do not hold at an efficient solution under fairly mild assumptions, whereas the Guignard constraint qualification was satisfied sometimes for mathematical programs with vanishing constraints. Mishra et al. [9] introduced suitable modifications of said constraint qualifications, established relationships, and derived the KKT-type necessary optimality conditions. Guu et al. [10] established strong KKT-type sufficient optimality conditions for nonsmooth multiobjective semi-infinite programming problems with vanishing constraints. Lai et al. [11] established Fritz–John and KKT-type stationary points conditions for nonsmooth semi-definite multiobjective mathematical programs with vanishing constraints.

Mehlitz [12] introduced the mathematical program with switching constraints (MPSC). It is not surprising that the issues involving the usual constraint qualifications for MPEC and MPVC also exist for MPSC. Mehlitz [12] showed that if an MPSC is treated as a nonlinear program, the Mangasarian–Fromovitz constraint qualifications fail at any feasible point for which there is a pair of switching functions with a value equal to zero. As a result, he introduced the concepts of weak, Mordukhovich (M-), and strong (S-) stationarity for MPSC and presented some constraint qualifications. Kanzow et al. [13] provided several relaxation methods from the numerical solutions of MPEC to MPSC. Liang and Ye [14] obtained various optimality conditions and local error bounds for MPSC. Pandey and Singh [15] studied several constraint qualifications and stationarity for multiobjective mathematical programs with switching constraints.

Uncertainty in the real world is inevitable. Therefore, imposing uncertainty in optimization problems becomes an interesting research topic. Interval-valued nonlinear programming is one such research area; see [16–19]. Lai et al. [20] established sufficient optimality conditions and duality results for semidifferentiable mathematical programming problems. Sharma et al. [21] established the Hermite–Hadamard inequalities for preinvex interval-valued functions. Su and Dinh [22] established duality results for interval-valued pseudoconvex optimization problems with equilibrium constraints with applications. Wang and Wang [23] obtained duality results for nondifferentiable semi-infinite interval-valued optimization problems with vanishing constraints.

The characterization of solution sets in mathematical programming is useful in understanding the development of solution methods for solving the problem. Mangasarian [24] introduced the concept of the characterization of solutions sets for convex programs, and Burke and Ferris [25] provided several characterizations of solution sets for nonsmooth convex programs. Jeyakumar et al. [26] provided Lagrange multiplier-based characterizations of solution sets of cone-constrained convex programs and semidefinite programs. Dinh et al. [27] studied Lagrange multiplier characterizations of solution sets of constrained pseudolinear optimization problems. Furthermore, Jeyakumar et al. [28] gave a dual characterization of the weak and proper solution sets. Jeyakumar et al. [28] discussed Lagrange multiplier characterizations of the solutions sets under regularity conditions. Lalitha and Mehta [29] derived Lagrange multiplier characterizations of solution sets for nonlinear mathematical programs with an h-convex objective and h-pseudolinear constraints. Several Lagrange multiplier characterizations of solution sets for a convex infinite programming problems are obtained in [30]. Mishra et al. [31] established several Lagrange multiplier characterizations of solution sets for constrained nonsmooth pseudolinear optimization problems. Recently, Sisarat and Wangkeeree [32] provided some characterizations of solution sets of constant pseudo Lagrangian-type functions and established Lagrange multiplier characterizations. Some recent developments of significant research on characterizations of solution sets are in [33–43] and references therein. Recently, Treanta [44] provided several characterizations of solution sets of interval-valued variational control problems and discussed its relationship with variational control problems.

Motivated by the above-mentioned work, firstly, we consider interval-valued mathematical programming with switching constraints (IVPSC). We introduce corresponding weak, Mordukhovich, and strong stationary conditions (W-stationary, M-stationary and S-stationary for short). We propose an interval-valued tightened nonlinear problem (IVTNP) associated with IVPSC. We provide several characterizations of solution sets for IVPSC with the help of the S-stationary condition and IVTNP. We construct the corresponding Lagrangian function for IVPSC. We use semiconvex functions introduced by Mifflin [45], extend for interval-valued nonsmooth functions and provide the properties of interval-valued semiconvex functions. Furthermore, we prove that the associated Lagrangian is constant under the S-stationary and semiconvexity conditions with a Clarke subdifferential. We also provide an example to support the theoretical findings.

2. Preliminaries

2.1. Interval Analysis

We collect some basic concepts and essential definitions related to interval-valued functions from Moore [46] and Wu [18].

We denote by $\mathcal{I}(\mathbb{R})$ the class of all closed intervals in $\mathbb{R}$. Let $U = [u^L, u^U]$, where u^L and u^U denote the lower and upper bounds of U, respectively. Let $U = [u^L, u^U]$ and $V = [v^L, v^U]$ be in $\mathcal{I}(\mathbb{R})$; then, we have

(i) $U + V = \{u + v : u \in U,\ v \in V\} = [u^L + v^L, u^U + v^U]$,

(ii) $-U = \{-u : u \in U\} = [-u^U, -u^L]$,

(iii) $U - V = U + (-V) = [u^L - v^U, u^U - v^L]$,

(iv) $tU = \{tu : u \in U\} = \begin{cases} [tu^L, tu^U] & \text{if } \ t \geq 0 \\ [tu^U, tu^L] & \text{for } \ t < 0 \end{cases}$ where t is a real number.

Let $U = [u^L, u^U]$ and $V = [v^L, v^U]$ be two closed intervals in $\mathbb{R}$. We write $U \preceq V$ if and only if $u^L \leq v^L$ and $u^U \leq v^U$. It means that U is inferior to V, or V is superior to U. It is easy to see that " $\preceq$ " is a partial ordering on $\mathcal{I}(\mathbb{R})$.

The function $f : \mathbb{R}^n \to \mathcal{I}$ is called an interval valued function; this means $f(u) = f(u_1, \cdots, u_n)$ is a closed interval in $\mathbb{R}$ for each $u \in \mathbb{R}^n$. f can be written as $f(u) = [f^L(u), f^U(u)]$, where f^L and f^U are two real valued functions defined on $\mathbb{R}^n$ such that $f^L(u) \leq f^U(u),\ \forall u \in \mathbb{R}^n$.

We write $U \prec_{LU} V$ if and only if $U \preceq_{LU} V$ and $U \neq V$. We say $U = (U_1, \cdots, U_p)$ is an interval valued vector if each component $U_k = [u_k^L, u_k^U]$ is a closed interval for $k = 1, \cdots, p$. Suppose $U = (U_1, \cdots, U_p)$ and $V = (V_1, \cdots, V_p)$ are two interval valued vectors. We write $U \preceq_{LU} V$ if and only if $U_k \preceq_{LU} V_k\ \forall k = 1, \cdots, p$, and $U \prec_{LU} V$ if and only if $U_k \preceq_{LU} V_k,\ \forall k = 1, \cdots, p$ and $U_q \prec_{LU} V_q$ for at least one q.

Definition 1 ([17]). *An interval-valued function $f(u) = [f^L(u), f^U(u)]$ defined on $X \subseteq \mathbb{R}^n$ is said to be LU-convex if $\forall u, v \in X,\ \lambda \in (0,1)$,*

$$f(\lambda u + (1-\lambda)v) \preceq_{LU} \lambda f(u) + (1-\lambda) f(v).$$

2.2. Generalized Derivatives

We collect the definitions and properties of generalized derivatives from Clarke [47]. Suppose $f : \mathbb{R}^n \to \mathbb{R}$ is a locally Lipschitz function at $u \in \mathbb{R}^n$. The generalized directional derivative of f at u in the direction $d \in \mathbb{R}^n$ is denoted by $f^c(u; d)$ and is defined by

$$f^c(u; d) := \limsup_{\substack{h \to 0 \\ t \downarrow 0}} \frac{f(u + h + td) - f(u + h)}{t}$$

and the Clarke's subdifferential of f at u, denoted by $\partial^c f(u)$, is defined by

$$\partial^c f(u) := \{u \in \mathbb{R}^n :\ f^c(u; d) \geq \langle u, d \rangle,\ \forall d \in \mathbb{R}^n\}.$$

We denote by $\langle u, v \rangle$ the usual inner product in n-dimensional real Euclidean space $\mathbb{R}^n$, i.e.,

$$\langle u, v \rangle = u^T v, \text{ for } u, v \in \mathbb{R}^n.$$

The directional derivatives of f at u in the direction of d, denoted by $f'(u; d)$, are defined by

$$\lim_{t \downarrow 0} \frac{f(u + td) - f(u)}{t} \text{ provided the limit exists.}$$

f is said to be regular at u in the Clarke sense if $f'(u;d)$ exists and is equal to $f^c(u;d)$ for every $d \in \mathbb{R}^n$ [48].

Consider $f : \mathbb{R}^n \to \mathcal{I}(\mathbb{R})$ is an interval-valued function; then, $f(u) = [f^L(u), f^U(u)]$ is regular if both the upper and lower bound functions f^L and f^U are regular.

Suppose M is the closed convex subset of $\mathbb{R}^n$. The normal cone [49] to M at u is

$$N(M,u) = \{\eta \in \mathbb{R}^n \, : \, \langle \eta, v-u \rangle \leq 0, \, \forall v \in M\}.$$

Definition 2 ([45])**.** *Suppose X is a nonempty subset of* $\mathbb{R}^n$. *A function* $f : \mathbb{R}^n \to \mathbb{R}$ *is said to be semiconvex at* $u \in X$ *if* f *is locally Lipschitz at* u *and regular at* u*, and it satisfies the following condition*

$$u + d \in X, d \in \mathbb{R}^n, f'(u;d) \geq 0 \implies f(u+d) \geq f(u).$$

The interval-valued function $f : \mathbb{R}^n \to \mathcal{I}(\mathbb{R})$ *is said to be semiconvex on X if* f^L *and* f^U *are semiconvex at every* $u \in X$.

We can easily see from the above definition that f is semiconvex at u if $\exists \, u \in \partial^c f(u) : \langle \eta, v-u \rangle \geq 0 \implies f(v) \geq f(u)$.

Mifflin [45] provided an important result on semiconvex functions, which can be further generalized for interval-valued functions.

Lemma 1. *Let the function* f *be semiconvex on a convex set* $X \subset \mathbb{R}^n$. *Then, for* $u \in X, d \in \mathbb{R}^n$ *with* $u + d \in X$*, we have*

$$f(u+d) \leq f(u) \implies f'(u;d) \leq 0.$$

The interval-valued function $f : \mathbb{R}^n \to \mathcal{I}(\mathbb{R})$ is semiconvex; then, for $u \in X \subset \mathbb{R}^n$, $d \in \mathbb{R}^n$ with $u + d \in X$, we have

$$f(u+d) \preceq_{LU} f(u) \implies f'(u;d) \preceq_{LU} 0.$$

This means that

$$\begin{aligned} f^L(u+d) \leq f^L(u) &\implies f^{L'}(u;d) \leq 0 \\ \text{and } f^U(u+d) \leq f^U(u) &\implies f^{U'}(u;d) \leq 0. \end{aligned}$$

2.3. *Interval-Valued Mathematical Programs with Switching Constraints (IVPSC)*

We consider the following interval-valued mathematical programs with switching constraints (IVPSC)

$$\begin{aligned} \min f(u) &= [f^L(u), f^U(u)] \quad (1) \\ \text{subject to } g_i(u) &\leq 0, \, \forall \, i = 1, \cdots, p, \\ h_j(u) &= 0, \, \forall \, j = 1, \cdots, q, \\ G_k(u) H_k(u) &= 0, \, \forall \, k = 1, \cdots r, \end{aligned}$$

where the functions f^L, g_i, h_j, G_k, $H_k : \mathbb{R}^n \to \mathbb{R}$ are continuously differentiable on $\mathbb{R}^n$. We say $G_k(u)H_k(u) = 0$, while the switching constraint since functions $G_k(u)$, $H_k(u)$ are active is at least one, $G_k(u) = 0$ or $H_k(u) = 0$ for all $k = 1, \cdots, r$, at any feasible point of IVPSC.

We denote the solution set of IVPSC by S.

$$\begin{aligned} S = \{u \in M : f^L(u) \leq f^L(v), \, f^U(u) \leq f^U(v), \, g(u) \leq 0, \\ h(u) = 0, \, G_k(u)H_k(u) = 0, \forall v \in M\}. \end{aligned}$$

2.4. Stationary Conditions

We need to mention some index sets to define stationary conditions at the feasible point $\bar{u}$ for IVPSC.

$$I_g(\bar{u}) := \{i \in \{1,\cdots,p\} : g_i(\bar{u}) = 0\},$$
$$I^G(\bar{u}) := \{k \in \{1,\cdots,r\} : G_k(\bar{u}) = 0 \text{ and } H_k(\bar{u}) \neq 0\},$$
$$I^H(\bar{u}) := \{k \in \{1,\cdots,r\} : G_k(\bar{u}) \neq 0 \text{ and } H_k(\bar{u}) = 0\},$$
$$I^{GH}(\bar{u}) := \{k \in \{1,\cdots,r\} : G_k(\bar{u}) = 0 \text{ and } H_k(\bar{u}) = 0\}.$$

We establish some stationary conditions in the Clarke subdifferential form motivated by Mehlitz [12]. In order to define the stationary conditions, we need to introduce the KKT system of IVPSC, which is as follows.

Definition 3. *(KKT-type conditions): A feasible point $\bar{u}$ of IVPSC is said to satisfy KKT-type conditions if there exist multipliers $\lambda^L, \lambda^U, \lambda_i (i \in \{1,\cdots,p\}), \lambda_j (j \in \{1,\cdots,q\}), \lambda_k, \mu_k (k \in \{1,\cdots,r\})$ such that the following conditions hold*

$$0 \in \lambda^L \partial^c f^L(\bar{u}) + \lambda^U \partial^c f^U(\bar{u}) + \sum_{i=1}^{p} \lambda_i \partial^c g_i(\bar{u}) + \sum_{j=1}^{q} \lambda_j \partial^c h_i(\bar{u})$$
$$+ \sum_{k=1}^{r} [\lambda_k \partial^c G_k(\bar{u}) + \mu_k \partial^c H_k(\bar{u})],$$
$$\lambda_i \geq 0 \,\forall\, i \in I_g(\bar{u}).$$

1. Weakly stationary point (W-stationary point): A feasible point $\bar{u}$ of IVPSC is called W-stationary if there exist multipliers $\lambda^L, \lambda^U, \lambda_i (i \in \{1,\cdots,p\}), \lambda_j (j \in \{1,\cdots,q\}), \lambda_k$, $\mu_k (k \in \{1,\cdots,r\})$ such that the following conditions hold

$$0 \in \lambda^L \partial^c f^L(\bar{u}) + \lambda^U \partial^c f^U(\bar{u}) + \sum_{i=1}^{p} \lambda_i \partial^c g_i(\bar{u}) + \sum_{j=1}^{q} \lambda_j \partial^c h_i(\bar{u})$$
$$+ \sum_{k=1}^{r} [\lambda_k \partial^c G_k(\bar{u}) + \mu_k \partial^c H_k(\bar{u})],$$
$$\lambda_i \geq 0 \,\forall\, i \in I_g(\bar{u}), \quad \lambda_k = 0 \,\forall\, k \in I^G(\bar{u}), \quad \mu_k = 0 \,\forall\, k \in I^H(\bar{u}).$$

2. Mordukhovich stationary point (M-stationary point): A feasible point $\bar{u}$ of IVPSC is called M-stationary if there exist multipliers $\lambda^L, \lambda^U, \lambda_i (i \in \{1,\cdots,p\}), \lambda_j (j \in \{1,\cdots,q\}), \lambda_k, \mu_k (k \in \{1,\cdots,r\})$ such that the following conditions hold

$$0 \in \lambda^L \partial^c f^L(\bar{u}) + \lambda^U \partial^c f^U(\bar{u}) + \sum_{i=1}^{p} \lambda_i \partial^c g_i(\bar{u}) + \sum_{j=1}^{q} \lambda_j \partial^c h_i(\bar{u})$$
$$+ \sum_{k=1}^{r} [\lambda_k \partial^c G_k(\bar{u}) + \mu_k \partial^c H_k(\bar{u})],$$
$$\lambda_i \geq 0 \,\forall\, i \in I_g(\bar{u}), \quad \lambda_k = 0 \,\forall\, k \in I^G(\bar{u}), \quad \mu_k = 0 \,\forall\, k \in I^H(\bar{u}),$$
$$\text{and } \lambda_k \mu_k = 0 \quad \forall\, k \in I^{GH}(\bar{u}).$$

3. Strong stationary point (S-stationary point): A feasible point $\bar{u}$ of IVPSC is called S-stationary if there exist multipliers $\lambda^L, \lambda^U, \lambda_i (i \in \{1,\cdots,p\}), \lambda_j (j \in \{1,\cdots,q\}), \lambda_k$, $\mu_k (k \in \{1,\cdots,r\})$ such that the following conditions hold

$$0 \in \lambda^L \partial^c f^L(\bar{u}) + \lambda^U \partial^c f^U(\bar{u}) + \sum_{i=1}^{p} \lambda_i \partial^c g_i(\bar{u}) + \sum_{j=1}^{q} \lambda_j \partial^c h_i(\bar{u})$$

$$+\sum_{k=1}^{r}[\lambda_k\partial^c G_k(\bar{u})+\mu_k\partial^c H_k(\bar{u})],$$
$$\lambda_i\geq 0\,\forall\, i\in I_g(\bar{u}),\quad \lambda_k=0\,\forall\, k\in I^G(\bar{u}),\quad \mu_k=0\,\forall\, k\in I^H(\bar{u}),$$
$$\text{and } \lambda_k=0,\ \mu_k=0\quad \forall\, k\in I^{GH}(\bar{u}).$$

We can easily see that the following relationship holds between the above stationary conditions.

S-stationary condition $\Longrightarrow$ M-stationary condition $\Longrightarrow$ W-stationary condition.

The W-stationary condition of IVPSC at one of its feasible points $\bar{u}$ is equivalent to KKT conditions of the following tightened nonlinear problem.

We consider the interval-valued tightened nonlinear problem (IVTNP) at $\bar{u}$.

$$\begin{aligned}(IVTNP)\qquad & \min f(\bar{u})=[f^L(\bar{u}),f^U(\bar{u})]\\ & \text{subject to } g_i(\bar{u})\leq 0,\ \forall\, i=1,\cdots,p,\\ & h_j(\bar{u})=0,\ \forall\, j=1,\cdots,q,\\ & G_k(\bar{u})=0,\ \forall\, k\in I^G(\bar{u})\cup I^{GH}(\bar{u}),\\ & H_k(\bar{u})=0,\ \forall\, k\in I^H(\bar{u})\cup I^{GH}(\bar{u}).\end{aligned}\tag{2}$$

The feasible set of IVTNP is a subset of the feasible set of IVPSC.

3. Lagrange Multiplier Characterization

We suppose that there exist multipliers $\lambda^L,\lambda^U,\lambda_i(i\in\{1,\cdots,p\}),\lambda_j(j\in\{1,\cdots,q\})$, $\lambda_k,\mu_k(k\in\{1,\cdots,r\})$ such the the following optimality conditions hold

$$\begin{aligned}0\in\ & \lambda^L\partial^c f^L(u)+\lambda^U\partial^c f^U(u)+\sum_{i=1}^{p}\lambda_i\partial^c g_i(u)+\sum_{j=1}^{q}\lambda_j\partial^c h_i(u)\\ & +\sum_{k=1}^{r}\Big(\lambda_k\partial^c G_k(u)+\mu_k\partial^c H_k(u)\Big)+N(M,u),\\ & \lambda_i g_i(u)=0,\forall i\in\{1,\cdots,p\},\ \lambda_j h_j(u)=0,\forall j\in\{1,\cdots,q\},\\ & \lambda_k G_k(u)=0,\forall k\in I^G(\bar{u})\cup I^{GH}(\bar{u}),\ \mu_k H_k(u)=0,\forall k\in I^H(\bar{u})\cup I^{GH}(\bar{u}).\end{aligned}\tag{3}$$

The addition of normal cone $N(M,u)$ in the above optimality condition is motivated by Theorem 5.1.6 of [50].

The Lagrangian function is defined by

$$\begin{aligned}L(u,\lambda,\mu)=\ & \lambda^L f^L(u)+\lambda^U f^U(u)+\sum_{i=1}^{p}\lambda_i g_i(u)+\sum_{j=1}^{q}\lambda_j h_i(u)\\ & +\sum_{k=1}^{r}\Big(\lambda_k G_k(u)+\mu_k H_k(u)\Big).\end{aligned}\tag{4}$$

Lemma 2. *Let $\bar{u}$ be the solution to the problem (IVTNP) such that the condition* (3) *and S-stationary condition hold. Suppose that the functions $f^L,f^U,g_i(i\in\{1,\cdots,p\}),h_j(j\in\{1,\cdots,q\})$, $G_k,H_k(k\in\{1,\cdots,r\})$ are regular at $\bar{u}$ and the Lagrangian function $L(\cdot,\lambda,\mu)$ is semiconvex at $\bar{u}$; then, $L(\cdot,\lambda.\mu)$ is constant on S.*

Proof. Let $\bar{u}\in S$, and there exist multipliers $\lambda^g,\lambda^h,\lambda^G,\lambda^H$ such that condition (3) holds. Then, there exist $u^L\in\partial^c f^L(\bar{u}),u^U\in\partial^c f^U(\bar{u}),w\in N(M,\bar{u}),v_g\in\partial^c g_i(\bar{u})(i\in\{1,\cdots,p\})$, $v_h\in\partial^c h_j(\bar{u})(j\in\{1,\cdots,q\}),v_G\in\partial^c G_k(\bar{u}),v_H\in\partial^c H_k(\bar{u})(k\in\{1,\cdots,r\})$, such that

$$\lambda^L u^L+\lambda^U u^U+\sum_{i=1}^{p}\lambda_i v_g+\sum_{j=1}^{q}\lambda_j v_h+\sum_{k=1}^{r}\Big(\lambda_k v_G+\mu_k v_H\Big)=-w.$$

As M is a closed convex subset of X, $\langle w, v-\bar{u}\rangle \leq 0\ \forall v \in M$, hence, we have

$$\left\langle \lambda^L u^L + \lambda^U u^U + \sum_{i=1}^{p} \lambda_i \nu_g + \sum_{j=1}^{q} \lambda_j \nu_h + \sum_{k=1}^{r} \Big(\lambda_k \nu_G + \mu_k \nu_H\Big), v-\bar{u} \right\rangle \geq 0. \tag{5}$$

Now, since $L(\cdot,\lambda,\mu)$ is regular at $\bar{u}$, we have

$$\begin{aligned} &\Big[\lambda^L f^L + \lambda^U f^U + \sum_{i\in I_g(\bar{u})} \lambda_i g_i + \sum_{j=1}^{q} \lambda_j h_j + \sum_{k=1}^{r} \Big(\lambda_k G_k + \mu_k H_k\Big)\Big]^c (\bar{u}, v-\bar{u}) \\ &= \Big[\lambda^L f^L + \lambda^U f^U + \sum_{i\in I_g(\bar{u})} \lambda_i g_i + \sum_{j=1}^{q} \lambda_j h_j + \sum_{k=1}^{r} \Big(\lambda_k G_k + \mu_k H_k\Big)\Big]' (\bar{u}, v-\bar{u}). \end{aligned} \tag{6}$$

Using the regularity of $f^L, f^U, g_i(i \in \{1,\cdots,p\}), h_j(j \in \{1,\cdots,q\}), G_k$, $H_k(k \in \{1,\cdots,r\})$ and from (5) and (6), we obtain

$$\Big[\lambda^L f^L + \lambda^U f^U + \sum_{i\in I_g(\bar{u})} \lambda_i g_i + \sum_{j=1}^{q} \lambda_j h_j + \sum_{k=1}^{r} \Big(\lambda_k G_k + \mu_k H_k\Big)\Big]' (\bar{u}, v-\bar{u}) \geq 0.$$

Since $L(\cdot,\lambda,\mu)$ is semiconvex at $\bar{u}$, we have

$$\begin{aligned} &\lambda f(\bar{u}) + \sum_{i\in I_g(\bar{u})} \lambda_i g_i(\bar{u}) + \sum_{j=1}^{q} \lambda_j h_j(\bar{u}) + \sum_{k=1}^{r} \Big(\lambda_k G_k(\bar{u}) + \mu_k H_k(\bar{u})\Big) \\ &\preceq_{LU} \lambda f(v)) + \sum_{i\in I_g(\bar{u})} \lambda_i g_i(v) + \sum_{j=1}^{q} \lambda_j h_j(v) + \sum_{k=1}^{r} \Big(\lambda_k G_k(v) + \mu_k H_k(v)\Big). \end{aligned}$$

This means

$$\begin{aligned} &\lambda^L f^L(v) + \lambda^U f^U(v) + \sum_{i\in I_g(\bar{u})} \lambda_i g_i(v) + \sum_{j=1}^{q} \lambda_j h_j(v) + \sum_{k=1}^{r} \Big(\lambda_k G_k(v) + \mu_k H_k(v)\Big) \\ &\geq \lambda^L f^L(\bar{u}) + \lambda^U f^U(\bar{u}) + \sum_{i\in I_g(\bar{u})} \lambda_i g_i(\bar{u}) + \sum_{j=1}^{q} \lambda_j h_j(\bar{u}) + \sum_{k=1}^{r} \Big(\lambda_k G_k(\bar{u}) + \mu_k H_k(\bar{u})\Big). \end{aligned} \tag{7}$$

Since condition (3) and S-stationary condition hold at $\bar{u}$, so

$$\begin{aligned} \lambda_i g_i(\bar{u}) = 0, \forall i \in \{1,\cdots,p\},\ &\lambda_j h_j(\bar{u}) = 0, \forall j \in \{1,\cdots,q\}, \\ &\lambda_k G_k(\bar{u}) = 0, \forall k \in I^G(\bar{u}) \cup I^{GH}(\bar{u}), \\ &\mu_k H_k(\bar{u}) = 0, \forall k \in I^H(\bar{u}) \cup I^{GH}(\bar{u}). \end{aligned}$$

Hence, (7) becomes

$$\begin{aligned} \lambda^L f^L(v) + \lambda^U f^U(v) + \sum_{i\in I_g(\bar{u})} \lambda_i g_i(v) + \sum_{j=1}^{q} \lambda_j h_j(v) + \sum_{k=1}^{r} \Big(\lambda_k G_k(v) + \mu_k H_k(v)\Big) \\ \geq \lambda^L f^L(\bar{u}) + \lambda^U f^U(\bar{u}). \end{aligned} \tag{8}$$

When $v \in S$, this means $v \in M$, $g_i(v) = 0\ \forall i \in I_g(\bar{u})$ and $\lambda^L f^L(v) + \lambda^U f^U(v) = \lambda^L f^L(\bar{u}) + \lambda^U f^U(\bar{u})$. Hence,

$$\lambda^L f^L(\bar{u}) + \lambda^U f^U(\bar{u}) = \lambda^L f^L(v) + \lambda^U f^U(v)$$

$$\geq \lambda^L f^L(v) + \lambda^U f^U(v) + \sum_{i \in I_g(\bar{u})} \lambda_i g_i(v) + \sum_{j=1}^{q} \lambda_j h_j(v)$$
$$+ \sum_{k=1}^{r} \Big(\lambda_k G_k(v) + \mu_k H_k(v) \Big)$$
$$\geq \lambda^L f^L(\bar{u}) + \lambda^U f^U(\bar{u}). \tag{9}$$

Then, it follows from (8) and (9) that

$$\sum_{i \in I_g(\bar{u})} \lambda_i g_i(v) = 0 \text{ i.e., } g_i = 0 \ (i \in I_g(\bar{u})),$$
$$\sum_{j=1}^{q} \lambda_j h_j(v) = 0 \text{ i.e., } h_j = 0 \ (j \in \{1, \cdots, q\}),$$
$$\sum_{k=1}^{r} \Big(\lambda_k G_k(v) + \mu_k H_k(v) \Big) = 0 \text{ i.e., } G_k = 0 = H_k \ (k \in \{1, \cdots, r\}.$$

Therefore, $L(\cdot, \lambda, \mu)$ is constant on S. □

Theorem 1. *Let $\bar{u}$ be the solution to the problem (IVTNP), such that the condition* (3) *and S-stationary condition hold. Suppose that the functions f^L, f^U are semiconvex on M and the Lagrangian function $L(\cdot, \lambda, \mu)$ is semiconvex at $\bar{u}$, and suppose that the functions f^L, f^U, $g_i (i \in \{1, \cdots, p\}), h_j (j \in \{1, \cdots, q\}), G_k, H_k (k \in \{1, \cdots, r\})$ are regular at $\bar{u}$. Then, $S = S_1 = S_1^{'}$, where*

$$S_1 = \Big\{ v \in M : \exists \eta \in \{\lambda^L \partial^c f^L(\bar{u}) + \lambda^U \partial^c f^U(\bar{u})\} \cap \{\lambda^L \partial^c f^L(v) + \lambda^U \partial^c f^U(v)\},$$
$$\langle \eta, \bar{u} - v \rangle = 0, g_i(v) = 0 \, \forall \, i \in I_g(\bar{u}), \; g_i(v) \leq 0 \, \forall \, i \in \{1, \cdots, p\} \setminus I_g(\bar{u}),$$
$$h_j(v) = 0 \, \forall \, j \in \{1, \cdots, q\}, G_k(v) = 0, \forall k \in I^G(\bar{u}) \cup I^{GH}(\bar{u}),$$
$$H_k(v) = 0, \forall k \in I^H(\bar{u}) \cup I^{GH}(\bar{u}) \Big\},$$
$$S_1^{'} = \Big\{ v \in M : \exists \eta \in \lambda^L \partial^c f^L(v) + \lambda^U \partial^c f^U(v), \langle \eta, \bar{u} - v \rangle = 0,$$
$$g_i(v) = 0 \, \forall \, i \in I_g(\bar{u}), \; g_i(v) \leq 0 \, \forall \, i \in \{1, \cdots, p\} \setminus I_g(\bar{u}),$$
$$h_j(v) = 0 \, \forall \, j \in \{1, \cdots, q\}, G_k(v) = 0, \forall k \in I^G(\bar{u}) \cup I^{GH}(\bar{u}),$$
$$H_k(v) = 0, \forall k \in I^H(\bar{u}) \cup I^{GH}(\bar{u}) \Big\}.$$

Proof. Clearly, $S_1 \subset S_1^{'}$, we claim that $S \subset S_1$ and $S_1^{'} \subset S$.

Let us suppose that $v \in S_1^{'}$, then $\exists \, \eta \in \lambda^L \partial^c f^L(v) + \lambda^U \partial^c f^U(v)$, such that $\langle \eta, \bar{u} - v \rangle = 0, g_i(v) = 0 \, \forall \, i \in I_g(\bar{u}), \; g_i(v) \leq 0 \, \forall \, i \in \{1, \cdots, p\} \setminus I_g(\bar{u}), h_j(v) = 0 \, \forall \, j \in \{1, \cdots, q\}, G_k(v) = 0, \forall k \in I^G(\bar{u}) \cup I^{GH}(\bar{u}), H_k(v) = 0, \forall k \in I^H(\bar{u}) \cup I^{GH}(\bar{u})$.

Since f^L and f^U are semiconvex on X, $f^L(\bar{u}) \geq f^L(v)$ and $f^U(\bar{u}) \geq f^U(v)$.

In addition, since $\bar{u}, v \in M$ and $\bar{u}$ is a solution to (IVPSC), $v \in S$.

Now, we claim that $S \subset S_1$. Suppose $v \in S$, it follows from Lemma 2 that we have $g_i(v) = 0 \, \forall \, i \in I_g(\bar{u}), \; g_i(v) \leq 0 \, \forall \, i \in \{1, \cdots, p\} \setminus I_g(\bar{u})$.
As $\bar{u}$ satisfies condition (3) with $\lambda_i \in \mathbb{R}_+$ and the S-stationary condition holds at $\bar{u}$, then there exists $u^L \in \partial^c f^L(\bar{u}), u^U \in \partial^c f^U(\bar{u}), w \in N(M, \bar{u}), v_g \in \partial^c g_i(\bar{u}) (i \in \{1, \cdots, p\})$, $v_h \in \partial^c h_j(\bar{u}) (j \in \{1, \cdots, q\}), v_G \in \partial^c G_k(\bar{u}), v_H \in \partial^c H_k(\bar{u}) (k \in \{1, \cdots, r\})$, such that

$$\lambda^L u^L + \lambda^U u^U + \sum_{i=1}^{p} \lambda_i v_g + \sum_{j=1}^{q} \lambda_j v_h + \sum_{k=1}^{r} \Big(\lambda_k v_G + \mu_k v_H \Big) = -w.$$

As M is a closed convex subset of X, $\langle w, v-\bar{u}\rangle \leq 0\ \forall v \in M$, therefore, for $v \in S \subseteq M$, we obtain

$$\left\langle \lambda^L u^L + \lambda^U u^U + \sum_{i=1}^{p} \lambda_i \nu_g + \sum_{j=1}^{q} \lambda_j \nu_h + \sum_{k=1}^{r} \Big(\lambda_k \nu_G + \mu_k \nu_H\Big), v-\bar{u} \right\rangle \geq 0.$$

i.e.,

$$\begin{aligned}\langle \lambda^L u^L + \lambda^U u^U, v-\bar{u}\rangle &\geq -\Big\langle \sum_{i=1}^{p} \lambda_i \nu_g + \sum_{j=1}^{q} \lambda_j \nu_h + \sum_{k=1}^{r} \Big(\lambda_k \nu_G + \mu_k \nu_H\Big), v-\bar{u} \Big\rangle \\ &= -\Big\langle \sum_{i \in I_g(\bar{u})} \lambda_i \nu_g + \sum_{j=1}^{q} \lambda_j \nu_h + \sum_{k=1}^{r} \Big(\lambda_k \nu_G + \mu_k \nu_H\Big), v-\bar{u} \Big\rangle. \end{aligned} \tag{10}$$

Since $\lambda_i g_i(\bar{u}) = 0, \forall i \in \{1,\cdots,p\}$, $\lambda_j h_j(\bar{u}) = 0, \forall j \in \{1,\cdots,q\}$ and S-stationary holds at $\bar{u}$,

$$(\lambda_i g_i)'(\bar{u}, v-\bar{u}) = \lim_{t\downarrow 0} \frac{\lambda_i g_i(\bar{u}+t(v-\bar{u})) - \lambda_i g_i(\bar{u})}{t} = \lim_{t\downarrow 0} \frac{\lambda_i g_i(\bar{u}+t(v-\bar{u}))}{t}, \tag{11}$$

$$(\lambda_j^h h_j)'(\bar{u}, v-\bar{u}) = \lim_{t\downarrow 0} \frac{\lambda_j^h h_j(\bar{u}+t(v-\bar{u})) - \lambda_j h_j(\bar{u})}{t} = \lim_{t\downarrow 0} \frac{\lambda_j^h h_j(\bar{u}+t(v-\bar{u}))}{t}, \tag{12}$$

$$(\lambda_k G_k)'(\bar{u}, v-\bar{u}) = \lim_{t\downarrow 0} \frac{\lambda_k G_k(\bar{u}+t(v-\bar{u})) - \lambda_k G_k(\bar{u})}{t} = \lim_{t\downarrow 0} \frac{\lambda_k G_k(\bar{u}+t(v-\bar{u}))}{t}, \tag{13}$$

$$(\mu_k H_k)'(\bar{u}, v-\bar{u}) = \lim_{t\downarrow 0} \frac{\mu_k H_k(\bar{u}+t(v-\bar{u})) - \mu_k H_k(\bar{u})}{t} = \lim_{t\downarrow 0} \frac{\mu_k H_k(\bar{u}+t(v-\bar{u}))}{t}. \tag{14}$$

Since M is a convex subset of M, we have $\bar{u} + t(v-\bar{u}) \in M$, provided $\bar{u}, v \in M$ and $t \in (0,1)$.

Hence,

$$\begin{aligned} \lambda_i g_i(\bar{u}+t(v-\bar{u})) &\leq 0, \forall i \in \{1,\cdots,p\}, \\ \lambda_j h_j(\bar{u}+t(v-\bar{u})) &= 0, \forall j \in \{1,\cdots,q\}, \\ \lambda_k G_k(\bar{u}+t(v-\bar{u})) &= 0, \forall k \in I^G(\bar{u}) \cup I^{GH}(\bar{u}), \\ \mu_k H_k(\bar{u}+t(v-\bar{u})) &= 0, \forall k \in I^H(\bar{u}) \cup I^{GH}(\bar{u}). \end{aligned}$$

From (11)–(14) and the above argument, we obtain

$$\begin{aligned} (\lambda_i g_i)'(\bar{u}, v-\bar{u}) &\leq 0, i \in \{1,\cdots,p\}, \\ (\lambda_j^h h_j)'(\bar{u}, v-\bar{u}) &= 0, j \in \{1,\cdots,q\}, \\ (\lambda_k G_k)'(\bar{u}, v-\bar{u}) &= 0, k \in \{1,\cdots,r\}, \\ (\mu_k H_k)'(\bar{u}, v-\bar{u}) &= 0, k \in \{1,\cdots,r\}. \end{aligned}$$

Since, g_i, h_j, G_k, H_k are regular at $\bar{u}$, i.e.,

$$\begin{aligned} (\lambda_i g_i)'(\bar{u}, v-\bar{u}) &= (\lambda_i g_i)^c(\bar{u}, v-\bar{u}), \\ (\lambda_j^h h_j)'(\bar{u}, v-\bar{u}) &= (\lambda_j^h h_j)^c(\bar{u}, v-\bar{u}), \\ (\lambda_k G_k)'(\bar{u}, v-\bar{u}) &= (\lambda_k G_k)^c(\bar{u}, v-\bar{u}), \end{aligned}$$

$$(\mu_k H_k)'(\bar{u}, v - \bar{u}) = (\mu_k H_k)^c(\bar{u}, v - \bar{u}).$$

Let $\nu_g \in \partial^c g_i(\bar{u})(i \in \{1, \cdots, p\}), \nu_h \in \partial^c h_j(\bar{u})(j \in \{1, \cdots, q\}), \nu_G \in \partial^c G_k(\bar{u}), \nu_H \in \partial^c H_k(\bar{u})(k \in \{1, \cdots, r\})$, such that

$$\begin{aligned} \langle \lambda_i \nu_g, v - \bar{u} \rangle &\leq 0, \forall\, i \in \{1, \cdots, p\}, \\ \langle \lambda_j \nu_h, v - \bar{u} \rangle &= 0, \forall\, j \in \{1, \cdots, q\}, \\ \langle \lambda_k \nu_G, v - \bar{u} \rangle &= 0, \forall\, k \in I^G(\bar{u}) \cup I^{GH}(\bar{u}), \\ \langle \mu_k \nu_H, v - \bar{u} \rangle &= 0, \forall\, k \in I^H(\bar{u}) \cup I^{GH}(\bar{u}). \end{aligned} \tag{15}$$

From (15) and (10), we obtain $\langle \lambda^L u^L + \lambda^U u^U, v - \bar{u} \rangle \geq 0$.
Now, since $f^L(v) = f^L(\bar{u})$ and $f^U(v) = f^U(\bar{u})$, and f^L, f^U are semiconvex at $\bar{u}$.
Lemma 1 implies that $f'(\bar{u}, v - \bar{u}) \preceq_{LU} 0$; this means $(\lambda^L f^L + \lambda^U f^U)'(\bar{u}, v - \bar{u}) \leq 0$.
Therefore,

$$\begin{aligned} \langle \lambda^L u^L + \lambda^U u^U, v - \bar{u} \rangle &\leq (\lambda^L f^L + \lambda^U f^U)^c(\bar{u}, v - \bar{u}) \\ &= (\lambda^L f^L + \lambda^U f^U)'(\bar{u}, v - \bar{u}) \leq 0, \\ &\text{where } u^L \in \partial^c f^L(\bar{u}), u^U \in \partial^c f^U(\bar{u}). \end{aligned}$$

Hence, $\langle \lambda^L u^L + \lambda^U u^U, v - \bar{u} \rangle = 0$.
Now, we have to prove that $\lambda^L u^L + \lambda^U u^U \in \lambda^L \partial f^L(\bar{u}) + \lambda^U \partial f^U(\bar{u}) \cap \lambda^L \partial f^L(v) + \lambda^U \partial f^U(v)$.
Since $\lambda^L u^L + \lambda^U u^U \in \lambda^L \partial f^L(\bar{u}) + \lambda^U \partial f^U(\bar{u})$, it remains to prove that $\lambda^L u^L + \lambda^U u^U \in \lambda^L \partial f^L(v) + \lambda^U \partial f^U(v)$.
f^L and f^U are regular at $\bar{u}$ and v, so we have

$$\begin{aligned} (\lambda^L f^L + \lambda^U f^U)^c(\bar{u}, d) &= (\lambda^L f^L + \lambda^U f^U)'(\bar{u}, d), \\ (\lambda^L f^L + \lambda^U f^U)^c(v, d) &= (\lambda^L f^L + \lambda^U f^U)'(v, d), \forall d \in \mathbb{R}^n. \end{aligned}$$

Now, we claim that there does not exist any $d_0 \in \mathbb{R}^n$ such that $(\lambda^L f^L + \lambda^U f^U)'(\bar{u}, d_0) < (\lambda^L f^L + \lambda^U f^U)'(v, d_0)$.
Suppose on contrary, there exists $d_0 \in \mathbb{R}^n$, such that $(\lambda^L f^L + \lambda^U f^U)'(\bar{u}, d_0) < (\lambda^L f^L + \lambda^U f^U)'(v, d_0)$, i.e.,

$$\begin{aligned} &\lim_{t_1 \downarrow 0} \frac{(\lambda^L f^L + \lambda^U f^U)(v + t_1 d_0) - (\lambda^L f^L + \lambda^U f^U)(v)}{t_1} \\ &- \lim_{t_2 \downarrow 0} \frac{(\lambda^L f^L + \lambda^U f^U)(\bar{u} + t_2 d_0) - (\lambda^L f^L + \lambda^U f^U)(\bar{u})}{t_2} < 0. \end{aligned}$$

Then

$$\begin{aligned} \lim_{t \downarrow 0} \Bigg[&\frac{(\lambda^L f^L + \lambda^U f^U)(v + t d_0) - (\lambda^L f^L + \lambda^U f^U)(v)}{t} \\ &- \frac{(\lambda^L f^L + \lambda^U f^U)(\bar{u} + t d_0) - (\lambda^L f^L + \lambda^U f^U)(\bar{u})}{t} \Bigg] < 0. \end{aligned}$$

Since $(\lambda^L f^L + \lambda^U f^U)(v) = (\lambda^L f^L + \lambda^U f^U)(\bar{u})$, we have

$$\lim_{t \downarrow 0} \frac{(\lambda^L f^L + \lambda^U f^U)(v + t d_0) - (\lambda^L f^L + \lambda^U f^U)(\bar{u} + t d_0)}{t} < 0.$$

Thus, $\exists t_0 \in (0,1)$ and $\epsilon > 0$ small enough such that

$$(\lambda^L f^L + \lambda^U f^U)(v + td_0) - (\lambda^L f^L + \lambda^U f^U)(\bar{u} + td_0) < -\epsilon < 0 \forall t \in (0, t_0). \quad (16)$$

Easily, we can see that $F(t) = (\lambda^L f^L + \lambda^U f^U)(v + td_0) - (\lambda^L f^L + \lambda^U f^U)(\bar{u} + td_0)$ is continuous at $t = 0$.

Letting $t \to 0$, we have $(\lambda^L f^L + \lambda^U f^U)(v) - (\lambda^L f^L + \lambda^U f^U)(\bar{u}) < 0$, which is a contradiction, hence, if

$$\lambda^L u^L(d) \leq (\lambda^L f^L + \lambda^U f^U)'(\bar{u}, d) = (\lambda^L f^L + \lambda^U f^U)^c(\bar{u}, d) \; \forall \, d \in \mathbb{R}^n,$$
$$\text{and } \lambda^U u^U(d) \leq (\lambda^L f^L + \lambda^U f^U)'(\bar{u}, d) = (\lambda^L f^L + \lambda^U f^U)^c(\bar{u}, d) \; \forall \, d \in \mathbb{R}^n.$$

This proves that $\lambda^L u^L + \lambda^U u^U \in \lambda^L \partial^c f^L(\bar{u}) + \lambda^U \partial^c f^U(\bar{u})$ implies $\lambda^L u^L + \lambda^U u^U \in \lambda^L \partial^c f^L(v)$ $+ \lambda^U \partial^c f^U(v)$. We have $\lambda^L u^L + \lambda^U u^U \in \lambda^L \partial f^L(\bar{u}) + \lambda^U \partial f^U(\bar{u}) \cap \lambda^L \partial f^L(v) + \lambda^U \partial f^U(v)$. Hence, $v \in S_1$. This completes the proof. □

Example 1. *Consider an interval-valued optimization problem (IVPSC)*

$$\begin{aligned} &\min f(u) \\ \textit{subject to } &u_1 - u_2 \leq 0, \\ &u_1 u_2 = 0. \end{aligned}$$

where $f : \mathbb{R}^2 \to \mathcal{I}(\mathbb{R})$ is defined by

$$f(u_1, u_2) = \left[u_2^2 - u_1^2, u_2^2\right].$$

As $f^L(u) = u_2^2 - u_1^2$ and $f^U(u) = u_2^2$ are differentiable convex functions so the coresponding subgradient and gradient are the same.
$\nabla f^L(u) = (-2u_1, 2u_2)^T$ and $\nabla f^U(u) = (0, 2u_2)^T$.

Consider a set $M = \{u = (u_1, u_2) : u_1 - u_2 \leq 0, u_1 u_2 = 0\}$. f is a LU-convex on the set

$$M = \{u = (u_1, u_2) : u_1 - u_2 \leq 0, u_1 u_2 = 0\}.$$

Lagrangian $L(\cdot, \lambda, \mu)(u) = \lambda^L(u_2^2 - u_1^2) + \lambda^U(u_2^2) + \lambda^g(u_1 - u_2) + \lambda u_1 + \mu u_2$.

Here, the solution set is $S = \{(0,0)\}$. Let $\bar{u} = (0,0)$ hold the condition (3) and $L(\cdot, \lambda, \mu)$ is convex.

We can easily see that the condition (3) holds for the above interval-valued problem

$$\lambda^L \begin{bmatrix} -2u_1 \\ 2u_2 \end{bmatrix} + \lambda^U \begin{bmatrix} 0 \\ 2u_2 \end{bmatrix} + \lambda_g \begin{bmatrix} 1 \\ -1 \end{bmatrix} + \lambda_G \begin{bmatrix} 1 \\ 0 \end{bmatrix} + \lambda_H \begin{bmatrix} 0 \\ 1 \end{bmatrix} = (0,0),$$

with $\lambda_g = \lambda_G = \lambda_H = 0$ and for any values of λ^L and λ^U at point $\bar{u} = (0,0)$. We can also see that the S-stationary condition holds for IVPSC.

Choosing $\eta = 0 \in \lambda^L \partial f^L(\bar{u}) + \lambda^U \partial f^U(\bar{u})$ such that $\langle \eta, \bar{u} - v \rangle = 0 \Leftrightarrow v = 0$.

Hence,

$$\begin{aligned} S_1' = \Big\{ &v \in M : \exists \eta \in \lambda^L \partial^c f^L(v) + \lambda^U \partial^c f^U(v), \langle \eta, \bar{u} - v \rangle = 0, \\ &g_i(v) = 0 \, \forall \, i \in I_g(\bar{u}), \; g_i(v) \leq 0 \, \forall \, i \in \{1, \cdots, p\} \setminus I_g(\bar{u}), \\ &h_j(v) = 0 \, \forall \, j \in \{1, \cdots, q\}, G_k(v) = 0, \forall k \in I^G(\bar{u}) \cup I^{GH}(\bar{u}), \\ &H_k(v) = 0, \forall k \in I^H(\bar{u}) \cup I^{GH}(\bar{u}) \Big\} = \{(0,0)\} = S. \end{aligned}$$

This verifies the above result.

Figure 1 represents the lower and upper bound function $f^L(u)$ and $f^U(u)$ of interval-valued objective function $f(u)$. Figure 2 shows the constraint functions $g_i(u)$ and switching constraints $G_k(u)H_k(u)$ for Example 1.

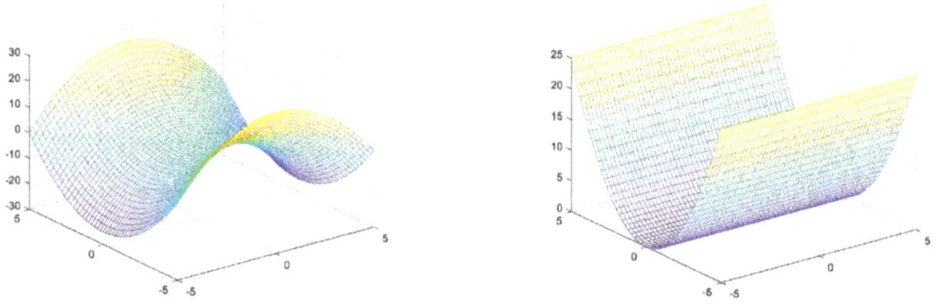

(a) $f^L(u)$ **(b)** $f^U(u)$

Figure 1. The lower and upper bound objective functions.

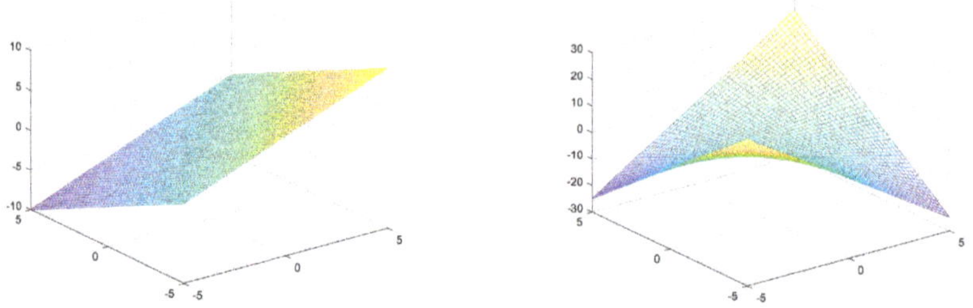

(a) $g_i(u)$ **(b)** $G_k(u)H_k(u)$

Figure 2. Constraints $g_i(u)$ and $G_k(u)H_k(u)$.

Corollary 1. *Let $\bar{u}$ be the solution to the problem (IVTNP) such that the condition* (3) *and S-stationary condition hold. Suppose that the functions $f^L, f^U, g_i(i \in \{1,\cdots,p\}), h_j(j \in \{1,\cdots,q\}), G_k, H_k(k \in \{1,\cdots,r\})$ are semiconvex on M and if the Lagrangian function $L(\cdot,\lambda,\mu)$ is semiconvex at $\bar{u}$, then $S = S_1 = S_1^{'}$, where*

$$
\begin{aligned}
S_1 = \Big\{& v \in M : \exists \eta \in \{\lambda^L \partial^c f^L(\bar{u}) + \lambda^U \partial^c f^U(\bar{u})\} \cap \{\lambda^L \partial^c f^L(v) + \lambda^U \partial^c f^U(v)\}, \\
& \langle \eta, \bar{u} - v \rangle = 0, g_i(v) = 0 \,\forall\, i \in I_g(\bar{u}),\ g_i(v) \le 0 \,\forall\, i \in \{1,\cdots,p\} \setminus I_g(\bar{u}), \\
& h_j(v) = 0 \,\forall\, j \in \{1,\cdots,q\}, G_k(v) = 0, \forall k \in I^G(\bar{u}) \cup I^{GH}(\bar{u}), \\
& H_k(v) = 0, \forall k \in I^H(\bar{u}) \cup I^{GH}(\bar{u}) \Big\}, \\
S_1^{'} = \Big\{& v \in M : \exists \eta \in \lambda^L \partial^c f^L(v) + \lambda^U \partial^c f^U(v), \langle \eta, \bar{u} - v \rangle = 0, \\
& g_i(v) = 0 \,\forall\, i \in I_g(\bar{u}),\ g_i(v) \le 0 \,\forall\, i \in \{1,\cdots,p\} \setminus I_g(\bar{u}), \\
& h_j(v) = 0 \,\forall\, j \in \{1,\cdots,q\}, G_k(v) = 0, \forall k \in I^G(\bar{u}) \cup I^{GH}(\bar{u}), \\
& H_k(v) = 0, \forall k \in I^H(\bar{u}) \cup I^{GH}(\bar{u}) \Big\}.
\end{aligned}
$$

We know that every convex function is semiconvex [51]. In the case where $f^L, f^U, g_i(i \in \{1,\cdots,p\}), h_j(j \in \{1,\cdots,q\}), G_k, H_k(k \in \{1,\cdots,r\})$ are convex functions, the Clarke subdifferential coincides with the subdifferential in the convex analysis.

Corollary 2. *Let $\bar{u}$ be the solution to the problem (IVTNP) such that the condition* (3) *and S-stationary condition hold. Suppose that the functions $f^L, f^U, g_i (i \in \{1, \cdots, p\}), h_j (j \in \{1, \cdots, q\}), G_k, H_k (k \in \{1, \cdots, r\})$ are convex; then, $S = S_2 = S_2'$, where*

$$S_2 = \Big\{v \in M : \exists \eta \in \{\lambda^L \partial f^L(\bar{u}) + \lambda^U \partial f^U(\bar{u})\} \cap \{\lambda^L \partial f^L(v) + \lambda^U \partial f^U(v)\},$$
$$\langle \eta, \bar{u} - v \rangle = 0, g_i(v) = 0 \,\forall\, i \in I_g(\bar{u}),\ g_i(v) \leq 0 \,\forall\, i \in \{1, \cdots, p\} \setminus I_g(\bar{u}),$$
$$h_j(v) = 0 \,\forall\, j \in \{1, \cdots, q\}, G_k(v) = 0, \forall k \in I^G(\bar{u}) \cup I^{GH}(\bar{u}),$$
$$H_k(v) = 0, \forall k \in I^H(\bar{u}) \cup I^{GH}(\bar{u})\Big\},$$
$$S_2' = \Big\{v \in M : \exists \eta \in \lambda^L \partial f^L(v) + \lambda^U \partial f^U(v), \langle \eta, \bar{u} - v \rangle = 0,$$
$$g_i(v) = 0 \,\forall\, i \in I_g(\bar{u}),\ g_i(v) \leq 0 \,\forall\, i \in \{1, \cdots, p\} \setminus I_g(\bar{u}),$$
$$h_j(v) = 0 \,\forall\, j \in \{1, \cdots, q\}, G_k(v) = 0, \forall k \in I^G(\bar{u}) \cup I^{GH}(\bar{u}),$$
$$H_k(v) = 0, \forall k \in I^H(\bar{u}) \cup I^{GH}(\bar{u})\Big\}.$$

We can easily see that

$$\Big[\bar{u} \in M, \sum_{i \in I_g(\bar{u})} \lambda_i g_i(v) + \sum_{j=1}^{q} \lambda_j h_j(v) + \sum_{k=1}^{r} \Big(\lambda_k G_k(v) + \mu_k H_k(v)\Big) = 0\Big]$$
$$\Leftrightarrow \Big[\bar{u} \in M, g_i(v) = 0 \,\forall\, i \in I_g(\bar{u}),\ g_i(v) \leq 0 \,\forall\, i \in \{1, \cdots, p\} \setminus I_g(\bar{u}),$$
$$h_j(v) = 0 \,\forall\, j \in \{1, \cdots, q\}, G_k(v) = 0, \forall k \in I^G(\bar{u}) \cup I^{GH}(\bar{u}),$$
$$H_k(v) = 0, \forall k \in I^H(\bar{u}) \cup I^{GH}(\bar{u}),\Big],$$

and by Lemma 2, $L(v, \lambda, \mu) = \lambda^L f^L(v) + \lambda^U f^U(v) \,\forall\, v \in S$.

Corollary 3. *Suppose that the functions $f^L, f^U, g_i (i \in \{1, \cdots, p\}), h_j (j \in \{1, \cdots, q\}), G_k, H_k (k \in \{1, \cdots, r\})$ and $L(\cdot, \lambda, \mu)$ are semiconvex on M, then $S = S_3 = S_3'$, where*

$$S_3 = \Big\{v \in M : \sum_{i \in I_g(\bar{u})} \lambda_i g_i(v) + \sum_{j=1}^{q} \lambda_j h_j(v) + \sum_{k=1}^{r} \Big(\lambda_k G_k(v) + \mu_k H_k(v)\Big) = 0,$$
$$\exists \eta \in \partial^c L(\cdot, \lambda^g, \lambda^h, \lambda^G, \lambda^H)(v),\ \langle \eta, \bar{u} - v \rangle = 0\Big\},$$
$$S_3' = \Big\{v \in M : \sum_{i \in I_g(\bar{u})} \lambda_i g_i(v) + \sum_{j=1}^{q} \lambda_j h_j(v) + \sum_{k=1}^{r} \Big(\lambda_k G_k(v) + \mu_k H_k(v)\Big) = 0,$$
$$\exists \eta \in \partial^c L(\cdot, \lambda^g, \lambda^h, \lambda^G, \lambda^H)(\bar{u}) \cap \partial^c L(\cdot, \lambda^g, \lambda^h, \lambda^G, \lambda^H)(v),\ \langle \eta, \bar{u} - v \rangle = 0\Big\}.$$

4. Conclusions and Future Remarks

We have considered the interval-valued mathematical programming problem with switching constraints (IVPSC) and studied the Lagrange multiplier characterizations of solution sets with the help of a semiconvex function and S-stationary condition. The S-stationary condition is stronger than the W-stationary and M-stationary conditions. We have proved that the associated Lagrangian function is constant for IVTNP withholding of the S-stationary condition. Thus, the W-stationary condition holds, too. Based on the proved by Mehlitz [12] condition, for the W-stationary condition, the feasible set of a tightened nonlinear problem (IVTNP) is a subset of the feasible set of the mathematical programs with switching constraints (IVPSC). Therefore, we have characterized the particular solutions sets for IVTNP. The IVPSC is a new class of optimization problems with significant applications. MPSC can be used for the discretized version of the optimal control problem with switching structure [12], and we can extend the results to interval-valued optimization problems from a practical point of view. The IVPSC can be reformulated as a mathematical program with disjunctive constraints (MPDC) [14]. We can introduce an alternative approach to LICQ and establish the first and second order optimality conditions for MPDC with interval-valued objective functions. To the best of our knowledge, there are a few papers related to characterizations of solution sets and interval-valued nonlinear optimization. This article can be extended for various nonlinear programming problems such as MPEC, MPVC, MPDC, and many more from the application point of view.

Author Contributions: Formal analysis, K.K.L., S.K.M., S.K.S. and M.H.; Funding acquisition, K.K.L.; Methodology, S.K.S. and M.H.; Supervision, S.K.M.; Validation, K.K.L., S.K.M., S.K.S. and M.H.; Writing—original draft, S.K.S.; Writing—review & editing, S.K.S. All authors have read and agreed to the published version of the manuscript.

Funding: The second author is financially supported by the "Research Grant for Faculty" (IoE Scheme) under Dev. Scheme No. 6031. The fourth author is financially supported by CSIR-UGC JRF, New Delhi, India, through Reference no.: 1009/(CSIR-UGC NET JUNE 2018).

Institutional Review Board Statement: Not applicable.

Informed Consent Statement: Not applicable.

Data Availability Statement: No data were used to support this study.

Acknowledgments: The authors are indebted to the anonymous reviewers for their valuable comments and remarks that helped to improve the presentation and quality of the manuscript.

Conflicts of Interest: The authors declare no conflict of interest.

References

1. Harker, P.T.; Pang, J.S. Existence of optimal solutions to mathematical programs with equilibrium constraints. *Oper. Res. Lett.* **1988**, *7*, 61–64. [CrossRef]
2. Achtziger, W.; Kanzow, C. Mathematical programs with vanishing constraints: Optimality conditions and constraint qualifications. *Math. Program.* **2008**, *114*, 69–99. [CrossRef]
3. Ben-Tal, A.; Jarre, F.; Kočvara, M.; Nemirovski, A.; Zowe, J. Optimal design of trusses under a nonconvex global buckling constraint. *Optim. Eng.* **2000**, *1*, 189–213. [CrossRef]
4. Singh, Y.; Pandey, Y.; Mishra, S.K. Saddle point optimality criteria for mathematical programming problems with equilibrium constraints. *Oper. Res. Lett.* **2017**, *45*, 254–258. [CrossRef]
5. Pandey, Y.; Mishra, S.K. Duality for nonsmooth optimization problems with equilibrium constraints, using convexificators. *J. Optim. Theory Appl.* **2016**, *171*, 694–707. [CrossRef]
6. Pandey, Y.; Mishra, S.K. Optimality conditions and duality for semi-infinite mathematical programming problems with equilibrium constraints, using convexificators. *Ann. Oper. Res.* **2018**, *69*, 549–564. [CrossRef]
7. Pandey, Y.; Mishra, S.K. On strong KKT type sufficient optimality conditions for nonsmooth multiobjective semi-infinite mathematical programming problems with equilibrium constraints. *Oper. Res. Lett.* **2016**, *44*, 148–151. [CrossRef]
8. Mishra, S.K.; Singh, V.; Laha, V. On duality for mathematical programs with vanishing constraints. *Ann. Oper. Res.* **2016**, *355*, 249–272. [CrossRef]
9. Mishra, S.K.; Singh, V.; Laha, V.; Mohapatra, R.N. On constraint qualifications for multiobjective optimization problems with vanishing constraints. In *Optimization Methods, Theory and Applications*; Springer: Berlin/Heidelberg, Germany, 2015; pp. 95–135.
10. Guu, S.M.; Singh, Y.; Mishra, S.K. On strong KKT type sufficient optimality conditions for multiobjective semi-infinite programming problems with vanishing constraints. *J. Ineq. Appl.* **2017**, *2017*, 282. [CrossRef]
11. Lai, K.K.; Hassan, M.; Singh, S.K.; Maurya, J.K.; Mishra, S.K. Semidefinite multiobjective mathematical programming problems with vanishing constraints using convexificators. *Fractal Fract.* **2022**, *6*, 3. [CrossRef]
12. Mehlitz, P. Stationarity conditions and constraint qualifications for mathematical programs with switching constraints. *Math. Program.* **2020**, *181*, 149–186. [CrossRef]
13. Kanzow, C.; Mehlitz, P.; Steck, D. Relaxation schemes for mathematical programmes with switching constraints. *Optim. Meth. Soft* **2019**, *36*, 1223–1258. [CrossRef]
14. Liang, Y.C.; Ye, J.J. Optimality conditions and exact penalty for mathematical programs with switching constraints. *J. Optim. Theory Appl.* **2021**, *190*, 1–31. [CrossRef]
15. Pandey, Y.; Singh, V. On Constraint Qualifications for Multiobjective Optimization Problems with Switching Constraints. In *Indo-French Seminar on Optimization, Variational Analysis and Applications*; Springer: Singapore, 2020; pp. 283–306.
16. Wu, H.C. On interval-valued nonlinear programming problems. *J. Math. Anal. Appl.* **2008**, *338*, 299–316. [CrossRef]

17. Wu, H.C. The Karush-Kuhn-Tucker optimality conditions in an optimization problem with interval-valued objective function. *Eur. J. Oper. Res.* **2007**, *176*, 46–59. [CrossRef]
18. Wu, H.C. The Karush-Kuhn-Tucker optimality conditions in multiobjective programming problems with interval-valued objective functions. *Eur. J. Oper. Res.* **2009**, *196*, 49–60. [CrossRef]
19. Zhang, J.; Zheng, Q.; Ma, X.; Li, L. Relationships between interval-valued vector optimization problems and vector variational inequalities. *Fuzzy Optim. Decis. Mak.* **2016**, *15*, 33–55. [CrossRef]
20. Lai, K.K.; Shahi, A.; Mishra, S.K. On semidifferentiable interval-valued programming problems. *J. Ineq. Appl.* **2021**, *2021*, 35. [CrossRef]
21. Sharma, N.; Singh, S.K.; Mishra, S.K.; Hamdi, A. Hermite-Hadamard-type inequalities for interval-valued preinvex functions via Riemann-Liouville fractional integrals. *J. Ineq. Appl.* **2021**, *2021*, 98. [CrossRef]
22. Van Su, T.; Dinh, D.H. Duality results for interval-valued pseudoconvex optimization problem with equilibrium constraints with applications. *Comput. Appl. Math.* **2020**, *39*, 127. [CrossRef]
23. Wang, H.; Wang, H. Duality theorems for nondifferentiable semi-infinite interval-valued optimization problems with vanishing constraints. *J. Ineq. Appl.* **2021**, *2021*, 182. [CrossRef]
24. Mangasarian, O.L. A simple characterization of solution sets of convex programs. *Oper. Res. Lett.* **1988**, *7*, 21–26. [CrossRef]
25. Burke, J.V.; Ferris, M.C. Characterization of solution sets of convex programs. *Oper. Res. Lett.* **1991**, *10*, 57–60. [CrossRef]
26. Jeyakumar, V.; Lee, G.M.; Dinh, N. Lagrange multiplier conditions characterizing optimal solution sets of cone-constrained convex programs. *J. Optim. Theory Appl.* **2004**, *123*, 83–103. [CrossRef]
27. Dinh, N.; Jeyakumar, V.; Lee, G.M. Lagrange multiplier characterizations of solution sets of constrained pseudolinear optimization problems. *Optimization* **2006**, *55*, 241–250. [CrossRef]
28. Jeyakumar, V.; Lee, G.M.; Dinh, N. Characterizations of solution sets of convex vector minimization problems. *Eur. J. Oper. Res.* **2006**, *174*, 1380–1395. [CrossRef]
29. Lalitha, C.S.; Mehta, M. Characterizations of solution sets of mathematical programs in terms of Lagrange multipliers. *Optimization* **2009**, *58*, 995–1007. [CrossRef]
30. Son, T.Q.; Dinh, N. Characterizations of optimal solution sets of convex infinite programs. *TOP* **2008**, *16*, 147–163. [CrossRef]
31. Mishra, S.K.; Upadhyay, B.B. Lagrange multiplier characterizations of solution sets of constrained nonsmooth pseudolinear optimization problems. *J. Optim. Theory Appl.* **2014**, *160*, 763–777. [CrossRef]
32. Sisarat, N.; Wangkeeree, R. Characterizing the solution set of convex optimization problems without convexity of constraints. *Optim. Lett.* **2020**, *14*, 1127–1144. [CrossRef]
33. Ivanov, V.I. Characterizations of solution sets of differentiable quasiconvex programming problems. *J. Optim. Theory Appl.* **2019**, *181*, 144–162. [CrossRef]
34. Jeyakumar, V.; Lee, G.M.; Li, G. Characterizing robust solution sets of convex programs under data uncertainty. *J. Optim. Theory Appl.* **2015**, *164* 407–435. [CrossRef]
35. Kim, D.S.; Son, T.Q. Characterizations of solutions sets of a class of nonconvex semi-infinite programmin problems. *J. Nonl. Convex Anal.* **2011**, *12*, 429–440.
36. Li, X.B.; Wang, S. Characterizations of robust solution set of convex programs with uncertain data. *Optim. Lett.* **2018**, *12*, 1387–1402. [CrossRef]
37. Long, X.J.; Liu, J.; Huang, N.J. Characterizing the solution set for nonconvex semi-infinite programs involving tangential subdifferentials. *Numer. Funct. Anal. Optim.* **2021**, *42*, 279–297. [CrossRef]
38. Sisarat, N.; Wangkeeree, R.; Lee, G.M. Some characterizations of robust solution sets for uncertain convex optimization problems with locally Lipschitz inequality constraints. *J. Ind. Manag. Optim.* **2020**, *16*, 469–493. [CrossRef]
39. Son, T.Q.; Kim, D.S. A new approach to characterize the solution set of a pseudoconvex programming problem. *J. Comput. Appl. Math.* **2014**, *261*, 333–340. [CrossRef]
40. Sun, X.K.; Teo, K.L. Long, X.J. Characterizations of robust ϵ-quasi optimal solutions for nonsmooth optimization problems with uncertain data. *Optimization* **2021**, *70*, 847–870. [CrossRef]
41. Sun, X.; Teo, K.L.; Tang, L. Dual approaches to characterize robust optimal solution sets for a class of uncertain optimization problems. *J. Optim. Theory Appl.* **2019**, *182*, 984–1000. [CrossRef]
42. Yang, X.M. On characterizing the solutions of pseudoinvex extremum problems. *J. Optim. Theory Appl.* **2009**, *140*, 537–542. [CrossRef]
43. Zhao, K.Q.; Yang, X.M. Characterizations of the solution set for a class of nonsmooth optimization problems. *Optim. Lett.* **2013**, *7*, 685–694. [CrossRef]
44. Treanta, S. Characterization results of solutions in interval-valued optimization problems with mixed constraints. *J. Glob. Optim.* **2021**, 951–964. [CrossRef]
45. Mifflin, R. Semismooth and semiconvex functions in constrained optimization. *SIAM J. Control Optim.* **1977**, *15*, 959–972. [CrossRef]
46. Moore, R.E. *Methods and Applications of Interval Analysis*; SIAM: Philadelphia, PA, USA, 1979.
47. Clarke, F.H. *Optimization and Nonsmooth Analysis*; Willey-Interscience: New York, NY, USA, 1983.
48. Clarke, F.H.; Yu S Ledyaev, J.S.S.; Wolenski, P.R. *Nonsmooth Analysis and Control Theory*; Springer: Berlin, Germany, 1998.
49. Rockafellar, R.T. *Convex Analysis*; Princeton University Press: Princeton, NJ, USA, 1970.

50. Makela, M.M.; Neittaanmaki, P. *Nonsmooth Optimization: Analysis and Algorithms with Applications to Optimal Control*; World Scientific Publishing: Singapore, 1992.
51. Loridan, P. Necessary Conditions for ϵ-Optimality. In *Optimality and Stability in Mathematical Programming*; Springer: Berlin/Heidelberg, Germany, 1982; pp. 140–152.

mathematics MDPI

Review

Recent Advances of Constrained Variational Problems Involving Second-Order Partial Derivatives: A Review

Savin Treanţă [1,2,3]

[1] Department of Applied Mathematics, University Politehnica of Bucharest, 060042 Bucharest, Romania; savin.treanta@upb.ro
[2] Academy of Romanian Scientists, 54 Splaiul Independentei, 050094 Bucharest, Romania
[3] Fundamental Sciences Applied in Engineering—Research Center (SFAI), University Politehnica of Bucharest, 060042 Bucharest, Romania

Abstract: This paper comprehensively reviews the nonlinear dynamics given by some classes of constrained control problems which involve second-order partial derivatives. Specifically, necessary optimality conditions are formulated and proved for the considered variational control problems governed by integral functionals. In addition, the well-posedness and the associated variational inequalities are considered in the present review paper.

Keywords: multi-time controlled Lagrangian of second-order; isoperimetric constraints; Euler–Lagrange equations; multiple integral; differential 1-form; curvilinear integral; variational inequalities

MSC: 49K15; 49K20; 49K21; 65K10

Citation: Treanţă, S. Recent Advances of Constrained Variational Problems Involving Second-Order Partial Derivatives: A Review. *Mathematics* **2021**, *10*, 2599. https://doi.org/10.3390/math10152599

Academic Editor: Yeol Je Cho

Received: 4 July 2022
Accepted: 25 July 2022
Published: 26 July 2022

1. Introduction

We all know that Calculus of Variations and Optimal Control Theory are two strongly connected mathematical fields. In this direction, several researchers have investigated these areas, achieving remarkable results (see Friedman [1], Hestenes [2], Kendall [3], Udrişte [4], Petrat and Tumulka [5], Treanţă [6] and Deckert and Nickel [7]). The problems (in several time variables) studied by the aforementioned researchers have been continued, in the last period, in the study of multi-dimensional optimization problems. These studies have many applications in different branches of mathematical sciences, web access problems, management science, portfolio selection, engineering design, query optimization in databases, game theory, and so on. In this respect, we mention the papers conducted by Mititelu and Treanţă [8], Treanţă [9–18], and Jayswal et al. [19]. For other connected but different ideas on this topic, the reader can consult Arisawa and Ishii [20], Lai and Motta [21], Shi et al. [22], An et al. [23], Zhao et al. [24], Hung et al. [25], Chen et al. [26], Antonsev and Shmarev [27], Cekic et al. [28], Chen et al. [29], Diening et al. [30], and Zhikov [31].

This review article is structured as follows. Section 2 introduces the second-order PDE-constrained optimal control problem under study (see Theorem 1). This result formulates the necessary conditions of optimality for the considered PDE-constrained optimization problem. Section 3 states the associated necessary optimality conditions for a new class of isoperimetric constrained control problems governed by multiple and curvilinear integrals. In Section 4, by using the pseudomonotonicity, hemicontinuity, and monotonicity of the considered integral functionals, we present the well-posedness of some variational inequality problems determined by partial derivatives of a second-order. Section 5 formulates some very important open problems to be investigated in the near future. Section 6 contains the conclusions of the paper.

2. Second-Order PDE-Constrained Control Problem

Let $\mathcal{H}_\zeta(b(t), b_\gamma(t), b_{\alpha\beta}(t), u(t), t),\ \zeta = \overline{1,m}$ be some functions of C^3-class, called *multi-time controlled Lagrangians of second order*, where $t = (t^\alpha) = (t^1, \cdots, t^m) \in \Lambda_{t_0,t_1} \subset \mathbb{R}^m_+$, $b = (b^i) = \left(b^1, \cdots, b^n\right) : \Lambda_{t_0,t_1} \to \mathbb{R}^n$ is a function of C^4-class (the *state variable*) and $u = (u^\vartheta) = \left(u^1, \cdots, u^k\right) : \Lambda_{t_0,t_1} \to \mathbb{R}^k$ is a piecewise continuous function (the *control variable*). In addition, denote $b_\alpha(t) := \dfrac{\partial b}{\partial t^\alpha}(t),\ b_{\alpha\beta}(t) := \dfrac{\partial^2 b}{\partial t^\alpha \partial t^\beta}(t),\ \alpha, \beta \in \{1, ..., m\}$ and consider $\Lambda_{t_0,t_1} = [t_0, t_1]$ (*multi-time interval* in $\mathbb{R}^m_+$) as a hyper-parallelepiped determined by the diagonally opposite points $t_0,\ t_1 \in \mathbb{R}^m_+$. Moreover, we assume that the previous multi-time controlled Lagrangians of second order determine a closed controlled Lagrange 1-form

$$\mathcal{H}_\zeta(b(t), b_\gamma(t), b_{\alpha\beta}(t), u(t), t) dt^\zeta$$

(see summation over the repeated indices), which provides the following curvilinear integral functional:

$$J(b(\cdot), u(\cdot)) = \int_{\Upsilon_{t_0,t_1}} \mathcal{H}_\zeta(b(t), b_\gamma(t), b_{\alpha\beta}(t), u(t), t) dt^\zeta, \tag{1}$$

where Υ_{t_0,t_1} is a smooth curve, included in Λ_{t_0,t_1}, joining $t_0,\ t_1 \in \mathbb{R}^m_+$.

Second-order PDE-constrained control problem. *Find the pair (b^*, u^*) that minimizes the aforementioned controlled path-independent curvilinear integral functional Equation* (1)*, among all the pair functions (b, u) satisfying*

$$b(t_0) = b_0, \quad b(t_1) = b_1, \quad b_\gamma(t_0) = \tilde{b}_{\gamma 0}, \quad b_\gamma(t_1) = \tilde{b}_{\gamma 1}$$

and the partial speed-acceleration constraints:

$$g^a_\zeta(b(t), b_\gamma(t), b_{\alpha\beta}(t), u(t), t) = 0, \quad a = 1, 2, \cdots, r \le n,\ \zeta = 1, 2, \cdots, m.$$

In order to investigate the above controlled optimization problem in Equation (1), associated with the aforementioned partial speed-acceleration constraints, we introduce the Lagrange multiplier $p = (p_a(t))$ and build new multi-time-controlled second-order Lagrangians (see summation over the repeated indices):

$$\mathcal{H}_{1\zeta}(b(t), b_\gamma(t), b_{\alpha\beta}(t), u(t), p(t), t) = \mathcal{H}_\zeta(b(t), b_\gamma(t), b_{\alpha\beta}(t), u(t), t)$$
$$+ p_a(t) g^a_\zeta(b(t), b_\gamma(t), b_{\alpha\beta}(t), u(t), t), \quad \zeta = \overline{1,m},$$

which change the initial controlled optimization problem (with second-order PDE constraints) into a partial speed-acceleration, unconstrained, controlled optimization problem:

$$\min_{(b(\cdot), u(\cdot),\ p(\cdot))} \int_{\Upsilon_{t_0,t_1}} \mathcal{H}_{1\zeta}(b(t), b_\gamma(t), b_{\alpha\beta}(t), u(t), p(t), t) dt^\zeta \tag{2}$$

$$b(t_q) = b_q, \quad b_\gamma(t_q) = \tilde{b}_{\gamma q}, \quad q = 0, 1,$$

if the Lagrange 1-form $\mathcal{H}_{1\zeta}(b(t), b_\gamma(t), b_{\alpha\beta}(t), u(t), p(t), t) dt^\zeta$ is completely integrable.

In accordance with Lagrange theory, an extreme point of Equation (1) is found among the extreme points of Equation (2).

To formulate the necessary optimality conditions associated with the aforementioned control problem, we shall introduce the Saunders's multi-index (Saunders [32], Treanţă [9–12]).

The following theorem represents the main result of this section (see Treanţă [12]). It establishes the necessary conditions of optimality associated with the considered second-order PDE-constrained control problem.

Theorem 1 (Treanţă [12]). *If $(b^*(\cdot),\ u^*(\cdot),\ p^*(\cdot))$ solves Equation (2), then*

$$(b^*(\cdot),\ u^*(\cdot),\ p^*(\cdot))$$

solves the following Euler–Lagrange system of PDEs:

$$\frac{\partial \mathcal{H}_{1\zeta}}{\partial b^i} - D_\gamma \frac{\partial \mathcal{H}_{1\zeta}}{\partial b^i_\gamma} + \frac{1}{\mu(\alpha,\beta)} D^2_{\alpha\beta} \frac{\partial \mathcal{H}_{1\zeta}}{\partial b^i_{\alpha\beta}} = 0, \quad i = \overline{1,n},\ \zeta = \overline{1,m}$$

$$\frac{\partial \mathcal{H}_{1\zeta}}{\partial u^\vartheta} - D_\gamma \frac{\partial \mathcal{H}_{1\zeta}}{\partial u^\vartheta_\gamma} + \frac{1}{\mu(\alpha,\beta)} D^2_{\alpha\beta} \frac{\partial \mathcal{H}_{1\zeta}}{\partial u^\vartheta_{\alpha\beta}} = 0, \quad \vartheta = \overline{1,k},\ \zeta = \overline{1,m}$$

$$\frac{\partial \mathcal{H}_{1\zeta}}{\partial p_a} - D_\gamma \frac{\partial \mathcal{H}_{1\zeta}}{\partial p_{a,\gamma}} + \frac{1}{\mu(\alpha,\beta)} D^2_{\alpha\beta} \frac{\partial \mathcal{H}_{1\zeta}}{\partial p_{a,\alpha\beta}} = 0, \quad a = \overline{1,r},\ \zeta = \overline{1,m},$$

where $p_{a,\gamma} := \dfrac{\partial p_a}{\partial t^\gamma},\ p_{a,\alpha\beta} := \dfrac{\partial^2 p_a}{\partial t^\alpha \partial t^\beta},\ u^\vartheta_{\alpha\beta} := \dfrac{\partial^2 u^\vartheta}{\partial t^\alpha \partial t^\beta},\ \alpha,\ \beta,\ \gamma \in \{1,2,...,m\}.$

Remark 1 (Treanţă [12]). *The system of Euler–Lagrange PDEs given in Theorem 1 becomes*

$$\frac{\partial \mathcal{H}_{1\zeta}}{\partial b^i} - D_\gamma \frac{\partial \mathcal{H}_{1\zeta}}{\partial b^i_\gamma} + \frac{1}{\mu(\alpha,\beta)} D^2_{\alpha\beta} \frac{\partial \mathcal{H}_{1\zeta}}{\partial b^i_{\alpha\beta}} = 0, \quad i = \overline{1,n},\ \zeta = \overline{1,m}$$

$$\frac{\partial \mathcal{H}_{1\zeta}}{\partial u^\vartheta} - D_\gamma \frac{\partial \mathcal{H}_{1\zeta}}{\partial u^\vartheta_\gamma} + \frac{1}{\mu(\alpha,\beta)} D^2_{\alpha\beta} \frac{\partial \mathcal{H}_{1\zeta}}{\partial u^\vartheta_{\alpha\beta}} = 0, \quad \vartheta = \overline{1,k},\ \zeta = \overline{1,m}$$

$$g^a_\zeta(b(t), b_\gamma(t), b_{\alpha,\beta}(t), u(t), t) = 0, \quad a = 1,2,\cdots,r \le n,\ \zeta = 1,2,\cdots,m.$$

Remark 2 (Treanţă [12]). *(i) The most general Lagrange* 1*-form that can be used in the previous problem is of the form:*

$$\mathcal{H}_{2\zeta}(b(t), b_\gamma(t), b_{\alpha\beta}(t), u(t), p(t), t) = \mathcal{H}_\zeta(b(t), b_\gamma(t), b_{\alpha\beta}(t), u(t), t)$$
$$+ p^\lambda_{a\zeta}(t) g^a_\lambda(b(t), b_\gamma(t), b_{\alpha\beta}(t), u(t), t).$$

(ii) The closeness conditions $D_\theta \mathcal{H}_\zeta = D_\zeta \mathcal{H}_\theta$ associated with the Lagrange 1*-form $\mathcal{H}_\zeta(b(t), b_\gamma(t), b_{\alpha\beta}(t), u(t), t)dt^\zeta$ are actually PDE constraints for the considered problem. The optimization problem of the controlled curvilinear integral cost functional $J(b(\cdot), u(\cdot))$, conditioned by $D_\theta \mathcal{H}_\zeta = D_\zeta \mathcal{H}_\theta$, can be studied by using the following Lagrange* 1*-form:*

$$\mathcal{H}_{3\zeta}(b(t), b_\gamma(t), b_{\alpha\beta}(t), u(t), p(t), t) = \mathcal{H}_\zeta(b(t), b_\gamma(t), b_{\alpha\beta}(t), u(t), t)$$
$$+ p^{\theta\lambda}_\zeta(t)(D_\theta \mathcal{H}_\lambda - D_\lambda \mathcal{H}_\theta).$$

Illustrative example. Minimize the following objective functional:

$$J(b(\cdot), u(\cdot)) = \int_{\Upsilon_{0,1}} \Big(b^2(t) + u^2(t)\Big)dt^1 + \Big(b^2(t) + u^2(t)\Big)dt^2$$

subject to $b_{t^1}(t) + b_{t^2}(t) = 0,\ b(0,0) = 0,\ b(1,1) = 0$, where $\Upsilon_{0,1}$ is a curve of C^1-class in $[0,1]^2$, joining $(0,0)$ and $(1,1)$.

Solution. The path-independence of the functional $J(b(\cdot), u(\cdot))$ gives:

$$b\Big(\frac{\partial b}{\partial t^2} - \frac{\partial b}{\partial t^1}\Big) = u\Big(\frac{\partial u}{\partial t^1} - \frac{\partial u}{\partial t^2}\Big).$$

Moreover, for the Lagrange 1-form (Remark 2), we obtain:

$$\Theta_{11} = b^2(t) + u^2(t) + \omega_1(t)(b_{t^1}(t) + b_{t^2}(t)),$$

$$\Theta_{12} = b^2(t) + u^2(t) + +\omega_2(t)(b_{t^1}(t) + b_{t^2}(t))$$

and the extreme points are formulated as below:

$$2s - \frac{\partial \omega_1}{\partial t^1} - \frac{\partial \omega_1}{\partial t^2} = 0, \quad 2s - \frac{\partial \omega_2}{\partial t^1} - \frac{\partial \omega_2}{\partial t^2} = 0,$$

$$2u = 0,$$

$$b_{t^1}(t) + b_{t^2}(t) = 0.$$

It follows that $(b^*, u^*) = (0,0)$ is the optimal point of the considered optimization problem, and satisfies $\dfrac{\partial \phi}{\partial t^1} + \dfrac{\partial \phi}{\partial t^2} = 0$, where $\phi := \omega_1 - \omega_2$.

3. Isoperimetric Constrained Controlled Optimization Problem

In this section, we use similar notations as in the previous section. We consider a C^3-class function $\mathcal{H}(b(t), b_\gamma(t), b_{\alpha\beta}(t), u(t), t)$, called *multi-time-controlled, second-order Lagrangian*, where $t = (t^\alpha) = (t^1, \cdots, t^m) \in \Lambda_{t_0,t_1} \subset \mathbb{R}^m_+$, $b = (b^i) = \left(b^1, \cdots, b^n\right) : \Lambda_{t_0,t_1} \to \mathbb{R}^n$ is a function of the C^4-class (the *state variable*), and $u = (u^\vartheta) = \left(u^1, \cdots, u^k\right) : \Lambda_{t_0,t_1} \to \mathbb{R}^k$ is a piecewise continuous function (the *control variable*). In addition, denote $b_\alpha(t) := \dfrac{\partial b}{\partial t^\alpha}(t)$, $b_{\alpha\beta}(t) := \dfrac{\partial^2 b}{\partial t^\alpha \partial t^\beta}(t)$, $\alpha, \beta \in \{1, ..., m\}$, and consider $\Lambda_{t_0,t_1} = [t_0, t_1]$ as a hyper-parallelepiped generated by the diagonally opposite points t_0, $t_1 \in \mathbb{R}^m_+$.

Isoperimetric constrained control problem. *Find the pair (b^*, u^*) that minimizes the following multiple integral functional:*

$$J(b(\cdot), u(\cdot)) = \int_{\Lambda_{t_0,t_1}} \mathcal{H}(b(t), b_\gamma(t), b_{\alpha\beta}(t), u(t), t) dt^1 \cdots dt^m \tag{3}$$

among all the pair functions (b, u) satisfying

$$b(t_0) = b_0, \quad b(t_1) = b_1, \quad b_\gamma(t_0) = \tilde{b}_{\gamma 0}, \quad b_\gamma(t_1) = \tilde{b}_{\gamma 1},$$

or

$$b(t)|_{\partial \Lambda_{t_0,t_1}} = given, \quad b_\gamma(t)|_{\partial \Lambda_{t_0,t_1}} = given$$

and the isoperimetric constraints (that is, constant level sets of some functionals) formulated as follows.

Isoperimetric Constraints Defined by Controlled Curvilinear Integral Functionals

Consider the isoperimetric constraints:

$$\int_{\Upsilon_{t_0,t_1}} g^a_\zeta(b(t), b_\gamma(t), b_{\alpha\beta}(t), u(t), t) dt^\zeta = l^a, \quad a = 1, 2, \cdots, r \le n,$$

where Υ_{t_0,t_1} is a smooth curve, included in Λ_{t_0,t_1}, joining the points t_0, $t_1 \in \mathbb{R}^m_+$, and

$$g^a_\zeta(b(t), b_\gamma(t), b_{\alpha\beta}(t), u(t), t) dt^\zeta, \quad a = 1, 2, \cdots, r$$

are completely integrable differential 1-forms, namely, $D_\gamma g_\zeta = D_\zeta g_\gamma, \gamma, \zeta \in \{1, \cdots, m\}$, $\gamma \neq \zeta$, with $D_\gamma := \dfrac{\partial}{\partial t^\gamma}$, $\gamma \in \{1, \cdots, m\}$.

In order to investigate the above controlled optimization problem in Equation (3), associated with the aforementioned isoperimetric constraints, we introduce the curve $\Upsilon_{t_0,t} \subset \Upsilon_{t_0,t_1}$ and the auxiliary variables:

$$y^a(t) = \int_{\Upsilon_{t_0,t}} g^a_\zeta(b(\tau), b_\gamma(\tau), b_{\alpha\beta}(\tau), u(\tau), \tau) d\tau^\zeta, \quad a = 1, 2, \cdots, r,$$

which satisfy $y^a(t_0) = 0,\ y^a(t_1) = l^a$. Consequently, the functions y^a fulfill the next first-order PDEs:

$$\frac{\partial y^a}{\partial t^\zeta}(t) = g^a_\zeta(b(t), b_\gamma(t), b_{\alpha\beta}(t), u(t), t), \quad y^a(t_1) = l^a.$$

Considering the Lagrange multiplier $p = \left(p^\zeta_a(t)\right)$ and by denoting $y = (y^a(t))$, we introduce a new multi-time-controlled Lagrangian of second order:

$$\mathcal{H}_1(b(t), b_\gamma(t), b_{\alpha\beta}(t), u(t), y(t), y_\zeta(t), p(t), t) = \mathcal{H}(b(t), b_\gamma(t), b_{\alpha\beta}(t), u(t), t)$$
$$+ p^\zeta_a(t)\left(g^a_\zeta(b(t), b_\gamma(t), b_{\alpha\beta}(t), u(t), t) - \frac{\partial y^a}{\partial t^\zeta}(t)\right)$$

that changes the initial control problem into an unconstrained control problem

$$\min_{b(\cdot), u(\cdot), y(\cdot), p(\cdot)} \int_{\Lambda_{t_0,t_1}} \mathcal{H}_1(b(t), b_\gamma(t), b_{\alpha\beta}(t), u(t), y(t), y_\zeta(t), p(t), t) dt^1 \cdots dt^m \tag{4}$$

$$b(t_q) = b_q, \quad b_\gamma(t_q) = \tilde{b}_{\gamma q}, \quad q = 0, 1$$
$$y(t_0) = 0, \quad y(t_1) = l.$$

In accordance with Lagrange theory, an extreme point of Equation (3) is found among the extreme points of Equation (4).

The following theorem (see Treanţă and Ahmad [13]) establishes the necessary conditions of optimality associated with the considered isoperimetric constrained control problem.

Theorem 2 (Treanţă and Ahmad [13]). *If $(b^*(\cdot),\ u^*(\cdot),\ y^*(\cdot),\ p^*(\cdot))$ solves Equation (4), then*

$$(b^*(\cdot),\ u^*(\cdot),\ y^*(\cdot),\ p^*(\cdot))$$

solves the following Euler–Lagrange system of PDEs:

$$\frac{\partial \mathcal{H}_1}{\partial b^i} - D_\gamma \frac{\partial \mathcal{H}_1}{\partial b^i_\gamma} + \frac{1}{\mu(\alpha, \beta)} D^2_{\alpha\beta} \frac{\partial \mathcal{H}_1}{\partial b^i_{\alpha\beta}} = 0, \quad i = \overline{1, n}$$

$$\frac{\partial \mathcal{H}_1}{\partial u^\vartheta} - D_\gamma \frac{\partial \mathcal{H}_1}{\partial u^\vartheta_\gamma} + \frac{1}{\mu(\alpha, \beta)} D^2_{\alpha\beta} \frac{\partial \mathcal{H}_1}{\partial u^\vartheta_{\alpha\beta}} = 0, \quad \vartheta = \overline{1, k}$$

$$\frac{\partial \mathcal{H}_1}{\partial y^a} - D_\zeta \frac{\partial \mathcal{H}_1}{\partial y^a_\zeta} + \frac{1}{\mu(\alpha, \beta)} D^2_{\alpha\beta} \frac{\partial \mathcal{H}_1}{\partial y^a_{\alpha\beta}} = 0, \quad a = \overline{1, r}$$

$$\frac{\partial \mathcal{H}_1}{\partial p^\zeta_a} - D_\gamma \frac{\partial \mathcal{H}_1}{\partial p^\zeta_{a,\gamma}} + \frac{1}{\mu(\alpha, \beta)} D^2_{\alpha\beta} \frac{\partial \mathcal{H}_1}{\partial p^\zeta_{a,\alpha\beta}} = 0,$$

where $p^\zeta_{a,\gamma} := \frac{\partial p^\zeta_a}{\partial t^\gamma},\ p^\zeta_{a,\alpha\beta} := \frac{\partial^2 p^\zeta_a}{\partial t^\alpha \partial t^\beta},\ u^\vartheta_{\alpha\beta} := \frac{\partial^2 u^\vartheta}{\partial t^\alpha \partial t^\beta},\ y^a_{\alpha\beta} := \frac{\partial^2 y^a}{\partial t^\alpha \partial t^\beta},\ \alpha, \beta, \gamma, \zeta \in \{1, 2, ..., m\}.$

Remark 3 (Treanţă and Ahmad [13]). *The system of Euler–Lagrange PDEs given in Theorem 2 becomes*

$$\frac{\partial \mathcal{H}_1}{\partial b^i} - D_\gamma \frac{\partial \mathcal{H}_1}{\partial b^i_\gamma} + \frac{1}{\mu(\alpha,\beta)} D^2_{\alpha\beta} \frac{\partial \mathcal{H}_1}{\partial b^i_{\alpha\beta}} = 0, \quad i = \overline{1,n}$$

$$\frac{\partial \mathcal{H}_1}{\partial u^\vartheta} - D_\gamma \frac{\partial \mathcal{H}_1}{\partial u^\vartheta_\gamma} + \frac{1}{\mu(\alpha,\beta)} D^2_{\alpha\beta} \frac{\partial \mathcal{H}_1}{\partial u^\vartheta_{\alpha\beta}} = 0, \quad \vartheta = \overline{1,k}$$

$$\frac{\partial p^\zeta_a}{\partial t^\zeta} = 0, \quad a = \overline{1,r}, \quad \zeta \in \{1,2,\cdots,m\}$$

$$\frac{\partial y^a}{\partial t^\zeta}(t) = g^a_\zeta(b(t), b_\gamma(t), b_{\alpha,\beta}(t), u(t), t).$$

In consequence, the Lagrange matrix multiplier p has null total divergence. Moreover, it is well determined only if the optimal solution is not an extreme for at least one of the functionals $\int_{\Upsilon_{t_0,t_1}} g^a_\zeta(b(t), b_\gamma(t), b_{\alpha,\beta}(t), u(t), t) dt^\zeta$, $a = \overline{1,r}$.

4. Well-Posedness of Some Variational Inequalities Involving Second-Order Partial Derivatives

In the following, in accordance with Treanţă [14–16], we consider: Λ_{s_1,s_2} as a compact set in $\mathbb{R}^m$; $\Lambda_{s_1,s_2} \ni s = (s^\zeta)$, $\zeta = \overline{1,m}$ as a multi-variate evolution parameter; $\Lambda_{s_1,s_2} \supset \Upsilon$ as a piecewise differentiable curve that links the points $s_1 = (s_1^1, \ldots, s_1^m)$, $s_2 = (s_2^1, \ldots, s_2^m)$ in Λ_{s_1,s_2}; $\mathcal{B}$ as the space of C^4-class *state* functions $b : \Lambda_{s_1,s_2} \to \mathbb{R}^n$; and $b_\kappa := \frac{\partial b}{\partial s^\kappa}$, $b_{\alpha\beta} := \frac{\partial^2 b}{\partial s^\alpha \partial s^\beta}$ denote the *partial speed* and *partial acceleration*, respectively. In addition, let $\mathbf{U}$ be the space of C^1-class *control* functions $u : \Lambda_{s_1,s_2} \to \mathbb{R}^k$ and assume that $B \times U$ is a (nonempty) convex and closed subset of $\mathcal{B} \times \mathbf{U}$, equipped with

$$\langle (b,u),(q,z) \rangle = \int_\Upsilon [b(s) \cdot q(s) + u(s) \cdot z(s)] ds^\zeta$$

$$= \int_\Upsilon [\sum_{i=1}^n b^i(s) q^i(s) + \sum_{j=1}^k u^j(s) z^j(s)] ds^\zeta$$

$$= \int_\Upsilon [\sum_{i=1}^n b^i(s) q^i(s) + \sum_{j=1}^k u^j(s) z^j(s)] ds^1 + \cdots + [\sum_{i=1}^n b^i(s) q^i(s) + \sum_{j=1}^k u^j(s) z^j(s)] ds^m,$$

$$\forall (b,u),(q,z) \in \mathcal{B} \times \mathbf{U}$$

and the norm induced by it.

Let $J^2(\mathbb{R}^m, \mathbb{R}^n)$ be the jet bundle of the second order of $\mathbb{R}^m$ and $\mathbb{R}^n$. Assume that the Lagrangians $w_\zeta : J^2(\mathbb{R}^m, \mathbb{R}^n) \times \mathbb{R}^k \to \mathbb{R}$, $\zeta = \overline{1,m}$ provide a closed controlled Lagrange 1-form

$$w_\zeta(s, b(s), b_\kappa(s), b_{\alpha\beta}(s), u(s)) ds^\zeta,$$

which gives the following integral functional:

$$W : \mathcal{B} \times \mathbf{U} \to \mathbb{R}, \quad W(b,u) = \int_\Upsilon w_\zeta(s, b(s), b_\kappa(s), b_{\alpha\beta}(s), u(s)) ds^\zeta$$

$$= \int_\Upsilon w_1(s, b(s), b_\kappa(s), b_{\alpha\beta}(s), u(s)) ds^1 + \cdots + w_m(s, b(s), b_\kappa(s), b_{\alpha\beta}(s), u(s)) ds^m.$$

In order to state the problem under study, we introduce the Saunders's multi-index (Saunders [32]).

Now, we introduce the variational problem: find $(b,u) \in B \times U$ such that

$$\int_Y \left[\frac{\partial w_\zeta}{\partial b}(\Psi_{b,u}(s))(q(s)-b(s)) + \frac{\partial w_\zeta}{\partial b_\kappa}(\Psi_{b,u}(s))D_\kappa(q(s)-b(s))\right]ds^\zeta \tag{5}$$

$$+\int_Y \left[\frac{1}{x(\alpha,\beta)}\frac{\partial w_\zeta}{\partial b_{\alpha\beta}}(\Psi_{b,u}(s))D^2_{\alpha\beta}(q(s)-b(s))\right]ds^\zeta$$

$$+\int_Y \left[\frac{\partial w_\zeta}{\partial u}(\Psi_{b,u}(s))(z(s)-u(s))\right]ds^\zeta \geq 0, \quad \forall (q,z) \in B \times U,$$

where $D_\kappa := \dfrac{\partial}{\partial s^\kappa}$ is the total derivative operator, $D^2_{\alpha\beta} := D_\alpha(D_\beta)$, and $(\Psi_{b,u}(s)) := (s, b(s), b_\kappa(s), b_{\alpha\beta}(s), u(s))$.

Let Ω be the feasible solution set of (5):

$$\begin{aligned}\Omega = \Big\{(b,u) \in B \times U : \int_Y &[(q(s)-b(s))\frac{\partial w_\zeta}{\partial b}(\Psi_{b,u}(s)) \\ &+ D_\kappa(q(s)-b(s))\frac{\partial w_\zeta}{\partial b_\kappa}(\Psi_{b,u}(s)) \\ &+ \frac{1}{x(\alpha,\beta)}D^2_{\alpha\beta}(q(s)-b(s))\frac{\partial w_\zeta}{\partial b_{\alpha\beta}}(\Psi_{b,u}(s)) \\ &+ (z(s)-u(s))\frac{\partial w_\zeta}{\partial u}(\Psi_{b,u}(s))]ds^\zeta \geq 0, \\ &\forall (q,z) \in B \times U\Big\}.\end{aligned}$$

Assumption 1. *The next working hypothesis is assumed:*

$$dG := D_\kappa\left[\frac{\partial w_\zeta}{\partial b_\kappa}(b-q)\right]ds^\zeta \tag{6}$$

as a total exact differential, with $G(s_1) = G(s_2)$.

According to Equation (6) and considering the notion of monotonicity associated with variational inequalities, we formulate (see Treanţă et al. [14]) the monotonicity and pseudomonotonicity for W.

Definition 1. *The functional W is monotone on $B \times U$ if*

$$\begin{aligned}\int_Y &\Big[(b(s)-q(s))\left(\frac{\partial w_\zeta}{\partial b}(\Psi_{b,u}(s)) - \frac{\partial w_\zeta}{\partial b}(\Psi_{q,z}(s))\right) \\ &+ (u(s)-z(s))\left(\frac{\partial w_\zeta}{\partial u}(\Psi_{b,u}(s)) - \frac{\partial w_\zeta}{\partial u}(\Psi_{q,z}(s))\right) \\ &+ D_\kappa(b(s)-q(s))\left(\frac{\partial w_\zeta}{\partial b_\kappa}(\Psi_{b,u}(s)) - \frac{\partial w_\zeta}{\partial b_\kappa}(\Psi_{q,z}(s))\right) \\ &+ \frac{1}{x(\alpha,\beta)}D^2_{\alpha\beta}(b(s)-q(s))\left(\frac{\partial w_\zeta}{\partial b_{\alpha\beta}}(\Psi_{b,u}(s)) - \frac{\partial w_\zeta}{\partial b_{\alpha\beta}}(\Psi_{q,z}(s))\right)\Big]ds^\zeta \geq 0,\end{aligned}$$

$$\forall (b,u), (q,z) \in B \times U$$

is satisfied.

Definition 2. *The functional W is pseudomonotone on $B \times U$ if*

$$\int_{\Upsilon}[(b(s)-q(s))\frac{\partial w_{\zeta}}{\partial b}(\Psi_{q,z}(s))+(u(s)-z(s))\frac{\partial w_{\zeta}}{\partial u}(\Psi_{q,z}(s))$$
$$+D_{\kappa}(b(s)-q(s))\frac{\partial w_{\zeta}}{\partial b_{\kappa}}(\Psi_{q,z}(s))$$
$$+\frac{1}{x(\alpha,\beta)}D^{2}_{\alpha\beta}(b(s)-q(s))\frac{\partial w_{\zeta}}{\partial b_{\alpha\beta}}(\Psi_{q,z}(s))]ds^{\zeta}\geq 0$$
$$\Rightarrow \int_{\Upsilon}[(b(s)-q(s))\frac{\partial w_{\zeta}}{\partial b}(\Psi_{b,u}(s))+(u(s)-z(s))\frac{\partial w_{\zeta}}{\partial u}(\Psi_{b,u}(s))$$
$$+D_{\kappa}(b(s)-q(s))\frac{\partial w_{\zeta}}{\partial b_{\kappa}}(\Psi_{b,u}(s))$$
$$+\frac{1}{x(\alpha,\beta)}D^{2}_{\alpha\beta}(b(s)-q(s))\frac{\partial w_{\zeta}}{\partial b_{\alpha\beta}}(\Psi_{b,u}(s))]ds^{\zeta}\geq 0,$$
$$\forall (b,u),(q,z)\in B\times U$$

is valid.

By using Usman and Khan [33], we introduce the following definition.

Definition 3. *W is hemicontinuous on $B \times U$ if*

$$\lambda \to \left\langle ((b(s),u(s))-(q(s),z(s)),\left(\frac{\delta_{\zeta}W}{\delta b_{\lambda}},\frac{\delta_{\zeta}W}{\delta u_{\lambda}}\right)\right\rangle, \quad 0\leq\lambda\leq 1$$

is continuous at 0^{+}, for $\forall(b,u),(q,z)\in B\times U$, where

$$\frac{\delta_{\zeta}W}{\delta b_{\lambda}}:=\frac{\partial w_{\zeta}}{\partial b}(\Psi_{b_{\lambda},u_{\lambda}}(s))-D_{\kappa}\frac{\partial w_{\zeta}}{\partial b_{\kappa}}(\Psi_{b_{\lambda},u_{\lambda}}(s))+\frac{1}{x(\alpha,\beta)}D^{2}_{\alpha\beta}\frac{\partial w_{\zeta}}{\partial b_{\alpha\beta}}(\Psi_{b_{\lambda},u_{\lambda}}(s))\in B,$$
$$\frac{\delta_{\zeta}W}{\delta u_{\lambda}}:=\frac{\partial w_{\zeta}}{\partial u}(\Psi_{b_{\lambda},u_{\lambda}}(s))\in U,$$
$$b_{\lambda}:=\lambda b+(1-\lambda)q,\quad u_{\lambda}:=\lambda u+(1-\lambda)z.$$

Lemma 1 (Treanţă et al. [14]). *Let the functional W be hemicontinuous and pseudomonotone on $B \times U$. A point $(b,u)\in B\times U$ solves Equation (5) if and only if $(b,u)\in B\times U$ solves:*

$$\int_{\Upsilon}[(q(s)-b(s))\frac{\partial w_{\zeta}}{\partial b}(\Psi_{q,z}(s))+(z(s)-u(s))\frac{\partial w_{\zeta}}{\partial u}(\Psi_{q,z}(s))$$
$$+D_{\kappa}(q(s)-b(s))\frac{\partial w_{\zeta}}{\partial b_{\kappa}}(\Psi_{q,z}(s))$$
$$+\frac{1}{x(\alpha,\beta)}D^{2}_{\alpha\beta}(q(s)-b(s))\frac{\partial w_{\zeta}}{\partial b_{\alpha\beta}}(\Psi_{q,z}(s))]ds^{\zeta}\geq 0,\quad \forall(q,z)\in B\times U.$$

Furthermore, according to Treanţă et al. [14], we present two well-posedness results associated with the considered variational inequality problem involving second-order PDEs.

Definition 4. *The sequence* $\{(b_n, u_n)\} \in B \times U$ *is called an approximating sequence of Equation (5) if there exists a sequence of positive real numbers* $\sigma_n \to 0$ *as* $n \to \infty$, *such that:*

$$\int_Y [(q(s) - b_n(s))\frac{\partial w_\zeta}{\partial b}(\Psi_{b_n,u_n}(s)) + (z(s) - u_n(s))\frac{\partial w_\zeta}{\partial u}(\Psi_{b_n,u_n}(s))$$

$$+D_\kappa(q(s) - b_n(s))\frac{\partial w_\zeta}{\partial b_\kappa}(\Psi_{b_n,u_n}(s))$$

$$+\frac{1}{x(\alpha,\beta)}D^2_{\alpha\beta}(q(s) - b_n(s))\frac{\partial w_\zeta}{\partial b_{\alpha\beta}}(\Psi_{b_n,u_n}(s))]ds^\zeta + \sigma_n \geq 0, \quad \forall (q,z) \in B \times U.$$

Definition 5. *The problem Equation (5) is called well-posed if:*

(i) *The problem in Equation (5) has one solution* (b_0, u_0);
(ii) *Each approximating sequence of Equation (5) converges to* (b_0, u_0).

The approximating solution set of Equation (5) is given as follows:

$$\Omega_\sigma = \Big\{(b,u) \in B \times U : \int_Y [(q(s) - b(s))\frac{\partial w_\zeta}{\partial b}(\Psi_{b,u}(s)) + (z(s) - u(s))\frac{\partial w_\zeta}{\partial u}(\Psi_{b,u}(s))$$
$$+ D_\kappa(q(s) - b(s))\frac{\partial w_\zeta}{\partial b_\kappa}(\Psi_{b,u}(s))$$
$$+ \frac{1}{x(\alpha,\beta)}D^2_{\alpha\beta}(q(s) - b(s))\frac{\partial w_\zeta}{\partial b_{\alpha\beta}}(\Psi_{b,u}(s))]ds^\zeta + \sigma \geq 0,\ \forall (q,z) \in B \times U\Big\}.$$

Remark 4. *We have:* $\Omega = \Omega_\sigma$, *when* $\sigma = 0$ *and* $\Omega \subseteq \Omega_\sigma$, $\forall \sigma > 0$.

Furthermore, for a set P, the diameter of P is defined as follows

$$diam\ P = \sup_{\phi,\eta \in P} \|\phi - \eta\|.$$

Theorem 3 (Treanţă et al. [14]). *Let the functional W be hemicontinuous and monotone on* $B \times U$. *The problem Equation (5) is well-posed if and only if:*

$$\Omega_\sigma \neq \emptyset, \forall \sigma > 0 \text{ and } diam\ \Omega_\sigma \to 0 \text{ as } \sigma \to 0.$$

Theorem 4 (Treanţă et al. [14]). *Let the functional W be hemicontinuous and monotone on* $B \times U$. *Then, Equation (5) is well-posed if and only if it has one solution.*

5. Open Problem

As in the previous sections, we start with $\mathcal{T}$ as a compact set in $\mathbb{R}^m$ and $\mathcal{T} \ni \zeta = (\zeta^\beta)$, $\beta = \overline{1,m}$, as a multi-variable. Let $\mathcal{T} \supset C : \zeta = \zeta(\varsigma), \varsigma \in [p,q]$ be a (piecewise) differentiable curve joining the following two fixed points $\zeta_1 = (\zeta_1^1, \ldots, \zeta_1^m)$, $\zeta_2 = (\zeta_2^1, \ldots, \zeta_2^m)$ in $\mathcal{T}$. In addition, we consider Λ as the space of (piecewise) smooth *state* functions $\sigma : \mathcal{T} \to \mathbb{R}^n$ and Ω as the space of *control* functions $\eta : \mathcal{T} \to \mathbb{R}^k$, which are considered to be piecewise continuous. Moreover, on the product space $\Lambda \times \Omega$, we consider the scalar product:

$$\langle(\sigma,\eta),(\pi,x)\rangle = \int_C \Big[\sigma(\zeta)\cdot\pi(\zeta) + \eta(\zeta)\cdot x(\zeta)\Big]d\zeta^\beta$$

$$= \int_C \Big[\sum_{i=1}^n \sigma^i(\zeta)\pi^i(\zeta) + \sum_{j=1}^k \eta^j(\zeta)x^j(\zeta)\Big]d\zeta^1$$

$$+\cdots+\Big[\sum_{i=1}^n \sigma^i(\zeta)\pi^i(\zeta) + \sum_{j=1}^k \eta^j(\zeta)x^j(\zeta)\Big]d\zeta^m, \quad (\forall)(\sigma,\eta),(\pi,x) \in \Lambda \times \Omega$$

together with the norm induced by it.

In the following, we introduce the vector functional defined by curvilinear integrals:

$$\Psi : \Lambda \times \Omega \to \mathbb{R}^p, \quad \Psi(\sigma, \eta) = \int_C \psi_\beta(\zeta, \sigma(\zeta), \sigma_\alpha(\zeta), \sigma_{ab}(\zeta), \eta(\zeta))d\zeta^\beta$$

$$= \left(\int_C \psi^1_\beta(\zeta, \sigma(\zeta), \sigma_\alpha(\zeta), \sigma_{ab}(\zeta), \eta(\zeta))d\zeta^\beta, \cdots, \int_C \psi^p_\beta(\zeta, \sigma(\zeta), \sigma_\alpha(\zeta), \sigma_{ab}(\zeta), \eta(\zeta))d\zeta^\beta \right),$$

where we used the vector-valued C^2-class functions $\psi_\beta = (\psi^l_\beta) : \mathcal{T} \times \mathbb{R}^n \times \mathbb{R}^{nm} \times \mathbb{R}^{nm^2} \times \mathbb{R}^k \to \mathbb{R}^p$, $\beta = \overline{1,m}$, $l = \overline{1,p}$. In addition, D_α, $\alpha \in \{1, \ldots, m\}$ represents the operator of total derivative, and the aforementioned 1-form densities

$$\psi_\beta = \left(\psi^1_\beta, \ldots, \psi^p_\beta\right) : \mathcal{T} \times \mathbb{R}^n \times \mathbb{R}^{nm} \times \mathbb{R}^{nm^2} \times \mathbb{R}^k \to \mathbb{R}^p, \quad \beta = \overline{1,m},$$

are closed ($D_\alpha \psi^l_\beta = D_\beta \psi^l_\alpha$, $\beta, \alpha = \overline{1,m}$, $\beta \neq \alpha$, $l = \overline{1,p}$). Throughout the paper, the following rules for equalities and inequalities are applied:

$$a = b \Leftrightarrow a^l = b^l, \quad a \leq b \Leftrightarrow a^l \leq b^l, \quad a < b \Leftrightarrow a^l < b^l, \quad a \preceq b \Leftrightarrow a \leq b,\ a \neq b, \quad l = \overline{1,p},$$

for all p-tuples, $a = \left(a^1, \cdots, a^p\right)$, $b = \left(b^1, \cdots, b^p\right)$ in $\mathbb{R}^p$.

Next, we formulate the partial differential equation/inequation constrained optimization problem:

$$(CP) \quad \min_{(\sigma,\eta)} \left\{ \Psi(\sigma, \eta) = \int_C \psi_\beta(\zeta, \sigma(\zeta), \sigma_\alpha(\zeta), \sigma_{ab}(\zeta), \eta(\zeta))d\zeta^\beta \right\} \text{ subject to } (\sigma, \eta) \in \mathcal{S},$$

where

$$\Psi(\sigma, \eta) = \int_C \psi_\beta(\zeta, \sigma(\zeta), \sigma_\alpha(\zeta), \sigma_{ab}(\zeta), \eta(\zeta))d\zeta^\beta$$

$$= \left(\int_C \psi^1_\beta(\zeta, \sigma(\zeta), \sigma_\alpha(\zeta), \sigma_{ab}(\zeta), \eta(\zeta))d\zeta^\beta, \cdots, \int_C \psi^p_\beta(\zeta, \sigma(\zeta), \sigma_\alpha(\zeta), \sigma_{ab}(\zeta), \eta(\zeta))d\zeta^\beta \right)$$

$$= \left(\Psi^1(\sigma, \eta), \ldots, \Psi^p(\sigma, \eta) \right)$$

and

$$\mathcal{S} = \Big\{ (\sigma, \eta) \in \Lambda \times \Omega \mid Z(\zeta, \sigma(\zeta), \sigma_\alpha(\zeta), \sigma_{ab}(\zeta), \eta(\zeta)) = 0,\ Y(\zeta, \sigma(\zeta), \sigma_\alpha(\zeta), \sigma_{ab}(\zeta), \eta(\zeta)) \leq 0,$$

$$\sigma|_{\zeta = \zeta_1, \zeta_2} = \text{given}, \ \sigma_\alpha|_{\zeta = \zeta_1, \zeta_2} = \text{given} \Big\}.$$

Above, we considered $Z = (Z^\iota) : \mathcal{T} \times \mathbb{R}^n \times \mathbb{R}^{nm} \times \mathbb{R}^{nm^2} \times \mathbb{R}^k \to \mathbb{R}^t$, $\iota = \overline{1,t}$, $Y = (Y^r) : \mathcal{T} \times \mathbb{R}^n \times \mathbb{R}^{nm} \times \mathbb{R}^{nm^2} \times \mathbb{R}^k \to \mathbb{R}^q$, $r = \overline{1,q}$ as C^2-class functions.

Definition 6. *A point $(\sigma^0, \eta^0) \in \mathcal{S}$ is called an efficient solution in (CP) if there exists no other $(\sigma, \eta) \in \mathcal{S}$ such that $\Psi(\sigma, \eta) \preceq \Psi(\sigma^0, \eta^0)$, or, equivalently, $\Psi^l(\sigma, \eta) - \Psi^l(\sigma^0, \eta^0) \leq 0$, $(\forall) l = \overline{1,p}$, with strict inequality for at least one l.*

Definition 7. *A point $(\sigma^0, \eta^0) \in \mathcal{S}$ is called a proper efficient solution in (CP) if $(\sigma^0, \eta^0) \in \mathcal{S}$ is an efficient solution in (CP) and there exists a positive real number M, such that, for all $l = \overline{1,p}$, we have*

$$\Psi^l(\sigma^0, \eta^0) - \Psi^l(\sigma, \eta) \leq M\left(\Psi^s(\sigma, \eta) - \Psi^s(\sigma^0, \eta^0)\right),$$

for some $s \in \{1, \cdots, p\}$ such that

$$\Psi^s(\sigma, \eta) > \Psi^s(\sigma^0, \eta^0),$$

whenever $(\sigma,\eta)\in\mathcal{S}$ *and*

$$\Psi^l(\sigma,\eta)<\Psi^l(\sigma^0,\eta^0).$$

Definition 8. *A point* $(\sigma^0,\eta^0)\in\mathcal{S}$ *is called a weak efficient solution in* (CP) *if there exists no other* $(\sigma,\eta)\in\mathcal{S}$ *such that* $\Psi(\sigma,\eta)<\Psi(\sigma^0,\eta^0)$, *or, equivalently,* $\Psi^l(\sigma,\eta)-\Psi^l(\sigma^0,\eta^0)<0$, $(\forall)l=\overline{1,p}$.

According to Treanţă [17,18], for $\sigma\in\Lambda$ *and* $\eta\in\Omega$, *we consider the vector functional*

$$K:\Lambda\times\Omega\to\mathbb{R}^p,\quad K(\sigma,\eta)=\int_C\kappa_\beta(\zeta,\sigma(\zeta),\sigma_\alpha(\zeta),\sigma_{ab}(\zeta),\eta(\zeta))d\zeta^\beta$$

and define the concepts of invexity and pseudoinvexity associated with K.

For examples of invex and/or pseudoinvex curvilinear integral functionals, the reader can consult Treanţă [17].

Definition 9 (Treanţă [18]). *We say that* $X\times Q\subset\Lambda\times\Omega$ *is invex with respect to* ϑ *and* v *if*

$$(\sigma^0,\eta^0)+\lambda\Big(\vartheta\big(\zeta,\sigma,\eta,\sigma^0,\eta^0\big),v\big(\zeta,\sigma,\eta,\sigma^0,\eta^0\big)\Big)\in X\times Q,$$

for all (σ,η), $(\sigma^0,\eta^0)\in X\times Q$ *and* $\lambda\in[0,1]$.

Now, we introduce the following (weak) vector controlled variational inequalities:

I. Find $(\sigma^0,\eta^0)\in\mathcal{S}$ *such that there exists no* $(\sigma,\eta)\in\mathcal{S}$ *satisfying*

$$(VI)\quad \Big(\int_C\Big[\frac{\partial\psi^1_\beta}{\partial\sigma}\big(\zeta,\sigma^0(\zeta),\sigma^0_\alpha(\zeta),\sigma^0_{ab}(\zeta),\eta^0(\zeta)\big)\vartheta+\frac{\partial\psi^1_\beta}{\partial\eta}\big(\zeta,\sigma^0(\zeta),\sigma^0_\alpha(\zeta),\sigma^0_{ab}(\zeta),\eta^0(\zeta)\big)v\Big]d\zeta^\beta$$

$$+\int_C\Big[\frac{\partial\psi^1_\beta}{\partial\sigma_\alpha}\big(\zeta,\sigma^0(\zeta),\sigma^0_\alpha(\zeta),\sigma^0_{ab}(\zeta),\eta^0(\zeta)\big)D_\alpha\vartheta\Big]d\zeta^\beta$$

$$+\frac{1}{x(a,b)}\int_C\Big[\frac{\partial\psi^1_\beta}{\partial\sigma_{ab}}\big(\zeta,\sigma^0(\zeta),\sigma^0_\alpha(\zeta),\sigma^0_{ab}(\zeta),\eta^0(\zeta)\big)D^2_{ab}\vartheta\Big]d\zeta^\beta,\cdots,$$

$$\int_C\Big[\frac{\partial\psi^p_\beta}{\partial\sigma}\big(\zeta,\sigma^0(\zeta),\sigma^0_\alpha(\zeta),\sigma^0_{ab}(\zeta),\eta^0(\zeta)\big)\vartheta+\frac{\partial\psi^p_\beta}{\partial\eta}\big(\zeta,\sigma^0(\zeta),\sigma^0_\alpha(\zeta),\sigma^0_{ab}(\zeta),\eta^0(\zeta)\big)v\Big]d\zeta^\beta$$

$$+\int_C\Big[\frac{\partial\psi^p_\beta}{\partial\sigma_\alpha}\big(\zeta,\sigma^0(\zeta),\sigma^0_\alpha(\zeta),\sigma^0_{ab}(\zeta),\eta^0(\zeta)\big)D_\alpha\vartheta\Big]d\zeta^\beta$$

$$+\frac{1}{x(a,b)}\int_C\Big[\frac{\partial\psi^p_\beta}{\partial\sigma_{ab}}\big(\zeta,\sigma^0(\zeta),\sigma^0_\alpha(\zeta),\sigma^0_{ab}(\zeta),\eta^0(\zeta)\big)D^2_{ab}\vartheta\Big]d\zeta^\beta\Big)\le 0;$$

II. Find $(\sigma^0,\eta^0)\in\mathcal{S}$ *such that there exists no* $(\sigma,\eta)\in\mathcal{S}$ *satisfying*

$$(WVI)\quad \Big(\int_C\Big[\frac{\partial\psi^1_\beta}{\partial\sigma}\big(\zeta,\sigma^0(\zeta),\sigma^0_\alpha(\zeta),\sigma^0_{ab}(\zeta),\eta^0(\zeta)\big)\vartheta+\frac{\partial\psi^1_\beta}{\partial\eta}\big(\zeta,\sigma^0(\zeta),\sigma^0_\alpha(\zeta),\sigma^0_{ab}(\zeta),\eta^0(\zeta)\big)v\Big]d\zeta^\beta$$

$$+\int_C\Big[\frac{\partial\psi^1_\beta}{\partial\sigma_\alpha}\big(\zeta,\sigma^0(\zeta),\sigma^0_\alpha(\zeta),\sigma^0_{ab}(\zeta),\eta^0(\zeta)\big)D_\alpha\vartheta\Big]d\zeta^\beta$$

$$+\frac{1}{x(a,b)}\int_C\Big[\frac{\partial\psi^1_\beta}{\partial\sigma_{ab}}\big(\zeta,\sigma^0(\zeta),\sigma^0_\alpha(\zeta),\sigma^0_{ab}(\zeta),\eta^0(\zeta)\big)D^2_{ab}\vartheta\Big]d\zeta^\beta,\cdots,$$

$$\int_C\Big[\frac{\partial\psi^p_\beta}{\partial\sigma}\big(\zeta,\sigma^0(\zeta),\sigma^0_\alpha(\zeta),\sigma^0_{ab}(\zeta),\eta^0(\zeta)\big)\vartheta+\frac{\partial\psi^p_\beta}{\partial\eta}\big(\zeta,\sigma^0(\zeta),\sigma^0_\alpha(\zeta),\sigma^0_{ab}(\zeta),\eta^0(\zeta)\big)v\Big]d\zeta^\beta$$

$$+\int_C \left[\frac{\partial \psi^p_\beta}{\partial \sigma_\alpha} \Big(\zeta, \sigma^0(\zeta), \sigma^0_\alpha(\zeta), \sigma^0_{ab}(\zeta), \eta^0(\zeta)\Big) D_\alpha \vartheta \right] d\zeta^\beta$$

$$+\frac{1}{x(a,b)} \int_C \left[\frac{\partial \psi^p_\beta}{\partial \sigma_{ab}} \Big(\zeta, \sigma^0(\zeta), \sigma^0_\alpha(\zeta), \sigma^0_{ab}(\zeta), \eta^0(\zeta)\Big) D^2_{ab} \vartheta \right] d\zeta^\beta \Big) < 0.$$

Note. *In the above formulation,* $\frac{1}{x(a,b)}$ *represents the Saunders's multi-index.*

Open Problem. *Taking into account the notion of an invex set with respect to some given functions, the Fréchet differentiability and invexity/pseudoinvexity of the considered curvilinear integral functionals (which are path-independent) state some relations between the solutions of the (weak) vector-controlled variational inequalities and (proper, weak) efficient solutions of the associated optimization problem.*

6. Conclusions

This paper presented the nonlinear dynamics generated by some classes of constrained controlled optimization problems involving second-order partial derivatives. More precisely, we have stated the necessary optimality conditions for the considered variational control problems given by integral functionals. In addition, the well-posedness and the associated variational inequalities have been considered in this review paper.

Funding: This research received no external funding.

Institutional Review Board Statement: Not applicable.

Informed Consent Statement: Not applicable.

Data Availability Statement: Not applicable.

Conflicts of Interest: The author declares no conflict of interest.

References

1. Friedman, A. The Cauchy problem in several time variables. *J. Math. Mech.* **1962**, *11*, 859–889.
2. Hestenes, M. *Calculus of Variations and Optimal Control Theory*; John Wiley & Sons: New York, NY, USA, 1966.
3. Kendall, W.S. Contours of Brownian processes with several-dimensional times. *Prob. Theory Rel. Fields* **1980**, *52*, 267–276. [CrossRef]
4. Udrişte, C.; Ţevy, I. Multi-time Euler-Lagrange-Hamilton theory. *WSEAS Trans. Math.* **2007**, *6*, 701–709.
5. Petrat, S.; Tumulka, R. Multi-time wave functions for quantum field theory. *Ann. Phys.* **2014**, *345*, 17–54. [CrossRef]
6. Treanţă, S. On a class of constrained interval-valued optimization problems governed by mechanical work cost functionals. *J. Optim. Theory Appl.* **2021**, *188*, 913–924. [CrossRef]
7. Deckert, D.A.; Nickel, L. Consistency of multi-time Dirac equations with general interaction potentials. *J. Math. Phys* **2016**, *57*, 072301. [CrossRef]
8. Mititelu, Ş.; Treantă, S.T. Efficiency conditions in vector control problems governed by multiple integrals. *J. Appl. Math. Comput.* **2018**, *57*, 647–665. [CrossRef]
9. Treanţă, S. Constrained variational problems governed by second-order Lagrangians. *Applic. Anal.* **2020**, *99*, 1467–1484. [CrossRef]
10. Treanţă, S. On a Class of Isoperimetric Constrained Controlled Optimization Problems. *Axioms* **2021**, *10*, 112. [CrossRef]
11. Treanţă, S. Second-order PDE constrained controlled optimization problems with application in mechanics. *Mathematics* **2021**, *9*, 1472. [CrossRef]
12. Treanţă, S.; Khan, M.B.; Saeed, T. Optimality for Control Problem with PDEs of Second-Order as Constraints. *Mathematics* **2022**, *10*, 977. [CrossRef]
13. Treanţă, S.; Ahmad, I. Controlled nonlinear dynamics generated by isoperimetric constrained optimization problems involving second-order partial derivatives. *Syst. Control. Lett.* **2022**, *submitted*.
14. Treanţă, S.; Khan, M.B.; Saeed, T. On Some Variational Inequalities Involving Second-Order Partial Derivatives. *Fractal Fract.* **2022**, *6*, 236. [CrossRef]
15. Treanţă, S. On well-posed isoperimetric-type constrained variational control problems. *J. Differ. Equ.* **2021**, **298**, 480–499. [CrossRef]
16. Treanţă, S.; Jha, S. On well-posedness associated with a class of controlled variational inequalities. *Math. Model. Nat. Phenom.* 2021, *16*, 52. [CrossRef]

17. Treanţă, S. On a modified optimal control problem with first-order PDE constraints and the associated saddle-point optimality criterion. *Eur. J. Control* **2020**, *51*, 1–9. [CrossRef]
18. Treanţă, S. On some vector variational inequalities and optimization problems. *AIMS Math.* **2022**, *7*, 14434–14443. [CrossRef]
19. Jayswal, A. An exact l1 penalty function method for multi-dimensional first-order PDE constrained control optimization problem. *European J. Control* **2020**, *52*, 34–41. [CrossRef]
20. Arisawa, M.; Ishii, H. Some properties of ergodic attractors for controlled dynamical systems. *Disc. Cont. Dyn. Syst.* **1998**, *4*, 43–54. [CrossRef]
21. Lai, A.C.; Motta, M. Stabilizability in optimization problems with unbounded data. *Disc. Cont. Dyna. Syst.* **2021**, *41*, 2447–2474.
22. Shi, L.Y.; Ansari, Q.H.; Wen, C.F.; Yao, J.C. Incremental gradient projection algorithm for constrained composite minimization problems. *J. Nonlinear Var. Anal.* **2017**, *1*, 253–264.
23. An, N.T.; Dong, P.D.; Qin, X. Robust feature selection via nonconvex sparsity-based methods *J. Nonlinear Var. Anal.* **2021**, *5*, 59–77.
24. Zhao, X.; Jolaoso, L.O.; Shehu, Y.; Yao, J.C. Convergence of a nonmonotone projected gradient method for nonconvex multiobjective optimization. *J. Nonlinear Var. Anal.* **2021**, **5**, 441–457.
25. Hung, N.V.; Dai, L.X.; Köbis, E.; Yao, J.C. The generic stability of solutions for vector quasi-equilibrium problems on Hadamard manifolds. *J. Nonlinear Var. Anal.* **2020**, *4*, 427–438.
26. Chen, J.W.; Köbis, E.; Kxoxbis, M.A.; Yao, J.C. Optimality conditions for solutions of constrained inverse vector variational inequalities by means of nonlinear scalarization. *J. Nonlinear Var. Anal.* **2017**, *1*, 145–158.
27. Antonsev, S.; Shmarev, S.A. A model porous medium equation with variable exponent of nonlinearity: Existence, uniqueness and localization properties of solutions. *Nonlinear Anal.* **2005**, *60*, 515–545. [CrossRef]
28. Cekic, B.; Kalinin, A.V.; Mashiyeva, R.A.; Avci, M. Lp(x)(Ω)-estimates of vector fields and some applications to magnetostatics problems. *J. Math. Anal. Appl.* **2012**, *389*, 838–851. [CrossRef]
29. Chen, Y.; Levine, S.; Rao, M. Variable exponent linear growth functionals in image restoration. *SIAM J. Appl. Math.* **2006**, *66*, 1383–1406. [CrossRef]
30. Diening, L.; Harjulehto, P.; Hästö, P.; Ružicka, M. *Lebesgue and Sobolev Spaces with Variable Exponents*; Springer: Berlin/Heidelberg, Germany, 2011.
31. Zhikov, V.V. Averaging of functionals of the calculus of variations and elasticity theory. *Math. USSR Izv.* **1987**, *29*, 33–66. [CrossRef]
32. Saunders, D.J. *The Geometry of Jet Bundles*; London Mathematical Society Lecture Note Series; Cambridge University Press: Cambridge, UK, 1989; Volume 142.
33. Usman, F.; Khan, S.A. A generalized mixed vector variational-like inequality problem. *Nonlinear Anal.* **2009**, *71*, 5354–5362. [CrossRef]

mathematics

Article

Interaction Behaviours between Soliton and Cnoidal Periodic Waves for Nonlocal Complex Modified Korteweg–de Vries Equation

Junda Peng , **Bo Ren** *, **Shoufeng Shen** and **Guofang Wang**

Department of Applied Mathematics, Zhejiang University of Technology, Hangzhou 310023, China; junda_peng@163.com (J.P.); mathssf@zjut.edu.cn (S.S.); 18815598139@163.com (G.W.)
* Correspondence: renbo@zjut.edu.cn

Abstract: The reverse space-time nonlocal complex modified Kortewewg–de Vries (mKdV) equation is investigated by using the consistent tanh expansion (CTE) method. According to the CTE method, a nonauto-Bäcklund transformation theorem of nonlocal complex mKdV is obtained. The interactions between one kink soliton and other different nonlinear excitations are constructed via the nonauto-Bäcklund transformation theorem. By selecting cnoidal periodic waves, the interaction between one kink soliton and the cnoidal periodic waves is derived. The specific Jacobi function-type solution and graphs of its analysis are provided in this paper.

Keywords: nonlocal modified Korteweg–de Vries equation; consistent tanh expansion method; parity-time symmetry

MSC: 35J60; 35N05; 35L05

Citation: Peng, J.D.; Ren, B.; Shen, S.F.; Wang G.F. Interaction Behaviours between Soliton and Cnoidal Periodic Waves for Nonlocal Complex Modified Korteweg-de Vries Equation. *Mathematics* **2022**, *10*, 1429. https://doi.org/10.3390/math10091429

Academic Editor: Savin Treanta

Received: 29 March 2022
Accepted: 21 April 2022
Published: 23 April 2022

1. Introduction

Physical systems exhibiting parity-time ($\mathcal{PT}$)-symmetries have received increasing attention since a family of non-Hermitian $\mathcal{PT}$-symmetric Hamiltonians with a real constant was first shown by Bender and Boettcher to admit entirely real spectra [1,2]. The study of $\mathcal{PT}$ symmetry in mathematics and physics can offer great research value and strong prospects for dynamical systems. $\mathcal{PT}$-symmetric nonlinear systems have become a major focus of nonlinear science, such as soliton theory, fluid mechanics, hydrodynamics and optical theory. Some effective methods have been developed to derive exact solutions of nonlinear integrable systems, such as the inverse scattering transform method [3,4], the dressing method [5], the Hirota direct method [6,7], the Darboux transformations [8–10] and the Bäcklund transformations [11–13], etc.

The modified Kortewewg–de Vries (mKdV) equation, which describes the evolutions of weakly dispersive wavelets in shallow water, is widely studied. The integrable nonlocal nonlinear Schrödinger equation proposed by Ablowitz and Musslimani [14] attracted many researchers because of its special property. Ablowitz and Musslimani proposed some new nonlocal nonlinear integrable equations, including the reverse space-time nonlocal complex mKdV equation [15]. In these new types of nonlocal equations; in addition to the terms at space-time point (x,t), there are terms at mirror image point $(-x,-t)$. The self-induced potential of the nonlocal complex mKdV equation is $V(x,t) = u(x,t)u^*(-x,-t)$ [15]. The PT-symmetry for the nonlocal complex mKdV equation amounts to the invariance of the self-induced potential in the case of classical optics, i.e., $V(x,t) = V^*(-x,-t)$, under the combined effect of parity and time reversal symmetry. A family of traveling solitary wave solutions including soliton, kink, periodic and singular solutions of the nonlocal mKdV equation is discussed [16].

The interaction between solitons and a periodic cnoidal wave of the Korteweg–de Vries equation and the cubic Schrödinger equation is discussed by using the inverse scattering technique [17,18]. Rogue waves on a periodic background and the nonlinear superposition of the two periodic solutions of mKdV equation are obtained by using the Darboux transformation [19,20]. The soliton excitation of the circular vortex motion can be constructed based on localized-induction approximation equations [21,22]. Recently, the consistent tanh expansion (CTE) method has been proposed to identify CTE-solvable systems [23,24]. The interaction between one soliton and other different nonlinear excitations such as cnoidal periodic waves can be obtained by using the CTE method. The method has been valid for classical integrable nonlinear systems, including the nonlinear Schrödinger system [25], the Broer–Kaup system [26], the higher-order KdV equation [27], etc. [28–30]. The application of the CTE method to nonlocal integrable systems with $\mathcal{PT}$-symmetric is deficient. Applying the CTE method to nonlocal $\mathcal{PT}$-symmetric integrable systems is innovative and convenient. In this paper, the CTE method is used to investigate the $\mathcal{PT}$-symmetric nonlocal complex mKdV equation and can construct the interaction solution of the soliton and cnoidal periodic waves.

This paper is organized as follows. In Section 2, a nonauto-Bäcklund transformation theorem is obtained by using the CTE method. The interactions between one kink soliton and other different nonlinear excitations are constructed by the nonauto-Bäcklund transformation theorem. Section 3 discusses the interaction between one kink soliton, and the Jacobi-elliptic function types are explicitly discussed both with analytical and graphical methods. Sections 4 and 5 include simple discussions and provide conclusions.

2. CTE Method for the Nonlocal Complex mKdV System

The reverse space-time nonlocal complex mKdV equation reads as follows [15]:

$$u_t(x,t) - 6\alpha u(x,t)u^*(-x,-t)u_x(x,t) + u_{xxx}(x,t) = 0, \tag{1}$$

where $u = u(x,t)$ is a complex function of real variables x and t, α is an arbitrary constant and $*$ denotes complex conjugation. The self-induced potential $V(x,t) = u(x,t)u^*(-x,-t)$ of (1) satisfies the $\mathcal{PT}$-symmetry condition $V(x,t) = V^*(-x,-t)$. The nonauto-Bäcklund transformations and the soliton phenomenology of the standard mKdV equation are systematically studied [31].

For the nonlocal complex mKdV system, one can take the generalized truncated tanh expansion form by using leading order analysis:

$$u = u_0 + u_1 \tanh(f), \tag{2}$$

where u_0 and u_1 are arbitrary functions of (x,t). f satisfies constraint $f(x,t) = f^*(-x,-t)$.

By substituting (2) into the nonlocal complex mKdV system (1), a complicated polynomial with respect to $\tanh(f)$ is obtained. Collecting coefficients of the powers of $\tanh^4(f)$ and $\tanh^3(f)$, we derive the following.

$$\alpha u_1(x,t)u_1^*(-x,-t) - f_x^2 = 0, \tag{3}$$

$$\alpha u_1^2(x,t)u_0^*(-x,-t)f_x + \alpha u_0(x,t)u_1^*(-x,-t)u_1(x,t)f_x - \alpha u_1(x,t)u_1^*(-x,-t)u_{1,x}(x,t) + u_1(x,t)f_xf_{xx} + u_{1,x}(x,t)f_x^2 = 0. \tag{4}$$

Substituting u_1 obtained by solving (3) into (4) and further solving for u_0, a set of solutions for u_1 and u_0 is derived as follows.

$$u_1 = \frac{1}{\sqrt{-\alpha}}f_x, \qquad u_0 = -\frac{1}{2\sqrt{-\alpha}}\frac{f_{xx}}{f_x}. \tag{5}$$

Substituting (5) into the complicated polynomial obtained before and collecting the coefficients of $\tanh^2(f)$, $\tanh^1(f)$ and $\tanh^0(f)$ via symbolic computation with the help of Maple, we obtain the following three over-determined systems.

$$\frac{3}{2}f_{xx}^2+2f_x^4-f_xf_{xxx}-f_xf_t=0, \tag{6}$$

$$\frac{3}{2}\frac{f_{xx}^3}{f_x^2}-3\frac{f_{xx}f_{xxx}}{f_x}-6f_x^2f_{xx}+f_{xt}+f_{xxxx}=0, \tag{7}$$

$$-\frac{3}{2}f_{xx}^2-2f_x^4-\frac{21}{4}\frac{f_{xx}^2f_{xxx}}{f_x^3}+\frac{9}{4}\frac{f_{xx}^4}{f_x^4}+f_xf_t+4f_xf_{xxx}+3f_{xx}^2-\frac{1}{2}\frac{f_{xxt}}{f_x}+\frac{1}{2}\frac{f_{xx}f_{xt}}{f_x^2}-\frac{1}{2}\frac{f_{xxxxx}}{f_x}+\frac{2f_{xxxx}f_{xx}}{f_x^2}+\frac{3}{2}\frac{f_{xxx}^2}{f_x^2}=0. \tag{8}$$

Moreover, the above three Equations (6)–(8) are consistent each other, meaning that if f satisfies one of the equations, it will be a solution for other two equations. According to above analysis, we derive the following nonauto-Bäcklund transformation theorem.

Nonauto-Bäcklund transformation theorem. If one finds that solution f satisfies (6), then u is obtained with the following:

$$u(x,t)=-\frac{1}{2\sqrt{-\alpha}}\frac{f_{xx}}{f_x}+\frac{1}{\sqrt{-\alpha}}f_x\tanh(f), \tag{9}$$

which is a solution of the reverse space-time nonlocal complex mKdV system (1).

The Miura transform is known as the transformation connection the solutions between KdV equation and mKdV equation. This nonauto-Bäcklund transformation can be treated as a form of Miura transformation. According to the above theorem, the exact solutions of the nonlocal complex mKdV system (1) are obtained by solving (6). Here are some interesting examples.

A quite trivial solution of (6) has the following form:

$$f=i(k_0x+w_0t),\quad w_0=-2k_0^3, \tag{10}$$

where k_0 is a free constant, and w_0 is determined by dispersion relations. Substituting the trivial solution (10) into (9), one kink soliton solution of the nonlocal complex mKdV system yields the following.

$$u=-\frac{1}{\sqrt{-\alpha}}k_0\tan(k_0x-2k_0^3t). \tag{11}$$

Some nontrivial solutions of the mKdV equation can be derived from a quite trivial solution of (10). To find interaction solutions between one kink soliton and other nonlinear excitations, we assume the interaction solution form as follows:

$$f=i(k_0x+w_0t)+F(X),\quad X=kx+wt, \tag{12}$$

where k_0, w_0, k and w are all free constants. Substituting expression (12) into (6), (6) becomes the following.

$$F_X^4+\frac{4ik}{k_0}F_X^3-\frac{12kk_0^2+w}{2k^3}F_X^2-\frac{i(8k_0^3k+kw_0+k_0w)}{2k^4}F_X-\frac{1}{2}F_XF_{XXX}+\frac{3}{4}F_{XX}^2-\frac{ik_0}{2k}F_{XXX}+\frac{2k_0^4+k_0w_0}{2k^4}=0. \tag{13}$$

Then, the following equation is obtained by using transformation $F_X=F_1$.

$$F_1^4+\frac{4ik_0}{k}F_1^3-\frac{12kk_0^2+w}{2k^3}F_1^2-\frac{i(8kk_0^3+kw_0+k_0w)}{2k^4}F_1+\frac{3}{4}F_{1,X}^2-\frac{1}{2}(F_1+\frac{ik_0}{k})F_{1,XX}+\frac{k_0(2k_0^3+w_0)}{2k^4}=0. \tag{14}$$

The CTE method is valid in many classical integrable systems. For the interaction between soliton and Jacobi periodic waves in classical integrable systems, one can obtain the standard Jacobi-elliptic function equation [32]. One only obtains Equation (14) rather than the standard Jacobi-elliptic function equation. In order to obtain the Jacobi periodic wave solution of (14), we assume that Equation (14) has a Jacobian elliptic function solution as $F_1(X)=c_1S_n(c_2X,m)$ [33]. Hence, the solution expressed by (9) is just the explicit exact interaction between one kink soliton and cnoidal periodic waves. To show more clearly this form of solution, we offer one special case for solving (14).

3. Interaction between Soliton and Cnoidal Periodic Waves

According to above analysis, the solution of (13) has the following form:

$$F(X) = \int c_1 S_n(c_2 X, m) dX = \frac{c_1 \ln[D_n(c_2 X, m) - mC_n(c_2 X, m)]}{c_2 m}, \tag{15}$$

where S_n, C_n and D_n are the Jacobian-elliptic functions with modulus m. Verified by Maple's symbolic calculation, (15) satisfies constraint $f(x,t) = f^*(-x,-t)$ and is a real even function. By substituting the undetermined parameter solution (15) into (13) and using symbolic computation with the help of Maple, the parameters satisfy the following.

$$c_1 = -\frac{c_2 m}{2}, \quad c_2 = 2\frac{ik_0}{k}, \quad w_0 = -2k_0^3(3m^2+1), \quad w = 2k_0^2 k(m^2-5). \tag{16}$$

The interaction between one kink soliton and the cnoidal wave of the nonlocal complex mKdV system (1) has the the following form.

$$u = \frac{2}{\sqrt{-\alpha}(c_1 S_n + ik_0)} \left[\tanh\left(\frac{c_1 \ln(D_n - mC_n) + ic_2 m(k_0 x + w_0 t)}{c_2 m}\right)\left(\frac{c_1^2 k^2}{2} S_n^2 + ic_1 k k_0 S_n - \frac{k_0^2}{2}\right) - \frac{c_1 c_2 k^2}{4} C_n D_n \right]. \tag{17}$$

The parameters c_1, c_2, w_0 and w have been given in (16).

We select the parameters as $\alpha = -1, k_0 = 0.4i, m = 0.4$ in Figures 1–3. Figures 1 and 2 plot the interaction solution between one kink soliton and the cnoidal wave in the patterns of three-dimensional and wave along x-axis. Field u exhibits one kink soliton propagating on the cnoidal wave's background. Figure 3 plots the status-only soliton or cnoidal wave at $t = 0$. The superpose status is just the interaction between one kink soliton and the cnoidal waves, which are depicted in Figure 2. The changes before and after superposition are displayed visually. There are some nonlinear waves including interactions between solitary waves and the cnoidal periodic waves, which can be described in certain ocean phenomena.

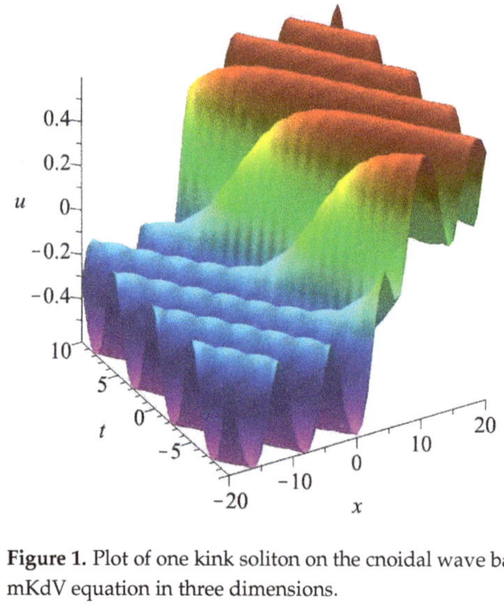

Figure 1. Plot of one kink soliton on the cnoidal wave background expressed by (17) of the nonlocal mKdV equation in three dimensions.

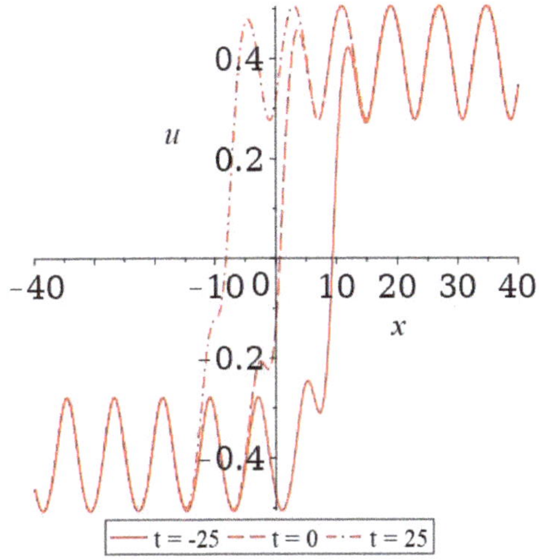

Figure 2. One dimensional image followed by $t = -25, 0, 25$.

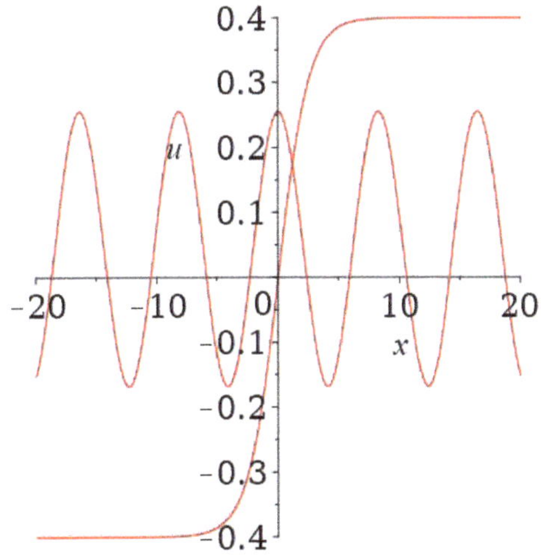

Figure 3. Plot of separate state for one kink soliton or the cnoidal wave expressed by (10) and (15) of the nonlocal mKdV equation at $t = 0$.

4. Discussion

Kuznetsov and Mikhailov discussed the interaction between solitons and a periodic cnoidal wave of the Korteweg–de Vries equation [17]. Gorshkov and Ostrovsky investigated the interaction between soliton and a periodic wave via the direct perturbation method [34]. The interaction between the Jacobi elliptic periodic wave and kink soliton for the complex mKdV equation is directly obtained by the CTE method in this paper. Compared with the previous two methods, the CTE method can obtain this type solution more directly and conveniently. Other reverse space-time nonlocal system is worthy of study by using the CTE method.

5. Conclusions

The reverse space-time nonlocal complex mKdV equation is investigated by using the CTE method. A nonauto-Bäcklund transformation theorem is constructed by using the CTE method. The interactions between one kink soliton and the cnoidal waves are derived by means of the nonauto-Bäcklund transformation theorem. The dynamics of the interactions are studied both with analytical and graphical methods. These types of interaction solutions can describe certain oceanic phenomena. The method is valid and promising for the $\mathcal{PT}$-symmetry models. The interactions between solitons and the cnoidal waves can be obtained by symmetry reductions related by nonlocal symmetry [27]. Symmetry reductions related by the nonlocal symmetry of the nonlocal complex mKdV equation will be studied in the future.

Author Contributions: Methodology, formal analysis and writing—original draft preparation, J.P.; Conceptualization, investigation, validation, software and writing—review and editing, B.R.; formal analysis, S.S.; formal analysis G.W. All authors have read and agreed to the published version of the manuscript.

Funding: This work is supported by the National Natural Science Foundation of China No. 11775146 and the Xinyuan Transportation Electronics Company Limited of Zhejiang Province of China Grant No. KYY-HX-20220005.

Institutional Review Board Statement: Not applicable.

Informed Consent Statement: Not applicable.

Data Availability Statement: Not applicable.

Conflicts of Interest: The authors declare no conflict of interest.

References

1. Bender, C.M.; Boettcher, S. Real spectra in non-Hermitian Hamiltonians having PT symmetry. *Phys. Rev. Lett.* **1998**, *80*, 5243. [CrossRef]
2. Bender, C.M.; Brody, D.C.; Jones, H.F.; Meister, B.K. Faster than Hermitian quantum mechanics. *Phys. Rev. Lett.* **2007**, *98*, 040403. [CrossRef]
3. Ma, W.X. Inverse scattering and soliton solutions of nonlocal complex reverse-spacetime mKdV equations. *J. Geom. Phys.* **2020**, *57*, 103845. [CrossRef]
4. Ablowitz, M.J.; Kaup, D.J.; Newell, A.C.; Segur, H. The inverse scattering transform-Fourier analysis for nonlinear problems. *Stud. Appl. Math.* **1974**, *53*, 249–315. [CrossRef]
5. Shabat, A.; Zakharov, V. Exact theory of two-dimensional self-focusing and one-dimensional self-modulation of waves in nonlinear media. *Sov. Phys. JETP* **1972**, *34*, 62.
6. Hirota, R. Exact solution of the modified Korteweg-de Vries equation for multiple collisions of solitons. *J. Phys. Soc. Jpn.* **1972**, *33*, 1456–1458. [CrossRef]
7. Hirota, R. *The Direct Method in Soliton Theory;* Cambridge University Press: Cambridge, UK, 2004.
8. Matveev, V.B.; Matveev, V.B. *Darboux Transformations and Solitons;* Springer: New York, NY, USA, 1991.
9. Nimmo, J.J.C. Darboux transformations and the discrete KP equation. *J. Phys. A Math. Gen.* **1997**, *30*, 8693. [CrossRef]
10. Cieśliński, J.L. Algebraic construction of the Darboux matrix revisited. *J. Phys. A Math. Theor.* **2009**, *42*, 404003. [CrossRef]
11. Rogers, C.; Shadwick, W.F. *Bäcklund Transformations and Their Applications;* Academic Press: New York, NY, USA, 1982.
12. Rogers, C.; Schief, W.K. *Bäcklund and Darboux Transformations: Geometry and Modern Applications in Soliton Theory;* Cambridge University Press: Cambridge, UK, 2002; Volume 30.
13. Lou, S.Y.; Hu, X.; Chen, Y. Nonlocal symmetries related to Bäcklund transformation and their applications. *J. Phys. A Math. Theor.* **2012**, *45*, 155209. [CrossRef]
14. Ablowitz, M.J.; Musslimani, Z.H. Integrable nonlocal nonlinear Schrödinger equation. *Phys. Rev. Lett.* **2013**, *110*, 064105. [CrossRef]
15. Ablowitz, M.J; Musslimani, Z.H. Integrable nonlocal nonlinear equations. *Stud. Appl. Math.* **2017**, *139*, 7–59. [CrossRef]
16. Wazwaz, A.M. Multiple complex soliton solutions for integrable negative-order KdV and integrable negative-order modified KdV equations. *Appl. Math. Lett.* **2019**, *88*, 1–7. [CrossRef]
17. Kuznetsov, E.A.; Mikhaĭlov, A.V. Stability of stationary waves in nonlinear weakly dispersive media. *Sov. Phys. JETP* **1975**, *40*, 855.
18. Ma, Y.C. The perturbed plane-wave solutions of the cubic Schrödinger equation. *Stud. Appl. Math.* **1979**, *60*, 43-58. [CrossRef]
19. Chen, J.; Pelinovsky, D.E. Rogue periodic waves of the modified KdV equation. *Nonlinearity* **2018**, *31*, 1955. [CrossRef]
20. Chowdury, A.; Ankiewicz, A.; Akhmediev, N. Periodic and rational solutions of modified Korteweg-de Vries equation. *Eur. Phys. J. D* **2016**, *70*, 104. [CrossRef]
21. Cieśliński, J.; Gragert, P.K.H.; Sym, A. Exact solution to localized-induction-approximation equation modeling smoke ring motion. *Phys. Rev. Lett.* **1986**, *57*, 1507. [CrossRef]
22. Sym, A. Vortex filament motion in terms of Jacobi theta functions. *Fluid. Dyn. Res.* **1988**, *3*, 151. [CrossRef]

23. Gao, X.N.; Lou, S.Y.; Tang, X.Y. Bosonization, singularity analysis, nonlocal symmetry reductions and exact solutions of supersymmetric KdV equation. *J. High Energy Phys.* **2013**, *2013*, 29. [CrossRef]
24. Lou, S.Y. Consistent Riccati expansion for integrable systems. *Stud. Appl. Math.* **2015**, *134*, 372–402. [CrossRef]
25. Lou, S.Y.; Cheng, X.P.; Tang, X.Y. Dressed dark solitons of the defocusing nonlinear Schrödinger equation. *Chin. Phys. Lett.* **2014**, *31*, 070201. [CrossRef]
26. Chen, C.L.; Lou, S.Y. CTE solvability and exact solution to the Broer-Kaup system. *Chin. Phys. Lett.* **2013**, *30*, 110202. [CrossRef]
27. Ren, B.; Liu, X.Z.; Liu, P. Nonlocal symmetry reductions, CTE method and exact solutions for higher-order KdV equation. *Commun. Theor. Phys.* **2015**, *163*, 125. [CrossRef]
28. Wang, Y.H.; Wang, H. Symmetry analysis and CTE solvability for the (2 + 1)-dimensional Boiti-Leon-Manna-Pempinelli equation. *Phys. Scr.* **2014**, *89*, 125203. [CrossRef]
29. Yang, D.; Lou, S.Y.; Yu, W.F. Interactions between solitons and cnoidal periodic waves of the Boussinesq equation. *Commun. Theor. Phys.* **2013**, *60*, 387. [CrossRef]
30. Ren, B.; Lin, J. Interaction behaviours between soliton and cnoidal periodic waves for the cubic generalised Kadomtsev-Petviashvili equation. *Z. Naturforsch. A* **2015**, *70*, 439–544. [CrossRef]
31. Calogero, F.; Degasperis, A. A modified modified Korteweg-de Vries equation. *Inverse Probl.* **1985**, *1*, 57. [CrossRef]
32. Ren, B. Interaction solutions for mKP equation with nonlocal symmetry reductions and CTE method. *Phys. Scr.* **2015**, *90*, 065206. [CrossRef]
33. Hu, X.R.; Lou, S.Y.; Chen, Y. Explicit solutions from eigenfunction symmetry of the Korteweg-de Vries equation. *Phys. Rev. E* **2012**, *85*, 056607. [CrossRef]
34. Gorshkov, K.A.; Ostrovsky, L. Interactions of solitons in nonintegrable systems: Direct perturbation method and applications. *Physica D* **1981**, *3*, 428–438. [CrossRef]

mathematics

MDPI

Article

Chaos Embed Marine Predator (CMPA) Algorithm for Feature Selection

Adel Fahad Alrasheedi [1], Khalid Abdulaziz Alnowibet [1], Akash Saxena [2,*], Karam M. Sallam [3] and Ali Wagdy Mohamed [4,5,*]

1 Statistics and Operations Research Department, College of Science, King Saud University, P.O. Box 2455, Riyadh 11451, Saudi Arabia; aalrasheedi@ksu.edu.sa (A.F.A.); knowibet@ksu.edu.sa (K.A.A.)
2 Swami Keshvanand Institute of Technology, Management & Gramothan, Jaipur 302017, India
3 School of IT and Systems, University of Canberra, Bruce, ACT 2601, Australia; karam.sallam@canberra.edu.au
4 Operations Research Department, Faculty of Graduate Studies for Statistical Research, Cairo University, Giza 12613, Egypt
5 Department of Mathematics and Actuarial Science School of Sciences Engineering, The American University in Cairo, Cairo 11835, Egypt
* Correspondence: aakash.saxena@hotmail.com (A.S.); aliwagdy@gmail.com (A.W.M.)

Abstract: Data mining applications are growing with the availability of large data; sometimes, handling large data is also a typical task. Segregation of the data for extracting useful information is inevitable for designing modern technologies. Considering this fact, the work proposes a chaos embed marine predator algorithm (CMPA) for feature selection. The optimization routine is designed with the aim of maximizing the classification accuracy with the optimal number of features selected. The well-known benchmark data sets have been chosen for validating the performance of the proposed algorithm. A comparative analysis of the performance with some well-known algorithms advocates the applicability of the proposed algorithm. Further, the analysis has been extended to some of the well-known chaotic algorithms; first, the binary versions of these algorithms are developed and then the comparative analysis of the performance has been conducted on the basis of mean features selected, classification accuracy obtained and fitness function values. Statistical significance tests have also been conducted to establish the significance of the proposed algorithm.

Keywords: metaheuristics; feature selection; classification

MSC: 68T01; 68T05; 68T07; 68T09; 68T20; 68T30

Citation: Alrasheedi, A.F.; Alnowibet, K.A.; Saxena, A.; Sallam, K.M.; Mohamed, A.W. Chaos Embed Marine Predator (CMPA) Algorithm for Feature Selection. *Mathematics* **2022**, *10*, 1411. https://doi.org/10.3390/math10091411

Academic Editor: Savin Treanta

Received: 12 March 2022
Accepted: 17 April 2022
Published: 22 April 2022

1. Introduction

In recent years, the application of optimization in the field of data-mining has been reported in many published approaches. Feature selection (FS) from a large data set is also one of the optimization problems. The FS problem has many industrial and healthcare-related applications. An effective FS technique can enhance the classification accuracy of the classifier and reduce the complexity of the system. The complexity of the system substantially enhanced with the dimension of the data. In other words, it speeds up the learning rate and improves the ability of a machine to anticipate the information pertaining to the data. The recent application of the FS technique in the field of healthcare is reported in [1], where an ensemble-based hybrid feature selection has been employed for the diagnosis of the brain tumor. The authors claimed that the proposed method is able to handle the imbalanced data. A network intrusion detection scheme based on the Least Square Support Vector Machine has been proposed by the authors [2]. The authors validated the approach on intrusion data sets. The problem of the high dimensionality of feature space pertaining to text characterization has been addressed in reference [3]. In this work, the authors proposed a novel Gini index for the classification and reduction of the features. Feature selection for the Brain Computer Interface (BCI) has been conducted with the help of information gain ranking, correlation-based feature selection, ReliefF, consistency-based feature selection and 1R ranking methods in the approach [4]. A brief classification of the feature selection algorithms are given in Figure 1.

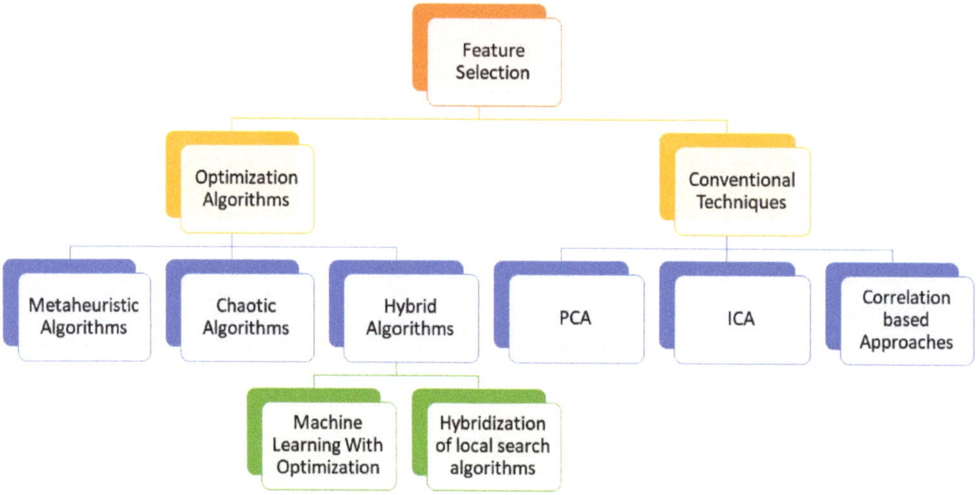

Figure 1. Classification of feature selection algorithms.

A very interesting approach on the path planning for the mobile robot is proposed in reference. For defining the obstacle, the situation of workers in the Artificial Bee Colony has been utilized and in the second phase, the shortest path is selected by Dijkstra's algorithm [5]. A very important application of the ABC algorithm has been reported for the identification of mechanical parameters of the Servo-drive system [6]. A novel approach of the Adaptive Procedure for Optimization Algorithms is proposed in reference [7]. Apart from these approaches, recent approaches based on the metaheuristic optimization motivated the author to employ the optimization algorithm in a feature selection task [8–10]. These references provide strong evidence of what optimization algorithms are capable of for dealing with complex engineering problems.

Apart from the application of metaheuristic optimization algorithms and evolution-based algorithms, there are many deterministic algorithms that are also employed for conducting feature selection tasks. Due to the deterministic nature or gradient-based mechanism, these algorithms are often stuck in a local minima trap and provide slow and premature convergence. For avoiding such problems and to provide a smooth and fast optimization environment, metaheuristic techniques are employed for executing feature selection problems. The recent trend is to apply the metaheuristic optimization algorithm for conducting this task; some of the fine approaches are depicted in the following references, where the application of the Hybrid Whale Optimization Algorithm (HWOA) [11] is explored with the amalgamation of the Whale Optimization Algorithm and Simulated annealing Algorithm (SA). A chaotic dragonfly algorithm has been proposed and applied on the feature selection task in reference [12].A similar approach based on the chaotic selfish heard optimizer has been proposed in reference [13]. A rich review of literature pertaining to the feature selection methods have been demonstrated in reference [14]. S-shaped and V-shaped functions are employed to create a binary search space in gaining and sharing a knowledge algorithm for the feature selection task in reference [15].

1.1. Some Recent Chaos-Based Approaches for Feature Selection

A chaotic optimization algorithm based on gaining and sharing knowledge-based optimization has been proposed in reference [16], as well as the the similar applications based on chaotic fruit fly optimization [17], chaotic crow search algorithms [18], chaotic multi verse optimizer [19] and chaotic salp swarm optimizers [20].

From these approaches, it is evident that the embedding chaos for making naive algorithms compatible for feature selection is a potential area of research. These approaches are strong evidence that by embedding chaos in the mechanism of algorithms, a substantial improvement can be achieved as far as classification accuracy and reduction in dimensionality is considered. Based on this discussion, the following subsection presents the research proposal for the work and objectives.

1.2. Research Objectives and Proposal

Recently, a new metaheuristic has been proposed [21] based on predatory behavior. The algorithm is known as the marine predator algorithm (MPA). The application of this algorithm in a multi-objective domain has been explored in reference [22]. A new improved model of MPA has been established in reference [23]. The paper touched the theme of introducing an opposition-based learning method, chaos map, self-adaption of population, and switching between exploration and exploitation phases. Application of this algorithm has been explored in the field of controller tuning. Further, a hybrid computational intelligence-based approach has been proposed for structural damage detection in reference [24].

Keeping these facts in mind, the work proposed in this paper addresses following objectives.

1. To propose a chaotic marine predator algorithm and develop a balance between the exploration and exploitation phase considering the binary search space.
2. To benchmark the proposed algorithm on a standard data set used in state-of-the-art classification tasks.
3. To evaluate the performance of the proposed algorithm with some recently proposed approaches in the feature selection domain.
4. To evaluate the performance of the proposed algorithm on certain evaluation criterion such as the statistical parameter calculation such as mean feature selected by algorithms, mean values of classification accuracy obtained in optimization runs and mean fitness values. Apart from these statistical attributes, a statistical test has also been conducted for showcasing the statistical significance of the algorithm.

The remaining part of this paper is organized as follows: in Section 2, brief details of the MPA are discussed. Section 3 presents the basic framework of the chaos embed marine predator algorithm (CMPA). Section 4 presents the problem formulation and details of the objective considered in this study. Section 5 presents the results and analysis of different tests. Section 6 concludes all major findings.

2. Marine Predator Algorithm: An Overview

The marine predator algorithm (MPA) [21] is a recently developed optimization technique that is based on the philosophy that while predator is searching for the prey, the prey also updates its position according to the location of food. The MPA presents a beautiful mimicry of a social life in terms of mathematical representations. This section briefly discuss the steps incorporated in the development of MPA. The different steps of MPA are as follows

1. Conceptualization of MPA: Like other nature-inspired algorithms, the initial population in MPA is equally scattered in the search region, which can be given as:

$$Y_0 = U_b + m(U_b - L_b) \tag{1}$$

Here, U_b and L_b are the minimum and maximum values of variables and r is an arbitrary number satisfying $0 < m < 1$.

Following the well-known Darwinian fittest theory in MPA, a group of best predators are selected as a final solution. In MPA, the initial location of the prey can be expressed as the following matrix of order $n \times d$, where n represents the number of search agents and d is the dimension of the problem.

$$TPR^{EM} = \begin{bmatrix} Y_{1,1}^{tp} & Y_{1,2}^{tp} & \cdots & Y_{1,d}^{tp} \\ Y_{2,1}^{tp} & Y_{2,2}^{tp} & \cdot & Y_{2,d}^{tp} \\ \vdots & \vdots & \ddots & \vdots \\ Y_{n,1}^{tp} & Y_{n,2}^{tp} & \cdots & Y_{n,d}^{tp} \end{bmatrix} \quad (2)$$

where $Y_{1,1}^{tp}$ represents the first top predator vector, which is replicated n times to construct the Elite matrix TPR^{EM}, which can be extended up to n times and d dimensions. In MPA, the prey is searching for food and the predator is searching for prey, hence both can be considered as search agents. The matrix TPM has taken initial solutions, and after every iteration, the position of prey has improved. This updated matrix is called the elite matrix TPR_{EM}. The prey matrix (TPM) is given by following expression.

$$TPM = \begin{bmatrix} Y_{1,1} & Y_{1,2} & \cdots & Y_{1,d} \\ Y_{2,1} & Y_{2,2} & \cdot & Y_{2,d} \\ \vdots & \vdots & \ddots & \vdots \\ Y_{n,1} & Y_{n,2} & \cdots & Y_{n,d} \end{bmatrix} \quad (3)$$

$Y_{i,j}$ denotes the location of i-th prey in the j-th dimension. It is to be noted that during the search process both prey and predators are search agents and they search for food.

1. Optimization steps: As predators and prey are two search agents of MPA, the whole optimization process depends on their proportional velocity. To illustrate the optimization process scientifically, it can be spilt up into three stages. Each stage predefined a natural order and time and was inspired by the natural behavior of the prey and predator. These stages are as follows:

    - Stage 1: If the velocity of predator is greater than prey. This case occurs in the initial steps or in intensification. When the proportion velocity is very high, i.e., ($\geq$10), then the predator is almost still. This can be mathematically written as when $t < T_{max}/3$,

    $$\vec{s}tep_i = \vec{R}_B \otimes (\vec{T}PR_i^{EM} - \vec{R}_B \otimes \overrightarrow{TP}_i) \quad (4)$$

    where t is the current iteration and T_{Max} maximum values of iteration.

    $$\overrightarrow{TPM}_i = \overrightarrow{TPM}_i + K.\vec{R} \otimes \vec{s}tep_i \quad (5)$$

    where $step_i$ = step size of i-th iteration, $\vec{R}_B$ = vector including arbitrary numbers related to Brownian motion, K = constant number taken as equal to 0.5 and $\vec{R}$ = a vector of arbitrary numbers $\in [0,1]$. This stage occurs in almost the first 33 percentage of the total iteration, when the intensification is high.
    - Stage 2: If the proportional velocity of predator and prey is almost the same, which indicates that the prey is looking for its food and the predator is looking for its prey. This case happens in middle iterations, when intensification is slowly converting into diversification. At this time, half of the part of the population, i.e., predator, is accountable for the intensification and the prey is responsible for the diversification. If the prey follows the Levy motion and the predator follows

the Brownian motion, then we get proportional velocity (≈1). Mathematically, when $\frac{1}{3}T_{max} < t < \frac{2}{3}T_{max}$. For the first part of the population:

$$\vec{s}tep_i = \vec{R}_L \otimes (\vec{T}PR_i^{EM} - \vec{R}_L \otimes \overrightarrow{TPM}_i) \tag{6}$$

$$\overrightarrow{TPM}_i = \overrightarrow{TPM}_i + K.\vec{R} \times \vec{s}tep_i \tag{7}$$

Here, the $\vec{R}_L$= vector includes arbitrary numbers related to the Levy motion. As in the Levy distribution, the step size is very small, hence this movement represents diversification.

In the second half population MPA consider

$$\vec{s}tep_i = \vec{R}_B \otimes (\vec{R}_B \otimes \vec{T}PR_i^{EM} - \overrightarrow{TPM}_i) \tag{8}$$

$$\overrightarrow{TPM}_i = \overrightarrow{TPM}_i + K.C \times \vec{s}_i \tag{9}$$

$C = \left(1 - \frac{t}{T_{max}}\right)^{\left(\frac{2t}{T_{max}}\right)}$ is a control parameter that commands the step size of movements of the predator. The predator moves according to the Brownian motion and the prey follow the predator for its position updates.

- Stage 3: If the proportional velocity ratio is low, i.e., the predator is moving faster in comparison to the prey. This situation occurs in the last iterations of optimization, and is related to diversification. The predator adopts the Levy motion in the case of low proportional velocity (=0.1). This can be given in the following way, if $t > \frac{2}{3}T_{max}$

$$\overrightarrow{step}_i = \vec{R}_L \otimes \left(\vec{R}_L \otimes \vec{T}PR_i^{EM} - \overrightarrow{TPM}_i\right) \; i = 1, ..., n \tag{10}$$

$$\overrightarrow{TPM}_i = \vec{T}PR_i^{EM} + K.C \times \overrightarrow{step}_i \tag{11}$$

These three stages present different steps of predators in finding their prey. According to their behaviour, we consider that the predator follows both the Brownian and Levy motion equally. In stage I, the predator is still, in stage II it follows the Brownian motion and in the last stage it moves in the Levy motion. These same things are also followed by the prey, as the prey is also a predator for some other marine creatures. For example, bony fish and marine invertebrates are prey for tuna fish and themselves a prey for silky sharks.

2. Fish Aggregating Device Effect (FAD): FAD is a floating device made by humans to find some specific marine creatures in tropical regions. It also affects marine animals in many other ways. According to [25], 80% of the lifespan of sharks has been spent around FAD and the rest in jumping in various dimensions to find prey. These FADs can be considered as local optima trapping agents of marine predators. The effect of FADs can be given mathematically as:

$$\overrightarrow{TPM}_i = \begin{cases} \overrightarrow{TPM}_i + C\left[\vec{L}_b + \vec{R} \times \left(\vec{U}_b - \vec{L}_b\right)\right] \times \vec{A} & if \; r \leq f \\ \overrightarrow{TPM}_i + [f(1-q) + q]\left(\overrightarrow{TPM}_{r_1} - \overrightarrow{TPM}_{r_2}\right) & if \; r > f \end{cases} \tag{12}$$

Here, f is the probability of the FAD effect on any optimizer and taken as $f = 0.2$, $q = a$ is the random number between 0 and 1, and r_1 and r_2 represent two arbitrary indexes of the prey matrix.

$$\vec{A} = \begin{matrix} 0 & if & r < 0.2 \\ 1 & if & r > 0.2 \end{matrix} \tag{13}$$

3. Memory of marine predators: Almost all marine predators are good at memorizing their location of successful foraging, which is referred to as the memory saving term in MPA. When the prey updates their location and the FAD effect is implemented, the fitness of the prey matrix has evaluated whether to update the elite matrix or not and the most fit matrix is chosen. This step also helpful in the improvement of the solution, according to [26].

3. Development of Chaos Embed Marine Predator Algorithm

This section presents the development of the chaos embed marine predator algorithm (CMPA). The following are the procedural steps for the development.

1. The MPA has been divided into three phases. During the first phase, the search agents take big leaps and try to acquire as much space as they can; hence, in a way it can be said that this phase is primarily governed by exploratory action. Likewise, during the final phase, the exploration virtue of the algorithm becomes weakened and the exploitation virtue becomes enhanced. In a way, the starting phase that governs 1/3 of the iterations and the last phase that governs last 1/3 phase of iterations is solely dedicated to the exploration and exploitation virtues. Hence, any modifications in these either enhance the exploration or exploitation virtue of MPA. Considering this fact, the authors are motivated to develop a new position update mechanism that can affect both virtues simultaneously.
2. During the intermediate phase, where the both processes are simultaneously progressing, a position update mechanism that can search alternative solutions is acutely required. Considering this argument, we propose a chaotic function-inspired position update mechanism that helps the algorithm to transit swiftly between exploration and exploitation phases.

(a) The generation of β-chaotic sequence through the initialization of the parameters (ν, μ, J_1, J_2) is carried out. A generalized equation for the β distribution, as given in following expression, is as follows:

$$\beta(J;\nu,\mu,J_1,J_2) = \begin{cases} \left(\frac{J-J_1}{J_c-J_1}\right)^{\nu}\left(\frac{J_2-J}{J_2-J_c}\right)^{\mu} & if\ J \in [J_1, J_2] \\ 0 & otherwise \end{cases} \tag{14}$$

where $(\nu, \mu, J_1, J_2) \in R$ and $J_1 < J_2$. The β-Chaotic sequence at any iteration t will be given as:

$$J_{t+1} = k\beta(J_t;\nu,\mu,J_1,J_2) \tag{15}$$

(b) For the first part of the population, during the second phase an update mechanism is introduced and represented as:

$$\vec{s}tep_i = \vec{R}_L \otimes (\vec{T}PR_i^{EM} - \vec{R}_L \otimes \overrightarrow{TPM}_i) \tag{16}$$

$$\overrightarrow{TPM}_i = \overrightarrow{TPM}_i + K.\vec{R} \times \vec{s}tep_i \tag{17}$$

Here, the $\vec{R}_L$= vector includes the arbitrary numbers related to the Levy motion. As in the Levy distribution the step size is very small, this movement represents diversification.

(c) More precisely, the update in prey position can be governed by by the following decision-making loop.

$$\overrightarrow{TPM}_i = \overrightarrow{TPM}_i + K.\vec{J} \times \vec{s}tep_i \tag{18}$$

In this modification, R has been replaced by Equation (15). This implies that for every iteration there will a new chaotic number is assigned for making a decision process. Hence, the decision for the position update is handled with the help of the chaotic function instead of a random function that is normally distributed. Pseudo code of the proposed algorithm is depicted in Algorithm 1.

Algorithm 1 Pseudo code of proposed CMPA.

```
Initialize the search agent number, maximum iteration T_max and FAD probability
while Termination criterion is not met, start the algorithm loop do
    if(t < T_max/3)
    Update prey based on phase 1 Equations (4) and (5).
else if(T_max/3 > t < 2 * T_max/3)
    Update prey based on phase 2 Equations (8), (9) and (15)–(18).
    Else update prey based on phase 3 Equations (10) and (11).
    End if loop
    Accomplish Memory saving and update TPR^EM
    Apply FAD effect and update based on the last phase as per Equations (12) and (13)
end while
Print the values of Fitness, Accuracy and Attributes.
```

Discussion

During stage 2, both prey and predator moves at the same pace; hence, there is a chance of local minima stagnation as the exploration and exploitation rates are almost same. Hence, to keep the exploration and exploitation phase alive the position update equation based on a random number has been replaced with chaotic numbers, which are obtained from the sequence generation as per the definition in Equations (14) and (15).

Embedding chaos at this stage, when the velocity of prey and predator is almost the same, is more meaningful because these search agents can be directed to a local minima spot without changing or exploring in the different direction. Hence, it is quite necessary to keep the gradient of the velocity agile. This fact also motivates the experimental investigation of embedding chaos in other phases. In this work, our focus is to embed chaos and observe the impact of this addition only on the optimization performance of the algorithm in the binary domain. The following section presents the problem formulation part for evaluation of the proposed CMPA.

4. Problem Formulation

From the evaluation perspective, the feature selection problem can be classified into two broad categories, in the first type of approach, which is based on filter-based methods, an effective subset of the feature is selected and its performance is evaluated; finally, the algorithm suggests the optimal subset. In this type of approach, the subset is not evaluated over the training samples. On the other hand, the wrapper feature selection-based approaches evaluate the feature subset and performance validation is conducted with testing and validation of the data sets. Feature selection is always considered as a multi objective optimization problem where objectives can be the maximization of the classification accuracy with the minimum number of feature subsets. It appears that both of the objectives are conflicting in nature. Hence, the objective function employed in this study is a weighted combination of these objectives.

$$ObjectiveFuncion(J) = w_1 \times Er(D) + w_2 \times \frac{R_c}{N} \tag{19}$$

where $Er(D)$ is the error in the classification rate of a given classifier; in this work, we have employed the K-nearest Neighbor classifier (KNN), and w_1 and w_2 are the weights where $w_1 = 1 - w_2$. The weighted combination philosophy has been adapted from reference [11].

5. Results and Discussions

For comparing the proposed variant we draw a comparison on the basis of the accuracy of the classification, fitness values obtained by algorithm and average attributes obtained from the optimization runs. In order to access the performance of the proposed algorithm, 17 classical data sets have been chosen. The details of data sets are shown in Table 1.

We have reported our results in two sets. In set-1, a comparison is made with contemporary algorithms, and in set-2 the chaotic algorithms are simulated and their comparative analysis is presented.

5.1. Experimental Details

Designing a mechanism that chooses the optimal feature from the given sets is a very important procedure, as the randomness can alter the results in a very effective manner; hence, a rigorous experimental analysis has been carried out for choosing the number of iterations, number of search agents and both chaotic marine algorithms, along with the marine algorithm, have been analyzed for many independent runs. We choose the Vote, Tic-Tac-Toe, Sonar, Penguin, Lymphography, Exactly, CongressEw and Breast Cancer for analysis. In this analysis, we change the values of search agents from (5, 10 and 20) and number of maximum iterations (20, 30, 50 and 70). From the analysis conducted in this experiment, we have adopted the numbers of search agents to be 10 and the maximum iteration number is 100. This analysis is conducted in such a manner that the parametric impact can be observed on the accuracy of classification and fitness values. We observe that in choosing these values of the parameters, the accuracy of the classification is not compromised and fitness values are also optimal. Further, the experimental details of this study has been shown in Figure 2.

Table 1. Data sets used for experimental verification.

S. No.	Data Set	No. of Attributes	No. of Objects
1	Breastcancer	9	699
2	Breast EW	30	569
3	CongressEw	16	435
4	Exactly	13	1000
5	Exactly2	13	1000
6	HeartEW	13	270
7	IonosphereEW	34	351
8	KrvskpEw	36	3196
9	Lymphography	18	148
10	Penguin	325	73
11	SonarEw	60	208
12	SpectEw	22	267
13	Tic-tac-toe	9	958
14	Vote	16	300
15	WaveformEw	40	5000
16	Wine	13	178
17	Zoo	16	101

Comparison with Previously Published Approaches

For investigation, the comparison is made with some of the previously reported approaches in the classification domain, where the objective function depicted in the previous section has been considered for dealing with the KNN classifier. The comparison results of the fitness values has been shown in Table 2. It is worth mentioning here that the simulation process is time consuming, hence the mean values of 10 runs are reported in the table. We observe that the fitness values for all the test data is optimal for the proposed

CMPA and in some cases these values are optimal. This fact establishes the applicability of CMPA in the binary domain. For example, in the case of CongressEw data, the fitness values are optimal for both CMPA and MPA.

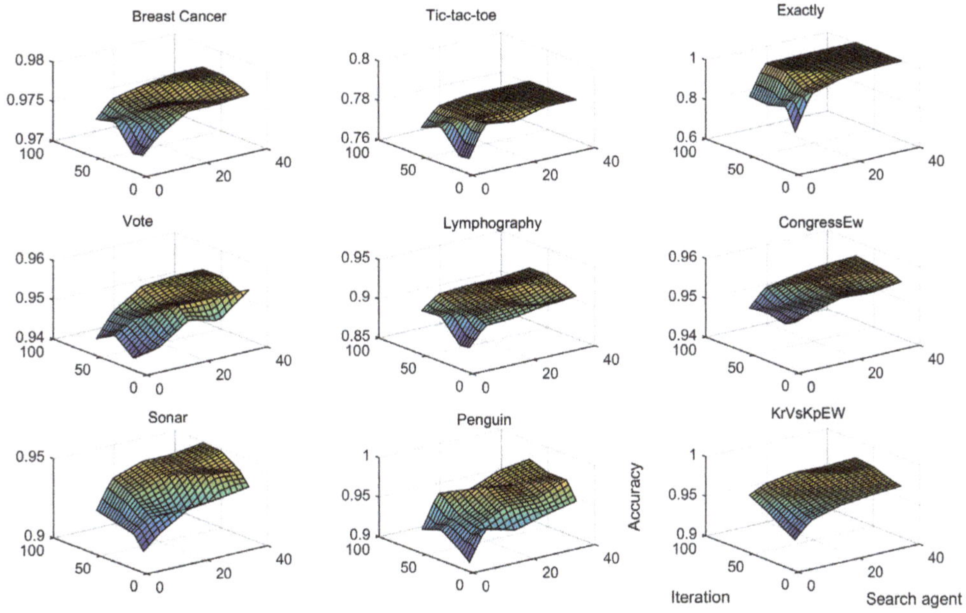

Figure 2. Classification of feature selection algorithms.

Table 2. Fitness value.

Data Set	MPA [21]	CMPA	ALO [27]	GA [28]	PSO [29]
Breastcancer	0.05	0.04	0.02	0.03	0.03
Breast EW	0.06	0.06	0.03	0.04	0.03
CongressEw	0.02	0.02	0.05	0.04	0.04
Exactly	0.16	0.12	0.29	0.28	0.28
Exactly2	0.21	0.21	0.24	0.25	0.25
HeartEW	0.19	0.19	0.12	0.14	0.15
IonosphereEW	0.07	0.07	0.11	0.13	0.14
KrvskpEw	0.03	0.03	0.05	0.07	0.05
Lymphography	0.13	0.13	0.14	0.17	0.19
Penguin	0.03	0.03	0.14	0.22	0.22
SonarEw	0.10	0.10	0.18	0.13	0.13
SpectEw	0.17	0.17	0.12	0.14	0.13
Tic-tac-toe	0.22	0.23	0.22	0.24	0.24
Vote	0.03	0.03	0.04	0.05	0.05
WaveformEw	0.21	0.21	0.021	0.2	0.22
Wine	0.03	0.03	0.02	0.01	0.02
Zoo	0.02	0.02	0.07	0.08	0.1

Further, the comparative analysis of the classification accuracy has also been conducted with previously published algorithms; we observed that the classification accuracy of the proposed algorithm is better than MPA and better than GA, PSO and ALO. These results are shown in Table 3. For example, in the case of the ZOO data base, we observed that the classification accuracy of the CMPA is about 98%, on the other hand, the classification accuracy has been substantially compromised in ALO (91%), GA (88%) and PSO (83%).

It is also important to showcase the fact that classification accuracy has been achieved without compromising feature size. Hence, the attributes (feature) selected by every algorithm in each run has been averaged and showcased in Table 4. These values are very important indicators, as it can be easily observed from the table that the number of features selected by the algorithm is optimal in many cases, and this happens without compromising the classification accuracy.

Table 3. Comparative analysis of classification accuracy.

Data Set	MPA	CMPA	ALO	GA	PSO
Breastcancer	0.96	0.96	0.96	0.96	0.95
Breast EW	0.94	0.94	0.93	0.94	0.94
CongressEw	0.98	0.98	0.93	0.94	0.94
Exactly	0.84	0.89	0.66	0.67	0.68
Exactly2	0.78	0.78	0.75	0.76	0.75
HeartEW	0.81	0.82	0.83	0.82	0.78
IonosphereEW	0.93	0.93	0.87	0.83	0.84
KrvskpEw	0.97	0.97	0.96	0.92	0.94
Lymphography	0.87	0.87	0.79	0.71	0.69
Penguin	0.97	0.97	0.63	0.7	0.72
SonarEw	0.90	0.90	0.74	0.73	0.74
SpectEw	0.83	0.83	0.8	0.78	0.77
Tic-tac-toe	0.78	0.78	0.73	0.71	0.73
Vote	0.97	0.97	0.92	0.89	0.89
WaveformEw	0.79	0.79	0.77	0.77	0.76
Wine	0.97	0.97	0.91	0.93	0.95
Zoo	0.98	0.98	0.91	0.88	0.83

Table 4. Optimized mean of attributes.

Data Set	MPA	CMPA	ALO	GA	PSO
Breastcancer	3.44	3.38	6.28	5.09	5.72
Breast EW	7.02	6.22	16.08	16.35	16.56
CongressEw	4.63	4.37	6.98	6.62	6.83
Exactly	4.75	5.61	6.62	10.82	9.75
Exactly2	2.10	2.05	10.7	6.18	6.18
HeartEW	5.07	5.73	10.31	9.49	7.94
IonosphereEW	7.39	6.88	9.42	17.31	19.18
KrvskpEw	18.82	15.94	24.7	22.43	20.81

Table 4. *Cont.*

Data Set	MPA	CMPA	ALO	GA	PSO
Lymphography	5.30	5.89	11.05	11.05	8.98
Penguin	63.83	60.43	164.13	177.13	178.75
SonarEw	20.78	16.23	37.92	33.3	31.2
SpectEw	5.29	5.00	16.15	11.75	12.5
Tic-tac-toe	5.60	5.53	6.99	6.85	6.61
Vote	3.81	3.61	9.52	6.62	8.8
WaveformEw	22.41	19.79	35.72	25.28	22.72
Wine	4.55	4.30	10.7	8.63	8.36
Zoo	4.92	4.78	13.97	10.11	9.74

5.2. Comparative Analysis of MPA and CMPA

For conducting this analysis, we have compared the optimization run results on the basis of attributes selected by the optimization algorithms, i.e., MPA and CMPA, on the basis of the fitness function values and on the basis of the classification accuracy achieved for different data sets. Table 5 showcases the results of the Wilcoxon rank-sum test [30] between MPA, and CMPA and the p-values are depicted in the table. This test is conducted with 95% confidence interval (5% significance level).

Table 5. Statistical significance test with MPA.

Data Set	Attributes	Fitness		Classification		Attributes	
		MPA	CMPA	MPA	CMPA	MPA	CMPA
Breastcancer	Mean Values	4.48×10^{-2}	4.52×10^{-2}	9.60×10^{-1}	9.60×10^{-1}	3.44	3.38
	p-values	1.00	5.82×10^{-1}	1.00	5.69×10^{-1}	1.00	9.03×10^{-1}
Breast EW	Mean Values	5.88×10^{-2}	6.13×10^{-2}	9.40×10^{-1}	9.40×10^{-1}	7.02	6.22
	p-values	1.00	4.32×10^{-1}	1.00	5.03×10^{-1}	1.00	1.81×10^{-1}
CongressEw	Mean Values	2.02×10^{-2}	2.12×10^{-2}	9.80×10^{-1}	9.80×10^{-1}	4.63	4.37
	p-values	1.00	3.48×10^{-1}	1.00	5.80×10^{-1}	1.00	5.08×10^{-1}
Exactly	Mean Values	1.16×10^{-1}	1.57×10^{-1}	8.40×10^{-1}	8.90×10^{-1}	4.75	5.61
	p-values	1.00	2.35×10^{-1}	1.00	2.35×10^{-1}	1.00	3.10×10^{-1}
Exactly2	Mean Values	2.15×10^{-1}	2.15×10^{-1}	7.80×10^{-1}	7.80×10^{-1}	2.10	2.05
	p-values	1.00	2.35×10^{-1}	1.00	2.35×10^{-1}	1.00	7.35×10^{-1}
HeartEW	Mean Values	1.86×10^{-1}	1.92×10^{-1}	8.10×10^{-1}	8.20×10^{-1}	5.07	5.73
	p-values	1.00	1.26×10^{-1}	1.00	1.10×10^{-1}	1.00	2.07×10^{-2}
IonosphereEW	Mean Values	6.60×10^{-2}	7.05×10^{-2}	9.30×10^{-1}	9.30×10^{-1}	7.39	6.88
	p-values	1.00	5.41×10^{-2}	1.00	6.39×10^{-2}	1.00	4.41×10^{-1}
KrvskpEw	Mean Values	3.41×10^{-2}	3.01×10^{-2}	9.70×10^{-1}	9.70×10^{-1}	1.88×10^{1}	1.59×10^{1}
	p-values	1.00	2.67×10^{-1}	1.00	1.55×10^{-1}	1.00	5.65×10^{-2}

Table 5. *Cont.*

Data Set	Attributes	Fitness		Classification		Attributes	
		MPA	CMPA	MPA	CMPA	MPA	CMPA
Lymphography	Mean Values	1.28×10^{-1}	1.29×10^{-1}	8.70×10^{-1}	8.70×10^{-1}	5.30	5.89
	p-values	1.00	6.62×10^{-1}	1.00	6.64×10^{-1}	1.00	2.18×10^{-1}
Penguin	Mean Values	2.66×10^{-2}	2.68×10^{-2}	9.70×10^{-1}	9.70×10^{-1}	6.38×10^{1}	6.04×10^{1}
	p-values	1.00	5.88×10^{-1}	1.00	1.00	1.00	4.57×10^{-1}
SonarEw	Mean Values	1.03×10^{-1}	1.03×10^{-1}	9.00×10^{-1}	9.00×10^{-1}	2.08×10^{1}	1.62×10^{1}
	p-values	1.00	5.43×10^{-1}	1.00	9.67×10^{-1}	1.00	3.97×10^{-3}
SpectEw	Mean Values	1.69×10^{-1}	1.66×10^{-1}	8.30×10^{-1}	8.30×10^{-1}	5.29	5.00
	p-values	1.00	4.80×10^{-1}	1.00	4.58×10^{-1}	1.00	6.36×10^{-1}
Tic-tac-toe	Mean Values	2.26×10^{-1}	2.20×10^{-1}	7.80×10^{-1}	7.80×10^{-1}	5.60	5.53
	p-values	1.00	3.19×10^{-1}	1.00	3.19×10^{-1}	1.00	5.79×10^{-1}
Vote	Mean Values	3.50×10^{-2}	3.19×10^{-2}	9.70×10^{-1}	9.70×10^{-1}	3.81	3.61
	p-values	1.00	1.73×10^{-1}	1.00	1.08×10^{-1}	1.00	8.39×10^{-1}
WaveformEw	Mean Values	2.11×10^{-1}	2.11×10^{-1}	7.90×10^{-1}	7.90×10^{-1}	2.24×10^{1}	1.98×10^{1}
	p-values	1.00	7.76×10^{-1}	1.00	9.89×10^{-1}	1.00	1.33×10^{-1}
Wine	Mean Values	3.33×10^{-2}	3.19×10^{-2}	9.70×10^{-1}	9.70×10^{-1}	4.55	4.30
	p-values	1.00	7.62×10^{-1}	1.00	7.41×10^{-1}	1.00	5.43×10^{-1}
Zoo	Mean Values	2.32×10^{-2}	2.21×10^{-2}	9.80×10^{-1}	9.80×10^{-1}	4.92	4.78
	p-values	1.00	4.22×10^{-1}	1.00	3.42×10^{-1}	1.00	5.43×10^{-1}

The column entry, which indicates value 1 in the *p*-values column, is considered as the native algorithm, from which the statistical comparison is executed. Here, MPA is considered as native algorithm and the rank-sum test calculation has been executed between MPA and the proposed CMPA. Hence, the results that obtained 0.05 were considered as a different distribution. From the entries depicted in the table, it has been observed that the CMPA provides competitive results when compared with MPA, and provides an optimal values of attributes, fitness function values and classification accuracies for almost all data sets. This fact advocates the applicability of a proposed algorithm on the feature selection problem.

5.3. Comparative Analysis of Performance of the Proposed CMPA with Other Chaotic Algorithms

Further, it has been an established fact that amending the chaos in the metaheuristic algorithms improvises the optimization efficiency in the binary domain. In order to investigate this fact, some recently published algorithms are considered for the evaluation of the performance of the proposed CMPA. These algorithms are the enhanced chaotic grasshopper optimization algorithm (ECGOA) (with sine map) [31], sinusoidal bridging mechanism-based grasshopper algorithm (with sine map) [32] and enhanced chaotic artificial bee colony algorithm (ECABC) (with sine map) [33]. The binary version of these chaotic algorithms are obtained, as per reference [11].

For showcasing the impact of chaos on the performance of these algorithms, the classification accuracy along with the mean fitness attribute selected by the algorithms is depicted in Table 6. From the table it has been observed that for majority of the data sets the classification accuracy is very competitive and that is with a smaller number of selected features.

Table 6. Comparative analysis of performance with chaotic algorithms.

Data Set	Parameter	MPA	CMPA	ECGOA [31]	SFECGOA [32]	ECABC [33]
Breastcancer	Mean (Feature)	3.44	3.38	3.54	3.65	6.74
	Classification	0.96	0.96	0.95	0.94	0.95
Breast EW	Mean (Feature)	7.02	6.22	7.29	7.56	7.25
	Classification	0.94	0.94	0.94	0.93	0.93
CongressEw	Mean (Feature)	4.63	4.37	4.44	4.56	4.92
	Classification	0.98	0.98	0.97	0.98	0.97
Exactly	Mean (Feature)	4.75	5.61	5.68	5.92	6.01
	Classification	0.84	0.89	0.85	0.84	0.83
Exactly2	Mean (Feature)	2.10	2.05	2.21	2.35	2.47
	Classification	0.78	0.78	0.77	0.78	0.79
HeartEW	Mean (Feature)	5.07	5.73	5.65	4.98	5.24
	Classification	0.81	0.82	0.8	0.8	0.8
IonosphereEW	Mean (Feature)	7.39	6.88	7.21	7.46	7.15
	Classification	0.93	0.93	0.92	0.91	0.93
KrvskpEw	Mean (Feature)	18.82	15.94	18.26	19.24	18.25
	Classification	0.97	0.97	0.95	0.96	0.96
Lymphography	Mean (Feature)	5.30	5.89	5.48	5.98	5.77
	Classification	0.87	0.87	0.86	0.86	0.86
Penguin	Mean (Feature)	63.83	60.43	64.25	64.98	69.32
	Classification	0.97	0.97	0.97	0.95	0.96
SonarEw	Mean (Feature)	20.78	16.23	21.56	23.87	25.36
	Classification	0.90	0.90	0.89	0.9	0.9
SpectEw	Mean (Feature)	5.29	5.00	5.24	5.63	5.41
	Classification	0.83	0.83	0.82	0.85	0.83
Tic-tac-toe	Mean (Feature)	5.60	5.53	5.98	5.72	5.69
	Classification	0.78	0.78	0.76	0.76	0.75
Vote	Mean (Feature)	3.81	3.61	3.89	3.95	3.63
	Classification	0.97	0.97	0.96	0.95	0.96
WaveformEw	Mean (Feature)	22.41	19.79	23.54	25.36	23.01
	Classification	0.79	0.79	0.77	0.78	0.78
Wine	Mean (Feature)	4.55	4.30	5.65	4.35	4.69
	Classification	0.97	0.97	0.96	0.96	0.96
Zoo	Mean (Feature)	4.92	4.78	4.98	4.65	4.79
	Classification	0.98	0.98	0.97	0.97	0.97

Further, as proof, the statistical significance test has been conducted for comparison of the proposed algorithm with other chaotic algorithms. The results of the mean feature obtained from the optimization runs along with the p-values of the rank-sum test have been showcased in Table 7. The following points are observed:

Table 7. Statistical significance analysis of CMPA with chaotic algorithms.

Data Set	Parameter	CMPA	ECGOA	SFECGOA	ECABC
Breastcancer	Mean (Feature)	3.38	3.54	3.65	6.74
	p-values	1.00	6.80×10^{-8}	6.80×10^{-8}	6.80×10^{-8}
Breast EW	Mean (Feature)	6.22	7.29	7.56	7.25
	p-values	1.00	6.80×10^{-8}	6.80×10^{-8}	6.80×10^{-8}
CongressEw	Mean (Feature)	4.37	4.44	4.56	4.92
	p-values	1.00	6.80×10^{-8}	6.80×10^{-8}	6.80×10^{-8}
Exactly	Mean (Feature)	5.61	5.68	5.92	6.01
	p-values	1.00	6.80×10^{-8}	6.80×10^{-8}	6.80×10^{-8}
Exactly2	Mean (Feature)	2.05	2.21	2.35	2.47
	p-values	1.00	6.80×10^{-8}	6.80×10^{-8}	6.80×10^{-8}
HeartEW	Mean (Feature)	5.73	5.65	4.98	5.24
	p-values	1.00	6.80×10^{-8}	6.80×10^{-8}	6.80×10^{-8}
IonosphereEW	Mean (Feature)	6.88	7.21	7.46	7.15
	p-values	1.00	6.80×10^{-8}	6.80×10^{-8}	6.80×10^{-8}
KrvskpEw	Mean (Feature)	15.94	18.26	19.24	18.25
	p-values	1.00	6.80×10^{-8}	6.80×10^{-8}	6.80×10^{-8}
Lymphography	Mean (Feature)	5.89	5.48	5.98	5.77
	p-values	1.00	4.40×10^{-8}	6.99×10^{-8}	1.80×10^{-8}
Penguin	Mean (Feature)	60.43	64.25	64.98	69.32
	p-values	1.00	2.18×10^{-8}	1.96×10^{-8}	2.80×10^{-8}
SonarEw	Mean (Feature)	16.23	21.56	23.87	25.36
	p-values	1.00	2.18×10^{-8}	1.96×10^{-8}	2.80×10^{-8}
SpectEw	Mean (Feature)	5.00	5.24	5.63	5.41
	p-values	1.00	6.80×10^{-8}	2.48×10^{-8}	6.80×10^{-8}
Tic-tac-toe	Mean (Feature)	5.53	5.98	5.72	5.69
	p-values	1.00	4.40×10^{-8}	2.48×10^{-8}	6.80×10^{-8}
Vote	Mean (Feature)	3.61	3.89	3.95	3.63
	p-values	1.00	6.80×10^{-8}	4.40×10^{-8}	2.48×10^{-8}
WaveformEw	Mean (Feature)	19.79	23.54	25.36	23.01
	p-values	1.00	2.48×10^{-8}	4.40×10^{-8}	6.80×10^{-8}
Wine	Mean (Feature)	4.30	5.65	4.35	4.69
	p-values	1.00	2.48×10^{-8}	2.80×10^{-8}	3.20×10^{-8}
Zoo	Mean (Feature)	4.78	4.98	4.65	4.79
	p-values	1.00	6.80×10^{-8}	6.80×10^{-8}	6.80×10^{-8}

- The mean values of features for 15 data sets are found optimal. Only the Zoo data set has optimal results for SFECGOA, and the HeartEW data set has the ECABC. This fact suggests that the selection of features without compromising accuracy can be possible with the proposed CMPA.
- Inspecting the p-values obtained from the Wilcoxon rank-sum test [30], it has been observed that all the algorithms have p-values less than 0.05. Hence, it can be said that a statistical significance exists in the results for obtaining the mean attributes. This fact indicates that if we repeat this experiment again with the same parameters, we will obtain the same results.
- The graphical analysis of the results obtained from the optimization process has been depicted with the help of bar charts in Figures 3 and 4. From these figures it is evident that the optimization capability of the proposed CMPA is superior to other algorithms.
- From the analysis conducted in this experiment, it has been observed that the chaotic position update mechanism in MPA yields better results as compared with the contemporary chaotic algorithms that uses chaos as a bridging mechanism. In short, the modification suggested in the MPA is meaningful and demonstrates a positive impact on the optimization performance of the proposed algorithm.

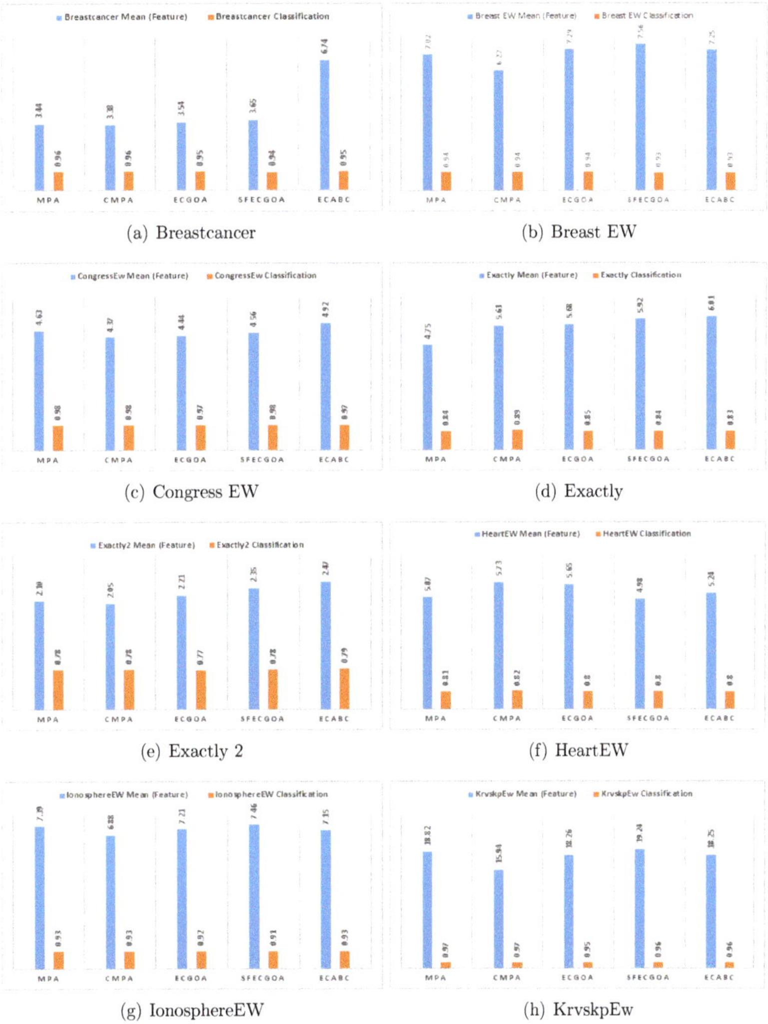

Figure 3. Graphical representation of the optimization results (set-1).

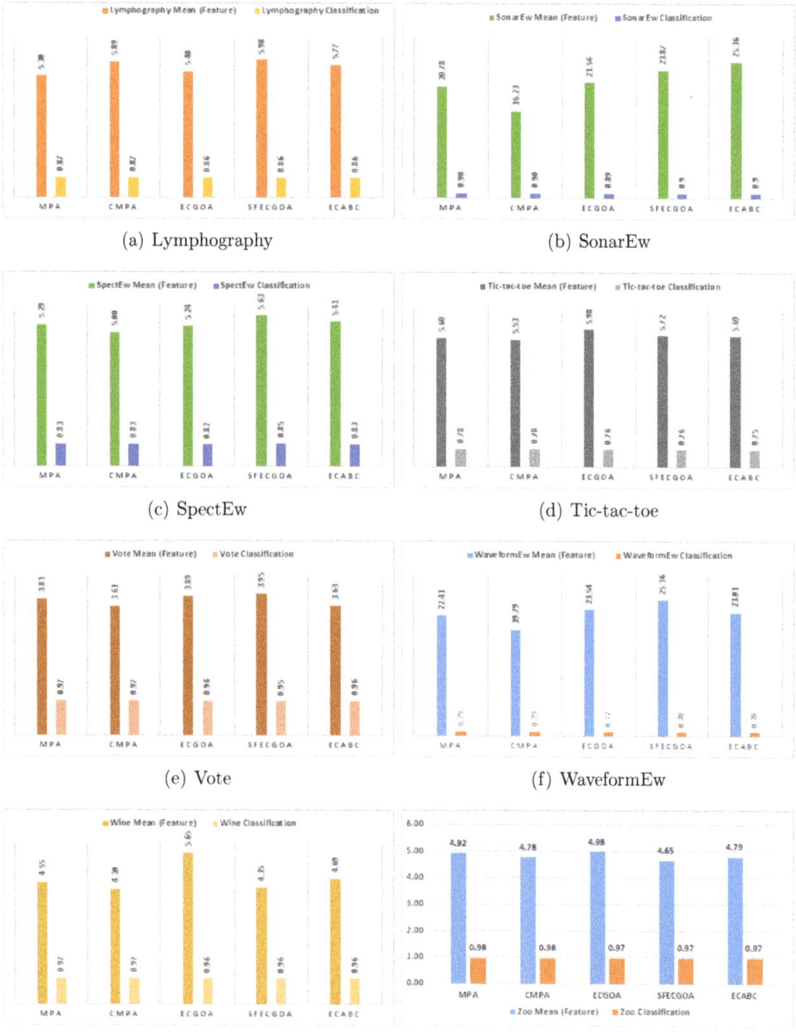

(a) Lymphography (b) SonarEw
(c) SpectEw (d) Tic-tac-toe
(e) Vote (f) WaveformEw
(g) Wine (h) Zoo

Figure 4. Graphical representation of the optimization results (set-2).

6. Conclusions

This paper reports an application of the chaotic marine predator algorithm in a feature selection task; a binary version of the chaotic MPA algorithm is proposed in this work by altering the decision making of the position update phase of stage-2 with a chaotic sequence. We have changed the decision process by inculcating chaotic numbers generated from a chaotic sequence. Further, the proposed binary algorithm has been tested over 17 data sets and the algorithm analysis has been performed with the native algorithm. We observed that the native algorithm is strong and robust but some modifications in the position update process make it more suitable for the feature selection task. The results are reported with the help of different analyses. The following are the major conclusions drawn from this work.

1. The algorithm analysis has been conducted on the basis of the number of search agents selected and the number of iterations selected for feature selection. After this

analysis, the optimal values of design parameters have been selected for executing the feature selection task.
2. A comparison with a recently published algorithm and state-of-the-art algorithms has been conducted to showcase the efficacy of the algorithm; the fitness value of the objective function along with classification accuracy have been reported in order to validate the efficacy of the proposed modification.
3. A comparison of some chaotic algorithms along with the proposed CMPA has also been reported to showcase the feasibility of CMPA. It is observed that the classification accuracy of the algorithm has not been compromised and the number of features obtained from the optimization runs are found optimal for the majority of cases.
4. Graphical analysis along with statistical comparison of the proposed algorithm with others revealed that a modification in the stage-2 of MPA algorithm has some positive implications on the optimization performance of MPA.

Application of chaos in multiple phases with normalization and scaled functions will be evaluated in the future.

Author Contributions: Conceptualization, K.M.S.; Data curation, K.A.A.; Formal analysis, A.S. and A.W.M.; Funding acquisition, A.F.A. and K.A.A.; Investigation, K.M.S.; Methodology, A.S.; Project administration, A.F.A.; Resources, K.A.A.; Supervision, A.W.M.; Writing—original draft, A.S.; Writing—review & editing, A.S. All authors have read and agreed to the published version of the manuscript.

Funding: This research is funded by the Researchers Supporting Program at King Saud University, Project number (RSP-2021/323).

Institutional Review Board Statement: Not applicable.

Informed Consent Statement: Not applicable.

Data Availability Statement: Not applicable.

Acknowledgments: The authors present their appreciation to King Saud University for funding this research through the Researchers Supporting Program (Project number RSP-2021/323), King Saud University, Riyadh, Saudi Arabia.

Conflicts of Interest: The authors declare no conflict of interest.

References

1. Huda, S.; Yearwood, J.; Jelinek, H.F.; Hassan, M.M.; Fortino, G.; Buckl, M. A hybrid feature selection with ensemble classification for imbalanced healthcare data: A case study for brain tumor diagnosis. *IEEE Access* **2016**, *4*, 9145–9154. [CrossRef]
2. Ambusaidi, M.A.; He, X.; Nanda, P.; Tan, Z. Building an intrusion detection system using a filter-based feature selection algorithm. *IEEE Trans. Comput.* **2016**, *65*, 2986–2998. [CrossRef]
3. Shang, W.; Huang, H.; Zhu, H.; Lin, Y.; Qu, Y.; Wang, Z. A novel feature selection algorithm for text categorization. *Expert Syst. Appl.* **2007**, *33*, 1–5. [CrossRef]
4. Koprinska, I. Feature selection for brain-computer interfaces. In *Pacific-Asia Conference on Knowledge Discovery and Data Mining*; Springer: Berlin/Heidelberg, Germany, 2009; pp. 106–117.
5. Szczepanski, R.; Tarczewski, T. Global path planning for mobile robot based on Artificial Bee Colony and Dijkstra's algorithms. In Proceedings of the 2021 IEEE 19th International Power Electronics and Motion Control Conference (PEMC), Gliwice, Poland, 25–29 April 2021; pp. 724–730.
6. Szczepanski, R.; Tarczewski, T.; Niewiara, L.J.; Stojic, D. Identification of mechanical parameters in servo-drive system. In Proceedings of the 2021 IEEE 19th International Power Electronics and Motion Control Conference (PEMC), Gliwice, Poland, 25–29 April 2021; pp. 566–573.
7. Szczepanski, R.; Tarczewski, T.; Grzesiak, L.M. Application of optimization algorithms to adaptive motion control for repetitive process. *ISA Trans.* **2021**, *115*, 192–205. [CrossRef] [PubMed]
8. Bangyal, W.H.; Ahmad, J.; Rauf, H.T. Optimization of neural network using improved bat algorithm for data classification. *J. Med. Imaging Health Inform.* **2019**, *9*, 670–681. [CrossRef]
9. Rukhsar, L.; Bangyal, W.H.; Nisar, K.; Nisar, S. Prediction of insurance fraud detection using machine learning algorithms. *Mehran Univ. Res. J. Eng. Technol.* **2022**, *41*, 33–40. [CrossRef]
10. Bangyal, W.H.; Ahmad, J.; Shafi, I.; Abbas, Q. A forward only counter propagation network-based approach for contraceptive method choice classification task. *J. Exp. Theor. Artif. Intell.* **2012**, *24*, 211–218. [CrossRef]

11. Mafarja, M.M.; Mirjalili, S. Hybrid whale optimization algorithm with simulated annealing for feature selection. *Neurocomputing* **2017**, *260*, 302–312. [CrossRef]
12. Sayed, G.I.; Tharwat, A.; Hassanien, A.E. Chaotic dragonfly algorithm: An improved metaheuristic algorithm for feature selection. *Appl. Intell.* **2019**, *49*, 188–205. [CrossRef]
13. Anand, P.; Arora, S. A novel chaotic selfish herd optimizer for global optimization and feature selection. *Artif. Intell. Rev.* **2020**, *53*, 1441–1486. [CrossRef]
14. Agrawal, P.; Abutarboush, H.F.; Ganesh, T.; Mohamed, A.W. Metaheuristic algorithms on feature selection: A survey of one decade of research (2009–2019). *IEEE Access* **2021**, *9*, 26766–26791. [CrossRef]
15. Agrawal, P.; Ganesh, T.; Oliva, D.; Mohamed, A.W. S-shaped and v-shaped gaining-sharing knowledge-based algorithm for feature selection. *Appl. Intell.* **2022**, *52*, 81–112. [CrossRef]
16. Agrawal, P.; Ganesh, T.; Mohamed, A.W. Chaotic gaining sharing knowledge-based optimization algorithm: An improved metaheuristic algorithm for feature selection. *Soft Comput.* **2021**, *25*, 9505–9528. [CrossRef]
17. Zhang, X.; Xu, Y.; Yu, C.; Heidari, A.A.; Li, S.; Chen, H.; Li, C. Gaussian mutational chaotic fruit fly-built optimization and feature selection. *Expert Syst. Appl.* **2020**, *141*, 112976. [CrossRef]
18. Sayed, G.I.; Hassanien, A.E.; Azar, A.T. Feature selection via a novel chaotic crow search algorithm. *Neural Comput. Appl.* **2019**, *31*, 171–188. [CrossRef]
19. Ewees, A.A.; El Aziz, M.A.; Hassanien, A.E. Chaotic multi-verse optimizer-based feature selection. *Neural Comput. Appl.* **2019**, *31*, 991–1006. [CrossRef]
20. Sayed, G.I.; Khoriba, G.; Haggag, M.H. A novel chaotic salp swarm algorithm for global optimization and feature selection. *Appl. Intell.* **2018**, *48*, 3462–3481. [CrossRef]
21. Faramarzi, A.; Heidarinejad, M.; Mirjalili, S.; Gandomi, A.H. Marine Predators Algorithm: A nature-inspired metaheuristic. *Expert Syst. Appl.* **2020**, *152*, 113377. [CrossRef]
22. Zhong, K.; Zhou, G.; Deng, W.; Zhou, Y.; Luo, Q. MOMPA: Multi-objective marine predator algorithm. *Comput. Methods Appl. Mech. Eng.* **2021**, *385*, 114029. [CrossRef]
23. Ramezani, M.; Bahmanyar, D.; Razmjooy, N. A new improved model of marine predator algorithm for optimization problems. *Arab. J. Sci. Eng.* **2021**, *46*, 8803–8826. [CrossRef]
24. Ho, L.V.; Nguyen, D.H.; Mousavi, M.; De Roeck, G.; Bui-Tien, T.; Gandomi, A.H.; Wahab, M.A. A hybrid computational intelligence approach for structural damage detection using marine predator algorithm and feedforward neural networks. *Comput. Struct.* **2021**, *252*, 106568. [CrossRef]
25. Filmalter, J.D.; Dagorn, L.; Cowley, P.D.; Taquet, M. First descriptions of the behavior of silky sharks, Carcharhinus falciformis, around drifting fish aggregating devices in the Indian Ocean. *Bull. Mar. Sci.* **2011**, *87*, 325–337. [CrossRef]
26. Parouha, R.P.; Das, K.N. A memory based differential evolution algorithm for unconstrained optimization. *Appl. Soft Comput.* **2016**, *38*, 501–517. [CrossRef]
27. Mirjalili, S. The ant lion optimizer. *Adv. Eng. Softw.* **2015**, *83*, 80–98. [CrossRef]
28. Harik, G.R.; Lobo, F.G.; Goldberg, D.E. The compact genetic algorithm. *IEEE Trans. Evol. Comput.* **2015**, *3*, 287–297. [CrossRef]
29. Kennedy, J.; Eberhart, R. Particle swarm optimization. In Proceedings of the ICNN'95-International Conference on Neural Networks, Perth, WA, Australia, 27 November–1 December 1995; Volume 4, pp. 1942–1948.
30. Wilcoxon, F. Individual comparisons by ranking methods. In *Breakthroughs in Statistics*; Springer: New York, NY, USA, 1992; pp. 196–202.
31. Saxena, A.; Shekhawat, S.; Kumar, R. Application and development of enhanced chaotic grasshopper optimization algorithms. *Model. Simul. Eng.* **2018**, *2018*, 4945157. [CrossRef]
32. Saxena, A. A comprehensive study of chaos embedded bridging mechanisms and crossover operators for grasshopper optimisation algorithm. *Expert Syst. Appl.* **2019**, *132*, 166–188. [CrossRef]
33. Saxena, A.; Shekhawat, S.; Sharma, A.; Sharma, H.; Kumar, R. Chaotic step length artificial bee colony algorithms for protein structure prediction. *J. Interdiscip. Math.* **2020**, *23*, 617–629. [CrossRef]

mathematics

Article

Guided Hybrid Modified Simulated Annealing Algorithm for Solving Constrained Global Optimization Problems

Khalid Abdulaziz Alnowibet [1], Salem Mahdi [2], Mahmoud El-Alem [3], Mohamed Abdelawwad [4] and Ali Wagdy Mohamed [5,6,*]

1 Statistics and Operations Research Department, College of Science, King Saud University, P.O. Box 2455, Riyadh 11451, Saudi Arabia; knowibet@ksu.edu.sa
2 Educational Research and Development Center Sanaa, Sanaa 31220, Yemen; samath2014@yahoo.com
3 Department of Mathematics & Computer Science, Faculty of Science, Alexandria University, Alexandria 21544, Egypt; mmelalem@alexu.edu.eg
4 Institute for Computer Architecture and System Programming, University of Kassel, 34127 Kassel, Germany; m.abdelawwad@uni-kassel.de
5 Operations Research Department, Faculty of Graduate Studies for Statistical Research, Cairo University, Giza 12613, Egypt
6 Department of Mathematics and Actuarial Science, School of Sciences Engineering, The American University in Cairo, Cairo 11835, Egypt
* Correspondence: aliwagdy@gmail.com

Abstract: In this paper, a hybrid gradient simulated annealing algorithm is guided to solve the constrained optimization problem. In trying to solve constrained optimization problems using deterministic, stochastic optimization methods or hybridization between them, penalty function methods are the most popular approach due to their simplicity and ease of implementation. There are many approaches to handling the existence of the constraints in the constrained problem. The simulated-annealing algorithm (SA) is one of the most successful meta-heuristic strategies. On the other hand, the gradient method is the most inexpensive method among the deterministic methods. In previous literature, the hybrid gradient simulated annealing algorithm (GLMSA) has demonstrated efficiency and effectiveness to solve unconstrained optimization problems. In this paper, therefore, the GLMSA algorithm is generalized to solve the constrained optimization problems. Hence, a new approach penalty function is proposed to handle the existence of the constraints. The proposed approach penalty function is used to guide the hybrid gradient simulated annealing algorithm (GLMSA) to obtain a new algorithm (GHMSA) that finds the constrained optimization problem. The performance of the proposed algorithm is tested on several benchmark optimization test problems and some well-known engineering design problems with varying dimensions. Comprehensive comparisons against other methods in the literature are also presented. The results indicate that the proposed method is promising and competitive. The comparison results between the GHMSA and the other four state-Meta-heuristic algorithms indicate that the proposed GHMSA algorithm is competitive with, and in some cases superior to, other existing algorithms in terms of the quality, efficiency, convergence rate, and robustness of the final result.

Keywords: nonlinear function; constrained optimization; hybrid algorithm; global optima; line search; gradient method; meta-heuristics; simulated annealing algorithm; constraint handling; penalty function; evolutionary computation; numerical comparisons

MSC: 65D05

Citation: Alnowibet, K.A.; Mahdi, S.; El-Alem, M.; Abdelawwad, M.; Mohamed, A.W. Guided Hybrid Modified Simulated Annealing Algorithm for Solving Constrained Global Optimization Problems. *Mathematics* **2022**, *10*, 1312. https://doi.org/10.3390/math10081312

Academic Editor: Savin Treanta

Received: 3 March 2022
Accepted: 11 April 2022
Published: 14 April 2022

1. Introduction

Optimization problems arise in different applications fields, such as technical sciences, industrial engineering, economics, networks, chemical engineering, etc. See for example [1–5]

In general, the constrained optimization problem can be formulated as follows:

$$\begin{aligned} \min_{x\in\mathbb{R}^n} \quad & f(x), \\ \text{s.t} \quad & g_l(x) \le 0, \quad l = 1,2,\dots,q, \\ & h_d(x) = 0, \quad d = 1,2,\dots,m, \quad m < n \\ & a_i \le x_i \le b_i, \; i = 1,2,\dots,n, \end{aligned} \tag{1}$$

where $a_i \in \{\mathbb{R} \cup \{-\infty\}\}$, and $b_i \in \{\mathbb{R} \cup \{\infty\}\}$.

The functions $f(x)$, $g_l(x)$, $h_j(x) : \mathbb{R}^n \rightarrow \mathbb{R}$ are real valued functions, n denotes the number of variables in x, q is the number of inequality constraints, m is the number of equality constraints, a is a lower bounded on x and b is an upper bounded on x. The objective function f, the inequality constraints $g_l, l = 1,2,\dots,q$, and the equality constraint $h_d, d = 1,2,\dots,m$, are assumed to be continuously differentiable nonlinear functions.

Recently, there has been great development of optimization algorithms that are proposed to find global solutions to optimization problems. See for example [2,6–8].

The global optimization methods are used to prevent convergence to local optima and increase the probability of finding the global optimum [9].

The numerical global optimization algorithms can be classified into two classes: deterministic and stochastic methods. In stochastic methods, the minimization process depends partly on probability. In deterministic methods, in contrast, no probabilistic information is used [9].

So, for finding the global minimum of the unconstrained problem by using deterministic methods, it needs an exhaustive search over the feasible region of the function f and additional assumptions for the function f. On the contrary, to find the global minimum of the unconstrained problems, by using stochastic methods, one can prove the asymptotic convergence in probability, i.e., these methods are asymptotically successful with probability 1, see for example [10–12]. In general, the computational results of the stochastic methods are better than those of the deterministic methods [13].

Due to those reasons, a meta-heuristics strategy (stochastic method) is used to guide the search process [13]. Hence a meta-heuristic is a technique designed for solving a problem more quickly when classic methods are too slow, or for finding an approximate solution when classic methods fail to find any exact or near-exact solution. This is achieved by trading optimality, completeness, accuracy, or precision for speed [14–16].

The simulated-annealing algorithm (SA) is one of the most successful meta-heuristic strategies. In fact, the numerical results display that the simulated annealing technique is very efficient and effective for finding the global minimizer. See, for example, [2,5,17–19].

On the other hand, the gradient method is the most inexpensive method for finding a local minimizer of a continuously differentiable function. It has been proved that the gradient algorithm converges locally to a local minimizer [20]. Therefore, if a line-search (L) is added to the gradient method (G) as a globalization strategy, the resulting algorithm is globally convergent to a local minimizer (GL) [9,21,22].

Hence, when the simulated-annealing algorithm (SA) as a global optimization algorithm is combined with the line-search gradient method (GL) as a globally convergent method, the result is the hybrid gradient simulated annealing algorithm (GLMSA) [23]. The idea behind this hybridization is to gain the benefits and advantages of both the GL algorithm and the MSA algorithm.

As a matter of fact, the numerical results demonstrated that the (GLMSA) algorithm is a very efficient, effective and strong competitor for finding the global minimizer. For example, Table 4 of [23] shows that the GL algorithm is able to reach the optimum point of all test problems whose objective functions have only one minimum point (no local minima except the global one. i.e., convex function) and it is stuck at a local minimum for test problems whose objective functions have several local minima (with one global minimum, i.e., non-convex function). Table 6 of [23] demonstrates that the SMA modified simulated annealing algorithm finds the global minimum of all test problems from any starting point of the feasible search space S. However, the GLMSA hybrid gradient simulated annealing algorithm is faster than MSA; also, GLMSA is efficient and effective compared to other meta-heuristic algorithms.

All the above have motivated and encouraged us to generalize the GLMSA algorithm to solve Problem (1).

The literature review analysis shows that the handling constraint which is based on a penalty function is considered the most popular implemented mechanism; this is due to its simplicity and ease of implementation [24–27]. A penalty technique transforms Problem (1) into an unconstrained problem by adding the penalty term of each constraint violation to the objective function value. The remainder of this paper is organized as follows. The next section provides a brief description of the GLMSA algorithm. Constraint handling, the penalty function method, proposed penalty method and interior-point algorithm are presented in Section 3. A guided hybrid simulated annealing algorithm to solve constrained problems is presented in Section 4. Numerical results are given in Section 5. Section 6 contains some concluding remarks.

Note: Section Abbreviations provides a list of the abbreviations and symbols which are used in this paper.

2. Summarized Description of GLMSA Algorithm

The GLMSA algorithm has been designed for solving unconstrained optimization problems; in this paper the GLMSA algorithm is generalized to solve Problem (1). The GLMSA algorithm contains two approaches to find a new step at each iteration, the first one is the gradient method. In this approach, a candidate point is generated and it might be accepted or rejected. If the objective function f is decreased at this point, then it will be accepted, otherwise, the second approach will be used to generate another point.

2.1. The First Approach (Gradient Method)

The gradient method solves an unconstrained optimization problem iteratively, such that at each iteration, a step in the direction of the negative gradient is computed and added to the current point as follows. Given an initial guess $x_0 \in \mathbb{R}^n$, the gradient method generates a sequence $\{x_k\}, k \geq 0$ of the objective function of the unconstrained optimization problem such that:

$$x_{k+1} = x_k + d_k, \tag{2}$$

where d_k is the first step, and it is defined by:

$$d_k = -|\alpha_k| g(x_k), \tag{3}$$

where $g(x_k)$ the gradient vector of the function f at point x_k and α_k is a step length along the negative gradient direction $(-g(x_k))$. The step length α_k along the $-g(x_k)$ is defined by:

$$\alpha_k = \frac{f(x_k)}{\| g(x_k) \|_2^2}. \tag{4}$$

The G gradient algorithm is listed in Algorithm 1 of [23]. The step length λ_k that is computed by the backtracking line-search approach is very important for global convergence of the gradient method. The following section presents a brief description of the backtracking line-search approach for globalizing the gradient method.

Globalizing the First Approach (Gradient Method)

To make the gradient method capable of finding a local minimizer x^* of the objective function of the unconstrained optimization problem from any starting point x_0, the G algorithm (gradient algorithm) is combined with the L algorithm (line-search algorithm) in order to obtain globally convergent algorithm GL. This algorithm is listed in Algorithm 1 below and it contains the first approach (gradient algorithm G) and the backtracking line-search algorithm L.

Algorithm 1 Line-Search Gradient Algorithm "GL"

Input: $f : \mathbb{R}^n \rightarrow \mathbb{R}, f \in C^1, \gamma \in (0,1), k = 0$, a starting point $x_k \in \mathbb{R}^n$ and $\varepsilon > 0$.
Output: $x^* = x_{ac}$ the local minimizer of f, $f(x^*)$, the value of f at x^*

```
Set x_ac = x_0.                                         ▷ x_ac is accepted solution.
Compute f_ac = f(x_ac), g_ac = g(x_ac) and d_k.
while ||g_ac||_2 > ε do   ▷ g_ac is the value of the gradient vector at the accepted point x_ac.
    Set k = k + 1.
    x_k = x_ac + d_k                      ▷ x_ac is the accepted point form the previous iteration.
    Compute f_k = f(x_k)
    Set λ = 1.
    while f_k > f_ac + γλ g_ac^T d_k do
        Set λ = λ/2
        x_k = x_ac − λ g_ac                     ▷ in this paper the value of γ is 10^−4.
        Compute f_k = f(x_k)
    end while
    Set x_ac ← x_k and f_ac ← f(x_k).
    Compute g_ac = g(x_ac) and d_k.
end while
return x_ac the local minimizer and its function value f_ac
```

For more details about the gradient method and the backtracking line-search approach see [23]. The second approach of the GLMSA algorithm is presented in the following subsection.

2.2. The Second Approach (Simulated Annealing SA)

It must be noted that the modified simulated annealing algorithm in [23] contains three alternatives to generate a new point, but in this paper, the first alternative is considered to generate a new point. This procedure is very important for reducing the function evaluations from three times at each iteration to one function evaluation for every iteration, because we need to allow for more inner iterations when solving constrained optimization problems. This procedure guarantees that the parameters of the penalty function are increasing enough because it is a necessary condition for non-stationary penalty functions [28], i.e., when $k \rightarrow \infty$, parameters must also go to infinity.

The second point is generated by

$$x_{k'+1} = x_{ac} + \psi_{k'}, \tag{5}$$

where x_{ac} is the best point which is accepted so far and $\psi_{k'}$ is the step of the second approach and computed by Algorithm 2 below.

The gradient line-search algorithm (GL) has been listed in Algorithm 1 and a modified simulated annealing algorithm (MSA) is illustrated by Algorithm 3.

Algorithm 2 The second approach to generate the step $\psi_{k'}$.

Step 1: Set $k' = 0$.
Step 2: Compute $\omega_{k'} = 10^{(0.1*k')}$.
Step 3: Generate a random vector $X'_k \in [-1,1]^n$.
Step 4: Compute $D^i_{k'} = \frac{-1+(1+\omega_{k'})^{|X^i_{k'}|}}{\omega_{k'}}$, $i = 1,2,\ldots,n$. ▷ n is the number of variables.
Step 5: Set $DX^i_{k'} = sign(X^i_{k'})$.
Step 6: Compute $DE^j_{k'} = D^i_{k'} * DX^j_{i}$.
Step 7: Compute $\psi^i_{k'} = b_i * DE^i_{k'}$. ▷ b_i is the upper bound of the feasible search space.
Step 8: $k' \leftarrow k' + 1$.
Step 9: Repeat steps 2–8 until $k' = N$. ▷ N is the number of iterations and it is given in advance.

Algorithm 3 Modified Simulated-Annealing "MSA".

Input: x_{ac}, f_{ac}, N and T. ▷ T control parameter (Temperature)
Output: x_{best} is the best point of N points and it value f_{best}

```
for k' = 0 → N do
    x_{k'} = x_ac + ψ_{k'}, using Equation (5).
    Compute Δf = f(x_{k'}) − f_ac.
    if Δf < 0 then
        Set x_{ac_{k'}} ← x_{k'}, f_{ac_{k'}} ← f(x_{k'}).
    else
        Generate a random number β ∈ (0,1)
        if β < e^{−Δf/T} then
            Set x_{ac_{k'}} ← x_{k'}, f_{ac_k} ← f(x_{k'}).
        end if
    end if
end for
return x_ac and its function value f_ac.            ▷ f_ac = f(x_ac).
```

where N is the maximum number of possible trials (Length Markov Chains of MSA) and T is the control parameter (temperature). For more details about the MSA algorithm, please, see [23].

For a detailed description of the simulated annealing algorithm SA see for example [18,29–31].

As we have mentioned above, Algorithm 1 (gradient line-search algorithm (GL)) is hybridized with Algorithm 3 (a modified simulated annealing algorithm (MSA)) to get the LGMSA algorithm that solves the unconstrained optimization problem.

In the next section, the LGMSA algorithm is guided to solve Problem (1) by using the penalty function method. There are many methods for handling the existence of the constraints in the constrained problem.

3. Constraints Handling

The algorithms which have been proposed to solve unconstrained optimization problems are unable to deal directly with constrained optimization problems. There are several approaches proposed to handle the existence of the constraints, see for example [27,32,33]. The most popular of them is the penalty function method.

The penalty function method is a successful technique for handling constraints [27,34,35].

3.1. Penalty Function Methods

The penalty methods have been most widely studied and used due to their simplicity in implementation. The major definition of the penalty function methods is the degree to which each constraint is penalized [28]. There are several types of penalty methods that are used to penalize the constraints in constrained optimization problems.

Three groups of penalty function methods are most popular; the first one is a group of methods of static penalties. In these methods, the penalty parameter does not depend on the current iteration, i.e., parameters remain constant through the evolutionary process [24,36].

The second one is a set of methods of dynamic penalties. In these methods the penalty parameters are usually dependent on the current iteration, in other words, the penalty parameters are functions in the iteration k, i.e., they are non-stationary. See [24,37,38].

The third is a set of methods of adaptive penalties; in this group penalty parameters are updated for every iteration [24].

The next section presents a suggested penalty function method with dynamic and adaptive parameters.

Proposed Penalty Function Method

This section shows how Problem (1) is transformed to an unconstrained optimization problem which is simple bounded as follows:

$$\begin{aligned} \min_{x\in\mathbb{R}^n} \quad & \theta(x,r) = f(x) + rp(x), \\ s.t \quad & a_i \leq x_i \leq b_i, \quad i = 1,2,\ldots,n, \end{aligned} \tag{6}$$

where $f(x)$ is the original objective function in Problem (1), r is a penalty parameter. The penalty term $p(x)$ is defined by:

$$p(x) = \sum_{l=1}^{q} (max\{0, g_l(x)\})^2 + \sum_{j=1}^{m} |h_j(x)|^2. \tag{7}$$

The difference between the penalty function methods is in the way of defining the penalty term and its parameter r [24].

The penalty function methods force infeasible points toward the feasible region by step-wise increasing the penalty; r is used in the penalizing function $p(x)$.

Therefore, the solution x^* minimizes the objective function of Problem (6) and also minimizes the objective function of Problem (1), i.e., as long as $k \to \infty$ and $r_k \to \infty$, x^* approaches the feasible region and $r_k p(x) \to 0$ [28].

In this paper, the penalty function method has two parameters—the first one is r which penalizes the inequality constraint that is violated , i.e., when $g_l(x) > 0$. The second parameter is t which penalizes the equality constraint $h_j(x)$ whose value is not equal to zero.

Accordingly, the $\theta(x,r)$ function is defined by:

$$\theta(x,r) = f(x) + \frac{r}{2} p_1(x) + \frac{t}{2} p_2(x), \tag{8}$$

where $p_1(x) = \sum_{l=1}^{q} (max\{0, g_l(x)\})^2$, $p_2(x) = \sum_{j=1}^{m} |h_j(x)|^2$ and r and t are the parameters for inequality and equality constraints respectively.

The parameters r and t are updated at each iteration k as follows.

$$\begin{aligned} r_{k+1} &= r_k + \varphi_k * \Phi_k, \\ t_{k+1} &= t_k + 1, \end{aligned} \tag{9}$$

where the parameter φ_k is updated by:

$$\varphi_k = \begin{cases} 0 & \text{if } g_l(x) \le 0, \\ 2 & \text{otherwise.} \end{cases} \tag{10}$$

The parameter φ_k is an adaptive parameter, i.e., when the candidate solutions are out of the feasible region then φ_k penalizes a violated constraint by multiplying the term Φ_k by 2, where $r_0 = 1$ is the initial value of r. The parameter Φ is updated as follows: $\Phi_{k+1} = \Phi_k + 1, t_0 = 1$.

Note: The equality constraint is more difficult than the inequality constraint because the size of the feasible region of the equality constraint is smaller than the size of the feasible region of the inequality constraint. For example, $f(x, y) = xy$ s.t $h(x, y) = x^2 + y^2 - 1 = 0$ and $f(x, y) = xy$ s.t $g(x, y) = x^2 + y^2 - 1 <= 0$. The first problem is much harder than the second because in the first problem the size of the feasible region is the circumference of the circle while in the second problem, the feasible region is the whole disk. So, the parameter $t(k)$ must be taken carefully.

3.2. Mechanism of Working of the Penalty Function Method

The penalty method solves the general Problem (1), during a succession of unconstrained optimization problems.

Let us discuss two examples in order to illustrate how the parameters of the penalty function are run.

The first example is very easy (one dimension); minimize $f(x) = x^2 - 3$ subject to $g(x) = 0.5 - 0.5x \le 0$, where $S = [-6, 6]$ is the search domain.

If we want to find the optimal solution of the objective function $f(x) = x^2 - 3$ as an unconstrained problem, it is clear that the global solution to this problem is the point $x^* = 0$, such that $f(x^*) = -3$, for $x \in \mathbb{R}$, but when we want to find the optimal solution of the objective function $f(x) = x^2 - 3$ subject to $g(x) \le 0$, in this case, the problem is very difficult because we have to find the point x^* that minimizes $f(x)$ and at the same time it must satisfy the condition of the constraint $g(x) \le 0$, which is why we need to apply the penalty function.

Hence, the problem $f(x) = x^2 - 3$ subject to $g(x) = 0.5 - 0.5x \le 0$ is transformed into $\theta(x, r) = x + \frac{r}{2}(\max\{0, (\frac{1}{2} - 0.5x)\}^2)$, if $g(x) > 0$; ($g(x)$ is violated), the first derivative is computed by the function $\theta(x, r)$; $\frac{d\theta(x,r)}{dx} = 1 - \frac{r}{2}(\frac{1}{2} - 0.5x)$, then $1 - \frac{r}{2}(\frac{1}{2} - 0.5x) = 0$; $x^* = 1 - \frac{4}{r}$, when $r = \{1, 2, 3, \ldots, \infty\}$, then $x^* = \{-3, -1, \frac{-1}{3}, \ldots, 1\}$, $f(x^*) = \{6, -2, \frac{-26}{9} \ldots, -2\}$ and $g(x^*) = \{2, 1, \frac{2}{3}, \ldots, 0\}$, i.e., when $r \to \infty$, $x^* \to 1$, $g(x^*) \to 0$, $rp(x^*) \to 0$, $f(x^*) \to -2$, and $\theta(x^*, r) \to -2$.

Hence, the optimal point is $x^* = 1$, such that $f(x^*) = -2$ and the constraint $g(x^*) = 0$ is satisfied.

Figure 1 illustrates the behavior of the penalty functions; $rp_1(x)$, $rp_2(x)$ and $rp_3(x)$ and the objective function $f(x)$ of the original problem (constrained problem) and the objective function $\theta(x, r)$ of the transformed problem (unconstrained problem) for all $x \in S = [-6, 6]$.

Example 2: minimize $-xy$ s.t $g(x, y) = x + 2y - 4 \le 0$; $\theta(x, y, r) = -xy + \frac{r}{2}(\max\{0, (x + 2y - 4)\}^2)$, if $g(x, y) > 0$; ($g(x, y)$ is violated), the gradient vector is computed by the function $\theta(x, y)$; $g(x, y) = [-y + r(x + 2y - 4), -x + 2r(x + 2y - 4)]$, hence, $(x^*, y^*) = (\frac{2}{1-\frac{1}{4r}}, \frac{1}{1-\frac{1}{4r}})$, then $(x^*, y^*) \to (2, 1)$ as $r \to \infty$; this is why it must allow for the parameters r_k and t_k to increase as long as there exists a violated constraint, i.e., when a process of searching for a solution is an infeasible region.

To ensure that the process of searching for the optimal solution remains within the search domain, the interior-point algorithm is used. Therefore, the next section presents a brief description of this technique.

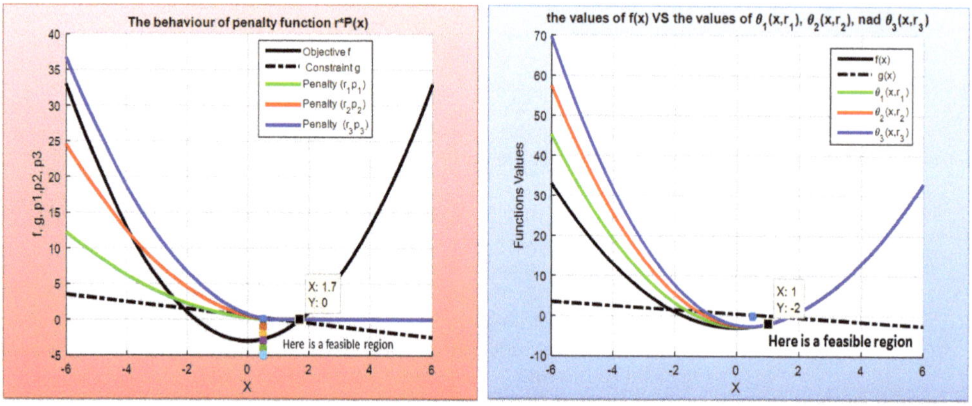

Figure 1. Penalty function $rp(x)$ converges to zero VS $f(x) \rightarrow -2$ and $\theta(r,x) \rightarrow -2$ that is the optimal solution of the constrained problem.

3.3. Interior-Point Method

The interior-point method is used in this paper, when a simple bounded exists in the test problem. Therefore, the interior point technique is used to ensure that the candidate solution lies inside a feasible region. This technique is used as follows at each iteration k, a damping parameter τ_k is applied to insure that x_{k+1} is feasible with respect to the limits $a_i \leq x_i \leq b_i, i = 1, 2, \ldots n$ and $k = 1, 2, \ldots M$ as the inner loop of Algorithm 4, ref. [39].

Algorithm 4 Guided Hybrid Modified Simulated-Annealing Algorithm (GHMSA).

Input: $f(x)$, $g_l(x)$ and $h_d(x) : \mathbb{R}^n \longrightarrow \mathbb{R}$, $x_0 \in \mathbb{R}^n$, $M, T, T_f, T_{out}, \varepsilon, r_0, \Phi_0$ and t_0.

set $x_{ac} = x_0$ ▷ at the beginning we accept the initial point x_0 as an optimal solution.
compute $\theta(x_{ac}) = f(x_{ac}) + \frac{r_k}{2} p_1(x_{ac}) + \frac{t_k}{2} p_2(x_{ac})$ ▷ Using Formula (8).
set $\theta_b = \theta(x_{ac})$ and $\theta_\delta = 1$. ▷ The values of θ_b and $\theta_\delta = 1$ are updated after M iterations.
while $\left(T > T_f \text{ and } \theta_\delta > \varepsilon\right) \text{or} \left(T > T_{out}\right)$ **do** ▷ $T_{out} < T_f \leq 10^{-4}$ are as stopping criteria.
    for $k = 0$ to M **do**
        compute $\theta(x_{ac}) = f(x_{ac}) + \frac{r_k}{2} p_1(x_{ac}) + \frac{t_k}{2} p_2(x_{ac})$.
        set $\theta_{ac} = \theta(x_{ac})$.
        compute $x_1 = x_{ac} + d_k$. ▷ d_k is competed by (16).
        go to Formula (8) to ensure that the point x_1 lies inside $[a, b]^n$ ▷ by Formula (14).
        compute $\Delta\theta = \theta(x_1) - \theta_{ac}$
        if $\Delta\theta < 0$ **then**
            go to Algorithm 1.
        else
            go to Formula (5) to generate other point.
        end if
    end for
    compute $\Phi_{k+1} = \Phi_k + 1$ ▷ here update penalty parameters.
    $T = r_T * T$ ▷ decrease temperature, where $r_T = 0.8$.
    compute $\theta_\delta = |\theta_b - \theta_{ac}|$ and $\theta_b \leftarrow \theta_{ac}$.▷ θ_δ is a stopping criterion when the solutions converge in the accumulation point for all iterations.
end while
Set $x_g \leftarrow x_{ac}, \theta_g \leftarrow \theta_{ac}$
return x_g the global minimizer and the value of the objective function $\theta(x_g)$ at x_g.

The damping parameter τ_k is defined to be:

$$\tau_k = \min\{1, \min_i\{u_k^i, v_k^i\}\}, \tag{11}$$

where

$$u_k^i = \begin{cases} \frac{[a^i - x_k^i]}{\Delta x_k^i} & \text{if } a^i > -\infty \text{ and } \Delta x_k^i < 0, \\ 1, & \text{otherwise,} \end{cases} \tag{12}$$

$$v_k^i = \begin{cases} \frac{[b^i - x_k^i]}{\Delta x_k^i} & \text{if } b^i < \infty \text{ and } \Delta x_k^i > 0, \\ 1 & \text{otherwise,} \end{cases} \tag{13}$$

where a^i and b^i are the lower and upper bounds of the domain of the problem respectively, $i = 1, 2, \ldots n$, n is the number of variables of function in problem, x_k^i is the component ith of variable x at iteration k and Δx_k denotes the steps which are obtained by either Formula (2) or by Formula (5).

Since the $\{x_k\}$ is always required to satisfy, for all k, $a < x_k < b$, and then the point x_{k+1} is computed by:

$$x_{k+1} = x_k + 0.99\tau_k \Delta x_k, \tag{14}$$

where the constant 0.99 is a damping parameter to ensure that x_k is feasible with respect to the domain of function in the problem.

4. The Proposed Algorithm for Solving Constrained Optimization Problems (GHMSA)

According to the above procedures the GLMSA Algorithm is capable of solving Problem (1) as a constrained optimization problem during the solving of Problem (6) as an unconstrained optimization problem, hence there are some changes to the objective function $\theta(x, r)$ in Problem (6) to fit with the first step of the GLMSA Algorithm as follows.

- the function $f(x)$ is replaced by the function $\theta(x, r)$ defined in Equation (8), and then calculate

$$\alpha_k = \frac{\theta(x_{ac})}{\| g(x_{ac}, r_k) \|_2^2}, \tag{15}$$

  where x_{ac} is the accepted solution at iteration k,

$$d_k = -|\alpha_k| g(x_{ac}, r_k), \tag{16}$$

  where the parameter r_k might denote r only or t only or both together according to a type of constrained optimization problem, for example, if the constraints contain mixed constraints inequality and equality, then $r_k = (r_k, t_k)$.
- if the constrained problem contains simple bounded, we use Formula (14) to limit the new point inside this simple bounded.

In light of the above procedures, we rename the GLMSA Algorithm the "Guided Hybrid Modified Simulated-Annealing Algorithm" with the abbreviation "GHMSA".

Setting Parameters of GHMSA Algorithm

The choice of a cooling schedule has an important impact on the performance of the simulated-annealing algorithm. The cooling schedule includes two terms: the initial value of the temperature T and the cooling coefficient r_T which is used to reduce T. Many suggestions have been proposed in the literature for determining the initial value of the temperature T and the cooling coefficient r_T, see for example [4,18,40–42].

In general, it is a unanimous fact that the initial temperature T must be sufficiently high (to ensure escape from local points) and $r_T \in (0.1, 1)$ [7,43,44]. In this section, we suggest that the initial value of T be related to the number of variables and the value of $f(x)$ at the starting point x_0. The cooling coefficient is taken to be $r_T \in [0.8, 1)$ to decrease the temperature T slowly.

Therefore, the parameters used in Algorithm 4 are presented as follows. M is the inner loop maximum number of iterations, T is the control parameter (Temperature), $Tout$ is a final value of T, r_T is the cooling coefficient and T_f is a final value of T if it is sufficiently small.

The setting of parameters is as follows: $T = 10^4$, $\varepsilon = 10^{-6}$, $T_f = 10^{-14}$, $T_{out} = 10^{-20}$, $r_T = 0.8$, and $M = 10\ n$.

5. Numerical Result

To test the effectiveness and efficiency of the proposed algorithm, the algorithm is run on some test problems. The test problems are divided into two sets. The first set of test problems are taken from [45]. They are 24 well-known constrained real-parameter optimization problems. The objective functions in these problems take different shapes and the number of variables is between 2 and 24. These test problems also contain four types of constraints as follows: (LI) denotes a linear inequality, (LE) is a linear equality, (NI) refers to a nonlinear inequality, and (NE) denotes a nonlinear equality. They are listed in Table 1, where $f(x^*)$ is the best known optimal function value and a denotes the active constraint number at the known optimal solution. "The information mentioned in Table 1 is taken from [46]".

Table 1. List of first and second types of test problems and their exact solutions.

pr	n	$f(x^*)$	Kind of Function	LI	NI	LE	NE	a
G1	13	−15	quadratic	9	0	0	0	6
G3	10	−1.0005001000	polynomial	0	0	0	1	1
G4	5	−30,665.5386717834	quadratic	0	6	0	0	2
G5	4	5126.4967140071	cubic	2	0	0	3	3
G6	2	−6961.8138755802	cubic	0	2	0	0	2
G7	10	24.3062090681	quadratic	3	5	0	0	6
G8	2	−0.0958250415	nonlinear	0	2	0	0	0
G9	7	680.6300573745	polynomial	0	4	0	0	2
G10	8	7049.2480205286	linear	3	3	0	0	6
G11	2	0.7499000000	quadratic	0	0	0	1	1
G12	3	−1.0000000000	quadratic	0	1	0	0	0
G13	5	0.0539415140	nonlinear	0	0	0	3	3
G14	10	−47.7648884595	nonlinear	0	0	3	0	3
G15	3	961.7150222899	quadratic	0	0	1	1	2
G16	5	−1.9051552586	nonlinear	4	34	0	0	4
G18	9	−0.8660254038	quadratic	0	13	0	0	6
G19	15	32.6555929502	nonlinear	0	5	0	0	0
G24	10	−5.5080132716	polynomial	0	0	0	1	1

The GHMSA Algorithm solved 18 test problems out of the 24 because the other problems are either not continuous or not differentiable. The second set of test problems contains four known non-linear engineering design optimization problems. These test problems do not have known exact solutions.

5.1. Results of "GHMSA" Algorithm

The GHMSA algorithm is programmed using MATLAB version 8.5.0.197613 (R2015a) and it is run on a personal laptop and the machine epsilon about 1×10^{-16}.

The results of our algorithm are compared against the results of the CB-ABC Algorithm in [47], the CCiALF Algorithm in [48], the NDE Algorithm in [49] and the CAMDE Algorithm in [50].

Liang et al. [45] suggested that the achieved function error values of the obtained optimal solution x after 5×10^3, 5×10^4 and 5×10^5 function evaluations (FES) are summarized in terms of {Best, Median, Worst, c, $\overline{v}$ ($\overline{v} = \frac{p(x)}{q+m}$, $p(x)$ is a penalty term in Equation (7)), Mean, s.d}.

The results are listed in Tables 2–4; where c is a concatenation of three numbers indicating the violated constraint number at the median solution by more than 1.0, between 0.01 and 1.0, and between 0.0001 and 0.1, respectively. $\overline{v}$ is the mean value of the violations of all constraints at the median solution. The numbers in the parenthesis after the error value of the Best, Median, Worst solution are the constraint numbers not satisfying the feasible condition of the Best, Median, and Worst solutions, respectively. Tables 2–4 denote that the GHMSA can determine feasible solutions at each run utilizing 5×10^3 FES for 12 test problems {G01, G03, G04, G06, G08, G09, G10, G12, G13, G16, G18, G24}. As for problems G11, G14 and G15, the GHMSA Algorithm finds feasible solutions by using 5×10^4 FES. For the other three test problems, {G05, G07, G19}, the GHMSA Algorithm is able to reach feasible solutions by using 5×10^5 FES.

Assume that if the result x is a feasible one satisfying $(f(x) - f(x^*) \leq 0.0001$, then x is in a neighborhood (near-optimal) of the optimal point $x^* = x_g$. Tables 2–4 indicate that the GHMSA Algorithm can get near-optimal points for six problems, { G01, G04, G06, G08, G12, G24,} by using only 5×10^3 FES, { G03, G11, G13, G14, G15, G16,G18} by using only 5×10^4 FES and { G07, G09, G13, G19} by using only 5×10^5 FES. However, the GHMSA Algorithm failed to satisfy $(f(x) - f(x^*) \leq 0.0001$, for two problems {G05, G10}. As suggested by [45], Table 5 presents the Best, Median, Worst, Mean, and s.d values of successful run, feasible rate, success rate, and success performance over 40 runs. Let us define the following:

Feasible run: A run through which at least one feasible solution is found in Max FES.
Successful run: A run during which the algorithm finds a feasible solution x satisfying $(f(x) - f(x^*) \leq 0.0001$.
Feasible rate (f.r) = (# of feasible runs)/ total runs.
Successrate(s.r) = (# of successful runs) / total runs.
Successperformance(s.p) = mean (FES for successful runs) × (# of total runs)/(# of successful runs).

Table 2. Error values achieved if FES = 5×10^3, FES = 5×10^4, FES = 5×10^5 for G1, G3, G4, G5, G6 and G7.

FES		G1	G3	G4	G5	G6	G7
	Best	1.93×10^{-05} (0)	2.70×10^{-04} (0)	2.68×10^{-09} (0)	0.02 (3)	8.00×10^{-08} (0)	−1.26 (8)
	Median	8.44×10^{-05} (0)	9.34×10^{-04} (0)	1.5×10^{-05} (0)	0.41 (3)	3.7×10^{-06} (0)	0.206 (8)
	Worst	9.99×10^{-05} (0)	1 (0)	4.25×10^{-05} (0)	13.18 (3)	2.89×10^{-04} (0)	28.16 (8)
5×10^3	c	0, 0, 0	0	0, 0, 0	0, 3, 3	0, 0, 0	0, 8, 8
	$\overline{v}$	0	4.22×10^{-04}	0	0.02	0	0.016
	Mean	8.15×10^{-05}	1.77×10^{-01}	1.9×10^{-05}	1.97	1.7×10^{-05}	6.644
	s.d	1.70×10^{-05}	0.380881	1.48×10^{-05}	3.44	5.5×10^{-05}	9.222
	Best	0 (0)	3.62×10^{-06} (0)	1.09×10^{-11} (0)	0.0016 (3)	8×10^{-08} (0)	−0.07 (4)
	Median	0 (0)	3.64×10^{-06} (0)	8.00×10^{-11} (0)	0.02 (3)	1×10^{-06} (0)	-4.55×10^{-03} (4)
	Worst	0 (0)	3.99×10^{-06} (0)	9.82×10^{-11} (0)	1.32 (3)	4×10^{-05} (0)	0.819 (4)
5×10^4	c	0, 0, 0	0, 0, 0	0, 0, 0	0, 0, 3	0, 0, 0	0, 0, 0, 4
	$\overline{v}$	0	1.51×10^{-06}	0	3.45×10^{-04}	0	2×10^{-04}
	Mean	0	3.71×10^{-06}	6.90×10^{-11}	0.166	5×10^{-06}	−0.04
	s.d	0	1.24×10^{-07}	2.86×10^{-11}	0.3237	8×10^{-06}	0.004
	Best	0 (0)	9.99×10^{-07} (0)	1.09×10^{-11} (0)	0.0016 (0)	8×10^{-08} (0)	-1×10^{-04} (0)
	Median	0 (0)	2.58×10^{-06} (0)	8.00×10^{-11} (0)	0.0233 (0)	1×10^{-06} (0)	-3×10^{-05} (0)
	Worst	0 (0)	8.50×10^{-06} (0)	9.82×10^{-11} (0)	1.3182 (0)	4×10^{-05} (0)	410^{-05} (0)
5×10^5	c	0, 0, 0	0, 0, 0	0, 0, 0	0, 0, 0	0, 0, 0	0, 0, 0
	$\overline{v}$	0	4.05×10^{-07}	0	3.45×10^{-05}	0	2.3×10^{-05}
	Mean	0	2.37×10^{-06}	6.90×10^{-11}	0.166	5×10^{-06}	-4×10^{-05}
	s.d	0	1.92×10^{-06}	2.86×10^{-11}	0.03237	8×10^{-06}	4×10^{-05}

Table 3. Error values achieved when FES = 5×10^3, FES = 5×10^4, FES = 5×10^5 for Problems G8, G9, G10, G11, G12 and G13.

FES		G8	G9	G10	G11	G12	G13
	Best	1.05×10^{-10} (0)	1.0467 (0)	4.77 (0)	1.9×10^{-04} (1)	0 (0)	1.25×10^{-04} (0)
	Median	6.52×10^{-09} (0)	1.494 (0)	17.67 (0)	1.04×10^{-03} (1)	0 (0)	3.83×10^{-03} (0)
	Worst	4.13×10^{-08} (0)	3.42 (0)	300.41 (0)	5.66×10^{-03} (1)	0 (0)	9.83×10^{-02} (0)
5×10^3	c	0, 0, 0	0, 0, 0	0, 0, 0	0, 0, 1	0, 0, 0	0, 0, 0
	$\overline{v}$	0	0	0	0.00173	0	7.27×10^{-05}
	Mean	9.24×10^{-09}	1.863	49.86	0.00161	0	0.01171
	Std	1.20×10^{-08}	0.9631	75.17	0.00151	0	0.02013
	Best	1.05×10^{-10} (0)	0.3489 (0)	0.10 (0)	6.67×10^{-05} (0)	0 (0)	8.96×10^{-06} (0)
	Median	6.52×10^{-09} (0)	4.98×10^{-01} (0)	0.35 (0)	9.60×10^{-05} (0)	0 (0)	6.93×10^{-05} (0)
	Worst	4.13×10^{-08} (0)	1.14 (0)	6.01 (0)	9.96×10^{-05} (0)	0 (0)	2.94×10^{-04} (0)
5×10^4	c	0, 0, 0	0, 0, 0	0, 0, 0	0, 0, 0	0, 0, 0	0, 0, 0
	$\overline{v}$	0	0	0	4.72×10^{-06}	0	2.02×10^{-06}
	Mean	9.24×10^{-09}	6.21×10^{-01}	1.00	9.60×10^{-05}	0	4.39×10^{-05}
	Std	1.20×10^{-08}	0.321034	1.50	1.70×10^{-06}	0	6.53×10^{-05}
	Best	1.05×10^{-10} (0)	6.58×10^{-05} (0)	0.02 (0)	6.67×10^{-05} (0)	0 (0)	8.50×10^{-06} (0)
	Median	6.52×10^{-09} (0)	8.53×10^{-05} (0)	0.09 (0)	9.60×10^{-05} (0)	0 (0)	5.70×10^{-05} (0)
	Worst	4.13×10^{-08} (0)	9.88×10^{-05} (0)	1.50 (0)	9.96×10^{-05} (0)	0 (0)	9.90×10^{-05} (0)
5×10^5	c	0, 0, 0	0, 0, 0	0, 0, 0	0, 0, 0	0, 0, 0	0, 0, 0
	$\overline{v}$	0	0	0	4.72×10^{-06}	0	4.90×10^{-07}
	Mean	9.24×10^{-09}	8.38×10^{-05}	0.25	9.60×10^{-05}	0	5.50×10^{-05}
	Std	1.20×10^{-08}	1.52×10^{-05}	0.38	1.70×10^{-06}	0	2.70×10^{-05}

Table 4. Error values achieved when FES = 5×10^3, FES = 5×10^4, FES = 5×10^5 for Problems G14, G15, G16, G18, G19 and G24.

FES		G14	G15	G16	G18	G19	G24
	Best	4.25×10^{-01} (3)	-5.83×10^{-02} (2)	4.31×10^{-04} (0)	0.01 (0)	-5.58×10^{-02} (3)	5.10×10^{-12} (0)
	Median	1.4 (3)	0.18 (2)	0.0064 (0)	0.21 (0)	4.28×10^{-01} (3)	9.05×10^{-12} (0)
	Worst	1.53 (3)	55.40 (2)	0.0181 (0)	0.79 (0)	27.6 (3)	9.99×10^{-12} (0)
5×10^3	c	0, 3, 3	0, 1, 2	0, 0, 0	0, 0, 0	0, 0, 3	0, 0, 0
	$\overline{v}$	2.62×10^{-02}	1.16×10^{-03}	0	0	9.80×10^{-03}	0
	Mean	1.23	2.60	0.0076	0.27	4.07	8.57×10^{-12}
	s.d	0.40	10.79	0.0046	0.21	7.69	1.32×10^{-12}
	Best	2.85×10^{-07} (0)	1.12×10^{-07} (0)	7.70×10^{-11} (0)	4.51×10^{-06} (0)	-5.58×10^{-03} (3)	5.10×10^{-12} (0)
	Median	4.68×10^{-05} (0)	6.96×10^{-06} (0)	8.40×10^{-11} (0)	7.97×10^{-05} (0)	4.28×10^{-02} (3)	9.05×10^{-12} (0)
	Worst	9.11×10^{-05} (0)	4.75×10^{-04} (0)	8.90×10^{-11} (0)	9.88×10^{-05} (0)	2.76 (3)	9.99×10^{-12} (0)
5×10^4	c	0, 0, 0	0, 0, 0	0, 0, 0	0, 0, 0	0, 0, 3	0, 0, 0
	$\overline{v}$	3.62×10^{-05}	8.10×10^{-06}	0	0	9.80×10^{-04}	0
	Mean	5.17×10^{-05}	5.08×10^{-05}	8.40×10^{-11}	6.83×10^{-05}	4.07×10^{-01}	8.57×10^{-12}
	s.d	2.42×10^{-05}	1.20×10^{-04}	3.40×10^{-12}	2.65×10^{-05}	0.76855	1.32×10^{-12}
	Best	2.85×10^{-07} (0)	1.12×10^{-07} (0)	7.70×10^{-11} (0)	4.51×10^{-06} (0)	-9.94×10^{-05} (0)	5.10×10^{-12} (0)
	Median	4.68×10^{-05} (0)	6.96×10^{-06} (0)	8.40×10^{-11} (0)	7.97×10^{-05} (0)	-3.21×10^{-05} (0)	9.05×10^{-12} (0)
	Worst	9.11×10^{-05} (0)	4.75×10^{-04} (0)	8.90×10^{-11} (0)	9.88×10^{-05} (0)	8.70×10^{-05} (0)	9.99×10^{-12} (0)
5×10^5	c	0, 0, 0	0, 0, 0	0, 0, 0	0, 0, 0	0, 0, 0	0, 0, 0
	$\overline{v}$	3.62×10^{-05}	8.10×10^{-06}	0	0	8.09×10^{-05}	0
	Mean	5.17×10^{-05}	5.08×10^{-05}	8.40×10^{-11}	6.83×10^{-05}	-1.86×10^{-05}	8.57×10^{-12}
	s.d	2.42×10^{-05}	1.20×10^{-04}	3.40×10^{-12}	2.65×10^{-05}	6.76×10^{-05}	1.32×10^{-12}

Table 5 shows that the GHMSA Algorithm obtains a 100% feasible rate and success rate for all 18 problems with the exception of problems G05 and G10.

Table 5. Number of FES to achieve the fixed accuracy level $((f(x) - f(x^*)) \leq 0.0001)$, success rate, feasible rate and success performance.

pr	Best	Median	Worst	Mean	s.d	f.r (%)	s.r (%)	s.p
G1	1964	2360	2748	2386.68	172.3774278	100	100	2386.68
G3	7681	11,558	13,545	11,566.82353	1167.105632	100	100	11,566.82353
G4	1906	4417	4924	4295.6	563.9451037	100	100	4295.6
G5	-	-	-	-	-	0	0	-
G6	3628	4455	5409	4388.851852	390.8762903	100	100	4388.851852
G7	34,773	210,502	500,559	259,738.33	224,164.15	100	100	259,738.33
G8	794	1108	1350	1109.9615	133.37526	100	100	1109.9615
G9	417,565	4.33×10^{05}	495,232	444,552.9	31,764.59	100	100	444,552.9
G10	-	-	-	-	-	0	0	-
G11	6248	8146	9877	8233.92	917.8058	100	100	8233.92
G12	117	230	339	226.6	57.190209	100	100	226.6
G13	12,800	37,261	80,814	42,242.04	17,190.94051	100	100	42242.04
G14	28,366	54,687	71,293	52,486.30769	16,047.27821	100	100	52,486.30769
G15	9258	25,435	90,720	30,647.44	19,355.55703	100	100	30,647.44
G16	5758	9199	11,398	8970.76	1060.014463	100	100	8970.76
G18	10,300	36,198	85,882	42,434.56	20,906.48809	100	100	42,434.56
G19	73,800	193,000	499,000	247,000	187,852.1	100	100	247,000
G24	537	755.5	999	744.846154	103.587456	100	100	744.846154

For achieving the success condition during the view of success performance in Table 5, the GHMSA Algorithm needs:

(1) $117 \leq \text{FES} \leq 4.924 \times 10^3$ for 5 problems i.e., {G01, G04, G08, G12, G24}.

(2) $3628 \leq \text{FES} \leq 1.4 \times 10^4$ for 4 problems i.e., {G03, G06, G11, G16}.

(3) $9258 \leq \text{FES} \leq 90{,}720$ for 4 problems i.e., {G13, G14, G15, G18}.

(4) $34{,}773 \leq \text{FES} \leq 500{,}559$ for 3 problems i.e., {G07, G09, G19}.

The GHMSA Algorithm failed to achieve the success condition for two problems, i.e., {G05, G10}. More information about the performance of the GHMSA Algorithm for solving these problems is given in Figures 2–4. We have plotted the relationship between $log_{10}(f(x) - f(x^*))$ and FES for showing the convergence of the GHMSA at the median run over 40 independent runs. So the convergence graphs of these problems in Figures 2–4 show that the error values decrease dramatically with increasing FES for all test problems.

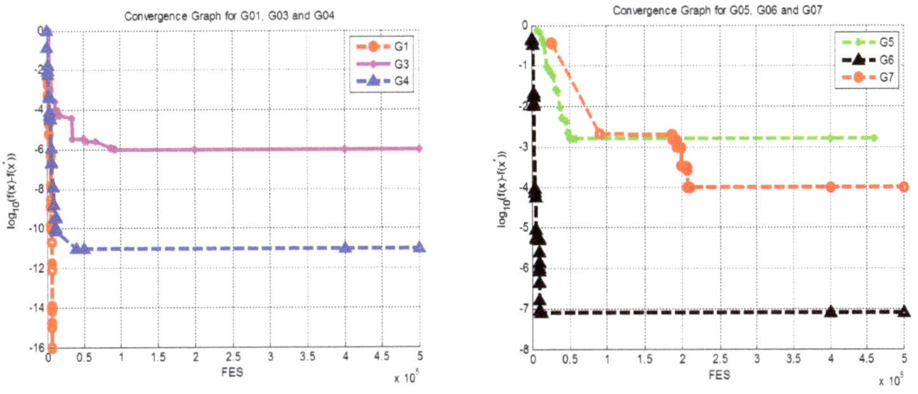

Figure 2. Convergence graph for G01 to G07.

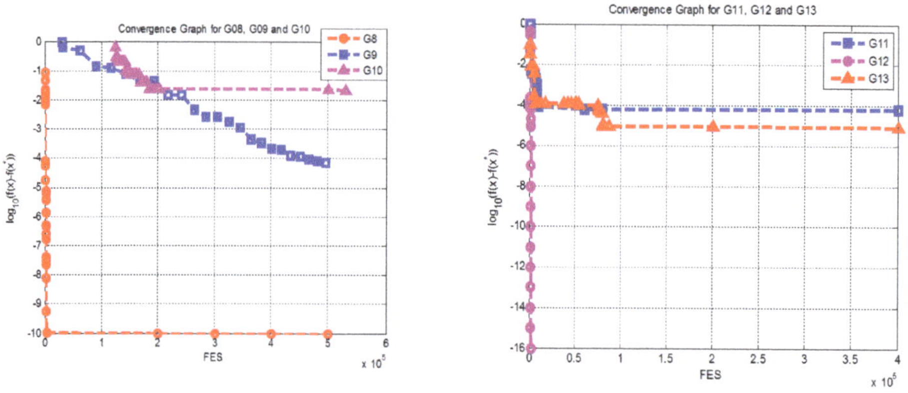

Figure 3. Convergence graph for G08 to G13.

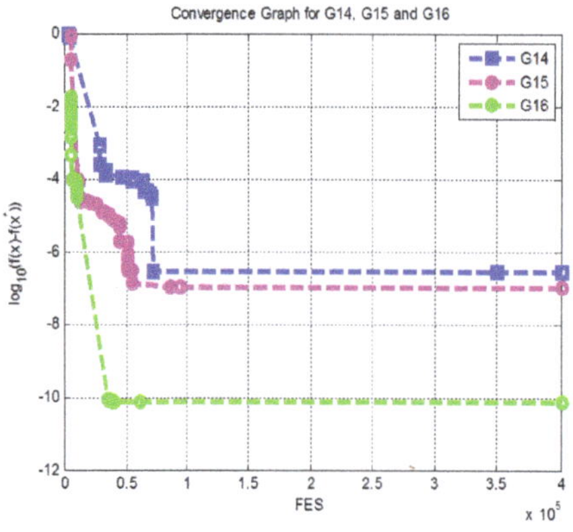

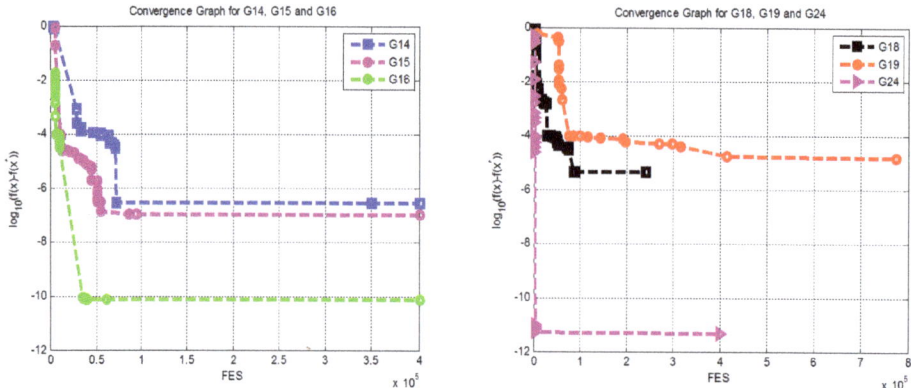

Figure 4. Convergence graph for G14 to G24.

5.2. Performance of GHMSA Algorithm Using Statistical Hypothesis Testing

In this section, we use statistical hypothesis testing to evaluate the efficiency of the GHMSA Algorithm versus the efficiency of the CB-ABC, the CCiALF, the NDE and the CAMDE Algorithms.

A statistical hypothesis is a surmise about a population parameter. This expectation might be true or false. The null hypothesis is denoted by H_0, and it is a statistical hypothesis that announces that there is no difference between a parameter and a specific value or that there is no difference between two parameters. The alternative hypothesis is indicated by H_a, and it is a statistical hypothesis that declares a specific difference between a parameter and a specific value or states that there is a difference between two parameters. Hypothesis testing is a form of inferential statistic which authorizes us to draw conclusions on a whole population based on a representative sample [51]. Parametric tests can provide trustworthy results with distributions that are skewed and non normal. Parametric analysis can produce reliable results even if the continuous data are non normally distributed. We just have to be sure that the sample size is greater than 30. A one sample t-test is one of the parametric tests that is used to compare the mean (Average) of a sample with a mean of the population. The important conditions for using the one-sample t-test are independence and normality (or sample size > 30). In our study the sample size is 50, i.e., the number of runs is 50 randomly (from any starting point) run; this criterion is suggested by [45]. The significance level in this study is 95%, i.e., $\alpha = 0.05$. Our hypotheses are formulated in the following:

H_0: the mean (average) of the results of the GHMSA Algorithm and the mean (average) of the results of other algorithms are equal.

H_a: the mean (average) of the results of the GHMSA Algorithm and the mean of the results of other algorithms are different.

The above hypotheses can be formulated in Equation (17).

$$\begin{aligned} H_0 &: Me_{GHMSA} = Me_{Algorithm_l}, \\ H_a &: Me_{GHMSA} \neq Me_{Algorithm_l}, \end{aligned} \tag{17}$$

where l denotes one of the algorithms, CB-ABC, CCiALF, NDE and CAMDE, and *Me* denotes the average results of the algorithms.

In order to compare the performance of the GHMSA Algorithm with the CB-ABC, the CCiALF, the NDE and the CAMDE Algorithms, the *t*-test with a significance level of $\alpha = 0.05$ is performed. To perform the *t*-test, the hypotheses in Equation (17) are considered.

Statistical processes are performed by using the SPSS Program. Rejecting or accepting H_0 is based on the value of the p-value (Sig. (2-tailed)) according to Column 1 of Table 6. While the performance of the algorithm based on the value of the *t*-test is in Column 3 of Table 6. So, Column 4 of Table 6 takes three values according to the probabilities in (18).

$$\text{Decision} = \begin{cases} 1 & \text{then } Me_{GHMSA} < Me_{Algorithm_{al}}, \\ -1 & \text{then } Me_{GHMSA} > Me_{Algorithm_l}, \\ 0 & \text{then } Me_{GHMSA} = Me_{Algorithm_l}. \end{cases} \tag{18}$$

The results of the GHMSA are compared to the results of the CB-ABC, the CCiALF, the NDE and the CAMDE Algorithms. The statistical hypotheses in Equation (17) are tested by using the *t*-test. Tables 7–10 present these results.

The results of the GHMSA are compared versus the four meta-heuristic algorithms in the literature. The results of statistical tests are presented in Tables 7, 9 and 10. In Table 7, Column 1 presents the abbreviation of the test problems denoted by pr. Column 2 presents the results of the s.t which include {b.s, mean, s.d, Decision }, where Decision denotes wins, losses and draws of the GHMSA compared with the other algorithms. Columns 3–7 give the results of the five algorithms. Tables 9 and 10 are similar to Table 7.

After executing the pairwise *t*-test for all algorithms, if the GHMSA Algorithm is superior, inferior or equal to the compared algorithm denoted by $algorithm_l$, then the decision is set to 1, −1 and 0 respectively, as we have shown in Table 6. The left of Figure 5 summarizes the results that are presented in Tables 7–10 regarding the decision. The left of Figure 5 shows that the GHMSA Algorithm was superior at {7, 6, 9, 5 } problems, equal at {6, 6, 3, 5 } problems and inferior at {4, 5, 5, 7 } problems compared to the CB-ABC, the CALF, the NDE and the CAMDE Algorithms, respectively. However, the GHMSA is inferior at seven problems compared to the CAMDE, but the GHMSA needs 1,590,905 as a total FES versus the CAMDE needing 4,320,000, as shown in Figure 6. To gain the success condition from the point of view of successful execution, the GHMSA needs less than 5×10^3 FES for five problems, i.e., {G01, G04, G08, G12, G24} versus the CAMDE needing at least 5×10^3 FES for two problems, i.e., {G08, G12}. We can say that the percentage of superior, equal and inferior of the GHMSA are 40%, 30%, 30% respectively.

Table 6. How the null hypothesis is rejected (or accepted) and the decision is made.

p-Value	H_0	t	Decision
$<\alpha$	reject	<0	1
$<\alpha$	reject	>0	−1
$>\alpha$	accept	-	0

Table 7. Comparison of results for test problems G01 to G08.

pr	s.t	CB-ABC	CCiALF	NDE	CAMDE	GHMSA
G1	b.s	−15	−15	−15	−15	−15
	mean	−15	−15	−15	−15	−15
	s.d	5.03×10^{-15}	2.39×10^{-08}	0	0	0
	decision	0	0	0	0	0
	FES	135,180	30,819	240,000	240,000	5773.84
G3	b.s	−1.0005	−1.000501	−1.0005001	−1.000500	−1.000009
	mean	−1.0005	−1.000501	−1.0005001	−1.000500	−1.000002
	s.d	3.64×10^{-07}	1.69×10^{-08}	0	6.80×10^{-16}	1.92×10^{-06}
	decision	‡	‡	‡	‡	
	FES	90,090	87,860	240,000	240,000	62,546.38462
G4	b.s	−30,665.54	−30,665.539	−30,665.539	−30,665.53867	−30,665.53867
	mean	−30,665.54	−30,665.539	−30,665.539	−30,665.53867	−30,665.53867
	s.d	8.72×10^{-11}	9.80×10^{-06}	0	3.71×10^{-12}	3.49×10^{-07}
	decision	0	0	0	0	
	FES	45,045	26,268	240,000	240,000	9671.32
G5	b.s	5126.50	5126.4967	5126.49671	5126.496710	5126.49833
	mean	5126.50	5126.497	5126.49671	5126.496710	5126.662712
	s.d	1.07×10^{-10}	9.17×10^{-08}	0	2.78×10^{-12}	0.03442
	decision	−1	−1	−1	−1	
	FES	135,180	156,248	240,000	240,000	33,917.7702
G6	b.s	−6961.81	−6961.814	−6961.813875	−6961.81388	−6961.813826
	mean	−6961.81	−6961.814	−6961.813875	−6961.81388	−6961.813811
	s.d	1.82×10^{-12}	5.19×10^{-11}	0	0	9.20×10^{-06}
	decision	1	0	1	1	
	FES	45,045	17,573	240,000	240,000	8921.518519
G7	b.s	24.3062	24.3062	24.306209	24.30621	24.30610911
	mean	24.3062	24.3062	24.306209	24.30621	24.30617
	s.d	4.16×10^{-07}	6.82×10^{-07}	1.35×10^{-14}	8.55×10^{-15}	4.34×10^{-05}
	decision	1	1	1	1	
	FES	135,180	8745	240,000	240,000	259,738.33
G8	b.s	−0.095825	−0.095825	−0.095825	−0.09583	−0.0958141
	mean	−0.095825	−0.095825	−0.095825	−0.09583	−0.0957819
	s.d	2.87×10^{-17}	1.07×10^{-15}	0	1.42×10^{-17}	2.58×10^{-05}
	decision	1	1	1	−1	
	FES	8000	4812	240,000	240, 000	2394.577

The mark ‡ means that we do not use G03 to compare the result of the GHMSA with results of the four algorithms because the $h(x^*) = 0.0001$, i.e., $\overline{v} = 0.0001$ in [45], but $\overline{v}$ for the GHMSA is 4.05×10^{-07}, see Tables 1, 2 and 8.

Table 8. Statistical results of "GHMSA" Algorithm for first set of test problems and four mechanical engineering problems.

pr	Best	Median	Worst	Mean	s.d	FES
G1	−15	−15	−15	−15	0	5773.84
G3	−1.000009	−1.000003	−1.000001	−1.000002	1.91679×10^{-06}	62,546.38462
G4	−30,665.538672	−30,665.538672	−30,665.53867	−30,665.538672	3.49×10^{-07}	9671.32
G5	5126.49833	5126.520053	5127.81491	5126.662712	0.03442	33,917.7702
G6	−6961.813826	−6961.813811	−6961.81377	−6961.813811	9.19642×10^{-06}	8921.518519
G7	24.30610911	24.30618042	24.30625377	24.30617	4.34×10^{-05}	259,738.33
G8	−0.0958141	−0.095824999	−0.09582499	−0.0957819	2.58×10^{-05}	2394.577
G9	680.6301232	680.6301426	680.6301562	680.6301412	1.52×10^{-05}	444,552.9
G10	7049.271862	7049.689888	7049.460323	7049.336552	2.69×10^{-02}	290,146
G11	0.74999176	0.749996	0.75	0.7499961	0.0000001	8233.92
G12	−1	−1	−1	−1	0	1515
G13	0.053950002	0.053998358	0.054040318	0.053996327	2.73×10^{-05}	53,754
G14	−47.76497953	−47.76493525	−47.76488874	−47.76494056	2.51×10^{-05}	52,486.30769
G15	961.71502	961.71502	961.715107	961.7149837	1.31×10^{-04}	38,609.24

Table 8. *Cont.*

pr	Best	Median	Worst	Mean	s.d	FES
G16	−1.905155259	−1.905155259	−1.905155259	−1.905155259	2.06×10^{-10}	36,346.76
G18	−0.866025404	−0.865945746	−0.865926597	−0.865958115	2.85×10^{-05}	42,434.56
G19	32.65549	32.65556	32.65568	32.6555744	6.76×10^{-05}	247,295.25
G24	−5.508013272	−5.508013272	−5.508013272	−5.508013272	1.09×10^{-10}	2460.038
Enp1	5885.332773	5885.332773	5885.332773	5885.332773	2.2×10^{-12}	32,129
Enp2	0.012665233	0.012665268	0.012665243	0.012665334	1.54×10^{-09}	9970
Enp3	1.724852306	1.724852306	1.724852306	1.724852306	1.33×10^{-16}	24,270
Enp4	2994.471066	2994.471066	2994.471066	2994.471066	4.27×10^{-15}	16,764

Table 9. Comparison of results for test problems G09 to G15.

pr	s.t	CB-ABC	CCiALF	NDE	CAMDE	GHMSA
G9	b.s	680.63	680.63	680.630057	680.63006	680.6301232
	mean	680.63	680.63	680.630057	680.63006	680.6301412
	s.d	2.77×10^{-09}	5.43×10^{-08}	0	2.32×10^{-13}	1.52×10^{-05}
	decision	0	0	−1	−1	
	FES	45,045	12,801	240,000	240,000	444,552.9
G10	b.s	7049.25	7049.248	7049.24802	7049.24802	7049.271862
	mean	7049.25	7049.248	7049.24802	7049.24802	7049.336552
	s.d	3.98×10^{-05}	6.04×10^{-07}	3.41×10^{-09}	4.39×10^{-12}	2.69×10^{-02}
	decision	−1	−1	−1	−1	
	FES	135,180	2858	240,000	240,000	240,146
G11	b.s	0.7499	0.749896	0.749999	0.749900	0.74999176
	mean	0.7499	0.749898	0.749999	0.749900	0.7499961
	s.d	1.29×10^{-10}	2.05×10^{-16}	0	1.13×10^{-16}	0.0000001
	decision	−1	−1	1	−1	
	FES	90,090	168,448	240,000	240,000	8233.92
G12	b.s	−1	−1	−1	−1	−1
	mean	−1	−1	−1	−1	−1
	s.d	0	7.76×10^{-11}	0	0	0
	decision	0	0	0	0	
	FES	13,500	17,892	240,000	240,000	1515
G13	b.s	0.053942	0.053942	0.0539415	0.05394	0.053950002
	mean	0.06677	0.053943	0.0539415	0.05394	0.053996327
	s.d	6.91×10^{-02}	4.03×10^{-06}	0	2.32×10^{-17}	2.73×10^{-05}
	decision	1	−1	−1	−1	
	FES	198,270	19,883	240,000	240,000	53,754
G14	b.s	−47.7649	−47.764900	−47.7648885	−47.764890	−47.76497953
	mean	−47.7649	−47.764900	−47.7648885	−47.764890	−47.76494056
	s.d	1.02×10^{-05}	4.04×10^{-08}	5.14×10^{-15}	2.21×10^{-14}	2.51×10^{-05}
	decision	1	1	1	1	
	FES	239,715	152,697	240,000	240,000	52,486.30769
G15	b.s	961.715	961.715	961.7150223	961.715020	961.71502
	mean	961.715	961.715	961.7150223	961.715020	961.7149837
	s.d	2.81×10^{-11}	1.86×10^{-08}	0	5.80×10^{-13}	1.31×10^{-04}
	decision	0	0	1	1	
	FES	135, 180	77, 910	240, 000	240, 000	38, 609.24

For the four engineering problems, we give a brief description. The pressure vessel problem is a practical problem that is often used as a benchmark problem for testing optimization algorithms [52]. The left of Figure 7 shows the structure of this issue, where a cylindrical pressure vessel is capped at both ends by hemispherical heads. The aim of the problem is to find the minimum total cost of fabrication, including costs from a combination of welding, material and forming. The thickness of the cylindrical skin,$x_1(Ts)$, thickness of the spherical head, $x_2(T_h)$, the inner radius, $x_3(R)$, and the length of the cylindrical segment of the vessel, $x_4(L)$, were included as the optimization design variables of the problem. The GHMSA Algorithm obtains these results: $x_{GHMSA} = \{0.778168641375105, 0.384649162627902, 40.3196187240987, 200\}$, i.e.,

$f(x_{GHMSA}) = 5885.332774$, c = {0, –3.8858 × 10^{-16}, 1.1642 × 10^{-97}, -40}, i.e., $\overline{v} = 0$; the left of Figure 8 shows a convergence graph of the GHMSA to the best solution for this problem.

Table 10. Comparison of results for test problems G16, G18, G19, G24 and Enp1-Enp4.

pr	s.t	CB-ABC	CCiALF	NDE	CAMDE	GHMSA
G16	b.s	−1.905	−1.905155	−1.90515525	−1.905160	−1.905155259
	mean	−1.905	−1.905155	−1.90515525	−1.905160	−1.905155259
	s.d	7.90×10^{-11}	9.77×10^{-09}	0	4.53×10^{-16}	2.06×10^{-10}
	decision	1	1	1	0	
	FES	45,045	196,196	240,000	240,000	36,346.76
G18	b.s	−0.866025	−0.866026	−0.8660254	−0.86603	−0.866025404
	mean	−0.866025	−0.866026	−0.8660254	−0.86603	−0.865958115
	s.d	1.72×10^{-08}	3.58×10^{-07}	0	4.53×10^{-17}	2.85×10^{-05}
	decision	−1	−1	−1	−1	
	FES	135,180	8742	240,000	240,000	42,434.56
G19	b.s	32.6556	32.655610	32.65559377	32.655590	32.65549
	mean	32.6556	32.660770	32.65562603	32.655590	32.6555744
	s.d	1.88×10^{-05}	2.35×10^{-04}	3.73×10^{-05}	7.11×10^{-15}	6.76×10^{-05}
	decision	0	1	1	0	
	FES	198,270	240,000	240,000	240,000	247,295.25
G24	b.s	−5.508	−5.508013	−5.50801327	−5.508010	−5.508013272
	mean	−5.508	−5.508013	−5.50801327	−5.508010	−5.508013272
	s.d	7.15×10^{-15}	1.30×10^{-08}	0	9.06×10^{-16}	1.09×10^{-10}
	decision	1	1	1	1	
	FES	27,000	6450	240,000	240,000	2460.038
Enp1	b.s	6059.71	6059.714335	6059.714335	6059.714335	5885.332773
	mean	6126.62	6059.714335	6059.714335	6059.714335	5885.332773
	s.d	1.14×10^{02}	1.01×10^{-11}	4.56×10^{-07}	1.22×10^{-06}	2.2×10^{-12}
	Decision	1	1	1	1	
	FES	15,000	12,000	20,000	10,000	32,1290
Enp2	b.s	0.012665	0.012665233	0.012665232	0.012665233	0.01266523
	mean	0.012671	0.012665251	0.012668899	0.012666981	0.01266533
	s.d	1.42×10^{-05}	9.87×10^{-08}	5.38×10^{-06}	3.65×10^{-06}	1.54×10^{-09}
	Decision	1	0	1	1	
	FES	15,000	5000	24,000	10,000	9970
Enp3	b.s	1.724852	1.724852	1.724852309	1.724852	1.724852
	mean	1.724852	1.724852	1.724852309	1.724852	1.724852
	s.d	0	5.11×10^{-07}	3.73×10^{-12}	2.32×10^{-13}	1.33×10^{-16}
	Decision	0	0	1	0	
	FES	15,000	10,000	8000	10,000	24,270
Enp4	b.s	2994.471066	2994.471066	2994.471066	2994.471066	2994.471065
	mean	2994.471066	2994.4710660	2994.47106610	2994.471066	2994.471065
	s.d	2.48×10^{-07}	2.31×10^{-12}	4.17×10^{-12}	2.20×10^{-12}	4.27×10^{-15}
	Decision	0	0	1	0	
	FES	15,000	10,000	18,000	10,000	16,764

Another well-known engineering optimization task is the design of a tension (compression spring) for a minimum weight. This problem has been studied by several authors. For example, [52]. The right of Figure 7 shows a tension (compression spring) with three design variables. It needs to minimize the weight of a tension (compression string) subject to constraints on minimum deflection, shear stress, surge frequency, limits on outside diameter and on design variables. The design variables are the wire diameter, $d(x_1)$, the mean coil diameter, $D(x_2)$, and the number of active coils, $P(x_3)$. The GHMSA obtains these results: x_{GHMSA} = {0.0516890825110813, 0.356718255308635, 11.2889355307237}, i.e., $f(x_{GHMSA}) = 0.01266523279$, c = {-1.55×10^{-10}, 4.44×10^{-16}, –4.05379, –0.72773}, i.e., $\overline{v} = 1.11 \times 10^{-16}$. The convergence graph for Engp2 is presented on the right of Figure 8. The welded beam design optimization problem has been solved by many researchers [52]. The left of Figure 9 shows the welded beam structure which consists of a beam A and the weld required to hold it to member B. The goal of this problem is to minimize the overall cost of fabrication, subject to some constraints. This problem has four design variables—x_1,

x_2, x_3 and x_4—with constraints of shear stress τ, bending stress in the beam σ, buckling load on the bar P_c, and end deflection on the beam δ. The GHMSA obtains these results: $x_{GHMSA} = \{0.205729642092758, 3.4704886133955, 9.03662391715327, 0.205729639752274\}$, i.e., $f(x_{GHMSA}) = 1.7248523060$, $c = \{-9.03 \times 10^{-08}, -4.02 \times 10^{-05}, 2.34 \times 10^{-09}, -3.43298, -0.08073, -0.23554, -8.73 \times 10^{-09}\}$, i.e., $\overline{v} = 3.3429 \times 10^{-10}$. The convergence graph for Engp3 is presented by the left of Figure 10.

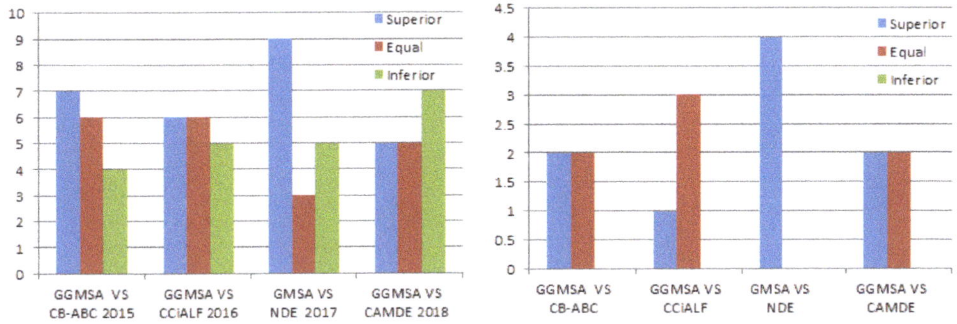

Figure 5. The number of "wins-draws-losses" of GHMSA compared with other algorithms for G01 to G24 and Enp1 to Enp4.

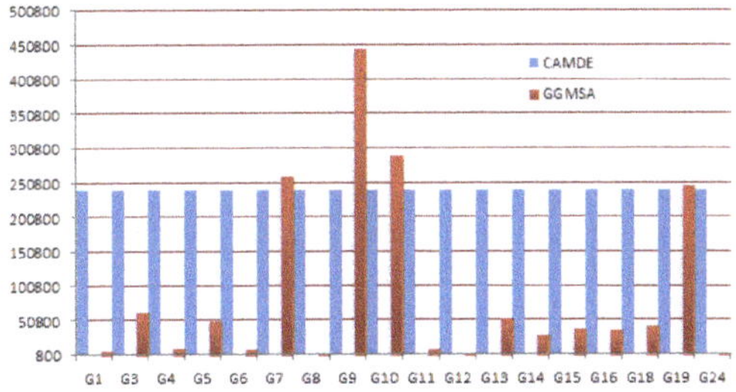

Figure 6. Comparison Between GHMSA With CAMDE Regarding FES.

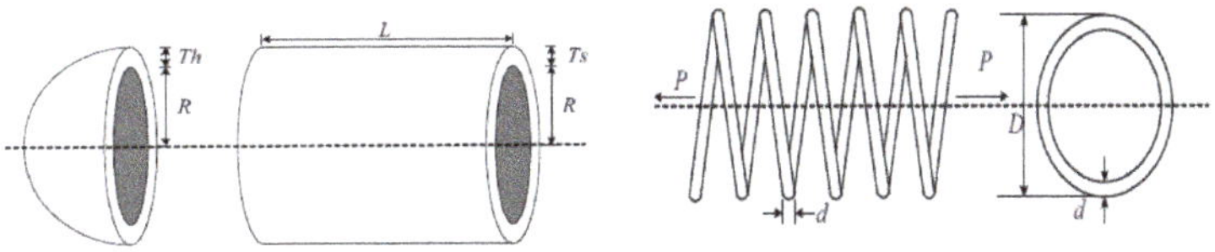

Figure 7. Design engineering problems (Engp1 and Engp2).

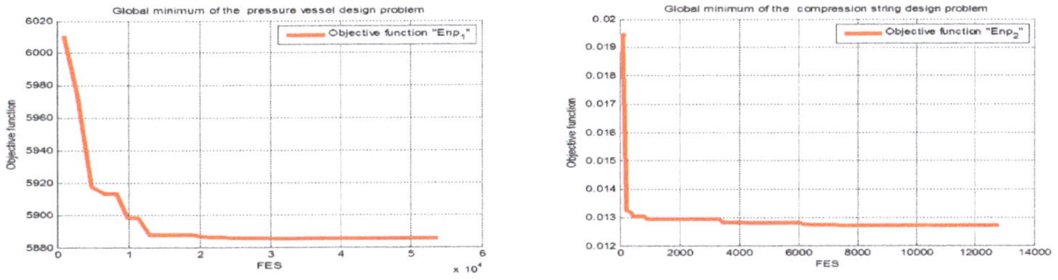

Figure 8. Convergence graph for engineering problems (Engp1 and Engp2).

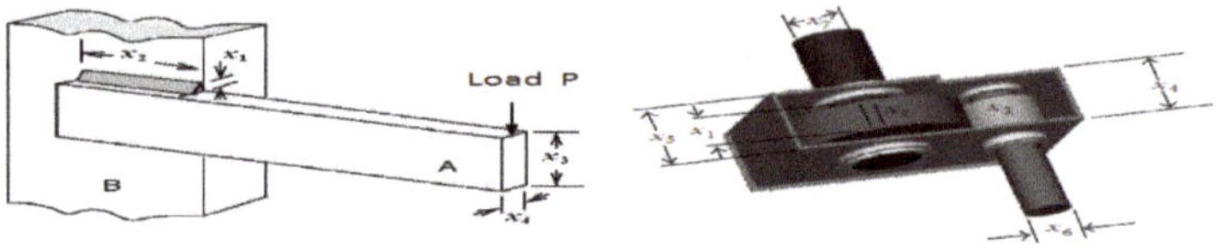

Figure 9. Design engineering problems (Engp3 and Engp4).

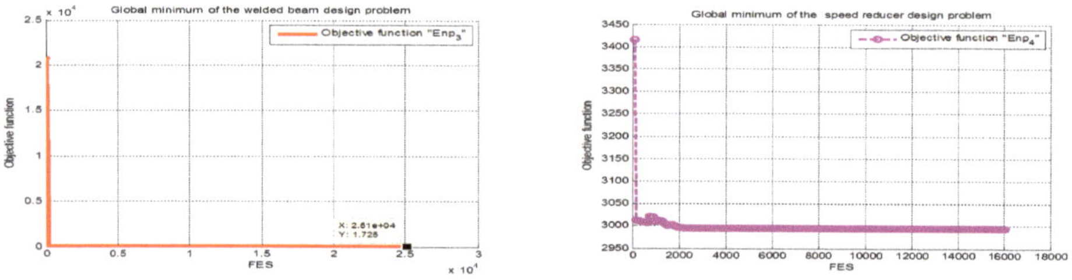

Figure 10. Convergence graph for engineering problems (Engp3 and Engp4).

The speed reducer design problem is one of the benchmark structural engineering problems [52]. It has seven design variables as described in the right of Figure 9, with the face width x_1, module of teeth x_2, number of teeth on pinion x_3, length of the first shaft between bearings x_4, length of the second shaft between bearings x_5, diameter of the first shaft x_6, and diameter of the first shaft x_7. The aim of this problem is to minimize the total weight of the decelerator. The GHMSA obtains these results: $x_{GHMSA} = \{3.499999999, 0.7, 17, 7.3, 7.715319913, 3.350214666, 5.286654465\}$, i.e., $f(x_{GHMSA}) = 2994.471066$, $c = \{-0.073915, -0.198, -0.49917, -0.90464, 8.6365 \times 10^{-11}, -1.0931 \times 10^{-11}, -0.7025, 2.86 \times 10^{-10}, -0.58333, -0.051326, -1.944210^{-10}\}$, i.e, $\overline{v} = 2.6 \times 10^{-11}$. The convergence graph for Engp4 is presented by the right of Figure 10. The four engineering problems are used to compare the performance of the GHMSA against the CB-ABC, the CCiALF, the NDE and the CAMDE Algorithms. Statistical hypotheses in Equation (17) are used to compare the mean of the GHMSA with means of the CB-ABC, the CCiALF, the NDE and the CAMDE Algorithms. Rows 22–41 of Table 10 present the statistical comparisons of the GHMSA versus the four Algorithms for engineering problems Enp1 to Enp4. The right of Figure 5 gives the number of "wins-draws-losses" of the GHMSA compared with the CB-ABC, the CCiALF, the NDE and the CAMDE for Enp1 to Enp4. Figure 11 shows the convergence graph of standard deviation for problems Enp1, Enp2, Enp3 and Enp4 for the five algorithms. The relation between the four engineering problems {Enp1, Enp2, Enp3 and Enp4} and their values for $log_{10}(s.d)$ are plotted. From the right of Figures 5 and 11, it can be said that the performance of the GHMSA algorithm is better than the other algorithms for problems Enp1 to Enp4, for the following reasons:

(1) The GHMSA obtains a minimum value of objective function (5885.332774) for engineering problem Enp1 (pressure vessel), the point minimum x^* is feasible; many of the algorithms obtained a value of objective function equal to or greater than 6059.71. see for example [48–50,52–58].

In addition to that, if $10 \leq x_4(L) < \infty$, then $f(x^*) = 5804.37621675626$, otherwise if $10 \leq x_4(L) < 208$, then $f(x^*) = 5866.99226593889$, where L is shown in the left of Figure 8.

(2) The right of Figure 5 shows that the GHMSA Algorithm does not fall at any problem versus the other algorithms.

(3) The GHMSA is superior at {2, 1, 4, 2} problems versus the CB-ABC Algorithm, the CCiALF Algorithm, the NDE and the CAMDE Algorithm, respectively.

(4) The GHMSA is equal at {2, 3, 0, 2} problems versus the CB-ABC Algorithm, the CCiALF Algorithm, the NDE and the CAMDE Algorithm, respectively.

(5) Figure 11 shows that the GHMSA Algorithm converges to zero for the standard deviation (s.d). See the green color.

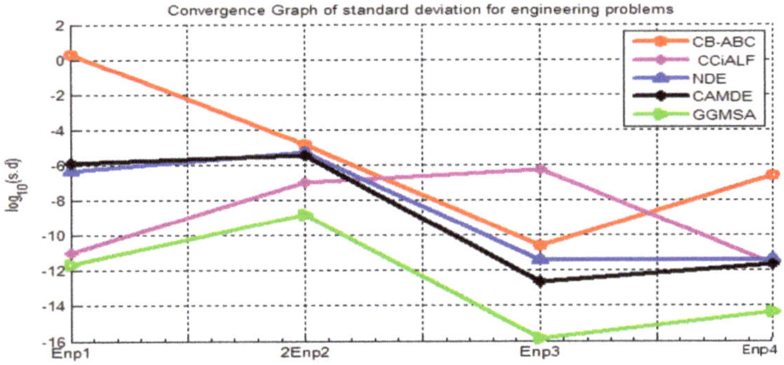

Figure 11. Convergence graph of standard deviation for Enp1 to Enp4.

6. Conclusions and Future Work

The unconstrained nonlinear optimization algorithms have been guided to find the global minimizer of the constrained optimization problem. A result, Algorithm "GHMSA", has been proposed for finding the global minimizer of the non-linear constrained optimization problem. Algorithm "GHMSA" contains a new technique that is applied to convert the constrained optimization problem into the unconstrained optimization problem. The results of the algorithm demonstrate that the proposed penalty function is a good technique to make the unconstrained algorithm able to deal with the constrained optimization problem. The interior-point algorithm keeps the candidate solutions inside the domain search. The results of some nonlinear constrained optimization problems and four nonlinear engineering optimization problems show that the GHMSA algorithm has superiority over the other four algorithms in some test problems. For the future work, the proposed algorithm can be enhanced and modified to solve the multi-objective function, and the convergence analysis of the modified simulated annealing algorithm will be performed.

Moreover, it will be considered in future work to propose a new free derivative to approximate the gradient vector that will be combined (hybridized) with a new simulated annealing algorithm to solve unconstrained optimization, constrained, or multi-objective optimization problems. Convergence analysis of the GMLSA and GHMAS algorithms will be considered in future work.

Author Contributions: M.E.-A.; Formal analysis, M.A.; Funding acquisition, K.A.A.; Investigation, M.A.; Methodology, A.W.M.; Project administration, K.A.A.; Resources, K.A.A.; Supervision, A.W.M.; Validation, M.E.-A.; Writing—original draft, S.M.; Writing—review & editing, S.M. All authors have read and agreed to the published version of the manuscript.

Funding: The Research is funded by Researchers Supporting Program at King Saud University, (Project# RSP-2021/305).

Institutional Review Board Statement: Not applicable.

Informed Consent Statement: Not applicable.

Data Availability Statement: Not applicable.

Acknowledgments: The authors present their appreciation to King Saud University for funding the publication of this research through Researchers Supporting Program (RSP-2021/305), King Saud University, Riyadh, Saudi Arabia.

Conflicts of Interest: The authors declare no conflict of interest.

Abbreviations

The following abbreviations are used in this manuscript:

CB-ABC	Crossover-Based Artificial Bee Colony Algorithm
CCiALF	Cooperative Coevolutionary Differential Evolution Algorithm
NDE	A novel Differential Evolution Algorithm
CAMDE	Adaptive Differential Evolution with Multi-Population-based Mutation Operators for Constrained Optimization
GLMSA	Gradient Line-Search Modified Simulated-Annealing Algorithm
GHMSA	Guided Hybrid Gradient Modified Simulated-Annealing Algorithm
Symbols	
T	Control Parameter (Temperature)
k	Number Iteration
n	Number of Variables
$V \in [-1,1]^n$	A random Vector of n Dimension in Interval $[-1,1]$
x_0	Starting Point
x_1	A point Computed by GHMSA Algorithm
x_2	A point Computed by GHMSA Algorithm
x_{ac}	the Best Point Accepted by Our Algorithm at Iteration k
θ_{ac}	Function Value at Point x_{ac}
θ_1	Function Value at Point x_1
θ_2	Function Value at Point x_2
$\triangle f$	the Difference Between the Value f_{ac} and f_1
M	the Inner Loop Maximum Number of Iterations
ψ	the Step Size which is Generated by First Approach in "EMSA" Algorithm
d	the Step Size which is Generated by GHMSA Algorithm
β	A random Number in $(0,1)$
r_T	the Cooling Coefficient
T_f	A final Value of T it is Sufficiently Small
T_{out}	A final Value of T; $T_{out} < T_{f_2}$
ε	A parameter has Small Value Used as A stopping Criterion
#pr	Number of Test Problems
x_g	Global Minimizer Found by GHMSA Algorithm
$\theta(x_g)$	Function Value at Global Minimum
$g(x)$	the gradient vector
$\parallel g(x_g) \parallel_2$	Norm of the gradient vector of θ at x_g
$p(x)$	Penalty Term
$g_i(x)$	Inequality Constraint
$h_j(x)$	Equality Constraint
q	A number of the Inequality Constraints
m	A number of the Equality Constraints
r	Penalty Parameter for the Inequality Constraints
t	Penalty Parameter for the Equality Constraints
U	Upper Feasible Region (Domain Search)
L	Lower Feasible Region (Domain Search)
$b.s$	the Best Solution Found by the Algorithm
$w.s$	the Worst Solution Found by the Algorithm
$s.d$	the Standard Deviation
$w.b$	Absolute Value Between the Worst Solution and the Best Denoted by $\lvert worst - best\rvert$
er	Absolute Value Between the Best Solution and the Exact Denoted by $\lvert best - exact\rvert$
$e.c$	Error Constraint where $e.c = \max\{0, g_i(x)\} + \max\{0, h_j(x)\}$
$e:v_1$	the Average of $\{s.d, w.b, er\}$
$e:v_2$	the Average of $\{s.d, w.b, e.c\}$

FES	Function Evaluation
c	A sequence of 3 Numbers Denoting the Violated Constraint Number at the Median solution
$\overline{v}$	Is the Mean Value of the Violations of All Constraints at the Median Solution
H_0	the Null Hypothesis
H_a	the Alternative Hypothesis
Me	the Average Results

References

1. Abdel-Baset, M.; Hezam, I. A Hybrid Flower Pollination Algorithm for Engineering Optimization Problems. *Int. J. Comput. Appl.* **2016**, *140*, 12. [CrossRef]
2. Ayumi, V.; Rere, L.; Fanany, M.I.; Arymurthy, A.M. Optimization of Convolutional Neural Network using Microcanonical Annealing Algorithm. *arXiv* **2016**, arXiv:1610.02306.
3. Rere, L.; Fanany, M.I.; Arymurthy, A.M. Metaheuristic Algorithms for Convolution Neural Network. *Comput. Intell. Neurosci.* **2016**, *2016*, 1537325. [CrossRef] [PubMed]
4. Rere, L.R.; Fanany, M.I.; Murni, A. Application of metaheuristic algorithms for optimal smartphone-photo enhancement. In Proceedings of the 2014 IEEE 3rd Global Conference on Consumer Electronics (GCCE), Tokyo, Japan, 7–10 October 2014; pp. 542–546.
5. Samora, I.; Franca, M.J.; Schleiss, A.J.; Ramos, H.M. Simulated annealing in optimization of energy production in a water supply network. *Water Resour. Manag.* **2016**, *30*, 1533–1547. [CrossRef]
6. Agrawal, P.; Ganesh, T.; Mohamed, A.W. A novel binary gaining–sharing knowledge-based optimization algorithm for feature selection. *Neural Comput. Appl.* **2021**, *33*, 5989–6008. [CrossRef]
7. Certa, A.; Lupo, T.; Passannanti, G. A New Innovative Cooling Law for Simulated Annealing Algorithms. *Am. J. Appl. Sci.* **2015**, *12*, 370. [CrossRef]
8. Mohamed, A.A.; Kamel, S.; Hassan, M.H.; Mosaad, M.I.; Aljohani, M. Optimal Power Flow Analysis Based on Hybrid Gradient-Based Optimizer with Moth–Flame Optimization Algorithm Considering Optimal Placement and Sizing of FACTS/Wind Power. *Mathematics* **2022**, *10*, 361. [CrossRef]
9. Nocedal, J.; Wright, S. *Numerical Optimization*; Springer Science & Business Media: Cham, Switzerland, 2006.
10. Aarts, E.; Korst, J. *Simulated Annealing and Boltzmann Machines: A Stochastic Approach to Combinatorial Optimization and Neural Computing*; John Wiley & Sons, Inc.: New York, NY, USA, 1989.
11. Hillier, F.S.; Price, C.C. *International Series in Operations Research & Management Science*; Springer: Berlin/Heidelberg, Germany, 2001.
12. Laarhoven, P.J.V.; Aarts, E.H. *Simulated Annealing: Theory and Applications*; Springer-Science + Business Media, B. V.: Berlin/Heidelberg, Germany, 1987.
13. Kan, A.R.; Timmer, G. Stochastic methods for global optimization. *Am. J. Math. Manag. Sci.* **1984**, *4*, 7–40. [CrossRef]
14. Ali, M. Some Modified Stochastic Global Optimization Algorithms with Applications. Ph.D. Thesis, Loughborough University, Loughborough, UK, 1994.
15. Blum, C.; Roli, A. Metaheuristics in combinatorial optimization: Overview and conceptual comparison. *ACM Comput. Surv.* **2003**, *35*, 268–308. [CrossRef]
16. Desale, S.; Rasool, A.; Andhale, S.; Rane, P. Heuristic and meta-heuristic algorithms and their relevance to the real world: A survey. *Int. J. Comput. Eng. Res. Trends* **2015**, *2*, 296–304.
17. Chakraborti, S.; Sanyal, S. An Elitist Simulated Annealing Algorithm for Solving Multi Objective Optimization Problems in Internet of Things Design. *Int. J. Adv. Netw. Appl.* **2015**, *7*, 2784.
18. Gonzales, G.V.; dos Santos, E.D.; Emmendorfer, L.R.; Isoldi, L.A.; Rocha, L.A.O.; Estrada, E.d.S.D. A Comparative Study of Simulated Annealing with different Cooling Schedules for Geometric Optimization of a Heat Transfer Problem According to Constructal Design. *Sci. Plena* **2015**, *11*. [CrossRef]
19. Poorjafari, V.; Yue, W.L.; Holyoak, N. A Comparison between Genetic Algorithms and Simulated Annealing for Minimizing Transfer Waiting Time in Transit Systems. *Int. J. Eng. Technol.* **2016**, *8*, 216. [CrossRef]
20. Armijo, L. Minimization of functions having lipschitz continuous first-partial derivatives. *Pac. J. Math.* **1966**, *16*, 187–192. [CrossRef]
21. Bertsekas, D.P. *Nonlinear Programming*; Athena Scientific Belmont: Belmont, MA, USA, 1999.
22. Dennis, J.E., Jr.; Schnabel, R.B. *Numerical Methods for Unconstrained Optimization and Nonlinear Equations*; Society for Industrial and Applied Mathematics: Philadelphia, PA, USA, 1996; Volume 16.
23. EL-Alem, M.; Aboutahoun, A.; Mahdi, S. Hybrid gradient simulated annealing algorithm for finding the global optimal of a nonlinear unconstrained optimization problem. *Soft Comput.* **2020**, *25*, 2325–2350. [CrossRef]
24. Ali, M.; Golalikhani, M.; Zhuang, J. A computational study on different penalty approaches for solving constrained global optimization problems with the electromagnetism-like method. *Optimization* **2014**, *63*, 403–419. [CrossRef]

25. Datta, R.; Deb, K. An adaptive normalization based constrained handling methodology with hybrid bi-objective and penalty function approach. In Proceedings of the 2012 IEEE Congress on Evolutionary Computation, Brisbane, QLD, Australia, 10–15 June 2012; pp. 1–8.
26. Deb, K. An efficient constraint handling method for genetic algorithms. *Comput. Methods Appl. Mech. Eng.* **2000**, *186*, 311–338. [CrossRef]
27. Jordehi, A.R. A review on constraint handling strategies in particle swarm optimization. *Neural Comput. Appl.* **2015**, *26*, 1265–1275. [CrossRef]
28. Joines, J.A.; Houck, C.R. On the Use of Non-Stationary Penalty Functions to Solve Nonlinear Constrained Optimization Problems with GA's. In Proceedings of the International Conference on Evolutionary Computation, Orlando, FL, USA, 27–29 June 1994; pp. 579–584.
29. Dekkers, A.; Aarts, E. Global Optimization and simulated-annealing algorithm. *Math. Program.* **1991**, *50*, 367–393. [CrossRef]
30. Ingber, L. Simulated Annealing: Practice versus Theory. *Mathl. Comput. Model.* **1993**, *18*, 29–57. [CrossRef]
31. Vidal, R. Applied Simulated Annealing (Lecture Notes in Economics and Mathematical Systems). In *Applied Simulated Annealing: Lecture Notes in Economics and Mathematical Systems*; Springer: Cham, Switzerland, 1993.
32. Kazarlis, S.; Petridis, V. Varying fitness functions in genetic algorithms: Studying the rate of increase of the dynamic penalty terms. In Proceedings of the International Conference on Parallel Problem Solving from Nature, Leiden, The Netherlands, 5–9 September 2020; Springer: Berlin/Heidelberg, Germany, 1998; pp. 211–220.
33. Michalewicz, Z.; Janikow, C.Z. Handling Constraints in Genetic Algorithms. In Proceedings of the 4th International Conference on Genetic Algorithms, San Diego, CA, USA, 13–16 July 1991; pp. 151–157.
34. Michalewicz, Z. A Survey of Constraint Handling Techniques in Evolutionary Computation Methods. *Evol. Program.* **1995**, *4*, 135–155.
35. Michalewicz, Z.; Schoenauer, M. Evolutionary algorithms for constrained parameter optimization problems. *Evol. Comput.* **1996**, *4*, 1–32. [CrossRef]
36. Homaifar, A.; Qi, C.X.; Lai, S.H. Constrained optimization via genetic algorithms. *Simulation* **1994**, *62*, 242–253. [CrossRef]
37. Parsopoulos, K.E.; Vrahatis, M.N. Particle swarm optimization method for constrained optimization problems. *Intell.-Technol.-Theory Appl. New Trends Intell. Technol.* **2002**, *76*, 214–220.
38. Petalas, Y.G.; Parsopoulos, K.E.; Vrahatis, M.N. Memetic particle swarm optimization. *Ann. Oper. Res.* **2007**, *156*, 99–127. [CrossRef]
39. El-Alem, M.; El-Sayed, S.; El-Sobky, B. Local convergence of the interior-point Newton method for general nonlinear programming. *J. Optim. Theory Appl.* **2004**, *120*, 487–502. [CrossRef]
40. Ali, M.M.; Gabere, M. A simulated annealing driven multi-start algorithm for bound constrained global optimization. *J. Comput. Appl. Math.* **2010**, *233*, 2661–2674. [CrossRef]
41. Kirkpatrick, S.; Gelatt, C.D.; Vecchi, M.P. Optimization by simulated annealing. *Science* **1983**, *220*, 671–680. [CrossRef]
42. Yarmohamadi, H.; Mirhosseini, S.H. A New Dynamic Simulated Annealing Algorithm for Global Optimization. *J. Math. Comput. Sci.* **2015**, *14*, 16–23. [CrossRef]
43. Corona, A.; Marchesi, M.; Martini, C.; Ridella, S. Minimizing multimodal functions of continuous variables with the simulated annealing algorithm. *ACM Trans. Math. Softw.* **1987**, *13*, 262–280. [CrossRef]
44. Metropolis, N.; Rosenbluth, A.W.; Rosenbluth, M.N.; Teller, A.H.; Teller, E. Equation of state calculations by fast computer machines. *J. Chem. Phys.* **1953**, *21*, 1087–1092. [CrossRef]
45. Liang, J.; Runarsson, T.P.; Mezura-Montes, E.; Clerc, M.; Suganthan, P.N.; Coello, C.C.; Deb, K. Problem definitions and evaluation criteria for the CEC 2006 special session on constrained real-parameter optimization. *J. Appl. Mech.* **2006**, *41*, 8–31.
46. Ma, H.; Simon, D. Blended biogeography-based optimization for constrained optimization. *Eng. Appl. Artif. Intell.* **2011**, *24*, 517–525. [CrossRef]
47. Brajevic, I. Crossover-based artificial bee colony algorithm for constrained optimization problems. *Neural Comput. Appl.* **2015**, *26*, 1587–1601. [CrossRef]
48. Ghasemishabankareh, B.; Li, X.; Ozlen, M. Cooperative coevolutionary differential evolution with improved augmented Lagrangian to solve constrained optimisation problems. *Inf. Sci.* **2016**, *369*, 441–456. [CrossRef]
49. Mohamed, A.W. A novel differential evolution algorithm for solving constrained engineering optimization problems. *J. Intell. Manuf.* **2018**, *29*, 659–692. [CrossRef]
50. Xu, B.; Tao, L.; Chen, X.; Cheng, W. Adaptive differential evolution with multi-population-based mutation operators for constrained optimization. *Soft Comput.* **2019**, *23*, 3423–3447. [CrossRef]
51. Sheskin, D.J. *Handbook of Parametric and Nonparametric Statistical Procedures*; CRC Press: Boca Raton, FL, USA, 2003.
52. Long, W.; Liang, X.; Cai, S.; Jiao, J.; Zhang, W. A modified augmented Lagrangian with improved grey wolf optimization to constrained optimization problems. *Neural Comput. Appl.* **2016**, *28*, 421–438. [CrossRef]
53. Lobato, F.S.; Steffen, V., Jr. Fish swarm optimization algorithm applied to engineering system design. *Lat. Am. J. Solids Struct.* **2014**, *11*, 143–156. [CrossRef]
54. Mazhoud, I.; Hadj-Hamou, K.; Bigeon, J.; Joyeux, P. Particle swarm optimization for solving engineering problems: A new constraint-handling mechanism. *Eng. Appl. Artif. Intell.* **2013**, *26*, 1263–1273. [CrossRef]

55. Mohamed, A.W.; Sabry, H.Z. Constrained optimization based on modified differential evolution algorithm. *Inf. Sci.* **2012**, *194*, 171–208. [CrossRef]
56. Rocha, A.M.A.; Fernandes, E.M.d.G. Self-Adaptive Penalties in the Electromagnetism-like Algorithm for Constrained Global Optimization Problems. In Proceedings of the 8th World Congress on Structural and Multidisciplinary Optimization, Lisbon, Portugal, 1–5 June 2009.
57. Yang, X.S.; Hossein Gandomi, A. Bat algorithm: A novel approach for global engineering optimization. *Eng. Comput.* **2012**, *29*, 464–483. [CrossRef]
58. Zhang, C.; Li, X.; Gao, L.; Wu, Q. An improved electromagnetism-like mechanism algorithm for constrained optimization. *Expert Syst. Appl.* **2013**, *40*, 5621–5634. [CrossRef]

mathematics MDPI

Article

Some New Versions of Integral Inequalities for Left and Right Preinvex Functions in the Interval-Valued Settings

Muhammad Bilal Khan [1], Savin Treanţă [2], Mohamed S. Soliman [3], Kamsing Nonlaopon [4,*] and Hatim Ghazi Zaini [5]

1 Department of Mathematics, COMSATS University Islamabad, Islamabad 44000, Pakistan; bilal42742@gmail.com
2 Department of Applied Mathematics, University Politehnica of Bucharest, 060042 Bucharest, Romania; savin.treanta@upb.ro
3 Department of Electrical Engineering, College of Engineering, Taif University, P.O. Box 11099, Taif 21944, Saudi Arabia; soliman@tu.edu.sa
4 Department of Mathematics, Faculty of Science, Khon Kaen University, Khon Kaen 40002, Thailand
5 Department of Computer Science, College of Computers and Information Technology, Taif University, P.O. Box 11099, Taif 21944, Saudi Arabia; h.zaini@tu.edu.sa
* Correspondence: nkamsi@kku.ac.th; Tel.: +668-6642-1582

Abstract: The principles of convexity and symmetry are inextricably linked. Because of the considerable association that has emerged between the two in recent years, we may apply what we learn from one to the other. In this paper, our aim is to establish the relation between integral inequalities and interval-valued functions (*IV-Fs*) based upon the pseudo-order relation. Firstly, we discuss the properties of left and right preinvex interval-valued functions (left and right preinvex *IV-Fs*). Then, we obtain Hermite–Hadamard ($\mathcal{H}$-$\mathcal{H}$) and Hermite–Hadamard–Fejér ($\mathcal{H}$-$\mathcal{H}$-Fejér) type inequality and some related integral inequalities with the support of left and right preinvex *IV-Fs* via pseudo-order relation and interval Riemann integral. Moreover, some exceptional special cases are also discussed. Some useful examples are also given to prove the validity of our main results.

Keywords: left and right preinvex interval-valued function; interval Riemann integral; Hermite–Hadamard type inequality; Hermite–Hadamard–Fejér type inequality

Citation: Khan, M.B.; Treanţă, S.; Soliman, M.S.; Nonlaopon, K.; Zaini, H.G. Some New Versions of Integral Inequalities for Left and Right Preinvex Functions in the Interval-Valued Settings. *Mathematics* **2022**, *10*, 611. https://doi.org/10.3390/math10040611

Academic Editors: Simeon Reich and Janusz Brzdęk

Received: 13 December 2021
Accepted: 15 February 2022
Published: 16 February 2022

1. Introduction

Hanson [1] defined the class of invex functions as one of the most significant extensions of convex functions. Weir and Mond [2], in 1988, used the notion of preinvex functions to demonstrate adequate optimality criteria and duality in nonlinear programming. For a differentiable mapping, the concept of fractional integral identities involving Riemann–Liouville fractional and Hadamard fractional integrals integrals was considered by Wang et al. [3], who identified some inequalities using standard convex, r-convex, m-convex, S-convex, (s, m)-convex, and (β, m)-convex. Moreover, Işcan [4] also used fractional integrals for preinvex functions to obtain various $\mathcal{H}$-$\mathcal{H}$ type inequalities. See [5–8] for other generalizations of the $\mathcal{H}$-$\mathcal{H}$ inequality.

For accurate solutions to various problems in practical mathematics, Moore [9] used interval arithmetic, *IV-Fs*, and integrals of *IV-Fs* to establish arbitrarily sharp upper and lower limits. Moore [9] showed that, if a real-valued mapping $Y(\varkappa)$ meets an ordinary Lipschitz condition in Y, $|Y(\varkappa) - Y(\omega)| \leq L|\varkappa - \omega|$, for ω, $\varkappa \in Y$, then, the united extension is a Lipschitz interval extension in Y. To combine the study of discrete and continuous dynamical systems, Hilger [10] introduced a time scales theory. The widespread use of dynamic equations and integral inequalities on time scales, in domains as diverse as electrical engineering, quantum physics, heat transfer, neural networks, combinatorics, and population dynamics [11], has highlighted the need for this theory. Young's inequality,

Minkoswki's inequality, Jensen's inequality, Hölder's inequality, $\mathcal{H}$-$\mathcal{H}$ inequality, Steffensen's inequality, Opial type inequality and Čhebyšhev's inequality were all explored by Agarwal et al. [11]. Srivastava et al. [12] discovered some generic time scale weighted Opial type inequalities in 2010. Srivastava et al. [13] also proposed several time-based expansions and generalizations of Maroni's inequality. Under certain proper conditions, some new local fractional integral analogue of Anderson's inequality on fractal space was introduced by Wei et al. [14], demonstrating that for classical Anderson's inequality, it was a novel extension on fractal space. Tunç et al. [15] also constructed an identity for local fractional integrals and derived numerous modifications of the well-known Steffensen's inequality for fractional integrals. The papers [11,16] and the references therein might be consulted for further information. Bhurjee and Panda [17] identified the parametric form of an *IV-F* and devised a technique to investigate the existence of a generic interval optimization issue solution. Using the notion of the generalized Hukuhara difference, Lupulescu [18] developed differentiability and integrability for *IV-Fs* on time scales. Cano et al. [19] developed a novel form of the Ostrowski inequality for gH differentiable *IV-Fs* in 2015 and achieved an extension of the class of real functions that are not always differentiable. For gH-differentiable *IV-Fs*, Cano et al. [19] found error limitations to quadrature rules. In addition, Roy and Panda [20] developed the idea of the -monotonic property of *IV-Fs* in the higher dimension and used extended Hukuhara differentiability to obtain various conclusions. We refer to [21–25], and the references therein, for further information on *IV-Fs*. An et al. [26] and Zhao et al. [27] recently proposed an (h1, h2)-convex *IV-F* and harmonically h-convex *IV-F*, respectively. Moreover, they found certain interval $\mathcal{H}$-$\mathcal{H}$ type inequalities. Budak et al. [28] also created the $\mathcal{H}$-$\mathcal{H}$ inequality for a convex *IV-F* and its product. For more information related to generalized convex functions and fractional inequalities in interval-valued settings, see [29–53] and the references therein.

Inspired by the ongoing research, we introduce the concept of left and right preinvex *IV-F* and establish the $\mathcal{H}$-$\mathcal{H}$ and $\mathcal{H}$-$\mathcal{H}$-Fejér inequality for left and right preinvex *IV-Fs* and the product of two left and right preinvex *IV-Fs* using Riemann integrals in interval-valued settings, which are motivated by the above studies and ideas. We also provide some examples to support our ideas.

2. Preliminaries

First, we offer some background information on interval-valued functions, the theory of convexity, interval-valued integration, and interval-valued fractional integration, which will be utilized throughout the article.

We offer some fundamental arithmetic regarding interval analysis in this paragraph, which will be quite useful throughout the article.

$$\mathcal{Z} = [\mathcal{Z}_*,\ \mathcal{Z}^*],\ \mathcal{Q} = [\mathcal{Q}_*,\ \mathcal{Q}^*]\ (\mathcal{Z}_* \leq \varkappa \leq\ \mathcal{Z}^*\ and\ \mathcal{Q}_* \leq z \leq\ \mathcal{Q}^*\varkappa\,,\ z \in \mathbb{R})$$
$$\mathcal{Z} + \mathcal{Q} = [\mathcal{Z}_*,\ \mathcal{Z}^*] + [\mathcal{Q}_*,\ \mathcal{Q}^*] = [\mathcal{Z}_* + \mathcal{Q}_*,\ \mathcal{Z}^* + \mathcal{Q}^*],$$
$$\mathcal{Z} - \mathcal{Q} = [\mathcal{Z}_*,\ \mathcal{Z}^*] - [\mathcal{Q}_*,\ \mathcal{Q}^*] = [\mathcal{Z}_* - \mathcal{Q}_*,\ \mathcal{Z}^* - \mathcal{Q}^*],$$
$$\min\mathcal{X} = \min\{\mathcal{Z}_*\mathcal{Q}_*,\ \mathcal{Z}^*\mathcal{Q}_*,\ \mathcal{Z}_*\mathcal{Q}^*,\ \mathcal{Z}^*\mathcal{Q}^*\},\ \max\mathcal{X} = \max\{\mathcal{Z}_*\mathcal{Q}_*,\ \mathcal{Z}^*\mathcal{Q}_*,\ \mathcal{Z}_*\mathcal{Q}^*,\ \mathcal{Z}^*\mathcal{Q}^*\}$$
$$\nu.[\mathcal{Z}_*,\ \mathcal{Z}^*] = \begin{cases} [\nu\mathcal{Z}_*,\ \nu\mathcal{Z}^*] \text{ if } \nu > 0, \\ \{0\} \text{ if } \nu = 0, \\ [\nu\mathcal{Z}^*, \nu\mathcal{Z}_*] \text{ if } \nu < 0. \end{cases}$$

Let $\mathcal{K}_C$, $\mathcal{K}_C^+$, $\mathcal{K}_C^-$ be the set of all closed intervals of $\mathbb{R}$, the set of all closed positive intervals of $\mathbb{R}$ and the set of all closed negative intervals of $\mathbb{R}$. Then, $\mathcal{K}_C$, $\mathcal{K}_C^+$, and $\mathcal{K}_C^-$ are defined as

$$\mathcal{K}_C = \{[\mathcal{Z}_*,\ \mathcal{Z}^*] : \mathcal{Z}_*,\ \mathcal{Z}^* \in \mathbb{R} \text{ and } \mathcal{Z}_* \leq\ \mathcal{Z}^*\}$$
$$\mathcal{K}_C^+ = \{[\mathcal{Z}_*,\ \mathcal{Z}^*] : \mathcal{Z}_*,\ \mathcal{Z}^* \in \mathcal{K}_C \text{ and } \mathcal{Z}_* > 0\}$$
$$\mathcal{K}_C^- = \{[\mathcal{Z}_*,\ \mathcal{Z}^*] : \mathcal{Z}_*,\ \mathcal{Z}^* \in \mathcal{K}_C \text{ and} \mathcal{Z}^* < 0\}$$

For $[\mathcal{Z}_*,\ \mathcal{Z}^*]$, $[\mathcal{Q}_*,\ \mathcal{Q}^*] \in \mathcal{K}_C$, the inclusion " $\subseteq$ " is defined by $[\mathcal{Z}_*,\ \mathcal{Z}^*] \subseteq [\mathcal{Q}_*,\ \mathcal{Q}^*]$, if and only if, $\mathcal{Q}_* \leq \mathcal{Z}_*$, $\mathcal{Z}^* \leq \mathcal{Q}^*$.

Remark 1. *[36] The relation " $\leq_p$ " defined on $\mathcal{K}_C$ by*

$$[\mathcal{Q}_*,\ \mathcal{Q}^*] \leq_p [\mathcal{Z}_*,\ \mathcal{Z}^*]\ if\ and\ only\ if\ \mathcal{Q}_* \leq \mathcal{Z}_*,\ \mathcal{Q}^* \leq \mathcal{Z}^*, \tag{1}$$

for all $[\mathcal{Q}_*,\ \mathcal{Q}^*],\ [\mathcal{Z}_*,\ \mathcal{Z}^*] \in \mathcal{K}_C$, *is a pseudo-order relation.*

Theorem 1. *[9] If* $Y : [\mu,\ v] \subset \mathbb{R} \to \mathcal{K}_C$ *is an IV-F, such that* $Y(\omega) = [Y_*(\omega),\ Y^*(\omega)]$, *then, Y is Riemann integrable over* $[\mu, v]$ *if and only if,* $Y_*(\omega)$ *and* $Y^*(\omega)$ *are both Riemann integrable over* $[\mu, v]$, *such that*

$$(IR)\int_{\mu}^{v} Y(\omega)d\omega = \left[(R)\int_{\mu}^{v} Y_*(\omega)d\omega,\ (R)\int_{\mu}^{v} Y^*(\omega)d\omega\right] \tag{2}$$

where $Y_*, Y^* : [\mu,\ v] \to \mathbb{R}$.

The collection of all Riemann integrable real valued functions and Riemann integrable *IV-Fs* is denoted by $\mathcal{R}_{[\mu,v]}$ and $\mathcal{IR}_{[\mu,v]}$, respectively.

Definition 1. *A set* $K \subset \mathbb{R}^n$ *is said to be a convex set, if, for all* $\omega, \varkappa \in K,\ \mathrm{t} \in [0,\ 1]$, *we have*

$$\mathrm{t}\varkappa + (1-\mathrm{t})\omega \in K,\ or\ \mathrm{t}\omega + (1-\mathrm{t})\varkappa \in K.$$

Definition 2. *[36] Let K be a convex set. Then, IV-F* $Y : K \to \mathcal{K}_C^+$ *is said to be left and right convex on K if*

$$Y(\mathrm{t}\omega + (1-\mathrm{t})\varkappa) \leq_p \mathrm{t}Y(\omega) + (1-\mathrm{t})Y(\varkappa), \tag{3}$$

for all $\omega, \varkappa \in K,\ \mathrm{t} \in [0,\ 1]$. *Y is called left and right concave on K if Equation (3) is reversed.*

Definition 3. *[7] A set* $A \subset \mathbb{R}^n$ *is said to be an invex set, if, for all* $\omega, \varkappa \in A,\ \mathrm{t} \in [0,\ 1]$, *we have*

$$\omega + (1-\mathrm{t})\zeta(\varkappa, \omega) \in A\ or\ \omega + \mathrm{t}\zeta(\varkappa, \omega) \in A,$$

where $\zeta : \mathbb{R}^n \times \mathbb{R}^n \to \mathbb{R}^n$.

Definition 4. *[6] Let A be an invex set. Then, IV-F* $Y : A \to \mathcal{K}_C^+$ *is said to be left and right preinvex on A with respect to* ζ *if*

$$Y(\omega + (1-\mathrm{t})\zeta(\varkappa, \omega)) \leq_p \mathrm{t}Y(\omega) + (1-\mathrm{t})Y(\varkappa), \tag{4}$$

for all $\omega, \varkappa \in A,\ \mathrm{t} \in [0,\ 1]$, *where* $\zeta : \mathbb{R}^n \times \mathbb{R}^n \to \mathbb{R}^n$. *Y is called left and right preincave on A with respect to* ζ *if inequality (4) is reversed. Y is called affine if Y is both convex and concave.*

Remark 2. *The left and right preinvex IV-Fs have some very nice properties similar to left and right convex IV-F:*

- *if Y is left and right preinvex IV-F, then,* θY *is also left and right preinvex for* $\theta \geq 0$.
- *if Y and* $\mathfrak{D}$ *both are left and right preinvex IV-Fs, then,* $max(Y(\omega), \mathfrak{D}(\omega))$ *is also left and right preinvex IV-Fs.*

  In the case of $\zeta(\varkappa, \omega) = -\omega$, *we obtain (4) from (3).*

The following outcome is very important in the field of interval-valued calculus because, by using this result, we can easily handle *IV-Fs*. Basically, Theorem 2 establishes the relation between *IV-F* $Y(\omega)$ and lower function $Y_*(\omega)$ and upper function $Y^*(\omega)$.

The following assumption will be required to prove the next result regarding the bifunction $\zeta : \mathbb{R}^n \times \mathbb{R}^n \to \mathbb{R}^n$, which is known as:

Condition C. *[7] Let A be an invex set with respect to ζ. For any $\varkappa, \omega \in A$ and $t \in [0, 1]$,*

$$\zeta(\omega, \omega + t\zeta(\varkappa, \omega)) = -t\zeta(\varkappa, \omega),$$
$$\zeta(\varkappa, \omega + t\zeta(\varkappa, \omega)) = (1-t)\zeta(\varkappa, \omega).$$

Clearly for $t = 0$, we have $\zeta(\varkappa, \omega) = 0$ if and only if, $\varkappa = \omega$, for all $\varkappa, \omega \in A$. For the applications of Condition C, see [26,30,34,35].

Theorem 2. *[6] Let A be an invex set and $Y : A \to \mathcal{K}_C^+$ be a IV-F such that*

$$Y(\omega) = [Y_*(\omega),\ Y^*(\omega)],\ \forall\, \omega \in A, \tag{5}$$

for all $\omega \in A$. Then, Y is left and right preinvex IV-F on A, if and only if, $Y_*(\omega)$ and $Y^*(\omega)$ both are preinvex functions.

Remark 3. *If $Y_*(\omega) = Y^*(\omega)$, then, from (4), one can acquire the following inequality, see [2]:*

$$Y(\omega + (1-t)\zeta(\varkappa, \omega)) \le tY(\omega) + (1-t)Y(\varkappa), \tag{6}$$

for all $\omega, \in A$, $t \in [0, 1]$, where $\zeta : \mathbb{R}^n \times \mathbb{R}^n \to \mathbb{R}^n$.

If $Y_*(\omega) = Y^*(\omega)$ with $\zeta(\varkappa, \omega) = \varkappa - \omega$, then, from (4), one can acquire the following inequality:

$$Y(t\omega + (1-t)\varkappa) \le tY(\omega) + (1-t)Y(\varkappa), \tag{7}$$

for all $\omega, \varkappa \in K$, $t \in [0, 1]$.

Example 1. *We consider the IV-F $Y : [0,1] \to \mathcal{K}_C^+$ defined by $Y(\omega) = [2, 4]\omega^2$. Since end point functions $Y_*(\omega)$, $Y^*(\omega)$ are preinvex functions with respect to $\zeta(\varkappa, \omega) = \varkappa - \omega$. Hence, $Y(\omega)$ is left and right preinvex IV-F.*

3. Main Results

In this section, we derive interval $\mathcal{H}$-$\mathcal{H}$ type inequalities for left and right preinvex functions in interval-valued settings. Moreover, we provide some nontrivial examples to verify the validity of the theory developed in this study.

Theorem 3. *Let $Y : [v,\ v + \zeta(\mu,\ v)] \to \mathcal{K}_C^+$ be a left and right preinvex IV-F such that $Y(\omega) = [Y_*(\omega),\ Y^*(\omega)]$ for all $\omega \in [v,\ v + \zeta(\mu,\ v)]$. If $Y \in \mathfrak{TR}_{([v,\ v+\zeta(\mu,\ v)])}$, then*

$$Y\left(\frac{2v + \zeta(\mu,\ v)}{2}\right) \le_p \frac{1}{\zeta(\mu,\ v)}\,(IR)\int_v^{v+\zeta(\mu,\ v)} Y(\omega)d\omega \le_p \frac{Y(v) + Y(v + \zeta(\mu,\ v))}{2} \le_p \frac{Y(v) + Y(\mu)}{2} \tag{8}$$

If Y is left and right preincave, then, we achieve the following coming inequality:

$$Y\left(\frac{2v + \zeta(\mu,\ v)}{2}\right) \ge_p \frac{1}{\zeta(\mu,\ v)}\,(IR)\int_v^{v+\zeta(\mu,\ v)} Y(\omega)d\omega \ge_p \frac{Y(v) + Y(v + \zeta(\mu,\ v))}{2} \le_p \frac{Y(v) + Y(\mu)}{2} \tag{9}$$

Proof. Let $Y : [v,\ v + \zeta(\mu,\ v)] \to \mathcal{K}_C^+$ be a left and right preinvex *IV-F*. Then, by hypothesis, we have

$$2Y\left(\frac{2v + \zeta(\mu,\ v)}{2}\right) \le_p Y(v + (1-t)\zeta(\mu,\ v)) + Y(v + t\zeta(\mu,\ v)).$$

Therefore, we have

$$2Y_*\left(\tfrac{2v+\zeta(\mu,\ v)}{2}\right) \le Y_*(v + (1-t)\zeta(\mu,\ v)) + Y_*(v + t\zeta(\mu,\ v)),$$
$$2Y^*\left(\tfrac{2v+\zeta(\mu,\ v)}{2}\right) \le Y^*(v + (1-t)\zeta(\mu,\ v)) + Y^*(v + t\zeta(\mu,\ v)).$$

Then

$$2\int_0^1 Y_*\left(\frac{2v+\zeta(\mu,v)}{2}\right)dt \le \int_0^1 Y_*(v+(1-t)\zeta(\mu,v))dt + \int_0^1 Y_*(v+t\zeta(\mu,v))dt,$$
$$2\int_0^1 Y^*\left(\frac{2v+\zeta(\mu,v)}{2}\right)dt \le \int_0^1 Y^*(v+(1-t)\zeta(\mu,v))dt + \int_0^1 Y^*(v+t\zeta(\mu,v))dt.$$

It follows that

$$Y_*\left(\frac{2v+\zeta(\mu,v)}{2}\right) \le \frac{1}{\zeta(\mu,v)}\int_v^{v+\zeta(\mu,v)} Y_*(\omega)d\omega,$$
$$Y^*\left(\frac{2v+\zeta(\mu,v)}{2}\right) \le \frac{2}{\zeta(\mu,v)}\int_v^{v+\zeta(\mu,v)} Y^*(\omega)d\omega.$$

That is

$$\left[Y_*\left(\frac{2v+\zeta(\mu,v)}{2}\right), Y^*\left(\frac{2v+\zeta(\mu,v)}{2}\right)\right] \le_p \frac{1}{\zeta(\mu,v)}\left[\int_v^{v+\zeta(\mu,v)} Y_*(\omega)d\omega, \int_v^{v+\zeta(\mu,v)} Y^*(\omega)d\omega\right].$$

Thus,

$$Y\left(\frac{2v+\zeta(\mu,v)}{2}\right) \le_p \frac{1}{\zeta(\mu,v)} (IR)\int_v^{v+\zeta(\mu,v)} Y(\omega)d\omega. \tag{10}$$

In a similar way to the above, we have

$$\frac{1}{\zeta(\mu,v)} (IR)\int_v^{v+\zeta(\mu,v)} Y(\omega)d\omega \le_p \frac{Y(v)+Y(\mu)}{2}. \tag{11}$$

Combining (10) and (11), we have

$$Y\left(\frac{2v+\zeta(\mu,v)}{2}\right) \le_p \frac{1}{\zeta(\mu,v)} (IR)\int_v^{v+\zeta(\mu,v)} Y(\omega)d\omega \le_p \frac{Y(v)+Y(\mu)}{2}.$$

This completes the proof. □

Remark 4. *If $\xi(\mu,v) = \mu - v$, then Theorem 3 reduces to the result for left and right convex IV-F, see [29]:*

$$Y\left(\frac{v+\mu}{2}\right) \le_p \frac{1}{\mu-v} (IR)\int_v^\mu Y(\omega)d\omega \le_p \frac{Y(v)+Y(\mu)}{2}. \tag{12}$$

If $Y_*(\omega) = Y^*(\omega)$, then Theorem 3 reduces to the result for the preinvex function, see [30]:

$$Y\left(\frac{2v+\zeta(\mu,v)}{2}\right) \le \frac{1}{\zeta(\mu,v)} (R)\int_v^{v+\zeta(\mu,v)} Y(\omega)d\omega \le [Y(v)+Y(\mu)]\int_0^1 t\,dt. \tag{13}$$

If $Y_*(\omega) = Y^*(\omega)$ with $\xi(\mu,v) = \mu - v$, then Theorem 3 reduces to the result for the convex function, see [31,32]:

$$Y\left(\frac{v+\mu}{2}\right) \le \frac{1}{\mu-v} (R)\int_v^\mu Y(\omega)d\omega \le \frac{Y(v)+Y(\mu)}{2}. \tag{14}$$

Example 2. *We consider the IV-F $Y: [v, v+\zeta(\mu,v)] = [0, \zeta(2,0)] \to \mathcal{K}_C^+$ defined by $Y(\omega) = [2\omega^2, 4\omega^2]$. Since end point functions $Y_*(\omega) = 2\omega^2$, $Y^*(\omega) = 4\omega^2$ are preinvex functions with respect to $\zeta(\mu,v) = \mu - v$. Hence, $Y(\omega)$ is left and right preinvex IV-F with respect to $\zeta(\mu,v) = \mu - v$. We now compute the following*

$$Y\left(\frac{2v+\zeta(\mu,v)}{2}\right) \le_p \frac{1}{\zeta(\mu,v)} (IR)\int_v^{v+\zeta(\mu,v)} Y(\omega)d\omega \le_p \frac{Y(v)+Y(\mu)}{2}.$$
$$Y_*\left(\frac{2v+\zeta(\mu,v)}{2}\right) = Y_*(1) = 2,$$
$$\frac{1}{\zeta(\mu,v)}\int_v^{v+\zeta(\mu,v)} Y_*(\omega)d\omega = \frac{1}{2}\int_0^2 2\omega^2 d\omega = \frac{8}{3},$$
$$\frac{Y_*(v)+Y_*(\mu)}{2} = 4,$$

that means

$$2 \leq \frac{8}{3} \leq 4.$$

Similarly, it can be easily shown that

$$Y^*\left(\frac{2v+\zeta(\mu,\ v)}{2}\right) \leq \frac{1}{\zeta(\mu,\ v)} \int_v^{v+\zeta(\mu,\ v)} Y^*(\omega)d\omega \leq \frac{Y^*(v)+Y^*(\mu)}{2}$$

such that

$$\begin{gathered} Y^*\left(\frac{2v+\zeta(\mu,\ v)}{2}\right) = Y_*(1) = 4, \\ \frac{1}{\zeta(\mu,\ v)} \int_v^{v+\zeta(\mu,\ v)} Y^*(\omega)d\omega = \frac{1}{2}\int_0^2 4\omega^2 d\omega = \frac{16}{3}, \\ \frac{Y^*(v)+Y^*(\mu)}{2} = 8. \end{gathered}$$

From which, it follows that

$$4 \leq \frac{16}{3} \leq 8,$$

that is

$$[2,\ 4] \ \leq_p \left[\frac{8}{3},\ \frac{16}{3}\right] \ \leq_p [4,\ 8]$$

hence,

$$Y\left(\frac{2v+\zeta(\mu,\ v)}{2}\right) \leq_p \frac{1}{\zeta(\mu,\ v)}\ (IR) \int_v^{v+\zeta(\mu,\ v)} Y(\omega)d\omega \leq_p \frac{Y(v)+Y(\mu)}{2}.$$

Theorem 4. *Let $Y, \mathfrak{D} : [v,\ v+\zeta(\mu,\ v)] \to \mathcal{K}_C^+$ be two left and right preinvex IV-F such that $Y(\omega) = [Y_*(\omega),\ Y^*(\omega)]$ and $\mathfrak{D}(\omega) = [\mathfrak{D}_*(\omega),\ \mathfrak{D}^*(\omega)]$ for all $\omega \in [v,\ v+\zeta(\mu,\ v)]$. If Y, $\mathfrak{D}$ and $Y \times \mathfrak{D} \in \mathfrak{TR}_{([v,\ v+\zeta(\mu,\ v)])}$, then*

$$\frac{1}{\zeta(\mu,\ v)}\ (IR) \int_v^{v+\zeta(\mu,\ v)} Y(\omega) \times \mathfrak{D}(\omega)d\omega \leq_p \frac{\mathcal{A}(v,\mu)}{3} + \frac{\mathcal{C}(v,\mu)}{6}, \tag{15}$$

where $\mathcal{A}(v,\mu) = Y(v) \times \mathfrak{D}(v) + Y(\mu) \times \mathfrak{D}(\mu)$, $\mathcal{C}(v,\mu) = Y(v) \times \mathfrak{D}(\mu) + Y(\mu) \times \mathfrak{D}(v)$, and $\mathcal{A}(v,\mu) = [\mathcal{A}_*((v,\mu)),\ \mathcal{A}^*((v,\mu))]$ and $\mathcal{C}(v,\mu) = [\mathcal{C}_*((v,\mu)),\ \mathcal{C}^*((v,\mu))]$.

Proof. Since $Y,\ \mathfrak{D} \in \mathcal{IR}_{([v,\ v+\zeta(\mu,\ v)])}$, then we have

$$\begin{gathered} Y_*(v+(1-t)\zeta(\mu,\ v)) \leq tY_*(v) + (1-t)Y_*(\mu), \\ Y^*(v+(1-t)\zeta(\mu,\ v)) \leq tY^*(v) + (1-t)Y^*(\mu). \end{gathered}$$

And

$$\begin{gathered} \mathfrak{D}_*(v+(1-t)\zeta(\mu,\ v)) \leq t\mathfrak{D}_*(v) + (1-t)\mathfrak{D}_*(\mu), \\ \mathfrak{D}^*(v+(1-t)\zeta(\mu,\ v)) \leq t\mathfrak{D}^*(v) + (1-t)\mathfrak{D}^*(\mu). \end{gathered}$$

From the definition of left and right preinvex *IV-F*, it follows that $0 \leq_p Y(\omega)$ and $0 \leq_p \mathfrak{D}(\omega)$, so

$$\begin{gathered} Y_*(v+(1-t)\zeta(\mu,\ v)) \times \mathfrak{D}_*(v+(1-t)\zeta(\mu,\ v)) \\ \leq \left(\ tY_*(v) + (1-t)Y_*(\mu)\ \right)\left(\ t\mathfrak{D}_*(v) + (1-t)\mathfrak{D}_*(\mu)\ \right) \\ = Y_*(v) \times \mathfrak{D}_*(v)t^2 + Y_*(\mu) \times \mathfrak{D}_*(\mu)t^2 + Y_*(v) \times \mathfrak{D}_*(\mu)t(1-t) \\ +Y_*(\mu) \times \mathfrak{D}_*(v)t(1-t), \\ Y^*(v+(1-t)\zeta(\mu,\ v)) \times \mathfrak{D}^*(v+(1-t)\zeta(\mu,\ v)) \\ \leq \left(\ tY^*(v) + (1-t)Y^*(\mu)\ \right)\left(\ t\mathfrak{D}^*(v) + (1-t)\mathfrak{D}^*(\mu)\ \right) \\ = Y^*(v) \times \mathfrak{D}^*(v)t^2 + Y^*(\mu) \times \mathfrak{D}^*(\mu)t^2 + Y^*(v) \times \mathfrak{D}^*(\mu)t(1-t) \\ +Y^*(\mu) \times \mathfrak{D}^*(v)t(1-t), \end{gathered}$$

Integrating both sides of the above inequality over [0,1], we obtain

$$\begin{aligned}
&\int_0^1 Y_*(v+(1-t)\zeta(\mu,\ v))\mathfrak{D}_*(v+(1-t)\zeta(\mu,\ v)) \\
&\quad = \tfrac{1}{\zeta(\mu,\ v)}\int_v^{v+\zeta(\mu,\ v)} Y_*(\omega)\mathfrak{D}_*(\omega)d\omega \\
&\quad \le (Y_*(v)\mathfrak{D}_*(v)+Y_*(\mu)\mathfrak{D}_*(\mu))\int_0^1 t^2dt \\
&\quad +(Y_*(v)\mathfrak{D}_*(\mu)+Y_*(\mu)\mathfrak{D}_*(v))\int_0^1 t(1-t)dt, \\
&\int_0^1 Y^*(v+(1-t)\zeta(\mu,\ v))\mathfrak{D}^*(v+(1-t)\zeta(\mu,\ v)) \\
&\quad = \tfrac{1}{\zeta(\mu,\ v)}\int_v^{v+\zeta(\mu,\ v)} Y^*(\omega)\mathfrak{D}^*(\omega)d\omega \\
&\quad \le (Y^*(v)\mathfrak{D}^*(v)+Y^*(\mu)\mathfrak{D}^*(\mu))\int_0^1 t^2dt \\
&\quad +(Y^*(v)\mathfrak{D}^*(\mu)+Y^*(\mu)\mathfrak{D}^*(v))\int_0^1 t(1-t)dt.
\end{aligned}$$

It follows that,

$$\begin{aligned}
&\tfrac{1}{\zeta(\mu,\ v)}\int_v^{v+\zeta(\mu,\ v)} Y_*(\omega)\mathfrak{D}_*(\omega)d\omega \le \mathcal{A}_*((v,\mu))\int_0^1 t^2dt + \mathcal{C}_*((v,\mu))\int_0^1 t(1-t)dt, \\
&\tfrac{1}{\zeta(\mu,\ v)}\int_v^{v+\zeta(\mu,\ v)} Y^*(\omega)\mathfrak{D}^*(\omega)d\omega \le \mathcal{A}^*((v,\mu))\int_0^1 t^2dt + \mathcal{C}^*((v,\mu))\int_0^1 t(1-t)dt,
\end{aligned}$$

that is

$$\begin{aligned}
&\tfrac{1}{\zeta(\mu,\ v)}\left[\int_v^{v+\zeta(\mu,\ v)} Y_*(\omega)\mathfrak{D}_*(\omega)d\omega,\ \int_v^{v+\zeta(\mu,\ v)} Y^*(\omega)\mathfrak{D}^*(\omega)d\omega\right] \\
&\quad \le_p \left[\tfrac{\mathcal{A}_*((v,\mu))}{3},\ \tfrac{\mathcal{A}^*((v,\mu))}{3}\right] + \left[\tfrac{\mathcal{C}_*((v,\mu))}{6},\ \tfrac{\mathcal{C}^*((v,\mu))}{6}\right].
\end{aligned}$$

Thus,

$$\frac{1}{\zeta(\mu,\ v)}\,(IR)\int_v^{v+\zeta(\mu,\ v)} Y(\omega)\mathfrak{D}(\omega)d\omega \le_p \frac{\mathcal{A}(v,\mu)}{3} + \frac{\mathcal{C}(v,\mu)}{6},$$

and the theorem has been established. □

Example 3. *We consider the IV-Fs* $Y,\ \mathfrak{D} : [v,\ v+\zeta(\mu,\ v)] = [0,\ \zeta(1,\ 0)] \to \mathcal{K}_C^+$ *defined by* $Y(\omega) = [2\omega^2, 4\omega^2]$ *and* $\mathfrak{D}(\omega) = [\omega, 2\omega]$*. Since end point functions* $Y_*(\omega) = 2\omega^2$*,* $Y^*(\omega) = 4\omega^2$ *and* $\mathfrak{D}_*(\omega) = \omega$*,* $\mathfrak{D}^*(\omega) = 2\omega$ *are preinvex functions with respect to* $\zeta(\mu,\ v) = \mu - v$*. Hence* $Y,\ \mathfrak{D}$ *both are left and right preinvex IV-Fs. We now compute the following*

$$\begin{aligned}
\tfrac{1}{\zeta(\mu,\ v)}\int_v^{v+\zeta(\mu,\ v)} Y_*(\omega)\times\mathfrak{D}_*(\omega)d\omega &= \tfrac{1}{2}, \\
\tfrac{1}{\zeta(\mu,\ v)}\int_v^{v+\zeta(\mu,\ v)} Y^*(\omega)\times\mathfrak{D}^*(\omega)d\omega &= 2, \\
\tfrac{\mathcal{A}_*((v,\mu))}{3} &= \tfrac{1}{3}, \\
\tfrac{\mathcal{A}^*((v,\mu))}{3} &= \tfrac{8}{3}, \\
\tfrac{\mathcal{C}_*((v,\mu))}{6} &= 0, \\
\tfrac{\mathcal{C}^*((v,\mu))}{6} &= 0,
\end{aligned}$$

that means

$$\tfrac{1}{2} \le \tfrac{2}{3},\ 2 \le \tfrac{8}{3}.$$

Hence, Theorem 4 is verified.

Theorem 5. *Let* $Y, \mathfrak{D} : [v,\ v+\zeta(\mu,\ v)] \to \mathcal{K}_C^+$ *be two left and right preinvex IV-Fs, such that* $Y(\omega) = [Y_*(\omega),\ Y^*(\omega)]$ *and* $\mathfrak{D}(\omega) = [\mathfrak{D}_*(\omega),\ \mathfrak{D}^*(\omega)]$ *for all* $\omega \in [v,\ v+\zeta(\mu,\ v)]$*. If* Y*,* $\mathfrak{D}$ *and* $Y\times\mathfrak{D} \in \mathfrak{IR}_{([v,\ v+\zeta(\mu,\ v)])}$ *and condition C hold for* ζ*, then*

$$2\,Y\left(\frac{2v+\zeta(\mu,\ v)}{2}\right)\times\mathfrak{D}\left(\frac{2v+\zeta(\mu,\ v)}{2}\right) \le_p \frac{1}{\zeta(\mu,\ v)}\,(IR)\int_v^{v+\zeta(\mu,\ v)} Y(\omega)\times\mathfrak{D}(\omega)d\omega + \frac{\mathcal{A}(v,\mu)}{6} + \frac{\mathcal{C}(v,\mu)}{3}, \quad (16)$$

where $\mathcal{A}(v,\mu) = Y(v)\times\mathfrak{D}(v) + Y(\mu)\times\mathfrak{D}(\mu)$, $\mathcal{C}(v,\mu) = Y(v)\times\mathfrak{D}(\mu) + Y(\mu)\times\mathfrak{D}(v)$, and $\mathcal{A}(v,\mu) = [\mathcal{A}_*((v,\mu)),\ \mathcal{A}^*((v,\mu))]$ and $\mathcal{C}(v,\mu) = [\mathcal{C}_*((v,\mu)),\ \mathcal{C}^*((v,\mu))]$.

Proof. Using condition C, we can write

$$v+\frac{1}{2}\zeta(\mu,\,v)=v+\mathrm{t}\zeta(\mu,\,v)+\frac{1}{2}\zeta(v+(1-\mathrm{t})\zeta(\mu,v),\,v+\mathrm{t}\zeta(\mu,v)).$$

By hypothesis, we have

$$\begin{aligned}
&Y_*\left(\tfrac{2v+\zeta(\mu,\,v)}{2}\right)\times\mathfrak{D}_*\left(\tfrac{2v+\zeta(\mu,\,v)}{2}\right)\\
&Y^*\left(\tfrac{2v+\zeta(\mu,\,v)}{2}\right)\times\mathfrak{D}^*\left(\tfrac{2v+\zeta(\mu,\,v)}{2}\right)\\
&=Y_*\left(v+\mathrm{t}\zeta(\mu,\,v)+\tfrac{1}{2}\zeta(v+(1-\mathrm{t})\zeta(\mu,v),\,v+\mathrm{t}\zeta(\mu,v))\right)\\
&\times\mathfrak{D}_*\left(v+\mathrm{t}\zeta(\mu,\,v)+\tfrac{1}{2}\zeta(v+(1-\mathrm{t})\zeta(\mu,v),\,v+\mathrm{t}\zeta(\mu,v))\right)\\
&=Y^*\left(v+\mathrm{t}\zeta(\mu,\,v)+\tfrac{1}{2}\zeta(v+(1-\mathrm{t})\zeta(\mu,v),\,v+\mathrm{t}\zeta(\mu,v))\right)\\
&\times\mathfrak{D}^*\left(v+\mathrm{t}\zeta(\mu,\,v)+\tfrac{1}{2}\zeta(v+(1-\mathrm{t})\zeta(\mu,v),\,v+\mathrm{t}\zeta(\mu,v))\right)\\
&\le\tfrac{1}{4}\begin{bmatrix}Y_*(v+(1-\mathrm{t})\zeta(\mu,\,v))\times\mathfrak{D}_*(v+(1-\mathrm{t})\zeta(\mu,\,v))\\+Y_*(v+(1-\mathrm{t})\zeta(\mu,\,v))\times\mathfrak{D}_*(v+\mathrm{t}\zeta(\mu,\,v))\end{bmatrix}\\
&\quad+\tfrac{1}{4}\begin{bmatrix}Y_*(v+\mathrm{t}\zeta(\mu,\,v))\times\mathfrak{D}_*(v+(1-\mathrm{t})\zeta(\mu,\,v))\\+Y_*(v+\mathrm{t}\zeta(\mu,\,v))\times\mathfrak{D}_*(v+\mathrm{t}\zeta(\mu,\,v))\end{bmatrix},\\
&\le\tfrac{1}{4}\begin{bmatrix}Y^*(v+(1-\mathrm{t})\zeta(\mu,\,v))\times\mathfrak{D}^*(v+(1-\mathrm{t})\zeta(\mu,\,v))\\+Y^*(v+(1-\mathrm{t})\zeta(\mu,\,v))\times\mathfrak{D}^*(v+\mathrm{t}\zeta(\mu,\,v))\end{bmatrix}\\
&\quad+\tfrac{1}{4}\begin{bmatrix}Y^*(v+\mathrm{t}\zeta(\mu,\,v))\times\mathfrak{D}^*(v+(1-\mathrm{t})\zeta(\mu,\,v))\\+Y^*(v+\mathrm{t}\zeta(\mu,\,v))\times\mathfrak{D}^*(v+\mathrm{t}\zeta(\mu,\,v))\end{bmatrix},\\
&\le\tfrac{1}{4}\begin{bmatrix}Y_*(v+(1-\mathrm{t})\zeta(\mu,\,v))\times\mathfrak{D}_*(v+(1-\mathrm{t})\zeta(\mu,\,v))\\+Y_*(v+\mathrm{t}\zeta(\mu,\,v))\times\mathfrak{D}_*(v+\mathrm{t}\zeta(\mu,\,v))\end{bmatrix}\\
&\quad+\tfrac{1}{4}\begin{bmatrix}(\mathrm{t}Y_*(v)+(1-\mathrm{t})Y_*(\mu))\times((1-\mathrm{t})\mathfrak{D}_*(v)+\mathrm{t}\mathfrak{D}_*(\mu))\\+((1-\mathrm{t})Y_*(v)+\mathrm{t}Y_*(\mu))\times(\mathrm{t}\mathfrak{D}_*(v)+(1-\mathrm{t})\mathfrak{D}_*(\mu))\end{bmatrix},\\
&\le\tfrac{1}{4}\begin{bmatrix}Y^*(v+(1-\mathrm{t})\zeta(\mu,\,v))\times\mathfrak{D}^*(v+(1-\mathrm{t})\zeta(\mu,\,v))\\+Y^*(v+\mathrm{t}\zeta(\mu,\,v))\times\mathfrak{D}^*(v+\mathrm{t}\zeta(\mu,\,v))\end{bmatrix}\\
&\quad+\tfrac{1}{4}\begin{bmatrix}(\mathrm{t}Y^*(v)+(1-\mathrm{t})Y^*(\mu))\times((1-\mathrm{t})\mathfrak{D}^*(v)+\mathrm{t}\mathfrak{D}^*(\mu))\\+((1-\mathrm{t})Y^*(v)+\mathrm{t}Y^*(\mu))\times(\mathrm{t}\mathfrak{D}^*(v)+(1-\mathrm{t})\mathfrak{D}^*(\mu))\end{bmatrix},\\
&=\tfrac{1}{4}\begin{bmatrix}Y_*(v+(1-\mathrm{t})\zeta(\mu,\,v))\times\mathfrak{D}_*(v+(1-\mathrm{t})\zeta(\mu,\,v))\\+Y_*(v+\mathrm{t}\zeta(\mu,\,v))\times\mathfrak{D}_*(v+\mathrm{t}\zeta(\mu,\,v))\end{bmatrix}\\
&\quad+\tfrac{1}{2}\begin{bmatrix}\left\{\mathrm{t}^2+(1-\mathrm{t})^2\right\}\mathcal{C}_*((v,\mu))\\+\{\mathrm{t}(1-\mathrm{t})+(1-\mathrm{t})\mathrm{t}\}\mathcal{A}_*((v,\mu))\end{bmatrix},\\
&=\tfrac{1}{4}\begin{bmatrix}Y^*(v+(1-\mathrm{t})\zeta(\mu,\,v))\times\mathfrak{D}^*(v+(1-\mathrm{t})\zeta(\mu,\,v))\\+Y^*(v+\mathrm{t}\zeta(\mu,\,v))\times\mathfrak{D}^*(v+\mathrm{t}\zeta(\mu,\,v))\end{bmatrix}\\
&\quad+\tfrac{1}{2}\begin{bmatrix}\left\{\mathrm{t}^2+(1-\mathrm{t})^2\right\}\mathcal{C}^*((v,\mu))\\+\{\mathrm{t}(1-\mathrm{t})+(1-\mathrm{t})\mathrm{t}\}\mathcal{A}^*((v,\mu))\end{bmatrix}.
\end{aligned}$$

Integrating over $[0,\,1]$, we have

$$\begin{aligned}
2\,Y_*\left(\tfrac{2v+\zeta(\mu,\,v)}{2}\right)\times\mathfrak{D}_*\left(\tfrac{2v+\zeta(\mu,\,v)}{2}\right)&\le\tfrac{1}{\zeta(\mu,\,v)}\int_v^{v+\zeta(\mu,\,v)}Y_*(\omega)\times\mathfrak{D}_*(\omega)d\omega+\tfrac{\mathcal{A}_*((v,\mu))}{6}+\tfrac{\mathcal{C}_*((v,\mu))}{3},\\
2\,Y^*\left(\tfrac{2v+\zeta(\mu,\,v)}{2}\right)\times\mathfrak{D}^*\left(\tfrac{2v+\zeta(\mu,\,v)}{2}\right)&\le\tfrac{1}{\zeta(\mu,\,v)}\int_v^{v+\zeta(\mu,\,v)}Y^*(\omega)\times\mathfrak{D}^*(\omega)d\omega+\tfrac{\mathcal{A}^*((v,\mu))}{6}+\tfrac{\mathcal{C}^*((v,\mu))}{3},
\end{aligned}$$

from which, we have

$$\begin{aligned}
&2\left[Y_*\left(\tfrac{2v+\zeta(\mu,\,v)}{2}\right)\times\mathfrak{D}_*\left(\tfrac{2v+\zeta(\mu,\,v)}{2}\right),\,Y^*\left(\tfrac{2v+\zeta(\mu,\,v)}{2}\right)\times\mathfrak{D}^*\left(\tfrac{2v+\zeta(\mu,\,v)}{2}\right)\right]\\
&\le\tfrac{1}{p\,\zeta(\mu,\,v)}\left[\int_v^{v+\zeta(\mu,\,v)}Y_*(\omega)\times\mathfrak{D}_*(\omega)d\omega,\,\int_v^{v+\zeta(\mu,\,v)}Y^*(\omega)\times\mathfrak{D}^*(\omega)d\omega\right]\\
&\quad+\left[\tfrac{\mathcal{A}_*((v,\mu))}{6},\,\tfrac{\mathcal{A}^*((v,\mu))}{6}\right]+\left[\tfrac{\mathcal{C}_*((v,\mu))}{3},\,\tfrac{\mathcal{C}^*((v,\mu))}{3}\right],
\end{aligned}$$

that is

$$2\,Y\left(\frac{2v+\zeta(\mu,\,v)}{2}\right)\times\mathfrak{D}\left(\frac{2v+\zeta(\mu,\,v)}{2}\right)\leq_p\frac{1}{\zeta(\mu,\,v)}\,(IR)\int_v^{v+\zeta(\mu,\,v)}Y(\omega)\times\mathfrak{D}(\omega)d\omega+\frac{\mathcal{A}(v,\mu)}{6}+\frac{\mathcal{C}(v,\mu)}{3}.$$

This completes the proof. □

Example 4. *We consider the IV-Fs* $Y,\,\mathfrak{D}:[v,\,v+\zeta(\mu,\,v)]=[0,\,\zeta(1,\,0)]\to\mathcal{K}_C^+$ *defined by,* $Y(\omega)=[2\omega^2,4\omega^2]$ *and* $\mathfrak{D}(\omega)=[1,2]\omega$*, and these functions fulfill all the assumptions of Theorem 5. Since* $Y(\omega)$*,* $\mathfrak{D}(\omega)$ *both are left and right preinvex IV-Fs with respect to* $\zeta(\mu,\,v)=\mu-v$*, we have* $Y_*(\omega)=2\omega^2$*,* $Y^*(\omega)=4\omega^2$ *and* $\mathfrak{D}_*(\omega)=\omega$*,* $\mathfrak{D}^*(\omega)=2\omega$*. We now compute the following*

$$\begin{gathered}2\,Y_*\left(\tfrac{2v+\zeta(\mu,\,v)}{2}\right)\times\mathfrak{D}_*\left(\tfrac{2v+\zeta(\mu,\,v)}{2}\right)=\tfrac{1}{2},\\ 2\,Y^*\left(\tfrac{2v+\zeta(\mu,\,v)}{2}\right)\times\mathfrak{D}^*\left(\tfrac{2v+\zeta(\mu,\,v)}{2}\right)=2,\\ \tfrac{1}{\zeta(\mu,\,v)}\int_v^{v+\zeta(\mu,\,v)}Y_*(\omega)\times\mathfrak{D}_*(\omega)d\omega=\tfrac{1}{2},\\ \tfrac{1}{\zeta(\mu,\,v)}\int_v^{v+\zeta(\mu,\,v)}Y^*(\omega)\times\mathfrak{D}^*(\omega)d\omega=2,\\ \tfrac{\mathcal{A}_*((v,\mu))}{6}=\tfrac{1}{3},\\ \tfrac{\mathcal{A}^*((v,\mu))}{6}=\tfrac{4}{3},\\ \tfrac{\mathcal{C}_*((v,\mu))}{3}=0,\\ \tfrac{\mathcal{C}^*((v,\mu))}{3}=0,\end{gathered}$$

that means

$$\begin{gathered}\tfrac{1}{2}\leq\tfrac{1}{2}+0+\tfrac{1}{3}=\tfrac{5}{6},\\ 2\leq 2+0+\tfrac{4}{3}=\tfrac{10}{3}.\end{gathered}$$

Hence, Theorem 5 is verified.

It is well known that classical $\mathcal{H}$-$\mathcal{H}$-Fejér inequality is a generalization of classical $\mathcal{H}$-$\mathcal{H}$ inequality. Now we derive $\mathcal{H}$-$\mathcal{H}$-Fejér inequality for left and right preinvex *IV-Fs* and then we will obtain the validity of this inequality with the help of a non-trivial example. Firstly, we obtain the second $\mathcal{H}$-$\mathcal{H}$-Fejér inequality for left and right preinvex *IV-F*.

Theorem 6. *Let* $Y:[v,\,v+\zeta(\mu,\,v)]\to\mathcal{K}_C^+$ *be a left and right preinvex IV-F with* $v<v+\zeta(\mu,\,v)$ *such that* $Y(\omega)=[Y_*(\omega),\,Y^*(\omega)]$ *for all* $\omega\in[v,\,v+\zeta(\mu,\,v)]$*. If* $Y\in\mathfrak{TR}_{([v,\,v+\zeta(\mu,\,v)])}$ *and* $\mathcal{S}:[v,\,v+\zeta(\mu,\,v)]\to\mathbb{R}$*,* $\mathcal{S}(\omega)\geq 0$*, symmetric with respect to* $v+\frac{1}{2}\zeta(\mu,\,v)$*, then*

$$\frac{1}{\zeta(\mu,\,v)}\,(IR)\int_v^{v+\zeta(\mu,\,v)}Y(\omega)\mathcal{S}(\omega)d\omega\leq_p[Y(v)+Y(\mu)]\int_0^1 \mathrm{t}\mathcal{S}(v+\mathrm{t}\zeta(\mu,\,v))d\mathrm{t}. \tag{17}$$

Proof. Let Y be a left and right preinvex *IV-F*. Then, we have

$$\begin{gathered}Y_*(v+(1-\mathrm{t})\zeta(\mu,v))\mathcal{S}(v+(1-\mathrm{t})\zeta(\mu,v))\\ \leq(\mathrm{t}Y_*(v)+(1-\mathrm{t})Y_*(\mu))\mathcal{S}(v+(1-\mathrm{t})\zeta(\mu,v)),\\ Y^*(v+(1-\mathrm{t})\zeta(\mu,v))\mathcal{S}(v+(1-\mathrm{t})\zeta(\mu,v))\\ \leq(\mathrm{t}Y^*(v)+(1-\mathrm{t})Y^*(\mu))\mathcal{S}(v+(1-\mathrm{t})\zeta(\mu,v)).\end{gathered} \tag{18}$$

And

$$\begin{gathered}Y_*(v+\mathrm{t}\zeta(\mu,\,v))\mathcal{S}(v+\mathrm{t}\zeta(\mu,\,v))\leq((1-\mathrm{t})Y_*(v)+\mathrm{t}Y_*(\mu))\mathcal{S}(v+\mathrm{t}\zeta(\mu,\,v)),\\ Y^*(v+\mathrm{t}\zeta(\mu,\,v))\mathcal{S}(v+\mathrm{t}\zeta(\mu,\,v))\leq((1-\mathrm{t})Y^*(v)+\mathrm{t}Y^*(\mu))\mathcal{S}(v+\mathrm{t}\zeta(\mu,\,v)).\end{gathered} \tag{19}$$

After adding (18) and (19), and integrating over $[0,\ 1]$, we get

$$\begin{aligned}
&\int_0^1 Y_*(v+(1-t)\zeta(\mu,v))\mathcal{S}(v+(1-t)\zeta(\mu,v))dt \\
&\quad+\int_0^1 Y_*(v+t\zeta(\mu,\ v))\mathcal{S}(v+t\zeta(\mu,\ v))dt \\
&\leq \int_0^1\left[\begin{array}{c} Y_*(v)\{t\mathcal{S}(v+(1-t)\zeta(\mu,v))+(1-t)\mathcal{S}(v+t\zeta(\mu,\ v))\} \\ +Y_*(\mu)\{(1-t)\mathcal{S}(v+(1-t)\zeta(\mu,v))+t\mathcal{S}(v+t\zeta(\mu,\ v))\}\end{array}\right]dt, \\
&\int_0^1 Y^*(v+t\zeta(\mu,\ v))\mathcal{S}(v+t\zeta(\mu,\ v))dt \\
&\quad+\int_0^1 Y^*(v+(1-t)\zeta(\mu,v))\mathcal{S}(v+(1-t)\zeta(\mu,v))dt \\
&\leq \int_0^1\left[\begin{array}{c} Y^*(v)\{t\mathcal{S}(v+(1-t)\zeta(\mu,v))+(1-t)\mathcal{S}(v+t\zeta(\mu,\ v))\} \\ +Y^*(\mu)\{(1-t)\mathcal{S}(v+(1-t)\zeta(\mu,v))+t\mathcal{S}(v+t\zeta(\mu,\ v))\}\end{array}\right]dt. \\
&= 2Y_*(v)\int_0^1\ t\mathcal{S}(v+(1-t)\zeta(\mu,v))\ dt+2Y_*(\mu)\int_0^1\ t\mathcal{S}(v+t\zeta(\mu,\ v))\ dt, \\
&= 2Y^*(v)\int_0^1\ t\mathcal{S}(v+(1-t)\zeta(\mu,v))\ dt+2Y^*(\mu)\int_0^1\ t\mathcal{S}(v+t\zeta(\mu,\ v))\ dt.
\end{aligned}$$

Since $\mathcal{S}$ is symmetric, then

$$\begin{aligned}
&= 2[Y_*(v)+Y_*(\mu)]\int_0^1\ t\mathcal{S}(v+t\zeta(\mu,\ v))\ dt, \\
&= 2[Y^*(v)+Y^*(\mu)]\int_0^1\ t\mathcal{S}(v+t\zeta(\mu,\ v))\ dt.
\end{aligned} \tag{20}$$

Since

$$\begin{aligned}
&\int_0^1 Y_*(v+(1-t)\zeta(u,v))\mathcal{S}(v+(1-t)\zeta(\mu,v))dt \\
&= \int_0^1 Y_*(v+t\zeta(u,v))\mathcal{S}(v+t\zeta(\mu,v))dt \\
&= \frac{1}{\zeta(\mu,\ v)}\int_v^{v+\zeta(\mu,\ v)} Y_*(\omega)\mathcal{S}(\omega)d\omega, \\
&\int_0^1 Y^*(v+t\zeta(u,v))\mathcal{S}(v+t\zeta(\mu,v))dt \\
&= \int_0^1 Y^*(v+(1-t)\zeta(u,v))\mathcal{S}(v+(1-t)\zeta(\mu,v))dt \\
&= \frac{1}{\zeta(\mu,\ v)}\int_v^{v+\zeta(\mu,\ v)} Y^*(\omega)\mathcal{S}(\omega)d\omega.
\end{aligned} \tag{21}$$

From (21), we have

$$\begin{aligned}
&\frac{1}{\zeta(\mu,\ v)}\int_v^{v+\zeta(\mu,\ v)} Y_*(\omega)\mathcal{S}(\omega)d\omega \leq [Y_*(v)+Y_*(\mu)]\int_0^1\ t\mathcal{S}(v+t\zeta(\mu,\ v))\ dt, \\
&\frac{1}{\zeta(\mu,\ v)}\int_v^{v+\zeta(\mu,\ v)} Y^*(\omega)\mathcal{S}(\omega)d\omega \leq [Y^*(v)+Y^*(\mu)]\int_0^1\ t\mathcal{S}(v+t\zeta(\mu,\ v))\ dt,
\end{aligned}$$

that is

$$\begin{aligned}
&\left[\frac{1}{\zeta(\mu,\ v)}\int_v^{v+\zeta(\mu,\ v)} Y_*(\omega)\mathcal{S}(\omega)d\omega,\ \frac{1}{\zeta(\mu,\ v)}\int_v^{v+\zeta(\mu,\ v)} Y^*(\omega)\mathcal{S}(\omega)d\omega\right] \\
&\leq_p [Y_*(v)+Y_*(\mu),\ Y^*(v)+Y^*(\mu)]\int_0^1\ t\mathcal{S}(v+t\zeta(\mu,\ v))\ dt
\end{aligned}$$

hence

$$\frac{1}{\zeta(\mu,\ v)}\ (IR)\int_v^{v+\zeta(\mu,\ v)} Y(\omega)\mathcal{S}(\omega)d\omega \leq_p [Y(v)+Y(\mu)]\int_0^1 t\mathcal{S}(v+t\zeta(\mu,\ v))dt.$$

□

Now, we present the succeeding reformative version of the generalized version of first $\mathcal{H}$-$\mathcal{H}$-Fejér inequalities for left and right preinvex *IV-Fs*.

Theorem 7. *Let $Y:[v,\ v+\zeta(\mu,\ v)]\to\mathcal{K}_C^+$ be a left and right preinvex IV-F with $v<v+\zeta(\mu,\ v)$ such that $Y(\omega)=[Y_*(\omega),\ Y^*(\omega)]$ for all $\omega\in[v,\ v+\zeta(\mu,\ v)]$. If $Y\in\mathfrak{TR}_{([v,\ v+\zeta(\mu,\ v)])}$ and $\mathcal{S}:[v,\ v+\zeta(\mu,\ v)]\to\mathbb{R}$, $\mathcal{S}(\omega)\geq 0$, symmetric with respect to $v+\frac{1}{2}\zeta(\mu,\ v)$, and $\int_v^{v+\zeta(\mu,\ v)}\mathcal{S}(\omega)d\omega>0$, and Condition C for ζ, then*

$$Y\left(v+\frac{1}{2}\zeta(\mu,\ v)\right)\leq_p \frac{1}{\int_v^{v+\zeta(\mu,\ v)}\mathcal{S}(\omega)d\omega}\ (IR)\int_v^{v+\zeta(\mu,\ v)} Y(\omega)\mathcal{S}(\omega)d\omega. \tag{22}$$

Proof. Using condition C, we can write

$$v+\frac{1}{2}\zeta(\mu,\ v)=v+\mathrm{t}\zeta(\mu,\ v)+\frac{1}{2}\zeta(v+(1-\mathrm{t})\zeta(\mu,v),\ v+\mathrm{t}\zeta(\mu,v)).$$

Since Y is a left and right preinvex, we have

$$\begin{aligned} Y_*\left(v+\tfrac{1}{2}\zeta(\mu,\ v)\right) &= Y_*\left(v+\mathrm{t}\zeta(\mu,\ v)+\tfrac{1}{2}\zeta(v+(1-\mathrm{t})\zeta(\mu,v),\ v+\mathrm{t}\zeta(\mu,v))\right)\\ &\le \tfrac{1}{2}(Y_*(v+(1-\mathrm{t})\zeta(\mu,v))+Y_*(v+\mathrm{t}\zeta(\mu,v))),\\ Y^*\left(v+\tfrac{1}{2}\zeta(\mu,\ v)\right) &= Y^*\left(v+\mathrm{t}\zeta(\mu,\ v)+\tfrac{1}{2}\zeta(v+(1-\mathrm{t})\zeta(\mu,v),\ v+\mathrm{t}\zeta(\mu,v))\right)\\ &\le (Y^*(v+(1-\mathrm{t})\zeta(\mu,v))+Y^*(v+\mathrm{t}\zeta(\mu,v))). \end{aligned} \tag{23}$$

By multiplying (23) by $\mathcal{S}(v+(1-\mathrm{t})\zeta(\mu,v))=\mathcal{S}(v+\mathrm{t}\zeta(\mu,v))$ and integrating it by t over $[0,\ 1]$, we obtain

$$\begin{aligned} & Y_*\left(v+\tfrac{1}{2}\zeta(\mu,\ v)\right)\int_0^1\mathcal{S}(v+\mathrm{t}\zeta(\mu,\ v))d\mathrm{t}\\ \le \tfrac{1}{2}&\begin{pmatrix}\int_0^1 Y_*(v+(1-\mathrm{t})\zeta(\mu,v))\mathcal{S}(v+(1-\mathrm{t})\zeta(\mu,\ v))d\mathrm{t}\\ +\int_0^1 Y_*(v+\mathrm{t}\zeta(\mu,v))d\mathrm{t}\mathcal{S}(v+\mathrm{t}\zeta(\mu,\ v))\end{pmatrix}\\ & Y^*\left(v+\tfrac{1}{2}\zeta(\mu,\ v)\right)\int_0^1\mathcal{S}(v+\mathrm{t}\zeta(\mu,\ v))d\mathrm{t}\\ \le \tfrac{1}{2}&\begin{pmatrix}\int_0^1 Y^*(v+(1-\mathrm{t})\zeta(\mu,v))\mathcal{S}(v+(1-\mathrm{t})\zeta(\mu,\ v))d\mathrm{t}\\ +\int_0^1 Y^*(v+\mathrm{t}\zeta(\mu,v))\mathcal{S}(v+\mathrm{t}\zeta(\mu,\ v))d\mathrm{t}\end{pmatrix}. \end{aligned} \tag{24}$$

Since

$$\begin{aligned} &\int_0^1 Y_*(v+(1-\mathrm{t})\zeta(\mu,v))\mathcal{S}(v+(1-\mathrm{t})\zeta(\mu,v))d\mathrm{t}\\ &=\int_0^1 Y_*(v+\mathrm{t}\zeta(\mu,\ v))\mathcal{S}(v+\mathrm{t}\zeta(\mu,\ v))d\mathrm{t}\\ &=\tfrac{1}{\zeta(\mu,\ v)}\int_v^{v+\zeta(\mu,\ v)}Y_*(\omega)\mathcal{S}(\omega)d\omega\\ &\int_0^1 Y^*(v+\mathrm{t}\zeta(\mu,\ v))\mathcal{S}(v+\mathrm{t}\zeta(\mu,\ v))d\mathrm{t}\\ &=\int_0^1 Y^*(v+(1-\mathrm{t})\zeta(\mu,v))\mathcal{S}(v+(1-\mathrm{t})\zeta(\mu,v))d\mathrm{t}\\ &=\tfrac{1}{\zeta(\mu,\ v)}\int_v^{v+\zeta(\mu,\ v)}Y^*(\omega)\mathcal{S}(\omega)d\omega. \end{aligned} \tag{25}$$

From (25), we have

$$\begin{aligned} Y_*\left(v+\tfrac{1}{2}\zeta(\mu,\ v)\right) &\le \frac{1}{\int_v^{v+\zeta(\mu,\ v)}\mathcal{S}(\omega)d\omega}\int_v^{v+\zeta(\mu,\ v)}Y_*(\omega)\mathcal{S}(\omega)d\omega,\\ Y^*\left(v+\tfrac{1}{2}\zeta(\mu,\ v)\right) &\le \frac{1}{\int_v^{v+\zeta(\mu,\ v)}\mathcal{S}(\omega)d\omega}\int_v^{v+\zeta(\mu,\ v)}Y^*(\omega)\mathcal{S}(\omega)d\omega. \end{aligned}$$

From which, we have

$$\begin{aligned} &\left[Y_*\left(v+\tfrac{1}{2}\zeta(\mu,\ v)\right),\ Y^*\left(v+\tfrac{1}{2}\zeta(\mu,\ v)\right)\right]\\ \le\ & {}_p\frac{1}{\int_v^{v+\zeta(\mu,\ v)}\mathcal{S}(\omega)d\omega}\left[\int_v^{v+\zeta(\mu,\ v)}Y_*(\omega)\mathcal{S}(\omega)d\omega,\ \int_v^{v+\zeta(\mu,\ v)}Y^*(\omega)\mathcal{S}(\omega)d\omega\right], \end{aligned}$$

that is

$$Y\left(v+\frac{1}{2}\zeta(\mu,\ v)\right)\le_p\frac{1}{\int_v^{v+\zeta(\mu,\ v)}\mathcal{S}(\omega)d\omega}(IR)\int_v^{v+\zeta(\mu,\ v)}Y(\omega)\mathcal{S}(\omega)d\omega.$$

This completes the proof. □

Remark 5. *If one considers taking $\zeta(\mu,\ v)=\mu-v$, then, by combining inequalities (17) and (22), we achieve the expected inequality.*

If one considers taking $Y_*(\omega)=Y^*(\omega)$, then, by combining inequalities (17) and (22), we achieve the classical $\mathcal{H}$-$\mathcal{H}$-Fejér inequality, see [30].

If one considers taking $Y_*(\omega) = Y^*\omega$ *and* $\zeta(\mu, v) = \mu - v$, *then, by combining inequalities (17) and (22), we acquire the classical* $\mathcal{H}$-$\mathcal{H}$*-Fejér inequality, see [33].*

Example 5. *We consider the IV-F* $Y : [1, 1 + \zeta(4, 1)] \to \mathcal{K}_C^+$ *defined by* $Y(\omega) = [2, 4]e^{\omega}$. *Since end point functions* $Y_*(\omega)$, $Y^*(\omega)$ *are preinvex functions* $\zeta(\varkappa, \omega) = \varkappa - \omega$, *then,* $Y(\omega)$ *is left and right preinvex IV-F. If*

$$\mathcal{S}(\omega) = \begin{cases} \omega - 1, \ \sigma \in \left[1, \frac{5}{2}\right], \\ 4 - \omega, \ \sigma \in \left(\frac{5}{2}, 4\right]. \end{cases}$$

Then, we have

$$\begin{aligned}
&\tfrac{1}{\zeta(4,\,1)} \int_1^{1+\,\zeta(4,\,1)} Y_*(\omega)\mathcal{S}(\omega)d\omega = \tfrac{1}{3}\int_1^4 Y_*(\omega)\mathcal{S}(\omega)d\omega \\
&\quad = \tfrac{1}{3}\int_1^{\frac{5}{2}} Y_*(\omega)\mathcal{S}(\omega)d\omega + \tfrac{1}{3}\int_{\frac{5}{2}}^4 Y_*(\omega)\mathcal{S}(\omega)d\omega, \\
&\tfrac{1}{\zeta(4,\,1)} \int_1^{1+\,\zeta(4,\,1)} Y^*(\omega)\mathcal{S}(\omega)d\omega = \tfrac{1}{3}\int_1^4 Y^*(\omega)\mathcal{S}(\omega)d\omega \\
&\quad = \tfrac{1}{3}\int_1^{\frac{5}{2}} Y^*(\omega)\mathcal{S}(\omega)d\omega + \tfrac{1}{3}\int_{\frac{5}{2}}^4 Y^*(\omega)\mathcal{S}(\omega)d\omega, \\
&\quad = \tfrac{2}{3}\int_1^{\frac{5}{2}} e^{\omega}(\omega - 1)d\omega + \tfrac{2}{3}\int_{\frac{5}{2}}^4 e^{\omega}(4 - \omega)d\omega \approx 22, \\
&\quad = \tfrac{4}{3}\int_1^{\frac{5}{2}} e^{\omega}(\omega - 1)d\omega + \tfrac{4}{3}\int_{\frac{5}{2}}^4 e^{\omega}(4 - \omega)d\omega \approx 44,
\end{aligned} \tag{26}$$

and

$$\begin{aligned}
&[Y_*(v) + Y_*(\mu)] \int_0^1 \ \mathrm{t}\mathcal{S}(v + \mathrm{t}\zeta(\mu,\, v)) \ dt \\
&[Y^*(v) + Y^*(\mu)] \int_0^1 \ \mathrm{t}\mathcal{S}(v + \mathrm{t}\zeta(\mu,\, v)) \ dt \\
&= 2\left[e + e^4\right]\left[\int_0^{\frac{1}{2}} 3\mathrm{t}^2 d\omega + \int_{\frac{1}{2}}^1 \mathrm{t}(3 - 3\mathrm{t})dt\right] \approx 43. \\
&= 4\left[e + e^4\right]\left[\int_0^{\frac{1}{2}} 3\mathrm{t}^2 d\omega + \int_{\frac{1}{2}}^1 \mathrm{t}(3 - 3\mathrm{t})dt\right] \approx 86.
\end{aligned} \tag{27}$$

From (26) and (27), we have

$$[22,\ 44] \ \leq_p [43,\ 86]$$

Hence, Theorem 6 is verified. For Theorem 7, we have

$$\begin{aligned}
Y_*\left(v + \tfrac{1}{2}\zeta(\mu,\, v)\right) &\approx \tfrac{122}{5}, \\
Y^*\left(v + \tfrac{1}{2}\zeta(\mu,\, v)\right) &\approx \tfrac{244}{5},
\end{aligned} \tag{28}$$

$$\int_v^{v+\zeta(\mu,\,v)} \mathcal{S}(\omega)d\omega = \int_1^{\frac{5}{2}} (\omega - 1)d\omega + \int_{\frac{5}{2}}^4 (4 - \omega)d\omega = \frac{9}{4},$$

$$\begin{aligned}
&\tfrac{1}{\int_v^{v+\zeta(\mu,\,v)} \mathcal{S}(\omega)d\omega} \int_1^4 Y_*(\omega)\mathcal{S}(\omega)d\omega \approx \tfrac{146}{5} \\
&\tfrac{1}{\int_v^{v+\zeta(\mu,\,v)} \mathcal{S}(\omega)d\omega} \int_1^4 Y^*(\omega)\mathcal{S}(\omega)d\omega \approx \tfrac{293}{5}
\end{aligned} \tag{29}$$

From (28) and (29), we have

$$\left[\frac{122}{5},\ 49\right] \ \leq_p \left[\frac{146}{5},\ \frac{293}{5}\right].$$

Hence, Theorem 7 is verified.

4. Conclusions and Prospective Results

In this study, the notion of left and right preinvex functions in interval-valued settings was presented. For left and right preinvex interval-valued functions, we constructed Hermite–Hadamard type inequalities, as well as for the product of two left and right preinvex interval-valued functions. We also established Hemite–Hadamard–Fejér type inequality. We also discussed some special cases and provided some examples to prove the validity of our main results. In future, we will seek to explore this concept by using different fractional integral operators, such as Riemann–Liouville fractional operators, Katugampola fractional operators and generalized K-fractional operators.

Finally, we think that our results may be relevant to other fractional calculus models having Mittag–Liffler functions in their kernels, such as Atangana–Baleanu and Prabhakar fractional operators. This consideration has been presented as an open problem for academics interested in this topic. Researchers who are interested might follow the steps outlined in the references [54,55].

Author Contributions: Conceptualization, M.B.K.; methodology, M.B.K.; validation, S.T., M.S.S. and H.G.Z.; formal analysis, K.N.; investigation, M.S.S.; resources, S.T.; data curation, H.G.Z.; writing—original draft preparation, M.B.K., K.N. and H.G.Z.; writing—review and editing, M.B.K. and S.T.; visualization, H.G.Z.; supervision, M.B.K. and M.S.S.; project administration, M.B.K.; funding acquisition, K.N., M.S.S. and H.G.Z. All authors have read and agreed to the published version of the manuscript.

Funding: The authors would like to thank the Rector, COMSATS University Islamabad, Islamabad, Pakistan, for providing excellent research support. This work was funded by Taif University Researchers Supporting Project number (TURSP-2020/345), Taif University, Taif, Saudi Arabia. In addition, this research has received funding support from the National Science, Research and Innovation Fund (NSRF), Thailand.

Institutional Review Board Statement: Not applicable.

Informed Consent Statement: Not applicable.

Data Availability Statement: Not applicable.

Conflicts of Interest: The authors declare no conflict of interest.

References

1. Hanson, M.A. On sufficiency of the Kuhn-Tucker conditions. *J. Math. Anal. Appl.* **1981**, *80*, 545–550. [CrossRef]
2. Weir, T.; Mond, B. Preinvex functions in multiple objective optimization. *J. Math. Anal. Appl.* **1988**, *136*, 29–38. [CrossRef]
3. Wang, J.; Feckan, M. *Fractional Hermite-Hadamard Inequalities*; De Gruyter: Berlin, Germany, 2018; p. 5.
4. İşcan, I. Hermite-Hadamard's inequalities for preinvex functions via fractional integrals and related fractional inequalities. *arXiv* **2012**, arXiv:1204.0272.
5. Macías-Díaz, J.E.; Khan, M.B.; Noor, M.A.; Abd Allah, A.M.; Alghamdi, S.M. Hermite-Hadamard inequalities for generalized convex functions in interval-valued calculus. *AIMS Math* **2022**, *7*, 4266–4292. [CrossRef]
6. Khan, M.B.; Zaini, H.G.; Treanţă, S.; Soliman, M.S.; Nonlaopon, K. Riemann–Liouville Fractional Integral Inequalities for Generalized Pre-Invex Functions of Interval-Valued Settings Based upon Pseudo Order Relation. *Mathematics* **2022**, *10*, 204. [CrossRef]
7. Mohan, S.R.; Neogy, S.K. On invex sets and preinvex functions. *J. Math. Anal. Appl.* **1995**, *189*, 901–908. [CrossRef]
8. Sharma, N.; Mishra, S.K.; Hamdi, A. A weighted version of Hermite-Hadamard type inequalities for strongly GA-convex functions. *Int. J. Adv. Appl. Sci.* **2020**, *7*, 113–118.
9. Moore, R.E. *Methods and Applications of Interval Analysis*; SIAM: Philadelphia, PA, USA, 1979.
10. Hilger, S. Ein Maßkettenkalkül mit Anwendung auf Zentrumsmannigfaltigkeiten. Ph.D. Thesis, Universitßt Würzburg, Würzburg, Germany, 1988.
11. Agarwal, R.; O'Regan, D.; Saker, S. *Dynamic Inequalities on Time Scales*; Springer: Berlin/Heidelberg, Germany, 2014.
12. Srivastava, H.M.; Tseng, K.-L.; Tseng, S.-J.; Lo, J.-C. Some weighted Opial type inequalities on time scales. *Taiwan. J. Math.* **2010**, *14*, 107–122. [CrossRef]
13. Srivastava, H.M.; Tseng, K.-L.; Tseng, S.-J.; Lo, J.-C. Some generalization of Maroni's inequality on time scales. *Math. Inequal. Appl.* **2011**, *14*, 469–480. [CrossRef]
14. Wei, W.; Srivastava, H.M.; Zhang, Y.; Wang, L.; Shan, P.; Zhang, T. A local fractional integral inequality on fractal space analogous to Anderson's inequality. *Abstr. Appl. Anal.* **2014**, *2014*, 5218–5229. [CrossRef]
15. Tunç, T.; Sarikaya, M.Z.; Srivastava, H.M. Some generalized Steffensen's inequalities via a new identity for local fractional integrals. *Int. J. Anal. Appl.* **2017**, *13*, 98–107.
16. Srivastava, H.M.; Zhang, Z.-H.; Wu, Y.-D. Some further refinements and extensions of the Hermite-Hadamard and Jensen inequalities in several variables. *Math. Comput. Model.* **2011**, *54*, 2709–2717. [CrossRef]
17. Bhurjee, A.K.; Panda, G. Efficient solution of interval optimization problem. *Math. Methods Oper. Res.* **2012**, *76*, 273–288. [CrossRef]

18. Lupulescu, V. Hukuhara differentiability of interval-valued functions and interval differential equations on time scales. *Inf. Sci.* **2013**, *248*, 50–67. [CrossRef]
19. Chalco-Cano, Y.; Lodwick, W.A.; Condori-Equice, W. Ostrowski type inequalities and applications in numerical integration for interval-valued functions. *Soft Comput.* **2015**, *19*, 3293–3300. [CrossRef]
20. Roy, P.; Panda, G. Expansion of generalized Hukuhara differentiable interval-valued function. *New Math. Nat. Comput.* **2019**, *15*, 553–570. [CrossRef]
21. Bhurjee, A.K.; Panda, G. Multi-objective interval fractional programming problems: An approach for obtaining efficient solutions. *Opsearch* **2015**, *52*, 156–167. [CrossRef]
22. Bhurjee, A.K.; Panda, G. Sufficient optimality conditions and duality theory for interval optimization problem. *Ann. Oper. Res.* **2016**, *243*, 335–348. [CrossRef]
23. Khan, M.B.; Noor, M.A.; Abdeljawad, T.; Mousa, A.A.A.; Abdalla, B.; Alghamdi, S.M. LR-Preinvex Interval-Valued Functions and Riemann–Liouville Fractional Integral Inequalities. *Fractal Fract.* **2021**, *5*, 243. [CrossRef]
24. Khan, M.B.; Noor, M.A.; Al-Bayatti, H.M.; Noor, K.I. Some New Inequalities for LR-Log-h-Convex Interval-Valued Functions by Means of Pseudo Order Relation. *Appl. Math.* **2021**, *15*, 459–470.
25. Lupulescu, V. Fractional calculus for interval-valued functions. *Fuzzy Sets Syst.* **2015**, *265*, 63–85. [CrossRef]
26. An, Y.; Ye, G.; Zhao, D.; Liu, W. Hermite-Hadamard type inequalities for interval (h_1, h_2)-convex functions. *Mathematics* **2019**, *7*, 436. [CrossRef]
27. Zhao, D.F.; An, T.Q.; Ye, G.J.; Torres, D.F.M. On Hermite-Hadamard type inequalities for harmonical h-convex interval-valued functions. *Math. Inequal. Appl.* **2020**, *23*, 95–105.
28. Budak, H.; Tunç, T.; Sarikaya, M.Z. Fractional Hermite-Hadamard-type inequalities for interval-valued functions. *Proc. Am. Math. Soc.* **2019**, *148*, 705–718. [CrossRef]
29. Khan, M.B.; Noor, M.A.; Noor, K.I.; Nisar, K.; Ismail, K.I.; Elfasakhany, A. Some Inequalities for LR-(h_1, h_2) h_1, h_2-Convex interval-valued functions by means of pseudo order relation. *Int. J. Comput. Intell. Syst.* **2021**, *14*, 1–15. [CrossRef]
30. Noor, M.A. Hermite–Hadamard integral inequalities for log-preinvex functions. *J. Math. Anal. Approx. Theory* **2007**, *5*, 126–131.
31. Hadamard, J. Étude sur les propriétés des fonctions entières et en particulier d'une fonction considérée par Riemann. *J. Mathématiques Pures Appliquées* **1893**, *5*, 171–215.
32. Hermite, C. Sur deux limites d'une intégrale définie. *Mathesis* **1883**, *3*, 1–82.
33. Pachpatte, B.G. On some inequalities for convex functions. *RGMIA Res. Rep. Coll.* **2003**, *6*, 1–9.
34. Noor, M.A. Fuzzy preinvex functions. *Fuzzy Sets Syst.* **1994**, *4*, 95–104. [CrossRef]
35. Noor, M.A.; Noor, K.I. On strongly generalized preinvex functions. *J. Inequ. Pure Appl. Math.* **2005**, *6*, 102.
36. Zhang, D.; Guo, C.; Chen, D.; Wang, G. Jensen's inequalities for set-valued and fuzzy set-valued functions. *Fuzzy Sets Syst.* **2020**, *2020*, 1–27. [CrossRef]
37. Khan, M.B.; Noor, M.A.; Noor, K.I.; Chu, Y.M. New Hermite-Hadamard type inequalities for -convex fuzzy-interval-valued functions. *Adv. Differ. Equ.* **2021**, *2021*, 6–20. [CrossRef]
38. Khan, M.B.; Mohammed, P.O.; Noor, M.A.; Baleanu, D.; Guirao, J. Some New Fractional Estimates of Inequalities for LR-p-Convex Interval-Valued Functions by Means of Pseudo Order Relation. *Axioms* **2021**, *10*, 175. [CrossRef]
39. Khan, M.B.; Treanţă, S.; Budak, H. Generalized p-Convex Fuzzy-Interval-Valued Functions and Inequalities Based upon the Fuzzy-Order Relation. *Fractal Fract.* **2022**, *6*, 63. [CrossRef]
40. Khan, M.B.; Srivastava, H.M.; Mohammed, P.O.; Macías-Díaz, J.E.; Hamed, Y.S. Some new versions of integral inequalities for log-preinvex fuzzy-interval-valued functions through fuzzy order relation. *Alex. Eng. J.* **2022**, *61*, 7089–7101. [CrossRef]
41. Khan, M.B.; Srivastava, H.M.; Mohammed, P.O.; Guirao, J.L.; Jawa, T.M. Fuzzy-interval inequalities for generalized preinvex fuzzy interval valued functions. *Math. Biosci. Eng.* **2022**, *19*, 812–835. [CrossRef]
42. Khan, M.B.; Mohammed, P.O.; Noor, M.A.; Hamed, Y.S. New Hermite-Hadamard inequalities in fuzzy-interval fractional calculus and related inequalities. *Symmetry* **2021**, *13*, 673. [CrossRef]
43. Khan, M.B.; Mohammed, P.O.; Noor, M.A.; Alsharif, A.M.; Noor, K.I. New fuzzy-interval inequalities in fuzzy-interval fractional calculus by means of fuzzy order relation. *AIMS Math* **2021**, *6*, 10964–10988. [CrossRef]
44. Khan, M.B.; Noor, M.A.; Mohammed, P.O.; Guirao, J.L.; Noor, K.I. Some Integral Inequalities for Generalized Convex Fuzzy-Interval-Valued Functions via Fuzzy Riemann Integrals. *Int. J. Comput. Intell. Syst.* **2021**, *14*, 1–15. [CrossRef]
45. Khan, M.B.; Noor, M.A.; Al-Shomrani, M.M.; Abdullah, L. Some novel inequalities for LR-h-convex interval-valued functions by means of pseudo-order relation. *Math. Methods Appl. Sci.* **2022**, *45*, 1310–1340. [CrossRef]
46. Khan, M.B.; Noor, M.A.; Abdullah, L.; Chu, Y.M. Some New Classes of Preinvex Fuzzy-Interval-Valued Functions and Inequalities. *Int. J. Comput. Intell. Syst.* **2021**, *14*, 1403–1418. [CrossRef]
47. Liu, P.; Khan, M.B.; Noor, M.A.; Noor, K.I. New Hermite-Hadamard and Jensen inequalities for log-s-convex fuzzy-interval-valued functions in the second sense. *Complex Intell. Syst.* **2021**, *2021*, 1–15. [CrossRef]
48. Sana, G.; Khan, M.B.; Noor, M.A.; Mohammed, P.O.; Chu, Y.M. Harmonically convex fuzzy-interval-valued functions and fuzzy-interval Riemann–Liouville fractional integral inequalities. *Int. J. Comput. Intell. Syst.* **2021**, *14*, 1809–1822. [CrossRef]
49. Khan, M.B.; Mohammed, P.O.; Noor, M.A.; Abualnaja, K.M. Fuzzy integral inequalities on coordinates of convex fuzzy interval-valued functions. *Math. Biosci. Eng.* **2021**, *18*, 6552–6580. [CrossRef]

50. Khan, M.B.; Treanţă, S.; Soliman, M.S.; Nonlaopon, K.; Zaini, H.G. Some Hadamard–Fejér Type Inequalities for LR-Convex Interval-Valued Functions. *Fractal Fract.* **2022**, *6*, 6. [CrossRef]
51. Khan, M.B.; Srivastava, H.M.; Mohammed, P.O.; Nonlaopon, K.; Hamed, Y.S. Some new Jensen, Schur and Hermite-Hadamard inequalities for log convex fuzzy interval-valued functions. *AIMS Math* **2022**, *7*, 4338–4358. [CrossRef]
52. Khan, M.B.; Mohammed, P.O.; Machado, J.A.T.; Guirao, J.L. Integral Inequalities for Generalized Harmonically Convex Functions in Fuzzy-Interval-Valued Settings. *Symmetry* **2021**, *13*, 2352. [CrossRef]
53. Khan, M.B.; Srivastava, H.M.; Mohammed, P.O.; Baleanu, D.; Jawa, T.M. Fuzzy-interval inequalities for generalized convex fuzzy-interval-valued functions via fuzzy Riemann integrals. *AIMS Math* **2022**, *7*, 1507–1535. [CrossRef]
54. Fernandez, A.; Mohammed, P. Hermite-Hadamard inequalities in fractional calculus defined using Mittag-Leffler kernels. *Math. Meth. Appl. Sci.* **2020**, *2020*, 1–18. [CrossRef]
55. Mohammed, P.O.; Abdeljawad, T. Integral inequalities for a fractional operator of a function with respect to another function with nonsingular kernel. *Adv. Differ. Equ.* **2020**, *2020*, 363. [CrossRef]

mathematics

Article

Hermite-Hadamard-Type Fractional Inclusions for Interval-Valued Preinvex Functions

Kin Keung Lai [1,*], Jaya Bisht [2], Nidhi Sharma [2] and Shashi Kant Mishra [2]

1 International Business School, Shaanxi Normal University, Xi'an 710119, China
2 Department of Mathematics, Institute of Science, Banaras Hindu University, Varanasi 221005, India; jaya.bisht10@bhu.ac.in (J.B.); nidhi.sharma10@bhu.ac.in (N.S.); shashikant.mishra@bhu.ac.in (S.K.M.)
* Correspondence: mskklai@outlook.com

Abstract: We introduce a new class of interval-valued preinvex functions termed as harmonically h-preinvex interval-valued functions. We establish new inclusion of Hermite–Hadamard for harmonically h-preinvex interval-valued function via interval-valued Riemann–Liouville fractional integrals. Further, we prove fractional Hermite–Hadamard-type inclusions for the product of two harmonically h-preinvex interval-valued functions. In this way, these findings include several well-known results and newly obtained results of the existing literature as special cases. Moreover, applications of the main results are demonstrated by presenting some examples.

Keywords: Hermite–Hadamard inequalities; harmonical convex functions; interval-valued functions; fractional integrals

Citation: Lai, K.K.; Bisht, J.; Sharma, N.; Mishra, S.K. Hermite-Hadamard-Type Fractional Inclusions for Interval-Valued Preinvex Functions. *Mathematics* **2022**, *10*, 264. https://doi.org/10.3390/math10020264

Academic Editor: Savin Treanta

Received: 22 December 2021
Accepted: 13 January 2022
Published: 16 January 2022

1. Introduction

It is well known that extensive literature on the class of integral inequalities is being introduced under various notions of convexity; see, for instance [1–6]. Inspired by the importance of convexity in multiple fields of pure and applied sciences, researchers generalized and extended the notion of convexity in various settings. A useful generalization of convex functions is introduced by Hanson [7] which is called invex functions. In 1986, Ben-Israel and Mond [8] proposed the notion of preinvex functions and showed that every differentiable preinvex function is invex, but the converse may not be true. Yang and Li [9] provided two conditions that determine the preinvexity of a function via an intermediate-point preinvexity check under conditions of upper and lower semicontinuity, respectively.

On the other hand, interval analysis was introduced to handle interval uncertainty in many mathematical or computer models of some deterministic real-world phenomena. Moore [10] was the first to propose the concept of interval analysis and extend the arithmetic of intervals to the computer. Moore et al. [11] discussed an arithmetic for intervals, integration of interval functions, and interval Newton methods. Bhurjee and Panda [12] provided a methodology to determine the efficient solution of general multi-objective interval fractional programming problem. Lupulescu [13] gave a theory of the fractional calculus for interval-valued functions using gH-difference for closed intervals. Further, Li et al. [14] introduced the concept of invexity using gH-derivative of interval-valued functions and derived Kuhn–Tucker optimality conditions for an interval-valued objective function. Interval analysis has applications in various fields such as experimental and computational physics, error analysis, computer graphics, robotics, numerical integration, and many other fields (see [15–19]).

2. Literature Survey

Işcan [20] proposed the concept of harmonically convex functions and presented some Hermite–Hadamard (H–H)-type inequalities for harmonically convex functions. Noor et al. [21] defined a new class of preinvex functions named h-preinvex functions and

Corollary 1 ([33]). *If $\psi : [\omega_1, \omega_2] \to X_I$ is an interval-valued function such that $\psi(u) = [\underline{\psi}(u), \overline{\psi}(u)]$ with $\underline{\psi}(u), \overline{\psi}(u) \in R_{([\omega_1,\omega_2])}$, then we have*

$$J^{\alpha}_{\omega_1^+}\psi(u) = [J^{\alpha}_{\omega_1^+}\underline{\psi}(u),\ J^{\alpha}_{\omega_1^+}\overline{\psi}(u)]$$

and

$$J^{\alpha}_{\omega_2^-}\psi(u) = [J^{\alpha}_{\omega_2^-}\underline{\psi}(u),\ J^{\alpha}_{\omega_2^-}\overline{\psi}(u)].$$

Definition 4 ([52]). *A set $I = [\omega_1, \omega_2] \subseteq \mathbb{R}\backslash\{0\}$ is called a harmonic convex set if*

$$\frac{uv}{tu + (1-t)v} \in I, \quad \forall u, v \in I, \quad t \in [0,1].$$

Definition 5 ([20]). *A function $\psi : I = [\omega_1, \omega_2] \subseteq \mathbb{R}\backslash\{0\} \to \mathbb{R}$ is called harmonic convex, if*

$$\psi\left(\frac{uv}{tu + (1-t)v}\right) \leq (1-t)\psi(u) + t\psi(v), \ \forall u, v \in I, \ t \in [0,1].$$

Now we consider some concepts for harmonic preinvex functions. Let $\psi : I \subseteq \mathbb{R}\backslash\{0\} \to \mathbb{R}$ and $\eta(.,.) : I \times I \to \mathbb{R}$ be continuous functions.

Definition 6 ([53]). *A set $I = [\omega_1, \omega_1 + \eta(\omega_2, \omega_1)] \subseteq \mathbb{R}\backslash\{0\}$ is called a harmonic invex with respect to $\eta(.,.)$, if*

$$\frac{u(u + \eta(v,u))}{u + (1-t)\eta(v,u)} \in I, \quad \forall u, v \in I, \quad t \in [0,1].$$

It is well known that every harmonic convex set is harmonic invex with respect to $\eta(v,u) = v - u$ but not conversely.

Definition 7 ([53]). *A function $\psi : I = [\omega_1, \omega_1 + \eta(\omega_2, \omega_1)] \subseteq \mathbb{R}\backslash\{0\} \to \mathbb{R}$ is said to be harmonic preinvex with respect to the bifunction $\eta(.,.)$, if*

$$\psi\left(\frac{u(u + \eta(v,u))}{u + (1-t)\eta(v,u)}\right) \leq (1-t)\psi(u) + t\psi(v), \ \forall u, v \in I, \ t \in [0,1].$$

Condition C [54]. Let $I \subseteq \mathbb{R}$ be an invex set with respect to $\eta(.,.)$. Then, function η holds the condition C if for any $t \in [0,1]$ and any $u, v \in I$,

$$\eta(v, v + t\eta(u,v)) = -t\eta(u,v),$$

$$\eta(u, v + t\eta(u,v)) = (1-t)\eta(u,v).$$

Note that $\forall\, t_1, t_2 \in [0,1],\ u, v \in I$ and from condition C, we have

$$\eta(v + t_2\eta(u,v), v + t_1\eta(u,v)) = (t_2 - t_1)\eta(u,v).$$

Theorem 2 ([55]). *Let $\psi : I = [\omega_1, \omega_1 + \eta(\omega_2, \omega_1)] \subseteq \mathbb{R} \to (0, \infty)$ be a preinvex function on I and $\omega_1, \omega_2 \in I$ with $\omega_1 < \omega_1 + \eta(\omega_2, \omega_1)$. Then*

$$\psi\left(\frac{2\omega_1 + \eta(\omega_2, \omega_1)}{2}\right) \leq \frac{1}{\eta(\omega_2, \omega_1)} \int_{\omega_1}^{\omega_1 + \eta(\omega_2, \omega_1)} \psi(u) du \leq \frac{\psi(\omega_1) + \psi(\omega_2)}{2},$$

which is called the H–H-Noor inequality.

Definition 8 ([41]). *If $I \subseteq \mathbb{R}$ is an invex set with respect to $\eta(.,.)$, $\psi(u) = [\underline{\psi}(u), \overline{\psi}(u)]$ is an interval-valued function on I. Then ψ is preinvex interval-valued function on I with respect to $\eta(.,.)$ if*

$$\psi(v + t\eta(u,v)) \supseteq t\psi(u) + (1-t)\psi(v), \ \forall\, t \in [0,1] \text{ and } \forall\, u, v \in I.$$

4. Main Results

In this section, first, we define harmonically h-preinvex interval-valued function and discuss some special cases of harmonically h-preinvex interval-valued function.

Definition 9. *Let $h : [0,1] \subseteq J \to \mathbb{R}$ be a non-negative function such that $h \not\equiv 0$, and $I \subseteq \mathbb{R}\backslash\{0\}$ be a harmonic invex set with respect to $\eta(.,.)$. Let $\psi : I \subseteq \mathbb{R}\backslash\{0\} \to X_I^+$ be an interval-valued function on set I, then ψ is called harmonically h-preinvex interval-valued function with respect to $\eta(.,.)$ if*

$$\psi\left(\frac{u(u + \eta(v,u))}{u + (1-t)\eta(v,u)}\right) \supseteq h(1-t)\psi(u) + h(t)\psi(v), \ \forall\, t \in [0,1] \text{ and } \forall\, u, v \in I.$$

Now, we consider some special cases of harmonically h-preinvex interval- valued functions.

For $h(t) = 1$, function ψ is called a harmonically $P-$preinvex interval-valued function.
For $h(t) = t$, function ψ is called a harmonically preinvex interval-valued function.
If $h(t) = t^s$, $s \in (0,1)$, then we find the definition of Breckner type of $s-$harmonically preinvex interval-valued functions.
If $h(t) = t^{-s}$, $s \in (0,1)$, then we find the definition of Godunova–Levin type of $s-$harmonically preinvex interval-valued functions.

Example 1. *Let $I = [1,2] \subset \mathbb{R}\backslash\{0\}$, $\psi(u) = \left[1 - \frac{1}{2u^2}, 1 + \frac{1}{2u}\right]$, $\eta(v,u) = v - 2u$, $h(t) = t$ then ψ is harmonically h-preinvex interval-valued function on I.*

Now, we establish fractional inclusion of H–H for harmonically h-preinvex interval-valued functions.

Theorem 3. *Let $h : [0,1] \to \mathbb{R}$ be a non-negative function such that $h(\frac{1}{2}) \neq 0$. Let $\psi : I = [\omega_1, \omega_1 + \eta(\omega_2,\omega_1)] \subseteq \mathbb{R}\backslash\{0\} \to X_I^+$ be a harmonically h-preinvex interval-valued function such that $\psi = [\underline{\psi}, \overline{\psi}]$ and $\omega_1, \omega_2 \in I$ with $\omega_1 < \omega_1 + \eta(\omega_2,\omega_1)$. If $\psi \in L[\omega_1, \omega_1 + \eta(\omega_2,\omega_1)]$, $\alpha > 0$ and η holds condition C, then*

$$\begin{aligned}
&\frac{1}{\alpha h(\frac{1}{2})}\psi\left(\frac{2\omega_1(\omega_1 + \eta(\omega_2,\omega_1))}{2\omega_1 + \eta(\omega_2,\omega_1)}\right) \\
&\supseteq \Gamma(\alpha)\left(\frac{\omega_1(\omega_1 + \eta(\omega_2,\omega_1))}{\eta(\omega_2,\omega_1)}\right)^{\alpha}\left[J^{\alpha}_{\left(\frac{1}{\omega_1 + \eta(\omega_2,\omega_1)}\right)^+}(\psi o \Omega)\left(\frac{1}{\omega_1}\right) + J^{\alpha}_{\left(\frac{1}{\omega_1}\right)^-}(\psi o \Omega)\left(\frac{1}{\omega_1 + \eta(\omega_2,\omega_1)}\right)\right] \\
&\supseteq [\psi(\omega_1) + \psi(\omega_1 + \eta(\omega_2,\omega_1))]\int_0^1 t^{\alpha-1}[h(t) + h(1-t)]dt,
\end{aligned}$$

where $\Omega(u) = \frac{1}{u}$ and $\psi o \Omega$ is defined by $\psi o \Omega(u) = \psi(\Omega(u))$, $\forall\, u \in \left[\frac{1}{\omega_1 + \eta(\omega_2,\omega_1)}, \frac{1}{\omega_1}\right]$.

Proof. As ψ is harmonically h-preinvex interval-valued function on $[\omega_1, \omega_1 + \eta(\omega_2,\omega_1)]$, we have

$$\frac{1}{h(\frac{1}{2})}\psi\left(\frac{2u(u + \eta(v,u))}{2u + \eta(v,u)}\right) \supseteq \psi(u) + \psi(v), \ \forall\, u, v \in [\omega_1, \omega_1 + \eta(\omega_2,\omega_1)]. \tag{1}$$

Let $u = \frac{\omega_1(\omega_1 + \eta(\omega_2,\omega_1))}{\omega_1 + (1-t)\eta(\omega_2,\omega_1)}$ and $v = \frac{\omega_1(\omega_1 + \eta(\omega_2,\omega_1))}{\omega_1 + t\eta(\omega_2,\omega_1)}$. Then, using Condition C in (1), we find

$$\frac{1}{h(\frac{1}{2})}\psi\left(\frac{2\omega_1(\omega_1+\eta(\omega_2,\omega_1))}{2\omega_1+\eta(\omega_2,\omega_1)}\right) \supseteq \psi\left(\frac{\omega_1(\omega_1+\eta(\omega_2,\omega_1))}{\omega_1+(1-t)\eta(\omega_2,\omega_1)}\right)+\psi\left(\frac{\omega_1(\omega_1+\eta(\omega_2,\omega_1))}{\omega_1+t\eta(\omega_2,\omega_1)}\right). \tag{2}$$

Multiplying (2) by $t^{\alpha-1}$, $\alpha>0$ and integrating over $[0,1]$ with respect to t, we have

$$\begin{aligned}\frac{1}{h(\frac{1}{2})}(IR)\int_0^1 t^{\alpha-1}\psi\left(\frac{2\omega_1(\omega_1+\eta(\omega_2,\omega_1))}{2\omega_1+\eta(\omega_2,\omega_1)}\right)dt &\supseteq (IR)\int_0^1 t^{\alpha-1}\psi\left(\frac{\omega_1(\omega_1+\eta(\omega_2,\omega_1))}{\omega_1+(1-t)\eta(\omega_2,\omega_1)}\right)dt\\ &+(IR)\int_0^1 t^{\alpha-1}\psi\left(\frac{\omega_1(\omega_1+\eta(\omega_2,\omega_1))}{\omega_1+t\eta(\omega_2,\omega_1)}\right)dt.\end{aligned} \tag{3}$$

Applying Theorem 1 in above relation, we find

$$\begin{aligned}&(IR)\int_0^1 t^{\alpha-1}\psi\left(\frac{2\omega_1(\omega_1+\eta(\omega_2,\omega_1))}{2\omega_1+\eta(\omega_2,\omega_1)}\right)dt\\ &=\left[(R)\int_0^1 t^{\alpha-1}\underline{\psi}\left(\frac{2\omega_1(\omega_1+\eta(\omega_2,\omega_1))}{2\omega_1+\eta(\omega_2,\omega_1)}\right)dt,(R)\int_0^1 t^{\alpha-1}\overline{\psi}\left(\frac{2\omega_1(\omega_1+\eta(\omega_2,\omega_1))}{2\omega_1+\eta(\omega_2,\omega_1)}\right)dt\right]\\ &=\left[\frac{1}{\alpha}\underline{\psi}\left(\frac{2\omega_1(\omega_1+\eta(\omega_2,\omega_1))}{2\omega_1+\eta(\omega_2,\omega_1)}\right),\frac{1}{\alpha}\overline{\psi}\left(\frac{2\omega_1(\omega_1+\eta(\omega_2,\omega_1))}{2\omega_1+\eta(\omega_2,\omega_1)}\right)\right]\\ &=\frac{1}{\alpha}\psi\left(\frac{2\omega_1(\omega_1+\eta(\omega_2,\omega_1))}{2\omega_1+\eta(\omega_2,\omega_1)}\right),\end{aligned} \tag{4}$$

$$\begin{aligned}&(IR)\int_0^1 t^{\alpha-1}\psi\left(\frac{\omega_1(\omega_1+\eta(\omega_2,\omega_1))}{\omega_1+(1-t)\eta(\omega_2,\omega_1)}\right)dt\\ &=\left[(R)\int_0^1 t^{\alpha-1}\underline{\psi}\left(\frac{\omega_1(\omega_1+\eta(\omega_2,\omega_1))}{\omega_1+(1-t)\eta(\omega_2,\omega_1)}\right)dt,(R)\int_0^1 t^{\alpha-1}\overline{\psi}\left(\frac{\omega_1(\omega_1+\eta(\omega_2,\omega_1))}{\omega_1+(1-t)\eta(\omega_2,\omega_1)}\right)dt\right]\\ &=\Gamma(\alpha)\left(\frac{\omega_1(\omega_1+\eta(\omega_2,\omega_1))}{\eta(\omega_2,\omega_1)}\right)^{\alpha}\left[J^{\alpha}_{\left(\frac{1}{\omega_1+\eta(\omega_2,\omega_1)}\right)^+}\underline{\psi}o\Omega\left(\frac{1}{\omega_1}\right),J^{\alpha}_{\left(\frac{1}{\omega_1+\eta(\omega_2,\omega_1)}\right)^+}\overline{\psi}o\Omega\left(\frac{1}{\omega_1}\right)\right]\\ &=\Gamma(\alpha)\left(\frac{\omega_1(\omega_1+\eta(\omega_2,\omega_1))}{\eta(\omega_2,\omega_1)}\right)^{\alpha}J^{\alpha}_{\left(\frac{1}{\omega_1+\eta(\omega_2,\omega_1)}\right)^+}(\psi o\Omega)\left(\frac{1}{\omega_1}\right).\end{aligned} \tag{5}$$

Similarly,

$$(IR)\int_0^1 t^{\alpha-1}\psi\left(\frac{\omega_1(\omega_1+\eta(\omega_2,\omega_1))}{\omega_1+t\eta(\omega_2,\omega_1)}\right)dt=\Gamma(\alpha)\left(\frac{\omega_1(\omega_1+\eta(\omega_2,\omega_1))}{\eta(\omega_2,\omega_1)}\right)^{\alpha}J^{\alpha}_{\left(\frac{1}{\omega_1}\right)^-}(\psi o\Omega)\left(\frac{1}{\omega_1+\eta(\omega_2,\omega_1)}\right). \tag{6}$$

Using (4)–(6) in (3), we have

$$\begin{aligned}\frac{1}{\alpha h(\frac{1}{2})}\psi\left(\frac{2\omega_1(\omega_1+\eta(\omega_2,\omega_1))}{2\omega_1+\eta(\omega_2,\omega_1)}\right) &\supseteq \Gamma(\alpha)\left(\frac{\omega_1(\omega_1+\eta(\omega_2,\omega_1))}{\eta(\omega_2,\omega_1)}\right)^{\alpha}\left[J^{\alpha}_{\left(\frac{1}{\omega_1+\eta(\omega_2,\omega_1)}\right)^+}(\psi o\Omega)\left(\frac{1}{\omega_1}\right)\right.\\ &\left.+J^{\alpha}_{\left(\frac{1}{\omega_1}\right)^-}(\psi o\Omega)\left(\frac{1}{\omega_1+\eta(\omega_2,\omega_1)}\right)\right].\end{aligned} \tag{7}$$

As ψ is an harmonically h-preinvex interval-valued function on $[\omega_1,\omega_1+\eta(\omega_2,\omega_1)]$, we have

$$\begin{aligned}\psi\left(\frac{\omega_1(\omega_1+\eta(\omega_2,\omega_1))}{\omega_1+(1-t)\eta(\omega_2,\omega_1)}\right) &= \psi\left(\frac{(\omega_1+\eta(\omega_2,\omega_1))(\omega_1+\eta(\omega_2,\omega_1)+\eta(\omega_1,\omega_1+\eta(\omega_2,\omega_1))}{\omega_1+\eta(\omega_2,\omega_1)+t\eta(\omega_1,\omega_1+\eta(\omega_2,\omega_1))}\right)\\ &\supseteq h(t)\psi(\omega_1+\eta(\omega_2,\omega_1))+h(1-t)\psi(\omega_1)\end{aligned} \tag{8}$$

and

$$\psi\left(\frac{\omega_1(\omega_1+\eta(\omega_2,\omega_1))}{\omega_1+t\eta(\omega_2,\omega_1)}\right)=\psi\left(\frac{(\omega_1+\eta(\omega_2,\omega_1))(\omega_1+\eta(\omega_2,\omega_1)+\eta(\omega_1,\omega_1+\eta(\omega_2,\omega_1))}{\omega_1+\eta(\omega_2,\omega_1)+(1-t)\eta(\omega_1,\omega_1+\eta(\omega_2,\omega_1))}\right)$$
$$\supseteq h(1-t)\psi(\omega_1+\eta(\omega_2,\omega_1))+h(t)\psi(\omega_1). \tag{9}$$

Adding (8) and (9), we have

$$\psi\left(\frac{\omega_1(\omega_1+\eta(\omega_2,\omega_1))}{\omega_1+(1-t)\eta(\omega_2,\omega_1)}\right)+\psi\left(\frac{\omega_1(\omega_1+\eta(\omega_2,\omega_1))}{\omega_1+t\eta(\omega_2,\omega_1)}\right)\supseteq[h(t)+h(1-t)][\psi(\omega_1)+\psi(\omega_1+\eta(\omega_2,\omega_1))]. \tag{10}$$

Multiplying (10) by $t^{\alpha-1}$ and integrating over $[0,1]$ with respect to t, we have

$$(IR)\int_0^1 t^{\alpha-1}\psi\left(\frac{\omega_1(\omega_1+\eta(\omega_2,\omega_1))}{\omega_1+(1-t)\eta(\omega_2,\omega_1)}\right)dt+(IR)\int_0^1 t^{\alpha-1}\psi\left(\frac{\omega_1(\omega_1+\eta(\omega_2,\omega_1))}{\omega_1+t\eta(\omega_2,\omega_1)}\right)dt$$
$$\supseteq(IR)\int_0^1 t^{\alpha-1}[h(t)+h(1-t)][\psi(\omega_1)+\psi(\omega_1+\eta(\omega_2,\omega_1))]dt.$$

This implies

$$\Gamma(\alpha)\left(\frac{\omega_1(\omega_1+\eta(\omega_2,\omega_1))}{\eta(\omega_2,\omega_1)}\right)^{\alpha}\left[J^{\alpha}_{\left(\frac{1}{\omega_1+\eta(\omega_2,\omega_1)}\right)^+}(\psi o\Omega)\left(\frac{1}{\omega_1}\right)+J^{\alpha}_{\left(\frac{1}{\omega_1}\right)^-}(\psi o\Omega)\left(\frac{1}{\omega_1+\eta(\omega_2,\omega_1)}\right)\right]$$
$$\supseteq[\psi(\omega_1)+\psi(\omega_1+\eta(\omega_2,\omega_1))]\int_0^1 t^{\alpha-1}[h(t)+h(1-t)]dt. \tag{11}$$

From (7) and (11), we find

$$\frac{1}{\alpha h(\frac{1}{2})}\psi\left(\frac{2\omega_1(\omega_1+\eta(\omega_2,\omega_1))}{2\omega_1+\eta(\omega_2,\omega_1)}\right)$$
$$\supseteq\Gamma(\alpha)\left(\frac{\omega_1(\omega_1+\eta(\omega_2,\omega_1))}{\eta(\omega_2,\omega_1)}\right)^{\alpha}\left[J^{\alpha}_{\left(\frac{1}{\omega_1+\eta(\omega_2,\omega_1)}\right)^+}(\psi o\Omega)\left(\frac{1}{\omega_1}\right)+J^{\alpha}_{\left(\frac{1}{\omega_1}\right)^-}(\psi o\Omega)\left(\frac{1}{\omega_1+\eta(\omega_2,\omega_1)}\right)\right]$$
$$\supseteq[\psi(\omega_1)+\psi(\omega_1+\eta(\omega_2,\omega_1))]\int_0^1 t^{\alpha-1}[h(t)+h(1-t)]dt.$$

□

Example 2. *Let $I=[\omega_1,\omega_1+\eta(\omega_2,\omega_1)]=[1,2]$, $\eta(\omega_2,\omega_1)=\omega_2-2\omega_1$. Let $\alpha=1$ and $h(t)=t\ \forall\ t\in[0,1]$,*
$\psi: I\to X_I^+$ be defined by

$$\psi(u)=\left[-\frac{1}{u}+2,\frac{1}{u}+2\right],\quad\forall\, u\in I.$$

We find

$$\frac{1}{\alpha h(\frac{1}{2})}\psi\left(\frac{2\omega_1(\omega_1+\eta(\omega_2,\omega_1))}{2\omega_1+\eta(\omega_2,\omega_1)}\right)=2\psi\left(\frac{4}{3}\right)=\left[\frac{5}{2},\frac{11}{2}\right], \tag{12}$$

$$\Gamma(\alpha)\left(\frac{\omega_1(\omega_1+\eta(\omega_2,\omega_1))}{\eta(\omega_2,\omega_1)}\right)^{\alpha}\left[J^{\alpha}_{\left(\frac{1}{\omega_1+\eta(\omega_2,\omega_1)}\right)^+}(\psi o\Omega)\left(\frac{1}{\omega_1}\right)+J^{\alpha}_{\left(\frac{1}{\omega_1}\right)^-}(\psi o\Omega)\left(\frac{1}{\omega_1+\eta(\omega_2,\omega_1)}\right)\right]$$
$$=\frac{2\omega_1(\omega_1+\eta(\omega_2,\omega_1))}{\eta(\omega_2,\omega_1)}\int_{\omega_1}^{\omega_1+\eta(\omega_2,\omega_1)}\frac{\psi(u)}{u^2}du=2\int_1^2\frac{1}{u^2}\left[-\frac{1}{u}+2,\frac{1}{u}+2\right]du=\left[\frac{5}{2},\frac{11}{2}\right] \tag{13}$$

and

$$[\psi(\omega_1)+\psi(\omega_1+\eta(\omega_2,\omega_1))]\int_0^1 t^{\alpha-1}[h(t)+h(1-t)]dt=[\psi+\psi]=\left[\frac{5}{2},\frac{11}{2}\right]. \tag{14}$$

From (12)–(14), we see Theorem 3 is verified.

Remark 1. *If we put $\eta(\omega_2,\omega_1)=\omega_2-\omega_1$ in the above theorem, we obtain Theorem 5 of [50].*

Remark 2. *If we put $\eta(\omega_2,\omega_1)=\omega_2-\omega_1$ and $\alpha=1$ in the above theorem, we obtain Theorem 1 of [38].*

Remark 3. *If we put $\eta(\omega_2,\omega_1)=\omega_2-\omega_1$ and $h(t)=t$ in the above theorem, we obtain Theorem 3.6 of [56].*

Now we present some particular cases of Theorem 3.

Corollary 2. *If $\alpha=1$, then Theorem 3 gives the following result:*

$$\frac{1}{h(\frac{1}{2})}\psi\left(\frac{2\omega_1(\omega_1+\eta(\omega_2,\omega_1))}{2\omega_1+\eta(\omega_2,\omega_1)}\right)\supseteq\frac{2\omega_1(\omega_1+\eta(\omega_2,\omega_1))}{\eta(\omega_2,\omega_1)}\int_{\omega_1}^{\omega_1+\eta(\omega_2,\omega_1)}\frac{\psi(u)}{u^2}du$$
$$\supseteq[\psi(\omega_1)+\psi(\omega_1+\eta(\omega_2,\omega_1))]\int_0^1[h(t)+h(1-t)]dt.$$

Corollary 3. *If $h(t)=t$, then Theorem 3 gives the following result:*

$$\psi\left(\frac{2\omega_1(\omega_1+\eta(\omega_2,\omega_1))}{2\omega_1+\eta(\omega_2,\omega_1)}\right)$$
$$\supseteq\frac{\Gamma(\alpha+1)}{2}\left(\frac{\omega_1(\omega_1+\eta(\omega_2,\omega_1))}{\eta(\omega_2,\omega_1)}\right)^{\alpha}\left[J^{\alpha}_{\left(\frac{1}{\omega_1+\eta(\omega_2,\omega_1)}\right)^+}\psi\left(\frac{1}{\omega_1}\right)+J^{\alpha}_{\left(\frac{1}{\omega_1}\right)^-}\psi\left(\frac{1}{\omega_1+\eta(\omega_2,\omega_1)}\right)\right]$$
$$\supseteq\frac{\psi(\omega_1)+\psi(\omega_1+\eta(\omega_2,\omega_1))}{2}.$$

Next, we prove fractional inclusions of H–H-type for the product of two harmonically h-preinvex interval-valued functions.

Theorem 4. *Let $h_1,h_2:[0,1]\to\mathbb{R}$ be non-negative functions and $h_1,h_2\not\equiv 0$. Let $\psi,\varphi:I=[\omega_1,\omega_1+\eta(\omega_2,\omega_1)]\subseteq\mathbb{R}\backslash\{0\}\to X_I^+$ be two harmonically h_1- and h_2-preinvex interval-valued functions, respectively, such that $\psi=[\underline{\psi},\overline{\psi}]$, $\varphi=[\underline{\varphi},\overline{\varphi}]$ and $\omega_1,\omega_2\in I$ with $\omega_1<\omega_1+\eta(\omega_2,\omega_1)$. If $\psi\varphi\in L[\omega_1,\omega_1+\eta(\omega_2,\omega_1)]$, $\alpha>0$ and η holds condition C, then*

$$\Gamma(\alpha)\left(\frac{\omega_1(\omega_1+\eta(\omega_2,\omega_1))}{\eta(\omega_2,\omega_1)}\right)^{\alpha}\left[J^{\alpha}_{\left(\frac{1}{\omega_1+\eta(\omega_2,\omega_1)}\right)^+}(\psi o\Omega)\left(\frac{1}{\omega_1}\right)(\varphi o\Omega)\left(\frac{1}{\omega_1}\right)\right.$$
$$\left.+J^{\alpha}_{\left(\frac{1}{\omega_1}\right)^-}(\psi o\Omega)\left(\frac{1}{\omega_1+\eta(\omega_2,\omega_1)}\right)(\varphi o\Omega)\left(\frac{1}{\omega_1+\eta(\omega_2,\omega_1)}\right)\right]$$
$$\supseteq F(\omega_1,\omega_1+\eta(\omega_2,\omega_1))\int_0^1[t^{\alpha-1}+(1-t)^{\alpha-1}]h_1(t)h_2(t)dt$$
$$+G(\omega_1,\omega_1+\eta(\omega_2,\omega_1))\int_0^1[t^{\alpha-1}+(1-t)^{\alpha-1}]h_1(1-t)h_2(t)]dt, \tag{15}$$

where $F(\omega_1,\omega_1+\eta(\omega_2,\omega_1))=\psi(\omega_1)\varphi(\omega_1)+\psi(\omega_1+\eta(\omega_2,\omega_1))\varphi(\omega_1+\eta(\omega_2,\omega_1))$, $N(\omega_1,\omega_1+\eta(\omega_2,\omega_1))=\psi(\omega_1)\varphi(\omega_1+\eta(\omega_2,\omega_1))+\psi(\omega_1+\eta(\omega_2,\omega_1))\varphi(\omega_1)$ and $\Omega(u)=\frac{1}{u}$.

Proof. As ψ and φ are two harmonically h_1- and h_2-preinvex interval-valued functions on $[\omega_1, \omega_1 + \eta(\omega_2, \omega_1)]$, respectively. Therefore,

$$\psi\left(\frac{\omega_1(\omega_1+\eta(\omega_2,\omega_1))}{\omega_1+(1-t)\eta(\omega_2,\omega_1)}\right) = \psi\left(\frac{(\omega_1+\eta(\omega_2,\omega_1))(\omega_1+\eta(\omega_2,\omega_1)+\eta(\omega_1,\omega_1+\eta(\omega_2,\omega_1))}{\omega_1+\eta(\omega_2,\omega_1)+t\eta(\omega_1,\omega_1+\eta(\omega_2,\omega_1))}\right)$$
$$\supseteq h_1(t)\psi(\omega_1+\eta(\omega_2,\omega_1)) + h_1(1-t)\psi(\omega_1) \tag{16}$$

and

$$\varphi\left(\frac{\omega_1(\omega_1+\eta(\omega_2,\omega_1))}{\omega_1+(1-t)\eta(\omega_2,\omega_1)}\right) = \varphi\left(\frac{(\omega_1+\eta(\omega_2,\omega_1))(\omega_1+\eta(\omega_2,\omega_1)+\eta(\omega_1,\omega_1+\eta(\omega_2,\omega_1))}{\omega_1+\eta(\omega_2,\omega_1)+t\eta(\omega_1,\omega_1+\eta(\omega_2,\omega_1))}\right)$$
$$\supseteq h_2(t)\varphi(\omega_1+\eta(\omega_2,\omega_1)) + h_2(1-t)\varphi(\omega_1). \tag{17}$$

As $\psi(u), \varphi(u) \in X_I^+$, $\forall\, u \in [\omega_1, \omega_1 + \eta(\omega_2, \omega_1)]$, then from (16) and (17), we obtain

$$\psi\left(\frac{\omega_1(\omega_1+\eta(\omega_2,\omega_1))}{\omega_1+(1-t)\eta(\omega_2,\omega_1)}\right)\varphi\left(\frac{\omega_1(\omega_1+\eta(\omega_2,\omega_1))}{\omega_1+(1-t)\eta(\omega_2,\omega_1)}\right)$$
$$\supseteq h_1(t)h_2(t)\psi(\omega_1+\eta(\omega_2,\omega_1))\varphi(\omega_1+\eta(\omega_2,\omega_1)) + h_1(1-t)h_2(1-t)\psi(\omega_1)\varphi(\omega_1)$$
$$+ h_1(t)h_2(1-t)\psi(\omega_1+\eta(\omega_2,\omega_1))\varphi(\omega_1) + h_1(1-t)h_2(t)\psi(\omega_1)\varphi(\omega_1+\eta(\omega_2,\omega_1)). \tag{18}$$

Similarly,

$$\psi\left(\frac{\omega_1(\omega_1+\eta(\omega_2,\omega_1))}{\omega_1+t\eta(\omega_2,\omega_1)}\right)\varphi\left(\frac{\omega_1(\omega_1+\eta(\omega_2,\omega_1))}{\omega_1+t\eta(\omega_2,\omega_1)}\right)$$
$$\supseteq h_1(1-t)h_2(1-t)\psi(\omega_1+\eta(\omega_2,\omega_1))\varphi(\omega_1+\eta(\omega_2,\omega_1)) + h_1(t)h_2(t)\psi(\omega_1)\varphi(\omega_1)$$
$$+ h_1(1-t)h_2(t)\psi(\omega_1+\eta(\omega_2,\omega_1))\varphi(\omega_1) + h_1(t)h_2(1-t)\psi(\omega_1)\varphi(\omega_1+\eta(\omega_2,\omega_1)). \tag{19}$$

Adding (18) and (19), we have

$$\psi\left(\frac{\omega_1(\omega_1+\eta(\omega_2,\omega_1))}{\omega_1+(1-t)\eta(\omega_2,\omega_1)}\right)\varphi\left(\frac{\omega_1(\omega_1+\eta(\omega_2,\omega_1))}{\omega_1+(1-t)\eta(\omega_2,\omega_1)}\right)$$
$$+ \psi\left(\frac{\omega_1(\omega_1+\eta(\omega_2,\omega_1))}{\omega_1+t\eta(\omega_2,\omega_1)}\right)\varphi\left(\frac{\omega_1(\omega_1+\eta(\omega_2,\omega_1))}{\omega_1+t\eta(\omega_2,\omega_1)}\right)$$
$$\supseteq [h_1(t)h_2(t) + h_1(1-t)h_2(1-t)][\psi(\omega_1)\varphi(\omega_1) + \psi(\omega_1+\eta(\omega_2,\omega_1))\varphi(\omega_1+\eta(\omega_2,\omega_1))]$$
$$+ [h_1(t)h_2(1-t) + h_1(1-t)h_2(t)][\psi(\omega_1+\eta(\omega_2,\omega_1))\varphi(\omega_1) + \psi(\omega_1)\varphi(\omega_1+(\omega_2,r))]$$
$$= F(\omega_1,\omega_1+\eta(\omega_2,\omega_1))[h_1(t)h_2(t) + h_1(1-t)h_2(1-t)]$$
$$+ G(\omega_1,\omega_1+\eta(\omega_2,\omega_1))[h_1(1-t)h_2(t) + h_1(t)h_2(1-t)]. \tag{20}$$

Multiplying (20) by $t^{\alpha-1}$ and integrating over $[0,1]$ with respect to t, we have

$$(IR)\int_0^1 t^{\alpha-1}\psi\left(\frac{\omega_1(\omega_1+\eta(\omega_2,\omega_1))}{\omega_1+(1-t)\eta(\omega_2,\omega_1)}\right)\varphi\left(\frac{\omega_1(\omega_1+\eta(\omega_2,\omega_1))}{\omega_1+(1-t)\eta(\omega_2,\omega_1)}\right)dt$$
$$+ (IR)\int_0^1 t^{\alpha-1}\psi\left(\frac{\omega_1(\omega_1+\eta(\omega_2,\omega_1))}{\omega_1+t\eta(\omega_2,\omega_1)}\right)\varphi\left(\frac{\omega_1(\omega_1+\eta(\omega_2,\omega_1))}{\omega_1+t\eta(\omega_2,\omega_1)}\right)dt$$
$$\supseteq (IR)\int_0^1 t^{\alpha-1}F(\omega_1,\omega_1+\eta(\omega_2,\omega_1))[h_1(t)h_2(t) + h_1(1-t)h_2(1-t)]dt$$
$$+ (IR)\int_0^1 t^{\alpha-1}G(\omega_1,\omega_1+\eta(\omega_2,\omega_1))[h_1(1-t)h_2(t) + h_1(t)h_2(1-t)]dt. \tag{21}$$

As

$$(IR)\int_0^1 t^{\alpha-1}\psi\left(\frac{\omega_1(\omega_1+\eta(\omega_2,\omega_1))}{\omega_1+(1-t)\eta(\omega_2,\omega_1)}\right)\varphi\left(\frac{\omega_1(\omega_1+\eta(\omega_2,\omega_1))}{\omega_1+(1-t)\eta(\omega_2,\omega_1)}\right)dt$$

$$= \Gamma(\alpha)\left(\frac{\omega_1(\omega_1+\eta(\omega_2,\omega_1))}{\eta(\omega_2,\omega_1)}\right)^{\alpha} J^{\alpha}_{\left(\frac{1}{\omega_1+\eta(\omega_2,\omega_1)}\right)^+}(\psi o\Omega)\left(\frac{1}{\omega_1}\right)(\varphi o\Omega)\left(\frac{1}{\omega_1}\right), \tag{22}$$

$$(IR)\int_0^1 t^{\alpha-1}\psi\left(\frac{\omega_1(\omega_1+\eta(\omega_2,\omega_1))}{\omega_1+t\eta(\omega_2,\omega_1)}\right)\varphi\left(\frac{\omega_1(\omega_1+\eta(\omega_2,\omega_1))}{\omega_1+t\eta(\omega_2,\omega_1)}\right)dt$$
$$= \Gamma(\alpha)\left(\frac{\omega_1(\omega_1+\eta(\omega_2,\omega_1))}{\eta(\omega_2,\omega_1)}\right)^{\alpha} J^{\alpha}_{\left(\frac{1}{\omega_1}\right)^-}(\psi o\Omega)\left(\frac{1}{\omega_1+\eta(\omega_2,\omega_1)}\right)(\varphi o\Omega)\left(\frac{1}{\omega_1+\eta(\omega_2,\omega_1)}\right). \tag{23}$$

Using (22), (23) in (21), we have

$$\Gamma(\alpha)\left(\frac{\omega_1(\omega_1+\eta(\omega_2,\omega_1))}{\eta(\omega_2,\omega_1)}\right)^{\alpha}\left[J^{\alpha}_{\left(\frac{1}{\omega_1+\eta(\omega_2,\omega_1)}\right)^+}(\psi o\Omega)\left(\frac{1}{\omega_1}\right)(\varphi o\Omega)\left(\frac{1}{\omega_1}\right)\right.$$
$$\left.+J^{\alpha}_{\left(\frac{1}{\omega_1}\right)^-}(\psi o\Omega)\left(\frac{1}{\omega_1+\eta(\omega_2,\omega_1)}\right)(\varphi o\Omega)\left(\frac{1}{\omega_1+\eta(\omega_2,\omega_1)}\right)\right]$$
$$\supseteq F(\omega_1,\omega_1+\eta(\omega_2,\omega_1))\int_0^1[t^{\alpha-1}+(1-t)^{\alpha-1}]h_1(t)h_2(t)dt$$
$$+G(\omega_1,\omega_1+\eta(\omega_2,\omega_1))\int_0^1[t^{\alpha-1}+(1-t)^{\alpha-1}]h_1(1-t)h_2(t)]dt.$$

□

Remark 4. *If we put $\eta(\omega_2,\omega_1)=\omega_2-\omega_1$ in the above theorem, we obtain Theorem 6 of [50].*

Remark 5. *If we put $\eta(\omega_2,\omega_1)=\omega_2-\omega_1$ and $\alpha=1$ in the above theorem, we obtain Theorem 3 of [38].*

Corollary 4. *If $\alpha=1$, then Theorem 4 gives the following result:*

$$\frac{\omega_1(\omega_1+\eta(\omega_2,\omega_1))}{\eta(\omega_2,\omega_1)}\int_{\omega_1}^{\omega_1+\eta(\omega_2,\omega_1)}\frac{\psi(u)\varphi(u)}{u^2}du$$
$$\supseteq F(\omega_1,\omega_1+\eta(\omega_2,\omega_1))\int_0^1 h_1(t)h_2(t)dt+G(\omega_1,\omega_1+\eta(\omega_2,\omega_1))\int_0^1 h_1(1-t)h_2(t)]dt.$$

Corollary 5. *If $h_1(t)=h_2(t)=t$, then Theorem 4 gives the following result:*

$$\Gamma(\alpha)\left(\frac{\omega_1(\omega_1+\eta(\omega_2,\omega_1))}{\eta(\omega_2,\omega_1)}\right)^{\alpha}\left[J^{\alpha}_{\left(\frac{1}{\omega_1+\eta(\omega_2,\omega_1)}\right)^+}(\psi o\Omega)\left(\frac{1}{\omega_1}\right)(\varphi o\Omega)\left(\frac{1}{\omega_1}\right)\right.$$
$$\left.+J^{\alpha}_{\left(\frac{1}{\omega_1}\right)^-}(\psi o\Omega)\left(\frac{1}{\omega_1+\eta(\omega_2,\omega_1)}\right)(\varphi o\Omega)\left(\frac{1}{\omega_1+\eta(\omega_2,\omega_1)}\right)\right]$$
$$\supseteq F(\omega_1,\omega_1+\eta(\omega_2,\omega_1))\int_0^1 t^2[t^{\alpha-1}+(1-t)^{\alpha-1}]dt$$
$$+G(\omega_1,\omega_1+\eta(\omega_2,\omega_1))\int_0^1 t(1-t)[t^{\alpha-1}+(1-t)^{\alpha-1}]dt$$
$$=\frac{\alpha^2+\alpha+2}{\alpha(\alpha+1)(\alpha+2)}F(\omega_1,\omega_1+\eta(\omega_2,\omega_1))+\frac{2}{(\alpha+1)(\alpha+2)}G(\omega_1,\omega_1+\eta(\omega_2,\omega_1))$$
$$=\frac{(\alpha^2+\alpha+2)F(\omega_1,\omega_1+\eta(\omega_2,\omega_1))+2\alpha G(\omega_1,\omega_1+\eta(\omega_2,\omega_1))}{\alpha(\alpha+1)(\alpha+2)}.$$

Theorem 5. *Let $h_1,h_2:[0,1]\to\mathbb{R}$ be non-negative functions and $h_1(\frac{1}{2})h_2(\frac{1}{2})\neq 0$. Let $\psi,\varphi: I=[\omega_1,\omega_1+\eta(\omega_2,\omega_1)]\subseteq\mathbb{R}\backslash\{0\}\to X_I^+$ be two harmonically h_1- and h_2-preinvex* *interval-valued functions, respectively, such that* $\psi = [\underline{\psi}, \overline{\psi}]$, $\varphi = [\underline{\varphi}, \overline{\varphi}]$ *and* $\omega_1, \omega_2 \in I$ *with* $\omega_1 < \omega_1 + \eta(\omega_2, \omega_1)$. *If* $\psi\varphi \in L[\omega_1, \omega_1 + \eta(\omega_2, \omega_1)]$, $\alpha > 0$ *and* η *holds condition C, then*

$$\begin{aligned}
&\frac{1}{\alpha h_1(\frac{1}{2})h_2(\frac{1}{2})}\psi\left(\frac{2\omega_1(\omega_1+\eta(\omega_2,\omega_1))}{2\omega_1+\eta(\omega_2,\omega_1)}\right)\varphi\left(\frac{2\omega_1(\omega_1+\eta(\omega_2,\omega_1))}{2\omega_1+\eta(\omega_2,\omega_1)}\right)\\
&\supseteq \Gamma(\alpha)\left(\frac{\omega_1(\omega_1+\eta(\omega_2,\omega_1))}{\eta(\omega_2,\omega_1)}\right)^{\alpha}\left[J^{\alpha}_{\left(\frac{1}{\omega_1+\eta(\omega_2,\omega_1)}\right)^+}(\psi o\Omega)\left(\frac{1}{\omega_1}\right)(\varphi o\Omega)\left(\frac{1}{\omega_1}\right)\right.\\
&\left.+J^{\alpha}_{\left(\frac{1}{\omega_1}\right)^-}(\psi o\Omega)\left(\frac{1}{\omega_1+\eta(\omega_2,\omega_1)}\right)(\varphi o\Omega)\left(\frac{1}{\omega_1+\eta(\omega_2,\omega_1)}\right)\right]\\
&+F(\omega_1,\omega_1+\eta(\omega_2,\omega_1))\int_0^1(t^{\alpha-1}+(1-t)^{\alpha-1})h_1(t)h_2(1-t)dt\\
&+G(\omega_1,\omega_1+\eta(\omega_2,\omega_1))\int_0^1(t^{\alpha-1}+(1-t)^{\alpha-1})h_1(t)h_2(t)dt,
\end{aligned}$$

where $F(\omega_1, \omega_1 + \eta(\omega_2, \omega_1))$ *and* $G(\omega_1, \omega_1 + \eta(\omega_2, \omega_1))$ *are defined as previous.*

Proof. As ψ is harmonically h_1-preinvex interval-valued function on $[\omega_1, \omega_1 + \eta(\omega_2, \omega_1)]$, we have

$$\frac{1}{h_1(\frac{1}{2})}\psi\left(\frac{2u(u+\eta(v,u))}{2u+\eta(v,u)}\right) \supseteq \psi(u)+\psi(v),\ \forall\, u,v \in [\omega_1,\omega_1+\eta(\omega_2,\omega_1)]. \tag{24}$$

Let $u = \frac{\omega_1(\omega_1+\eta(\omega_2,\omega_1))}{\omega_1+(1-t)\eta(\omega_2,\omega_1)}$ and $v = \frac{\omega_1(\omega_1+\eta(\omega_2,\omega_1))}{\omega_1+t\eta(\omega_2,\omega_1)}$. Then, using Condition C in (24), we find

$$\frac{1}{h_1(\frac{1}{2})}\psi\left(\frac{2\omega_1(\omega_1+\eta(\omega_2,\omega_1))}{2\omega_1+\eta(\omega_2,\omega_1)}\right) \supseteq \psi\left(\frac{\omega_1(\omega_1+\eta(\omega_2,\omega_1))}{\omega_1+(1-t)\eta(\omega_2,\omega_1)}\right)+\psi\left(\frac{\omega_1(\omega_1+\eta(\omega_2,\omega_1))}{\omega_1+t\eta(\omega_2,\omega_1)}\right). \tag{25}$$

Similarly,

$$\frac{1}{h_2(\frac{1}{2})}\varphi\left(\frac{2\omega_1(\omega_1+\eta(\omega_2,\omega_1))}{2\omega_1+\eta(\omega_2,\omega_1)}\right) \supseteq \varphi\left(\frac{\omega_1(\omega_1+\eta(\omega_2,\omega_1))}{\omega_1+(1-t)\eta(\omega_2,\omega_1)}\right)+\varphi\left(\frac{\omega_1(\omega_1+\eta(\omega_2,\omega_1))}{\omega_1+t\eta(\omega_2,\omega_1)}\right). \tag{26}$$

From (25) and (26), we find

$$\begin{aligned}
&\frac{1}{h_1(\frac{1}{2})h_2(\frac{1}{2})}\psi\left(\frac{2\omega_1(\omega_1+\eta(\omega_2,\omega_1))}{2\omega_1+\eta(\omega_2,\omega_1)}\right)\varphi\left(\frac{2\omega_1(\omega_1+\eta(\omega_2,\omega_1))}{2\omega_1+\eta(\omega_2,\omega_1)}\right)\\
&\supseteq \left[\psi\left(\frac{\omega_1(\omega_1+\eta(\omega_2,\omega_1))}{\omega_1+(1-t)\eta(\omega_2,\omega_1)}\right)+\psi\left(\frac{\omega_1(\omega_1+\eta(\omega_2,\omega_1))}{\omega_1+t\eta(\omega_2,\omega_1)}\right)\right]\\
&\times\left[\varphi\left(\frac{\omega_1(\omega_1+\eta(\omega_2,\omega_1))}{\omega_1+(1-t)\eta(\omega_2,\omega_1)}\right)+\varphi\left(\frac{\omega_1(\omega_1+\eta(\omega_2,\omega_1))}{\omega_1+t\eta(\omega_2,\omega_1)}\right)\right]\\
&=\psi\left(\frac{\omega_1(\omega_1+\eta(\omega_2,\omega_1))}{\omega_1+(1-t)\eta(\omega_2,\omega_1)}\right)\varphi\left(\frac{\omega_1(\omega_1+\eta(\omega_2,\omega_1))}{\omega_1+(1-t)\eta(\omega_2,\omega_1)}\right)\\
&+\psi\left(\frac{\omega_1(\omega_1+\eta(\omega_2,\omega_1))}{\omega_1+t\eta(\omega_2,\omega_1)}\right)\varphi\left(\frac{\omega_1(\omega_1+\eta(\omega_2,\omega_1))}{\omega_1+t\eta(\omega_2,\omega_1)}\right)\\
&+\left[\psi\left(\frac{\omega_1(\omega_1+\eta(\omega_2,\omega_1))}{\omega_1+(1-t)\eta(\omega_2,\omega_1)}\right)\varphi\left(\frac{\omega_1(\omega_1+\eta(\omega_2,\omega_1))}{\omega_1+t\eta(\omega_2,\omega_1)}\right)\right.\\
&\left.+\psi\left(\frac{\omega_1(\omega_1+\eta(\omega_2,\omega_1))}{\omega_1+t\eta(\omega_2,\omega_1)}\right)\varphi\left(\frac{\omega_1(\omega_1+\eta(\omega_2,\omega_1))}{\omega_1+(1-t)\eta(\omega_2,\omega_1)}\right)\right].
\end{aligned} \tag{27}$$

As $\psi(u)$ and $\varphi(u) \in X_I^+$, $\forall u \in [\omega_1, \omega_1 + \eta(\omega_2, \omega_1)]$ are two harmonically h_1- and h_2-preinvex interval-valued functions, respectively. Therefore,

$$\begin{aligned}
&\psi\left(\frac{\omega_1(\omega_1+\eta(\omega_2,\omega_1))}{\omega_1+(1-t)\eta(\omega_2,\omega_1)}\right)\varphi\left(\frac{\omega_1(\omega_1+\eta(\omega_2,\omega_1))}{\omega_1+t\eta(\omega_2,\omega_1)}\right)\\
&\supseteq h_1(t)h_2(t)\psi(\omega_1+\eta(\omega_2,\omega_1))\varphi(\omega_1)+h_1(1-t)h_2(1-t)\psi(\omega_1)\varphi(\omega_1+\eta(\omega_2,\omega_1))\\
&\quad+h_1(t)h_2(1-t)\psi(\omega_1+\eta(\omega_2,\omega_1))\varphi(\omega_1+\eta(\omega_2,\omega_1))+h_1(1-t)h_2(t)\psi(\omega_1)\varphi(\omega_1).
\end{aligned}\tag{28}$$

Similarly,

$$\begin{aligned}
&\psi\left(\frac{\omega_1(\omega_1+\eta(\omega_2,\omega_1))}{\omega_1+t\eta(\omega_2,\omega_1)}\right)\varphi\left(\frac{\omega_1(\omega_1+\eta(\omega_2,\omega_1))}{\omega_1+(1-t)\eta(\omega_2,\omega_1)}\right)\\
&\supseteq h_1(t)h_2(t)\psi(\omega_1)\varphi(\omega_1+\eta(\omega_2,\omega_1))+h_1(1-t)h_2(1-t)\psi(\omega_1+\eta(\omega_2,\omega_1))\varphi(\omega_1)\\
&\quad+h_1(t)h_2(1-t)\psi(\omega_1)\varphi(\omega_1)+h_1(1-t)h_2(t)\psi(\omega_1+\eta(\omega_2,\omega_1))\varphi(\omega_1+\eta(\omega_2,\omega_1)).
\end{aligned}\tag{29}$$

Adding (28) and (29), we obtain

$$\begin{aligned}
&\psi\left(\frac{\omega_1(\omega_1+\eta(\omega_2,\omega_1))}{\omega_1+(1-t)\eta(\omega_2,\omega_1)}\right)\varphi\left(\frac{\omega_1(\omega_1+\eta(\omega_2,\omega_1))}{\omega_1+t\eta(\omega_2,\omega_1)}\right)\\
&\quad+\psi\left(\frac{\omega_1(\omega_1+\eta(\omega_2,\omega_1))}{\omega_1+t\eta(\omega_2,\omega_1)}\right)\varphi\left(\frac{\omega_1(\omega_1+\eta(\omega_2,\omega_1))}{\omega_1+(1-t)\eta(\omega_2,\omega_1)}\right)\\
&\supseteq G(\omega_1,\omega_1+\eta(\omega_2,\omega_1))[h_1(t)h_2(t)+h_1(1-t)h_2(1-t)]\\
&\quad+F(\omega_1,\omega_1+\eta(\omega_2,\omega_1))[h_1(1-t)h_2(t)+h_1(t)h_2(1-t)].
\end{aligned}\tag{30}$$

From (27) and (30), we have

$$\begin{aligned}
&\frac{1}{h_1(\frac{1}{2})h_2(\frac{1}{2})}\psi\left(\frac{2\omega_1(\omega_1+\eta(\omega_2,\omega_1))}{2\omega_1+\eta(\omega_2,\omega_1)}\right)\varphi\left(\frac{2\omega_1(\omega_1+\eta(\omega_2,\omega_1))}{2\omega_1+\eta(\omega_2,\omega_1)}\right)\\
&\supseteq\psi\left(\frac{\omega_1(\omega_1+\eta(\omega_2,\omega_1))}{\omega_1+(1-t)\eta(\omega_2,\omega_1)}\right)\varphi\left(\frac{\omega_1(\omega_1+\eta(\omega_2,\omega_1))}{\omega_1+(1-t)\eta(\omega_2,\omega_1)}\right)\\
&\quad+\psi\left(\frac{\omega_1(\omega_1+\eta(\omega_2,\omega_1))}{\omega_1+t\eta(\omega_2,\omega_1)}\right)\varphi\left(\frac{\omega_1(\omega_1+\eta(\omega_2,\omega_1))}{\omega_1+t\eta(\omega_2,\omega_1)}\right)\\
&\quad+G(\omega_1,\omega_1+\eta(\omega_2,\omega_1))[h_1(t)h_2(t)+h_1(1-t)h_2(1-t)]dt\\
&\quad+F(\omega_1,\omega_1+\eta(\omega_2,\omega_1))[h_1(1-t)h_2(t)+h_1(t)h_2(1-t)]dt.
\end{aligned}\tag{31}$$

Multiplying (31) by $t^{\alpha-1}$, then integrating over $[0,1]$ with respect to t, we find

$$\begin{aligned}
&\frac{1}{h_1(\frac{1}{2})h_2(\frac{1}{2})}(IR)\int_0^1 t^{\alpha-1}\psi\left(\frac{2\omega_1(\omega_1+\eta(\omega_2,\omega_1))}{2\omega_1+\eta(\omega_2,\omega_1)}\right)\varphi\left(\frac{2\omega_1(\omega_1+\eta(\omega_2,\omega_1))}{2\omega_1+\eta(\omega_2,\omega_1)}\right)dt\\
&\supseteq(IR)\int_0^1 t^{\alpha-1}\psi\left(\frac{\omega_1(\omega_1+\eta(\omega_2,\omega_1))}{\omega_1+(1-t)\eta(\omega_2,\omega_1)}\right)\varphi\left(\frac{\omega_1(\omega_1+\eta(\omega_2,\omega_1))}{\omega_1+(1-t)\eta(\omega_2,\omega_1)}\right)dt\\
&\quad+(IR)\int_0^1 t^{\alpha-1}\psi\left(\frac{\omega_1(\omega_1+\eta(\omega_2,\omega_1))}{\omega_1+t\eta(\omega_2,\omega_1)}\right)\varphi\left(\frac{\omega_1(\omega_1+\eta(\omega_2,\omega_1))}{\omega_1+t\eta(\omega_2,\omega_1)}\right)dt\\
&\quad+G(\omega_1,\omega_1+\eta(\omega_2,\omega_1))(IR)\int_0^1 t^{\alpha-1}[h_1(t)h_2(t)+h_1(1-t)h_2(1-t)]dt\\
&\quad+F(\omega_1,\omega_1+\eta(\omega_2,\omega_1))(IR)\int_0^1 t^{\alpha-1}[h_1(1-t)h_2(t)+h_1(t)h_2(1-t)]dt.
\end{aligned}$$

This implies

$$\frac{1}{\alpha h_1(\frac{1}{2})h_2(\frac{1}{2})}\psi\left(\frac{2\omega_1(\omega_1+\eta(\omega_2,\omega_1))}{2\omega_1+\eta(\omega_2,\omega_1)}\right)\varphi\left(\frac{2\omega_1(\omega_1+\eta(\omega_2,\omega_1))}{2\omega_1+\eta(\omega_2,\omega_1)}\right)$$

$$\supseteq \Gamma(\alpha)\left(\frac{\omega_1(\omega_1+\eta(\omega_2,\omega_1))}{\eta(\omega_2,\omega_1)}\right)^{\alpha}\left[J^{\alpha}_{\left(\frac{1}{\omega_1+\eta(\omega_2,\omega_1)}\right)^{+}}(\psi o\Omega)\left(\frac{1}{\omega_1}\right)\varphi o\Omega\left(\frac{1}{\omega_1}\right)\right.$$
$$\left.+J^{\alpha}_{\left(\frac{1}{\omega_1}\right)^{-}}(\psi o\Omega)\left(\frac{1}{\omega_1+\eta(\omega_2,\omega_1)}\right)(\varphi o\Omega)\left(\frac{1}{\omega_1+\eta(\omega_2,\omega_1)}\right)\right]$$
$$+F(\omega_1,\omega_1+\eta(\omega_2,\omega_1))\int_0^1(t^{\alpha-1}+(1-t)^{\alpha-1})h_1(t)h_2(1-t)]dt$$
$$+G(\omega_1,\omega_1+\eta(\omega_2,\omega_1))\int_0^1(t^{\alpha-1}+(1-t)^{\alpha-1})h_1(t)h_2(t)dt.$$

□

Remark 6. *If we put $\eta(\omega_2,\omega_1)=\omega_2-\omega_1$ in the above theorem, we obtain Theorem 7 of [50].*

Remark 7. *If we put $\eta(\omega_2,\omega_1)=\omega_2-\omega_1$ and $\alpha=1$ in the above theorem, we obtain Theorem 4 of [38].*

Corollary 6. *If $\alpha=1$, then Theorem 5 gives the following result:*

$$\frac{1}{2h_1(\frac{1}{2})h_2(\frac{1}{2})}\psi\left(\frac{2\omega_1(\omega_1+\eta(\omega_2,\omega_1))}{2\omega_1+\eta(\omega_2,\omega_1)}\right)\varphi\left(\frac{2\omega_1(\omega_1+\eta(\omega_2,\omega_1))}{2\omega_1+\eta(\omega_2,\omega_1)}\right)$$
$$\supseteq\frac{\omega_1(\omega_1+\eta(\omega_2,\omega_1))}{\eta(\omega_2,\omega_1)}\int_{\omega_1}^{\omega_1+\eta(\omega_2,\omega_1))}\frac{\psi(u)\varphi(u)}{u^2}du+F(\omega_1,\omega_1+\eta(\omega_2,\omega_1))\int_0^1 h_1(t)h_2(1-t)dt$$
$$+G(\omega_1,\omega_1+\eta(\omega_2,\omega_1))\int_0^1 h_1(t)h_2(t)dt.$$

Corollary 7. *If $h_1(t)=h_2(t)=t$, then Theorem 5 gives the following result:*

$$\frac{4}{\alpha}\psi\left(\frac{2\omega_1(\omega_1+\eta(\omega_2,\omega_1))}{2\omega_1+\eta(\omega_2,\omega_1)}\right)\varphi\left(\frac{2\omega_1(\omega_1+\eta(\omega_2,\omega_1))}{2\omega_1+\eta(\omega_2,\omega_1)}\right)$$
$$\supseteq \Gamma(\alpha)\psi\left(\frac{\omega_1(\omega_1+\eta(\omega_2,\omega_1))}{\eta(\omega_2,\omega_1)}\right)^{\alpha}\left[J^{\alpha}_{\left(\frac{1}{\omega_1+\eta(\omega_2,\omega_1)}\right)^{+}}(\psi o\Omega)\left(\frac{1}{\omega_1}\right)\varphi o\Omega\left(\frac{1}{\omega_1}\right)\right.$$
$$\left.+J^{\alpha}_{\left(\frac{1}{\omega_1}\right)^{-}}(\psi o\Omega)\left(\frac{1}{\omega_1+\eta(\omega_2,\omega_1)}\right)(\varphi o\Omega)\left(\frac{1}{\omega_1+\eta(\omega_2,\omega_1)}\right)\right]$$
$$+F(\omega_1,\omega_1+\eta(\omega_2,\omega_1))\int_0^1 t(1-t)(t^{\alpha-1}+(1-t)^{\alpha-1})dt$$
$$+G(\omega_1,\omega_1+\eta(\omega_2,\omega_1))\int_0^1 t^2(t^{\alpha-1}+(1-t)^{\alpha-1})dt$$
$$=\Gamma(\alpha)\psi\left(\frac{\omega_1(\omega_1+\eta(\omega_2,\omega_1))}{\eta(\omega_2,\omega_1)}\right)^{\alpha}\left[J^{\alpha}_{\left(\frac{1}{\omega_1+\eta(\omega_2,\omega_1)}\right)^{+}}(\psi o\Omega)\left(\frac{1}{\omega_1}\right)\varphi o\Omega\left(\frac{1}{\omega_1}\right)\right.$$
$$\left.+J^{\alpha}_{\left(\frac{1}{\omega_1}\right)^{-}}(\psi o\Omega)\left(\frac{1}{\omega_1+\eta(\omega_2,\omega_1)}\right)(\varphi o\Omega)\left(\frac{1}{\omega_1+\eta(\omega_2,\omega_1)}\right)\right]$$
$$+\frac{2}{(\alpha+1)(\alpha+2)}F(\omega_1,\omega_1+\eta(\omega_2,\omega_1))+\frac{\alpha^2+\alpha+2}{\alpha(\alpha+1)(\alpha+2)}G(\omega_1,\omega_1+\eta(\omega_2,\omega_1))$$
$$=\Gamma(\alpha)\psi\left(\frac{\omega_1(\omega_1+\eta(\omega_2,\omega_1))}{\eta(\omega_2,\omega_1)}\right)^{\alpha}\left[J^{\alpha}_{\left(\frac{1}{\omega_1+\eta(\omega_2,\omega_1)}\right)^{+}}(\psi o\Omega)\left(\frac{1}{\omega_1}\right)\varphi o\Omega\left(\frac{1}{\omega_1}\right)\right.$$
$$\left.+J^{\alpha}_{\left(\frac{1}{\omega_1}\right)^{-}}(\psi o\Omega)\left(\frac{1}{\omega_1+\eta(\omega_2,\omega_1)}\right)(\varphi o\Omega)\left(\frac{1}{\omega_1+\eta(\omega_2,\omega_1)}\right)\right]$$

$$+\frac{2\alpha F(\omega_1,\omega_1+\eta(\omega_2,\omega_1))+(\alpha^2+\alpha+2)G(\omega_1,\omega_1+\eta(\omega_2,\omega_1))}{\alpha(\alpha+1)(\alpha+2)}.$$

5. Results and Discussions

After illustrating the concept of interval-valued functions, this paper proposes a new definition of harmonically h-preinvex interval-valued functions. Further, with the help of the proposed harmonically h-preinvexity for interval-valued functions, we have proven H–H-type inclusions for interval-valued R–L fractional integrals. From the definition of harmonically h-preinvex interval-valued function, we can see that every harmonical h-convex interval-valued function is harmonically h-preinvex interval-valued function with respect to $\eta(v,u)=v-u$. The results obtained in this paper are generalization of the results of Zhao et al. [38] and Shi et al. [50]. Moreover, some particular cases of our main outcomes are considered.

6. Conclusions and Future Directions

In this paper, we have introduced harmonically h-preinvex interval-valued functions which include harmonical h-convex interval-valued functions and harmonical convex interval-valued functions as special cases. We have obtained H–H-type fractional inclusions for harmonically h-preinvex interval-valued functions. After that, we have proven fractional H–H-type inclusions for the product of two harmonically h-preinvex interval-valued functions. The results obtained in this paper may be extended for other kinds of interval-valued fractional integrals including harmonically h-preinvex interval-valued functions. In the future, we can investigate the interval-valued preinvexity on coordinates and establish new inclusions of H–H-type for interval-valued coordinated preinvex functions. It is expected that current work will motivate researchers working in fractional calculus, interval analysis, and other related areas.

Author Contributions: Formal analysis, K.K.L., J.B., N.S. and S.K.M.; funding acquisition, K.K.L.; investigation, S.K.M.; methodology, J.B., N.S. and S.K.M.; supervision, S.K.M.; validation, N.S.; writing—original draft, J.B.; writing—review and editing, K.K.L., J.B. and N.S. All authors have read and agreed to the published version of the manuscript.

Funding: Second author is financially supported by the Ministry of Science and Technology, Department of Science and Technology, New Delhi, India, through Registration No. DST/INSPIRE Fellowship/[IF190355] and the fourth author is financially supported by "Research Grant for Faculty" (IoE Scheme) under Dev. Scheme NO. 6031 and Department of Science and Technology, SERB, New Delhi, India through grant no.: MTR/2018/000121.

Institutional Review Board Statement: Not applicable.

Informed Consent Statement: Not applicable.

Data Availability Statement: No data were used to support this study.

Acknowledgments: The authors are indebted to the anonymous reviewers for their valuable comments and remarks that helped to improve the presentation and quality of the manuscript.

Conflicts of Interest: The authors declare no conflict of interest.

References

1. İşcan, I. Hermite-Hadamard's inequalities for preinvex functions via fractional integrals and related fractional inequalities. *arXiv* **2012**, arXiv:1204.0272.
2. Noor, M.A. Hadamard integral inequalities for product of two preinvex functions. *Nonlinear Anal. Forum.* **2009**, *14*, 167–173.
3. Sharma, N.; Bisht, J.; Mishra, S.K. Hermite–Hadamard-type inequalities for functions whose derivatives are strongly η-convex via fractional integrals. In *Indo-French Seminar on Optimization, Variational Analysis and Applications*; Springer: Berlin/Heidelberg, Germany, 2020; pp. 83–102.
4. Sharma, N.; Bisht, J.; Mishra, S.K.; Hamdi, A. Some majorization integral inequalities for functions defined on rectangles via strong convexity. *J. Inequal. Spec. Funct.* **2019**, *10*, 21–34.

5. Sharma, N.; Mishra, S.K.; Hamdi, A. A weighted version of Hermite-Hadamard-type inequalities for strongly GA-convex functions. *Int. J. Adv. Appl. Sci.* **2020**, *7*, 113–118.
6. Wu, X.; Wang, J.; Zhang, J. Hermite–Hadamard-type inequalities for convex functions via the fractional integrals with exponential kernel. *Mathematics* **2019**, *7*, 845. [CrossRef]
7. Hanson, M.A. On sufficiency of the kuhn-tucker conditions. *J. Math. Anal. Appl.* **1981**, *80*, 545–550. [CrossRef]
8. Ben-Israel, A.; Mond, B. What is invexity? *ANZIAM J.* **1986**, *28*, 1–9. [CrossRef]
9. Yang, X.M.; Li, D. On properties of preinvex functions. *J. Math. Anal. Appl.* **2001**, *256*, 229–241. [CrossRef]
10. Moore, R.E. *Interval Analysis*; Prentice-Hall: Englewood Cliffs, NJ, USA, 1966.
11. Moore, R.E.; Kearfott, R.B.; Cloud, M.J. *Introduction to Interval Analysis*; SIAM: Philadelphia, PA, USA, 2009.
12. Bhurjee, A.K.; Panda, G. Multi-objective interval fractional programming problems: An approach for obtaining efficient solutions. *Opsearch* **2015**, *52*, 156–167. [CrossRef]
13. Lupulescu, V. Fractional calculus for interval-valued functions. *Fuzzy Sets Syst.* **2015**, *265*, 63–85. [CrossRef]
14. Li, L.; Liu, S.; Zhang, J. On interval-valued invex mappings and optimality conditions for interval-valued optimization problems. *J. Inequal. Appl.* **2015**, *2015*, 179. [CrossRef]
15. Chalco-Cano, Y.; Lodwick, W.A.; Condori-Equice, W. Ostrowski type inequalities and applications in numerical integration for interval-valued functions. *Soft Comput.* **2015**, *19*, 3293–3300. [CrossRef]
16. Guo, Y.; Ye, G.; Zhao, D.; Liu, W. $gH-$symmetrically derivative of interval-valued functions and applications in interval-valued optimization. *Symmetry* **2019**, *11*, 1203. [CrossRef]
17. Moore, R.E. *Methods and Applications of Interval Analysis*; SIAM: Philadelphia, PA, USA, 1979.
18. Rothwell, E.J.; Cloud, M.J. Automatic error analysis using intervals. *IEEE Trans. Educ.* **2011**, *55*, 9–15. [CrossRef]
19. Snyder, J.M. Interval analysis for computer graphics. In Proceedings of the 19th Annual Conference on Computer Graphics and Interactive Techniques, Chicago, IL, USA, 27–31 July 1992; pp. 121–130.
20. İşcan, I. Hermite-Hadamard-type inequalities for harmonically convex functions. *Hacet. J. Math. Stat.* **2014**, *43*, 935–942. [CrossRef]
21. Noor, M.A.; Noor, K.I.; Awan, M.U.; Li, J. On Hermite-Hadamard inequalities for h-preinvex functions. *Filomat* **2014**, *28*, 1463–1474. [CrossRef]
22. Noor, M.A.; Noor, K.I.; Iftikhar, S. Fractional ostrowski inequalities for harmonic h-preinvex functions. *Facta Univ. Ser. Math. Inform.* **2016**, *31*, 417–445.
23. Deng, Y.; Kalsoom, H.; Wu, S. Some new quantum Hermite–Hadamard-type estimates within a class of generalized $(s,m)-$preinvex functions. *Symmetry* **2019**, *11*, 1283. [CrossRef]
24. Kashuri, A.; Set, E.; Liko, R. Some new fractional trapezium-type inequalities for preinvex functions. *Fractal Fract.* **2019**, *3*, 12. [CrossRef]
25. Mehmood, S.; Zafar, F.; Yasmin, N. Hermite-Hadamard-Fejér Type Inequalities for Preinvex Functions Using Fractional Integrals. *Mathematics* **2019**, *7*, 467. [CrossRef]
26. Noor, M.A.; Noor, K.I.; Rashid, S. Some new classes of preinvex functions and inequalities. *Mathematics* **2019**, *7*, 29. [CrossRef]
27. Rashid, S.; Latif, M.A.; Hammouch, Z.; Chu, Y.M. Fractional integral inequalities for strongly h-preinvex functions for a kth order differentiable functions. *Symmetry* **2019**, *11*, 1448. [CrossRef]
28. Sial, I.B.; Ali, M.A.; Murtaza, G.; Ntouyas, S.K.; Soontharanon, J.; Sitthiwirattham, T. On Some New Inequalities of Hermite–Hadamard Midpoint and Trapezoid Type for Preinvex Functions in (p, q)-Calculus. *Symmetry* **2021**, *13*, 1864. [CrossRef]
29. Sitho, S.; Ali, M.A.; Budak, H.; Ntouyas, S.K.; Tariboon, J. Trapezoid and Midpoint Type Inequalities for Preinvex Functions via Quantum Calculus. *Mathematics* **2021**, *9*, 1666. [CrossRef]
30. Tariq, M.; Ahmad, H.; Budak, H.; Sahoo, S.K.; Sitthiwirattham, T.; Reunsumrit, J. A Comprehensive Analysis of Hermite–Hadamard Type Inequalities via Generalized Preinvex Functions. *Axioms* **2021**, *10*, 328 [CrossRef]
31. Chalco-Cano, Y.; Flores-Franulič, A.; Román-Flores, H. Ostrowski type inequalities for interval-valued functions using generalized Hukuhara derivative. *Comput. Appl. Math.* **2012**, *31*, 457–472.
32. Zhao, D.; Ye, G.; Liu, W.; Torres, D.F.M. Some inequalities for interval-valued functions on time scales. *Soft Comput.* **2019**, *23*, 6005–6015. [CrossRef]
33. Budak, H.; Tunç, T.; Sarikaya, M.Z. Fractional Hermite-Hadamard-type inequalities for interval-valued functions. *Proc. Am. Math. Soc.* **2020**, *148*, 705–718. [CrossRef]
34. Lou, T.; Ye, G.; Zhao, D.F.; Liu, W. Iq-Calculus and $Iq-$Hermite–Hadamard inequalities for interval-valued functions. *Adv. Differ. Equ.* **2020**, *2020*, 446. [CrossRef]
35. Tariboon, J.; Ali, M.A.; Budak, H.; Ntouyas, S.K. Hermite–Hadamard Inclusions for Co-Ordinated Interval-Valued Functions via Post-Quantum Calculus. *Symmetry* **2021**, *13*, 1216. [CrossRef]
36. Wannalookkhee, F.; Nonlaopon, K.; Tariboon, J.; Ntouyas, S.K. On Hermite-Hadamard-type inequalities for coordinated convex functions via (p,q)-calculus. *Mathematics* **2021**, *9*, 698. [CrossRef]
37. Ali, M.A.; Budak, H.; Murtaza, G.; Chu, Y.M. Post-quantum Hermite–Hadamard type inequalities for interval-valued convex functions. *J. Inequal. Appl.* **2021**, *2021*, 84. [CrossRef]
38. Zhao, D.; An, T.; Ye, G.; Torres, D.F.M. On Hermite-Hadamard type inequalities for harmonical h-convex interval-valued functions. *Math. Inequal. Appl.* **2020**, *23*, 95–105.

39. Zhao, D.; Ali, M.A.; Murtaza, G.; Zhang, Z. On the Hermite–Hadamard inequalities for interval-valued coordinated convex functions. *Adv. Differ. Equ.* **2020**, *2020*, 570. [CrossRef]
40. Zhao, D.; Zhao, G.; Ye, G.; Liu, W.; Dragomir, S.S. On Hermite–Hadamard-type Inequalities for Coordinated h-Convex Interval-Valued Functions. *Mathematics* **2021**, *9*, 2352. [CrossRef]
41. Sharma, N.; Singh, S.K.; Mishra, S.K.; Hamdi, A. Hermite-Hadamard-type inequalities for interval-valued preinvex functions via Riemann–Liouville fractional integrals. *J. Inequal. Appl.* **2021**, *2021*, 98. [CrossRef]
42. Zhou, H.; Saleem, M.S.; Nazeer, W.; Shah, A.F. Hermite-Hadamard-type inequalities for interval-valued exponential type preinvex functions via Riemann-Liouville fractional integrals. *AIMS Math.* **2021**, *7*, 2602–2617. [CrossRef]
43. Román-Flores, H.; Chalco-Cano, Y.; Lodwick, W.A. Some integral inequalities for interval-valued functions. *Comput. Appl. Math.* **2018**, *37*, 1306–1318. [CrossRef]
44. Shi, F.; Ye, G.; Zhao, D.; Liu, W. Some fractional Hermite–Hadamard-type inequalities for interval-valued coordinated functions. *Adv. Differ. Equ.* **2021**, *2021*, 32. [CrossRef]
45. Zhao, D.; An, T.; Ye, G.; Liu, W. Chebyshev type inequalities for interval-valued functions. *Fuzzy Sets Syst.* **2020**, *396*, 82–101. [CrossRef]
46. An, Y.; Ye, G.; Zhao, D.; Liu, W. Hermite-Hadamard-type inequalities for interval $(h_1, h_2)-$convex functions. *Mathematics* **2019**, *7*, 436. [CrossRef]
47. Kalsoom, H.; Latif, M.A.; Khan, Z.A.; Vivas-Cortez, M. Some New Hermite-Hadamard-Fejér Fractional Type Inequalities for h-Convex and Harmonically h-Convex Interval-Valued Functions. *Mathematics* **2021**, *10*, 74. [CrossRef]
48. Kara, H.; Ali, M.A.; Budak, H. Hermite-Hadamard-type inequalities for interval-valued coordinated convex functions involving generalized fractional integrals. *Math. Methods Appl. Sci.* **2021**, *44*, 104–123. [CrossRef]
49. Khan, M.B.; Noor, M.A.; Abdeljawad, T.; Mousa, A.A.A.; Abdalla, B.; Alghamdi, S.M. LR-Preinvex Interval-Valued Functions and Riemann–Liouville Fractional Integral Inequalities. *Fractal Fract.* **2021**, *5*, 243. [CrossRef]
50. Shi, F.; Ye, G.; Zhao, D.; Liu, W. Some fractional Hermite-Hadamard type inequalities for interval-valued functions. *Mathematics* **2020**, *8*, 534. [CrossRef]
51. Kilbas, A.A.; Srivastava, H.M.; Trujillo, J.J. *Theory and Applications of Fractional Differential Equations;* North-Holland Mathematics Studies; Elsevier: Amsterdam, The Netherlands, 2006; Volume 204.
52. Anderson, G.D.; Vamanamurthy, M.K.; Vuorinen, M. Generalized convexity and inequalities. *J. Math. Anal. Appl.* **2007**, *335*, 1294–1308. [CrossRef]
53. Noor, M.A.; Noor, K.I.; Iftikhar, S. Hermite-Hadamard inequalities for harmonic preinvex functions. *Saussurea* **2016**, *6*, 34–53.
54. Mohan, S.R.; Neogy, S.K. On invex sets and preinvex functions. *J. Math. Anal. Appl.* **1995**, *189*, 901–908. [CrossRef]
55. Noor, M.A. Hermite-Hadamard integral inequalities for log-preinvex functions. *J. Math. Anal. Approx. Theory* **2007**, *2*, 126–131.
56. Liu, X.L.; Ye, G.J.; Zhao, D.F.; Liu, W. Fractional Hermite-Hadamard-type inequalities for interval-valued functions. *J. Inequal. Appl.* **2019**, *2019*, 266. [CrossRef]

mathematics

Article

Riemann–Liouville Fractional Integral Inequalities for Generalized Pre-Invex Functions of Interval-Valued Settings Based upon Pseudo Order Relation

Muhammad Bilal Khan [1], Hatim Ghazi Zaini [2], Savin Treanţă [3], Mohamed S. Soliman [4] and Kamsing Nonlaopon [5,*]

1 Department of Mathematics, COMSATS University Islamabad, Islamabad 45550, Pakistan; bilal42742@gmail.com
2 Department of Computer Science, College of Computers and Information Technology, Taif University, P.O. Box 11099, Taif 21944, Saudi Arabia; h.zaini@tu.edu.sa
3 Department of Applied Mathematics, University Politehnica of Bucharest, 060042 Bucharest, Romania; savin.treanta@upb.ro
4 Department of Electrical Engineering, College of Engineering, Taif University, P.O. Box 11099, Taif 21944, Saudi Arabia; soliman@tu.edu.sa
5 Department of Mathematics, Faculty of Science, Khon Kaen University, Khon Kaen 40002, Thailand
* Correspondence: nkamsi@kku.ac.th; Tel.: +66-866-421-582

Abstract: The concepts of convex and non-convex functions play a key role in the study of optimization. So, with the help of these ideas, some inequalities can also be established. Moreover, the principles of convexity and symmetry are inextricably linked. In the last two years, convexity and symmetry have emerged as a new field due to considerable association. In this paper, we study a new version of interval-valued functions (*I-V·Fs*), known as left and right χ-pre-invex interval-valued functions (LR-χ-pre-invex *I-V·Fs*). For this class of non-convex *I-V·Fs*, we derive numerous new dynamic inequalities interval Riemann–Liouville fractional integral operators. The applications of these repercussions are taken into account in a unique way. In addition, instructive instances are provided to aid our conclusions. Meanwhile, we'll discuss a few specific examples that may be extrapolated from our primary findings.

Keywords: LR-χ-pre-invex interval-valued function; interval Riemann–Liouville fractional integral operator; Hermite–Hadamard inequality; Hermite–Hadamard Fejér inequality

Citation: Khan, M.B.; Zaini, H.G.; Treanţă, S.; Soliman, M.S.; Nonlaopon, K. Riemann–Liouville Fractional Integral Inequalities for Generalized Pre-Invex Functions of Interval-Valued Settings Based upon Pseudo Order Relation. *Mathematics* **2022**, *10*, 204. https://doi.org/10.3390/math10020204

Academic Editor: Sitnik Sergey

Received: 7 December 2021
Accepted: 7 January 2022
Published: 10 January 2022

1. Introduction

The Hermite–Hadamard inequality (see [1,2], p. 137) is a well-known inequality in convex function theory, with a geometrical explanation and a wide range of applications. Hermite–Hadamard inequality (*H-H* inequality) is a development of the concept of convexity, and it logically follows from Jensen's inequality. In recent years, the *H-H* inequality for convex functions has sparked a lot of attention, and several refinements and extensions have been investigated; see [3–14] and the references therein.

On the other hand, interval analysis is a subset of set-valued analysis and is concerned with the study of intervals in the context of mathematical analysis and topology. It was developed as a means of dealing with interval uncertainty, which is included in many mathematical or computer models of deterministic real-world systems. A historical example of an interval enclosure is Archimedes' method for calculating the circumference of a circle. In 1966, Moore [15] released the first book on interval analysis. Moore is recognized as being the first usage of intervals in computer mathematics. Following the release of his book, a lot of scientists began to study interval arithmetic's theory and applications. Because of its universality, interval analysis is currently a useful approach in a range of sectors that are interested in ambiguous data. Moreover, interval analysis has also applications in different fields like in error analysis, computer graphics, error analysis, experimental and computational physics, and many more.

Numerous significant inequalities for *I-V·Fs* (Hermite–Hadamard, Ostrowski, etc.) have been investigated in recent years. In [16,17], Chalco–Cano et al. constructed Ostrowski type inequalities for *I-V·Fs* using the Hukuhara derivative for *I-V·Fs*. Román-Flores et al. developed Minkowski and Beckenbach's inequality for *I-V·Fs* in [18]. For more information, see [18–22] and the references therein. Moreover, inequalities can be examined for the more general set-valued mappings for example, Sadowska [23] introduced the *H-H* inequality general set-valued mappings. Similarly, for generalized inequalities, we refer to the following articles, see [24,25] and the references therein. Recently, Khan et al. extended the interval *H-H* inequalities in terms of fuzzy interval *H-H* inequalities using fuzzy Riemannian and fuzzy Riemann–Liouville fractional integral operators such as in [26]. Khan et al. also presented the new class of convex fuzzy mappings known as (χ_1, χ_2)-convex fuzzy-interval-valued functions ((χ_1, χ_2)-convex *F-I-V·F*) and obtained the new version of *H-H* inequalities for (χ_1, χ_2)-convex *F-I-V·Fs*. Moreover, Khan et al. introduced new notions of generalized convex *F-I-V·Fs*, and derived new fractional *H-H* type and *H-H* type inequalities for convex *F-I-V·Fs* [27–32]. For more analysis and applications of *F-I-V·Fs*, see [33–50] and the references therein.

This study is organized as follows: Section 2 presents preliminary and new concepts and results in interval space, and convex analysis. Section 3 obtains interval *H-H* inequalities and *H-H* Fejér inequalities for LR-χ-pre-invex *I-V·Fs* via interval Riemann–Liouville fractional integral operators. In addition, some interesting examples are also given to verify our results. Section 4 gives conclusions and future plans.

2. Preliminaries

Let $\mathcal{K}_C$ stand for the collection of all closed and bounded intervals of $\mathbb{R}$. We use $\mathcal{K}_C^+$ to represent the set of all positive intervals. The collections of all Riemann integrable real valued functions and Riemann integrable *I-V-F* are denoted by $\mathcal{R}_{[\mu,\omega]}$ and $\mathcal{IR}_{[\mu,\omega]}$, respectively. For more conceptions on *I-V·Fs*, see [36]. Moreover, we have:

Remark 1. [35] *(i) The relation "* $\leq_p$ *" defined on* $\mathcal{K}_C$ *by:*

$$[\mathfrak{U}_*,\ \mathfrak{U}^*] \leq_p [\mathcal{Z}_*,\ \mathcal{Z}^*] \text{ if and only if } \mathfrak{U}_* \leq \mathcal{Z}_*,\ \mathfrak{U}^* \leq \mathcal{Z}^*, \tag{1}$$

for all $[\mathfrak{U}_*,\ \mathfrak{U}^*],\ [\mathcal{Z}_*,\ \mathcal{Z}^*] \in \mathcal{K}_C$*, it is a pseudo-order relation. For given* $[\mathfrak{U}_*,\ \mathfrak{U}^*],\ [\mathcal{Z}_*,\ \mathcal{Z}^*] \in \mathcal{K}_C$*, we say that* $[\mathfrak{U}_*,\ \mathfrak{U}^*] \leq_p [\mathcal{Z}_*,\ \mathcal{Z}^*]$ *if and only if* $\mathfrak{U}_* \leq \mathcal{Z}_*,\ \mathfrak{U}^* \leq \mathcal{Z}^*$ *or* $\mathfrak{U}_* \leq \mathcal{Z}_*,\ \mathfrak{U}^* < \mathcal{Z}^*$*. The relation* $[\mathfrak{U}_*,\ \mathfrak{U}^*] \leq_p [\mathcal{Z}_*,\ \mathcal{Z}^*]$ *coincident to* $[\mathfrak{U}_*,\ \mathfrak{U}^*] \leq [\mathcal{Z}_*,\ \mathcal{Z}^*]$ *on* $\mathcal{K}_C$*.*

(ii) It can be easily seen that " $\leq_p$ *" looks like "left and right" on the real line* $\mathbb{R}$*, so we call "* $\leq_p$ *" "left and right" (or "LR" order, in short).*

The concept of the Riemann integral for *I-V-F* first introduced by Moore [15] is defined as follows:

Theorem 1. [15] *If* $\mathfrak{S} : [\mu,\omega] \subset \mathbb{R} \to \mathcal{K}_C$ *is an I-V·F on* $[\mu,\omega]$ *such that* $\mathfrak{S}(x) = [\mathfrak{S}_*(x),\ \mathfrak{S}^*(x)]$*, then* $\mathfrak{S}$ *is Riemann integrable over* $[\mu,\omega]$ *if and only if,* $\mathfrak{S}_*(x)$ *and* $\mathfrak{S}^*(x)$ *both are Riemann integrable over* $[\mu,\omega]$ *such that:*

$$(IR)\int_\mu^\omega \mathfrak{S}(x)dx = \left[(R)\int_\mu^\omega \mathfrak{S}_*(x)dx,\ (R)\int_\mu^\omega \mathfrak{S}^*(x)dx\right] \tag{2}$$

Lupulescu and Budak et al. [36,37] introduced the following interval Riemann–Liouville fractional integral operators:

Let $\alpha > 0$ and $L([\mu,\ \omega], \mathcal{K}_C^+)$ be the collection of all Lebesgue measurable I-V-Fs on $[\mu, \omega]$. Then the interval left and right Riemann–Liouville fractional integrals of $\mathfrak{S} \in L([\mu,\ \omega], \mathcal{K}_C^+)$ with order $\alpha > 0$ are defined by:

$$\mathcal{I}_{\mu^+}^{\alpha}\ \mathfrak{S}(x) = \frac{1}{\Gamma(\alpha)} \int_{\mu}^{x} (x - \varsigma)^{\alpha - 1} \mathfrak{S}(\varsigma) d\varsigma, \quad (x > \mu), \tag{3}$$

and:

$$\mathcal{I}_{\omega^-}^{\alpha}\ \mathfrak{S}(x) = \frac{1}{\Gamma(\alpha)} \int_{x}^{\omega} (\varsigma - x)^{\alpha - 1} \mathfrak{S}(\varsigma) d\varsigma, \quad (x < \omega) \tag{4}$$

respectively, where $\Gamma(x) = \int_0^{\infty} \varsigma^{x-1} e^{-\varsigma} d\varsigma$ is the Euler gamma function.

Definition 1. [34] *A real-valued function $\mathfrak{S} : [\mu,\ \omega] \to \mathbb{R}^+$ is named as convex function if:*

$$\mathfrak{S}(\varsigma x + (1 - \varsigma) z) \leq \varsigma \mathfrak{S}(x) + (1 - \varsigma) \mathfrak{S}(z), \tag{5}$$

for all $x,\ z \in [\mu,\ \omega],\ \varsigma \in [0,\ 1]$. If (5) is reversed, then $\mathfrak{S}$ is named as concave.

Definition 2. [40] *A real valued function $\mathfrak{S} : [\mu,\ \omega] \to \mathbb{R}^+$ is named as pre-invex function if:*

$$\mathfrak{S}(x + (1 - \varsigma)\varphi(z, x)) \leq \varsigma \mathfrak{S}(x) + (1 - \varsigma) \mathfrak{S}(z), \tag{6}$$

for all $x,\ z \in [\mu,\ \omega],\ \varsigma \in [0,\ 1]$, where $\varphi : [\mu, \omega] \times [\mu, \omega] \to \mathbb{R}$. If (6) is reversed, then $\mathfrak{S}$ is named as pre-incave.

Definition 3. [35] *The I-V·F $\mathfrak{S} : [\mu,\ \omega] \to \mathcal{K}_C^+$ is named as LR-convex I-V·F on $[\mu,\ \omega]$ if:*

$$\mathfrak{S}(\varsigma x + (1 - \varsigma) z) \leq_p \varsigma \mathfrak{S}(x) + (1 - \varsigma) \mathfrak{S}(z), \tag{7}$$

for all $x,\ z \in [\mu,\ \omega],\ \varsigma \in [0,\ 1]$. If (7) is reversed, then $\mathfrak{S}$ is named as LR-concave I-V·F on $[\mu,\ \omega]$. $\mathfrak{S}$ is affine, if and only if it is both LR-convex and LR-concave I-V·F.

Definition 4. [41] *The I-V·F $\mathfrak{S} : [\mu,\ \omega] \to \mathcal{K}_C^+$ is named as LR-pre-invex I-V·F on invex interval $[\mu,\ \omega]$ if:*

$$\mathfrak{S}(x + (1 - \varsigma)\varphi(z, x)) \leq_p \varsigma \mathfrak{S}(x) + (1 - \varsigma) \mathfrak{S}(z), \tag{8}$$

for all $x,\ z \in [\mu,\ \omega],\ \varsigma \in [0,\ 1]$, where $\varphi : [\mu, \omega] \times [\mu, \omega] \to \mathbb{R}$. If (8) is reversed then, $\mathfrak{S}$ is named as LR-pre-incave I-V·F on $[\mu,\ \omega]$. $\mathfrak{S}$ is a LR-affine if and only if, it is both LR-pre-invex and LR-pre-incave I-V·Fs.

Definition 5. *Let $\chi\ : [0,\ 1] \subseteq [\mu, \omega] \to \mathbb{R}^+$ such that $\chi 0$. Then, I-V·F $\mathfrak{S} : [\mu, \omega] \to \mathcal{K}_C^+$ is said to be LR-χ-pre-invex I-V·F on $[\mu, \omega]$ if:*

$$\mathfrak{S}(x + (1 - \varsigma)\varphi(x, z)) \leq_p \chi(\varsigma) \mathfrak{S}(x) + \chi(1 - \varsigma) \mathfrak{S}(z), \tag{9}$$

for all $x,\ z \in [\mu, \omega],\ \varsigma \in [0,\ 1]$, where $\varphi : [\mu, \omega] \times [\mu, \omega] \to \mathbb{R}$. If $\mathfrak{S}$ is LR-χ-pre-incave on $[\mu, \omega]$, then inequality (9) is reversed.

Remark 2. *If $\chi(\varsigma) = \varsigma$, then LR-$\chi$-pre-invex I-V·F becomes LR-pre-invex I-V·F. If $\chi(\varsigma) \equiv 1$, then LR-χ-pre-invex I-V·F becomes LR-P I-V·F, that is:*

$$\mathfrak{S}(x + (1 - \varsigma)\varphi(x, z)) \leq_p \mathfrak{S}(x) + \mathfrak{S}(z),\ \forall\ x,\ z \in [\mu, \omega],\ \varsigma \in [0,\ 1]. \tag{10}$$

Theorem 2. *Let $\chi : [0,\ 1] \subseteq [\mu, \omega] \to \mathbb{R}$ be a non-negative real valued function such that $\chi 0$ and let $\mathfrak{S} : [\mu, \omega] \to \mathcal{K}_C^+$ be a I-V·F such that:*

$$\mathfrak{S}(z) = [\mathfrak{S}_*(z),\ \mathfrak{S}^*(z)], \tag{11}$$

for all $z \in [\mu, \omega]$. Then, $\mathfrak{S}(z)$ is LR-χ-pre-invex I-V·F on $[\mu, \omega]$, if and only if, $\mathfrak{S}_*(z)$ and $\mathfrak{S}^*(z)$ both are χ-pre-invex.

Proof. Assume that, $\mathfrak{S}_*(x)$ and $\mathfrak{S}^*(x)$ are χ-pre-invex on $[\mu, \omega]$. Then from (6), we have:

$$\mathfrak{S}_*(x + (1-\varsigma)\varphi(x,z)) \le \chi(\varsigma)\mathfrak{S}_*(x) + \chi(1-\varsigma)\mathfrak{S}_*(z),\ \forall\ x,z \in [\mu, \omega],\ \varsigma \in [0,\ 1],$$

and:

$$\mathfrak{S}^*(x + (1-\varsigma)\varphi(x,z)) \le \chi(\varsigma)\mathfrak{S}^*(x) + \chi(1-\varsigma)\mathfrak{S}^*(z), \forall\ x,z \in [\mu, \omega],\ \varsigma \in [0,\ 1].$$

Then by (11), we obtain:

$$\begin{aligned}\mathfrak{S}(x + (1-\varsigma)\varphi(x,z)) &= [\mathfrak{S}_*(x + (1-\varsigma)\varphi(x,z)),\ \mathfrak{S}^*(x + (1-\varsigma)\varphi(x,z))], \\ &\le [\chi(\varsigma)\mathfrak{S}_*(x),\ \chi(\varsigma)\mathfrak{S}^*(x)] + [\chi(1-\varsigma)\mathfrak{S}_*(z),\ \chi(1-\varsigma)\mathfrak{S}^*(z)],\end{aligned}$$

that is:

$$\mathfrak{S}(x + (1-\varsigma)\varphi(x,z)) \le_p \chi(\varsigma)\mathfrak{S}(x) + \chi(1-\varsigma)\mathfrak{S}(z), \forall\ x,z \in [\mu, \omega],\ \varsigma \in [0,\ 1].$$

Hence, $\mathfrak{S}$ is LR-χ-pre-invex IVF on $[\mu, \omega]$.

Conversely, let $\mathfrak{S}$ be a LR-χ-pre-invex IVF on $[\mu, \omega]$. Then for all $x, z \in [\mu, \omega]$ and $\varsigma \in [0,\ 1]$, we have:

$$\mathfrak{S}(x + (1-\varsigma)\varphi(x,z)) \le_p \chi(\varsigma)\mathfrak{S}(x) + \chi(1-\varsigma)\mathfrak{S}(z).$$

Therefore, from (11), we have:

$$\mathfrak{S}(x + (1-\varsigma)\varphi(x,z)) = [\mathfrak{S}_*(x + (1-\varsigma)\varphi(x,z)),\ \mathfrak{S}^*(x + (1-\varsigma)\varphi(x,z))].$$

Again, from (11), we obtain:

$$\chi(\varsigma)\mathfrak{S}(x) + \chi(1-\varsigma)\mathfrak{S}(x) = [\chi(\varsigma)\mathfrak{S}_*(x),\ \chi(\varsigma)\mathfrak{S}^*(x)] + [\chi(1-\varsigma)\mathfrak{S}_*(z),\ \chi(1-\varsigma)\mathfrak{S}^*(z)],$$

for all $x, z \in [\mu, \omega]$ and $\varsigma \in [0,\ 1]$. Then by LR-χ-pre-invexity of $\mathfrak{S}$, we have for all $x, z \in [\mu, \omega]$ and $\varsigma \in [0,\ 1]$ such that:

$$\mathfrak{S}_*(x + (1-\varsigma)\varphi(x,z)) \le \chi(\varsigma)\mathfrak{S}_*(x) + \chi(1-\varsigma)\mathfrak{S}_*(z),$$

and:

$$\mathfrak{S}^*(x + (1-\varsigma)\varphi(x,z)) \le \chi(\varsigma)\mathfrak{S}^*(x) + \chi(1-\varsigma)\mathfrak{S}^*(z),$$

hence, the result follows. □

Example 1. *We consider $\chi(\varsigma) = \varsigma$, for $\varsigma \in [0,\ 1]$ and the I-V·F $\mathfrak{S} : [0,\ 4] \to \mathcal{K}_C^+$ defined by $\mathfrak{S}(z) = \left[z, 2e^{z^2}\right]$. Since end point functions $\mathfrak{S}_*(z)$, $\mathfrak{S}^*(z)$ are χ-pre-invex functions with respect to $\varphi(x,z) = x - z$. Hence $\mathfrak{S}(z)$ is LR-χ-pre-invex I-V·F.*

Remark 3. *If $\chi(\varsigma) \equiv \varsigma$ and $\mathfrak{S}_*(z) = \mathfrak{S}^*(z)$, then from (8), we obtain the inequality (6).*

If $\chi(\varsigma) \equiv \varsigma$ and $\mathfrak{S}_*(z) = \mathfrak{S}^*(z)$ and $\varphi(x,z) = x - z$, then from (8), we obtain the inequality (5).

We'll need to make the following assumption about the function $\varphi : [\mu, \omega] \times [\mu, \omega] \to \mathbb{R}$, which will be crucial in the major findings.

Condition C. [40]

$$\varphi(x, z + \varsigma\varphi(x,z)) = (1-\varsigma)\varphi(x,z),$$
$$\varphi(z, z + \varsigma\varphi(x,z)) = -\varsigma\varphi(x,z).$$

Note that $\forall\, z,\ x \in [\mu, \omega]$ and $\varsigma \in [0,\ 1]$, then from condition C we have

$$\varphi(z + \varsigma_2\varphi(x,z), z + \varsigma_1\varphi(x,z)) = (\varsigma_2 - \varsigma_1)\varphi(x,z)$$

Clearly for $\varsigma = 0$, we have $\varphi(x,z) = 0$ if and only if $x = z$, for all $z,\ x \in [\mu, \omega]$. For the application of condition C, see [40,41].

3. Interval Fractional Hermite–Hadamard Inequalities

In this section, we will prove some new *H-H* type inequalities for LR-χ-pre-invex *I-V·Fs* via Riemann–Liouville fractional integral operators. In the next results, we will denote $L([\mu,\ \mu + \varphi(\omega,\mu)], \mathcal{K}_C^+)$ as the family of Lebesgue measurable *I-V·Fs*.

Theorem 3. *Let* $\mathfrak{S} : [\mu,\ \mu + \varphi(\omega,\mu)] \to \mathcal{K}_C^+$ *be a LR--pre-invex I-V·F on* $[\mu,\ \mu + \varphi(\omega,\mu)]$ *such that* $\mathfrak{S}(z) = [\mathfrak{S}_*(z),\ \mathfrak{S}^*(z)]$ *for all* $z \in [\mu,\ \mu + \varphi(\omega,\mu)]$. *If* φ *satisfies condition C and* $\mathfrak{S} \in L([\mu,\ \mu + \varphi(\omega,\mu)], \mathcal{K}_C^+)$, *then:*

$$\begin{aligned}\frac{1}{\alpha\chi\left(\frac{1}{2}\right)}\mathfrak{S}\left(\frac{2\mu+\varphi(\omega,\mu)}{2}\right) &\leq_p \frac{\Gamma(\alpha)}{(\varphi(\omega,\mu))^\alpha}\left[\mathcal{I}_{\mu^+}^\alpha\ \mathfrak{S}(\mu+\varphi(\omega,\mu)) + \mathcal{I}_{\mu+\varphi(\omega,\mu)^-}^\alpha\ \mathfrak{S}(\mu)\right] \\ &\leq_p (\mathfrak{S}(\mu) + \mathfrak{S}(\mu+\varphi(\omega,\mu)))\int_0^1 \varsigma^{\alpha-1}[\chi(\varsigma) - \chi(1-\varsigma)]d\varsigma \\ &\leq_p (\mathfrak{S}(\mu) + \mathfrak{S}(\omega))\int_0^1 \varsigma^{\alpha-1}[\chi(\varsigma) - \chi(1-\varsigma)]d\varsigma\end{aligned} \tag{12}$$

If $\mathfrak{S}(z)$ *is pre-incave I-V·F, then:*

$$\begin{aligned}\frac{1}{\alpha\chi\left(\frac{1}{2}\right)}\mathfrak{S}\left(\frac{2\mu+\varphi(\omega,\mu)}{2}\right) &\geq_p \frac{\Gamma(\alpha)}{(\varphi(\omega,\mu))^\alpha}\left[\mathcal{I}_{\mu^+}^\alpha\ \mathfrak{S}(\mu+\varphi(\omega,\mu)) + \mathcal{I}_{\mu+\varphi(\omega,\mu)^-}^\alpha\ \mathfrak{S}(\mu)\right] \\ &\geq_p (\mathfrak{S}(\mu) + \mathfrak{S}(\mu+\varphi(\omega,\mu)))\int_0^1 \varsigma^{\alpha-1}[\chi(\varsigma) - \chi(1-\varsigma)]d\varsigma \\ &\geq_p (\mathfrak{S}(\mu) + \mathfrak{S}(\omega))\int_0^1 \varsigma^{\alpha-1}[\chi(\varsigma) - \chi(1-\varsigma)]d\varsigma\end{aligned} \tag{13}$$

Proof. Let $\mathfrak{S} : [\mu,\ \mu + \varphi(\omega,\mu)] \to \mathcal{K}_C^+$ be a LR--pre-invex *I-V·F*. If condition C holds then, by hypothesis, we have:

$$\frac{1}{\chi\left(\frac{1}{2}\right)}\mathfrak{S}\left(\frac{2\mu+\varphi(\omega,\mu)}{2}\right) \leq_p \mathfrak{S}(\mu + (1-\varsigma)\varphi(\omega,\mu)) + \mathfrak{S}(\mu + \varsigma\varphi(\omega,\mu)).$$

Therefore, we have:

$$\begin{aligned}\frac{1}{\chi\left(\frac{1}{2}\right)}\mathfrak{S}_*\left(\frac{2\mu+\varphi(\omega,\mu)}{2}\right) &\leq \mathfrak{S}_*(\mu + (1-\varsigma)\varphi(\omega,\mu)) + \mathfrak{S}_*(\mu + \varsigma\varphi(\omega,\mu)), \\ \frac{1}{\chi\left(\frac{1}{2}\right)}\mathfrak{S}^*\left(\frac{2\mu+\varphi(\omega,\mu)}{2}\right) &\leq \mathfrak{S}^*(\mu + (1-\varsigma)\varphi(\omega,\mu)) + \mathfrak{S}^*(\mu + \varsigma\varphi(\omega,\mu)).\end{aligned}$$

Multiplying both sides by $\varsigma^{\alpha-1}$ and integrating the obtained result with respect to ς over $(0,1)$, we have

$$\begin{aligned}\frac{1}{\chi\left(\frac{1}{2}\right)}\int_0^1 \varsigma^{\alpha-1}\mathfrak{S}_*\left(\frac{2\mu+\varphi(\omega,\mu)}{2}\right)d\varsigma &\leq \int_0^1 \varsigma^{\alpha-1}\mathfrak{S}_*(\mu + (1-\varsigma)\varphi(\omega,\mu))d\varsigma + \int_0^1 \varsigma^{\alpha-1}\mathfrak{S}_*(\mu + \varsigma\varphi(\omega,\mu))d\varsigma, \\ \frac{1}{\chi\left(\frac{1}{2}\right)}\int_0^1 \varsigma^{\alpha-1}\mathfrak{S}^*\left(\frac{2\mu+\varphi(\omega,\mu)}{2}\right)d\varsigma &\leq \int_0^1 \varsigma^{\alpha-1}\mathfrak{S}^*(\mu + (1-\varsigma)\varphi(\omega,\mu))d\varsigma + \int_0^1 \varsigma^{\alpha-1}\mathfrak{S}^*(\mu + \varsigma\varphi(\omega,\mu))d\varsigma.\end{aligned}$$

Let $x = \mu + (1 - \varsigma)\varphi(\omega, \mu)$ and $x = \mu + \varsigma\varphi(\omega, \mu)$. Then, we have:

$$\begin{aligned}
\frac{1}{\alpha\chi\left(\frac{1}{2}\right)}\mathfrak{S}_*\left(\frac{2\mu+\varphi(\omega,\mu)}{2}\right) &\leq \frac{1}{(\varphi(\omega,\mu))^\alpha} \int_\mu^{\mu+\varphi(\omega,\mu)} (\mu + \varphi(\omega, \mu) - x)^{\alpha-1}\mathfrak{S}_*(x)dx \\
&+ \frac{1}{(\varphi(\omega,\mu))^\alpha} \int_\mu^{\mu+\varphi(\omega,\mu)} (z - \mu)^{\alpha-1}\mathfrak{S}_*(z)dz \\
\frac{1}{\alpha\chi\left(\frac{1}{2}\right)}\mathfrak{S}^*\left(\frac{2\mu+\varphi(\omega,\mu)}{2}\right) &\leq \frac{1}{(\varphi(\omega,\mu))^\alpha} \int_\mu^{\mu+\varphi(\omega,\mu)} (\mu + \varphi(\omega, \mu) - x)^{\alpha-1}\mathfrak{S}^*(x)dx \\
&+ \frac{1}{(\varphi(\omega,\mu))^\alpha} \int_\mu^{\mu+\varphi(\omega,\mu)} (z - \mu)^{\alpha-1}\mathfrak{S}^*(z)dz, \\
&\leq \frac{\Gamma(\alpha)}{(\varphi(\omega,\mu))^\alpha}\left[\mathcal{I}_{\mu^+}^\alpha\ \mathfrak{S}_*(\mu + \varphi(\omega, \mu)) + \mathcal{I}_{\mu+\varphi(\omega,\mu)^-}^\alpha\ \mathfrak{S}_*(\mu)\right] \\
&\leq \frac{\Gamma(\alpha)}{(\varphi(\omega,\mu))^\alpha}\left[\mathcal{I}_{\mu^+}^\alpha\ \mathfrak{S}^*(\mu + \varphi(\omega, \mu)) + \mathcal{I}_{\mu+\varphi(\omega,\mu)^-}^\alpha\ \mathfrak{S}^*(\mu)\right],
\end{aligned}$$

that is:

$$\begin{aligned}
&\frac{1}{\alpha\chi\left(\frac{1}{2}\right)}\left[\mathfrak{S}_*\left(\frac{2\mu+\varphi(\omega,\mu)}{2}\right), \mathfrak{S}^*\left(\frac{2\mu+\varphi(\omega,\mu)}{2}\right)\right] \\
&\leq_p \frac{\Gamma(\alpha)}{(\varphi(\omega,\mu))^\alpha}\left[\mathcal{I}_{\mu^+}^\alpha\ \mathfrak{S}_*(\mu + \varphi(\omega, \mu)) + \mathcal{I}_{\mu+\varphi(\omega,\mu)^-}^\alpha\ \mathfrak{S}_*(\mu),\ \mathcal{I}_{\mu^+}^\alpha\ \mathfrak{S}^*(\mu + \varphi(\omega, \mu)) + \mathcal{I}_{\mu+\varphi(\omega,\mu)^-}^\alpha\ \mathfrak{S}^*(\mu)\right]
\end{aligned}$$

thus,

$$\frac{1}{\alpha\chi\left(\frac{1}{2}\right)}\ \mathfrak{S}\left(\frac{2\mu + \varphi(\omega, \mu)}{2}\right) \leq_p \frac{\Gamma(\alpha)}{(\varphi(\omega, \mu))^\alpha}\left[\mathcal{I}_{\mu^+}^\alpha\ \mathfrak{S}(\mu + \varphi(\omega, \mu)) + \mathcal{I}_{\mu+\varphi(\omega,\mu)^-}^\alpha\ \mathfrak{S}(\mu)\right]. \tag{14}$$

In a similar way as above, we have:

$$\begin{aligned}
&\frac{\Gamma(\alpha)}{(\varphi(\omega,\mu))^\alpha}\left[\mathcal{I}_{\mu^+}^\alpha\ \mathfrak{S}(\mu + \varphi(\omega, \mu)) + \mathcal{I}_{\mu+\varphi(\omega,\mu)^-}^\alpha\ \mathfrak{S}(\mu)\right] \\
&\leq_p [\mathfrak{S}(\mu) + \mathfrak{S}(\mu + \varphi(\omega, \mu))] \int_0^1 \varsigma^{\alpha-1}[\chi(\varsigma) - \chi(1 - \varsigma)]d\varsigma.
\end{aligned} \tag{15}$$

Combining (14) and (15), we have:

$$\begin{aligned}
\frac{1}{\alpha\chi\left(\frac{1}{2}\right)}\mathfrak{S}\left(\frac{2\mu+\varphi(\omega,\mu)}{2}\right) &\leq_p \frac{\Gamma(\alpha)}{(\varphi(\omega,\mu))^\alpha}\left[\mathcal{I}_{\mu^+}^\alpha\ \mathfrak{S}(\mu + \varphi(\omega, \mu)) + \mathcal{I}_{\mu+\varphi(\omega,\mu)^-}^\alpha\ \mathfrak{S}(\mu)\right] \\
&\leq_p [\mathfrak{S}(\mu) + \mathfrak{S}(\mu + \varphi(\omega, \mu))] \int_0^1 \varsigma^{\alpha-1}[\chi(\varsigma) - \chi(1 - \varsigma)]d\varsigma \\
&\leq_p [\mathfrak{S}(\mu) + \mathfrak{S}(\omega)] \int_0^1 \varsigma^{\alpha-1}[\chi(\varsigma) - \chi(1 - \varsigma)]d\varsigma
\end{aligned}$$

hence, the required result. □

Remark 4. *From Theorem 3 we clearly see that:*

If $\varphi(\omega, \mu) = \omega - \mu$, then from Theorem 3, we get the following new result in fractional calculus, see [42].

$$\mathfrak{Q}\left(\frac{\mu + \omega}{2}\right) \leq_p \frac{\Gamma(\alpha + 1)}{2(\omega - \mu)^\alpha}\left[\mathcal{I}_{\mu^+}^\alpha\ \mathfrak{Q}(\omega) + \mathcal{I}_{\omega^-}^\alpha\ \mathfrak{Q}(\mu)\right] \leq_p \frac{\mathfrak{Q}(\mu) + \mathfrak{Q}(\omega)}{2} \tag{16}$$

If $\alpha = 1$, then from Theorem 3, we obtain the following results for LR--pre-invex I-V·F, which are also new ones:

$$\begin{aligned}
&\frac{1}{2\chi\left(\frac{1}{2}\right)}\ \mathfrak{S}\left(\frac{2\mu+\varphi(\omega,\mu)}{2}\right) \leq_p \frac{1}{\varphi(\omega,\mu)}\ (FR) \int_\mu^{\mu+\varphi(\omega,\mu)} \mathfrak{S}(z)dz \\
&\leq_p [\mathfrak{S}(\mu) + \mathfrak{S}(\mu + \varphi(\omega, \mu))] \int_0^1 \chi(\varsigma)d\varsigma.
\end{aligned} \tag{17}$$

If $\chi(\varsigma) = \varsigma$, then Theorem 3 reduces to the result for LR-pre-invex I-V·F, see [41]*:*

$$\mathfrak{S}\left(\frac{2\mu + \varphi(\omega, \mu)}{2}\right) \leq_p \frac{\Gamma(\alpha + 1)}{2(\varphi(\omega, \mu))^\alpha}\left[\mathcal{I}_{\mu^+}^\alpha\ \mathfrak{S}(\mu + \varphi(\omega, \mu)) + \mathcal{I}_{\mu+\varphi(\omega,\mu)^-}^\alpha\ \mathfrak{S}(\mu)\right] \leq_p \frac{\mathfrak{S}(\mu) + \mathfrak{S}(\mu + \varphi(\omega, \mu))}{2} \tag{18}$$

Let $\alpha = 1$ *and* $\chi(\varsigma) = \varsigma$. *Then, Theorem 3 reduces to the result for LR-pre-invex-I-V·F, see* [41]:

$$\mathfrak{S}\left(\frac{2\mu + \varphi(\omega, \mu)}{2}\right) \leq_p \frac{1}{\varphi(\omega, \mu)}\,(FR)\int_{\mu}^{\mu+\varphi(\omega,\mu)} \mathfrak{S}(z)dz \leq_p \frac{\mathfrak{S}(\mu) + \mathfrak{S}(\omega)}{2} \quad (19)$$

Example 2. $\alpha = \frac{1}{2}, \chi(\varsigma) = \varsigma$, *for all* $\varsigma \in [0, 1]$ *and the I-V·F* $\mathfrak{S} : [\mu, \mu + \varphi(\omega, \mu)] = [2, 2 + \varphi(3,2)] \to \mathcal{K}_C^+$, *defined by* $\mathfrak{S}(z) = [1,2]\left(2 - z^{\frac{1}{2}}\right)$. *Since left and right end-point functions* $\mathfrak{S}_*(z) = \left(2 - z^{\frac{1}{2}}\right)$, $\mathfrak{S}^*(z) = 2\left(2 - z^{\frac{1}{2}}\right)$, *are LR-*$\chi$*-pre-invex functions, then* $\mathfrak{S}(z)$ *is LR-*χ*-pre-invex I-V·F. We clearly see that* $\mathfrak{S} \in L([\mu, \mu + \varphi(\omega, \mu)], \mathcal{K}_C^+)$ *and:*

$$\frac{1}{\alpha\chi\left(\frac{1}{2}\right)}\mathfrak{S}_*\left(\frac{2\mu + \varphi(\omega, \mu)}{2}\right) = \mathfrak{S}_*\left(\frac{5}{2}\right) = \frac{4 - \sqrt{10}}{8}$$

$$\frac{1}{\alpha\chi\left(\frac{1}{2}\right)}\mathfrak{S}^*\left(\frac{2\mu + \varphi(\omega, \mu)}{2}\right) = \mathfrak{S}^*\left(\frac{5}{2}\right) = \frac{4 - \sqrt{10}}{4},$$

$$\frac{\mathfrak{S}_*(\mu) + \mathfrak{S}_*(\mu + \varphi(\omega, \mu))}{2}\int_0^1 \varsigma^{\alpha-1}[\chi(\varsigma) - \chi(1-\varsigma)]d\varsigma = \left(4 - \sqrt{2} - \sqrt{3}\right)$$

$$\frac{\mathfrak{S}^*(\mu) + \mathfrak{S}^*(\mu + \varphi(\omega, \mu))}{2}\int_0^1 \varsigma^{\alpha-1}[\chi(\varsigma) - \chi(1-\varsigma)]d\varsigma = 2\left(4 - \sqrt{2} - \sqrt{3}\right).$$

Note that:

$$\begin{aligned}
&\frac{\Gamma(\alpha)}{(\varphi(\omega,\mu))^{\alpha}}\left[\mathcal{I}_{\mu^+}^{\alpha}\ \mathfrak{S}_*(\mu + \varphi(\omega, \mu)) + \mathcal{I}_{\mu+\varphi(\omega,\mu)^-}^{\alpha}\ \mathfrak{S}_*(\mu)\right] \\
&= \frac{\Gamma\left(\frac{1}{2}\right)}{2}\frac{1}{\sqrt{\pi}}\int_2^3 (3 - z)^{\frac{-1}{2}} \cdot \left(2 - z^{\frac{1}{2}}\right)dz \\
&+ \frac{\Gamma\left(\frac{1}{2}\right)}{2}\frac{1}{\sqrt{\pi}}\int_2^3 (z - 2)^{\frac{-1}{2}} \cdot \left(2 - z^{\frac{1}{2}}\right)dz \\
&= \frac{1}{2}\left[\frac{7393}{10{,}000} + \frac{9501}{10{,}000}\right] \\
&= \frac{8447}{20{,}000}.
\end{aligned}$$

$$\begin{aligned}
&\frac{\Gamma(\alpha)}{(\varphi(\omega,\mu))^{\alpha}}\left[\mathcal{I}_{\mu^+}^{\alpha}\ \mathfrak{S}^*(\mu + \varphi(\omega, \mu)) + \mathcal{I}_{\mu+\varphi(\omega,\mu)^-}^{\alpha}\ \mathfrak{S}^*(\mu)\right] \\
&\frac{\Gamma(\alpha)}{(\varphi(\omega,\mu))^{\alpha}}\left[\mathcal{I}_{\mu^+}^{\alpha}\ \mathfrak{S}^*(\mu + \varphi(\omega, \mu)) + \mathcal{I}_{\mu+\varphi(\omega,\mu)^-}^{\alpha}\ \mathfrak{S}^*(\mu)\right] \\
&+ \frac{\Gamma\left(\frac{1}{2}\right)}{2}\frac{1}{\sqrt{\pi}}\int_2^3 (z - 2)^{\frac{-1}{2}} \cdot 2\left(2 - z^{\frac{1}{2}}\right)dz \\
&= \left[\frac{7393}{10{,}000} + \frac{9501}{10{,}000}\right] \\
&= \frac{8447}{10{,}000}.
\end{aligned}$$

Therefore:

$$\left[\frac{4 - \sqrt{10}}{8}, \frac{4 - \sqrt{10}}{4}\right] \leq_p \left[\frac{8447}{20{,}000}, \frac{8447}{10{,}000}\right] \leq_p \left[\left(4 - \sqrt{2} - \sqrt{3}\right), 2\left(4 - \sqrt{2} - \sqrt{3}\right)\right]$$

and Theorem 3 is verified.

From Theorems 4 and 5, we obtain some interval fractional integral inequalities related to interval fractional *H-H* inequalities.

Theorem 4. *Let $\mathfrak{S}, \mathcal{H} : [\mu,\ \mu+\varphi(\omega,\mu)] \to \mathcal{K}_C^+$ be LR-χ_1-pre-invex and LR-χ_2-pre-invex I-V·Fs on $[\mu,\ \mu+\varphi(\omega,\mu)]$, respectively, such that $\mathfrak{S}(z) = [\mathfrak{S}_*(z),\ \mathfrak{S}^*(z)]$ and $\mathcal{H}(z) = [\mathcal{H}_*(z),\ \mathcal{H}^*(z)]$ for all $z \in [\mu,\ \mu+\varphi(\omega,\mu)]$. If φ satisfies condition C and $\mathfrak{S} \times \mathcal{H} \in L([\mu,\ \mu+\varphi(\omega,\mu)], \mathcal{K}_C^+)$, then:*

$$\begin{array}{l}\frac{\Gamma(\alpha)}{(\varphi(\omega,\mu))^{\alpha}}\left[\mathcal{I}_{\mu^+}^{\alpha}\ \mathfrak{S}(\mu+\varphi(\omega,\mu)) \times \mathcal{H}(\mu+\varphi(\omega,\mu)) + \mathcal{I}_{\mu+\varphi(\omega,\mu)^-}^{\alpha}\mathfrak{S}(\mu) \times \mathcal{H}(\mu)\right] \\ \quad \leq_p \xi(\mu,\mu+\varphi(\omega,\mu)) \int_0^1 \varsigma^{\alpha-1}[\chi_1(\varsigma)\chi_2(\varsigma) + \chi_1(1-\varsigma)\chi_2(1-\varsigma)]d\varsigma \\ \quad +\partial(\mu,\mu+\varphi(\omega,\mu)) \int_0^1 \varsigma^{\alpha-1}[\chi_1(\varsigma)\chi_2(1-\varsigma) + \chi_1(1-\varsigma)\chi_2(\varsigma)]d\varsigma.\end{array} \tag{20}$$

where $\xi(\mu,\mu+\varphi(\omega,\mu)) = \mathfrak{S}(\mu) \times \mathcal{H}(\mu) + \mathfrak{S}(\mu+\varphi(\omega,\mu)) \times \mathcal{H}(\mu+\varphi(\omega,\mu))$, $\partial(\mu,\mu+\varphi(\omega,\mu)) = \mathfrak{S}(\mu) \times \mathcal{H}(\mu+\varphi(\omega,\mu)) + \mathfrak{S}(\mu+\varphi(\omega,\mu)) \times \mathcal{H}(\mu)$, *and* $\xi(\mu,\mu+\varphi(\omega,\mu)) = [\xi_*((\mu,\mu+\varphi(\omega,\mu))),\ \xi^*((\mu,\mu+\varphi(\omega,\mu)))]$ *and* $\partial(\mu,\mu+\varphi(\omega,\mu)) = [\partial_*(\mu,\mu+\varphi(\omega,\mu)),\ \partial^*(\mu,\mu+\varphi(\omega,\mu))]$.

Proof. Since $\mathfrak{S}$, $\mathcal{H}$ both are LR-χ_1-pre-invex and LR-χ_2-pre-invex *I-V·F* then, we have:

$$\begin{aligned}\mathfrak{S}_*(\mu+(1-\varsigma)\varphi(\omega,\mu)) &= \mathfrak{S}_*(\mu+\varphi(\omega,\mu)+\varsigma\varphi(\mu,\mu+\varphi(\omega,\mu))) \\ &\leq \chi_1(\varsigma)\mathfrak{S}_*(\mu) + \chi_1(1-\varsigma)\mathfrak{S}_*(\mu+\varphi(\omega,\mu)) \\ \mathfrak{S}^*(\mu+(1-\varsigma)\varphi(\omega,\mu)) &= \mathfrak{S}^*(\mu+\varphi(\omega,\mu)+\varsigma\varphi(\mu,\mu+\varphi(\omega,\mu))) \\ &\leq \chi_1(\varsigma)\mathfrak{S}^*(\mu) + \chi_1(1-\varsigma)\mathfrak{S}^*(\mu+\varphi(\omega,\mu)).\end{aligned}$$

and:

$$\begin{aligned}\mathcal{H}_*(\mu+(1-\varsigma)\varphi(\omega,\mu)) &= \mathcal{H}_*(\mu+(1-\varsigma)\varphi(\omega,\mu)) \\ &\leq \chi_2(\varsigma)\mathcal{H}_*(\mu) + \chi_2(1-\varsigma)\mathcal{H}_*(\mu+\varphi(\omega,\mu)) \\ \mathcal{H}^*(\mu+(1-\varsigma)\varphi(\omega,\mu)) &= \mathcal{H}^*(\mu+(1-\varsigma)\varphi(\omega,\mu)) \\ &\leq \chi_2(\varsigma)\mathcal{H}^*(\mu) + \chi_2(1-\varsigma)\mathcal{H}^*(\mu+\varphi(\omega,\mu)).\end{aligned}$$

From the definition of LR--pre-invex *I-V·F*, we have:

$$\begin{array}{l}\mathfrak{S}_*(\mu+(1-\varsigma)\varphi(\omega,\mu)) \times \mathcal{H}_*(\mu+(1-\varsigma)\varphi(\omega,\mu)) \\ \quad \leq \chi_1(\varsigma)\chi_2(\varsigma)\mathfrak{S}_*(\mu) \times \mathcal{H}_*(\mu) + \chi_1(1-\varsigma)\chi_2(1-\varsigma)\mathfrak{S}_*(\mu+\varphi(\omega,\mu)) \times \mathcal{H}_*(\mu+\varphi(\omega,\mu)) \\ \quad +\chi_1(\varsigma)\chi_2(1-\varsigma)\mathfrak{S}_*(\mu) \times \mathcal{H}_*(\mu+\varphi(\omega,\mu)) + \chi_1(1-\varsigma)\chi_2(\varsigma)\mathfrak{S}_*(\mu+\varphi(\omega,\mu)) \times \mathcal{H}_*(\mu) \\ \mathfrak{S}^*(\mu+(1-\varsigma)\varphi(\omega,\mu)) \times \mathcal{H}^*(\mu+(1-\varsigma)\varphi(\omega,\mu)) \\ \quad \leq \chi_1(\varsigma)\chi_2(\varsigma)\mathfrak{S}^*(\mu) \times \mathcal{H}^*(\mu) + \chi_1(1-\varsigma)\chi_2(1-\varsigma)\mathfrak{S}^*(\mu+\varphi(\omega,\mu)) \times \mathcal{H}^*(\mu+\varphi(\omega,\mu)) \\ \quad +\chi_1(\varsigma)\chi_2(1-\varsigma)\mathfrak{S}^*(\mu) \times \mathcal{H}^*(\mu+\varphi(\omega,\mu)) + \chi_1(1-\varsigma)\chi_2(\varsigma)\mathfrak{S}^*(\mu+\varphi(\omega,\mu)) \times \mathcal{H}^*(\mu).\end{array} \tag{21}$$

Analogously, we have:

$$\begin{array}{l}\mathfrak{S}_*(\mu+\varsigma\varphi(\omega,\mu))\mathcal{H}_*(\mu+\varsigma\varphi(\omega,\mu)) \\ \quad \leq \chi_1(1-\varsigma)\chi_2(1-\varsigma)\mathfrak{S}_*(\mu) \times \mathcal{H}_*(\mu) + \chi_1(\varsigma)\chi_2(\varsigma)\mathfrak{S}_*(\mu+\varphi(\omega,\mu)) \times \mathcal{H}_*(\mu+\varphi(\omega,\mu)) \\ \quad +\chi_1(1-\varsigma)\chi_2(\varsigma)\mathfrak{S}_*(\mu) \times \mathcal{H}_*(\mu+\varphi(\omega,\mu)) + \chi_1(\varsigma)\chi_2(1-\varsigma)\mathfrak{S}_*(\mu+\varphi(\omega,\mu)) \times \mathcal{H}_*(\mu) \\ \mathfrak{S}^*(\mu+\varsigma\varphi(\omega,\mu)) \times \mathcal{H}^*(\mu+\varsigma\varphi(\omega,\mu)) \\ \quad \leq \chi_1(1-\varsigma)\chi_2(1-\varsigma)\mathfrak{S}^*(\mu) \times \mathcal{H}^*(\mu) + \chi_1(\varsigma)\chi_2(\varsigma)\mathfrak{S}^*(\mu+\varphi(\omega,\mu)) \times \mathcal{H}^*(\mu+\varphi(\omega,\mu)) \\ \quad +\chi_1(1-\varsigma)\chi_2(\varsigma)\mathfrak{S}^*(\mu) \times \mathcal{H}^*(\mu+\varphi(\omega,\mu)) + \chi_1(\varsigma)\chi_2(1-\varsigma)\mathfrak{S}^*(\mu+\varphi(\omega,\mu)) \times \mathcal{H}^*(\mu).\end{array} \tag{22}$$

Adding (21) and (22), we have:

$$\begin{aligned}
&\mathfrak{S}_*(\mu+(1-\varsigma)\varphi(\omega,\mu)) \times \mathcal{H}_*(\mu+(1-\varsigma)\varphi(\omega,\mu)) + \mathfrak{S}_*(\mu+\varsigma\varphi(\omega,\mu)) \times \mathcal{H}_*(\mu+\varsigma\varphi(\omega,\mu)) \\
&\quad \le \begin{bmatrix} \chi_1(\varsigma)\chi_2(\varsigma) \\ +\chi_1(1-\varsigma)\chi_2(1-\varsigma) \end{bmatrix} [\mathfrak{S}_*(\mu) \times \mathcal{H}_*(\mu) + \mathfrak{S}_*(\mu+\varphi(\omega,\mu)) \times \mathcal{H}_*(\mu+\varphi(\omega,\mu))] \\
&\quad + \begin{bmatrix} \chi_1(\varsigma)\chi_2(1-\varsigma) \\ +\chi_1(1-\varsigma)\chi_2(\varsigma) \end{bmatrix} [\mathfrak{S}_*(\mu+\varphi(\omega,\mu)) \times \mathcal{H}_*(\mu) + \mathfrak{S}_*(\mu) \times \mathcal{H}_*(\mu+\varphi(\omega,\mu))] \\
&\mathfrak{S}^*(\mu+(1-\varsigma)\varphi(\omega,\mu)) \times \mathcal{H}^*(\mu+(1-\varsigma)\varphi(\omega,\mu)) + \mathfrak{S}^*(\mu+\varsigma\varphi(\omega,\mu)) \times \mathcal{H}^*(\mu+\varsigma\varphi(\omega,\mu)) \\
&\quad \le \begin{bmatrix} \chi_1(\varsigma)\chi_2(\varsigma) \\ +\chi_1(1-\varsigma)\chi_2(1-\varsigma) \end{bmatrix} [\mathfrak{S}^*(\mu) \times \mathcal{H}^*(\mu) + \mathfrak{S}^*(\mu+\varphi(\omega,\mu)) \times \mathcal{H}^*(\mu+\varphi(\omega,\mu))] \\
&\quad + \begin{bmatrix} \chi_1(\varsigma)\chi_2(1-\varsigma) \\ +\chi_1(1-\varsigma)\chi_2(\varsigma) \end{bmatrix} [\mathfrak{S}^*(\mu+\varphi(\omega,\mu)) \times \mathcal{H}^*(\mu) + \mathfrak{S}^*(\mu) \times \mathcal{H}^*(\mu+\varphi(\omega,\mu))].
\end{aligned} \tag{23}$$

Taking multiplication of (23) with $\varsigma^{\alpha-1}$ and integrating the obtained result with respect to ς over (0,1), we have:

$$\begin{aligned}
&\int_0^1 \varsigma^{\alpha-1}\mathfrak{S}_*(\mu+(1-\varsigma)\varphi(\omega,\mu)) \times \mathcal{H}_*(\mu+(1-\varsigma)\varphi(\omega,\mu)) \\
&\qquad + \varsigma^{\alpha-1}\mathfrak{S}_*(\mu+\varsigma\varphi(\omega,\mu)) \times \mathcal{H}_*(\mu+\varsigma\varphi(\omega,\mu))d\varsigma \\
&\quad \le \xi_*((\mu,\mu+\varphi(\omega,\mu))) \int_0^1 \varsigma^{\alpha-1}[\chi_1(\varsigma)\chi_2(\varsigma)+\chi_1(1-\varsigma)\chi_2(1-\varsigma)]d\varsigma \\
&\quad +\partial_*((\mu,\mu+\varphi(\omega,\mu))) \int_0^1 \varsigma^{\alpha-1}[\chi_1(\varsigma)\chi_2(1-\varsigma)+\chi_1(1-\varsigma)\chi_2(\varsigma)]d\varsigma \\
&\int_0^1 \varsigma^{\alpha-1}\mathfrak{S}^*(\mu+(1-\varsigma)\varphi(\omega,\mu)) \times \mathcal{H}^*(\mu+(1-\varsigma)\varphi(\omega,\mu)) \\
&\qquad + \varsigma^{\alpha-1}\mathfrak{S}^*(\mu+\varsigma\varphi(\omega,\mu)) \times \mathcal{H}^*(\mu+\varsigma\varphi(\omega,\mu))d\varsigma \\
&\quad \le \xi^*((\mu,\mu+\varphi(\omega,\mu))) \int_0^1 \varsigma^{\alpha-1}[\chi_1(\varsigma)\chi_2(\varsigma)+\chi_1(1-\varsigma)\chi_2(1-\varsigma)]d\varsigma \\
&\quad +\partial^*((\mu,\mu+\varphi(\omega,\mu))) \int_0^1 \varsigma^{\alpha-1}[\chi_1(\varsigma)\chi_2(1-\varsigma)+\chi_1(1-\varsigma)\chi_2(\varsigma)]d\varsigma.
\end{aligned}$$

It follows that:

$$\begin{aligned}
&\frac{\Gamma(\alpha)}{(\varphi(\omega,\mu))^\alpha}\Big[\mathcal{I}^\alpha_{\mu^+}\ \mathfrak{S}_*(\mu+\varphi(\omega,\mu)) \times \mathcal{H}_*(\mu+\varphi(\omega,\mu)) + \mathcal{I}^\alpha_{\mu+\varphi(\omega,\mu)^-}\ \mathfrak{S}_*(\mu) \times \mathcal{H}_*(\mu)\Big] \\
&\quad \le \xi_*((\mu,\mu+\varphi(\omega,\mu))) \int_0^1 \varsigma^{\alpha-1}[\chi_1(\varsigma)\chi_2(\varsigma)+\chi_1(1-\varsigma)\chi_2(1-\varsigma)]d\varsigma \\
&\quad +\partial_*((\mu,\mu+\varphi(\omega,\mu))) \int_0^1 \varsigma^{\alpha-1}[\chi_1(\varsigma)\chi_2(1-\varsigma)+\chi_1(1-\varsigma)\chi_2(\varsigma)]d\varsigma \\
&\frac{\Gamma(\alpha)}{(\varphi(\omega,\mu))^\alpha}\Big[\mathcal{I}^\alpha_{\mu^+}\ \mathfrak{S}^*(\mu+\varphi(\omega,\mu)) \times \mathcal{H}^*(\mu+\varphi(\omega,\mu)) + \mathcal{I}^\alpha_{\mu+\varphi(\omega,\mu)^-}\ \mathfrak{S}^*(\mu) \times \mathcal{H}^*(\mu)\Big] \\
&\quad \le \xi^*((\mu,\mu+\varphi(\omega,\mu))) \int_0^1 \varsigma^{\alpha-1}[\chi_1(\varsigma)\chi_2(\varsigma)+\chi_1(1-\varsigma)\chi_2(1-\varsigma)]d\varsigma \\
&\quad +\partial^*((\mu,\mu+]\varphi(\omega,\mu))) \int_0^1 \varsigma^{\alpha-1}[\chi_1(\varsigma)\chi_2(1-\varsigma)+\chi_1(1-\varsigma)\chi_2(\varsigma)]d\varsigma.
\end{aligned}$$

It results that:

$$\begin{aligned}
&\frac{\Gamma(\alpha)}{(\varphi(\omega,\mu))^\alpha}\Big[\mathcal{I}^\alpha_{\mu^+}\ \mathfrak{S}_*(\mu+\varphi(\omega,\mu)) \times \mathcal{H}_*(\mu+\varphi(\omega,\mu)) + \mathcal{I}^\alpha_{\mu+\varphi(\omega,\mu)^-}\ \mathfrak{S}_*(\mu) \times \mathcal{H}_*(\mu),\ \mathcal{I}^\alpha_{\mu^+}\ \mathfrak{S}^*(\mu+\varphi(\omega,\mu)) \times \mathcal{H}^*(\mu+\varphi(\omega,\mu)) + \mathcal{I}^\alpha_{\mu+\varphi(\omega,\mu)^-}\ \mathfrak{S}^*(\mu) \times \mathcal{H}^*(\mu)\Big] \\
&\le_p [\xi_*((\mu,\mu+\varphi(\omega,\mu))),\ \xi^*((\mu,\mu+\varphi(\omega,\mu)))] \int_0^1 \varsigma^{\alpha-1}[\chi_1(\varsigma)\chi_2(\varsigma)+\chi_1(1-\varsigma)\chi_2(1-\varsigma)]d\varsigma \\
&+[\partial_*((\mu,\mu+\varphi(\omega,\mu))),\ \partial^*((\mu,\mu+\varphi(\omega,\mu)))] \int_0^1 \varsigma^{\alpha-1}[\chi_1(\varsigma)\chi_2(1-\varsigma)+\chi_1(1-\varsigma)\chi_2(\varsigma)]d\varsigma
\end{aligned}$$

that is:

$$\begin{aligned}
&\frac{\Gamma(\alpha)}{(\varphi(\omega,\mu))^\alpha}\Big[\mathcal{I}^\alpha_{\mu^+}\ \mathfrak{S}(\mu+\varphi(\omega,\mu)) \times \mathcal{H}(\mu+\varphi(\omega,\mu)) + \mathcal{I}^\alpha_{\mu+\varphi(\omega,\mu)^-}\mathfrak{S}(\mu) \times \mathcal{H}(\mu)\Big] \\
&\quad \le_p \xi(\mu,\mu+\varphi(\omega,\mu)) \int_0^1 \varsigma^{\alpha-1}[\chi_1(\varsigma)\chi_2(\varsigma)+\chi_1(1-\varsigma)\chi_2(1-\varsigma)]d\varsigma \\
&\quad +\partial(\mu,\mu+\varphi(\omega,\mu)) \int_0^1 \varsigma^{\alpha-1}[\chi_1(\varsigma)\chi_2(1-\varsigma)+\chi_1(1-\varsigma)\chi_2(\varsigma)]d\varsigma
\end{aligned}$$

and the theorem has been established. □

Theorem 5. *Let $\mathfrak{S}$, $\mathcal{H}$: $[\mu,\ \mu+\varphi(\omega,\mu)] \to \mathcal{K}_C^+$ be two LR-χ_1-pre-invex and LR-χ_2-pre-invex I-V·Fs, respectively, such that $\mathfrak{S}(z) = [\mathfrak{S}_*(z),\ \mathfrak{S}^*(z)]$ and $\mathcal{H}(z) = [\mathcal{H}_*(z),\ \mathcal{H}^*(z)]$ for all $z \in [\mu,\ \mu+\varphi(\omega,\mu)]$. If φ satisfies condition C and $\mathfrak{S} \times \mathcal{H} \in L([\mu,\ \mu+\varphi(\omega,\mu)], \mathcal{K}_C^+)$, then:*

$$\begin{aligned}
&\frac{1}{\alpha\chi_1\left(\frac{1}{2}\right)\chi_2\left(\frac{1}{2}\right)}\,\mathfrak{S}\left(\frac{2\mu+\varphi(\omega,\mu)}{2}\right)\times\mathcal{H}\left(\frac{2\mu+\varphi(\omega,\mu)}{2}\right)\\
&\leq_p \frac{\Gamma(\alpha)}{(\varphi(\omega,\mu))^{\alpha}}\left[\mathcal{I}^{\alpha}_{\mu^+}\,\mathfrak{S}(\mu+\varphi(\omega,\mu))\times\mathcal{H}(\omega)+\mathcal{I}^{\alpha}_{\mu+\varphi(\omega,\mu)^-}\,\mathfrak{S}(\mu)\times\mathcal{H}(\mu)\right]\\
&\quad+\partial(\mu,\mu+\varphi(\omega,\mu))\int_0^1\left[\varsigma^{\alpha-1}+(1-\varsigma)^{\alpha-1}\right]\chi_1(\varsigma)\chi_2(1-\varsigma)d\varsigma\\
&\quad+\xi(\mu,\mu+\varphi(\omega,\mu))\int_0^1\left[\varsigma^{\alpha-1}+(1-\varsigma)^{\alpha-1}\right]\chi_1(1-\varsigma)\chi_2(1-\varsigma)d\varsigma,
\end{aligned}\tag{24}$$

where $\xi(u,u+\varphi(v,u)) = \mathfrak{S}(u)\times\mathcal{H}(u)+\mathfrak{S}(\mu+\varphi(\omega,\mu))\times\mathcal{H}(\mu+\varphi(\omega,\mu))$, $\partial(\mu,\mu+\varphi(\omega,\mu)) = \mathfrak{S}(\mu)\times\mathcal{H}(\mu+\varphi(\omega,\mu))+\mathfrak{S}(\mu+\varphi(\omega,\mu))\times\mathcal{H}(\mu)$, *and* $\xi(\mu,\mu+\varphi(\omega,\mu)) = [\xi_*(\mu,\mu+\varphi(\omega,\mu)),\ \xi^*(\mu,\mu+\varphi(\omega,\mu))]$ *and* $\partial(\mu,\mu+\varphi(\omega,\mu)) = [\partial_*((\mu,\mu+\varphi(\omega,\mu))),\ \partial^*(\mu,\mu+\varphi(\omega,\mu))]$.

Proof. Consider $\mathfrak{S},\mathcal{H}\ :[\mu,\ \mu+\varphi(\omega,\mu)]\to\mathcal{K}_C^+$. are LR-$\chi_1$-pre-invex and LR-$\chi_2$-pre-invex *I-V·Fs*. Then, by hypothesis, we have:

$$\begin{aligned}
&\mathfrak{S}_*\left(\frac{2\mu+\varphi(\omega,\mu)}{2}\right)\times\mathcal{H}_*\left(\frac{2\mu+\varphi(\omega,\mu)}{2}\right)\\
&\mathfrak{S}^*\left(\frac{2\mu+\varphi(\omega,\mu)}{2}\right)\times\mathcal{H}^*\left(\frac{2\mu+\varphi(\omega,\mu)}{2}\right)\\
&\leq\chi_1\left(\tfrac{1}{2}\right)\chi_2\left(\tfrac{1}{2}\right)\left[\begin{array}{c}\mathfrak{S}_*(\mu+(1-\varsigma)\varphi(\omega,\mu))\times\mathcal{H}_*(\mu+(1-\varsigma)\varphi(\omega,\mu))\\+\mathfrak{S}_*(\mu+(1-\varsigma)\varphi(\omega,\mu))\times\mathcal{H}_*(\mu+\varsigma\varphi(\omega,\mu))\end{array}\right]\\
&\quad+\chi_1\left(\tfrac{1}{2}\right)\chi_2\left(\tfrac{1}{2}\right)\left[\begin{array}{c}\mathfrak{S}_*(\mu+\varsigma\varphi(\omega,\mu))\times\mathcal{H}_*(\mu+(1-\varsigma)\varphi(\omega,\mu))\\+\mathfrak{S}_*(\mu+\varsigma\varphi(\omega,\mu))\times\mathcal{H}_*(\mu+\varsigma\varphi(\omega,\mu))\end{array}\right]\\
&\leq\chi_1\left(\tfrac{1}{2}\right)\chi_2\left(\tfrac{1}{2}\right)\left[\begin{array}{c}\mathfrak{S}^*(\mu+(1-\varsigma)\varphi(\omega,\mu))\times\mathcal{H}^*(\mu+(1-\varsigma)\varphi(\omega,\mu))\\+\mathfrak{S}^*(\mu+(1-\varsigma)\varphi(\omega,\mu))\times\mathcal{H}^*(\mu+\varsigma\varphi(\omega,\mu))\end{array}\right]\\
&\quad+\chi_1\left(\tfrac{1}{2}\right)\chi_2\left(\tfrac{1}{2}\right)\left[\begin{array}{c}\mathfrak{S}^*(\mu+\varsigma\varphi(\omega,\mu))\times\mathcal{H}^*(\mu+(1-\varsigma)\varphi(\omega,\mu))\\+\mathfrak{S}^*(\mu+\varsigma\varphi(\omega,\mu))\times\mathcal{H}^*(\mu+\varsigma\varphi(\omega,\mu))\end{array}\right],\\
&\leq\chi_1\left(\tfrac{1}{2}\right)\chi_2\left(\tfrac{1}{2}\right)\left[\begin{array}{c}\mathfrak{S}_*(\mu+(1-\varsigma)\varphi(\omega,\mu))\times\mathcal{H}_*(\mu+(1-\varsigma)\varphi(\omega,\mu))\\+\mathfrak{S}_*(\mu+\varsigma\varphi(\omega,\mu))\times\mathcal{H}_*(\mu+\varsigma\varphi(\omega,\mu))\end{array}\right]\\
&\quad+\chi_1\left(\tfrac{1}{2}\right)\chi_2\left(\tfrac{1}{2}\right)\left[\begin{array}{c}(\chi_1(\varsigma)\mathfrak{S}_*(\mu)+\chi_1(1-\varsigma)\mathfrak{S}_*(\mu+\varphi(\omega,\mu),))\\\times(\chi_2(1-\varsigma)\mathcal{H}_*(\mu)+\chi_2(\varsigma)\mathcal{H}_*(\mu+\varphi(\omega,\mu),))\\+(\chi_1(1-\varsigma)\mathfrak{S}_*(\mu)+\chi_1(\varsigma)\mathfrak{S}_*(\mu+\varphi(\omega,\mu),))\\\times(\chi_2(\varsigma)\mathcal{H}_*(\mu)+\chi_2(1-\varsigma)\mathcal{H}_*(\mu+\varphi(\omega,\mu),))\end{array}\right]\\
&\leq\chi_1\left(\tfrac{1}{2}\right)\chi_2\left(\tfrac{1}{2}\right)\left[\begin{array}{c}\mathfrak{S}^*(\mu+(1-\varsigma)\varphi(\omega,\mu))\times\mathcal{H}^*(\mu+(1-\varsigma)\varphi(\omega,\mu))\\+\mathfrak{S}^*(\mu+\varsigma\varphi(\omega,\mu))\times\mathcal{H}^*(\mu+\varsigma\varphi(\omega,\mu))\end{array}\right]\\
&\quad+\chi_1\left(\tfrac{1}{2}\right)\chi_2\left(\tfrac{1}{2}\right)\left[\begin{array}{c}(\chi_1(\varsigma)\mathfrak{S}^*(\mu)+\chi_1(1-\varsigma)\mathfrak{S}^*(\mu+\varphi(\omega,\mu),))\\\times(\chi_2(1-\varsigma)\mathcal{H}^*(\mu)+\chi_2(\varsigma)\mathcal{H}^*(\mu+\varphi(\omega,\mu),))\\+(\chi_1(1-\varsigma)\mathfrak{S}^*(\mu)+\chi_1(\varsigma)\mathfrak{S}^*(\mu+\varphi(\omega,\mu),))\\\times(\chi_2(\varsigma)\mathcal{H}^*(\mu)+\chi_2(1-\varsigma)\mathcal{H}^*(\mu+\varphi(\omega,\mu),))\end{array}\right],\\
&=\chi_1\left(\tfrac{1}{2}\right)\chi_2\left(\tfrac{1}{2}\right)\left[\begin{array}{c}\mathfrak{S}_*(\mu+(1-\varsigma)\varphi(\omega,\mu))\times\mathcal{H}_*(\mu+(1-\varsigma)\varphi(\omega,\mu))\\+\mathfrak{S}_*(\mu+\varsigma\varphi(\omega,\mu))\times\mathcal{H}_*(\mu+\varsigma\varphi(\omega,\mu))\end{array}\right]\\
&\quad+\chi_1\left(\tfrac{1}{2}\right)\chi_2\left(\tfrac{1}{2}\right)\left[\begin{array}{c}\{\chi_1(\varsigma)\chi_2(1-\varsigma)+\chi_1(1-\varsigma)\chi_2(\varsigma)\}\partial_*((\mu,\mu+\varphi(\omega,\mu)))\\+\{\chi_1(\varsigma)\chi_2(\varsigma)+\chi_1(1-\varsigma)\chi_2(1-\varsigma)\}\xi_*((\mu,\mu+\varphi(\omega,\mu)))\end{array}\right]\\
&=\chi_1\left(\tfrac{1}{2}\right)\chi_2\left(\tfrac{1}{2}\right)\left[\begin{array}{c}\mathfrak{S}^*(\mu+(1-\varsigma)\varphi(\omega,\mu))\times\mathcal{H}^*(\mu+(1-\varsigma)\varphi(\omega,\mu))\\+\mathfrak{S}^*(\mu+\varsigma\varphi(\omega,\mu))\times\mathcal{H}^*(\mu+\varsigma\varphi(\omega,\mu))\end{array}\right]\\
&\quad+\chi_1\left(\tfrac{1}{2}\right)\chi_2\left(\tfrac{1}{2}\right)\left[\begin{array}{c}\{\chi_1(\varsigma)\chi_2(1-\varsigma)+\chi_1(1-\varsigma)\chi_2(\varsigma)\}\partial^*(\mu,\mu+\varphi(\omega,\mu))\\+\{\chi_1(\varsigma)\chi_2(\varsigma)+\chi_1(1-\varsigma)\chi_2(1-\varsigma)\}\xi^*(\mu,\mu+\varphi(\omega,\mu))\end{array}\right].
\end{aligned}\tag{25}$$

Taking multiplication of (25) with $\varsigma^{\alpha-1}$ and integrating over $(0,\ 1)$, we get:

$$\begin{aligned}
&\frac{1}{\alpha\chi_1\left(\frac{1}{2}\right)\chi_2\left(\frac{1}{2}\right)}\mathfrak{S}_*\left(\frac{2\mu+\varphi(\omega,\mu)}{2}\right)\times\mathcal{H}_*\left(\frac{2\mu+\varphi(\omega,\mu)}{2}\right)\\
&\quad\le\frac{\Gamma(\alpha)}{(\varphi(\omega,\mu))^{\alpha}}\left[\mathcal{I}^{\alpha}_{\mu^+}\ \mathfrak{S}_*(\mu+\varphi(\omega,\mu))\times\mathcal{H}_*(\mu+\varphi(\omega,\mu))+\mathcal{I}^{\alpha}_{\mu+\varphi(\omega,\mu)^-}\ \mathfrak{S}_*(\mu)\times\mathcal{H}_*(\mu)\right]\\
&\quad+\partial_*(\mu,\mu+\varphi(\omega,\mu))\int_0^1\left[\varsigma^{\alpha-1}+(1-\varsigma)^{\alpha-1}\right]\chi_1(\varsigma)\chi_2(1-\varsigma)d\varsigma b\\
&\quad+\xi_*(\mu,\mu+\varphi(\omega,\mu))\int_0^1\left[\varsigma^{\alpha-1}+(1-\varsigma)^{\alpha-1}\right]\chi_1(1-\varsigma)\chi_2(1-\varsigma)d\varsigma\\
&\frac{1}{\alpha\chi_1\left(\frac{1}{2}\right)\chi_2\left(\frac{1}{2}\right)}\mathfrak{S}^*\left(\frac{2\mu+\varphi(\omega,\mu)}{2}\right)\times\mathcal{H}^*\left(\frac{2\mu+\varphi(\omega,\mu)}{2}\right)\\
&\quad\le\frac{\Gamma(\alpha)}{(\varphi(\omega,\mu))^{\alpha}}\left[\mathcal{I}^{\alpha}_{\mu^+}\ \mathfrak{S}^*(\mu+\varphi(\omega,\mu))\times\mathcal{H}^*(\mu+\varphi(\omega,\mu))+\mathcal{I}^{\alpha}_{\mu+\varphi(\omega,\mu)^-}\ \mathfrak{S}^*(\mu)\times\mathcal{H}^*(\mu)\right]\\
&\quad+\partial^*(\mu,\mu+\varphi(\omega,\mu))\int_0^1\left[\varsigma^{\alpha-1}+(1-\varsigma)^{\alpha-1}\right]\chi_1(\varsigma)\chi_2(1-\varsigma)d\varsigma\\
&\quad+\xi^*(\mu,\mu+\varphi(\omega,\mu))\int_0^1\left[\varsigma^{\alpha-1}+(1-\varsigma)^{\alpha-1}\right]\chi_1(1-\varsigma)\chi_2(1-\varsigma)d\varsigma.
\end{aligned}$$

It follows that:

$$\begin{aligned}
&\frac{1}{\alpha\chi_1\left(\frac{1}{2}\right)\chi_2\left(\frac{1}{2}\right)}\ \mathfrak{S}\left(\frac{2\mu+\varphi(\omega,\mu)}{2}\right)\times\mathcal{H}\left(\frac{2\mu+\varphi(\omega,\mu)}{2}\right)\\
&\le_p\ \frac{\Gamma(\alpha)}{(\varphi(\omega,\mu))^{\alpha}}\left[\mathcal{I}^{\alpha}_{\mu^+}\ \mathfrak{S}(\mu+\varphi(\omega,\mu))\times\mathcal{H}(\mu+\varphi(\omega,\mu))\right.\\
&\qquad\left.+\mathcal{I}^{\alpha}_{\mu+\varphi(\omega,\mu)^-}\ \mathfrak{S}(\mu)\times\mathcal{H}(\mu)\right]\\
&\quad+\partial(\mu,\mu+\varphi(\omega,\mu))\int_0^1\left[\varsigma^{\alpha-1}+(1-\varsigma)^{\alpha-1}\right]\chi_1(\varsigma)\chi_2(1-\varsigma)d\varsigma\\
&\quad+\xi(\mu,\mu+\varphi(\omega,\mu))\int_0^1\left[\varsigma^{\alpha-1}+(1-\varsigma)^{\alpha-1}\right]\chi_1(1-\varsigma)\chi_2(1-\varsigma)d\varsigma
\end{aligned}$$

Hence, the required result. □

Now, we present the successful reformative version of the generalized version of interval *H-H* inequality on invex set for LR-χ-pre-invex *I-V·F* via interval Riemann–Liouville fractional integral.

Theorem 6. *(Second fractional H-H Fejér inequality) Let* $\mathfrak{S}:[\mu,\ \mu+\varphi(\omega,\mu)]\to\mathcal{K}_C^+$ *be a LR-*χ*-pre-invex I-V·F with* $\mu<\mu+\varphi(\omega,\mu)$*, such that* $\mathfrak{S}(z)=[\mathfrak{S}_*(z),\ \mathfrak{S}^*(z)]$ *for all* $z\in[\mu,\ \mu+\varphi(\omega,\mu)]$*. If* $\mathfrak{S}\in L([\mu,\ \mu+\varphi(\omega,\mu)],\mathcal{K}_C^+)$ *and* $\mathcal{D}:[\mu,\ \mu+\varphi(\omega,\mu)]\to\mathbb{R}$, $\mathcal{D}(z)\ge0$, *symmetric with respect to* $\frac{2\mu+\varphi(\omega,\mu)}{2}$*, then:*

$$\begin{aligned}
&\frac{\Gamma(\alpha)}{(\varphi(\omega,\mu))^{\alpha}}\left[\mathcal{I}^{\alpha}_{\mu^+}\ \mathfrak{S}\mathcal{D}(\mu+\varphi(\omega,\mu))+\mathcal{I}^{\alpha}_{\mu+\varphi(\omega,\mu)^-}\ \mathfrak{S}\mathcal{D}(\mu)\right]\\
&\le_p(\mathfrak{S}(\mu)+\mathfrak{S}(\mu+\varphi(\omega,\mu)))\int_0^1\ \varsigma^{\alpha-1}[\chi(\varsigma)+\chi(1-\varsigma)]D(\mu+\varsigma\varphi(\omega,\mu))d\varsigma\ .
\end{aligned}\tag{26}$$

If $\mathfrak{S}$ *is pre-incave I-V·F, then inequality (26) is reversed.*

Proof. Let $\mathfrak{S}$ be a LR-χ-pre-invex *I-V·F* and $\varsigma^{\alpha-1}\mathcal{D}(\mu+(1-\varsigma)\varphi(\omega,\mu))\ge0$. Then, we have:

$$\begin{aligned}
&\varsigma^{\alpha-1}\mathfrak{S}_*(\mu+(1-\varsigma)\varphi(\omega,\mu))\mathcal{D}(\mu+(1-\varsigma)\varphi(\omega,\mu))\\
&\quad\le\varsigma^{\alpha-1}(\chi(\varsigma)\mathfrak{S}_*(\mu)+\chi(1-\varsigma)\mathfrak{S}_*(\mu+\varphi(\omega,\mu)))\mathcal{D}(\mu+(1-\varsigma)\varphi(\omega,\mu))\\
&\varsigma^{\alpha-1}\mathfrak{S}^*(\mu+(1-\varsigma)\varphi(\omega,\mu))\mathcal{D}(\mu+(1-\varsigma)\varphi(\omega,\mu))\\
&\quad\le\varsigma^{\alpha-1}(\chi(\varsigma)\mathfrak{S}^*(\mu)+\chi(1-\varsigma)\mathfrak{S}^*(\mu+\varphi(\omega,\mu)))\mathcal{D}(\mu+(1-\varsigma)\varphi(\omega,\mu)),
\end{aligned}\tag{27}$$

and:

$$\begin{aligned}
&\varsigma^{\alpha-1}\mathfrak{S}_*(\mu+\varsigma\varphi(\omega,\mu))\mathcal{D}(\mu+\varsigma\varphi(\omega,\mu))\\
&\quad\le\varsigma^{\alpha-1}(\chi(1-\varsigma)\mathfrak{S}_*(\mu)+\chi(\varsigma)\mathfrak{S}_*(\mu+\varphi(\omega,\mu)))\mathcal{D}(\mu+\varsigma\varphi(\omega,\mu))\\
&\varsigma^{\alpha-1}\mathfrak{S}^*(\mu+\varsigma\varphi(\omega,\mu))\mathcal{D}(\mu+\varsigma\varphi(\omega,\mu))\\
&\quad\le\varsigma^{\alpha-1}(\chi(1-\varsigma)\mathfrak{S}^*(\mu)+\chi(\varsigma)\mathfrak{S}^*(\mu+\varphi(\omega,\mu)))\mathcal{D}(\mu+\varsigma\varphi(\omega,\mu)).
\end{aligned}\tag{28}$$

After adding (27) and (28), and integrating over $[0,\ 1]$, we get:

$$\begin{aligned}
&\int_0^1 \varsigma^{\alpha-1}\mathfrak{S}_*(\mu+(1-\varsigma)\varphi(\omega,\mu))\mathcal{D}(\mu+(1-\varsigma)\varphi(\omega,\mu))d\varsigma \\
&\quad+\int_0^1 \varsigma^{\alpha-1}\mathfrak{S}_*(\mu+\varphi(\omega,\mu))\mathcal{D}(\mu+\varsigma\varphi(\omega,\mu))d\varsigma \\
&\le \int_0^1 \begin{bmatrix} \varsigma^{\alpha-1}\mathfrak{S}_*(\mu)\{\chi(\varsigma)\mathcal{D}(\mu+(1-\varsigma)\varphi(\omega,\mu))+\chi(1-\varsigma)\mathcal{D}(\mu+\varsigma\varphi(\omega,\mu))\} \\ +\varsigma^{\alpha-1}\mathfrak{S}_*(\mu+\varphi(\omega,\mu))\{\chi(1-\varsigma)\mathcal{D}(\mu+(1-\varsigma)\varphi(\omega,\mu))+\chi(\varsigma)\mathcal{D}(\mu+\varsigma\varphi(\omega,\mu))\} \end{bmatrix} d\varsigma, \\
&\quad=\mathfrak{S}_*(\mu)\int_0^1 \varsigma^{\alpha-1}[\chi(\varsigma)+\chi(1-\varsigma)]D(\mu+(1-\varsigma)\varphi(\omega,\mu))\ d\varsigma \\
&\quad+\mathfrak{S}_*(\mu+\varphi(\omega,\mu))\int_0^1 \varsigma^{\alpha-1}[\chi(\varsigma)+\chi(1-\varsigma)]D(\mu+\varsigma\varphi(\omega,\mu))\ d\varsigma, \\
&\int_0^1 \varsigma^{\alpha-1}\mathfrak{S}^*(\mu+\varsigma\varphi(\omega,\mu))\mathcal{D}(\mu+\varsigma\varphi(\omega,\mu))d\varsigma \\
&\quad+\int_0^1 \varsigma^{\alpha-1}\mathfrak{S}^*(\mu+(1-\varsigma)\varphi(\omega,\mu))\mathcal{D}(\mu+(1-\varsigma)\varphi(\omega,\mu))d\varsigma \\
&\le \int_0^1 \begin{bmatrix} \varsigma^{\alpha-1}\mathfrak{S}^*(\mu)\{\chi(\varsigma)\mathcal{D}(\mu+(1-\varsigma)\varphi(\omega,\mu))+\chi(1-\varsigma)\mathcal{D}(\mu+\varsigma\varphi(\omega,\mu))\} \\ +\varsigma^{\alpha-1}\mathfrak{S}^*(\mu+\varphi(\omega,\mu))\{\chi(1-\varsigma)\mathcal{D}(\mu+(1-\varsigma)\varphi(\omega,\mu))+\chi(\varsigma)\mathcal{D}(\mu+\varsigma\varphi(\omega,\mu))\} \end{bmatrix} d\varsigma, \\
&\quad=\mathfrak{S}^*(\mu)\int_0^1 \varsigma^{\alpha-1}[\chi(\varsigma)+\chi(1-\varsigma)]D(\mu+(1-\varsigma)\varphi(\omega,\mu))\ d\varsigma \\
&\quad+\mathfrak{S}^*(\mu+\varphi(\omega,\mu))\int_0^1 \varsigma^{\alpha-1}[\chi(\varsigma)+\chi(1-\varsigma)]D(\mu+\varsigma\varphi(\omega,\mu))\ d\varsigma.
\end{aligned} \tag{29}$$

Taking the right hand side of inequality (29), we have:

$$\begin{aligned}
&\int_0^1 \varsigma^{\alpha-1}\mathfrak{S}_*(\mu+(1-\varsigma)\varphi(\omega,\mu))\mathcal{D}(\mu+\varsigma\varphi(\omega,\mu))d\varsigma \\
&\quad+\int_0^1 \varsigma^{\alpha-1}\mathfrak{S}_*(\mu+\varsigma\varphi(\omega,\mu))\mathcal{D}(\mu+\varsigma\varphi(\omega,\mu))d\varsigma \\
&=\frac{1}{(\varphi(\omega,\mu))^\alpha}\int_\mu^{\mu+\varphi(\omega,\mu)}(z-\mu)^{\alpha-1}\mathfrak{S}_*(2\mu+\varphi(\omega,\mu)-z)\mathcal{D}(z)dz \\
&\quad+\frac{1}{(\varphi(\omega,\mu))^\alpha}\int_\mu^{\mu+\varphi(\omega,\mu)}(z-\mu)^{\alpha-1}\mathfrak{S}_*(z)\mathcal{D}(z)dz \\
&=\frac{1}{(\varphi(\omega,\mu))^\alpha}\int_\mu^{\mu+\varphi(\omega,\mu)}(\mu+\varphi(\omega,\mu)-z)^{\alpha-1}\mathfrak{S}_*(z)\mathcal{D}(2\mu+\varphi(\omega,\mu)-z)dz \\
&\quad+\frac{1}{(\varphi(\omega,\mu))^\alpha}\int_\mu^{\mu+\varphi(\omega,\mu)}(z-\mu)^{\alpha-1}\mathfrak{S}_*(z)\mathcal{D}(z)dz \\
&=\frac{\Gamma(\alpha)}{(\varphi(\omega,\mu))^\alpha}\left[\mathcal{I}_{\mu^+}^\alpha\ \mathfrak{S}_*\mathcal{D}(\mu+\varphi(\omega,\mu))+\mathcal{I}_{\mu+\varphi(\omega,\mu)^-}^\alpha\ \mathfrak{S}_*\mathcal{D}(\mu)\right], \\
&\int_0^1 \varsigma^{\alpha-1}\mathfrak{S}^*(\mu+(1-\varsigma)\varphi(\omega,\mu))\mathcal{D}(\mu+\varsigma\varphi(\omega,\mu))d\varsigma \\
&\quad+\int_0^1 \varsigma^{\alpha-1}\mathfrak{S}^*(\mu+\varsigma\varphi(\omega,\mu))\mathcal{D}(\mu+\varsigma\varphi(\omega,\mu))d\varsigma \\
&=\frac{\Gamma(\alpha)}{(\varphi(\omega,\mu))^\alpha}\left[\mathcal{I}_{\mu^+}^\alpha\ \mathfrak{S}^*\mathcal{D}(\mu+\varphi(\omega,\mu))+\mathcal{I}_{\mu+\varphi(\omega,\mu)^-}^\alpha\ \mathfrak{S}^*\mathcal{D}(\mu)\right]
\end{aligned} \tag{30}$$

From (30), we have:

$$\begin{aligned}
&\frac{\Gamma(\alpha)}{(\varphi(\omega,\mu))^\alpha}\left[\mathcal{I}_{\mu^+}^\alpha\ \mathfrak{S}_*\mathcal{D}(\mu+\varphi(\omega,\mu))+\mathcal{I}_{\mu+\varphi(\omega,\mu)^-}^\alpha\ \mathfrak{S}_*\mathcal{D}(\mu)\right] \\
&\quad\le(\mathfrak{S}_*(\mu)+\mathfrak{S}_*(\mu+\varphi(\omega,\mu)))\int_0^1 \varsigma^{\alpha-1}\begin{bmatrix}\chi(\varsigma)\\+\chi(1-\varsigma)\end{bmatrix}D(\mu+\varsigma\varphi(\omega,\mu)) \\
&\frac{\Gamma(\alpha)}{(\varphi(\omega,\mu))^\alpha}\left[\mathcal{I}_{\mu^+}^\alpha\ \mathfrak{S}^*\mathcal{D}(\mu+\varphi(\omega,\mu))+\mathcal{I}_{\mu+\varphi(\omega,\mu)^-}^\alpha\ \mathfrak{S}^*\mathcal{D}(\mu)\right] \\
&\quad\le(\mathfrak{S}^*(\mu)+\mathfrak{S}^*(\mu+\varphi(\omega,\mu)))\int_0^1 \varsigma^{\alpha-1}\begin{bmatrix}\chi(\varsigma)\\+\chi(1-\varsigma)\end{bmatrix}D(\mu+\varsigma\varphi(\omega,\mu)),
\end{aligned}$$

that is:

$$\begin{aligned}
&\frac{\Gamma(\alpha)}{(\varphi(\omega,\mu))^\alpha}\left[\mathcal{I}_{\mu^+}^\alpha\ \mathfrak{S}_*\mathcal{D}(\mu+\varphi(\omega,\mu))+\mathcal{I}_{\mu+\varphi(\omega,\mu)^-}^\alpha\ \mathfrak{S}_*\mathcal{D}(\mu),\ \mathcal{I}_{\mu^+}^\alpha\ \mathfrak{S}^*\mathcal{D}(\mu+\varphi(\omega,\mu))+\mathcal{I}_{\mu+\varphi(\omega,\mu)^-}^\alpha\ \mathfrak{S}^*\mathcal{D}(\mu)\right] \\
&\le_p[\mathfrak{S}_*(\mu)+\mathfrak{S}_*(\mu+\varphi(\omega,\mu)),\ \mathfrak{S}^*(\mu)+\mathfrak{S}^*(\mu+\varphi(\omega,\mu))]\int_0^1 \varsigma^{\alpha-1}[\chi(\varsigma)+\chi(1-\varsigma)]D(\mu+\varsigma\varphi(\omega,\mu))d\varsigma
\end{aligned}$$

Hence,

$$\begin{aligned}
&\frac{\Gamma(\alpha)}{(\varphi(\omega,\mu))^\alpha}\left[\mathcal{I}_{\mu^+}^\alpha\ \mathfrak{S}\mathcal{D}(\mu+\varphi(\omega,\mu))+\mathcal{I}_{\mu+\varphi(\omega,\mu)^-}\ \mathfrak{S}\mathcal{D}(\mu)\right] \\
&\le_p(\mathfrak{S}(\mu)+\mathfrak{S}(\omega))\int_0^1 \varsigma^{\alpha-1}[\chi(\varsigma)+\chi(1-\varsigma)]D(\mu+\varsigma\varphi(\omega,\mu))d\varsigma
\end{aligned}$$

□

Now, we propose the first *H-H* Fejér inequality for LR--pre-invex *I-V·F* using the interval Riemann–Liouville fractional integral. Then we will prove the validity of Theorem 6 and Theorem 7 with a nontrivial Example 3.

Theorem 7. *(First fractional H-H Fejér inequality) Let $\mathfrak{S} : [\mu,\ \mu + \varphi(\omega, \mu)] \to \mathcal{K}_C^+$ be a LR--pre-invex I-V·F such that $\mathfrak{S}(z) = [\mathfrak{S}_*(z),\ \mathfrak{S}^*(z)]$ for all $z \in [\mu,\ \mu + \varphi(\omega, \mu)]$. Let $\mathfrak{S} \in L([\mu,\ \mu + \varphi(\omega, \mu)], \mathcal{K}_C^+)$ and $\mathcal{D} : [\mu,\ \mu + \varphi(\omega, \mu)] \to \mathbb{R}$, $\mathcal{D}(z) \geq 0$, symmetric with respect to $\frac{2\mu+\varphi(\omega,\mu)}{2}$. If φ satisfies condition C, then:*

$$\begin{aligned} &\frac{1}{2\chi\left(\frac{1}{2}\right)}\mathfrak{S}\left(\frac{2\mu+\varphi(\omega,\mu)}{2}\right)\left[\mathcal{I}_{\mu^+}^{\alpha}\ \mathcal{D}(\mu + \varphi(\omega, \mu)) + \mathcal{I}_{\mu+\varphi(\omega,\mu)^-}^{\alpha}\ \mathcal{D}(\mu)\right] \\ &\quad \leq_p \left[\mathcal{I}_{\mu^+}^{\alpha}\ \mathfrak{S}\mathcal{D}(\mu + \varphi(\omega, \mu)) + \mathcal{I}_{\mu+\varphi(\omega,\mu)^-}^{\alpha}\ \mathfrak{S}\mathcal{D}(\mu)\right] \end{aligned} \tag{31}$$

If $\mathfrak{S}$ is pre-incave I-V·F, then inequality (31) is reversed.

Proof. Since $\mathfrak{S}$ is a LR-χ-pre-invex *I-V·F* then, we have:

$$\begin{aligned} \mathfrak{S}_*\left(\frac{2\mu+\varphi(\omega,\mu)}{2}\right) &\leq \chi\left(\tfrac{1}{2}\right)(\mathfrak{S}_*(\mu + (1-\varsigma)\varphi(\omega, \mu)) + \mathfrak{S}_*(\mu + \varsigma\varphi(\omega, \mu))) \\ \mathfrak{S}^*\left(\frac{2\mu+\varphi(\omega,\mu)}{2}\right) &\leq \chi\left(\tfrac{1}{2}\right)(\mathfrak{S}^*(\mu + (1-\varsigma)\varphi(\omega, \mu)) + \mathfrak{S}^*(\mu + \varsigma\varphi(\omega, \mu))). \end{aligned} \tag{32}$$

Since $\mathcal{D}(\mu + (1-\varsigma)\varphi(\omega, \mu)) = \mathcal{D}(\mu + \varsigma\varphi(\omega, \mu))$, then by multiplying (32) by $\varsigma^{\alpha-1}\mathcal{D}(\mu + \varsigma\varphi(\omega, \mu))$ and integrate it with respect to ς over $[0,\ 1]$, we obtain:

$$\begin{aligned} &\mathfrak{S}_*\left(\frac{2\mu+\varphi(\omega,\mu)}{2}\right)\int_0^1 \varsigma^{\alpha-1}\mathcal{D}(\mu + \varsigma\varphi(\omega, \mu))d\varsigma \\ &\quad \leq \chi\left(\tfrac{1}{2}\right)\left(\begin{array}{c} \int_0^1 \varsigma^{\alpha-1}\mathfrak{S}_*(\mu + (1-\varsigma)\varphi(\omega, \mu))\mathcal{D}(\mu + \varsigma\varphi(\omega, \mu))d\varsigma \\ + \int_0^1 \varsigma^{\alpha-1}\mathfrak{S}_*(\mu + \varsigma\varphi(\omega, \mu))\mathcal{D}(\mu + \varsigma\varphi(\omega, \mu))d\varsigma \end{array}\right), \\ &\mathfrak{S}^*\left(\frac{2\mu+\varphi(\omega,\mu)}{2}\right)\int_0^1 \varsigma^{\alpha-1}\mathcal{D}(\mu + \varsigma\varphi(\omega, \mu))d\varsigma \\ &\quad \leq \chi\left(\tfrac{1}{2}\right)\left(\begin{array}{c} \int_0^1 \varsigma^{\alpha-1}\mathfrak{S}^*(\mu + (1-\varsigma)\varphi(\omega, \mu))\mathcal{D}(\mu + \varsigma\varphi(\omega, \mu))d\varsigma \\ + \int_0^1 \varsigma^{\alpha-1}\mathfrak{S}^*(\mu + \varsigma\varphi(\omega, \mu))\mathcal{D}(\mu + \varsigma\varphi(\omega, \mu))d\varsigma \end{array}\right). \end{aligned} \tag{33}$$

Let $x = \mu + \varsigma\varphi(\omega, \mu)$. Then, on the right hand side of inequality (33), we have:

$$\begin{aligned} &\int_0^1 \varsigma^{\alpha-1}\mathfrak{S}_*(\mu + (1-\varsigma)\varphi(\omega, \mu))\mathcal{D}(\mu + \varsigma\varphi(\omega, \mu))d\varsigma \\ &\quad + \int_0^1 \varsigma^{\alpha-1}\mathfrak{S}_*(\mu + \varsigma\varphi(\omega, \mu))\mathcal{D}(\mu + \varsigma\varphi(\omega, \mu))d\varsigma \\ &\quad = \frac{1}{(\varphi(\omega,\mu))^{\alpha}}\int_{\mu}^{\mu+\varphi(\omega,\mu)}(z-\mu)^{\alpha-1}\mathfrak{S}_*(2\mu + \varphi(\omega, \mu) - z)\mathcal{D}(z)dz \\ &\quad + \frac{1}{(\varphi(\omega,\mu))^{\alpha}}\int_{\mu}^{\mu+\varphi(\omega,\mu)}(z-\mu)^{\alpha-1}\mathfrak{S}_*(z)\mathcal{D}(z)dz \\ &\quad = \frac{1}{(\varphi(\omega,\mu))^{\alpha}}\int_{\mu}^{\mu+\varphi(\omega,\mu)}(z-\mu)^{\alpha-1}\mathfrak{S}_*(z)\mathcal{D}(\mu - \omega - z)dz \\ &\quad + \frac{1}{(\varphi(\omega,\mu))^{\alpha}}\int_{\mu}^{\mu+\varphi(\omega,\mu)}(z-\mu)^{\alpha-1}\mathfrak{S}_*(z)\mathcal{D}(z)dz \\ &\quad = \frac{\Gamma(\alpha)}{(\varphi(\omega,\mu))^{\alpha}}\left[\mathcal{I}_{\mu^+}^{\alpha}\ \mathfrak{S}_*\mathcal{D}(\mu + \varphi(\omega, \mu)) + \mathcal{I}_{\mu+\varphi(\omega,\mu)^-}^{\alpha}\ \mathfrak{S}_*\mathcal{D}(\mu)\right], \\ &\int_0^1 \varsigma^{\alpha-1}\mathfrak{S}^*(\mu + (1-\varsigma)\varphi(\omega, \mu))\mathcal{D}(\mu + \varsigma\varphi(\omega, \mu))d\varsigma \\ &\quad + \int_0^1 \varsigma^{\alpha-1}\mathfrak{S}^*(\mu + \varsigma\varphi(\omega, \mu))\mathcal{D}(\mu + \varsigma\varphi(\omega, \mu))d\varsigma \\ &\quad = \frac{\Gamma(\alpha)}{(\varphi(\omega,\mu))^{\alpha}}\left[\mathcal{I}_{\mu^+}^{\alpha}\ \mathfrak{S}^*\mathcal{D}(\mu + \varphi(\omega, \mu)) + \mathcal{I}_{\mu+\varphi(\omega,\mu)^-}^{\alpha}\ \mathfrak{S}^*\mathcal{D}(\mu)\right]. \end{aligned} \tag{34}$$

Then from (34), we have:

$$\begin{aligned} &\frac{1}{2\chi\left(\frac{1}{2}\right)}\mathfrak{S}_*\left(\frac{2\mu+\varphi(\omega,\mu)}{2}\right)\left[\mathcal{I}_{\mu^+}^{\alpha}\ \mathcal{D}(\mu + \varphi(\omega, \mu)) + \mathcal{I}_{\mu+\varphi(\omega,\mu)^-}^{\alpha}\ \mathcal{D}(\mu)\right] \\ &\quad \leq \left[\mathcal{I}_{\mu^+}^{\alpha}\ \mathfrak{S}_*\mathcal{D}(\mu + \varphi(\omega, \mu)) + \mathcal{I}_{\mu+\varphi(\omega,\mu)^-}^{\alpha}\ \mathfrak{S}_*\mathcal{D}(\mu)\right] \\ &\frac{1}{2\chi\left(\frac{1}{2}\right)}\mathfrak{S}^*\left(\frac{2\mu+\varphi(\omega,\mu)}{2}\right)\left[\mathcal{I}_{\mu^+}^{\alpha}\ \mathcal{D}(\mu + \varphi(\omega, \mu)) + \mathcal{I}_{\mu+\varphi(\omega,\mu)^-}^{\alpha}\ \mathcal{D}(\mu)\right] \\ &\quad \leq \left[\mathcal{I}_{\mu^+}^{\alpha}\ \mathfrak{S}^*\mathcal{D}(\mu + \varphi(\omega, \mu)) + \mathcal{I}_{\mu+\varphi(\omega,\mu)^-}^{\alpha}\ \mathfrak{S}^*\mathcal{D}(\mu)\right], \end{aligned}$$

from which, we have:

$$\frac{1}{2\chi\left(\frac{1}{2}\right)}\left[\mathfrak{S}_*\left(\frac{2\mu+\varphi(\omega,\mu)}{2}\right),\ \mathfrak{S}^*\left(\frac{2\mu+\varphi(\omega,\mu)}{2}\right)\right]\left[\mathcal{I}^{\alpha}_{\mu^+}\ \mathcal{D}(\mu+\varphi(\omega,\mu))+\mathcal{I}^{\alpha}_{\mu+\varphi(\omega,\mu)^-}\ \mathcal{D}(\mu)\right]$$
$$\leq\ _p\left[\mathcal{I}^{\alpha}_{\mu^+}\ \mathfrak{S}_*\mathcal{D}(\mu+\varphi(\omega,\mu))+\mathcal{I}^{\alpha}_{\mu+\varphi(\omega,\mu)^-}\ \mathfrak{S}_*\mathcal{D}(\mu),\ \mathcal{I}^{\alpha}_{\mu^+}\ \mathfrak{S}^*\mathcal{D}(\mu+\varphi(\omega,\mu))+\mathcal{I}^{\alpha}_{\mu+\varphi(\omega,\mu)^-}\ \mathfrak{S}^*\mathcal{D}(\mu)\right],$$

and it follows that:

$$\frac{1}{2\chi\left(\frac{1}{2}\right)}\mathfrak{S}\left(\frac{2\mu+\varphi(\omega,\mu)}{2}\right)\left[\mathcal{I}^{\alpha}_{\mu^+}\ \mathcal{D}(\mu+\varphi(\omega,\mu))+\mathcal{I}^{\alpha}_{\mu+\varphi(\omega,\mu)^-}\ \mathcal{D}(\mu)\right]$$
$$\leq\ _p\left[\mathcal{I}^{\alpha}_{\mu^+}\ \mathfrak{S}\mathcal{D}(\mu+\varphi(\omega,\mu))+\mathcal{I}^{\alpha}_{\mu+\varphi(\omega,\mu)^-}\ \mathfrak{S}\mathcal{D}(\mu)\right]$$

This completes the proof. □

Remark 5. *If $\mathcal{D}(z)=1$, then from (26) and (31), we get Theorem 3.*

If $\chi(\varsigma)=\varsigma$, then from (26) and (31), we achieve the following coming inequality, see [42]*:*

$$\begin{aligned}&\mathfrak{S}\left(\frac{2\mu+\varphi(\omega,\mu)}{2}\right)\left[\mathcal{I}^{\alpha}_{\mu^+}\ \mathcal{D}(\mu+\varphi(\omega,\mu))+\mathcal{I}^{\alpha}_{\mu+\varphi(\omega,\mu)^-}\ \mathcal{D}(\mu)\right]\\ &\leq_p\left[\mathcal{I}^{\alpha}_{\mu^+}\ \mathfrak{S}\mathcal{D}(\mu+\{\varphi(\omega,\mu))+\mathcal{I}^{\alpha}_{\mu+\varphi(\omega,\mu)^-}\ \mathfrak{S}\mathcal{D}(\mu)\right]\\ &\leq_p\frac{\mathfrak{S}(\mu)+\mathfrak{S}(\mu+\varphi(\omega,\mu))}{2}\left[\mathcal{I}^{\alpha}_{\mu^+}\ \mathcal{D}(\mu+\varphi(\omega,\mu))+\mathcal{I}^{\alpha}_{\mu+\varphi(\omega,\mu)^-}\ \mathcal{D}(\mu)\right]\\ &\leq_p\frac{\mathfrak{S}(\mu)+\mathfrak{S}(\omega)}{2}\left[\mathcal{I}^{\alpha}_{\mu^+}\ \mathcal{D}(\mu+\varphi(\omega,\mu))+\mathcal{I}^{\alpha}_{\mu+\varphi(\omega,\mu)^-}\ \mathcal{D}(\mu)\right]\end{aligned} \tag{35}$$

Let $\chi(\varsigma)=\varsigma$ and $\alpha=1$. Then, from (26) and (31), we achieve the following coming inequality:

$$\mathfrak{S}\left(\frac{2\mu+\varphi(\omega,\mu)}{2}\right)\leq_p\frac{1}{\int_{\mu}^{\mu+\varphi(\omega,\mu)}\mathcal{D}(z)dz}\,(FR)\int_{\mu}^{\mu+\varphi(\omega,\mu)}\mathfrak{S}(z)\mathcal{D}(z)dz\leq_p\frac{\mathfrak{S}(\mu)+\mathfrak{S}(\omega)}{2} \tag{36}$$

If $\mathfrak{S}_*(z)=\mathfrak{S}^*(z)$ and $\chi(\varsigma)=\varsigma$, then from (26) and (31), we achieve the following coming inequality:

$$\begin{aligned}&\mathfrak{S}\left(\frac{2\mu+\varphi(\omega,\mu)}{2}\right)\left[\mathcal{I}^{\alpha}_{\mu^+}\ \mathcal{D}(\omega)+\mathcal{I}^{\alpha}_{\omega^-}\ \mathcal{D}(\mu)\right]\leq\left[\mathcal{I}^{\alpha}_{\mu^+}\ \mathfrak{S}\mathcal{D}(\mu+\varphi(\omega,\mu))+\mathcal{I}^{\alpha}_{\mu+\varphi(\omega,\mu)^-}\ \mathfrak{S}\mathcal{D}(\mu)\right]\\ &\leq\frac{\mathfrak{S}(\mu)+\mathfrak{S}(\mu+\varphi(\omega,\mu))}{2}\left[\mathcal{I}^{\alpha}_{\mu^+}\ \mathcal{D}(\mu+\varphi(\omega,\mu))+\mathcal{I}^{\alpha}_{\mu+\varphi(\omega,\mu)^-}\ \mathcal{D}(\mu)\right]\\ &\leq\frac{\mathfrak{S}(\mu)+\mathfrak{S}(\omega)}{2}\left[\mathcal{I}^{\alpha}_{\mu^+}\ \mathcal{D}(\mu+\varphi(\omega,\mu))+\mathcal{I}^{\alpha}_{\mu+\varphi(\omega,\mu)^-}\ \mathcal{D}(\mu)\right]\end{aligned} \tag{37}$$

If $\mathfrak{S}_*(z)=\mathfrak{S}^*(z)$ and $\alpha=1$ and $\chi(\varsigma)=\varsigma$, then from (26) and (31), we acquire the classical H-H Fejér inequality.

If $\mathfrak{S}_*(z)=\mathfrak{S}^*(z)$ and $\mathcal{D}(z)=\alpha=1$ and $\chi(\varsigma)=\varsigma$, then from (26) and (31), we acquire the classical H-H inequality.

Example 3. *We consider the I-V·F $\mathfrak{S}:[0,\ \varphi(2,0)]\to\mathcal{K}_C^+$ defined by, $\mathfrak{S}(z)=[1,2](2-\sqrt{z})$. Since end-point functions $\mathfrak{S}_*(z)$, $\mathfrak{S}^*(z)$ are LR-χ-pre-invex functions, then $\mathfrak{S}(z)$ is LR-χ-pre-invex I-V·F.*

If:

$$\mathcal{D}(z)=\begin{cases}\sqrt{z}, & \sigma\in[0,1],\\ \sqrt{2-z}, & \sigma\in(1,\ 2],\end{cases}$$

then $\mathcal{D}(2-z)=\mathcal{D}(z)\geq 0$, for all $z\in[0,\ 2]$. Since $\mathfrak{S}_*(z)=(2-\sqrt{z})$ and $\mathfrak{S}^*(z)=2(2-\sqrt{z})$. If $\chi(\varsigma)=\varsigma$ and $\alpha=\frac{1}{2}$, then we compute the following:

$$\begin{aligned}\frac{\mathfrak{S}_*(\mu)+\mathfrak{S}_*(\mu+\varphi(\omega,\mu))}{2}\int_0^1\varsigma^{\alpha-1}[\chi(\varsigma)+\chi(1-\varsigma)]D(\mu+\varsigma\varphi(\omega,\mu)) &=\frac{\pi}{\sqrt{2}}\left(\frac{4-\sqrt{2}}{2}\right),\\ \frac{\mathfrak{S}^*(\mu)+\mathfrak{S}^*(\mu+\varphi(\omega,\mu))}{2}\int_0^1\varsigma^{\alpha-1}[\chi(\varsigma)+\chi(1-\varsigma)]D(\mu+\varsigma\varphi(\omega,\mu)) &=\frac{\pi}{\sqrt{2}}\left(4-\sqrt{2}\right),\end{aligned} \tag{38}$$

$$\begin{aligned}
\frac{\mathfrak{S}_*(\mu)+\mathfrak{S}_*(\mu+\varphi(\mu+\varphi(\omega,\mu),\mu))}{2}\int_0^1 \varsigma^{\alpha-1}[\chi(\varsigma)+\chi(1-\varsigma)]D(\mu+\varsigma\varphi(\omega,\mu)) &= \frac{\pi}{\sqrt{2}}\left(\frac{4-\sqrt{2}}{2}\right),\\
\frac{\mathfrak{S}^*(\mu)+\mathfrak{S}^*(\mu+\varphi(\omega,\mu))}{2}\int_0^1 \varsigma^{\alpha-1}[\chi(\varsigma)+\chi(1-\varsigma)]D(\mu+\varsigma\varphi(\omega,\mu)) &= \frac{\pi}{\sqrt{2}}\left(4-\sqrt{2}\right),\\
\frac{\Gamma(\alpha)}{(\varphi(\omega,\mu))^\alpha}\left[\mathcal{I}^\alpha_{\mu^+}\ \mathfrak{S}_*\mathcal{D}(\mu+\varphi(\omega,\mu))+\mathcal{I}^\alpha_{\mu+\varphi(\omega,\mu)^-}\ \mathfrak{S}_*\mathcal{D}(\mu)\right] &= \frac{1}{\sqrt{\pi}}\left(2\pi+\frac{4-8\sqrt{2}}{3}\right),\\
\frac{\Gamma(\alpha)}{(\varphi(\omega,\mu))^\alpha}\left[\mathcal{I}^\alpha_{\mu^+}\ \mathfrak{S}^*\mathcal{D}(\mu+\varphi(\omega,\mu))+\mathcal{I}^\alpha_{\mu+\varphi(\omega,\mu)^-}\ \mathfrak{S}^*\mathcal{D}(\mu)\right] &= \frac{2}{\sqrt{\pi}}\left(2\pi+\frac{4-8\sqrt{2}}{3}\right).
\end{aligned} \tag{39}$$

From (38) and (39), we have:

$$\frac{1}{\sqrt{\pi}}\left[\left(2\pi+\frac{4-8\sqrt{2}}{3}\right), 2\left(2\pi+\frac{4-8\sqrt{2}}{3}\right)\right] \quad \leq_p \quad \frac{\pi}{\sqrt{2}}\left[\frac{4-\sqrt{2}}{2}, 4-\sqrt{2}\right].$$

Hence, Theorem 6 is verified.
For Theorem 7, we have:

$$\begin{aligned}
&\mathcal{I}^\alpha_{\mu^+}\ \mathfrak{S}_*\mathcal{D}(\mu+\varphi(\omega,\mu))+\mathcal{I}^\alpha_{\mu+\varphi(\omega,\mu)^-}\ \mathfrak{S}_*\mathcal{D}(\mu)\\
&\quad= \frac{1}{\sqrt{\pi}}\int_0^2 (2-z)^{\frac{-1}{2}}\ \mathcal{D}(z)(2-\sqrt{z})dz+\frac{1}{\sqrt{\pi}}\int_0^2 (z)^{\frac{-1}{2}}\ \mathcal{D}(z)(2-\sqrt{z})dz\\
&\quad= \frac{1}{\sqrt{\pi}}\left(\pi+\frac{8-8\sqrt{2}}{3}\right)+\frac{1}{\sqrt{\pi}}\left(\pi-\frac{4}{3}\right)=\frac{1}{\sqrt{\pi}}\left(2\pi+\frac{4-8\sqrt{2}}{3}\right)\\
&\mathcal{I}^\alpha_{\mu^+}\ \mathfrak{S}^*\mathcal{D}(\mu+\varphi(\omega,\mu))+\mathcal{I}^\alpha_{\mu+\varphi(\omega,\mu)^-}\ \mathfrak{S}^*\mathcal{D}(\mu)\\
&\quad= \frac{2}{\sqrt{\pi}}\int_0^2 (2-z)^{\frac{-1}{2}}\ \mathcal{D}(z)(2-\sqrt{z})dz+\frac{2}{\sqrt{\pi}}\int_0^2 (z)^{\frac{-1}{2}}\ \mathcal{D}(z)(2-\sqrt{z})dz\\
&\quad= \frac{2}{\sqrt{\pi}}\left(\pi+\frac{8-8\sqrt{2}}{3}\right)+\frac{2}{\sqrt{\pi}}\left(\pi-\frac{4}{3}\right)=\frac{2}{\sqrt{\pi}}\left(2\pi+\frac{4-8\sqrt{2}}{3}\right).
\end{aligned} \tag{40}$$

$$\begin{aligned}
\frac{1}{2\chi\left(\frac{1}{2}\right)}\mathfrak{S}_*\left(\frac{2\mu+\varphi(\omega,\mu)}{2}\right)\left[\mathcal{I}^\alpha_{\mu^+}\ \mathcal{D}(\mu+\varphi(\omega,\mu))+\mathcal{I}^\alpha_{\mu+\varphi(\omega,\mu)^-}\ \mathcal{D}(\mu)\right] &= \sqrt{\pi},\\
\frac{1}{2\chi\left(\frac{1}{2}\right)}\mathfrak{S}^*\left(\frac{2\mu+\varphi(\omega,\mu)}{2}\right)\left[\mathcal{I}^\alpha_{\mu^+}\ \mathcal{D}(\mu+\varphi(\omega,\mu))+\mathcal{I}^\alpha_{\mu+\varphi(\omega,\mu)^-}\ \mathcal{D}(\mu)\right] &= 2\sqrt{\pi}.
\end{aligned} \tag{41}$$

4. Conclusions

We have proposed the class of LR-χ-pre-invexity for *I-V·Fs*. By using this class, we have presented several interval *H-H* inequalities and interval *H-H* Fejér inequalities using interval Riemann–Liouville fractional integral operators. Useful examples that illustrate the applicability of theory developed in this study are also presented. In future, we intend to discuss generalized LR-χ-pre-invex *I-V·Fs*. We hope that this concept will be helpful for other authors to play their roles in different fields of sciences.

Author Contributions: Conceptualization, M.B.K.; methodology, M.B.K.; validation, S.T., M.S.S. and H.G.Z.; formal analysis, K.N.; investigation, M.S.S.; resources, S.T.; data curation, H.G.Z.; writing—original draft preparation, M.B.K., K.N. and H.G.Z.; writing—review and editing, M.B.K. and S.T.; visualization, H.G.Z.; supervision, M.B.K. and M.S.S.; project administration, M.B.K.; funding acquisition, K.N., M.S.S. and H.G.Z. All authors have read and agreed to the published version of the manuscript.

Funding: This research received no external funding.

Institutional Review Board Statement: Not applicable.

Informed Consent Statement: Not applicable.

Acknowledgments: The authors would like to thank the Rector, COMSATS University Islamabad, Islamabad, Pakistan, for providing excellent research. This work was funded by Taif University Researchers Supporting Project number (TURSP-2020/345), Taif University, Taif, Saudi Arabia. Moreover, this research has also received funding support from the National Science, Research and Innovation Fund (NSRF), Thailand.

Conflicts of Interest: The authors declare no conflict of interest.

References

1. Hermite, C. Sur deux limites d'une intégrale définie. *Mathesis* **1883**, *3*, 82–97.
2. Hadamard, J. Étude sur les propriétés des fonctions entières et en particulier d'une fonction considérée par Riemann. *J. Mathématiques Pures Appliquées* **1893**, *7*, 171–215.
3. Dragomir, S.; Pearce, C. *Selected Topics on Hermite–Hadamard Inequalities and Applications*; RGMIA Monographs; Victoria University: Melbourne, Australia, 2004.
4. Peajcariaac, J.E.; Tong, Y.L. *Convex Functions, Partial Orderings, and Statistical Applications*; Academic Press: Bostan, MA, USA, 1992.
5. Chen, F. A note on Hermite–Hadamard inequalities for products of convex functions. *J. Appl. Math.* **2013**, *2013*, 1–6. [CrossRef]
6. Dragomir, S.S. Inequalities of Hermite–Hadamard type for h-convex functions on linear spaces. *Proyecciones* **2015**, *34*, 323–341. [CrossRef]
7. Dragomir, S.S. Two mappings in connection to Hadamard's inequalities. *J. Math. Anal. Appl.* **1992**, *167*, 49–56. [CrossRef]
8. Dragomir, S.J.; Pecaric, L.-E. Persson, Some inequalities of Hadamard type. *Soochow J. Math.* **1995**, *21*, 335–341.
9. Pachpatte, B. On some inequalities for convex functions. *RGMIA Res. Rep. Collect.* **2003**, *6*, 1–9.
10. Wang, J.; Li, X.; Zhu, C. Refinements of Hermite–Hadamard type inequalities involving fractional integrals. *Bull. Belg. Math. Soc. Simon Stevin* **2013**, *20*, 655–666. [CrossRef]
11. Sarikaya, M.Z.; Ertugral, F. On the generalized Hermite–Hadamard inequalities. *Ann. Univ. Craioval Math. Comput. Sci. Ser.* **2017**, *47*, 193–213.
12. Sarikaya, M.; Yildirim, H. On generalization of the Riesz potential. *Indian J. Math. Math. Sci.* **2007**, *3*, 231–235.
13. Ertugral, F.; Sarikaya, M.Z. Simpson type integral inequalities for generalized fractional integral. *Rev. R. Acad. Cienc. Exactas Fís. Nat. Ser. A Mat.* **2019**, *113*, 3115–3124. [CrossRef]
14. Tseng, K.L.; Hwang, S.R. New Hermite–Hadamard-type inequalities and their applications. *Filomat* **2016**, *30*, 3667–3680. [CrossRef]
15. Moore, R.E. *Interval Analysis*; Prentice Hall: Englewood Cliffs, NJ, USA, 1966.
16. Chalco-Cano, Y.; Flores-Franulic, A.; Román-Flores, H. Ostrowski type inequalities for interval-valued functions using generalized Hukuhara derivative. *Comput. Appl. Math.* **2012**, *31*, 457–472.
17. Chalco-Cano, Y.; Lodwick, W.A.; Condori-Equice, W. Ostrowski type inequalities and applications in numerical integration for interval-valued functions. *Soft Comput.* **2015**, *19*, 3293–3300. [CrossRef]
18. Román-Flores, H.; Chalco-Cano, Y.; Lodwick, W. Some integral inequalities for interval-valued functions. *Comput. Appl. Math.* **2018**, *37*, 1306–1318. [CrossRef]
19. Costa, T. Jensen's inequality type integral for fuzzy-interval-valued functions. *Fuzzy Sets Syst.* **2017**, *327*, 31–47. [CrossRef]
20. Costa, T.; Román-Flores, H. Some integral inequalities for fuzzy-interval-valued functions. *Inf. Sci.* **2017**, *420*, 110–125. [CrossRef]
21. Flores-Franulic, A.; Chalco-Cano, Y.; Román-Flores, H. An Ostrowski type inequality for interval-valued functions. In Proceedings of the 2013 Joint IFSA World Congress and NAFIPS Annual Meeting (IFSA/NAFIPS), Edmonton, AB, Canada, 24–28 June 2013; pp. 1459–1462.
22. Román-Flores, H.; Chalco-Cano, Y.; Silva, G.N. A note on Gronwall type inequality for interval-valued functions. In Proceedings of the 2013 Joint IFSA World Congress and NAFIPS Annual Meeting (IFSA/NAFIPS), Edmonton, AB, Canada, 24–28 June 2013; pp. 1455–1458.
23. Sadowska, E. Hadamard inequality and a refinement of Jensen inequality for set valued functions. *Results Math.* **1997**, *32*, 332–337. [CrossRef]
24. Mitroi, F.-C.; Nikodem, K.; Wasowicz, S. Hermite–Hadamard inequalities for convex set-valued functions. *Demonstr. Math.* **2013**, *46*, 655–662. [CrossRef]
25. Nikodem, K.; Sanchez, J.L.; Sanchez, L. Jensen and Hermite–Hadamard inequalities for strongly convex set-valued maps. *Math. Aeterna* **2014**, *4*, 979–987.
26. Khan, M.B.; Noor, M.A.; Noor, K.I.; Chu, Y.M. New Hermite-Hadamard type inequalities for (h1, h2)-convex fuzzy-interval-valued functions. *Adv. Differ. Equ.* **2021**, *2021*, 6–20. [CrossRef]
27. Khan, M.B.; Mohammed, P.O.; Noor, M.A.; Hamed, Y.S. New Hermite-Hadamard inequalities in fuzzy-interval fractional calculus and related inequalities. *Symmetry* **2021**, *13*, 673. [CrossRef]
28. Khan, M.B.; Mohammed, P.O.; Noor, M.A.; Alsharif, A.M.; Noor, K.I. New fuzzy-interval inequalities in fuzzy-interval fractional calculus by means of fuzzy order relation. *AIMS Math.* **2021**, *6*, 10964–10988. [CrossRef]
29. Khan, M.B.; Noor, M.A.; Abdullah, L.; Chu, Y.M. Some new classes of preinvex fuzzy-interval-valued functions and inequalities. *Int. J. Comput. Intell. Syst.* **2021**, *14*, 1403–1418. [CrossRef]
30. Liu, P.; Khan, M.B.; Noor, M.A.; Noor, K.I. New Hermite-Hadamard and Jensen inequalities for log-s-convex fuzzy-interval-valued functions in the second sense. *Complex Intell. Syst.* **2021**, *2021*, 1–15. [CrossRef]
31. Khan, M.B.; Noor, M.A.; Al-Bayatti, H.M.; Noor, K.I. Some new inequalities for LR-log-h-convex interval-valued functions by means of pseudo order relation. *Appl. Math. Inf. Sci.* **2021**, *15*, 459–470.
32. Sana, G.; Khan, M.B.; Noor, M.A.; Mohammed, P.O.; Chu, Y.M. Harmonically convex fuzzy-interval-valued functions and fuzzy-interval Riemann–Liouville fractional integral inequalities. *Int. J. Comput. Intell. Syst.* **2021**, *14*, 1809–1822. [CrossRef]
33. Khan, M.B.; Mohammed, P.O.; Noor, M.A.; Abualnaja, K.M. Fuzzy integral inequalities on coordinates of convex fuzzy interval-valued functions. *Math. Biosci. Eng.* **2021**, *18*, 6552–6580. [CrossRef]

34. Niculescu, C.P.; Persson, L.E. *Convex Functions and Their Applications*; Springer: New York, NY, USA, 2006.
35. Zhang, D.; Guo, C.; Chen, D.; Wang, G. Jensen's inequalities for set-valued and fuzzy set-valued functions. *Fuzzy Sets Syst.* **2020**, *2020*, 1–27. [CrossRef]
36. Lupulescu, V. Fractional calculus for interval-valued functions. *Fuzzy Sets Syst.* **2015**, *265*, 63–85. [CrossRef]
37. Budak, H.; Tunç, T.; Sarikaya, M. Fractional Hermite-Hadamard-type inequalities for interval-valued functions. *Proc. Am. Math. Soc.* **2020**, *148*, 705–718. [CrossRef]
38. Khan, M.B.; Noor, M.A.; Noor, K.I. Some Inequalities for LR-(h_1,h_2)-Convex Interval-Valued Functions by Means of Pseudo Order Relation. *Int. J. Comput. Intell. Syst.* **2021**, *14*, 180. [CrossRef]
39. Khan, M.B.; Mohammed, P.O.; Noor, M.A.; Baleanu, D.; Guirao, J. Some New Fractional Estimates of Inequalities for LR-p-Convex Interval-Valued Functions by Means of Pseudo Order Relation. *Axioms* **2021**, *10*, 175. [CrossRef]
40. Mohan, S.R.; Neogy, S.K. On invex sets and preinvex functions. *J. Math. Anal. Appl.* **1995**, *189*, 901–908. [CrossRef]
41. Khan, M.B.; Noor, M.A.; Abdeljawad, T.; Mousa, A.A.A.; Abdalla, B.; Alghamdi, S.M. LR-Preinvex Interval-Valued Functions and Riemann–Liouville Fractional Integral Inequalities. *Fractal Fract.* **2021**, *5*, 243. [CrossRef]
42. Khan, M.B.; Treanţă, S.; Soliman, M.S.; Nonlaopon, K.; Zaini, H.G. Some Hadamard–Fejér Type Inequalities for LR-Convex Interval-Valued Functions. *Fractal Fract.* **2022**, *6*, 6. [CrossRef]
43. Awan, M.U.; Noor, M.A.; Mihai, M.V.; Noor, K.I. Generalized Coordinated Nonconvex Functions and Integral Inequalities. *Appl. Math.* **2008**, *12*, 337–344. [CrossRef]
44. Khan, M.B.; Srivastava, H.M.; Mohammed, P.O.; Nonlaopon, K.; Hamed, Y.S. Some new Jensen, Schur and Hermite-Hadamard inequalities for log convex fuzzy interval-valued functions. *AIMS Math.* **2022**, *7*, 4338–4358. [CrossRef]
45. Khan, M.B.; Mohammed, P.O.; Machado, J.A.T.; Guirao, J.L. Integral Inequalities for Generalized Harmonically Convex Functions in Fuzzy-Interval-Valued Settings. *Symmetry* **2021**, *13*, 2352. [CrossRef]
46. Khan, M.B.; Srivastava, H.M.; Mohammed, P.O.; Baleanu, D.; Jawa, T.M. Fuzzy-interval inequalities for generalized convex fuzzy-interval-valued functions via fuzzy Riemann integrals. *AIMS Math.* **2022**, *7*, 1507–1535. [CrossRef]
47. Awan, M.U.; Noor, M.A.; Noor, K.I. Hermite-Hadamard inequalities for exponentially convex functions. *Appl. Math. Inf. Sci.* **2018**, *12*, 405–409. [CrossRef]
48. Macías-Díaz, J.E.; Khan, M.B.; Noor, M.A.; Abd Allah, A.M.; Alghamdi, S.M. Hermite-Hadamard inequalities for generalized convex functions in interval-valued calculus. *AIMS Math.* **2022**, *7*, 4266–4292. [CrossRef]
49. Saleem, N.; Abbas, M.; Raza, Z. Optimal coincidence best approximation solution in non-Archimedean Fuzzy Metric Spaces. *Iran. J. Fuzzy Syst.* **2016**, *13*, 113–124.
50. Saleem, N.; Zhou, M.; Bashir, S.; Husnine, S.M. Some new generalizations of F-contraction type mappings that weaken certain conditions on Caputo fractional type differential equations. *AIMS Math.* **2021**, *6*, 12718. [CrossRef]

mathematics

Article

Optimality Conditions and Duality for a Class of Generalized Convex Interval-Valued Optimization Problems

Yating Guo [1], Guoju Ye [1], Wei Liu [1,*], Dafang Zhao [2] and Savin Treanţă [3]

[1] College of Science, Hohai University, Nanjing 210098, China; yatingguogyt@163.com or yatingguo@hhu.edu.cn (Y.G.); yegj@hhu.edu.cn (G.Y.)
[2] School of Mathematics and Statistics, Hubei Normal University, Huangshi 435002, China; dafangzhao@163.com or dafangzhao@hbnu.edu.cn
[3] Department of Applied Mathematics, University Politehnica of Bucharest, 060042 Bucharest, Romania; savin.treanta@upb.ro
* Correspondence: liuwhhu@163.com or liuw626@hhu.edu.cn; Tel.: +86-182-6005-7068

Abstract: This paper is devoted to derive optimality conditions and duality theorems for interval-valued optimization problems based on gH-symmetrically derivative. Further, the concepts of symmetric pseudo-convexity and symmetric quasi-convexity for interval-valued functions are proposed to extend above optimization conditions. Examples are also presented to illustrate corresponding results.

Keywords: gH-symmetrically derivative; optimality conditions; wolfe duality; symmetric pseudo-convexity; symmetric quasi-convexity

Citation: Guo, Y.; Ye, G.; Liu, W.; Zhao, D.; Treanţă, S. Optimality Conditions and Duality for a Class of Generalized Convex Interval-Valued Optimization Problems. *Mathematics* **2021**, *9*, 2979. https://doi.org/10.3390/math9222979

Academic Editor: Armin Fügenschuh

Received: 25 October 2021
Accepted: 20 November 2021
Published: 22 November 2021

1. Introduction

Due to the complexity of the environment and the inherent ambiguity of human cognition, the information data in real world optimization problems are usually uncertain. More often, we can not ignore the fact that small uncertainties in data may lead to a completely meaningless of the usual optimal solutions from a practical viewpoint. Therefore, much interest has been paid to the uncertain optimization problems, see [1–4].

There are various approaches used to tackle the optimization problems with uncertainty, such as stochastic process [5], fuzzy set theory [6] and interval analysis [7]. Among them, the method of interval analysis is to express an uncertain variable as a real interval or an interval-valued function (IVF), which has been applied to many fields, such as, the models involving inexact linear programming problems [8], data envelopment analysis [9], optimal control [10], goal programming [11], minimax regret solutions [12] and multi-period portfolio selection problems [13] etc. Up to now, we can find many works involving interval-valued optimization problems (IVOPs) (see [14,15]).

In classical optimization theory, the derivative is the most frequently used one. It plays an important role in the study of optimality conditions and duality theorems in constrained optimization problems. To date, various notions of IVF's derivative have been proposed, see [16–23]. One famous concept is H-derivative defined in [16]. However, the H-derivative is restrictive. In 2009, Stefanini and Bede presented the gH-derivative [23] to overcome the disadvantages of H-derivative. Furthermore, in [24], Guo et al. proposed the gH-symmetrically derivative which is more general than gH-derivative. Researchers of optimal problems have largely used these derivatives of IVFs. For instance, Wu [25] considered the Karush–Kuhn–Tucker (KKT) conditions for nonlinear IVOPs using H-derivative. In [26,27], Wolfe type dual problems of IVOPs were investigated. Later, more general KKT optimality conditions has been proposed by Chalco-Cano et al. [28,29] based on gH-derivative. Besides, Jayswal et al. [30] extended optimality conditions and duality theorems for IVOPs with the generalized convexity. Antczak et al. [31] studied the optimality conditions and duality results for nonsmooth vector optimization problems with multiple IVFs [32]. In

2019, Ghosh [33] have extended the KKT condition for constrained IVOPs. In addition, Van [34] investigated the duality results for interval-valued pseudoconvex optimization problems with equilibrium constraints.

Based on the fact that the IVOPs have been extensively studied on optimality condition and duality by many researchers in recent years, in this paper, we continue to study and develop these results on optimality conditions and Wolfe duality of IVOPs on the basis of the gH-symmetrically derivative. In addition, we are going to introduce more appropriate concepts of symmetric pseudo-convexity and symmetric quasi-convexity to weak the convexity hypothesis.

The remaining of the paper is as follows: In Section 2, we give preliminaries and recall some main concepts. In Section 3, we propose the directional gH-symmetrically derivative and more appropriate concepts of generalized convexity. Section 4 establishes the necessary optimality conditions and Wolfe duality theorems. In Section 5, we apply the generalized convexities to investigate the content in Section 4. Our results are properly wider than the results in [28–30].

2. Preliminaries

Theorem 1 ([35])**.** *Suppose that $f : M \to \mathbb{R}$ is symmetrically differentiable on M and N is an open convex subset of M. Then f is convex on N if and only if*

$$f(t) - f(t^*) \geq f^s(t^*)^T(t - t^*),\ \text{for all}\ t, t^* \in N. \tag{1}$$

Theorem 2 ([36])**.** *Let A be a $m \times n$ real matrix and let $c \in \mathbb{R}^n$ be a column vector. Then the implication*

$$At \leq 0 \Rightarrow c^T t \leq 0 \tag{2}$$

holds for all $t \in \mathbb{R}^n$ if and only if

$$\exists u \geq 0 :\ u^T A = c^T, \tag{3}$$

where $u \in \mathbb{R}^m$.

Let $\mathbb{I}$ be the set of all bounded and closed intervals in $\mathbb{R}$, i.e.,

$$\mathbb{I} = \{a = [\underline{a}, \overline{a}] | \underline{a}, \overline{a} \in \mathbb{R} \text{ and } \underline{a} \leq \overline{a}\}.$$

For $a = [\underline{a}, \overline{a}]$, $b = [\underline{b}, \overline{b}]$, $c = [\underline{c}, \overline{c}] \in \mathbb{I}$ and $k \in \mathbb{R}$, we have

$$a + b = [\underline{a}, \overline{a}] + [\underline{b}, \overline{b}] = [\underline{a} + \underline{b}, \overline{a} + \overline{b}],$$

$$k \cdot a = k \cdot [\underline{a}, \overline{a}] = \begin{cases} [k\underline{a}, k\overline{a}], \text{if } k > 0; \\ [k\overline{a}, k\underline{a}], \text{if } k \leq 0. \end{cases}$$

In [23], Stefanini and Bede presented the gH-difference:

$$a \ominus_g b = c \Leftrightarrow \begin{cases} a = b + c; \\ \text{or } b = a + (-1)c. \end{cases}$$

In addition, this difference between two intervals always exists, i.e.,

$$a \ominus_g b = \left[\min\{\underline{a} - \underline{b}, \overline{a} - \overline{b}\},\ \max\{\underline{a} - \underline{b}, \overline{a} - \overline{b}\}\right].$$

Furthermore, the partial order relation "$\preceq_{LU}$" on $\mathbb{I}$ is determined as follows:

$$[\underline{a}, \overline{a}] \preceq_{LU} [\underline{b}, \overline{b}] \Leftrightarrow \underline{a} \leq \underline{b} \text{ and } \overline{a} \leq \overline{b},$$

$$[\underline{a}, \overline{a}] \prec_{LU} [\underline{b}, \overline{b}] \Leftrightarrow [\underline{a}, \overline{a}] \preceq_{LU} [\underline{b}, \overline{b}] \text{ and } [\underline{a}, \overline{a}] \neq [\underline{b}, \overline{b}],$$

a and b are said to be comparable if and only if $a \preceq_{LU} b$ or $a \succeq_{LU} b$.

Let $\mathbb{R}^n$ be the n-dimensional Euclidean space, and $T \subset \mathbb{R}^n$ is an open set. We call the function $F : T \to \mathbb{I}$ an IVF, i.e., $F(t)$ is a closed interval in $\mathbb{R}$ for every $t \in T$. The IVF F can also be denoted as $F = [\underline{F}, \overline{F}]$, where $\underline{F}$ and $\overline{F}$ are real functions and $\underline{F} \leq \overline{F}$ on T. Moreover, $\underline{F}, \overline{F}$ are called the endpoint functions of F.

Definition 1 ([24]). *Let $F : T \to \mathbb{I}$. Then F is said to be gH-symmetrically differentiable at $t^0 \in T$ if there exists $F^s(t^0) \in \mathbb{I}$ such that:*

$$\lim_{||h|| \to 0} \frac{F(t^0 + h) \ominus_g F(t^0 - h)}{||h||} = F^s(t^0). \tag{4}$$

Definition 2 ([24]). *Let $F : T \to \mathbb{I}$ and $t^0 \in T$. If the IVF $\varphi(t_i) = F(t_1^0, \ldots, t_{i-1}^0, t_i, t_{i+1}^0, \ldots, t_n^0)$ is gH-symmetrically differentiable at t_i^0, then we say that F has the ith partial gH-symmetrically derivative $(\frac{\partial^s F}{\partial t_i})_g(t^0)$ at t^0 and*

$$(\frac{\partial^s F}{\partial t_i})_g(t^0) = \varphi^s(t_i^0).$$

Definition 3 ([24]). *Let $F : T \to \mathbb{I}$ be an IVF, and $\partial^s_{t_i} F$ stands for the partial gH-symmetrically derivative with respect to the ith variable t_i. If $\partial^s_{t_i} F(t^0)$ $(i = 1, \ldots, n)$ exist on some neighborhoods of t^0 and are continuous at t^0, then F is said to be gH-symmetrically differentiable at $t^0 \in T$. Moreover, we denote by*

$$\nabla^s F(t^0) = (\partial^s_{t_1} F(t^0), \ldots, \partial^s_{t_n} F(t^0))$$

the symmetric gradient of F at t^0.

Theorem 3 ([24]). *Let the IVF $F : T \to \mathbb{I}$ be continuous in $(t^0 - \delta, t^0 + \delta)$ for some $\delta > 0$. Then F is gH-symmetrically differentiable at $t^0 \in T$ if and only if $\underline{F}$ and $\overline{F}$ are symmetrically differentiable at t^0.*

Definition 4 ([28]). *Let $F = [\underline{F}, \overline{F}]$ be an IVF defined on T. We say that F is LU-convex at t^* if*

$$F(\theta t^* + (1 - \theta)t) \preceq_{LU} \theta F(t^*) + (1 - \theta)F(t)$$

for every $\theta \in [0, 1]$ and $t \in T$.

Now, we introduce the following IVOP :

$$\begin{aligned} \min \quad & F(t) \\ \text{subject to} \quad & g_i(t) \leq 0, \quad i = 1, \ldots, m, \end{aligned} \tag{5}$$

where $F : M \to \mathbb{I}$, $g_i : M \to \mathbb{R}$ $(i = 1, \ldots, m)$, and $M \subset \mathbb{R}^n$ is an open and convex set. Let

$$\mathcal{X} = \{t \in \mathbb{R}^n : t \in M \text{ and } g_i(t) \leq 0,\ i = 1, \ldots, m\}$$

be the collection of feasible points of Problem (5), and the set of objective values of primal Problem (5) is indicated by:

$$O_P(F, \mathcal{X}) = \{F(t) : t \in \mathcal{X}\}. \tag{6}$$

Moreover, we review the definition of non-dominated solution to the Problem (5):

Definition 5 ([27]). *Let t^* be a feasible solution of Problem (5), i.e., $t^* \in \mathcal{X}$. Then t^* is said to be a non-dominated solution of Problem (5) if there exists no $t \in \mathcal{X} \setminus \{t^*\}$ such that: $F(t) \prec_{LU} F(t^*)$.*

The KKT sufficient optimality conditions of Problem (5) have been obtained in [24]:

Theorem 4 ([24], Sufficient optimality condition). *Assume that $F : M \to \mathbb{I}$ is LU-convex and gH-symmetrically differentiable at t^*, $g : M \to \mathbb{R}^n$ is convex and symmetrically differentiable at t^*. If there exist (Lagrange) multipliers $0 \leq \mu_i \in \mathbb{R}$, $i = 1, \ldots, m$ such that*

$$\begin{aligned} &\nabla^s \underline{F}(t^*) + \nabla^s \overline{F}(t^*) + \sum_{i=1}^{m} \mu_i \nabla^s g_i(t^*) = 0; \\ &\sum_{i=1}^{m} \mu_i g_i(t^*) = 0, \text{where } \mu = (\mu_1, \ldots, \mu_m)^T, \end{aligned} \tag{7}$$

then t^* is a non-dominated solution to Problem (5).

Example 1. *Consider the IVOP as below:*

$$\begin{aligned} \min \quad & F(t) \\ \text{subject to} \quad & g_1(t) \leq 0, \\ & g_2(t) \leq 0, \end{aligned} \tag{8}$$

where

$$F(t) = \begin{cases} [4t^2 + 2t - 3, 3t^2 + 3t], & \text{if } t \in (-1, 0); \\ [3t - 3, 3t], & \text{if } t \in [0, 1), \end{cases}$$

and

$$g_1(t) = -t; \;\; g_2(t) = t - 1.$$

By simple calculation, F is LU-convex and gH-symmetrically differentiable at $t = 0$ and

$$\nabla^s F(0) = [\frac{5}{2}, 3], \; g_1^s(0) = -1, \text{ and } g_2^s(0) = 1.$$

The condition (7) in Theorem 4 is satisfied at $t = 0$ when $\mu_1 = \frac{11}{2}$, and $\mu_2 = 0$.

On the other hand, it can be easily verified that $t = 0$ is a non-dominated solution of Problem (8). Hence, Theorem 4 is verified.

Noted that F is not gH-differentiable at $t = 0$, the sufficient conditions in [24] are properly wider than those in [28].

3. Generalized Convexity of gH-Symmetrically Differentiable IVFs

The LU-convexity assumption in [28] may be restrictive. For example, the IVF

$$F(t) = \begin{cases} [t, 2t], & \text{if } t \geq 0; \\ [2t, t], & \text{if } t < 0, \end{cases}$$

is not LU-convex at $t = 0$. Inspired by this, we introduce the directional gH-symmetrically derivative and the concepts of generalized convexity for IVFs which will be used in Section 4.

Definition 6. *Let $F : T \to \mathbb{I}$ be an IVF and $h \in \mathbb{R}^n$. Then F is called directional gH-symmetrically differentiable at t^0 in the direction h if $D^s F(t^0 : h) \in \mathbb{I}$ exists and*

$$D^s F(t^0 : h) = \lim_{\alpha \to 0^+} \frac{F(t^0 + \alpha h) \ominus_g F(t^0 - \alpha h)}{2\alpha}. \tag{9}$$

If $t = (t_1, \ldots, t_n)^T$ and $e_i = (0, \ldots, \overset{i}{1}, \ldots, 0)$, then $D^s F(t : e^i)$ is the partial gH-symmetrically derivative of F with respect to t_i at t.

Theorem 5. *If $F : T \to \mathbb{I}$ is gH-symmetrically differentiable at $t \in T$ and $h \in \mathbb{R}^n$, then the directional gH-symmetrically derivative exists and*

$$D^s F(t : h) = F^s(t)^T h.$$

Proof. Since, by hypothesis, F is gH-symmetrically differentiable at t, then there exists $F^s(t) \in \mathbb{I}$ such that:

$$\lim_{\alpha h \to 0} \frac{F(t + \alpha h) \ominus_g F(t - \alpha h)}{2\alpha h} = F^s(t).$$

Then, we have:

$$\lim_{\alpha \to 0} D\Big(\frac{F(t + \alpha h) \ominus_g F(t - \alpha h)}{2\alpha}, F^s(t)h\Big) = 0.$$

i.e.,

$$D^s F(t : h) = F^s(t)h.$$

Thus, we complete the proof. □

Definition 7. *The IVF $F : T \to \mathbb{I}$ is called symmetric pseudo-convex (SP-convex) at $t^0 \in T$, if F is gH-symmetrically differentiable at t^0 and*

$$F^s(t^0)(t - t^0) \succeq_{LU} 0 \text{ implies } F(t) \succeq_{LU} F(t^0),$$

for all $t \in T$.

F is said to be symmetric pseudo-concave (SP-concave) at t^0 if $-F$ is SP-convex at t^0.

Definition 8. *The IVF $F : T \to \mathbb{I}$ is called symmetric quasi-convex (SQ-convex) at $t^0 \in T$, if F is gH-symmetrically differentiable at t^0 and*

$$F(t) \preceq_{LU} F(t^0) \text{ implies } F^s(t^0)(t - t^0) \preceq_{LU} 0,$$

for all $t \in T$.

F is said to be symmetric quasi-concave (SQ-concave) at t^0 if $-F$ is SQ-convex at t^0.

Remark 1. *When $\underline{F} = \overline{F}$, i.e., F degenerates to a real function, the concepts of SQ-convexity and SP-convexity will degenerate to s-quasiconvexity and s-pseudoconvexity in [35].*

4. KKT Necessary Conditions

The necessary optimality conditions are an important part of the optimization theory, because these conditions can be used to exclude all the feasible solutions which are not optimal solutions, i.e., they can identify all options for solving the problem. From this point, using gH-symmetrically derivative, we establish a KKT necessary optimality condition which is more general than [28,29].

In order to obtain the necessary condition of Problem (5), we shall use the Slater's constraint qualification [37]. Such condition is:

$$\exists t^0 \in \mathcal{X} \text{ such that } g_i(t^0) < 0,\ i = 1, \ldots, m. \tag{10}$$

Theorem 6 (Necessary optimality condition). *Assume that $F : M \to \mathbb{I}$ is LU-convex and gH-symmetrically differentiable, $g_i : M \to \mathbb{R}(i = 1, \ldots, m)$ are symmetrically differentiable and convex on M. Suppose $H = \{i : g_i(t^*) = 0\}$. If t^* is a non-dominated solution to Problem (5) and the following conditions are satisfied:*

(*A*1) *For every* $i \in H$ *and for all* $y \in \mathbb{R}^n$, *there exist some positive real numbers* ξ_i, *when* $0 < \xi < \xi_i$ *and* $\nabla^s g_i(t^*)^T y < 0$, *we have:*

$$\nabla^s g_i(t^* + \xi y)^T y < 0;$$

(*A*2) *The set* $\mathcal{X}$ *satisfies the Slater's constraint qualification. For* $i \in H$ *and for all* $h \in \mathbb{R}^n$, $D^+\underline{F}(t^* : h) \geq 0$ *implies that* $D^s\underline{F}(t^* : h) \geq 0$ *or* $D^+\overline{F}(t^* : h) \geq 0$ *implies that* $D^s\overline{F}(t^* : h) \geq 0$;

where $D^+\underline{F}$ *and* $D^-\underline{F}$ ($D^+\overline{F}$ *and* $D^-\overline{F}$) *are the right-sided and left-sided directional derivative of* $\underline{F}$ ($\overline{F}$). *Then, there exists* $u^* \in \mathbb{R}^m_+$ *such that condition (7) in Theorem 4 holds.*

Proof. Suppose the above conditions are satisfied. Assume there exists $w \in \mathbb{R}^n$ such that:

$$\begin{aligned} & w^T \nabla^s g_i(t^*) \leq 0, \\ \text{and} \quad & w^T \nabla^s \underline{F}(t^*) < 0, \quad w^T \nabla^s \overline{F}(t^*) < 0, \quad (\forall i \in H). \end{aligned} \tag{11}$$

Since $\mathcal{X}$ satisfies the Slater's constraint qualification, by Equation (10), there exists $t^0 \in \mathcal{X}$ such that $g_i(t^0) < 0$ $(i = 1, \ldots, m)$. Then we have:

$$g_i(t^0) - g_i(t^*) < 0, \quad (\forall i \in H),$$

Combining Theorem 1 and the convexity of g_i, we have

$$\nabla^s g_i(t^*)(t^0 - t^*) < 0, \quad (\forall i \in H).$$

by inequality (11), we get

$$\nabla^s g_i(t^*)[w + \rho(t^0 - t^*)] < 0, \quad (\forall i \in H)$$

for all $\rho > 0$. By hypothesis in (*A*1), there exists $\xi_i > 0$ such that

$$g_i(t^* + \xi[w + \rho(t^0 - t^*)] < 0, \quad (\forall i \in H)$$

for $0 < \xi < \xi_i$. Therefore, we have: $t^* + \xi[w + \rho(t^0 - t^*)] \in \mathcal{X}$.

Since t^* is a non-dominated solution to Problem (5), there exists no feasible solution t such that: $F(t) \prec F(t^*)$, i.e.,

$$\begin{aligned} & \underline{F}(t^* + \xi[w + \rho(t^0 - t^*)]) \geq \underline{F}(t^*), \\ \text{or} \quad & \overline{F}(t^* + \xi[w + \rho(t^0 - t^*)]) \geq \overline{F}(t^*). \end{aligned}$$

By hypothesis (A2), we have

$$\begin{aligned} & [w + \rho(t^0 - t^*)] \nabla^s \underline{F}(t^*) \geq 0, \\ \text{or} \quad & [w + \rho(t^0 - t^*)] \nabla^s \overline{F}(t^*) \geq 0, \end{aligned}$$

for all $\rho > 0$. When $\rho \to 0^+$, we obtain

$$w^T \nabla^s \underline{F}(t^*) \geq 0, \text{ or } w^T \nabla^s \overline{F}(t^*) \geq 0, \tag{12}$$

which contradicts to the inequality (11).

Thus, inequality (11) has no solution. By Theorem 2, there exists $0 \leq \mu_i^* \in \mathbb{R}$ such that

$$\nabla^s \underline{F}(t^*) + \nabla^s \overline{F}(t^*) + \sum_{i=1}^{m} \mu_i^* \nabla^s g_i(t^*) = 0.$$

For $i \notin H$, let $\mu_i = 0$, then we have $\sum_{i=1}^{m} \mu_i g_i(t^*) = 0$. The proof is complete. □

Example 2. *Continued from Example 1, note that $g_1(0) = 0$ and $g_1^s(t) \equiv -1$. Moreover, M satisfies the Slater's condition. For $h \in \mathbb{R}^n$ we have:*

$$D^+\underline{F}(0:h) = \lim_{\alpha \to 0^+} \frac{\underline{F}(0+\alpha h) - \underline{F}(0)}{\alpha} = \begin{cases} 3h, \, h > 0; \\ 2h, \, h \leq 0. \end{cases}$$

$$D^-\underline{F}(0:h) = \lim_{\alpha \to 0^-} \frac{\underline{F}(0+\alpha h) - \underline{F}(0)}{\alpha} = 3h.$$

Obviously, $D^+\underline{F}(t^*:h) \geq 0$ implies that

$$D^+\underline{F}(t^*:h) + D^-\underline{F}(t^*:h) \geq 0.$$

Thus, the conditions in Theorem 6 hold at $t = 0$.
On the other hand, we have:

$$\begin{aligned} &\nabla^s \underline{F}(0) + \nabla^s \overline{F}(0) + \sum_{i \in H} \mu_i^* \nabla^s g_i(0) \\ =&\frac{5}{2} + 3 + \mu_1 \cdot (-1) + \mu_2 \cdot 1 = 0 \end{aligned} \tag{13}$$

when $\mu_1 = \frac{11}{2}$, $\mu_2 = 0$. Hence, Theorem 6 is verified.

5. Wolfe Type Duality

In this section, we consider the Wolfe dual Problem (14) of Problem (5) as follows:

$$\begin{aligned} \max \quad & F(t) + \sum_{i=1}^{m} \mu_i g_i(t) \\ \text{subject to} \quad & \nabla^s \underline{F}(t) + \nabla^s \overline{F}(t) + \sum_{i=1}^{m} \mu_i \nabla^s g_i(t) = 0, \\ & \mu = (\mu_1, \ldots, \mu_m) \geq 0. \end{aligned} \tag{14}$$

For convenience, we write:

$$L(t, \mu) = F(t) + \sum_{i=1}^{m} \mu_1 g_i(t). \tag{15}$$

We denote by

$$\mathcal{Y} = \{(t, \mu) \in \mathbb{R}^n \times \mathbb{R}^m : \nabla^s \underline{F}(t) + \nabla^s \overline{F}(t) + \sum_{i=1}^{m} \mu_i \nabla^s g_i(t) = 0\} \tag{16}$$

the feasible set of dual Problem (14) and

$$O_D(L, \mathcal{Y}) = \{L(t, \mu) : (t, \mu) \in \mathcal{Y}\} \tag{17}$$

the set of all objective values of Problem (14).

Definition 9. *Let (t^*, μ^*) be a feasible solution to Problem (14), i.e., $(t^*, \mu^*) \in \mathcal{Y}$. (t^*, μ^*) is said to be a non-dominated solution to Problem (14), if there is no $(t, \mu) \in \mathcal{Y}$ such that $L(t^*, \mu^*) \prec_{LU} L(t, \mu)$.*

Next, we discuss the solvability for Wolfe primal and dual problems.

Lemma 1. *Assume that* $F : M \to \mathbb{I}$ *is LU-convex and gH-symmetrically differentiable,* $g_i : M \to \mathbb{R}(i = 1, \ldots, m)$ *are symmetrically differentiable and convex on M. Furthermore,* $H = \{i : g_i(t^*) = 0\}$*. If* $\hat{t}$*,* (t, μ) *are feasible solutions to Problems* (5) *and* (14)*, respectively, then the following statements hold true:*

(B1) If $\underline{F}(t) \geq \underline{F}(\hat{t})$*, then* $\overline{F}(\hat{t}) \geq \overline{L}(t, \mu)$*;*

(B2) If $\overline{F}(t) \geq \overline{F}(\hat{t})$*, then* $\underline{F}(\hat{t}) \geq \underline{L}(t, \mu)$*.*

Moreover, the statements still hold true under strict inequality.

Proof. Suppose $\hat{t}$, (t, μ) are feasible solutions to Problem (5) and (14), respectively. Since F is LU-convex, we have:

$$\begin{aligned}\overline{F}(\hat{t}) &\geq \overline{F}(t) + \nabla^s \overline{F}(t)(\hat{t} - t) \\ &= \overline{F}(t) - \nabla^s \underline{F}(t)(\hat{t} - t) - \sum_{i=1}^{m} \nabla^s g_i(t)(\hat{t} - t) \\ &\geq \overline{F}(t) + \underline{F}(t) - \underline{F}(\hat{t}) + \sum_{i=1}^{m} [g_i(t) - g_i(\hat{t})].\end{aligned}$$

If $\underline{F}(t) - \underline{F}(\hat{t}) \geq 0$, it follows that

$$\overline{F}(\hat{t}) \geq \overline{F}(t) + \sum_{i=1}^{m} g_i(t) = \overline{L}(t, \mu).$$

Thus, the statement $(B1)$ holds true. On the other hand, if $\underline{F}(t) - \underline{F}(\hat{t}) > 0$, then

$$\overline{F}(\hat{t}) > \overline{F}(t) + \sum_{i=1}^{m} g_i(t) = \overline{L}(t, \mu).$$

The other statements can also be proof by using similar arguments. □

Lemma 2. *Under the same assumption to Lemma 1, if* $\hat{t}$*,* (t, μ) *are feasible solutions to Problems* (5) *and* (14)*, respectively, then the following statements hold true:*

(C1) If $\overline{F}(t) \leq \overline{F}(\hat{t})$*, then* $\overline{F}(\hat{t}) \geq \overline{L}(t, \mu)$*;*

(C2) If $\underline{F}(t) \leq \underline{F}(\hat{t})$*, then* $\underline{F}(\hat{t}) \geq \underline{L}(t, \mu)$*.*

Moreover, the statements still hold true under strict inequality.

Proof. Suppose $\overline{F}(t) \leq \overline{F}(\hat{t})$, then we have:

$$\begin{aligned}&\overline{F}(\hat{t}) - \overline{L}(t, \mu) \\ =&\overline{F}(\hat{t}) - \overline{F}(t) - \sum_{i=1}^{m} \mu_i g_i(t) \\ \geq&\overline{F}^s(t)(\hat{t} - t) + [-\sum_{i=1}^{m} \mu_i g_i(\hat{t}) + \sum_{i=1}^{m} \mu_i g_i(\hat{t}) - \sum_{i=1}^{m} \mu_i g_i(t)] \\ \geq&\overline{F}^s(t)(\hat{t} - t) + [-\sum_{i=1}^{m} \mu_i g_i(\hat{t}) + \sum_{i=1}^{m} \mu_i g_i^s(t)(\hat{t} - t)] \\ =&[\overline{F}^s(t) + \sum_{i=1}^{m} \mu_i g_i^s(t)](\hat{t} - t) - \sum_{i=1}^{m} \mu_i g_i(\hat{t}) \\ =&-\underline{F}^s(\hat{t} - t) - \sum_{i=1}^{m} \mu_i g_i(\hat{t}) \\ \geq&\underline{F}(t) - \underline{F}(\hat{t}) - \sum_{i=1}^{m} \mu_i g_i(\hat{t})\end{aligned}$$

$$=\underline{F}(t)-\underline{L}(\hat{t},\mu)$$
$$\geq 0.$$

Thus, the statement (C1) holds true. On the other hand, if $\overline{F}(t)<\overline{F}(\hat{t})$, then:

$$\overline{F}(\hat{t})>\overline{L}(t,\mu).$$

The proof of (C2) is similar to (C1), so we omit it. □

Theorem 7. *(Weak duality) Under the same assumption of Lemma 1, if $\hat{t}$, (t,μ) are feasible solutions to Problems* (5) *and* (14)*, respectively, then the following statements hold true:*
(D1) If $F(t)$ and $F(\hat{t})$ are comparable, then $F(\hat{t})\succeq L(t,\mu)$.
(D2) If $F(t)$ and $F(\hat{t})$ are not comparable, then $\underline{F}(\hat{t})>\underline{L}(t,\mu)$ or $\overline{F}(\hat{t})>\overline{L}(t,\mu)$.

Proof. If $F(t)$ and $F(\hat{t})$ are comparable, by Lemmas 1 and 2, we can obtain the statement $(D1)$; If $F(t)$, $F(\hat{t})$ are not comparable, then we have:

$$F(\hat{t})\subset F(t),\text{ or } F(\hat{t})\supset F(t).$$

By Lemmas 1 and 2, we obtain that:

$$\underline{F}(\hat{t})>\underline{L}(t,\mu),\text{ or } \overline{F}(\hat{t})>\overline{L}(t,\mu).$$

The proof is complete. □

Example 3. *Consider the optimization problem in Example 1. The corresponding Wolfe duality problem is:*

$$\begin{aligned} \max\quad & F(t)+\mu_1 g_1(t)+\mu_2 g_2(t) \\ \textit{subject to}\quad & \nabla^s\underline{F}(t)+\nabla^s\overline{F}(t)+\mu_1\nabla^s g_1(t)+\mu_2\nabla^s g_2(t)=0, \\ & \mu=(\mu_1,\mu_2)\geq 0. \end{aligned} \tag{18}$$

Clearly, $\hat{t}=0$ is a feasible solution of the Problem (8) *and the objective value is $[-3,0]$. Moreover, $(t,\mu_1,\mu_2)=(-\frac{1}{2},0,2)$ is a feasible solution to the Problem* (18)*, and objective value is $[-6,-\frac{15}{4}]$.*
We observe that

$$F(0)\succ L(-\frac{1}{2},0,2). \tag{19}$$

Hence, Theorem 7 is verified.

Theorem 8. *(Solvability) Under the same assumption of Lemma 1, if $(t^*,\mu^*)\in\mathcal{Y}$ and $L(t^*,\mu^*)\in O_P(F,\mathcal{X})$, then (t^*,μ^*) solves the Problem* (14)*.*

Proof. Suppose (t^*,μ^*) is not a non-dominated solution to Problem (14), then there exists $(t,\mu)\in\mathcal{Y}$ so that:

$$L(t^*,\mu^*)\prec L(t,\mu).$$

Since $L(t^*,\mu^*)\in O_P(F,\mathcal{X})$, there exists $\hat{t}\in\mathcal{X}$ such that:

$$F(\hat{t})=L(t^*,\mu^*)\prec L(t,\mu). \tag{20}$$

According to Theorem 7, if $F(t)$, $F(\hat{t})$ are comparable, then we have

$$F(\hat{t})\succeq L(t,\mu).$$

If $F(t)$, $F(\hat{t})$ are not comparable, then:

$$\underline{F}(\hat{t}) > \underline{L}(t,\mu),\ \text{or}\ \overline{F}(\hat{t}) > \overline{L}(t,\mu).$$

These two results are contradict to Equation (20). Thus, we complete the proof. □

Theorem 9. *(Solvability) Under the same assumption of Lemma 1, if $\hat{t} \in \mathcal{X}$ is a feasible solution to Problem* (5) *and $F(\hat{t}) \in O_D(L, \mathcal{Y})$, then $\hat{t}$ solves the Problem* (5).

Proof. The proof is similar to Theorem 8, so we omit it. □

Corollary 1. *Under the same assumption of Lemma 1, if $\hat{t}$, (t^*, μ^*) are feasible solutions to Problems* (5) *and* (14)*, respectively, moreover, if $F(\hat{t}) = L(t^*, \mu^*)$, then $\hat{t}$ solves Problem* (5) *and (t^*, μ^*) solves the Problem* (14).

Proof. The proof follows Theorem 8 and Theorem 9. □

Theorem 10. *(Strong duality) Under the same assumption of Lemma 1, if F, g_i $(i = 1, \ldots, m)$ satisfy the conditions (A1) and (A2) at t^*, then there exists $\mu^* \in \mathbb{R}^m_+$ such that (t^*, μ^*) is a solution of Problem* (14) *and*

$$L(t^*, \mu^*) = F(t^*).$$

Proof. By Theorem 6, there exists $\mu^* \in \mathbb{R}^m_+$ such that:

$$\nabla^s \underline{F}(t^*) + \nabla^s \overline{F}(t^*) + \sum_{i=1}^{m} \mu_i^* \nabla^s g_i(t^*) = 0, \tag{21}$$

and $\sum_{i=1}^{m} g_i(t^*) = 0$. It can be shown that $L(t^*, \mu^*) \in O_D(L, \mathcal{Y})$ and

$$L(t^*, \mu^*) = F(t^*).$$

By Corollary 1, there exists $\mu^* \in \mathbb{R}^m_+$ such that (t^*, μ^*) is a solution to Problem (14). The proof is complete. □

Example 4. *Continued from Example 2, after calculation, the non-dominated solution to Problem* (18) *is $(0, \frac{11}{2}, 0)$ and the objective value is $[-6, 0]$; While $t = 0$ is also a non-dominated solution to Problem* (8) *and the objective value is $[-6, 0]$. Then we have:*

$$L(0, \frac{7}{2}, 0) = F(0).$$

On the other hand, the IVF F in Example 2 satisfies the conditions (A1) and (A2), which verifies Theorem 10.

6. The optimality Conditions with Generalized Convexity

In this section, we use the concepts of SP-convexity and SQ-convexity which are less restrictive than LU-convexity to obtain some generalized optimality theorems of Problem (5).

Theorem 11. *(Sufficient condition) Suppose F is SP-convex and g_i is s-quasiconvex at t^* for $i \in H$. If $t^* \in \mathcal{X}$, and for some $\mu^* \in \mathbb{R}^n_+$ condition* (7) *in Theorem 4 holds, then t^* is a non-dominated solution to Problem* (5).

Proof. Assume for some $\mu^* \geq 0$, condition (7) in Theorem 4 holds. We have $\sum_{i=1}^{m} \mu_i^* g_i(t^*) = 0$, where $\mu_i^* = 0$ when $i \notin H$. Since $g_i(t) \leq g_i(t^*)$ and g_i is s-quasiconvex at t^* for $i \in H$, we obtain $g_i^s(t^*)(t - t^*) \leq 0$. Thus:

$$\sum_{i=1}^{m} \mu_i^* g_i^s(t^*)(t - t^*) \leq 0, \quad \text{for all } t \in \mathcal{X},$$

which implies:

$$\nabla^s(\underline{F}(t^*) + \overline{F}(t^*))(t - t^*) \geq 0 \text{ for all } t \in \mathcal{X}.$$

Thanks to the SP-convexity of F, we have:

$$\underline{F}(t) + \overline{F}(t) \geq \underline{F}(t^*) + \overline{F}(t^*) \text{ for all } t \in \mathcal{X}. \tag{22}$$

Then t^* is an optimal solution to the real-valued objective function $\underline{F} + \overline{F}$ subject to the same constraints of Problem (5). Suppose t^* is not a non-dominated solution of Problem (5), there exists $t \in \mathcal{X}$ such that:

$$F(t) \prec F(t^*)$$

which contradicts Equation (22). The proof is complete. □

Example 5. *Consider the following optimization:*

$$\begin{aligned} \min \quad & F(t) \\ \textit{subject to} \quad & g_1(t) \leq 0, \\ & g_2(t) \leq 0. \end{aligned} \tag{23}$$

where:

$$F(t) = \begin{cases} [t^3 + t, 2t^3 + t], & \text{if } t \geq 0; \\ [2t, 1.5t], & \text{if } t < 0, \end{cases}$$

and $g_1(t) = -t$, $g_2(t) = t - 1$.

We observe that F is not gH-differentiable at $t = 0$*, and F is not LU-convex at* $t = 0$ *with:*

$$F(0) \not\preceq \frac{2}{3}F(\frac{1}{4}) + \frac{1}{3}F(-\frac{1}{2}).$$

However, F is SP-convex at $t = 0$ *and* g_i *is s-quasiconvex at* $t = 0$ *for* $i \in H$*. Furthermore, F is gH-symmetrically differentiable at* $t = 0$ *with*

$$F^s(0) = [\frac{5}{4}, \frac{3}{2}].$$

Moreover, we have:

$$\begin{aligned} & \nabla^s \underline{F}(0) + \nabla^s \overline{F}(0) + \sum_{i=1}^{m} \mu_i \nabla^s g_i(0) = 0; \\ & \sum_{i=1}^{m} \mu_i g_i(0) = 0, \textit{where } \mu = (\frac{11}{4}, 0)^T. \end{aligned} \tag{24}$$

On the other hand, $t = 0$ *is a non-dominated solution to Problem* (23)*, which verifies Theorem* 11.

Theorem 12. *(Necessary condition) Suppose F is SQ-concave at* t^* *and* g_i *is s-pseudoconcave at* t^* *for* $i \in H$*. If* t^* *is a non-dominated solution to Problem* (5) *and* g_i *is lower semicontinuous on M for all* $i \notin H$*, then* (t^*, μ^*) *satisfies condition* (7) *in Theorem* 4 *with some* $\mu^* \geq 0$.

Proof. Assume $\mathcal{X}_1 = \{t \in \mathcal{X} : g_i(t) < 0 \text{ for all } i \notin H\}$. The set $\mathcal{X}_1$ is relatively open since g_i is lower semicontinuous on M for each $i \notin H$. Since $t^* \in \mathcal{X}_1$, there is some α_0 such that for any $y \in E^n$, $t^* + \alpha y \in \mathcal{X}_1$ when: $0 < \alpha < \alpha_0$.

Suppose $0 < \alpha < \alpha_0$ and for $i \in H$ we have $g_i^s(t^*)^T y \leq 0$, then $g_i^s(t^*)^T \alpha y \leq 0$ for $i \in H$. According to the s-pseudoconcavity of g_i at t^*, we have:

$$g_i(t^* + \alpha y) \leq g_i(t^*).$$

Since t^* solves Problem (5), we have: $F(t^*) \preceq_{LU} F(t^* + \alpha y)$. The SQ-concavity of F at t^* implies that

$$(\nabla^s \underline{F}(t^*) + \nabla^s \overline{F}(t^*))(\alpha y) \geq 0.$$

Thus:

$$g_i^s(t^*)^T y \leq 0, \ (\nabla^s \underline{F}(t^*) + \nabla^s \overline{F}(t^*))y < 0$$

has no solution y in $\mathbb{R}^n$. Hence, by Farkas' lemma, there exist $\mu_i^* \geq 0$ such that:

$$\nabla^s \underline{F}(t^*) + \nabla^s \overline{F}(t^*) + \sum_{i=1}^{m} \mu_i^* \nabla^s g_i(t^*) = 0.$$

□

Example 6. *Note that in Example 5, $t = 0$ is a non-dominated solution. F is SQ-concave at $t = 0$, and $g_1(t) = -t$ is s-pseudoconcave at $t = 0$, $g_2(t) = t - 1$ is lower semicontinuous on $\mathbb{R}$.*

On the other hand, for $\mu = (\frac{11}{4}, 0)$, the condition (7) *is satisfied at $t = 0$ which verifies Theorem 12.*

Theorem 13. *(Weak duality) Suppose for each μ such that $(t, \mu) \in \mathbb{R}$, $L(\cdot, \mu)$ is SP-convex on $\mathcal{X}$. Then for all $\hat{t} \in \mathcal{X}$ and $(t, \mu) \in \mathcal{Y}$, $L(t, \mu) \preceq_{LU} F(\hat{t})$.*

Proof. Consider $\hat{t} \in \mathcal{X}$ and $(t, \mu) \in \mathcal{Y}$. Then we have: $L_t^s(t, \mu) = 0$. Since $L(\cdot, \mu)$ is SP-convex on $\mathcal{X}$, we obtain $L(\hat{t}, \mu) \succeq L(t, \mu)$. Therefore,

$$F(\hat{t}) + \sum_{i=1}^{m} u_i g_i(\hat{t}) \succeq L(t, \mu).$$

The proof is complete. □

Example 7. *Continued the problem of Example 5, $t = 0$ is a feasible solution to Problem* (23) *and the objective value is $F(0) = 0$.*

Moreover, $(t, \mu) = (1, 11, 0)$ is a feasible solution to the Wolfe problem of Problem (23) *and the objective value is $[-9, -8]$. Furthermore, we have*

$$F(0) \succ L(1, 11, 0),$$

which verifies Theorem 13.

Theorem 14. *(Strong duality) Suppose F, g_i $(i = 1, \ldots, m)$ and t^* satisfy the conditions of Theorem 12. Furthermore, for each μ such that $(t, \mu) \in \mathbb{R}$, $L(\cdot, \mu)$ is SP-convex on $\mathcal{X}$. Then there exists a $\mu^* \geq 0$ such that (t^*, μ^*) solves Problem* (14) *and $L(t^*, \mu^*) = F(t^*)$.*

Proof. The proof is similar to the proof of Theorem 10. □

Example 8. *Continued from Example 5, the non-dominated solution to Wolfe dual of Problem* (23) *is $(0, \frac{11}{4}, 0)$ and the objective value is $L(0, \frac{11}{4}, 0) = 0$.*

While $t = 0$ *is also a non-dominated solution of Problem* (23) *and the objective value is* $F(0) = 0$. *Then we have:*

$$L(0, \frac{11}{4}, 0) = F(0).$$

On the other hand, the IVF F in Example 5 satisfies the conditions of Theorem 14, which verifies Theorem 14.

7. Conclusions

The IVOP is an interesting topic with many real world applications. The nondifferentiable counterpart of this problem is an interesting topic too. In this work, we newly investigate a topic on gH-symmetrically differentiable IVOPs and obtain the KKT conditions and duality theorems which are properly wider than those in [28]. Additionally, more appropriate concepts of generalized convexity are introduced to extend the optimality conditions in [24]. Some developments of the results presented in this paper, which will be investigated in future papers, are given by the study of the saddle-point optimality criteria for the considered class of IVOPs.

Author Contributions: Funding acquisition, G.Y., W.L. and D.Z.; writing—original draft, Y.G.; writing—review and editing, G.Y., W.L., D.Z. and S.T. All authors have read and agreed to the published version of the manuscript.

Funding: This research was funded by the National Key Research and Development Program of China (2018YFC1508100), Natural Science Foundation of Jiangsu Province (BK20180500), Key Projects of Educational Commission of Hubei Province of China (D20192501), and Philosophy and Social Sciences of Educational Commission of Hubei Province of China (20Y109).

Institutional Review Board Statement: Not applicable.

Informed Consent Statement: Not applicable.

Data Availability Statement: Not applicable.

Acknowledgments: This work has been supported by the National Key Research and Development Program of China (2018YFC1508100), Natural Science Foundation of Jiangsu Province (BK20180500), Key Projects of Educational Commission of Hubei Province of China (D20192501), and Philosophy and Social Sciences of Educational Commission of Hubei Province of China (20Y109).

Conflicts of Interest: The authors declare no conflict of interest.

References

1. Abel, A.B. Optimal investment under uncertainty. *Am. Econ. Rev.* **1983**, *73*, 228–233.
2. Chuong, T.D. Robust Optimality and Duality in Multiobjective Optimization Problems under Data Uncertainty. *SIAM J. Optim.* **2020**, *30*, 1501–1526. [CrossRef]
3. Mehdi, D.; Hamid, M.A.; Perrin, F. Robustness and optimality of linear quadratic controller for uncertain systems. *Automatica* **1996**, *32*, 1081–1083. [CrossRef]
4. Engau, A.; Sigler, D. Pareto solutions in multicriteria optimization under uncertainty. *Eur. J. Oper. Res.* **2020**, *281*, 357–368. [CrossRef]
5. Fu, Y.; Xiao, H.; Lee, L.H.; Huang, M. Stochastic optimization using grey wolf optimization with optimal computing budget allocation. *Appl. Soft. Comput.* **2021**, *103*, 107154. [CrossRef]
6. Zhang, S.; Chen, M.; Zhang, W.; Zhuang, X. Fuzzy optimization model for electric vehicle routing problem with time windows and recharging stations. *Expert Syst. Appl.* **2020**, *145*, 113123. [CrossRef]
7. Steuer, R.E. Algorithms for linear programming problems with interval objective function coefficients. *Math. Oper. Res.* **1981**, *6*, 333–348. [CrossRef]
8. Charnes, A.; Granot, F.; Phillips, F. An algorithm for solving interval linear programming problems. *Oper. Res.* **1977**, *25*, 688–695. [CrossRef]
9. Despotis, D.K.; Smirlis, Y.G. Data envelopment analysis with imprecise data. *Eur. J. Oper. Res.* **2002**, *140*, 24–36. [CrossRef]
10. Treanţă, S. Efficiency in uncertain variational control problems. *Neural. Comput. Appl.* **2021**, *33*, 5719–5732. [CrossRef]
11. Inuiguchi, M.; Kume, Y. Goal programming problems with interval coefficients and target intervals. *Eur. J. Oper. Res.* **1991**, *52*, 345–360. [CrossRef]

12. Li, Y.P.; Huang, G.H.; Chen, X. An interval-valued minimax-regret analysis approach for the identification of optimal greenhouse-gas abatement strategies under uncertainty. *Energy Policy* **2011**, *39*, 4313–4324. [CrossRef]
13. Lai, K.K.; Wang, S.Y.; Xu, J.P.; Zhu, S.S.; Fang, Y. A class of linear interval programming problems and its application to portfolio selection. *IEEE Trans. Fuzzy Syst.* **2002**, *10*, 698–704. [CrossRef]
14. Urli, B.; Nadeau, R. An interactive method to multiobjective linear programming problems with interval coefficients. *INFOR Inf. Syst. Oper. Res.* **1992**, *30*, 127–137. [CrossRef]
15. Oliveira, C.; Antunes, C.H. Multiple objective linear programming models with interval coefficients-an illustrated overview. *Eur. J. Oper. Res.* **2007**, *181*, 1434–1463. [CrossRef]
16. Hukuhara, M. Integration des applications mesurables dont la valeur est un compact convexe. *Funkcial. Ekvac.* **1967**, *10*, 205–223.
17. Markov, S. Calculus for interval functions of a real variable. *Computing* **1979**, *22*, 325–337. [CrossRef]
18. Stefanini, L. A generalization of Hukuhara difference and division for interval and fuzzy arithmetic. *Fuzzy Sets Syst.* **2020**, *161*, 1564–1584. [CrossRef]
19. Malinowski, M.T. Interval differential equations with a second type Hukuhara derivative. *Appl. Math. Lett.* **2011**, *24*, 2118–2123. [CrossRef]
20. Chalco-Cano, Y.; Román-Flores, H.; Jiménez-Gamero, M.D. Generalized derivative and π-derivative for set-valued functions. *Inform. Sci.* **2011**, *181*, 2177–2188. [CrossRef]
21. Malinowski, M.T. Interval Cauchy problem with a second type Hukuhara derivative. *Inform. Sci.* **2012**, *213*, 94–105. [CrossRef]
22. Chalco-Cano, Y.; Maqui-Huamán, G.G.; Silva, G.N.; Jiménez-Gamero, M.D. Algebra of generalized Hukuhara differentiable interval-valued functions: review and new properties. *Fuzzy Sets Syst.* **2019**, *375*, 53–69. [CrossRef]
23. Stefanini, L.; Bede, B. Generalized Hukuhara differentiability of interval-valued functions and interval differential equations. *Nonlinear-Anal-Theory Methods Appl.* **2009**, *71*, 1311–1328. [CrossRef]
24. Guo, Y.; Ye, G.; Zhao, D.; Liu, W. gH-symmetrically derivative of interval-valued functions and applications in interval-valued optimization. *Symmetry* **2019**, *11*, 1203. [CrossRef]
25. Wu, H.C. The Karush-Kuhn-Tucker optimality conditions in an optimization problem with interval-valued objective function. *Eur. J. Oper. Res.* **2007**, *176*, 46–59. [CrossRef]
26. Wu, H.C. On interval-valued nonlinear programming problems. *J. Math. Anal. Appl.* **2008**, *338*, 299–316. [CrossRef]
27. Wu, H.C. Wolfe duality for interval-valued optimization. *J. Optim. Theory Appl.* **2008**, *138*, 497. [CrossRef]
28. Chalco-Cano, Y.; Lodwick, W.A.; Rufian-Lizana, A. Optimality conditions of type KKT for optimization problem with interval-valued objective function via generalized derivative. *Fuzzy Optim. Decis. Mak.* **2013**, *12*, 305–322. [CrossRef]
29. Osuna-Gomez, R.; Chalco-Cano, Y.; Hernandez-Jimenez, B.; Ruiz-Garzon, G. Optimality conditions for generalized differentiable interval-valued functions. *Inf. Sci.* **2015**, *321*, 136–146. [CrossRef]
30. Jayswal, A.; Stancu-Minasian, I.; Ahmad, I. On sufficiency and duality for a class of interval-valued programming problems. *Appl. Math. Comput.* **2011**, *218*, 4119–4127. [CrossRef]
31. Antczak, T. Optimality conditions and duality results for nonsmooth vector optimization problems with the multiple interval-valued objective function. *Acta. Math. Sci.* **2017**, *37*, 1133–1150. [CrossRef]
32. Dar, B.A.; Jayswal, A.; Singh, D. Optimality, duality and saddle point analysis for interval-valued nondifferentiable multiobjective fractional programming problems. *Optimization* **2021**, *70*, 1275–1305. [CrossRef]
33. Ghosh, D.; Singh, A.; Shukla, K.K.; Manchanda, K. Extended Karush-Kuhn-Tucker condition for constrained interval optimization problems and its application in support vector machines. *Inf. Sci.* **2019**, *504*, 276–292. [CrossRef]
34. Van, S.T.; Dinh, D.H. Duality results for interval-valued pseudoconvex optimization problem with equilibrium constraints with applications. *Comput. Appl. Math.* **2020**, *39*, 1–24. [CrossRef]
35. Minch, R.A. Applications of symmetric derivatives in mathematical programming. *Math. Program.* **1971**, *1*, 307–320. [CrossRef]
36. Farkas, J. Theorie der einfachen Ungleichungen. *J. Reine. Angew. Math.* **1902**, *1902*, 1–27.
37. Slater, M. *Lagrange Multipliers Revisited: A Contribution to NONLINEAR Programming*; Cowles Comission Discussion Paper No. 80: Mathematics 403; Cowles Foundation for Research in Economics: New Haven, CO, USA, 1950.

mathematics

Article

On Well-Posedness of Some Constrained Variational Problems

Savin Treanţă

Department of Applied Mathematics, University Politehnica of Bucharest, 060042 Bucharest, Romania; savin.treanta@upb.ro

Abstract: By considering the new forms of the notions of lower semicontinuity, pseudomonotonicity, hemicontinuity and monotonicity of the considered scalar multiple integral functional, in this paper we study the well-posedness of a new class of variational problems with variational inequality constraints. More specifically, by defining the set of approximating solutions for the class of variational problems under study, we establish several results on well-posedness.

Keywords: constrained variational problem; well-posedness; multiple integral functional

Citation: Treanţă, S. On Well-Posedness of Some Constrained Variational Problems. *Mathematics* **2021**, *9*, 2478. https://doi.org/10.3390/math9192478

Academic Editor: Simeon Reich

Received: 20 September 2021
Accepted: 1 October 2021
Published: 4 October 2021

1. Introduction

The concept of well-posedness is a very useful mathematical tool in the study of optimization problems. Thus, beginning with the work of Tykhonov [1], many types of well-posedness associated with variational problems have been introduced (Levitin–Polyak well-posedness [2–5], α-well-posedness [6,7], extended well-posedness [8–16], L-well-posedness [17]). Additionally, this mathematical tool can be used to study some related problems: variational inequality problems [18–20], complementary problems [21], equilibrium problems [22,23], fixed point problems [24], hemivariational inequality problems [25], Nash equilibrium problems [26], and so on. The well-posedness of generalized variational inequalities and the corresponding optimization problems have been analyzed by Jayswal and Shalini [27]. Moreover, an interesting and important extension of variational inequality problem is the multidimensional variational inequality problem and the associated multi-time optimization problems (see [28–33]). Recently, Treanţă [30] investigated the well-posed isoperimetric-type constrained variational control problems. For other different but connected ideas, the reader is directed to Dridi and Djebabla [34] and Jana [35].

In this paper, motivated and inspired by the above research papers, we study the well-posedness property for new constrained variational problems, implying second-order multiple integral functionals and partial derivatives. In this regard, we formulate new forms of monotonicity, lower semicontinuity, hemicontinuity, and pseudomonotonicity for the considered multiple integral-type functional. Further, we introduce the set of approximating solutions for the constrained optimization problem under study and establish several theorems on well-posedness. The previous research works in this scientific area did not take into account the new form of the notions mentioned above. In essence, the results derived here can be considered as dynamic generalizations of the corresponding static results already existing in the literature. In this paper, the framework is based on function spaces of infinite-dimension and multiple integral-type functionals. This element is completely new for the well-posed optimization problems.

The present paper is structured as follows: In Section 2, we formulate the problem under study and introduce the new forms of monotonicity, lower semicontinuity, hemicontinuity, and pseudomonotonicity for the considered multiple integral-type functional. Additionally, an auxiliary lemma is provided. In Section 3, we study the well-posedness for the considered constrained variational problem. More precisely, we prove that well-posedness is equivalent with the existence and uniqueness of a solution in the aforesaid problem. Finally, Section 4 concludes the paper and provides further developments.

2. Preliminaries and Problem Formulation

In this paper, we consider the following notations and mathematical tools: denote by K a compact domain in $\mathbb{R}^m$ and consider the point $K \ni \zeta = (\zeta^\alpha)$, $\alpha = \overline{1,m}$; let $\mathcal{E}$ denote the space of *state* functions of C^4-class $s : K \to \mathbb{R}^n$ and $s_\alpha := \dfrac{\partial s}{\partial \zeta^\alpha}$, $s_{\beta\gamma} := \dfrac{\partial^2 s}{\partial \zeta^\beta \partial \zeta^\gamma}$ denote the *partial speed* and *partial acceleration*, respectively; consider $E \subseteq \mathcal{E}$ as a nonempty, closed and convex subset, with $s|_{\partial K} =$ given, equipped with the inner product

$$\langle s, z\rangle = \int_K \left[s(\zeta)\cdot z(\zeta)\right] d\zeta = \int_K \left[\sum_{i=1}^n s^i(\zeta) z^i(\zeta)\right] d\zeta, \quad \forall s, z \in \mathcal{E}$$

and the induced norm, where $d\zeta = d\zeta^1 \cdots d\zeta^m$ is the element of volume on $\mathbb{R}^m$.

Let $J^2(\mathbb{R}^m, \mathbb{R}^n)$ be the second-order jet bundle for $\mathbb{R}^m$ and $\mathbb{R}^n$. By using the real-valued continuously differentiable function $f : J^2(\mathbb{R}^m, \mathbb{R}^n) \to \mathbb{R}$, we define the multiple integral-type functional:

$$F : \mathcal{E} \to \mathbb{R}, \quad F(s) = \int_K f(\zeta, s(\zeta), s_\alpha(\zeta), s_{\beta\gamma}(\zeta)) d\zeta.$$

By using the above mathematical framework, we formulate the *constrained variational problem* (in short, CVP) $((\pi_s(\zeta)) := (\zeta, s(\zeta), s_\alpha(\zeta), s_{\beta\gamma}(\zeta)))$:

$$\text{(CVP)} \qquad \text{Minimize} \int_K f(\pi_s(\zeta)) d\zeta \quad \text{subject to} \quad s \in \Omega,$$

where Ω stands for the set of solutions for the *variational inequality problem* (in short, VIP): *find $s \in E$ such that*

$$\text{(VIP)} \quad \int_K \left[\frac{\partial f}{\partial s}(\pi_s(\zeta))(z(\zeta) - s(\zeta)) + \frac{\partial f}{\partial s_\alpha}(\pi_s(\zeta)) D_\alpha(z(\zeta) - s(\zeta)) \right.$$
$$\left. + \frac{1}{n(\beta,\gamma)} \frac{\partial f}{\partial s_{\beta\gamma}}(\pi_s(\zeta)) D^2_{\beta\gamma}(z(\zeta) - s(\zeta))\right] d\zeta \geq 0, \quad \forall z \in E,$$

where $D^2_{\beta\gamma} := D_\beta(D_\gamma)$, and $n(\beta,\gamma)$ represents the multi-index notation (Saunders [36], Treanţă [33]).

More precisely, the set of all feasible solutions of (VIP) is defined as

$$\Omega = \left\{ s \in E : \int_K \left[(z(\zeta) - s(\zeta)) \frac{\partial f}{\partial s}(\pi_s(\zeta)) + D_\alpha(z(\zeta) - s(\zeta)) \frac{\partial f}{\partial s_\alpha}(\pi_s(\zeta)) \right.\right.$$
$$\left.\left. + \frac{1}{n(\beta,\gamma)} D^2_{\beta\gamma}(z(\zeta) - s(\zeta)) \frac{\partial f}{\partial s_{\beta\gamma}}(\pi_s(\zeta))\right] d\zeta \geq 0,\ \forall z \in E \right\}.$$

Definition 1. *The functional $F(s) = \int_K f(\pi_s(\zeta)) d\zeta$ is monotone on E if the inequality holds:*

$$\int_K \left[(s(\zeta) - z(\zeta)) \left(\frac{\partial f}{\partial s}(\pi_s(\zeta)) - \frac{\partial f}{\partial s}(\pi_z(\zeta)) \right) \right.$$
$$+ D_\alpha(s(\zeta) - z(\zeta)) \left(\frac{\partial f}{\partial s_\alpha}(\pi_s(\zeta)) - \frac{\partial f}{\partial s_\alpha}(\pi_z(\zeta)) \right)$$
$$\left. + \frac{1}{n(\beta,\gamma)} D^2_{\beta\gamma}(s(\zeta) - z(\zeta)) \left(\frac{\partial f}{\partial s_{\beta\gamma}}(\pi_s(\zeta)) - \frac{\partial f}{\partial s_{\beta\gamma}}(\pi_z(\zeta)) \right) \right] d\zeta \geq 0,$$

for $\forall s, z \in E$.

Definition 2. *The functional* $F(s) = \int_K f(\pi_s(\zeta))d\zeta$ *is pseudomonotone on* E *if the implication holds:*

$$\int_K \Big[(s(\zeta)-z(\zeta))\frac{\partial f}{\partial s}(\pi_z(\zeta)) + D_\alpha(s(\zeta)-z(\zeta))\frac{\partial f}{\partial s_\alpha}(\pi_z(\zeta))$$
$$+\frac{1}{n(\beta,\gamma)}D^2_{\beta\gamma}(s(\zeta)-z(\zeta))\frac{\partial f}{\partial s_{\beta\gamma}}(\pi_z(\zeta))\Big]d\zeta \geq 0$$
$$\Rightarrow \int_K \Big[(s(\zeta)-z(\zeta))\frac{\partial f}{\partial s}(\pi_s(\zeta)) + D_\alpha(s(\zeta)-z(\zeta))\frac{\partial f}{\partial s_\alpha}(\pi_s(\zeta))$$
$$+\frac{1}{n(\beta,\gamma)}D^2_{\beta\gamma}(s(\zeta)-z(\zeta))\frac{\partial f}{\partial s_{\beta\gamma}}(\pi_s(\zeta))\Big]d\zeta \geq 0,$$

for $\forall s, z \in E$.

Example 1. *Consider* $m = 2,\ n = 1$, *and* $K = [0,3]^2$. *Additionally, we define*

$$f(\pi_s(\zeta)) = 2\sin s(\zeta) + s(\zeta)e^{s(\zeta)}.$$

The functional $F(s) = \int_K f(\pi_s(\zeta))d\zeta$ *is pseudomonotone on* $E = C^4(K, [-1,1])$,

$$\int_K \Big[(s(\zeta)-z(\zeta))\frac{\partial f}{\partial s}(\pi_z(\zeta)) + D_\alpha(s(\zeta)-z(\zeta))\frac{\partial f}{\partial s_\alpha}(\pi_z(\zeta))$$
$$+\frac{1}{n(\beta,\gamma)}D^2_{\beta\gamma}(s(\zeta)-z(\zeta))\frac{\partial f}{\partial s_{\beta\gamma}}(\pi_z(\zeta))\Big]d\zeta$$

$$= \int_K \Big[(s(\zeta)-z(\zeta))(2\cos z(\zeta) + e^{z(\zeta)} + z(\zeta)e^{z(\zeta)})\Big]d\zeta \geq 0$$
$$\forall s, z \in E$$

$$\Rightarrow \int_K \Big[(s(\zeta)-z(\zeta))\frac{\partial f}{\partial s}(\pi_s(\zeta)) + D_\alpha(s(\zeta)-z(\zeta))\frac{\partial f}{\partial s_\alpha}(\pi_s(\zeta))$$
$$+\frac{1}{n(\beta,\gamma)}D^2_{\beta\gamma}(s(\zeta)-z(\zeta))\frac{\partial f}{\partial s_{\beta\gamma}}(\pi_s(\zeta))\Big]d\zeta$$

$$= \int_K \Big[(s(\zeta)-z(\zeta))(2\cos s(\zeta) + e^{s(\zeta)} + s(\zeta)e^{s(\zeta)})\Big]d\zeta \geq 0$$
$$\forall s, z \in E.$$

By direct computation, we obtain

$$\int_K \Big[(s(\zeta)-z(\zeta))\Big(\frac{\partial f}{\partial s}(\pi_s(\zeta)) - \frac{\partial f}{\partial s}(\pi_z(\zeta))\Big)$$
$$+ D_\alpha(s(\zeta)-z(\zeta))\Big(\frac{\partial f}{\partial s_\alpha}(\pi_s(\zeta)) - \frac{\partial f}{\partial s_\alpha}(\pi_z(\zeta))\Big)$$
$$+ \frac{1}{n(\beta,\gamma)}D^2_{\beta\gamma}(s(\zeta)-z(\zeta))\Big(\frac{\partial f}{\partial s_{\beta\gamma}}(\pi_s(\zeta)) - \frac{\partial f}{\partial s_{\beta\gamma}}(\pi_z(\zeta))\Big)\Big]d\zeta$$
$$= \int_K \Big[(s(\zeta)-z(\zeta))[2(\cos s(\zeta) - \cos z(\zeta)) + s(\zeta)e^{s(\zeta)} + e^{s(\zeta)} - z(\zeta)e^{z(\zeta)} - e^{z(\zeta)}]\Big]d\zeta \ngeq 0,$$
$$\forall s, z \in E,$$

which implies that the functional $F(s) = \int_K f(\pi_s(\zeta))d\zeta$ *is not monotone on E (in the sense of Definition 1).*

By considering the work of Usman and Khan [37], we provide the following definition.

Definition 3. *The functional* $F(s) = \int_K f(\pi_s(\zeta))d\zeta$ *is hemicontinuous on E if the application*

$$\lambda \to \left\langle s(\zeta) - z(\zeta), \frac{\delta F}{\delta s_\lambda}(\zeta) \right\rangle, \quad 0 \le \lambda \le 1$$

is continuous at 0^+*, for* $\forall s, z \in E$*, where*

$$\frac{\delta F}{\delta s_\lambda}(\zeta) := \frac{\partial f}{\partial s}(\pi_{s_\lambda}(\zeta)) - D_\alpha \frac{\partial f}{\partial s_\alpha}(\pi_{s_\lambda}(\zeta)) + \frac{1}{n(\beta,\gamma)} D^2_{\beta\gamma} \frac{\partial f}{\partial s_{\beta\gamma}}(\pi_{s_\lambda}(\zeta)) \in E,$$

$$s_\lambda := \lambda s + (1-\lambda)z.$$

Lemma 1. *Consider the functional* $F(s) = \int_K f(\pi_s(\zeta))d\zeta$ *as hemicontinuous and pseudomonotone on E. Then, the function* $s \in E$ *solves (VIP) if and only if it solves the variational inequality*

$$\int_K \Big[(z(\zeta) - s(\zeta)) \frac{\partial f}{\partial s}(\pi_z(\zeta)) + D_\alpha (z(\zeta) - s(\zeta)) \frac{\partial f}{\partial s_\alpha}(\pi_z(\zeta))$$

$$+ \frac{1}{n(\beta,\gamma)} D^2_{\beta\gamma} (z(\zeta) - s(\zeta)) \frac{\partial f}{\partial s_{\beta\gamma}}(\pi_z(\zeta)) \Big] d\zeta \ge 0, \quad \forall z \in E.$$

Proof. Firstly, let us consider that the function $s \in E$ solves (VIP). In consequence, it follows

$$\int_K \Big[(z(\zeta) - s(\zeta)) \frac{\partial f}{\partial s}(\pi_s(\zeta)) + D_\alpha (z(\zeta) - s(\zeta)) \frac{\partial f}{\partial s_\alpha}(\pi_s(\zeta))$$

$$+ \frac{1}{n(\beta,\gamma)} D^2_{\beta\gamma} (z(\zeta) - s(\zeta)) \frac{\partial f}{\partial s_{\beta\gamma}}(\pi_s(\zeta)) \Big] d\zeta \ge 0, \quad \forall z \in E.$$

By using the pseudomonotonicity property of $F(s) = \int_K f(\pi_s(\zeta))d\zeta$, the previous inequality involves

$$\int_K \Big[(z(\zeta) - s(\zeta)) \frac{\partial f}{\partial s}(\pi_z(\zeta)) + D_\alpha (z(\zeta) - s(\zeta)) \frac{\partial f}{\partial s_\alpha}(\pi_z(\zeta))$$

$$+ \frac{1}{n(\beta,\gamma)} D^2_{\beta\gamma} (z(\zeta) - s(\zeta)) \frac{\partial f}{\partial s_{\beta\gamma}}(\pi_z(\zeta)) \Big] d\zeta \ge 0, \quad \forall z \in E.$$

Conversely, assume that

$$\int_K \Big[(z(\zeta) - s(\zeta)) \frac{\partial f}{\partial s}(\pi_z(\zeta)) + D_\alpha (z(\zeta) - s(\zeta)) \frac{\partial f}{\partial s_\alpha}(\pi_z(\zeta))$$

$$+ \frac{1}{n(\beta,\gamma)} D^2_{\beta\gamma} (z(\zeta) - s(\zeta)) \frac{\partial f}{\partial s_{\beta\gamma}}(\pi_z(\zeta)) \Big] d\zeta \ge 0, \quad \forall z \in E.$$

For $z \in E$ and $\lambda \in (0,1]$, we define

$$z_\lambda = (1-\lambda)s + \lambda z \in E.$$

Therefore, the above inequality can be rewritten as follows

$$\int_K \Big[(z_\lambda(\zeta) - s(\zeta))\frac{\partial f}{\partial s}(\pi_{z_\lambda}(\zeta)) + D_\alpha(z_\lambda(\zeta) - s(\zeta))\frac{\partial f}{\partial s_\alpha}(\pi_{z_\lambda}(\zeta))$$

$$+\frac{1}{n(\beta,\gamma)}D^2_{\beta\gamma}(z_\lambda(\zeta) - s(\zeta))\frac{\partial f}{\partial s_{\beta\gamma}}(\pi_{z_\lambda}(\zeta))\Big]d\zeta \geq 0, \quad z \in E.$$

By considering $\lambda \to 0$ (and the hemicontinuity property of $F(s) = \int_K f(\pi_s(\zeta))d\zeta$), it results that

$$\int_K \Big[(z(\zeta) - s(\zeta))\frac{\partial f}{\partial s}(\pi_s(\zeta)) + D_\alpha(z(\zeta) - s(\zeta))\frac{\partial f}{\partial s_\alpha}(\pi_s(\zeta))$$

$$+\frac{1}{n(\beta,\gamma)}D^2_{\beta\gamma}(z(\zeta) - s(\zeta))\frac{\partial f}{\partial s_{\beta\gamma}}(\pi_s(\zeta))\Big]d\zeta \geq 0, \quad \forall z \in E,$$

which shows that s is solution for (VIP). The proof of this lemma is now complete. □

Definition 4. *The functional* $F(s) = \int_K f(\pi_s(\zeta))d\zeta$ *is lower semicontinuous at* $s_0 \in E$ *if*

$$\int_K f(\pi_{s_0}(\zeta))d\zeta \leq \liminf_{s \to s_0} \int_K f(\pi_s(\zeta))d\zeta.$$

3. Well-Posedness Associated with (CVP)

In this section, we analyze the well-posedness property for the constrained variational problem (CVP). To this aim, we provide the following mathematical tools.

Let us denote by $\mathcal{S}$ the *set of all solutions* for (CVP), that is,

$$\mathcal{S} = \Big\{s \in E \mid \int_K f(\pi_s(\zeta))d\zeta \leq \inf_{z\in\Omega}\int_K f(\pi_z(\zeta))d\zeta \text{ and}$$
$$\int_K \Big[(z(\zeta) - s(\zeta))\frac{\partial f}{\partial s}(\pi_s(\zeta)) + D_\alpha(z(\zeta) - s(\zeta))\frac{\partial f}{\partial s_\alpha}(\pi_s(\zeta))$$
$$+\frac{1}{n(\beta,\gamma)}D^2_{\beta\gamma}(z(\zeta) - s(\zeta))\frac{\partial f}{\partial s_{\beta\gamma}}(\pi_s(\zeta))\Big]d\zeta \geq 0, \ \forall z \in E\Big\}.$$

Additionally, for $\theta, \vartheta \geq 0$, we define the *set of approximating solutions* for (CVP) as

$$\mathcal{S}(\theta,\vartheta) = \Big\{s \in E \mid \int_K f(\pi_s(\zeta))d\zeta \leq \inf_{z\in\Omega}\int_K f(\pi_z(\zeta))d\zeta + \theta \text{ and}$$
$$\int_K \Big[(z(\zeta) - s(\zeta))\frac{\partial f}{\partial s}(\pi_s(\zeta)) + D_\alpha(z(\zeta) - s(\zeta))\frac{\partial f}{\partial s_\alpha}(\pi_s(\zeta))$$
$$+\frac{1}{n(\beta,\gamma)}D^2_{\beta\gamma}(z(\zeta) - s(\zeta))\frac{\partial f}{\partial s_{\beta\gamma}}(\pi_s(\zeta))\Big]d\zeta + \vartheta \geq 0, \ \forall z \in E\Big\}.$$

Remark 1. *For* $(\theta,\vartheta) = (0,0)$*, we have* $\mathcal{S} = \mathcal{S}(\theta,\vartheta)$ *and, for* $(\theta,\vartheta) > (0,0)$*, we obtain* $\mathcal{S} \subseteq \mathcal{S}(\theta,\vartheta)$.

Definition 5. *If there exists a sequence of positive real numbers* $\vartheta_n \to 0$ *as* $n \to \infty$*, such that the following inequalities*

$$\limsup_{n\to\infty} \int_K f(\pi_{s_n}(\zeta))d\zeta \leq \inf_{z\in\Omega}\int_K f(\pi_z(\zeta))d\zeta$$

and

$$\int_K \Big[(z(\zeta) - s_n(\zeta))\frac{\partial f}{\partial s}(\pi_{s_n}(\zeta)) + D_\alpha(z(\zeta) - s_n(\zeta))\frac{\partial f}{\partial s_\alpha}(\pi_{s_n}(\zeta))$$

$$+\frac{1}{n(\beta,\gamma)}D^2_{\beta\gamma}(z(\zeta)-s_n(\zeta))\frac{\partial f}{\partial s_{\beta\gamma}}(\pi_{s_n}(\zeta))\Big]d\zeta+\vartheta_n\geq 0,\quad \forall z\in E$$

are fulfilled, then the sequence $\{s_n\}$ is called an approximating sequence of (CVP).

Definition 6. *The problem (CVP) is called well-posed if:*

(i) *It has a unique solution s_0;*

(ii) *Each approximating sequence of (CVP) will converge to this unique solution s_0.*

Further, the symbol "diam B" stands for the diameter of B. Moreover, it is defined by

$$diam\ B=\sup_{x,y\in B}\|x-y\|.$$

Theorem 1. *Consider the functional $F(s)=\int_K f(\pi_s(\zeta))d\zeta$ as lower semicontinuous, hemicontinuous and monotone on E. Then, the problem (CVP) is well-posed if and only if*

$$\mathcal{S}(\theta,\vartheta)\neq\emptyset,\forall\theta,\vartheta>0\ and\ diam\ \mathcal{S}(\theta,\vartheta)\to 0\ as\ (\theta,\vartheta)\to(0,0).$$

Proof. Let us consider the case that (CVP) is well-posed. Therefore, it admits a unique solution $\bar{s}\in\mathcal{S}$. Since $\mathcal{S}\subseteq\mathcal{S}(\theta,\vartheta)$, $\forall\theta,\vartheta>0$, we obtain $\mathcal{S}(\theta,\vartheta)\neq\emptyset$, $\forall\theta,\vartheta>0$. Contrary to the result, let us suppose that diam $\mathcal{S}(\theta,\vartheta)\nrightarrow 0$ as $(\theta,\vartheta)\to(0,0)$. Then, there exists $r>0$, a positive integer m, $\theta_n,\vartheta_n>0$ with $\theta_n,\vartheta_n\to 0$, and $s_n,\ s_n'\in\mathcal{S}(\theta_n,\vartheta_n)$ such that

$$\|s_n-s_n'\|>r,\quad \forall n\geq m. \tag{1}$$

Since $s_n,\ s_n'\in\mathcal{S}(\theta_n,\vartheta_n)$, we obtain

$$\int_K f(\pi_{s_n}(\zeta))d\zeta\leq\inf_{z\in\Omega}\int_K f(\pi_z(\zeta))d\zeta+\theta_n,$$

$$\int_K\Big[(z(\zeta)-s_n(\zeta))\frac{\partial f}{\partial s}(\pi_{s_n}(\zeta))+D_\alpha(z(\zeta)-s_n(\zeta))\frac{\partial f}{\partial s_\alpha}(\pi_{s_n}(\zeta))$$

$$+\frac{1}{n(\beta,\gamma)}D^2_{\beta\gamma}(z(\zeta)-s_n(\zeta))\frac{\partial f}{\partial s_{\beta\gamma}}(\pi_{s_n}(\zeta))\Big]d\zeta+\vartheta_n\geq 0,\quad \forall z\in E$$

and

$$\int_K f(\pi_{s_n'}(\zeta))d\zeta\leq\inf_{z\in\Omega}\int_K f(\pi_z(\zeta))d\zeta+\theta_n,$$

$$\int_K\Big[(z(\zeta)-s_n'(\zeta))\frac{\partial f}{\partial s}(\pi_{s_n'}(\zeta))+D_\alpha(z(\zeta)-s_n'(\zeta))\frac{\partial f}{\partial s_\alpha}(\pi_{s_n'}(\zeta))$$

$$+\frac{1}{n(\beta,\gamma)}D^2_{\beta\gamma}(z(\zeta)-s_n'(\zeta))\frac{\partial f}{\partial s_{\beta\gamma}}(\pi_{s_n'}(\zeta))\Big]d\zeta+\vartheta_n\geq 0,\quad \forall z\in E.$$

It results that $\{s_n\}$ and $\{s_n'\}$ are approximating sequences of (CVP) which tend to $\bar{s}$ (the problem (CVP) is well-posed, by hypothesis). By direct computation, it follows that

$$\|s_n-s_n'\|=\|s_n-\bar{s}+\bar{s}-s_n'\|$$

$$\leq\|s_n-\bar{s}\|+\|\bar{s}-s_n'\|\leq\vartheta,$$

which contradicts (1) for some $\vartheta=r$. In consequence, diam $\mathcal{S}(\theta,\vartheta)\to 0$ as $(\theta,\vartheta)\to(0,0)$.

Conversely, let us consider that $\{s_n\}$ is an approximating sequence of (CVP). Then there exists a sequence of positive real numbers $\vartheta_n\to 0$ as $n\to\infty$ such that the inequalities

$$\limsup_{n\to\infty}\int_K f(\pi_{s_n}(\zeta))d\zeta\leq\inf_{z\in\Omega}\int_K f(\pi_z(\zeta))d\zeta, \tag{2}$$

$$\int_K \Big[(z(\zeta)-s_n(\zeta))\frac{\partial f}{\partial s}(\pi_{s_n}(\zeta)) + D_\alpha(z(\zeta)-s_n(\zeta))\frac{\partial f}{\partial s_\alpha}(\pi_{s_n}(\zeta))$$
$$+\frac{1}{n(\beta,\gamma)}D^2_{\beta\gamma}(z(\zeta)-s_n(\zeta))\frac{\partial f}{\partial s_{\beta\gamma}}(\pi_{s_n}(\zeta))\Big]d\zeta + \vartheta_n \geq 0, \quad \forall z \in E \tag{3}$$

hold, including $s_n \in \mathcal{S}(\theta_n, \vartheta_n)$, for a sequence of positive real numbers $\theta_n \to 0$ as $n \to \infty$. Since diam $\mathcal{S}(\theta_n, \vartheta_n) \to 0$ as $(\theta_n, \vartheta_n) \to (0,0)$, $\{s_n\}$ is a Cauchy sequence which converges to some $\bar{s} \in E$ as E is a closed set.

By hypothesis, the multiple integral functional $\int_K f(\pi_s(\zeta))d\zeta$ is monotone on E. Therefore, by Definition 1, for $\bar{s}, z \in E$, we have

$$\int_K \Big[(\bar{s}(\zeta)-z(\zeta))\Big(\frac{\partial f}{\partial s}(\pi_{\bar{s}}(\zeta)) - \frac{\partial f}{\partial s}(\pi_z(\zeta))\Big)$$
$$+D_\alpha(\bar{s}(\zeta)-z(\zeta))\Big(\frac{\partial f}{\partial s_\alpha}(\pi_{\bar{s}}(\zeta)) - \frac{\partial f}{\partial s_\alpha}(\pi_z(\zeta))\Big)$$
$$+\frac{1}{n(\beta,\gamma)}D^2_{\beta\gamma}(\bar{s}(\zeta)-z(\zeta))\Big(\frac{\partial f}{\partial s_{\beta\gamma}}(\pi_{\bar{s}}(\zeta)) - \frac{\partial f}{\partial s_{\beta\gamma}}(\pi_z(\zeta))\Big)\Big]d\zeta \geq 0,$$

or, equivalently,

$$\int_K \Big[(\bar{s}(\zeta)-z(\zeta))\frac{\partial f}{\partial s}(\pi_{\bar{s}}(\zeta)) + D_\alpha(\bar{s}(\zeta)-z(\zeta))\frac{\partial f}{\partial s_\alpha}(\pi_{\bar{s}}(\zeta))$$
$$+\frac{1}{n(\beta,\gamma)}D^2_{\beta\gamma}(\bar{s}(\zeta)-z(\zeta))\frac{\partial f}{\partial s_{\beta\gamma}}(\pi_{\bar{s}}(\zeta))\Big]d\zeta$$
$$\geq \int_K \Big[(\bar{s}(\zeta)-z(\zeta))\frac{\partial f}{\partial s}(\pi_z(\zeta)) + D_\alpha(\bar{s}(\zeta)-z(\zeta))\frac{\partial f}{\partial s_\alpha}(\pi_z(\zeta))$$
$$+\frac{1}{n(\beta,\gamma)}D^2_{\beta\gamma}(\bar{s}(\zeta)-z(\zeta))\frac{\partial f}{\partial s_{\beta\gamma}}(\pi_z(\zeta))\Big]d\zeta. \tag{4}$$

Taking limit in inequality (3), we have

$$\int_K \Big[(\bar{s}(\zeta)-z(\zeta))\frac{\partial f}{\partial s}(\pi_{\bar{s}}(\zeta)) + D_\alpha(\bar{s}(\zeta)-z(\zeta))\frac{\partial f}{\partial s_\alpha}(\pi_{\bar{s}}(\zeta))$$
$$+\frac{1}{n(\beta,\gamma)}D^2_{\beta\gamma}(\bar{s}(\zeta)-z(\zeta))\frac{\partial f}{\partial s_{\beta\gamma}}(\pi_{\bar{s}}(\zeta))\Big]d\zeta \leq 0. \tag{5}$$

On combining (4) and (5), we obtain

$$\int_K \Big[(z(\zeta)-\bar{s}(\zeta))\frac{\partial f}{\partial s}(\pi_z(\zeta)) + D_\alpha(z(\zeta)-\bar{s}(\zeta))\frac{\partial f}{\partial s_\alpha}(\pi_z(\zeta))$$
$$+\frac{1}{n(\beta,\gamma)}D^2_{\beta\gamma}(z(\zeta)-\bar{s}(\zeta))\frac{\partial f}{\partial s_{\beta\gamma}}(\pi_z(\zeta))\Big]d\zeta \geq 0.$$

Further, taking into account Lemma 1, it follows that

$$\int_K \Big[(z(\zeta)-\bar{s}(\zeta))\frac{\partial f}{\partial s}(\pi_{\bar{s}}(\zeta)) + D_\alpha(z(\zeta)-\bar{s}(\zeta))\frac{\partial f}{\partial s_\alpha}(\pi_{\bar{s}}(\zeta))$$
$$+\frac{1}{n(\beta,\gamma)}D^2_{\beta\gamma}(z(\zeta)-\bar{s}(\zeta))\frac{\partial f}{\partial s_{\beta\gamma}}(\pi_{\bar{s}}(\zeta))\Big]d\zeta \geq 0, \tag{6}$$

which implies that $\bar{s} \in \Omega$.

Since the functional $\int_K f(\pi_s(\zeta))d\zeta$ is lower semicontinuous, it results that

$$\int_K f(\pi_{\bar{s}}(\zeta))d\zeta \leq \liminf_{n\to\infty} \int_K f(\pi_{s_n}(\zeta))d\zeta \leq \limsup_{n\to\infty} \int_K f(\pi_{s_n}(\zeta))d\zeta.$$

By using (2), the above inequality reduces to

$$\int_K f(\pi_{\bar{s}}(\zeta))d\zeta \leq \inf_{z\in\Omega} \int_K f(\pi_z(\zeta))d\zeta. \tag{7}$$

Thus, from (6) and (7), we conclude that $\bar{s}$ solves (CVP).

Now, let us prove that $\bar{s}$ is the unique solution of (CVP). Suppose that s_1, s_2 are two distinct solutions of (CVP). Then,

$$0 < \|s_1 - s_2\| \leq \operatorname{diam} \mathcal{S}(\theta, \vartheta) \to 0 \text{ as } (\theta, \vartheta) \to (0, 0),$$

and the proof is complete. □

Theorem 2. *Consider the functional $F(s) = \int_K f(\pi_s(\zeta))d\zeta$ as lower semicontinuous, hemicontinuous and monotone on E. Then, the problem (CVP) is well-posed if and only if it has a unique solution.*

Proof. Let us consider that (CVP) is well-posed. Thus, it possesses a unique solution s_0. Conversely, let us consider that (CVP) has a unique solution s_0, that is,

$$\int_K f(\pi_{s_0}(\zeta))d\zeta \leq \inf_{z\in\Omega} \int_K f(\pi_z(\zeta))d\zeta,$$

$$\int_K \Big[(z(\zeta) - s_0(\zeta))\frac{\partial f}{\partial s}(\pi_{s_0}(\zeta)) + D_\alpha(z(\zeta) - s_0(\zeta))\frac{\partial f}{\partial s_\alpha}(\pi_{s_0}(\zeta))$$
$$+\frac{1}{n(\beta,\gamma)} D^2_{\beta\gamma}(z(\zeta) - s_0(\zeta))\frac{\partial f}{\partial s_{\beta\gamma}}(\pi_{s_0}(\zeta))\Big]d\zeta \geq 0, \quad \forall z \in E, \tag{8}$$

but it is not well-posed. Therefore, by Definition 6, there exists an approximating sequence $\{s_n\}$ of (CVP), which does not converge to s_0, such that the following inequalities

$$\limsup_{n\to\infty} \int_K f(\pi_{s_n}(\zeta))d\zeta \leq \inf_{z\in\Omega} \int_K f(\pi_z(\zeta))d\zeta$$

and

$$\int_K \Big[(z(\zeta) - s_n(\zeta))\frac{\partial f}{\partial s}(\pi_{s_n}(\zeta)) + D_\alpha(z(\zeta) - s_n(\zeta))\frac{\partial f}{\partial s_\alpha}(\pi_{s_n}(\zeta))$$
$$+\frac{1}{n(\beta,\gamma)} D^2_{\beta\gamma}(z(\zeta) - s_n(\zeta))\frac{\partial f}{\partial s_{\beta\gamma}}(\pi_{s_n}(\zeta))\Big]d\zeta + \vartheta_n \geq 0, \quad \forall z \in E \tag{9}$$

are fulfilled. Further, we proceed by contradiction to prove the boundedness of $\{s_n\}$. Contrary to the result, we suppose that $\{s_n\}$ is not bounded; consequently, $\|s_n\| \to +\infty$ as $n \to +\infty$. We define $\delta_n = \dfrac{1}{\|s_n - s_0\|}$ and $\mathrm{s}_n = s_0 + \delta_n[s_n - s_0]$. We observe that $\{\mathrm{s}_n\}$ is bounded in E. Therefore, if necessary, passing to a subsequence, we may consider that

$$\mathrm{s}_n \to \mathrm{s} \text{ weakly in } E \neq (s_0).$$

It is not difficult to see that $\mathrm{s} \neq s_0$ due to $\|\delta_n[s_n - s_0]\| = 1$, for all $n \in \mathbb{N}$. Since s_0 is a solution of (CVP), the inequalities (8) are verified. By using Lemma 1, it follows that

$$\int_K f(\pi_{s_0}(\zeta))d\zeta \leq \inf_{z\in\Omega} \int_K f(\pi_z(\zeta))d\zeta,$$

$$\int_K \Big[(z(\zeta) - s_0(\zeta))\frac{\partial f}{\partial s}(\pi_z(\zeta)) + D_\alpha(z(\zeta) - s_0(\zeta))\frac{\partial f}{\partial s_\alpha}(\pi_z(\zeta))$$
$$+\frac{1}{n(\beta,\gamma)}D^2_{\beta\gamma}(z(\zeta) - s_0(\zeta))\frac{\partial f}{\partial s_{\beta\gamma}}(\pi_z(\zeta))\Big]d\zeta \geq 0, \quad \forall z \in E. \tag{10}$$

By considering the monotonicity property of the functional $\int_K f(\pi_s(\zeta))d\zeta$, for $s_n, z \in E$, we obtain

$$\int_K \Big[(s_n(\zeta) - z(\zeta))\Big(\frac{\partial f}{\partial s}(\pi_{s_n}(\zeta)) - \frac{\partial f}{\partial s}(\pi_z(\zeta))\Big)$$
$$+D_\alpha(s_n(\zeta) - z(\zeta))\Big(\frac{\partial f}{\partial s_\alpha}(\pi_{s_n}(\zeta)) - \frac{\partial f}{\partial s_\alpha}(\pi_z(\zeta))\Big)$$
$$+\frac{1}{n(\beta,\gamma)}D^2_{\beta\gamma}(s_n(\zeta) - z(\zeta))\Big(\frac{\partial f}{\partial s_{\beta\gamma}}(\pi_{s_n}(\zeta)) - \frac{\partial f}{\partial s_{\beta\gamma}}(\pi_z(\zeta))\Big)\Big]d\zeta \geq 0,$$

or, equivalently,

$$\int_K \Big[(z(\zeta) - s_n(\zeta))\frac{\partial f}{\partial s}(\pi_{s_n}(\zeta)) + D_\alpha(z(\zeta) - s_n(\zeta))\frac{\partial f}{\partial s_\alpha}(\pi_{s_n}(\zeta))$$
$$+\frac{1}{n(\beta,\gamma)}D^2_{\beta\gamma}(z(\zeta) - s_n(\zeta))\frac{\partial f}{\partial s_{\beta\gamma}}(\pi_{s_n}(\zeta))\Big]d\zeta$$
$$\leq \int_K \Big[(z(\zeta) - s_n(\zeta))\frac{\partial f}{\partial s}(\pi_z(\zeta)) + D_\alpha(z(\zeta) - s_n(\zeta))\frac{\partial f}{\partial s_\alpha}(\pi_z(\zeta))$$
$$+\frac{1}{n(\beta,\gamma)}D^2_{\beta\gamma}(z(\zeta) - s_n(\zeta))\frac{\partial f}{\partial s_{\beta\gamma}}(\pi_z(\zeta))\Big]d\zeta. \tag{11}$$

Combining with (9) and (11), we have

$$\int_K \Big[(z(\zeta) - s_n(\zeta))\frac{\partial f}{\partial s}(\pi_z(\zeta)) + D_\alpha(z(\zeta) - s_n(\zeta))\frac{\partial f}{\partial s_\alpha}(\pi_z(\zeta))$$
$$+\frac{1}{n(\beta,\gamma)}D^2_{\beta\gamma}(z(\zeta) - s_n(\zeta))\frac{\partial f}{\partial s_{\beta\gamma}}(\pi_z(\zeta))\Big]d\zeta \geq -\vartheta_n, \quad \forall z \in E.$$

Next, we can take $n_0 \in \mathbb{N}$ be large enough such that $\delta_n < 1$, for all $n \geq n_0$ (because of $\delta_n \to 0$ as $n \to \infty$). Multiplying the above inequality and (10) by $\delta_n > 0$ and $1 - \delta_n > 0$, respectively, we obtain

$$\int_K \Big[(z(\zeta) - \mathsf{s}_n(\zeta))\frac{\partial f}{\partial s}(\pi_z(\zeta)) + D_\alpha(z(\zeta) - \mathsf{s}_n(\zeta))\frac{\partial f}{\partial s_\alpha}(\pi_z(\zeta))$$
$$+\frac{1}{n(\beta,\gamma)}D^2_{\beta\gamma}(z(\zeta) - \mathsf{s}_n(\zeta))\frac{\partial f}{\partial s_{\beta\gamma}}(\pi_z(\zeta))\Big]d\zeta \geq -\vartheta_n, \quad \forall z \in E,\ \forall n \geq n_0.$$

By using $\mathsf{s}_n \to \mathsf{s} \neq s_0$ and $\mathsf{s}_n = s_0 + \mathbf{s}_n[s_n - s_0]$, we obtain

$$\int_K \Big[(z(\zeta) - \mathsf{s}(\zeta))\frac{\partial f}{\partial s}(\pi_z(\zeta)) + D_\alpha(z(\zeta) - \mathsf{s}(\zeta))\frac{\partial f}{\partial s_\alpha}(\pi_z(\zeta))$$
$$+\frac{1}{n(\beta,\gamma)}D^2_{\beta\gamma}(z(\zeta) - \mathsf{s}(\zeta))\frac{\partial f}{\partial s_{\beta\gamma}}(\pi_z(\zeta))\Big]d\zeta$$
$$= \lim_{n\to\infty} \int_K \Big[(z(\zeta) - \mathsf{s}_n(\zeta))\frac{\partial f}{\partial s}(\pi_z(\zeta)) + D_\alpha(z(\zeta) - \mathsf{s}_n(\zeta))\frac{\partial f}{\partial s_\alpha}(\pi_z(\zeta))$$
$$+\frac{1}{n(\beta,\gamma)}D^2_{\beta\gamma}(z(\zeta) - \mathsf{s}_n(\zeta))\frac{\partial f}{\partial s_{\beta\gamma}}(\pi_z(\zeta))\Big]d\zeta$$

$$\geq -\lim_{n\to\infty} \vartheta_n = 0, \quad \forall z \in E.$$

Taking into account Lemma 1 and by using the lower semicontinuity property, we obtain

$$\int_K f(\pi_{\mathrm{s}}(\zeta))d\zeta \leq \inf_{z\in\Omega} \int_K f(\pi_z(\zeta))d\zeta,$$

$$\int_K \Big[(z(\zeta) - \mathrm{s}(\zeta))\frac{\partial f}{\partial s}(\pi_{\mathrm{s}}(\zeta)) + D_\alpha(z(\zeta) - \mathrm{s}(\zeta))\frac{\partial f}{\partial s_\alpha}(\pi_{\mathrm{s}}(\zeta))$$
$$+\frac{1}{n(\beta,\gamma)}D^2_{\beta\gamma}(z(\zeta) - \mathrm{s}(\zeta))\frac{\partial f}{\partial s_{\beta\gamma}}(\pi_{\mathrm{s}}(\zeta))\Big]d\zeta \geq 0, \quad \forall z \in E. \tag{12}$$

This involves that s solves (CVP), contradiction with the uniqueness of s_0. Therefore, $\{s_n\}$ is a bounded sequence having a convergent subsequence $\{s_{n_k}\}$, which converges to $\bar{s} \in E$ as $k \to \infty$. Now, for $s_{n_k}, z \in E$, we obtain (see (11))

$$\int_K \Big[(z(\zeta) - s_{n_k}(\zeta))\frac{\partial f}{\partial s}(\pi_{s_{n_k}}(\zeta)) + D_\alpha(z(\zeta) - s_{n_k}(\zeta))\frac{\partial f}{\partial s_\alpha}(\pi_{s_{n_k}}(\zeta))$$
$$+\frac{1}{n(\beta,\gamma)}D^2_{\beta\gamma}(z(\zeta) - s_{n_k}(\zeta))\frac{\partial f}{\partial s_{\beta\gamma}}(\pi_{s_{n_k}}(\zeta))\Big]d\zeta$$
$$\leq \int_K \Big[(z(\zeta) - s_{n_k}(\zeta))\frac{\partial f}{\partial s}(\pi_z(\zeta)) + D_\alpha(z(\zeta) - s_{n_k}(\zeta))\frac{\partial f}{\partial s_\alpha}(\pi_z(\zeta))$$
$$+\frac{1}{n(\beta,\gamma)}D^2_{\beta\gamma}(z(\zeta) - s_{n_k}(\zeta))\frac{\partial f}{\partial s_{\beta\gamma}}(\pi_z(\zeta))\Big]d\zeta. \tag{13}$$

Additionally, by (9), we can write

$$\lim_{k\to\infty}\int_K \Big[(z(\zeta) - s_{n_k}(\zeta))\frac{\partial f}{\partial s}(\pi_{s_{n_k}}(\zeta)) + D_\alpha(z(\zeta) - s_{n_k}(\zeta))\frac{\partial f}{\partial s_\alpha}(\pi_{s_{n_k}}(\zeta))$$
$$+\frac{1}{n(\beta,\gamma)}D^2_{\beta\gamma}(z(\zeta) - s_{n_k}(\zeta))\frac{\partial f}{\partial s_{\beta\gamma}}(\pi_{s_{n_k}}(\zeta))\Big]d\zeta \geq 0. \tag{14}$$

By (13) and (14), we have

$$\lim_{k\to\infty}\int_K \Big[(z(\zeta) - s_{n_k}(\zeta))\frac{\partial f}{\partial s}(\pi_z(\zeta)) + D_\alpha(z(\zeta) - s_{n_k}(\zeta))\frac{\partial f}{\partial s_\alpha}(\pi_z(\zeta))$$
$$+\frac{1}{n(\beta,\gamma)}D^2_{\beta\gamma}(z(\zeta) - s_{n_k}(\zeta))\frac{\partial f}{\partial s_{\beta\gamma}}(\pi_z(\zeta))\Big]d\zeta \geq 0$$
$$\Rightarrow \int_K \Big[(z(\zeta) - \bar{s}(\zeta))\frac{\partial f}{\partial s}(\pi_z(\zeta)) + D_\alpha(z(\zeta) - \bar{s}(\zeta))\frac{\partial f}{\partial s_\alpha}(\pi_z(\zeta))$$
$$+\frac{1}{n(\beta,\gamma)}D^2_{\beta\gamma}(z(\zeta) - \bar{s}(\zeta))\frac{\partial f}{\partial s_{\beta\gamma}}(\pi_z(\zeta))\Big]d\zeta \geq 0.$$

Using Lemma 1 and the lower semicontinuity property of the considered functional, we obtain

$$\int_K f(\pi_{\bar{s}}(\zeta))d\zeta \leq \inf_{z\in\Omega} \int_K f(\pi_z(\zeta))d\zeta,$$

$$\int_K \Big[(z(\zeta) - \bar{s}(\zeta))\frac{\partial f}{\partial s}(\pi_{\bar{s}}(\zeta)) + D_\alpha(z(\zeta) - \bar{s}(\zeta))\frac{\partial f}{\partial s_\alpha}(\pi_{\bar{s}}(\zeta))$$
$$+\frac{1}{n(\beta,\gamma)}D^2_{\beta\gamma}(z(\zeta) - \bar{s}(\zeta))\frac{\partial f}{\partial s_{\beta\gamma}}(\pi_{\bar{s}}(\zeta))\Big]d\zeta \geq 0,$$

which shows that $\bar{s}$ is a solution of (CVP). Hence, $s_{n_k} \to \bar{s}$, that is, $s_{n_k} \to s_0$, involving $s_n \to s_0$ and the proof is complete. □

Example 2. *We consider $n = 1$ and $K = [0,2]^2 = [0,2] \times [0,2]$. Let us minimize the mass of K having the density (that depends on the current point) $f(\zeta, s(\zeta), s_\alpha(\zeta), s_{\beta\gamma}(\zeta)) = e^{s(\zeta)} - s(\zeta)$, such that the following behavior (positivity property)*

$$\iint_K (z(\zeta) - s(\zeta))(e^{s(\zeta)} - 1)d\zeta^1 d\zeta^2 \geq 0,$$

$$\forall z \in E = C^1(K, [-15, 15]),\ s|_{\partial K} = 0,$$

is satisfied.

To solve the previous practical problem, we consider the following constrained optimization problem:

$$(CVP1) \qquad \text{Minimize} \iint_K [e^{s(\zeta)} - s(\zeta)]d\zeta^1 d\zeta^2$$
$$\text{subject to} \quad s \in \Omega,$$

where Ω is the solution set of the following inequality problem

$$\iint_K (z(\zeta) - s(\zeta))(e^{s(\zeta)} - 1)d\zeta^1 d\zeta^2 \geq 0,$$

$$\forall z \in E = C^1(K, [-15, 15]),\ s|_{\partial K} = 0.$$

Clearly, $\mathcal{S} = \{0\}$ and the functional $\int_K e^{s(\zeta)} - s(\zeta))d\zeta$ is hemicontinuous, monotone and lower semicontinuous on E. Thus, all the hypotheses of Theorem 2 hold and, in consequence, the problem (CVP1) is well-posed. Additionally, $\mathcal{S}(\theta, \vartheta) = \{0\}$ and, therefore, $\mathcal{S}(\theta, \vartheta) \neq \emptyset$ and diam $\mathcal{S}(\theta, \vartheta) \to 0$ as $(\theta, \vartheta) \to (0,0)$. In conclusion, by Theorem 1, the variational problem (CVP1) is well-posed.

4. Conclusions

In this paper, we have studied the well-posedness property of new constrained variational problems governed by second-order partial derivatives. More precisely, by using the concepts of lower semicontinuity, monotonicity, hemicontinuity and pseudomonotonicity of considered multiple integral-type functional, we have proved that the well-posedness property of the problem under study is described in terms of existence and uniqueness of solution.

Funding: This research received no external funding.

Institutional Review Board Statement: Not applicable.

Informed Consent Statement: Not applicable.

Data Availability Statement: Not applicable.

Conflicts of Interest: The author declares no conflict of interest.

References

1. Tykhonov, A.N. On the stability of the functional optimization problems. *USSR Comput. Math. Math. Phys.* **1966**, *6*, 631–634. [CrossRef]
2. Hu, R.; Fang, Y.P. Levitin-Polyak well-posedness by perturbations of inverse variational inequalities. *Optim. Lett.* **2013**, *7*, 343–359. [CrossRef]
3. Jiang, B.; Zhang, J.; Huang, X.X. Levitin-Polyak well-posedness of generalized quasivariational inequalities with functional constraints. *Nonlinear Anal. Theory Methods Appl.* **2009**, *70*, 1492–1503. [CrossRef]
4. Lalitha, C.S.; Bhatia, G. Levitin-Polyak well-posedness for parametric quasivariational inequality problem of the Minty type. *Positivity* **2012**, *16*, 527–541. [CrossRef]
5. Levitin, E.S.; Polyak, B.T. Convergence of minimizing sequences in conditional extremum problems. *Sov. Math. Dokl.* **1996**, *7*, 764–767.
6. Lignola, M.B.; Morgan, J. *Approximate Solutions and α-Well-Posedness for Variational Inequalities and Nash Equilibria, Decision and Control in Management Science*; Zaccour, G., Ed.; Kluwer Academic Publishers: Dordrecht, The Netherlands, 2002; pp. 367–378.

7. Virmani, G.; Srivastava, M. On Levitin-Polyak α-well-posedness of perturbed variational-hemivariational inequality. *Optimization* **2015**, *64*, 1153–1172. [CrossRef]
8. Čoban, M.M.; Kenderov, P.S.; Revalski, J.P. Generic well-posedness of optimization problems in topological spaces. *Mathematika* **1989**, *36*, 301–324. [CrossRef]
9. Dontchev, A.L.; Zolezzi, T. *Well-Posed Optimization Problems*; Springer: Berlin, Germany, 1993.
10. Furi, M.; Vignoli, A. A characterization of well-posed minimum problems in a complete metric space. *J. Optim. Theory Appl.* **1970**, *5*, 452–461. [CrossRef]
11. Huang, X.X. Extended and strongly extended well-posedness of set-valued optimization problems. *Math. Methods Oper. Res.* **2001**, *53*, 101–116. [CrossRef]
12. Huang, X.X.; Yang, X.Q. Generalized Levitin-Polyak well-posedness in constrained optimization. *SIAM J. Optim.* **2006**, *17*, 243–258. [CrossRef]
13. Lignola, M.B.; Morgan, J. Well-posedness for optimization problems with constraints defined by variational inequalities having a unique solution. *J. Glob. Optim.* **2000**, *16*, 57–67. [CrossRef]
14. Lin, L.J.; Chuang, C.S. Well-posedness in the generalized sense for variational inclusion and disclusion problems and well-posedness for optimization problems with constraint. *Nonlinear Anal.* **2009**, *70*, 3609–3617. [CrossRef]
15. Lucchetti, R. *Convexity and Well-Posed Problems*; Springer: New York, NY, USA, 2006.
16. Zolezzi, T. Extended well-posedness of optimization problems. *J. Optim. Theory Appl.* **1996**, *91*, 257–266. [CrossRef]
17. Lignola, M.B. Well-posedness and L-well-posedness for quasivariational inequalities. *J. Optim. Theory. Appl.* **2006**, *128*, 119–138. [CrossRef]
18. Ceng, L.C.; Hadjisavvas, N.; Schaible, S.; Yao, J.C. Well-posedness for mixed quasivariational-like inequalities. *J. Optim. Theory Appl.* **2008**, *139*, 109–125. [CrossRef]
19. Fang, Y.P.; Hu, R. Estimates of approximate solutions and well-posedness for variational inequalities. *Math. Meth. Oper. Res.* **2007**, *65*, 281–291. [CrossRef]
20. Lalitha, C.S.; Bhatia, G. Well-posedness for parametric quasivariational inequality problems and for optimization problems with quasivariational inequality constraints. *Optimization* **2010**, *59*, 997–1011. [CrossRef]
21. Heemels, P.M.H.; Camlibel, M.K.C.; Schaft, A.J.V.; Schumacher, J.M. Well-posedness of the complementarity class of hybrid systems. In Proceedings of the IFAC 15th Triennial World Congress, Barcelona, Spain, 21–26 July 2002.
22. Chen, J.W.; Wang, Z.; Cho, Y.J. Levitin-Polyak well-posedness by perturbations for systems of set-valued vector quasi-equilibrium problems. *Math. Meth. Oper. Res.* **2013**, *77*, 33–64. [CrossRef]
23. Fang, Y.P.; Hu, R.; Huang, N.J. Well-posedness for equilibrium problems and for optimization problems with equilibrium constraints. *Comput. Math. Appl.* **2008**, *55*, 89–100. [CrossRef]
24. Ceng, L.C.; Yao, J.C. Well-posedness of generalized mixed variational inequalities, inclusion problems and fixed-point problems. *Nonlinear Anal.* **2008**, *69*, 4585–4603. [CrossRef]
25. Xiao, Y.B.; Yang, X.M.; Huang, N.J. Some equivalence results for well-posedness of hemivariational inequalities. *Glob. Optim.* **2015**, *61*, 789–802. [CrossRef]
26. Lignola, M.B.; Morgan, J. α-Well-posedness for Nash equilibria and for optimization problems with Nash equilibrium constraints. *Glob. Optim.* **2006**, *36*, 439–459. [CrossRef]
27. Jayswal, A.; Jha, S. Well-posedness for generalized mixed vector variational-like inequality problems in Banach space. *Math. Commun.* **2017**, *22*, 287–302.
28. Treanţă, S. A necessary and sufficient condition of optimality for a class of multidimensional control problems. *Optim. Control Appl. Meth.* **2020**, *41*, 2137–2148. [CrossRef]
29. Treanţă, S. Well-posedness of new optimization problems with variational inequality constraints. *Fractal Fract.* **2021**, *5*, 123. [CrossRef]
30. Treanţă, S. On well-posed isoperimetric-type constrained variational control problems. *J. Diff. Eq.* **2021**, *298*, 480–499. [CrossRef]
31. Treanţă, S. Second-order PDE constrained controlled optimization problems with application in mechanics. *Mathematics* **2021**, *9*, 1472. [CrossRef]
32. Treanţă, S. On a class of second-order PDE&PDI constrained robust modified optimization problems. *Mathematics* **2021**, *9*, 1473.
33. Treanţă, S. On a class of isoperimetric constrained controlled optimization problems. *Axioms* **2021**, *10*, 112. [CrossRef]
34. Dridi, H.; Djebabla, A. Timoshenko system with fractional operator in the memory and spatial fractional thermal effect. *Rend. Circ. Mat. Palermo II. Ser.* **2021**, *70*, 593–621. [CrossRef]
35. Jana, S. Equilibrium problems under relaxed α-monotonicity on Hadamard manifolds. *Rend. Circ. Mat. Palermo II. Ser.* **2021**. [CrossRef]
36. Saunders, D.J. *The Geometry of Jet Bundles*; London Math. Soc. Lecture Notes Series, 142; Cambridge Univ. Press: Cambridge, UK, 1989.
37. Usman, F.; Khan, S.A. A generalized mixed vector variational-like inequality problem. *Nonlinear Anal.* **2009**, *71*, 5354–5362. [CrossRef]

mathematics

MDPI

Article

A Remark on the Change of Variable Theorem for the Riemann Integral

Alexander Kuleshov [1,2]

1 Department of Computational Mathematics and Cybernetics, Lomonosov Moscow State University, 119991 Moscow, Russia; kuleshov@cs.msu.ru or kuleshov.a.a@yandex.ru; Tel.: +7-985-210-4280
2 Moscow Center for Fundamental and Applied Mathematics, 119991 Moscow, Russia

Abstract: In 1961, Kestelman first proved the change in the variable theorem for the Riemann integral in its modern form. In 1970, Preiss and Uher supplemented his result with the inverse statement. Later, in a number of papers (Sarkhel, Výborný, Puoso, Tandra, and Torchinsky), the alternative proofs of these theorems were given within the same formulations. In this note, we show that one of the restrictions (namely, the boundedness of the function f on its entire domain) can be omitted while the change of variable formula still holds.

Keywords: real analysis; Riemann integral; change of variable

Citation: Kuleshov, A. A Remark on the Change of Variable Theorem for the Riemann Integral. *Mathematics* **2021**, *9*, 1899. https://doi.org/10.3390/math9161899

Academic Editor: Denis N. Sidorov

Received: 25 July 2021
Accepted: 8 August 2021
Published: 10 August 2021

Publisher's Note: MDPI stays neutral with regard to jurisdictional claims in published maps and institutional affiliations.

1. Introduction

Throughout this paper, we denote $[a, b]$ as the closed interval connecting the points $a, b \in \mathbb{R}$, and denote $R[a, b]$ as the class of all Riemann-integrable real functions on $[a, b]$. In 1961, Kestelman (see [1]) first proved the following fundamental theorem for the Riemann integral.

Theorem 1. *Suppose that* $g \in R[\alpha, \beta]$, $c \in \mathbb{R}$,

$$G(t) := \int_{\alpha}^{t} g(y)dy + c \tag{1}$$

and $f \in R(G([\alpha, \beta]))$. *Then,* $(f \circ G)g \in R[\alpha, \beta]$ *and the following* ***change of variable formula*** *holds:*

$$\int_{G(\alpha)}^{G(\beta)} f(x)dx = \int_{\alpha}^{\beta} f(G(t))g(t)dt \tag{2}$$

In 1970, Preiss and Uher (see [2]) supplemented this result with the following statement.

Theorem 2. *Suppose that* $g \in R[\alpha, \beta]$, G *is defined by* (1), f *is bounded on* $[c, d] := G([\alpha, \beta])$ *and* $(f \circ G)g \in R[\alpha, \beta]$. *Then* $f \in R[c, d] \subset R[G(\alpha), G(\beta)]$ *and the change of variable Formula* (2) *holds.*

Later, in a number of papers (see [3–6]), the alternative Proofs of Theorems 1 and 2 were given within the same formulations. The main goal of this note is to abandon the requirement of boundedness of the function f on $[c, d] := G([\alpha, \beta])$ in Theorem 2. At the same time, the condition for the boundedness of the function f on $[G(\alpha), G(\beta)]$ is essential for the existence of the integral on the left-hand side of (2) and does not follow from other conditions of the theorem, which are shown by the example at the end of [3]. Let us now proceed to formulating the main result.

2. The Main Result

Theorem 3. *Suppose that $g \in R[\alpha, \beta]$, G is defined by* (1)*, f is bounded on $I := [G(\alpha), G(\beta)]$ and $(f \circ G)g \in R[\alpha, \beta]$. Then, $f \in R(I)$ and the change of variable Formula* (2) *holds.*

For the proof of Theorem 3, we need the following lemma.

Lemma 1. *If $g, gh \in R[\alpha, \beta]$, then $g|h| \in R[\alpha, \beta]$.*

Proof. By Lebesgue's criterion, the functions g and gh are both continuous a.e. on $[\alpha, \beta]$. Let $x_0 \in [\alpha, \beta]$ be the point of their mutual continuity. If h is continuous at x_0, then $g|h|$ is continuous at x_0. If h is discontinuous at x_0, then the equality $g(x_0) = 0$ must hold because otherwise, h must be continuous at x_0 as a quotient of continuous functions gh and g. Then, we have the following:

$$g(x)h(x) \to g(x_0)h(x_0) = 0,$$

and therefore,

$$g(x)|h(x)| = g(x)h(x)\text{sgn}(h(x)) \to 0 = g(x_0)|h(x_0)|$$

as $x \to x_0$, which means the continuity of $g|h|$ at x_0, and thus, its continuity a.e. on $[\alpha, \beta]$. Thus, $g|h| \in R[\alpha, \beta]$ by Lebesgue's criterion. □

Proof of Theorem 3. By the hypothesis of the theorem, there is $M_1 > 0$ such that $|f(x)| \leq M_1$ for all $x \in I$. For all $n \in \mathbb{N}$, let $c_n := M_1 + n$ and define for all $x \in [c, d] := G([\alpha, \beta])$ the following function:

$$f_n(x) := \begin{cases} f(x), \text{ if } |f(x)| \leq c_n; \\ c_n, \text{ if } f(x) > c_n; \\ -c_n, \text{ if } f(x) < -c_n. \end{cases}$$

From the given definition for all $n \in \mathbb{N}$, we obtain the boundedness of f_n as well as the following equality:

$$f_n|_I = f|_I. \tag{3}$$

Additionally, for every $n \in \mathbb{N}$ for all $x \in [c, d]$, we obtain the following:

$$|f_n(x)| \leq |f(x)|, \tag{4}$$

and for all $x \in [c, d]$, we have the following:

$$f_n(x) \to f(x) \tag{5}$$

as $n \to \infty$. Next, we show that $(f_n \circ G)g \in R[\alpha, \beta]$ for all $n \in \mathbb{N}$. For each $n \in \mathbb{N}$, we have the following explicit formula:

$$f_n = \min\{\max\{f, -c_n\}, c_n\} = \frac{1}{4}(f - c_n - |f - c_n| + |3c_n + f - |f - c_n||),$$

from which, for $h := f \circ G$, we obtain the following equality:

$$(f_n \circ G)g = \frac{1}{4}(h - c_n - |h - c_n| + |3c_n + h - |h - c_n||)g. \tag{6}$$

Since by the hypothesis of the theorem $g, gh \in R[\alpha, \beta]$, then by Lemma 1, we have $g|h - c_n| \in R[\alpha, \beta]$, and thus, $g|3c_n + h - |h - c_n|| \in R[\alpha, \beta]$ by the same lemma. Finally, (6) implies that $(f_n \circ G)g \in R[\alpha, \beta]$ for all $n \in \mathbb{N}$.

Since the function $(f \circ G)g$ is integrable (and, thus, bounded), there exists $M_2 > 0$ such that for all $n \in N, t \in [\alpha, \beta]$ holds the inequality as follows:

$$|f_n(G(t))g(t)| \overset{(4)}{\leq} |f(G(t))g(t)| \leq M_2,$$

Additionally, for all $t \in [\alpha, \beta]$ as $n \to \infty$, we have the following:

$$f_n(G(t))g(t) \overset{(5)}{\to} f(G(t))g(t).$$

By virtue of (3), using Theorem 2 and Arzela's bounded convergence theorem for the Riemann integral (see [7]), as $n \to \infty$ we obtain the following:

$$\int_{G(\alpha)}^{G(\beta)} f(x)dx \overset{(3)}{=} \int_{G(\alpha)}^{G(\beta)} f_n(x)dx \overset{\text{Th. 2}}{=} \int_{\alpha}^{\beta} f_n(G(t))g(t)dt \to \int_{\alpha}^{\beta} f(G(t))g(t)dt,$$

which completes the verification of (2) and the proof of the theorem. □

3. Some applications

The following example illustrates Theorem 3 in use: let $\alpha := -1$, $\beta := 2$, $g(t) := 2t$, $G(t) := t^2$ and

$$f(x) := \begin{cases} \dfrac{1}{\sqrt{x}} \text{ if } x > 0; \\ 0 \text{ if } x = 0. \end{cases}$$

Clearly, f is unbounded on $G([-1,2]) = [0,4]$, but there exists

$$\int_1^4 \frac{dx}{\sqrt{x}} = \int_{G(\alpha)}^{G(\beta)} f(x)dx \overset{\text{Th. 3}}{=} \int_{\alpha}^{\beta} f(G(t))g(t)dt = \int_{-1}^{2} 2\,\mathrm{sgn}(t)dt = 2.$$

To illustrate some other applications of our result, we obtain as a consequence the theorem on the change of a variable in an improper integral (in one direction) under quite general conditions.

Corollary 1 (of Theorem 3). *Suppose that $a < b$, $\alpha < \beta$, f is bounded on $[a, c]$ for all $c \in (a, b)$, $g \in R[\alpha, \gamma]$ for all $\gamma \in (\alpha, \beta)$,*

$$G(t) := \int_{\alpha}^{t} g(y)dy + a \xrightarrow{t \to \beta-} b-$$

and

$$\lim_{z \to \beta-} \int_{\alpha}^{z} f(G(t))g(t)dt = I.$$

Then, the following holds:

$$\lim_{x \to b-} \int_{a}^{x} f(s)ds = I.$$

Funding: This work was funded by a grant of the Government of the Russian Federation (project No. 161 14.W03.31.0031).

Institutional Review Board Statement: Not applicable.

Informed Consent Statement: Not applicable.

Data Availability Statement: No new data were created or analyzed in this study. Data sharing is not applicable to this article.

Conflicts of Interest: The authors declare no conflict of interest. The funders had no role in the design of the study; in the collection, analyses, or interpretation of data; in the writing of the manuscript, or in the decision to publish the results.

References

1. Kestelman, H. Change of variable in Riemann integration. *Math. Gaz.* **1961**, *45*, 17–23. [CrossRef]
2. Preiss, D.; Uher, J. Poznámka k větě o substituci pro Riemannův integrál. *Časopis PěStováNí Mat.* **1970**, *95*, 345–347. [CrossRef]
3. Sarkhel, D.N.; Výborný, R. A change of variables theorem for the Riemann integral. *Real Anal. Exch.* **1996**, *22*, 390–395. [CrossRef]
4. Puoso, R.L. Riemann integration via primitives for a new proof to the change of variable theorem. *arXiv* **2011**, arXiv:1105.5938v1.
5. Tandra, H. A new proof of the change of variable theorem for the Riemann Integral. *Amer. Math. Monthly* **2015**, *122*, 795–799. [CrossRef]
6. Torchinsky, A. The change of variable formula for the Riemann integral. *arXiv* **2019**, arXiv:1904.07446v1.
7. Gordon, R.A. The bounded convergence theorem for the Riemann integral. *Real Anal. Exch.* **1998**, *24*, 25–28. [CrossRef]

mathematics

Article
On Robust Saddle-Point Criterion in Optimization Problems with Curvilinear Integral Functionals

Savin Treanţă [1,*] and **Koushik Das** [2]

[1] Department of Applied Mathematics, University Politehnica of Bucharest, 060042 Bucharest, Romania
[2] Department of Mathematics, Taki Government College, Taki 743429, India; koushikdas.maths@gmail.com
* Correspondence: savin.treanta@upb.ro

Abstract: In this paper, we introduce a new class of multi-dimensional robust optimization problems (named (P)) with mixed constraints implying second-order partial differential equations (PDEs) and inequations (PDIs). Moreover, we define an auxiliary (modified) class of robust control problems (named $(P)_{(\bar{b},\bar{c})}$), which is much easier to study, and provide some characterization results of (P) and $(P)_{(\bar{b},\bar{c})}$ by using the notions of normal weak robust optimal solution and robust saddle-point associated with a Lagrange functional corresponding to $(P)_{(\bar{b},\bar{c})}$. For this aim, we consider path-independent curvilinear integral cost functionals and the notion of convexity associated with a curvilinear integral functional generated by a controlled closed (complete integrable) Lagrange 1-form.

Keywords: Lagrange 1-form; second-order Lagrangian; normal weak robust optimal solution; modified objective function method; robust saddle-point

Citation: Treanţă, S.; Das, K. On Robust Saddle-Point Criterion in Optimization Problems with Curvilinear Integral Functionals. *Mathematics* **2021**, *9*, 1790. https://doi.org/10.3390/math9151790

Academic Editor: Simeon Reich

Received: 6 July 2021
Accepted: 27 July 2021
Published: 28 July 2021

1. Introduction

As we all know, partial differential equations (PDEs) and partial differential inequations (PDIs) are essential in modeling and investigating many processes in engineering and science. In this respect, many researchers have taken a special interest in their study. We specify, for example, the research works of Mititelu [1], Treanţă [2–4], Mititelu and Treanţă [5], Olteanu and Treanţă [6], Preeti et al. [7], and Jayswal et al. [8] on the study of some optimization problems with ODE, PDE, or isoperimetric constraints. In order to reduce the complexity of the considered optimization problems, some auxiliary optimization problems were formulated to investigate the initial problems more easily (Treanţă [9–12]). Nevertheless, since the real-life processes and phenomena often imply uncertainty in initial data, many researchers have turned their attention to optimization issues governed by first- and second-order PDEs, isoperimetric restrictions, stochastic PDEs, uncertain data, or a combination thereof. In this context, we mention the following research papers: Wei et al. [13], Liu and Yuan [14], Jeyakumar et al. [15], Sun et al. [16], Preeti et al. [7], Lu et al. [17], and Treanţă [18]. The structure of approximate solutions associated with some autonomous variational problems on large finite intervals was studied by Zaslavski [19]. Furthermore, Geldhauser and Valdinoci [20] investigated an optimization problem with SPDE constraints, with the peculiarity that the control parameter s is the s-th power of the diffusion operator in the state equation. In [21], Babamiyi et al. focused on identifying a distributed parameter in a saddle point problem with application to the elasticity imaging inverse problem. Very recently, Debnath and Qin [22], investigated the robust optimality and duality for minimax fractional programming problems with support functions.

Motivated and inspired by previous research works, in this paper, we introduce and study new classes of robust optimization problems. More exactly, by taking curvilinear integral objective functionals with mixed (equality and inequality) constraints implying data uncertainty and second-order partial derivatives, we introduce the robust control problems under study. Further, by using the concept of convexity associated with curvilinear integral functionals and the notion of robust saddle-point associated with a Lagrange functional corresponding to the modified robust optimization problem, we formulate and prove some characterization results for the considered classes of control problems. The novelty elements included in the paper, in comparison with other research papers in this field, are provided by the presence of uncertain data both in the objective functional and in the constraint functionals and also by the presence of second-order partial derivatives. Moreover, the proofs associated with the main results are established in an innovative way. Furthermore, since the mathematical framework introduced here is appropriate for various scientific approaches and viewpoints on complex spatial behaviors, the current paper could be seen as a definitive research work for a large community of researchers in engineering and science.

The paper is structured as follows. Section 2 provides the preliminary and necessary mathematical tools, which will be used in the next sections. Section 3 includes the main results of this paper. Under convexity assumption of the cost functional, the first main result establishes a connection between a robust saddle point of the Lagrange functional associated with the associated modified problem $(P)_{(\bar{b},\bar{c})}$ and a weak robust optimal solution of (P). By assuming the convexity hypotheses of the constraint functionals, the converse of the first main result is presented in the second main result. In Section 4, we formulate the conclusions and further development.

2. Preliminaries

In this paper, we use the following working hypotheses and notations:

- Consider $\mathbb{R}^p, \mathbb{R}^q, \mathbb{R}^r$ and $\mathbb{R}^n$ as Euclidean spaces of dimension p, q, r and n, respectively;
- Consider $\Theta \subset \mathbb{R}^p$ as a compact domain and the point $t = (t^\alpha) \in \Theta$ as a *multi-parameter of evolution* or *multi-time*;
- Consider $\Gamma \subset \Theta$ as a piecewise smooth curve joining the points t_0 and t_1 in Θ;
- $\mathcal{B}$ is the space of C^4-class state functions $b = (b^\tau) : \Theta \to \mathbb{R}^q$ and $b_\alpha := \dfrac{\partial b}{\partial t^\alpha}$, $b_{\alpha\beta} := \dfrac{\partial^2 b}{\partial t^\alpha \partial t^\beta}$ denote the *partial speed* and *partial acceleration*, respectively;
- $\mathcal{C}$ is the space of C^1-class control functions $c = (c^j) : \Theta \to \mathbb{R}^r$;
- Consider T as the transpose for a given vector;
- Consider the following convention for inequalities and equalities of any two vectors $x, y \in \mathbb{R}^n$:

  (*i*) $x < y \Leftrightarrow x_i < y_i, \ \forall i = \overline{1,n},$
  (*ii*) $x = y \Leftrightarrow x_i = y_i, \ \forall i = \overline{1,n},$
  (*iii*) $x \leqq y \Leftrightarrow x_i \leq y_i, \ \forall i = \overline{1,n},$
  (*iv*) $x \leq y \Leftrightarrow x_i \leq y_i, \ \forall i = \overline{1,n}$ and $x_i < y_i$ for some i.

In the following, we consider $g = (g_1, \dots, g_m) = (g_l) : J^2\left(\Theta, \mathbb{R}^q\right) \times \mathcal{C} \times \mathcal{U}_l \to \mathbb{R}^m$, $l = \overline{1,m}$, $f_\kappa : J^2\left(\Theta, \mathbb{R}^q\right) \times \mathcal{C} \times \mathcal{W}_\kappa \to \mathbb{R}$, $\kappa = \overline{1,p}$, $h = (h_1, \dots, h_n) = (h_\zeta) : J^2\left(\Theta, \mathbb{R}^q\right) \times \mathcal{C} \times \mathcal{V}_\zeta \to \mathbb{R}^n, \zeta = \overline{1,n}$, are C^3-class functionals. Furthermore, let us assume that $w = (w_\kappa), u = (u_l)$ and $v = (v_\zeta)$ are the uncertain parameters for some convex compact subsets $\mathcal{W} = (\mathcal{W}_\kappa) \subset \mathbb{R}^p, \mathcal{U} = (\mathcal{U}_l) \subset \mathbb{R}^m$ and $\mathcal{V} = (\mathcal{V}_\zeta) \subset \mathbb{R}^n$, respectively. Denote by $J^2\left(\Theta, \mathbb{R}^q\right)$ the second-order jet bundle associated with Θ and $\mathbb{R}^q$. Furthermore, assume that the previous multi-time-controlled second-order Lagrangians f_κ determine a controlled closed (complete integrable) Lagrange 1-form (see summation over the repeated indices, Einstein summation):

$$f_\kappa(t, b(t), b_\sigma(t), b_{\alpha\beta}(t), c(t), w)dt^\kappa,$$

which generates the following controlled path-independent curvilinear integral functional:

$$\int_{\Gamma} f_{\kappa}(t, b(t), b_{\sigma}(t), b_{\alpha\beta}(t), c(t), w)dt^{\kappa}.$$

The second-order PDE and PDI constrained variational control problem with uncertainty in the objective and constraint functionals is defined as follows:

$$(P) \qquad \min_{(b(\cdot),c(\cdot))} \int_{\Gamma} f_{\kappa}(t, b(t), b_{\sigma}(t), b_{\alpha\beta}(t), c(t), w)dt^{\kappa}$$

subject to

$$g(t, b(t), b_{\sigma}(t), b_{\alpha\beta}(t), c(t), u) \leqq 0, \quad t \in \Theta$$
$$h(t, b(t), b_{\sigma}(t), b_{\alpha\beta}(t), c(t), v) = 0, \quad t \in \Theta$$
$$b(t_0) = b_0,\ b(t_1) = b_1,\ b_{\sigma}(t_0) = b_{\sigma 0},\ b_{\sigma}(t_1) = b_{\sigma 1}.$$

The associated robust counterpart of the aforementioned variational control problem (P) is defined as:

$$(RP) \qquad \min_{(b(\cdot),c(\cdot))} \int_{\Gamma} \max_{w \in \mathcal{W}} f_{\kappa}(t, b(t), b_{\sigma}(t), b_{\alpha\beta}(t), c(t), w)dt^{\kappa}$$

subject to

$$g(t, b(t), b_{\sigma}(t), b_{\alpha\beta}(t), c(t), u) \leqq 0, \quad t \in \Theta, \forall u \in \mathcal{U}$$
$$h(t, b(t), b_{\sigma}(t), b_{\alpha\beta}(t), c(t), v) = 0, \quad t \in \Theta, \forall vs. \in \mathcal{V}$$
$$b(t_0) = b_0,\ b(t_1) = b_1,\ b_{\sigma}(t_0) = b_{\sigma 0},\ b_{\sigma}(t_1) = b_{\sigma 1}.$$

Further, denote by

$$\mathcal{D} = \{(b,c) \in \mathcal{B} \times \mathcal{C} :\ g(t, b(t), b_{\sigma}(t), b_{\alpha\beta}(t), c(t), u) \leqq 0,$$
$$h(t, b(t), b_{\sigma}(t), b_{\alpha\beta}(t), c(t), v) = 0,\ b(t_0) = b_0,\ b(t_1) = b_1,$$
$$b_{\sigma}(t_0) = b_{\sigma 0},\ b_{\sigma}(t_1) = b_{\sigma 1},\ t \in \Theta, u \in \mathcal{U},\ vs. \in \mathcal{V}\}$$

the feasible solution set in (RP), and we call it the *robust feasible solution set* of (P).

To simplify the presentation, we use the following notation:

$$\pi = (t, b(t), b_{\sigma}(t), b_{\alpha\beta}(t), c(t)).$$

The associated first-order partial derivatives of f_{κ}, $\kappa = \overline{1,p}$, are defined as

$$\frac{\partial f_{\kappa}}{\partial b} = \left(\frac{\partial f_{\kappa}}{\partial b^1}, \dots, \frac{\partial f_{\kappa}}{\partial b^q}\right), \quad \frac{\partial f_{\kappa}}{\partial c} = \left(\frac{\partial f_{\kappa}}{\partial c^1}, \dots, \frac{\partial f_{\kappa}}{\partial c^r}\right).$$

In the same manner, we have $g_b := \dfrac{\partial g}{\partial b}$ and $g_c := \dfrac{\partial g}{\partial c}$ by using matrices with m rows and $h_b := \dfrac{\partial h}{\partial b}$ and $h_c := \dfrac{\partial h}{\partial c}$ by using matrices with n rows.

Further, in accordance to Treanţă [3], we define the notion of a weak robust optimal solution of the considered class of constrained variational control problems. This notion will be used to establish the associated robust necessary conditions of optimality and the main results derived in the paper.

Definition 1. *A pair $(\bar{b}, \bar{c}) \in \mathcal{D}$ is said to be a weak robust optimal solution to (P) if there does not exist another point $(b,c) \in \mathcal{D}$ such that*

$$\int_{\Gamma} \max_{w \in \mathcal{W}} f_{\kappa}(\pi, w)dt^{\kappa} < \int_{\Gamma} \max_{w \in \mathcal{W}} f_{\kappa}(\bar{\pi}, w)dt^{\kappa}.$$

Next, we shall use the Saunders's multi-index notation (Saunders [23], Treanţă [3,24]) to formulate the concept of convexity and the robust necessary optimality conditions for (P).

Definition 2. *A curvilinear integral functional*

$$F(b,c,\bar{w}) = \int_{\Gamma} f_{\kappa}(t,b(t),b_{\sigma}(t),b_{\alpha\beta}(t),c(t),\bar{w})dt^{\kappa} = \int_{\Gamma} f_{\kappa}(\pi,\bar{w})dt^{\kappa}$$

is said to be convex at $(\bar{b},\bar{c}) \in \mathcal{B} \times \mathcal{C}$ *if the following inequality*

$$F(b,c,\bar{w}) - F(\bar{b},\bar{c},\bar{w}) \geq \int_{\Gamma} \frac{\partial f_{\kappa}}{\partial b}(\bar{\pi},\bar{w})[b(t)-\bar{b}(t)]dt^{\kappa}$$
$$+\int_{\Gamma} \frac{\partial f_{\kappa}}{\partial b_{\sigma}}(\bar{\pi},\bar{w})[b_{\sigma}(t)-\bar{b}_{\sigma}(t)]dt^{\kappa}$$
$$+\frac{1}{n(\alpha,\beta)}\int_{\Gamma} \frac{\partial f_{\kappa}}{\partial b_{\alpha\beta}}(\bar{\pi},\bar{w})[b_{\alpha\beta}(t)-\bar{b}_{\alpha\beta}(t)]dt^{\kappa}$$
$$+\int_{\Gamma} \frac{\partial f_{\kappa}}{\partial c}(\bar{\pi},\bar{w})[c(t)-\bar{c}(t)]dt^{\kappa}$$

holds for all $(b,c) \in \mathcal{B} \times \mathcal{C}$.

According to Treanţă [24], we formulate the robust necessary optimality conditions for (P).

Theorem 1. *If* $(\bar{b},\bar{c}) \in \mathcal{D}$ *is a weak robust optimal solution to* (P) *and* $\max_{w\in\mathcal{W}} f_{\kappa}(\pi,w) = f_{\kappa}(\pi,\bar{w})$, $\kappa = \overline{1,p}$, *then there exist the scalar* $\bar{\mu} \in \mathbb{R}$, *the piecewise smooth functions* $\bar{v} = (\bar{v}_l(t)) \in \mathbb{R}^m_+, \bar{\gamma} = (\bar{\gamma}_{\zeta}(t)) \in \mathbb{R}^n$, *and the uncertainty parameters* $\bar{u} \in \mathcal{U}$ *and* $\bar{v} \in \mathcal{V}$ *such that the following conditions*

$$\bar{\mu}\frac{\partial f_{\kappa}}{\partial b}(\bar{\pi},\bar{w}) + \bar{v}^T g_b(\bar{\pi},\bar{u}) + \bar{\gamma}^T h_b(\bar{\pi},\bar{v}) \tag{1}$$
$$-D_{\sigma}\left[\bar{\mu}\frac{\partial f_{\kappa}}{\partial b_{\sigma}}(\bar{\pi},\bar{w}) + \bar{v}^T g_{b_{\sigma}}(\bar{\pi},\bar{u}) + \bar{\gamma}^T h_{b_{\sigma}}(\bar{\pi},\bar{v})\right]$$
$$+\frac{1}{n(\alpha,\beta)}D^2_{\alpha\beta}\left[\bar{\mu}\frac{\partial f_{\kappa}}{\partial b_{\alpha\beta}}(\bar{\pi},\bar{w}) + \bar{v}^T g_{b_{\alpha\beta}}(\bar{\pi},\bar{u}) + \bar{\gamma}^T h_{b_{\alpha\beta}}(\bar{\pi},\bar{v})\right] = 0, \quad \kappa = \overline{1,p}$$

$$\bar{\mu}\frac{\partial f_{\kappa}}{\partial c}(\bar{\pi},\bar{w}) + \bar{v}^T g_c(\bar{\pi},\bar{u}) + \bar{\gamma}^T h_c(\bar{\pi},\bar{v}) = 0, \quad \kappa = \overline{1,p} \tag{2}$$

$$\bar{v}^T g(\bar{\pi},\bar{u}) = 0,\ \bar{v} \geqq 0, \tag{3}$$

$$\bar{\mu} \geq 0 \tag{4}$$

hold for all $t \in \Theta$, *except at discontinuities.*

Remark 1. *The robust necessary optimality conditions of* (P) *are given by the conditions (1)–(4).*

Definition 3. *A pair* $(\bar{b},\bar{c}) \in \mathcal{D}$ *is said to be a normal weak robust optimal solution to* (P) *if* $\bar{\mu} > 0$ *in Theorem 1. We can consider* $\bar{\mu} = 1$ *without loss of generality.*

Next, we use the modified objective function method to reduce the complexity of (P). In this direction, let $(\bar{b},\bar{c})$ be an arbitrary given robust feasible solution to (P). The modified multi-dimensional variational control problem associated with the original optimization problem (P) is defined as:

$$(P)_{(\bar{b},\bar{c})} \quad \min_{(b(\cdot),c(\cdot))} \int_\Gamma \Big\{ \frac{\partial f_\kappa}{\partial b}(\bar{\pi},w)(b(t)-\bar{b}(t)) + \frac{\partial f_\kappa}{\partial b_\sigma}(\bar{\pi},w)(b_\sigma(t)-\bar{b}_\sigma(t))$$

$$+\frac{1}{n(\alpha,\beta)}\frac{\partial f_\kappa}{\partial b_{\alpha\beta}}(\bar{\pi},w)(b_{\alpha\beta}(t)-\bar{b}_{\alpha\beta}(t)) + \frac{\partial f_\kappa}{\partial c}(\bar{\pi},w)(c(t)-\bar{c}(t))\Big\}dt^\kappa$$

subject to

$$g(\pi,u) \leqq 0, \quad t\in\Theta$$

$$h(\pi,v) = 0, \quad t\in\Theta$$

$$b(t_0)=b_0,\ b(t_1)=b_1,\ b_\sigma(t_0)=b_{\sigma 0},\ b_\sigma(t_1)=b_{\sigma 1},$$

where the functionals g, f_κ and h are given as in (P).

The associated robust counterpart of the modified multi-dimensional variational control problem $(P)_{(\bar{b},\bar{c})}$ is defined as:

$$(RP)_{(\bar{b},\bar{c})} \quad \min_{(b(\cdot),c(\cdot))} \int_\Gamma \max_{w\in\mathcal{W}} \Big\{ \frac{\partial f_\kappa}{\partial b}(\bar{\pi},w)(b(t)-\bar{b}(t)) + \frac{\partial f_\kappa}{\partial b_\sigma}(\bar{\pi},w)(b_\sigma(t)-\bar{b}_\sigma(t))$$

$$+\frac{1}{n(\alpha,\beta)}\frac{\partial f_\kappa}{\partial b_{\alpha\beta}}(\bar{\pi},w)(b_{\alpha\beta}(t)-\bar{b}_{\alpha\beta}(t)) + \frac{\partial f_\kappa}{\partial c}(\bar{\pi},w)(c(t)-\bar{c}(t))\Big\}dt^\kappa$$

subject to

$$g(\pi,u) \leqq 0, \quad t\in\Theta,\ \forall u\in\mathcal{U}$$

$$h(\pi,v) = 0, \quad t\in\Theta,\ \forall vs. \in\mathcal{V}$$

$$b(t_0)=b_0,\ b(t_1)=b_1,\ b_\sigma(t_0)=b_{\sigma 0},\ b_\sigma(t_1)=b_{\sigma 1}.$$

Remark 2. *The robust feasible solution set of the problem $(P)_{(\bar{b},\bar{c})}$ is the same as in (P). Consequently, it is also denoted by $\mathcal{D}$.*

Definition 4. *A pair $(\hat{b},\hat{c}) \in \mathcal{D}$ is said to be a weak robust optimal solution to $(P)_{(\bar{b},\bar{c})}$ if there does not exist another point $(b,c)\in\mathcal{D}$ such that*

$$\int_\Gamma \max_{w\in\mathcal{W}} \Big[\frac{\partial f_\kappa}{\partial b}(\bar{\pi},w)(b-\bar{b}) + \frac{\partial f_\kappa}{\partial b_\sigma}(\bar{\pi},w)(b_\sigma-\bar{b}_\sigma)$$

$$+\frac{1}{n(\alpha,\beta)}\frac{\partial f_\kappa}{\partial b_{\alpha\beta}}(\bar{\pi},w)(b_{\alpha\beta}-\bar{b}_{\alpha\beta}) + \frac{\partial f_\kappa}{\partial c}(\bar{\pi},w)(c-\bar{c})\Big]dt^\kappa$$

$$< \int_\Gamma \max_{w\in\mathcal{W}} \Big[\frac{\partial f_\kappa}{\partial b}(\bar{\pi},w)(\hat{b}-\bar{b}) + \frac{\partial f_\kappa}{\partial b_\sigma}(\bar{\pi},w)(\hat{b}_\sigma-\bar{b}_\sigma)$$

$$+\frac{1}{n(\alpha,\beta)}\frac{\partial f_\kappa}{\partial b_{\alpha\beta}}(\bar{\pi},w)(\hat{b}_{\alpha\beta}-\bar{b}_{\alpha\beta}) + \frac{\partial f_\kappa}{\partial c}(\bar{\pi},w)(\hat{c}-\bar{c})\Big]dt^\kappa.$$

3. Saddle-Point Optimality Criterion

In this section, under some convexity assumptions, we establish some connections between a weak robust optimal solution of (P) and a *robust saddle-point* associated with a Lagrange functional (Lagrangian) corresponding to the modified multi-dimensional variational control problem $(P)_{(\bar{b},\bar{c})}$. In this regard, in accordance with Treanţă [9,11,12] and Preeti et al. [7], we formulate the next definitions.

Definition 5. *The Lagrange functional $L((b,c),\nu,\gamma,w,u,v) : \mathcal{B}\times\mathcal{C}\times\mathbb{R}^m_+\times\mathbb{R}^n\times\mathcal{W}\times\mathcal{U}\times\mathcal{V}\to\mathbb{R}$ associated with the modified variational control problem $(P)_{(\bar{b},\bar{c})}$ is defined as*

$$L((b,c),\nu,\gamma,w,u,v) = \int_\Gamma \Big\{ \max_{w\in\mathcal{W}} \Big[(b(t)-\bar{b}(t))\frac{\partial f_\kappa}{\partial b}(\bar{\pi},w) + (b_\sigma(t)-\bar{b}_\sigma(t))\frac{\partial f_\kappa}{\partial b_\sigma}(\bar{\pi},w)$$

$$+\frac{1}{n(\alpha,\beta)}(b_{\alpha\beta}(t)-\bar{b}_{\alpha\beta}(t))\frac{\partial f_\kappa}{\partial b_{\alpha\beta}}(\bar{\pi},w) + (c(t)-\bar{c}(t))\frac{\partial f_\kappa}{\partial c}(\bar{\pi},w)\Big]$$

$$+\nu^T(t)g(\pi,u) + \gamma^T(t)h(\pi,v)\Big\} dt^\kappa.$$

Definition 6. *A point $((\bar{b},\bar{c}),\bar{\nu},\bar{\gamma},\bar{w},\bar{u},\bar{v}) \in \mathcal{D}\times\mathbb{R}^m_+\times\mathbb{R}^n\times\mathcal{W}\times\mathcal{U}\times\mathcal{V}$ is said to be a robust saddle-point for the Lagrange functional $L((b,c),\nu,\gamma,w,u,v)$ associated with the modified multi-dimensional variational control problem $(P)_{(\bar{b},\bar{c})}$ if the following relations are fulfilled:*

(i) $L((\bar{b},\bar{c}),\nu,\gamma,w,u,v) \le L((\bar{b},\bar{c}),\bar{\nu},\bar{\gamma},w,\bar{u},\bar{v}),\ \forall\nu\in\mathbb{R}^m_+,\ \forall\gamma\in\mathbb{R}^n,\ \forall(u,v)\in\mathcal{U}\times\mathcal{V},$
(ii) $L((b,c),\bar{\nu},\bar{\gamma},w,\bar{u},\bar{v}) \ge L((\bar{b},\bar{c}),\bar{\nu},\bar{\gamma},w,\bar{u},\bar{v}),\ \forall(b,c)\in\mathcal{B}\times\mathcal{C}.$

Now, taking into account the above definitions, we establish the following two main results of this paper.

Theorem 2. *Let $(\bar{b},\bar{c})$ be a robust feasible solution to (P). Assume that $\max_{w\in\mathcal{W}} f_\kappa(\pi,w) = f_\kappa(\pi,\bar{w})$, $\kappa=\overline{1,p}$, and the objective functional $\int_\Gamma f_\kappa(\pi,\bar{w})dt^\kappa$ is convex at $(\bar{b},\bar{c})$. If the point $((\bar{b},\bar{c}),\bar{\nu},\bar{\gamma},\bar{w},\bar{u},\bar{v})$ is a robust saddle-point for the Lagrange functional $L((b,c),\nu,\gamma,w,u,v)$ associated with the modified multi-dimensional variational control problem $(P)_{(\bar{b},\bar{c})}$, then $(\bar{b},\bar{c})$ is a weak robust optimal solution to (P).*

Proof. By reductio ad absurdum, let us assume that $(\bar{b},\bar{c})$ is not a weak robust optimal solution to (P). Therefore, by using the convexity property of the objective functional $\int_\Gamma f_\kappa(\pi,\bar{w})dt^\kappa$, we get

$$\int_\Gamma \max_{w\in\mathcal{W}} \Big[(\tilde{b}-\bar{b})\frac{\partial f_\kappa}{\partial b}(\bar{\pi},w) + (\tilde{b}_\sigma-\bar{b}_\sigma)\frac{\partial f_\kappa}{\partial b_\sigma}(\bar{\pi},w) \tag{5}$$

$$+\frac{1}{n(\alpha,\beta)}(\tilde{b}_{\alpha\beta}-\bar{b}_{\alpha\beta})\frac{\partial f_\kappa}{\partial b_{\alpha\beta}}(\bar{\pi},w) + (\tilde{c}-\bar{c})\frac{\partial f_\kappa}{\partial c}(\bar{\pi},w)\Big] dt^\kappa$$

$$< \int_\Gamma \max_{w\in\mathcal{W}} \Big[(\bar{b}-\bar{b})\frac{\partial f_\kappa}{\partial b}(\bar{\pi},w) + (\bar{b}_\sigma-\bar{b}_\sigma)\frac{\partial f_\kappa}{\partial b_\sigma}(\bar{\pi},w)$$

$$+\frac{1}{n(\alpha,\beta)}(\bar{b}_{\alpha\beta}-\bar{b}_{\alpha\beta})\frac{\partial f_\kappa}{\partial b_{\alpha\beta}}(\bar{\pi},w) + (\bar{c}-\bar{c})\frac{\partial f_\kappa}{\partial c}(\bar{\pi},w)\Big] dt^\kappa,$$

for some $(\tilde{b},\tilde{c}) \in \mathcal{D}$.

From the feasibility of $(\tilde{b},\tilde{c})$ to the problem (P) and $\bar{\nu}\in\mathbb{R}^m_+$, we get

$$\int_\Gamma \bar{\nu}^T g(\tilde{\pi},\bar{u})dt^\kappa \le 0. \tag{6}$$

On the other hand, since $((\bar{b},\bar{c}),\bar{\nu},\bar{\gamma},\bar{w},\bar{u},\bar{v})$ is a robust saddle-point for the Lagrange functional $L((b,c),\nu,\gamma,w,u,v)$ associated with the modified multi-dimensional variational control problem $(P)_{(\bar{b},\bar{c})}$, by using Definition 6 (i), we have

$$L((\bar{b},\bar{c}),\nu,\gamma,w,u,v) \le L((\bar{b},\bar{c}),\bar{\nu},\bar{\gamma},w,\bar{u},\bar{v}),\ \forall\nu\in\mathbb{R}^m_+, \forall\gamma\in\mathbb{R}^n, \forall u\in\mathcal{U}, \forall vs.\in\mathcal{V},$$

which, using of the definition of Lagrange functional, can be rewritten as

$$\int_\Gamma \Big\{ \max_{w\in\mathcal{W}} \Big[(\bar{b}(t)-\bar{b}(t))\frac{\partial f_\kappa}{\partial b}(\bar{\pi},w) + (\bar{b}_\sigma(t)-\bar{b}_\sigma(t))\frac{\partial f_\kappa}{\partial b_\sigma}(\bar{\pi},w)$$

$$+\frac{1}{n(\alpha,\beta)}(\bar{b}_{\alpha\beta}(t)-\bar{b}_{\alpha\beta}(t))\frac{\partial f_\kappa}{\partial b_{\alpha\beta}}(\bar{\pi},w)+(\bar{c}(t)-\bar{c}(t))\frac{\partial f_\kappa}{\partial c}(\bar{\pi},w)\Big]$$

$$+\nu^T(t)g(\bar{\pi},u)+\gamma^T(t)h(\bar{\pi},v)\Big\}dt^\kappa$$

$$\leq\int_\Gamma\Big\{\max_{w\in\mathcal{W}}\Big[(\bar{b}(t)-\bar{b}(t))\frac{\partial f_\kappa}{\partial b}(\bar{\pi},w)+(\bar{b}_\sigma(t)-\bar{b}_\sigma(t))\frac{\partial f_\kappa}{\partial b_\sigma}(\bar{\pi},w)$$

$$+\frac{1}{n(\alpha,\beta)}(\bar{b}_{\alpha\beta}(t)-\bar{b}_{\alpha\beta}(t))\frac{\partial f_\kappa}{\partial b_{\alpha\beta}}(\bar{\pi},w)+(\bar{c}(t)-\bar{c}(t))\frac{\partial f_\kappa}{\partial c}(\bar{\pi},w)\Big]$$

$$+\bar{v}^T(t)g(\bar{\pi},\bar{u})+\bar{\gamma}^T(t)h(\bar{\pi},\bar{v})\Big\}dt^\kappa.$$

Since $\max_{w\in\mathcal{W}}f_\kappa(\pi,w)=f_\kappa(\pi,\bar{w})$, $\kappa=\overline{1,p}$, it follows that

$$\int_\Gamma\Big\{(\bar{b}(t)-\bar{b}(t))\frac{\partial f_\kappa}{\partial b}(\bar{\pi},\bar{w})+(\bar{b}_\sigma(t)-\bar{b}_\sigma(t))\frac{\partial f_\kappa}{\partial b_\sigma}(\bar{\pi},\bar{w})$$

$$+\frac{1}{n(\alpha,\beta)}(\bar{b}_{\alpha\beta}(t)-\bar{b}_{\alpha\beta}(t))\frac{\partial f_\kappa}{\partial b_{\alpha\beta}}(\bar{\pi},\bar{w})+(\bar{c}(t)-\bar{c}(t))\frac{\partial f_\kappa}{\partial c}(\bar{\pi},\bar{w})$$

$$+\nu^T(t)g(\bar{\pi},u)+\gamma^T(t)h(\bar{\pi},v)\Big\}dt^\kappa$$

$$\leq\int_\Gamma\Big\{(\bar{b}(t)-\bar{b}(t))\frac{\partial f_\kappa}{\partial b}(\bar{\pi},\bar{w})+(\bar{b}_\sigma(t)-\bar{b}_\sigma(t))\frac{\partial f_\kappa}{\partial b_\sigma}(\bar{\pi},\bar{w})$$

$$+\frac{1}{n(\alpha,\beta)}(\bar{b}_{\alpha\beta}(t)-\bar{b}_{\alpha\beta}(t))\frac{\partial f_\kappa}{\partial b_{\alpha\beta}}(\bar{\pi},\bar{w})+(\bar{c}(t)-\bar{c}(t))\frac{\partial f_\kappa}{\partial c}(\bar{\pi},\bar{w})$$

$$+\bar{v}^T(t)g(\bar{\pi},\bar{u})+\bar{\gamma}^T(t)h(\bar{\pi},\bar{v})\Big\}dt^\kappa.$$

If we set $\nu=0$ and $\gamma=0$ in the above inequality, we obtain

$$\int_\Gamma\bar{v}^Tg(\bar{\pi},\bar{u})dt^\kappa\geq 0. \tag{7}$$

From (6) and (7), it follows that

$$\int_\Gamma\bar{v}^Tg(\tilde{\pi},\tilde{u})dt^\kappa\leq\int_\Gamma\bar{v}^Tg(\bar{\pi},\bar{u})dt^\kappa,$$

which, along with the inequality (5), gives

$$\int_\Gamma\Big\{\max_{w\in\mathcal{W}}\Big[(\tilde{b}-\bar{b})\frac{\partial f_\kappa}{\partial b}(\bar{\pi},w)+(\tilde{b}_\sigma-\bar{b}_\sigma)\frac{\partial f_\kappa}{\partial b_\sigma}(\bar{\pi},w)$$

$$+\frac{1}{n(\alpha,\beta)}(\tilde{b}_{\alpha\beta}-\bar{b}_{\alpha\beta})\frac{\partial f_\kappa}{\partial b_{\alpha\beta}}(\bar{\pi},w)+(\tilde{c}-\bar{c})\frac{\partial f_\kappa}{\partial c}(\bar{\pi},w)\Big]+\bar{v}^Tg(\tilde{\pi},\tilde{u})\Big\}dt^\kappa$$

$$<\int_\Gamma\Big\{\max_{w\in\mathcal{W}}\Big[(\tilde{b}-\bar{b})\frac{\partial f_\kappa}{\partial b}(\bar{\pi},w)+(\tilde{b}_\sigma-\bar{b}_\sigma)\frac{\partial f_\kappa}{\partial b_\sigma}(\bar{\pi},w)$$

$$+\frac{1}{n(\alpha,\beta)}(\tilde{b}_{\alpha\beta}-\bar{b}_{\alpha\beta})\frac{\partial f_\kappa}{\partial b_{\alpha\beta}}(\bar{\pi},w)+(\tilde{c}-\bar{c})\frac{\partial f_\kappa}{\partial c}(\bar{\pi},w)\Big]+\bar{v}^Tg(\bar{\pi},\bar{u})\Big\}dt^\kappa,$$

equivalently with

$$\int_\Gamma\Big\{\max_{w\in\mathcal{W}}\Big[(\tilde{b}-\bar{b})\frac{\partial f_\kappa}{\partial b}(\bar{\pi},w)+(\tilde{b}_\sigma-\bar{b}_\sigma)\frac{\partial f_\kappa}{\partial b_\sigma}(\bar{\pi},w)$$

$$+\frac{1}{n(\alpha,\beta)}(\tilde{b}_{\alpha\beta}-\bar{b}_{\alpha\beta})\frac{\partial f_\kappa}{\partial b_{\alpha\beta}}(\bar{\pi},w)+(\tilde{c}-\bar{c})\frac{\partial f_\kappa}{\partial c}(\bar{\pi},w)\Big]+\bar{v}^Tg(\tilde{\pi},\tilde{u})+\bar{\gamma}^Th(\tilde{\pi},\tilde{v})\Big\}dt^\kappa$$

$$< \int_\Gamma \Big\{ \max_{w\in W} \Big[(\tilde{b}-\bar{b})\frac{\partial f_\kappa}{\partial b}(\bar{\pi},w) + (\tilde{b}_\sigma - \bar{b}_\sigma)\frac{\partial f_\kappa}{\partial b_\sigma}(\bar{\pi},w)$$

$$+\frac{1}{n(\alpha,\beta)}(\tilde{b}_{\alpha\beta}-\bar{b}_{\alpha\beta})\frac{\partial f_\kappa}{\partial b_{\alpha\beta}}(\bar{\pi},w) + (\tilde{c}-\bar{c})\frac{\partial f_\kappa}{\partial c}(\bar{\pi},w)\Big] + \bar{v}^T g(\bar{\pi},\bar{u}) + \bar{\gamma}^T h(\bar{\pi},\bar{v})\Big\} dt^\kappa,$$

or

$$L((\bar{b},\bar{c}),\bar{v},\bar{\gamma},\bar{w},\bar{u},\bar{v}) < L((\tilde{b},\tilde{c}),\bar{v},\bar{\gamma},\bar{w},\bar{u},\bar{v}), \quad (\tilde{b},\tilde{c}) \in \mathcal{B}\times\mathcal{C},$$

which contradicts Definition 6, and the proof is completed. □

Theorem 3. *Let $(\bar{b},\bar{c})$ be a normal weak robust optimal solution to (P). Assume that $\max_{w\in W}$ $f_\kappa(\pi,w) = f_\kappa(\pi,\bar{w})$, $\kappa = \overline{1,p}$, and the constraint functionals*

$$\int_\Gamma \bar{v}^T g(\pi,\bar{u}) dt^\kappa, \ \int_\Gamma \bar{\gamma}^T h(\pi,\bar{v}) dt^\kappa$$

are convex at $(\bar{b},\bar{c})$. Then, $((\bar{b},\bar{c}),\bar{v},\bar{\gamma},\bar{w},\bar{u},\bar{v})$ is a robust saddle-point for the Lagrange functional $L((b,c),v,\gamma,w,u,v)$ associated with the modified variational control problem $(P)_{(\bar{b},\bar{c})}$.

Proof. Since the relations (1)–(4), with $\bar{\mu}=1$, are satisfied for all $t \in \Theta$, except at discontinuities, the conditions (1) and (2) yield

$$\int_\Gamma (b-\bar{b})\{\frac{\partial f_\kappa}{\partial b}(\bar{\pi},\bar{w}) + \bar{v}^T g_b(\bar{\pi},\bar{u}) + \bar{\gamma}^T h_b(\bar{\pi},\bar{v}) \tag{8}$$

$$-D_\sigma\Big[\frac{\partial f_\kappa}{\partial b_\sigma}(\bar{\pi},\bar{w}) + \bar{v}^T g_{b_\sigma}(\bar{\pi},\bar{u}) + \bar{\gamma}^T h_{b_\sigma}(\bar{\pi},\bar{v})\Big]$$

$$+\frac{1}{n(\alpha,\beta)}D^2_{\alpha\beta}\Big[\frac{\partial f_\kappa}{\partial b_{\alpha\beta}}(\bar{\pi},\bar{w}) + \bar{v}^T g_{b_{\alpha\beta}}(\bar{\pi},\bar{u}) + \bar{\gamma}^T h_{b_{\alpha\beta}}(\bar{\pi},\bar{v})\Big]\} dt^\kappa$$

$$+\int_\Gamma (c-\bar{c})\{\frac{\partial f_\kappa}{\partial c}(\bar{\pi},\bar{w}) + \bar{v}^T g_c(\bar{\pi},\bar{u}) + \bar{\gamma}^T h_c(\bar{\pi},\bar{v})\} dt^\kappa$$

$$= \int_\Gamma \Big[(b-\bar{b})\{\frac{\partial f_\kappa}{\partial b}(\bar{\pi},\bar{w}) + \bar{v}^T g_b(\bar{\pi},\bar{u}) + \bar{\gamma}^T h_b(\bar{\pi},\bar{v})\}$$

$$+(b_\sigma - \bar{b}_\sigma)\{\frac{\partial f_\kappa}{\partial b_\sigma}(\bar{\pi},\bar{w}) + \bar{v}^T g_{b_\sigma}(\bar{\pi},\bar{u}) + \bar{\gamma}^T h_{b_\sigma}(\bar{\pi},\bar{v})\}$$

$$+\frac{1}{n(\alpha,\beta)}(b_{\alpha\beta}-\bar{b}_{\alpha\beta})\{\frac{\partial f_\kappa}{\partial b_{\alpha\beta}}(\bar{\pi},\bar{w}) + \bar{v}^T g_{b_{\alpha\beta}}(\bar{\pi},\bar{u}) + \bar{\gamma}^T h_{b_{\alpha\beta}}(\bar{\pi},\bar{v})\}\Big] dt^\kappa$$

$$+\int_\Gamma (c-\bar{c})\{\frac{\partial f_\kappa}{\partial c}(\bar{\pi},\bar{w}) + \bar{v}^T g_c(\bar{\pi},\bar{u}) + \bar{\gamma}^T h_c(\bar{\pi},\bar{v})\} dt^\kappa = 0,$$

where we used the formula of integration by parts, the result "*A total divergence is equal to a total derivative*" (see Treanţă [4]) and the boundary conditions formulated in the considered problem.

Further, taking into account the assumption of convexity for the following multiple integral functionals $\int_\Gamma \bar{v}^T g(\pi,\bar{u}) dt^\kappa$, $\int_\Gamma \bar{\gamma}^T h(\pi,\bar{v}) dt^\kappa$ at $(\bar{b},\bar{u})$, we obtain

$$\int_\Gamma \Big\{\bar{v}^T g(\pi,\bar{u}) - \bar{v}^T g(\bar{\pi},\bar{u})\Big\} dt^\kappa \geq \int_\Gamma (b-\bar{b})\bar{v}^T g_b(\bar{\pi},\bar{u}) dt^\kappa$$

$$+\int_\Gamma (b_\sigma - \bar{b}_\sigma)\bar{v}^T g_{b_\sigma}(\bar{\pi},\bar{u}) dt^\kappa + \frac{1}{n(\alpha,\beta)}\int_\Gamma (b_{\alpha\beta}-\bar{b}_{\alpha\beta})\bar{v}^T g_{b_{\alpha\beta}}(\bar{\pi},\bar{u}) dt^\kappa$$

$$+\int_\Gamma (c-\bar{c})\bar{v}^T g_c(\bar{\pi},\bar{u}) dt^\kappa,$$

$$\int_{\Gamma}\left\{\bar{\gamma}^T h(\pi,\bar{v}) - \bar{\gamma}^T h(\bar{\pi},\bar{v})\right\}dt^\kappa \geq \int_{\Gamma}(b-\bar{b})\bar{\gamma}^T h_b(\bar{\pi},\bar{v})dt^\kappa$$
$$+\int_{\Gamma}(b_\sigma - \bar{b}_\sigma)\bar{\gamma}^T h_{b_\sigma}(\bar{\pi},\bar{v})dt^\kappa + \frac{1}{n(\alpha,\beta)}\int_{\Gamma}(b_{\alpha\beta} - \bar{b}_{\alpha\beta})\bar{\gamma}^T h_{b_{\alpha\beta}}(\bar{\pi},\bar{v})dt^\kappa$$
$$+\int_{\Gamma}(c-\bar{c})\bar{\gamma}^T h_c(\bar{\pi},\bar{v}s.)dt^\kappa,$$

implying

$$\int_{\Gamma}\left\{\bar{v}^T g(\pi,\bar{u}) + \bar{\gamma}^T h(\pi,\bar{v})\right\}dt^\kappa - \int_{\Gamma}\left\{\bar{v}^T g(\bar{\pi},\bar{u}) + \bar{\gamma}^T h(\bar{\pi},\bar{v})\right\}dt^\kappa$$
$$\geq \int_{\Gamma}(b-\bar{b})\left[\bar{v}^T g_b(\bar{\pi},\bar{u}) + \gamma^T h_b(\bar{\pi},\bar{v})\right]dt^\kappa$$
$$+\int_{\Gamma}(b_\sigma - \bar{b}_\sigma)\left[\bar{v}^T g_{b_\sigma}(\bar{\pi},\bar{u}) + \bar{\gamma}^T h_{b_\sigma}(\bar{\pi},\bar{v})\right]dt^\kappa$$
$$+\frac{1}{n(\alpha,\beta)}\int_{\Gamma}(b_{\alpha\beta} - \bar{b}_{\alpha\beta})\left[\bar{v}^T g_{b_{\alpha\beta}}(\bar{\pi},\bar{u}) + \bar{\gamma}^T h_{b_{\alpha\beta}}(\bar{\pi},\bar{v})\right]dt^\kappa$$
$$+\int_{\Gamma}(c-\bar{c})\left[\bar{v}^T g_c(\bar{\pi},\bar{u}) + \bar{\gamma}^T h_c(\bar{\pi},\bar{v}s.)\right]dt^\kappa$$
$$= -\int_{\Gamma}(b-\bar{b})\frac{\partial f_\kappa}{\partial b}(\bar{\pi},\bar{w})dt^\kappa - \int_{\Gamma}(b_\sigma - \bar{b}_\sigma)\frac{\partial f_\kappa}{\partial b_\sigma}(\bar{\pi},\bar{w})dt^\kappa$$
$$-\frac{1}{n(\alpha,\beta)}\int_{\Gamma}(b_{\alpha\beta} - \bar{b}_{\alpha\beta})\frac{\partial f_\kappa}{\partial b_{\alpha\beta}}(\bar{\pi},\bar{w})dt^\kappa - \int_{\Gamma}(c-\bar{c})\frac{\partial f_\kappa}{\partial c}(\bar{\pi},\bar{w})dt^\kappa,$$

by considering (8). The previous inequality can be formulated as follows

$$\int_{\Gamma}(b-\bar{b})\frac{\partial f_\kappa}{\partial b}(\bar{\pi},\bar{w})dt^\kappa + \int_{\Gamma}(b_\sigma - \bar{b}_\sigma)\frac{\partial f_\kappa}{\partial b_\sigma}(\bar{\pi},\bar{w})dt^\kappa$$
$$+\frac{1}{n(\alpha,\beta)}\int_{\Gamma}(b_{\alpha\beta} - \bar{b}_{\alpha\beta})\frac{\partial f_\kappa}{\partial b_{\alpha\beta}}(\bar{\pi},\bar{w})dt^\kappa + \int_{\Gamma}(c-\bar{c})\frac{\partial f_\kappa}{\partial c}(\bar{\pi},\bar{w})dt^\kappa$$
$$+\int_{\Gamma}\left\{\bar{v}^T g(\pi,\bar{u}) + \bar{\gamma}^T h(\pi,\bar{v})\right\}dt^\kappa$$
$$\geq \int_{\Gamma}(\bar{b}-\bar{b})\frac{\partial f_\kappa}{\partial b}(\bar{\pi},\bar{w})dt^\kappa + \int_{\Gamma}(\bar{b}_\sigma - \bar{b}_\sigma)\frac{\partial f_\kappa}{\partial b_\sigma}(\bar{\pi},\bar{w})dt^\kappa$$
$$+\frac{1}{n(\alpha,\beta)}\int_{\Gamma}(\bar{b}_{\alpha\beta} - \bar{b}_{\alpha\beta})\frac{\partial f_\kappa}{\partial b_{\alpha\beta}}(\bar{\pi},\bar{w})dt^\kappa + \int_{\Gamma}(\bar{c}-\bar{c})\frac{\partial f_\kappa}{\partial c}(\bar{\pi},\bar{w})dt^\kappa$$
$$+\int_{\Gamma}\left\{\bar{v}^T g(\bar{\pi},\bar{u}) + \bar{\gamma}^T h(\bar{\pi},\bar{v})\right\}dt^\kappa,$$

which involves the inequality

$$L((b,c),\bar{v},\bar{\gamma},w,\bar{u},\bar{v}) \geq L((\bar{b},\bar{c}),\bar{v},\bar{\gamma},w,\bar{u},\bar{v}), \quad \forall (b,c) \in \mathcal{B}\times\mathcal{C}. \tag{9}$$

Furthermore, the following inequality is satisfied

$$\int_{\Gamma} v^T g(\bar{\pi},u)dt^\kappa + \int_{\Gamma}\gamma^T h(\bar{\pi},v)dt^\kappa \leq 0$$

for all $(v,\gamma) \in \mathbb{R}^m_+ \times \mathbb{R}^n$, $(u,v) \in \mathcal{U}\times\mathcal{V}$ and, using the feasibility of $(\bar{b},\bar{u})$, we obtain

$$\int_{\Gamma} v^T g(\bar{\pi},u)dt^\kappa + \int_{\Gamma}\gamma^T h(\bar{\pi},v)dt^\kappa$$
$$\leq \int_{\Gamma}\bar{v}^T g(\bar{\pi},\bar{u})dt^\kappa + \int_{\Gamma}\bar{\gamma}^T h(\bar{\pi},\bar{v})dt^\kappa,$$

or, equivalently,

$$\int_{\Gamma}(\bar{b}-\bar{b})\frac{\partial f_{\kappa}}{\partial b}(\bar{\pi},\bar{w})dt^{\kappa}+\int_{\Gamma}(\bar{b}_{\sigma}-\bar{b}_{\sigma})\frac{\partial f_{\kappa}}{\partial b_{\sigma}}(\bar{\pi},\bar{w})dt^{\kappa}$$

$$+\frac{1}{n(\alpha,\beta)}\int_{\Gamma}(\bar{b}_{\alpha\beta}-\bar{b}_{\alpha\beta})\frac{\partial f_{\kappa}}{\partial b_{\alpha\beta}}(\bar{\pi},\bar{w})dt^{\kappa}+\int_{\Gamma}(\bar{c}-\bar{c})\frac{\partial f_{\kappa}}{\partial c}(\bar{\pi},\bar{w})dt^{\kappa}$$

$$\int_{\Gamma}\nu^{T}g(\bar{\pi},u)dt^{\kappa}+\int_{\Gamma}\gamma^{T}h(\bar{\pi},v)dt^{\kappa}$$

$$\leq\int_{\Gamma}(\bar{b}-\bar{b})\frac{\partial f_{\kappa}}{\partial b}(\bar{\pi},\bar{w})dt^{\kappa}+\int_{\Gamma}(\bar{b}_{\sigma}-\bar{b}_{\sigma})\frac{\partial f_{\kappa}}{\partial b_{\sigma}}(\bar{\pi},\bar{w})dt^{\kappa}$$

$$+\frac{1}{n(\alpha,\beta)}\int_{\Gamma}(\bar{b}_{\alpha\beta}-\bar{b}_{\alpha\beta})\frac{\partial f_{\kappa}}{\partial b_{\alpha\beta}}(\bar{\pi},\bar{w})dt^{\kappa}+\int_{\Gamma}(\bar{c}-\bar{c})\frac{\partial f_{\kappa}}{\partial c}(\bar{\pi},\bar{w})dt^{\kappa}$$

$$\int_{\Gamma}\bar{\nu}^{T}g(\bar{\pi},\bar{u})dt^{\kappa}+\int_{\Gamma}\bar{\gamma}^{T}h(\bar{\pi},\bar{v})dt^{\kappa},$$

involving

$$L((\bar{b},\bar{c}),\nu,\gamma,w,u,v)\leq L((\bar{b},\bar{c}),\bar{\nu},\bar{\gamma},w,\bar{u},\bar{v}),\ \forall\nu\in\mathbb{R}^{m}_{+},\ \forall\gamma\in\mathbb{R}^{n},\quad\forall(u,v)\in\mathcal{U}\times\mathcal{V}. \tag{10}$$

Consequently, by (9) and (10), we conclude that $((\bar{b},\bar{c}),\bar{\nu},\bar{\gamma},\bar{w},\bar{u},\bar{v})$ is a robust saddle-point for the Lagrange functional $L((b,c),\nu,\gamma,w,u,v)$ associated with the modified multi-dimensional variational control problem $(P)_{(\bar{b},\bar{c})}$, and the proof is completed. □

Illustrative application. Let us minimize the mechanical work performed by the variable force $\bar{\mathcal{F}}(c^2(t)+w_1,c^2(t)+w_2)$, including the uncertain parameters $w_\kappa\in\mathcal{W}_\kappa=[0,1]$, $\kappa=1,2$, to move its point of application along the piecewise smooth curve Γ, contained in $\Theta=[0,3]^2=[0,3]\times[0,3]$ and joining the points $t_0=(0,0)$ and $t_1=(3,3)$, such that the following constraints

$$u_1(b-2)(b+2)\leq 0,\quad t=(t^1,t^2)\in\Theta$$

$$\frac{\partial b}{\partial t^1}=3-c+v_1,\quad t=(t^1,t^2)\in\Theta$$

$$\frac{\partial b}{\partial t^2}=3-c+v_2,\quad t=(t^1,t^2)\in\Theta$$

$$b(0,0)=1,\quad b(3,3)=2,$$

are satisfied, where $v_\zeta\in\mathcal{V}_\zeta=[1,2]$, $\zeta=1,2$ and $u_1\in\mathcal{U}_1=\left[\frac{1}{2},1\right]$.

To solve the previous problem, for $m=1$, $n=p=2$, we consider

$$f_\kappa(\pi,w)dt^\kappa=f_1(\pi,w)dt^1+f_2(\pi,w)dt^2=(c^2+w_1)(t)dt^1+(c^2+w_2)dt^2$$

and the constrained robust control problem:

$$(P1)\qquad\min_{(b(\cdot),c(\cdot))}\int_{\Gamma}f_\kappa(\pi,w)dt^\kappa$$

subject to

$$u_1(b-2)(b+2)\leq 0,\quad t=(t^1,t^2)\in\Theta \tag{11}$$

$$\frac{\partial b}{\partial t^1}=3-c+v_1,\quad t=(t^1,t^2)\in\Theta \tag{12}$$

$$\frac{\partial b}{\partial t^2}=3-c+v_2,\quad t=(t^1,t^2)\in\Theta \tag{13}$$

$$b(0,0)=1, \quad b(3,3)=2. \tag{14}$$

The robust counterpart of $(P1)$ is formulated as follows:

$$(RP1) \qquad \min_{(b(\cdot),c(\cdot))} \int_\Gamma \max_{w\in\mathcal{W}} f_\kappa(\pi,w)dt^\kappa$$

subject to

$$u_1(b-2)(b+2)\leq 0, \quad \forall u_1\in\mathcal{U}_1,\ t=(t^1,t^2)\in\Theta$$

$$\frac{\partial b}{\partial t^1}=3-c+v_1, \quad \forall v_1\in\mathcal{V}_1,\ t=(t^1,t^2)\in\Theta$$

$$\frac{\partial b}{\partial t^2}=3-c+v_2, \quad \forall v_2\in\mathcal{V}_2,\ t=(t^1,t^2)\in\Theta$$

$$b(0,0)=1, \quad b(3,3)=2.$$

Clearly, the set of all feasible solutions in $(RP1)$ is

$$\mathcal{D}=\{(b,c)\in\mathcal{S}\times\mathcal{C}:-2\leq b\leq 2,\ \frac{\partial b}{\partial t^1}=\frac{\partial b}{\partial t^2},\ b(0,0)=1,\ b(3,3)=2,$$

$$t\in\Theta,\ u_1\in\mathcal{U}_1,\ v_\zeta\in\mathcal{V}_\zeta,\ \zeta=1,2\}.$$

Now, we are interested in finding a weak robust optimal solution to the problem $(P1)$. This means that we must find the control function $\bar{c}:\Theta\to\mathbb{R}$ (that determines the state function $\bar{b}:\Theta\to\mathbb{R}$), which satisfies the dynamical system (11), (12) and (13) with respect to the boundary conditions (14). Additionally, we assume that the state function is affine.

Let $(\bar{b},\bar{c})\in\mathcal{D}$ be a weak robust optimal solution to the problem $(P1)$ and consider $\max_{w\in\mathcal{W}} f_\kappa(\pi,w)=f_\kappa(\pi,\bar{w}), \kappa=\overline{1,2}$. Then, according to Theorem 1, there exists the scalar $\bar{\mu}\in\mathbb{R}$, the piecewise smooth functions $\bar{v}=\bar{v}_1(t)\in\mathbb{R}_+, \bar{\gamma}=(\bar{\gamma}_1(t),\bar{\gamma}_2(t))\in\mathbb{R}^2$, and the uncertainty parameters $\bar{u}_1\in\mathcal{U}_1$ and $\bar{v}_\zeta\in\mathcal{V}_\zeta$, $\zeta=1,2$, such that the following conditions

$$2\bar{v}_1\bar{u}_1\bar{b}+\frac{\partial\bar{\gamma}_1}{\partial t^1}+\frac{\partial\bar{\gamma}_2}{\partial t^2}=0, \tag{15}$$

$$2\bar{\mu}\bar{c}-\bar{\gamma}_1-\bar{\gamma}_2=0, \tag{16}$$

$$\bar{v}_1\bar{u}_1(\bar{b}^2-4)=0, \quad \bar{v}_1\geq 0, \quad \bar{\mu}\geq 0 \tag{17}$$

hold for all $t\in\Theta$, except at discontinuities.

One can easily verify that the robust necessary optimality conditions (15)–(17) are satisfied at $(\bar{b},\bar{c})=\left(\frac{1}{6}(t^1+t^2)+1,\frac{29}{6}\right)$, with the Lagrange multipliers $\bar{\mu}=1,\bar{v}_1=0,\bar{\gamma}_1+\bar{\gamma}_2=d_1+d_2$ (with $d_1+d_2=\bar{\mu}\left(\frac{17}{3}+\bar{v}_1+\bar{v}_2\right)$) and the uncertain parameters $\bar{w}_1=w_2=\bar{u}_1=1,\bar{v}_1=\bar{v}_2=2\in[1,2]$. Further, it can also be easily verified that the objective functional $\int_\Gamma f_\kappa(\pi,\bar{w})dt^\kappa$ is convex at $(\bar{b},\bar{c})$ and that $((\bar{b},\bar{c}),\bar{v},\bar{\gamma},\bar{w},\bar{u},\bar{v})$ is a robust saddle-point for the Lagrange functional $L((b,c),v,\gamma,w,u,v)$ associated with the modified multi-dimensional variational control problem

$$(P1)_{(\bar{b},\bar{c})} \qquad \min_{(b(\cdot),c(\cdot))}\int_\Gamma\left(\frac{29}{3}+w_1\right)\left(c-\frac{29}{6}\right)dt^1+\left(\frac{29}{3}+w_2\right)\left(c-\frac{29}{6}\right)dt^2$$

subject to

$$u_1(b-2)(b+2)\leq 0, \quad t=(t^1,t^2)\in\Theta$$

$$\frac{\partial b}{\partial t^1}=3-c+v_1, \quad t=(t^1,t^2)\in\Theta$$

$$\frac{\partial b}{\partial t^2}=3-c+v_2, \quad t=(t^1,t^2)\in\Theta$$

$$b(0,0) = 1, \quad b(3,3) = 2.$$

Hence, all the conditions of Theorem 2 are satisfied, which ensures that $(\bar{b}, \bar{c}) = \left(\frac{1}{6}(t^1 + t^2) + 1, \frac{29}{6}\right)$ is a weak robust optimal solution to the problem $(P1)$.

4. Conclusions and Further Development

In this paper, by considering path-independent curvilinear integral cost functionals with mixed (equality and inequality) constraints implying data uncertainty and second-order partial derivatives, we have introduced new classes of robust optimization problems. More precisely, by using the notion of convexity for curvilinear integral functionals, the concept of a normal weak robust optimal solution and the robust saddle-point of a considered Lagrange functional, we have established some characterization results of the problems under study.

As an immediate subsequent development of the results presented in this paper, the author mentions the study of well-posedness for the considered classes of robust control problems.

Author Contributions: Conceptualization, S.T.; Methodology, K.D. Both authors have read and agreed to the published version of the manuscript.

Funding: This research received no external funding.

Data Availability Statement: Not applicable.

Conflicts of Interest: The authors declare no conflict of interest.

References

1. Mititelu, Ş. Optimality and duality for invex multi-dimensional control problems with mixed constraints. *J. Adv. Math. Stud.* **2009**, *2*, 25–34.
2. Treanţă, S. Second-Order PDE Constrained Controlled Optimization Problems With Application in Mechanics. *Mathematics* **2021**, *9*, 1472. [CrossRef]
3. Treanţă, S. On a Class of Second-Order PDE&PDI Constrained Robust Modified Optimization Problems. *Mathematics* **2021**, *9*, 1473.
4. Treanţă, S. On a class of isoperimetric constrained controlled optimization problems. *Axioms* **2021**, *10*, 112. [CrossRef]
5. Mititelu, Ş.; Treanţă, S. Efficiency conditions in vector control problems governed by multiple integrals. *J. Appl. Math. Comput.* **2018**, *57*, 647–665. [CrossRef]
6. Olteanu, O.; Treanţă, S. *Convexity, Optimization and Approximation, with Some Applications*; LAP Lambert Academic Publishing: Chisinau, Republic of Moldova, 2018; ISBN 978-613-9-87683-9.
7. Preeti; Jayswal, A.; Arana-Jiménez, M. Robust saddle-point criteria for multi-dimensional optimization problems with data uncertainty. *Int. J. Control* **2020**. [CrossRef]
8. Jayswal, A.; Antczak, T.; Jha, S. On equivalence between a variational problem and its modified variational problem with the η-objective function under invexity. *Int. Trans. Oper. Res.* **2019**, *26*, 2053–2070. [CrossRef]
9. Treanţă, S. Saddle-point optimality criteria in modified variational control problems with PDE constraints. *Optim. Control Appl. Meth.* **2020**, *41*, 1160–1175. [CrossRef]
10. Treanţă, S. On modified interval-valued variational control problems with first-order PDE constraints. *Symmetry* **2020**, *12*, 472. [CrossRef]
11. Treanţă, S. On a modified optimal control problem with first-order PDE constraints and the associated saddle-point optimality criterion. *Eur. J. Control* **2020**, *51*, 1–9. [CrossRef]
12. Treanţă, S. Saddle-point optimality criteria involving (ρ, b, d)-invexity and (ρ, b, d)-pseudoinvexity in interval-valued optimization problems. *Int. J. Control* **2021**. [CrossRef]
13. Wei, H.Z.; Chen, C.R.; Li, S.J. Characterizations for optimality conditions of general robust optimization problems. *J. Optim. Theory Appl.* **2018**, *177*, 835–856. [CrossRef]
14. Liu, X.W.; Yuan, Y.X. A robust algorithm for optimization with general equality and inequality constraints. *SIAM J. Sci. Comput.* **2000**, *22*, 517–534. [CrossRef]
15. Jeyakumar, V.; Wang, J.H.; Li, G. Lagrange multiplier characterizations of robust best approximations under constraint data uncertainty. *J. Math. Anal. Appl.* **2012**, *393*, 285–297. [CrossRef]
16. Sun, X.K.; Teo, K.L.; Zeng, J.; Guo, X.L. On approximate solutions and saddle point theorems for robust convex optimization. *Optim. Lett.* **2020**, *14*, 1711–1730. [CrossRef]

17. Lu, Z.; Zhu, Y.; Lu, Q. Stability analysis of nonlinear uncertain fractional differential equations with Caputo derivative. *Fractals* **2021**, *29*, 2150057. [CrossRef]
18. Treanţă, S. Efficiency in uncertain variational control problems. *Neural Comput. Appl.* **2021**, *33*, 5719–5732. [CrossRef]
19. Zaslavski, A.J. Convergence of extremals of variational problems on large intervals. *Adv. Nonlinear Stud.* **2015**, *15*, 221–240. [CrossRef]
20. Geldhauser, C.; Valdinoci, E. Optimizing the fractional power in a model with stochastic PDE constraints. *Adv. Nonlinear Stud.* **2018**, *18*, 649–669. [CrossRef]
21. Babaniyi, O.; Jadamba, B.; Khan, A.A.; Richards, M.; Sama, M.; Tammer, C. Three optimization formulations for an inverse problem in saddle point problems with applications to elasticity imaging of locating tumor in incompressible medium. *J. Nonlinear Var. Anal.* **2020**, *4*, 301–318.
22. Debnath, I.P.; Qin, X. Robust optimality and duality for minimax fractional programming problems with support functions. *J. Nonlinear Funct. Anal.* **2021**, *2021*, 5.
23. Saunders, D.J. *The Geometry of Jet Bundles*; London Mathematical Society Lecture Note Series, 142; Cambridge University Press: Cambridge, UK, 1989.
24. Treanţă, S. Constrained variational problems governed by second-order Lagrangians. *Appl. Anal.* **2020**, *99*, 1467–1484. [CrossRef]

MDPI
St. Alban-Anlage 66
4052 Basel
Switzerland
Tel. +41 61 683 77 34
Fax +41 61 302 89 18
www.mdpi.com

Mathematics Editorial Office
E-mail: mathematics@mdpi.com
www.mdpi.com/journal/mathematics

www.ingramcontent.com/pod-product-compliance
Lightning Source LLC
LaVergne TN
LVHW070405100526
838202LV00014B/1394
* 9 7 8 3 0 3 6 5 6 5 8 9 7 *